Sustainable Happin

Today's greatest health challenges, the so-called diseases of civilization—trauma, depression, obesity, cancer—are now known in large part to reflect our inability to tame stress reflexes gone wild and to empower instead the peaceful, healing and sociable part of our nature that adapts us to civilized life. The same can be said of the economic challenges posed by the stress-reactive cycles of boom and bust, driven by addictive greed and compulsive panic. As current research opens up new horizons of stress-cessation, empathic intelligence, peak performance, and shared happiness, it has also encountered Asian methods of self-healing and interdependence more effective and teachable than any known in the West.

Sustainable Happiness is the first book to make Asia's most rigorous and complete system of contemplative living, hidden for centuries in Tibet, accessible to help us all on our shared journey towards sustainable well-being, altruism, inspiration, and happiness.

Joe Loizzo, MD, PhD, is a psychotherapist and the founder of the Nalanda Institute for Contemplative Science, a non-profit contemplative learning community that helps people find sustainable ways of living in today's complex world. On faculty at the Weill Cornell Center for Integrative Medicine and the Columbia University Center for Buddhist Studies, Dr. Loizzo lectures widely on the role of contemplative science in the future of health, education, and contemporary life, and teaches regular public classes and workshops at Nalanda Institute, New York Open Center, and Tibet House US.

Sustainable Happiness

The Mind Science of Well-Being, Altruism, and Inspiration

Joe Loizzo

Routledge
Taylor & Francis Group
NEW YORK AND LONDON

First published 2012
by Routledge
711 Third Avenue, New York, NY 10017

Simultaneously published in the UK
by Routledge
27 Church Road, Hove, East Sussex BN3 2FA

Routledge is an imprint of the Taylor & Francis Group, an informa business

Library of Congress Cataloging in Publication Data
Loizzo, Joe.
Sustainable happiness : the mind science of well-being, altruism, and inspiration / Joe Loizzo.
p. cm.
Includes bibliographical references and index
1. Happiness. 2. Well-being. 3. Mind and body. I. Title.
BF575.H27L65 2012
158—dc23
2011047690

ISBN: 978-0-415-87815-9 (hbk)
ISBN: 978-0-415-87816-6 (pbk)
ISBN: 978-0-203-85481-5 (ebk)

Typeset in Minion
by EvS Communication Networx, Inc.

SFI Certified Sourcing
www.sfiprogram.org
SFI-00453

Printed and bound in the United States of America
by Edwards Brothers, Inc.

In loving memory of my mother,
Carmela Paula Napoli Loizzo (1917–2009) and
Venerable Tshanzhab Serkong Rinpoche (1914–1983),
Who met by chance on the fourth of July, 1979,
at her home in Old Westbury, New York

Like a geometer wholly dedicated
To squaring the circle, but who cannot find,
Think as he may, the principle indicated—
So did I study the supernal face.
I yearned to know just how our image merges
Into that circle, and how it there finds place;
But mine were not the wings for such a flight.
Yet as I wished, the truth I wished for came
Cleaving my mind in a great flash of light.
Here my powers rest from their high fantasy,
But already I could feel my being turned—
Instinct and intellect balanced equally
As in a wheel whose motion nothing jars—
By the love that moves the sun and the other stars.

—Dante Alighieri, *Paradiso*, Canto XXXIII,
From the Divine Comedy
My father gave my mother,
On his twenty-sixth birthday,
After his safe return from war,
May 13, 1945

Contents

Illustrations

Full-Color Illustrations

Buddhological Foreword

In our current era of global crisis and transition, there is no proven, civilizing, cultural tradition that holds more promise for helping humanity find sustainable happiness than the rich spiritual, scientific, and artistic civilization of Tibet. Over the last three decades, the enormous potential of this highly evolved tradition has increasingly been recognized in the West, leading to thousands of Tibetan spiritual teaching centers all over the world, a cascading spread of Tibetan cultural and artistic manifestations, and an ongoing dialogue between Western natural scientists and their Tibetan spiritual science counterparts. A great advocate of this dialogue, His Holiness the Dalai Lama has repeatedly pointed to two of the cultural gems of Tibetan civilization he considers most beneficial and precious: its integrative system of medicine and its comprehensive, contemplative science. In fact, His Holiness often speaks of these two sciences as Tibet's great gifts to the human body and mind.

Where these two gemlike human sciences converge is in the related disciplines some call Tibetan psychiatry and neuroscience. In fact, these are not separate disciplines, but twin faces of one definitive science and technology of self-healing and self-transformation developed in Buddhist India and preserved in Tibet. While this integral mind/body science—embedded in the rich contemplative and ritual arts of the Tantras—is distinctive to the Tibetan tradition, it also preserves and integrates the arts and sciences of personal liberation and enlightened altruism we associate with the more familiar Buddhist traditions of South and East Asia.

This comprehensive approach, preserving all Buddhist teaching in a gradual curriculum integrated with Tantric psychiatry and neuroscience, was developed at the Buddhist monastic University of Nālandā in North India and transplanted into the monastic colleges and universities of Tibet. It is most fully and clearly articulated in the futuristic vision and multidisciplinary science of the *Kālacakra* or *Wheel of Time*, the most modern system of Tantric, Vajrayāna Buddhist culture, of which His Holiness the Dalai Lama is the greatest living master.

According to the vision of the *Wheel of Time*, the future of humanity and our living planet lies in the global cultivation and spread of a science of lasting happiness, based on a system of contemplative learning and self-mastery meant to teach all humans to tap and harness our natural potential for heroic altruism inspired by unwavering bliss. As an integral part of that science, this synthetic tradition includes the whole gradual path of the Nālandā curriculum, since renunciation based on mindfulness and compassionate openness based on quiescence are vital prerequisites for Tantric practice, especially for the definitive arts of the Unexcelled Yoga Tantras, like the *Wheel of Time*. In addition to the familiar methods of mindfulness and compassion, the comprehensive curriculum of the *Wheel of Time* includes two extraordinary arts: the archetypal imagery of the Unexcelled Yoga creation stage; and the bliss-void intuition of the Unexcelled Yoga perfection stage.

It is my pleasure to share with you *Sustainable Happiness*, the first complete introduction to Tibetan mind science that locates all four of its systems of self-healing and self-transformation in the context of current developments in medicine, psychology, and neuroscience. This groundbreaking work takes the growing convergence of Western psychology and Buddhist contemplative science to the next level. It advances the dialogue not just by presenting the distinctive Tibetan approaches to mindfulness and loving-kindness, transcendent insight and altruistic compassion, but also by making the definitive arts of Tantric imagery and inspiration accessible in light of the classical system of the *Esoteric Community* (*Guhyasamāja*), the synthetic teachings of the *Wheel of Time*, and the latest developments in Western therapy and neuroscience.

I know of no one better prepared to make this remarkable gift of Tibetan civilization accessible to a wider audience than the author of *Sustainable Happiness*, my former student and close colleague, Dr. Joe Loizzo. Dr. Loizzo studied intensively with me at Amherst College, where he wrote a prize-winning Independent Study thesis, *Wittgenstein and the Madhyamika: Preparatory Studies for a Critical Psychology*. After receiving his medical degree and completing his psychiatry training at Harvard, he picked up his Tibetan studies with me at Columbia University, where he completed his doctoral dissertation, *Chandrakīrti and the Moon-Flower of Nālandā: Objectivity and Self-Correction in India's Central Therapeutic Philosophy of Language*. Since then, in addition to his translation study, *Nāgārjuna's Reason Sixty with Chandrakīrti's Commentary*, Dr. Loizzo has published key articles on the evolutionary psychology of *karma*, and the history of science at Nālandā and in the *Kālachakra* tradition. He is currently working on a translation of the crucial wisdom chapter of Khay Drub Je's *Great Wheel of Time Commentary*. In addition to his work as a Tibetan scholar, he is both a practicing Buddhist psychotherapist and the main teacher for the *Nalanda Institute Series in Contemplative Science* at Tibet House US.

To help unpack the four systems of the gradual curriculum, Dr. Loizzo has framed them in terms of the sacred architecture of the *Wheel of Time*, in which the mind/body process is mapped in four concentric spheres called the body wheel, speech wheel, mind wheel and bliss wheel. He has aligned these with the aims of Theravāda, Mahāyāna, Tantric Creation Stage and Perfection

Stage practice, which he terms personal healing, social healing, cultural healing and natural healing. And he explains how these aims are linked with the four contemplative systems developed to realize them: mindfulness or natural mind practice, which he calls "deep mindfulness"; mind-training, called "mind-clearing;" archetypal imagery, called "role-modeling imagery;" and bliss-void intuition, called "sublimation."

Throughout the book, Dr. Loizzo draws on classical sources, following the distinctive Tibetan tradition of integrating all vehicles of contemplative learning into one gradual path to perfect enlightenment, finally conceived in Tantric terms as the perfectly integrated altruism of a Vajra Master. He also takes the dialogue between Western and Buddhist science one step further, with thoughtful comparisons which show how Tibet's unique synthesis of all Buddhist psychology with the subtle-body model and mind/body methods of the Tantras anticipates and advances our fledgling brain-based approaches to psychiatry and psychotherapy.

Though traditionally the core disciplines of Vajrayāna Buddhism were guarded in secrecy, the modern system of the *Wheel of Time* sought to clarify their potential for all who had a sincere interest; and it also predicted a time when they would need to be introduced widely to the world. Now, given the proliferation of popular misconceptions about the Tantras, His Holiness has encouraged Tibetan and Western scholars to make reliable information about them widely available, even though their advanced practice ultimately requires extensive preparatory training, well-developed altruistic motivation, sound understanding (such as provided in this book), and special blessings and initiations.

At this crucial time, when our troubled world needs both a realistic vision and accessible methods of sustainable living, I am happy to recommend *Sustainable Happiness* to all who seek guidance from the wisdom of Tibet. The comprehensive system of contemplative living and learning introduced in this book holds enormous promise for helping us all develop the well-being, altruism and inspiration we need now more than ever. I am immensely proud of Dr. Joe Loizzo's great accomplishment, and absolutely delighted to welcome this magisterial work of his into the light of today!

Robert A. F. Thurman
Je Tsong Khapa Professor of Indo-Tibetan Buddhist Studies,
Columbia University
President, Tibet House, U.S.

Interpersonal Neurobiological Foreword

We are all in great need of a new way of being—in ourselves, in our schools, and in our society. Our modern culture has evolved in recent times to create a troubled world with individuals suffering from alienation, schools failing to inspire and to connect with students; in short, we live in a contemporary society often devoid of a moral compass to help clarify how we can move forward in our global community to create a more meaningful, sustainable, and compassionate way of living. As a physician, psychiatrist, psychotherapist, scientist, and educator, and as a father, husband, and son, I have been saddened and dismayed to find a firm grounding in the healthy mind absent even from our professional education and our work. After surveying over one hundred thousand mental health clinicians and nearly ten thousand teachers, the results are in that over 95 percent of these professionals focusing on helping others develop the mind have never been offered a working definition of what the mind is!

In the field in which I work called "interpersonal neurobiology," we combine over a dozen branches of science to address the question of what a working definition of the mind might be, and then on what a healthy mind is. Part of that journey of finding the universal principles across scientific disciplines has led us to explore the mechanisms of strengthening our mental skills through the attentional training of ancient meditative practices. One of these traditions comes from what is sometimes considered a "religion" but at other times is seen as a form of practical "mind science," the contemplative tradition of Buddhism. One facet of Buddhist meditation is the cultivation of a quality of attention that enhances the ability to be aware of present moment experience and free oneself from the burden of often self-created anxiety, despair, and isolation. In many ways, learning to train the mind to become more mindful has been demonstrated in a range of scientific studies to enhance immune function, improve cardiovascular health, increase the enzyme that maintains the ends of chromosomes (telomerase), balance emotions, decrease fear and anxiety, increase empathy, and even strengthen self-compassion. Being mindfully aware, attending to the richness of here-and-now experiences, creates scientifically recognized enhancements in our physiology, our mental functions, and in our interpersonal relationships. Being fully present in our awareness opens our lives to new possibilities of well-being. In addition, what is called "interpersonal attunement," focusing attention on the internal world of another, harnesses neural circuitry that enables two people to "feel felt" by one another, promoting longevity and resilience. Mindfulness may in fact be a form of "internal attunement" in which an observing self-function approaches a more directly experiencing self with curiosity, openness, acceptance, and love. This internal attunement may lead the brain to grow in ways that promote balanced self-regulation via the process of neural integration, which enables flexibility and self-understanding, empathy and compassion.

Almost all cultures have practices that help people develop awareness of the moment and what we can see enables attunement toward self and others. Each of the major religions of the world utilizes some method to enable individuals to focus their attention and feel connected to their inner and outer worlds, from meditation to prayer, yoga to *tai'chi*. Among these cultures, the Buddhist traditions of Asia have received growing attention from researchers and clinicians in recent years, in part because they approach our human needs for reflection and attunement as a science and healing art of individual and communal well-being. "The Buddha" was a man who sought a new way of living free from the self-created suffering that drove him to explore his inner world. The realization of a way to view suffering as inherent in the human condition and to outline the path to alleviate that suffering is the "awakening" that came with his journey. "Buddha" means the awakened one, and this awakening, this shedding light on a universal human condition, is the essence of Buddhist philosophy and practice.

After the Buddha's death, his followers ultimately travelled throughout Asia, and the various permutations of this original teaching have taken the form of specific traditions. The Theravada Buddhist tradition of South Asia has been enormously influential in the world, especially the West, offering time-tested methods of teaching and practicing mindfulness and loving-kindness, which have been increasingly integrated into a range of mindfulness- and acceptance-based approaches to psychotherapy. The Mahayana Buddhism of East and Southeast Asia, though less influential in the West, has also made itself felt in the form of the Zen-inspired methodology of Marsha Linnehan's Dialectical Behavior Therapy, as well as in the work of psychoanalysts like Jeremy Safran and Jeffery Rubin. Of all Buddhist traditions, the Vajrayana Buddhism of Central Asia, newest on the scene, is only now coming to our awareness through dialogues between Western researchers and the Dalai Lama, as well as through laboratory studies of expert Tibetan meditators by Herbert Benson, Richard Davidson and others.

Now we come to the book you hold in your hands: *Sustainable Happiness*. This is the first systematic look at the rich contemplative science of Tibetan Buddhism, as seen from the perspective of its potential contributions to popular psychology, psychotherapy and neuroscience. This in-depth introduction makes clear that Tibet, through its long isolation, has preserved the most comprehensive of Buddhist psychological traditions. We learn in this fascinating book that its comprehensive approach begins with the basic science of mindfulness, but adds to it three more advanced systems of building attunement specifically meant for people seeking to live more contemplative lives in the everyday world. While there are many overlaps, naturally, with other Buddhist teachings, this approach reveals an intricate exploration of mind that illuminates layers of what our mental lives are like and what we can do to explore, expand, and cultivate them to promote well-being.

Beyond offering unique ways of teaching and practicing mindfulness to lay people in our active lives, this tradition also offers a system of social emotional self-regulation like loving kindness and Zen, but tailored for facing stressful social relationships and building social leadership outside the monastery. Finally, the Tibetan tradition is further distinguished by adding to these more familiar methods two more powerful systems for deepening self-regulation and social attunement, based on the use of transformational imagery and narrative, and also by the induction of euphoric flow states. These techniques are little known and poorly understood in the West, though they seem to hold enormous potential to help busy people make quicker, more profound changes in perceptions of self and other, emotional regulation and visceral response style.

The key is that the way we learn to focus our attention, in this case using imagery, affirmations and breath control, can prime new neural patterns of activation and ultimately stimulate the growth of new synaptic connections in the brain itself. This is how we use the focus of attention with awareness—a function of the mind—to change the structure of the brain. Such tools of training attention may be especially helpful in bringing mindfulness and attunement to high performance social roles and intimate relationships. In many ways, these are "mindsight skills" that enable us to see our own and others' minds with more clarity and depth, and then to transform this energy and information flow in our bodies and in our relationships toward a process called integration—the linkage of differentiated parts of a system. Modern science can be interpreted to suggest that physiological, interpersonal, and psychological health emerge from such integration, experienced as harmony and flexibility. Ancient contemplative practices may reveal a rigorous form of mental training that ultimately can be seen to promote such integrative states in body, mind, and relationships. Also intriguing is the fact that these powerful methods from the Tibetan tradition are taught and practiced with the help of an explicit contemplative model of the nervous system, which explains mental states and functions in terms of neural energies, pathways, complexes and what are called chemical drops. In fact, within this model, as in our own current science, the conscious mastery of differentiated elements brought about by these rigorous methods of mind training is viewed as catalyzing a deep form of integration across many layers of mental life.

Tibet's comprehensive approach to contemplative science, called the gradual path or gradual curriculum, is ably introduced by Dr. Joe Loizzo, who is a Tibetan Buddhist scholar, an integrative psychiatrist, and a contemplative psychotherapist all rolled into one deeply thoughtful and integrative practitioner. Dr. Loizzo is uniquely qualified to present the Tibetan approach to the emerging field of contemplative science, explaining its links with current stress research, psychotherapy and neuroscience, as well as its potential contributions to public health and well-being, interpersonal relationships, and even the well-being of our global community. Linking the Tibetan psychology of social engagement to current evolutionary models of altruism, he explores how this ancient view is consistent with emerging scientific discoveries for the role of the prefrontal cortex in the development of empathy, social attunement, and higher neural integration. He also links the uniquely Tibetan contemplative discipline of transformational imagery and euphoric states to Stephen Kosslyn's groundbreaking work on mental imagery and Stephen Porges' polyvagal theory.

Throughout *Sustainable Happiness*, Dr. Loizzo balances traditional teachings on the four great Buddhist psychological systems or "vehicles" of contemplative life with frequent references to classical Buddhist texts, cutting edge science and a range of approaches to modern psychotherapy. Each of the book's four main parts explores more than meditation, diving deeply into the complementary disciplines of cognitive self-analysis and affective-behavioral transformation. The result of this carefully constructed scholarly journey is an unusual confluence of both a traditional and a contemporary science of mind that offers a glimpse into the enormous potential and promise of the ongoing dialogue and cross-fertilization between these two very distinct disciplines of discovery.

Given the challenges we face throughout our global community in cultivating well-being in this troubled and alienated world, it is vital to our future well-being, and even our very existence, that we preserve and explore all human strategies to strengthen self-regulation and promote the internal and interpersonal integration needed to help us build our natural capacities for deep self-awareness and interpersonal attunement. Integration can ultimately shift the pathway of cultural evolution in a positive direction—and a strengthened capacity for mindful awareness may be the essential starting place to cultivate such an intentional shift, helping our increasingly interconnected and rapidly changing world to survive and even thrive as we move into this new digital era.

Science brings knowledge and technology but not necessarily wisdom. If we take our human family's accomplishments in exploring the nature of our mental lives, it is natural to then seek a weaving of the important contributions of all the sciences with the deep understanding of our subjective mental lives in the wisdom traditions of contemplation. Among the methods available to us today, the comprehensive curriculum preserved in the contemplative discipline of Tibet holds great promise for us all, both because it can be tailored to life in the everyday world and because it offers a wide range of attention training tools of the mind that expand and deepen our capacity for empathic attunement and proactive social engagement. Such moral living does not arise from a vacuum, but can be cultivated with integrative practices. Integration is the source of well-being and health that provides a secular ethic around which we can focus our efforts to bring the world to a scientifically grounded place of positive growth. Integration made visible is kindness and compassion. Whether we come to such integrative practices as individuals seeking lasting happiness through caring relationships in the world, or as professionals seeking to heal, teach or lead, the insights and methods introduced in *Sustainable Happiness* can inspire us all and offer vitally relevant strategies to all walks of humanity, and to the future of the world, this fragile and precious Earth, the home we all share.

Daniel J. Siegel, MD
Co-Director, Mindful Awareness Research Institute;
Co-Investigator, Foundation for Psychocultural Research/
UCLA Center for Culture, Brain and Development;
and Clinical Professor of Psychiatry, UCLA School of Medicine
Executive Director, Mindsight Institute

Preface and Acknowledgments

Can human happiness be truly sustainable? Can it really be known or explained by science? Only decades ago, the answer most of our great minds would have given to both these questions was no. Expressing the consensus of modern science, Freud concluded our nature was so unfit for civilized life that our minds would always be plagued by discontent. Our twentieth century philosophers urged us to face the absurdity of our unnatural condition, and our scientists and economists portrayed our environment and marketplace as natural battlegrounds in which only the fiercest competitors can win happiness and dwindling resources. Against this backdrop, as the first decade of the new millennium has plunged us into a multi-dimensional crisis of global proportion, compounding economic collapse, rising inequity, international terror, preventable epidemics, exploding health costs, and irreversible climate change, it would seem that our prospects for lasting happiness are literally going up in smoke.

Just when things couldn't look bleaker, the quiet consensus from five decades of groundbreaking science has literally turned our view of ourselves and our world inside out. As the challenges facing humanity and life on our planet put more and more pressure on our capacity to live together in sustainable ways, new breakthroughs are helping us see our nature, brains and minds as far more equipped to enjoy peace and share happiness than even our most idealistic modern traditions dreamed. But this is not another book about the quantum universe, the brain's amazing plasticity, our deeply empathic intelligence, or the optimistic findings of positive psychology. Of course, it *is* about all these promising new fields, but only incidentally, not essentially so.

I see *Sustainable Happiness* less as a book than as a record. It is the record of a personal journey that began in my father's psychotherapy office. It is a journey that led by way of the least scientific of psychoanalysts—Carl Jung—to my first world religion class at Amherst College, where I entered into the time-machine of Tibetan Buddhism, in the person and through the genius of Robert Thurman, then an obscure former monk and newly minted professor of Indian studies. Were it not for Thurman, who had walked across the Middle East into a Tibetan refugee camp in North India ten years earlier, only to find his way back to Harvard and Amherst, my journey would no doubt have lead far closer home. Perhaps it would have taken me to Jung's library, a few hours from where I grew up in Switzerland, where my dad studied medicine and psychiatry. Or perhaps to the source of Freud's vision of humanity as torn between love and war: to the pre-Socratic Greek philosopher-scientist Empedocles, who lived and taught in Agrigento, Sicily, a few miles from my mother's childhood home.

Instead, thanks to Bob's genius for translation, I heard and saw the archetypes of transcendent wisdom and love Jung spoke of in his essays on Tibetan Buddhism come to life in the same sleepy valley where Emily Dickinson wrote her awakened poems. Inspired by Tibet's timeless synthesis of such poetic visions with the deconstructive philosophy of emptiness, the depth-psychology of unconditional love, and the contemplative neuroscience of blissful self-regulation, my journey with Bob eventually lead to India and the living masters of the transplanted universities of occupied Tibet. It was there that I met Bob's mentors, including His Holiness the Dalai Lama and his philosophy tutor, the Venerable Tsanzhab Serkong Rinpoche. Though I didn't realize it until decades later, my journey had taken me into the time-machine mentioned in the contemplative science tradition of the *Wheel of Time*, back to the ancient Buddhist university of Nalanda, in the footsteps of thousands of students and scholars from around Asia who had visited there in its heyday, from the sixth to the thirteenth century.

It was in the time-portable version of that university—in the futuristic vision, scientific theories and contemplative methods of the *Wheel of Time* embodied in His Holiness and his *Time-Wheel* mentor, Serkong—that I found the inspiration for this book: the living reality of a pure, contemplative science of lasting, blissful happiness, accessible and teachable to all citizens of our endangered planet. It was also there, in the least likely of places, that my mind was prepared to receive and embrace the revolutionary shifts in modern science that aligned quantum relativity and systems ecology with sociobiology, the neuroscience of plasticity, the neurobiology of empathy and the new psychology of happiness. That was 1979, when the colleagues I had not yet met—Jon Kabat-Zinn, Sharon Salzberg, Mark Epstein, Dan Siegel, Dan Goleman, Richie Davidson, Chris Germer, and Paul Fulton—were all struggling to find their own way into new fields we had all been told by our Western guides not even to think about. As I followed the advice of my Buddhist mentors to return to medical school and pursue psychiatry, it was in the certainty that our world *had* to change, and that the arts and sciences we needed to change it were close at hand.

What made me so certain that everything I'd learned and was learning in school *had* to give? Thinking back, I see now, this certainty also began with my father. Only not just as a hero, a man lucky in love who was also impassioned about his rare line of work, a simple practice of dialogue which seemed to offer our ailing world much needed drops of humanity and real rays of hope. My father was also my anti-hero. As I watched him struggle with poor health and burnout, with blocks to assuming his place as a community leader and to nurturing and being nurtured by his wife and family, I vowed that the only way I'd follow in his footsteps was if I could find a parallel path with the power to heal his demons and dispel his shadow. So I didn't take Jung's lead over that of his more scientifically grounded and philosophically critical mentor Freud because I was "in search of a soul." Between my old world teaching mom and my existentialist dad, my home reeked of soul. What was missing was the baby Freud threw out with the bathwater of creationism: the contemplative arts and sciences I found on the other side of our globe and our time.

Fast forward to the present. Now that my colleagues have made mindfulness and loving-kindness household words, and not just the new normal in psychotherapy but the focus of a whole new growth field incredibly called "contemplative neuroscience," what's left to add? The answer, remarkably enough, is: the full curriculum, spanning the next seven centuries of scientific progress, pedagogic innovation and technical advancement. As I'll explain in detail in the pages to follow, the science of mindfulness and art of loving kindness we know, along with *Hatha* yoga, belong to the first of four complete systems of scientific psychology and contemplative arts that make up the cumulative curriculum developed at Nalanda. And this expanded curriculum, unlike the one we now know and love, was specifically designed with lay practitioners in mind, with built-in power-tools for living a contemplative life in a stress-driven world. Most of this is news to us since that curriculum was kept essentially hidden from the world until 1959, when the Dalai Lama and most of his master teachers fled Tibet.

Over the years, as I've gotten more and more hopeful watching the work of my colleagues transform our world, I've had to galvanize my patience by reminding myself that my work unpacking the time-capsule of the Nalanda tradition for a wider audience must not be rushed. As one small measure of the enormity of the task I'd taken on, consider this: while the literature of the mindfulness tradition has been elegantly condensed into three volumes, the three libraries of Nalanda held thousands of texts and commentaries in all five of the classical Buddhist arts and sciences. Of the vast ocean of timeless wisdom and healing arts preserved in Tibet—as many as fifteen thousand classical volumes alone—most have not even been transcribed into modern formats, and only a few drops have been translated. This is why, when my fellow travellers were reaching out in groundbreaking ways, I went back into the time-machine with my mentor, Bob Thurman, finally at Columbia University, to complete a doctorate in Sanskrit and Tibetan studies. As my new colleagues in Buddhology—Ryuichi Abe, Christian Wedemeyer, Vesna Wallace, David Gray, Tom Yarnall, John Campbell and others—had only just begun, with Bob, to offer the first authoritative translations of the advanced process-oriented contemplative science of Tibet, once again I was reminded that there truly was no rushing the *Wheel of Time*. I am especially grateful for the recent translations of Christian Wedemeyer, Tom Yarnall, and Bob Thurman, which illumine Tibet's unique, process-oriented teaching tradition, just as Bob's *Essence of True Eloquence* did the engaged teaching tradition it shares with East Asia.

In addition to giving my translation skills and Western Tibetan studies time to ripen, my time at Columbia allowed for another key dimension of my work to take root. Thanks to receptive colleagues in the psychiatry department—Mary Scuitto, Ellen Stevenson, and Ina Becker—I was able to start not just translating the Nalanda curriculum but also *transplanting* its living practice, in much the same way that transcendental meditation and mindfulness practice had been some years earlier by my friends Herbert Benson and Jon Kabat-Zinn. The result, The Center for Meditation and Healing at Columbia-Presbyterian Hospital, seed of the Nalanda Institute for Contemplative Science, was the first such center founded in a major psychiatry department, and the first to incorporate Tibetan techniques into Jon's new paradigm of mindfulness-based stress reduction. In addition, thanks to one of my first students, Kathleen Walas, then the director of the Avon Foundation, as well as the vision and rigor of my research collaborators—Mary Charlson and Janey Peterson at Weill Cornell and Alyson Model at Albert Einstein—I was able to put my transplanted Tibetan approach to the test in a series of very promising pilot studies involving women with breast cancer, a group after angioplasty and a circle of stressed, for-profit and non-profit CEO's.

This final delay brings us to one last point about the way I've chosen to translate and transplant the Nalanda tradition. Among the many contexts in which Buddhist contemplative science is being transplanted into the West, this book assumes my development at Nalanda Institute of a multidisciplinary, multi-modal teaching method which I believe best replicates the blend of liberal arts content, therapeutic logic, and transferential pedagogy that earmarks Buddhist teaching, especially in the process-oriented tradition of Tibet. Though not wholly new, the mix of cognitive and behavioral coursework with group meditation instruction and individual mentoring bonds assumed in this book crosses disciplinary lines and combines methodologies in ways some may find challenging. My fellow Buddhologists and Buddhist practitioners may fear my reliance on current evolutionary psychology, neuroscience and psychotherapy risk over-translating traditional teaching and over-simplifying traditional practice. Likewise, my fellow medical researchers and clinical practitioners may fear my reliance on traditional Buddhist evolutionary psychology, contemplative neuroscience, and self-healing techniques risk confounding cultural beliefs with modern science and cultural practices with clinical methods.

Of course, I very strongly share these concerns with my colleagues on both sides of the cross-cultural dialogue. And this is yet another reason why I've subjected this system of translated teaching and transplanted practice to every possible test, delaying rather than pushing the publication of my work. On the other hand, on the flip side of due diligence and abundant care lies the error of neglecting to share insights and methods that may help speed the transmission and insure the preservation of this incomparable treasury of human know-how. However promising the current shifts underway in modern science, medicine, and psychotherapy are, the time-machine of the Nalanda tradition offers not just invaluable cross-cultural validation of tentative new directions, but also an unparalleled wealth of methods of teaching and practice that would otherwise take decades if not centuries to reinvent. Given the dire urgency and overwhelming complexity of the global crisis facing human civilization and life on earth, it would be truly reckless for concerned minds from either tradition to pull back from a rigorous effort to renew this legacy in our day and try to make it as widely accessible as mindfulness and loving-kindness have become.

Since closing a chapter on a journey that has guided me though most of my life feels as much like a death as a birth, I found myself awakened one night, remembering the kindness of the many individuals whose help and encouragement have made this work possible, as if I was reviewing my life history. After my parents and sisters, Patricia, Mary Jean, Barbara, and Margaret, I must acknowledge the inspiration of Western contemplatives Father Phillip Eichner and Brother Marion at Chaminade, the local Marianist high school for boys, who not only helped me read Jung, but also introduced me to global contemplative Thomas Merton, the existential analyst Victor Frankl and the romantic poetry of E.E. Cummings and T.S. Eliot. Alongside Bob Thurman, I am deeply grateful to Nena Thurman and my erstwhile siblings, Ganden, Uma, Dechen, and Mipham, who all allowed me to pursue my studies with Bob by welcoming me into the family at Amherst, in Woodstock, and in India.

In India and back in the states, I could not have found my way or stayed on track without the example and human kindness of Bob's Tibetan mentors, His Holiness the Dalai Lama, Ganden Tripa Kyabje Lingtsang Rinpoche, Tshanshab Serkong Rinpoche, and Kyabje Gelek Rinpoche. My frequent opportunities to dialogue with His Holiness on topics from Buddhist psychology to modern neuroscience, Tibetan medicine to quantum physics, combined with his teachings on the *Wheel of Time*, the art of mentoring, the wisdom of emptiness and the history of Nalanda worked to clear the gloom from my mind and light the fire of real happiness. I am deeply indebted to his senior tutor, the Venerable Ling Rinpoche, for sealing that fire in the crucible of the Father Tantras, embodying the wisdom of Nagarjuna. I feel enormous affection for Gelek Rinpoche, who gave me a spiritual home and introduced me to the blissful openness of the Mother Tantras, embodying the compassion of Asanga. I'm also truly grateful to Yeshi Donden, for manifesting the incomparable *mandala* of the Medicine Buddha, Lama Anagarika Govinda, for guiding me through the labyrinth of Buddhist psychology, and to Masatoshi Nagatomi and Geshe Losang Jamspal, for offering living examples of pure altruist-scholars.

On my return to medical school, I soon found my way to Herb Benson's lab at Harvard, where I felt my first sense of community in medicine with Joan Borysenko, Ilan Kutz, and Mark Epstein. Thanks to Tom Paolino, I then entered one of the last bastions of psychotherapy training left, at Cambridge

Hospital. There I worked closely with fellow Buddhist psychologist Dan Brown, as well as a full spectrum of great minds from the whole range of analytic and research schools, including Leston Havens, Hal Boris, Al Margulies, Myron Sharaf, Judith Herman, and Bessel Van der Kolk. In my time off, I compared notes with fellow travellers David Sloss, Chris Germer, and Paul Fulton. Of course, I went deepest in my seven years with the iconoclastic Rolf Arvidson, the unconventional Freudian-Jungian-Reichian analyst who for me will always personify the art. This broad and firm foundation in analytic insight therapy was expanded into the realm of deep transformational affect work in another seven years working closely with the super-gifted affect theorist and couples therapist, my dear friend Robert Rosenthal.

As you will see, Buddhist psychology, neuropsychiatry, and psychotherapy did not exhaust the disciplines I would need to draw on to translate the Tibetan arts of role-modeling imagery and affirmation. So I am eternally grateful to the friendship and guidance of my poetry mentors, Mary Karr, Heather McHugh, Marie Howe, and Ellen Bryant-Voigt, as well as my guides through the high peaks and exquisite plains of Tibetan and Sanskrit grammar, the gracious Indira Shetterly, the angelic Losang Jamspal, and the sublime Gary Tubb.

Of course, none of the work of transplanting the practice of the Nalanda tradition would have come to fruition without the excitement and involvement of my colleagues at Nalanda Institute. I'm especially grateful for the vision, encouragement, and energy of my assistant director Miles Neale; the patient rigor of my research director Emily Wolf; and the congeniality of members of both the board and the faculty, Elizabeth Rovere of the New School, and my old friends Ingrid Kemperman and Erin Olivo, leaders in New York's Dialectical Behavior Therapy community. I am grateful for the enduring support of the Zen psychoanalyst Edward Kenny and of yoga faculty member, couples therapist Arthur Greenberg. I've thoroughly enjoyed my collaboration with a key member of our coaching faculty, my good friend Michael McDermott. I thank the Lord Bhairava for another of our yoga faculty, my dear friend Mary Reilly Nichols, who keeps us awake in retreats and uplifts us all as only a true incarnation of Muktananda could.

Nalanda could not have developed as an institution without the informatics wizardry and design genius of Tom Damrauer and Diane Bertolo of Lotus and Pixel, or the organizational genius of Buddhist executive coach Elazar Aslan, non-profit genius Peggy Neu and fearless entrepreneur Brian O'Kelley. For validation of the research behind our comparative scientific translations, I owe a very great debt to the fastidious pioneering work of faculty members William Bushell and Niel Thiese. And finally, I am forever indebted to the director of our textbook project, Rich Kennedy, and our transcribing and editing team including Maria Perez, Yuria Celidwen, Laura Pintchik, John Wencz, and Emily Wolf, for their work developing a Nalanda textbook series which treats each of the four horizons of the Nalanda curriculum in a simple, accessible class dialogue format.

My gratitude list would be far from complete if I left out my many supervisees, clients, and students now and over the years, who daily teach me how deeply necessary this work is and how vital it is to get it just right. Also I want to thank the many friends who've freely shared their enthusiasm and expertise as formal or informal advisors, including Dan Goleman, Vasant Lad, Jon Kabat-Zinn, Mary Pearl, Jeff Walker, Beth Dembitzer, Randy Glatt, Mary Esbjornson, Richard and Andrea Tomasetti, Sander Tideman, Anders Fergusson, Jennifer McCrea, and Peter Miscovitch. I am deeply grateful for the circle of congenial teachers and guides who inspire me to keep learning, growing and changing, including Sharon Salzberg, Mark Epstein, Chris Germer, Paul Fulton, Jeffery Rubin, Pilar Jennings, Richard Brown, Patricia Gerbarg, and Diane Fosha. And last but not least, this book would not have been possible without the pioneers who have helped create the new scientific disciplines on which our translation depends, including Dan Siegel, Richie Davidson, Stephen Porges, Bruce McEwan, and Bessel van der Kolk.

This book would not have seen the light of day without my close friend and colleague, Miles Neale, who introduced me to my editor Anna Moore. Anna instantly saw the potential of making the Nalanda tradition accessible, quietly marshalled the book through the Routledge review process, and patiently tolerated my quirks as a writer. I also want to thank Lynn Nesbit for her generous support, especially for connecting me with her daughter, Priscilla Gilman, who put her genius as a writer and her skills as a literature professor together with her publishing savvy to find the best home for *Sustainable Happiness.* In addition, I am deeply appreciative of the generous encouragement and discerning eye of Ted Arnold, who served as my first reader and editor for the manuscript; and truly grateful for the generous feedback of my second readers, Adrienne Jamiel and Annette Barbasch. And I also thank Tom Damrauer and Diane Bertolo for their extraordinary work locating, acquiring, creating and editing all of the images, line drawings and diagrams in the book, including the artwork of Andy Weber.

Finally, I owe much if not all my lasting happiness in this life to my wife, Gerardine Hearne Loizzo, my partner in all things, including the development of Nalanda Institute and the writing of *Sustainable Happiness.* More than my Gemlike Yogini, I celebrate Geri's loving role as the mother-goddess to our two most challenging and adorable teachers, our sons Maitreya Dante and Ananda Rowan. As for our sons, I'm deeply grateful that they were born just in time to know their grandma Carmela's love, and that they recognize Serkhong Rinpoche as "the real Yoda," the model for the 900-year-old Jedi Master in George Lucas's *Star Wars.*

Before we embark on our journey together, I should add a few technical notes for my professional colleagues and non-scholarly readers. Fellow scholars will notice that I've refrained from leaving technical terms of any kind in Sanskrit or Tibetan in the text, and for the sake of non-scholarly readers, have omitted Sanskrit diacriticals and phonetically transcribed the names and few terms left untranslated, such as "Shakyamuni" and "*chakra.*" For your convenience I've included a glossary of key technical terms, listing the Sanskrit and Tibetan terms alongside the English translation you'll find in the text. I've also found it necessary to translate technical terms left in Sanskrit in passages cited from scholarly translations, and have very rarely substituted my translations for another translator's in passages where the conflicting terms would confuse, following the system found in the glossary. I've adapted these scholarly conventions in this context solely for the sake of reducing the learning curve imposed on non-scholarly readers. Wherever possible, in offering my own translations of selected verses or passages, I've cited the passage in the source language in a footnote, unless my translation has been previously published.

My scientific and clinical colleagues will notice that I've referenced a great deal of evidence to support the translations and interpretations I suggest in the book, including journal articles from a broad range of fields as well as books that review or interpret original research. Whenever possible, I've referenced prior review articles of mine which survey broad areas of research or interpretation, all of which can be downloaded from the resource library of the Nalanda Institute website. Finally, although I included case vignettes in each chapter in early drafts, they had to be edited out of the final manuscript to make room to clearly and concisely present the ideas and methods at hand. Hopefully, these vignettes will appear in a later manual on clinical practice of the four systems of guided self-analysis and self-healing combined in this comprehensive curriculum. On the other hand, I have kept most of the guided meditations I offer as experiments to help readers practically engage the material, following the experiential learning methods of the Buddhist scientific tradition. These can obviously be skipped by readers who prefer a mainly cognitive learning experience, although I strongly encourage trying at least some of the experiments. If listening to audio guided meditations might work better, these can also be downloaded from the resource library of the *Nalanda Institute* website.

Of course, if despite the guidance and help of all my mentors and friends, there remain any errors or omissions, I take full responsibility for them. May my kind mentors, inseparable from *Sheer Brilliance*, protect me! And may any merit or intuition that comes of writing and offering *Sustainable Happiness* help open the eyes and melt the hearts of all beings through the furthest reaches of space and time.

I've dedicated this book to an unlikely couple—Grandma Carmela and Lama Serkong—in part because a chance encounter between them has forever embodied for me the happy confluence of cultures I hope you'll find in this book. Detoured by a late landing at JFK on his first trip to the Americas, Serkong chose to stay at my mom's nearby home rather than drive straight to Woodstock. As they met on the front stoop, I was shocked to see tears run down Rinpoche's cheek, as if he was reuniting with his own long lost sister or mother. In the same breath as he stopped to wipe his tears, holding my mother's eyes in his smiling gaze, he reached out his hand to stroke her cheek, bringing her to tears and sending chills up my spine. In that moment I felt—and still feel, thanks to Serkong—our blue-green world, my mom's grieving family, and my whole body-mind, somehow dissolved into one clear drop of human kindness.

If it's true, as the great process adepts of India and Tibet often say, that the open word-matter and great inspiration of unwavering bliss hide like a jewel in the palms of all our hands, then, in the words of another lover of negative capability, John Keats, I offer *this* book as a *living hand—see, here it is—I hold it towards you.*

September 12, 2011
The Cliff Haven
Riverside Drive
Manhattan, New York

Introduction

Recent Breakthroughs, Timeless Methods

> And now, I think, the meaning of the evolution of civilization is no longer obscure to us. It must present the struggle between Eros and Death, between the instinct of life and the instinct of destruction, as it works itself out in the human species.
>
> (Sigmund Freud, *Civilization and its Discontents*[1])

Our Global Challenge: Lasting Happiness, One Heart at a Time

At the dawn of a new millennium, the twenty-first century has brought us face to face with the awesome challenge and promise of a new, global age. In healthcare, the economy, the environment, and daily life, we and our fellow citizens the world over are caught in the grips of a crisis of global scale and inexorable scope that seems to threaten not just our dreams but our whole way of life. The problems we face as individuals, societies, and as a planet seem so complex and intertwined that the old adage, "In crisis lies opportunity," seems hollow to many right now. Is there a thread that ties together the runaway cost of healthcare, the epidemic rise of obesity and school violence, the bursting of the latest financial bubble, and the present dangers of terrorism and global warming? If the challenges before us have no obvious precedent in our lifetimes or those of our forebears, where do we turn to find our way?

As a physician and psychotherapist, I see something similar to today's global crisis on the individual scale every time someone new comes to me with their hopes dashed by a life-threatening illness, a heart-wrenching divorce, or a career dead-end. I specialize in meditative maps and tools that help people find ways to heal, grow, and change, just when their lives seem to be falling apart. My work is to teach the insights and skills they need to clear a path through their trauma towards a new way of being. Time and again, I've seen people gradually arrive at a new way of life better than any they've known or could have dreamed possible. At historic points like these, when the whole world seems to be on the verge of a global meltdown, I feel incredibly lucky to have over twenty years of such uplifting experience to fall back on; twenty years and a thousand stories that have given me an unshakable confidence in the truly boundless potential we human beings have to heal ourselves and transform our lives.

I've written *Sustainable Happiness* as a crash course of sorts, meant to introduce a broader audience to what I believe may be humanity's most complete and systematic approach to finding optimal health and lasting happiness in complex lives like ours. It makes accessible the healing insights, skills, and life-strategies I use to help individuals navigate cataclysmic change, in the awareness that the global solutions we need today must begin and end with solutions on the human scale: one mind, one heart, one life at a time. The book answers two questions that were once issues just for the few, but are now everyone's daily business. "Is lasting happiness possible in an age of shrinking resources, growing interdependence, and inexorable human limits?" "Is there a reliable way anyone and everyone on this shrinking planet can reach and sustain such true happiness?" This book gives affirmative answers, based on my life's work integrating the latest science of human life and well-being with a science almost as old as history itself.

The new science I explain here is actually the convergence of several promising lines of research around a single hub: a surprisingly hopeful new view of humans and our environment as naturally prepared to exist in stable harmony and interdependence. The new brain science, new views of human evolution, research on stress and the benefits of meditation, the new behavioral economics, and the complex science of global sustainability have begun to come together like the pieces of a world puzzle that promises to provide a clear map of where we've gone wrong and what needs to change. The difficulty with this puzzle is that there is still no clear consensus on exactly how the pieces come together, much less on how to read and apply the new perspective to chart a course-correction for our personal lives and for civilization as a whole.

Back to the Future: The Time-Machine of Indic Contemplative Science

Fortunately for us all, the last decades have introduced us to more than one kind of new science. Although we moderns have lost touch with our own traditional wisdom and life arts, growing access to the cultures of India, East Asia, and Tibet has opened a whole new route to ancient traditions of contemplative science that anticipated in startling detail the new view of human nature and happiness we have only recently stumbled upon in the West. While these timeless sciences differ from ours in their language and methods, their surprising agreement with our latest breakthroughs lends support to our new science, while also offering a time-machine of sorts that allows us to glimpse what it might look like centuries from now. Those of us who have been lucky enough to take that time machine into the future by studying the precocious sciences of classical India and modern Tibet have been able to bring to the current crisis of health and happiness the perspective and technical mastery that normally comes of centuries of gradual advancement. My senior colleagues in this journey, Herbert Benson, Jon Kabat-Zinn, Daniel Goleman, and Marsha Linehan, have translated the most basic insights and skills of India's contemplative science into the young disciplines of mind/body medicine,[2] mindfulness-based psychotherapy,[3] and emotional intelligence.[4]

In this book I share the fruits of my own time-travel: a program in sustainable living that integrates the emerging new science of human happiness with a rare Indic tradition of contemplative science that holds enormous promise for us all. Although all the first civilizations from Greece to China shared a fascination with contemplative states, it was India that made contemplation into a science and healing art. Of all human cultures, India long ago foresaw the need for teaching the art of contemplative living not just to spiritual elites but to average people of all inclinations, backgrounds, and walks of life. This is why ancient Indian practices like yoga and mindfulness meditation have gone mainstream so quickly in the West. Fortunately for us all, these now popular practices represent only the first installment from the vast time-capsule of the world's most complete and accessible systems of contemplative living and learning. While my colleagues have focused on skills like mindfulness, developed for monastic living, my work and this book are based on an exceptional tradition tailored to lay students facing the challenges of everyday life in the world. This tradition evolved at Nalanda, a world-renowned teaching center in North India that hosted the world's first university a millennium before the first universities in the West, open to all students: secular and religious, lay and professional, national and international.[5]

Over time, Nalanda's masters combined the most effective meditation skills, healing insights and life strategies into a step-by-step system of lifelong self-healing called the gradual path.[6] Before Nalanda was destroyed by invaders, this unique system was fully transplanted into Tibet, where it thrived for centuries. Because Tibet was so isolated until the Chinese forced the Dalai Lama and others to flee in 1959, this world class approach to self-healing has come to our attention only in recent years. Prophetically, the most modern form of this rare tradition is called the *Time Machine* or *Wheel of Time*.[7] According to legend, the art and science of the *Wheel of Time* have been preserved in a time-capsule: the mountain kingdom hidden in Central Asia called Shambhala (depicted as Shangrila in the classic film *Lost Horizons*). To prime your imagination, see the image of the *Wheel of Time* in the color insert, the main figure framed by its living role-model, the Dalai Lama, and flanking Shambhala rulers Manju Yashas and Rudra Chakri (above), as well as by twin protective archetytpes, the *Fierce Mother* and *Diamond Thunderbolt* (below). As the prophecy goes, the crown jewel of the kingdom, its system for teaching contemplative life in a world torn by stress, trauma, and violence, will help spark the dawn of a new global era of inner and outer peace for all humanity when the world is ready. The program spelled out in *Sustainable Happiness* is the fruit of decades of work distilling the essentials of this unique system of contemplative living into a form that is both accessible and effective for contemporary minds and lives.

An Ancient Wisdom More Modern than Modern Science

At the heart of this program is the *Wheel of Time's* vision of the future of human science and civilization, based on surprisingly current views of our inner and outer environments. Anticipating the breakthroughs of quantum physics and systems theory, the natural science of the *Wheel of Time* views the world around us as a cosmic clockwork, in which all things and events unfold in harmonic waves of total, mutual interdependence. Anticipating the breakthroughs of social evolution and the mind/body connection, the life science of the *Wheel of Time* views humanity as inseparable from nature, and as thriving in personal and social harmony through the cohesive forces of inner peace and loving interdependence. Based on this scientific vision, the *Wheel of Time* views the progress of human individuals and societies as guided and advanced by a timeless, contemplative science that teaches all humans how to adapt our body, speech, mind, and intuition to the future of global interdependence. The keys to this science are the meditative skills, insights and life-strategies that help us tame the biology of stress and the psychology of trauma which block our instincts for peaceful living and civilized happiness. These keys are the very insights and arts that have been tailored to the demands of everyday life in the gradual path teachings I've woven into the program presented in this book.

While the *Wheel of Time's* vision for our planet sounds refreshingly hopeful, is it realistic or just wishful thinking? Does it really square with what modern science has taught us about the nature of reality and human potential? In struggling with this question over the years, I arrived at a conclusion that initially hit me with the disorienting force of a culture shock. After decades of following breaking developments in seemingly unrelated frontiers of science, it began to dawn on me that much of the science I'd learned in grade school, college, and medical school was already outdated. As the pieces of the new frontier science began to fit together, a decidedly different view of nature and life began to emerge. I began to realize that what I'd been taught was not just science, but science woven into a cultural view of the world based on assumptions that were now centuries old. The view that our world is made of atoms in a void, and is nothing like mind, came as much from the philosophy of Aristotle and Democritus as it did from the discoveries of Galileo and Newton. The view of nature as hostile to life, as a place where beings evolve accidentally and thrive only by constant struggle came as much from the philosophy of Epicurius and Lucretius as it did from the discoveries of Darwin. And finally, the view of human history and society as a war of all against all, a competition for scarce resources which only the most aggressive and self-seeking win, grows as much from the philosophy of Gorgias and Hobbes as it does out of the "classical" economics of Malthus and Adam Smith. Woven together into a fabric that was part science, part philosophy, these views painted a picture of the world as made of atomic bits of matter and life, all forced to collide into one another with a violence more likely to cause mutual destruction than stable bonding.

Enter the new science of the last half century. Quantum physics gives us a world in which matter is made of energy and space, more intangible by far than the stuff dreams are made of.[8] Sociobiology and neuroscience provide a new picture of evolution and development, as intricate, living webs of interdependence and social connectivity.[9] And social ecology and behavioral economics give us the imperative that humanity must progress towards a sustainable future that can support the global pursuit of happiness.[10] Woven together into a fabric that is part science, part futuristic vision, these views paint a picture of the world as made of waves of energy and life that we all must learn to conserve and cultivate. So the bottom line is this: the teachings of the *Wheel of Time* can look like wishful thinking or visionary science depending on the lens through which we read them. If we choose the science that shaped our parents' and teachers' view of the world as a lens, the *Wheel of Time* will read like a fable straight out of *Alice in Wonderland*. But if we use the mind-expanding science of the twenty-first century as a lens, the *Wheel of Time* reads like an encyclopedia of science for the next generation, brought back from the future by time machine.

Even assuming that the *Wheel of Time's* optimism is closer to current research than the science most of us learned in school, we naturally wonder, "Can such an ancient, contemplative vision truly be relevant to our technological culture and complex way of life?" The answer to this question lies in another question. How do we understand the demands that make our lives feel so stressful and our future so uncertain? As part of our modern view of history, most of us attribute the predicament we're in today to what's happened in the last few decades, if not the last few hours or minutes. Our modern faith in progress teaches us not to look further back into the past, but to dismiss as irrelevant most if not all of what humanity has confronted and learned in the course of its history. We attribute the stress in our lives to a recent health challenge, a setback at work, or conflict in a primary relationship. If we're really stretching, we may point to our iPhone or Blackberry, the recent financial crisis, global outsourcing, or larger concerns like terrorism and the environment—all things that have never happened before in human history. Yet such common complaints barely scratch the surface of our predicament. In effect, they confuse what *triggers* stress with its root causes.

We now know that the overwhelming majority of the harm done by stress is not directly caused by external events, but by the internal cascade of responses those events can trigger in our minds and bodies.[11] It doesn't take a laboratory to prove this. Experience teaches us that one man's stress is another's passion; and that what stresses us royally today may roll off our back tomorrow. So what is it in us that takes the bait of a trigger and gets us trapped in a heart-pounding nightmare of self-defeating fear, rage or shame? In most cases, what gets us to take the bait is our ingrained habit of worst-case thinking, backed up by memories of prior trauma; and what gets us trapped in reliving those traumas is the biology of the stress response, a self-protective reflex pre-programmed into the oldest, reptilian part of our brains.

In the chapters that follow, we will explore the psychology and biology of these internal forces, along with the contemplative insights and skills we need to master them. For now, I mention them to underscore a point. The root causes of the all-too common feeling we have that our lives are overwhelming and unmanageable are not the latest gadgetry and complexities of our age, but certain elements of our nature that reach beyond the dawn of civilization, beyond the birth of humanity, almost as far back as the origins of life on earth. Viewed in light of the natural history of these causes, the recorded history of civilization is less than an eye-blink. This is why the wisdom of great sages like Socrates, Buddha, Isaiah, Zoroaster, and Confucius, who taught in the so-called axial age when humanity was first turning to civilization, still speaks to us quite directly today. And this is why the Buddha's diagnosis and prescription for the human condition, compounded with centuries of refinement into the time-release formula of the *Wheel of Time*, can be as relevant and beneficial here and now as it was in twelfth century India and Tibet.

Life on the Fence: Human Nature in an Unnatural World

What exactly is Shakyamuni Buddha's diagnosis of the human condition? And how do the healing teachings of the Nalanda tradition, preserved in the *Wheel of Time*, provide practical solutions for our predicament today? In light of contemporary biology, the inexorable stresses and strains of the great majority of humans who live in civilization is the result of an evolutionary mismatch. While our early human and pre-human ancestors evolved over hundreds of millions of years to survive in the wild, we and our civilized forbears have increasingly been living in an unnatural environment less than ten thousand years old. As a result, our nature is simply not that well matched to the challenges of our daily lives. The problem is that for almost the entirety of our natural history, we humans and our mammalian ancestors have had to straddle two very different environments. On the one hand, we've had to survive the life-or-death challenges of being part of the food chain and the natural order, always vulnerable to fiercer predators and natural cycles or disasters. On the other hand, as mammals we also evolved to create and thrive in social environments of unnatural safety and abundance, produced as a result of ever-widening circles of ever more intelligent cooperation.

To meet the polar challenges of these two divergent environments, early mammals built on the binary nature of the reptilian brain. One mode of that brain supported the work of survival: seeking out food and shelter, fighting, flying, or freezing in the face of predators or prey. The opposite mode of the reptilian brain supported the work of abundance: resting and digesting, healing and growing, exploring and playing, mating, and tending offspring. The early mammalian brain added an extra layer or cortex that enhanced the complexity, range, and scope of both these binary modes.[12] Enhanced attachment and panic responses allowed our highly vulnerable yet collaborative mammal ancestors to engage others in the work of survival. Enhanced capacities for empathy and communication allowed our highly sociable and teachable mammal ancestors to engage others in nurturing the young, social learning and play. Further enhancements along the same lines were made possible by the evolution of another layer, the new cortex, in higher mammals like our primate ancestors. Yet throughout the entire fifty million years of their evolution, except for the eye-blink of the last several thousand years of human history, our mammalian ancestors had to be ready to turn on a predator's growl or a sudden windfall from one mode to the other.

Not surprisingly, then, our nature remains perpetually on the fence, ever alert to the shifting winds of survival or abundance. Meanwhile, the rise of complex social systems, animal husbandry, and sustainable agriculture finally tipped the primeval balance of life in the wild towards the advent of civilization. Increasingly over the last ten millennia, humans have lived in an environment that was more and more artificial, less and less natural. By the time of the axial age, around five hundred years before the common era, advances in agriculture and social organization had created unprecedented and unnatural conditions of more or less continuous security and abundance. This was especially true for those living in the first city-states around the great river valleys of Eurasia.[13] Humanity quickly rose to the top of the food chain, making the survival mode and its primitive fight-flight responses all but obsolete. Finally, civilized living gave free reign to the abundance mode, supporting the lifelong development and fullest use of humanity's incomparably social and creative brain.

Yet, as humanity experienced this revolutionary change for the better in its average expected living environment, human nature didn't change one *iota*. We humans have remained on the fence, ever on the look-out for the next life-threatening predator or disaster. And since human ingenuity tamed one predator, one force of nature after another, we turned our fear, rage, and shame onto ourselves and projected them onto other members of our own species. Enhanced by our powerful brains, something as artificial and arbitrary as a deadline can easily be mistaken for a death-threat, triggering our traumatic memories of childhood helplessness, which in turn trigger the mindless reflex of the stress-response.[14]

This would all be just a nightmare were it not for the fact that, under perceived life or death stress, the reptilian brain prepares us to face the physical threat of a predator by overriding and shutting down the mammalian brain. Tragically, this reptilian override shuts down not just bells and whistles but precisely those higher faculties we need to navigate the complex social stresses of civilized life. So it is that our binary nature keeps us feeling perpetually on edge, leaving our higher mammalian brain ever vulnerable to being hijacked by our own inner reptile, like a dinosaur stomping through the china shop of our daily lives. To make matters worse, the damage done by our inner dinosaur can pile up. If our time spent hijacked by stress outweighs our time recharging in abundance mode, the wear and tear literally eats away at us from within. Over time, our natural systems of immunity, healing, learning, and collaboration erode, predisposing us to what some call the diseases of civilization: addiction, obesity, heart disease, cancer, anxiety, and depression, not to mention compulsive behaviors like boom-and-bust risk taking, compulsive hoarding, and explosive violence.[15]

The on-the-fence syndrome of civilized humanity largely explains why smart, able people living in unprecedented leisure and opportunity can still feel and react like cornered animals so much of the time. And there's one more rub. The trouble caused by the mismatch between our binary nature and our unnatural lifestyle is aggravated by the self-protective bias evolution has pre-programmed into our nervous system. Given this bias, the aversive conditioning of stress and trauma seems to have a greater grip on our mindset and responses than the positive reinforcement of security and happiness.[16] Of course, this makes good intuitive sense. As a fail-safe, it's more crucial to our survival that we cling to the memory of any remotely life-threatening event than that we recall even the most abundant windfall. As a result of this bias, it takes an unwavering certainty and many decisive acts of will to get us off the fence, to unequivocally let go of our inner dinosaur and choose instead to live in sustainable abundance as totally committed mammals.

An Endless Web with One Root: The Fractal Logic of Our Discontent

Is it really possible for one evolutionary mismatch to cause the many, seemingly unrelated problems that make up our current global crisis? The idea runs counter to the analytic logic of modern science and medicine. This logic teaches us to look for the origins of problems—and hence their solution—by isolating problems and reducing their elements to the minutest particulars. This is the logic that seeks to reveal the mysteries of the universe by smashing atoms into more and more ungraspable fragments and searching through them for an "elementary particle" or "fundamental structure" of matter. It is the logic that seeks to unravel the intricacies of life by reducing complex living systems to the molecular blueprint of DNA. And it is also the logic that seeks to diagnose and treat all illnesses, physical, mental, behavioral, and environmental, by reducing them to the molecular level of biochemistry and eventually to single genes. At the heart of this logic we recognize the atomistic assumptions of the paradigm of modern science we inherited from the likes of Galileo, Newton, and Darwin.

In stark contrast to this approach is the new paradigm of interdependence, weaving together quantum physics, systems biology, ecology, and medical anthropology with current research in physiology, neuroscience, and functional medicine.[17] Representative of this paradigm is the new science of stress, inflammation and neuroimmunology, which seeks to understand illness and health by mapping complex interactions that coordinate all body systems in response to the challenges of an individual's changing mindset, behavior, and lifestyle.[18] This new science has clarified linkages between disorders long thought to be quite distinct, from atherosclerosis and obesity to cancer and autoimmune syndromes.[19] In the realm of neuropsychology, researchers have mapped most of the disorders in modern psychiatry—from anxiety and depression to addiction, post-traumatic stress, and even schizophrenia—along a spectrum of progressive wear and tear caused by the brain's chronic exposure to the corrosive effects of stress hormones and inflammatory cytokines.[20]

Finally, the findings of mind/body medicine, the latest research on violence, and the emerging field of neuroeconomics allow us to extend this web of linkages to public health epidemics like obesity, domestic abuse, and school violence, as well as global crises like our boom-and-bust markets, international terrorism and global warming, tying them all to one root: the neuropsychology of stress and trauma.[21] These linkages should not be surprising when we consider that stress and trauma affect the whole organism, mind and body; and that, since we are such social animals, the stress and trauma of relationships—between individuals and between social groups—is hands down the single greatest source of stress affecting humanity. Since understanding these linkages is crucial, we will examine them in more depth in the chapters that follow. I mention them here to help dispel the skepticism with which we tend to view any approach that tackles problems by connecting the dots or fleshing out the big picture of our lives and world. The fact that contemporary research is inexorably heading towards a big picture very much like the one drawn by ancient contemplative science should help reassure us that that ancient science may well help us see the forest for the tress, despite its exotic origins.

The Global Legacy of Shakyamuni, Our Luckiest Sage

So it is that my colleagues and I have increasingly begun to turn for ideas and tools to humanity's timeless contemplative traditions and the civilizing wisdom of the axial age. From time immemorial, human spiritual traditions around the world have taught our ancestors the importance of choosing our abundance instincts for peace, care, and love over survival instincts for fear, rage, and shame. Born in the cradles of civilization, the great sages saw its rise and spread as the inevitable future for all humanity. Enlightened by that vision, they tried in various ways to prepare their students to fully adapt to civilized living, teaching people to cut through instinctive confusion and disarm the destructive emotions that fuel stress and trauma. Since the secular mainstream of the modern West has steadily drifted further and further from that ancient vision, it not only has fallen prey to the corrosive effects of stress and violence, but also has tragically lost the civilizing wisdom and arts of its own contemplative traditions. Fortunately for us all, other cultures have carefully preserved and refined the teachings of the axial age. The luckiest and most successful of humanity's ancient sages was Shakyamuni, the sage of the Shakya clan, also known as Buddha, meaning someone awakened or enlightened.

Unlike his contemporaries elsewhere in the world, Shakyamuni had the benefit of access to India's yogic contemplative arts as well as the support of a wealthy, tolerant, and enlightened community that embraced him and his teachings. After six years of meditating in the wilderness, the former prince realized he had personally ended the repetitive cycle of senseless suffering that plagued his people and all humanity. His first public teaching of four noble truths diagnosed the human condition as one of mindless, self-destructive compulsion, caused by a cycle of repetitive, traumatic actions and reactions, rooted in our instinctive confusion and destructive emotions.[22] In the optimistic conviction that all of us have the potential to end this cycle and cut its roots, he taught a way to heal our traumatic condition and to re-learn how to live in peace, care, and love.

Shakyamuni believed that we humans, along with our animal ancestors, are endowed with two kinds of instincts between which we must choose: violent self-protective instincts that drive traumatic development and compulsive life; and non-violent, self-transcendent instincts that foster peaceful development and benevolent life. In the course of his enlightenment, he came to see the natural history of his own self-transcendence as a series of many lives in which his prior incarnations, both human and mammal, chose to respond to life-or-death challenges by renouncing violent reactions in favor of peaceful acts of compassion and altruism. The way he taught was a path of self-healing powered by the liberating forces of wisdom, contemplation, and ethics. Working in synergy, the healing disciplines he prescribed foster the self-knowledge, will-power, and self-mastery that enable ordinary humans to take the decisive actions needed to cut our ties to our violent memories and instincts, and to commit to the peaceful, benevolent side of our nature, one breath at a time.

So it is that, as strange as it seems, the great sage of ancient India, along with his colleagues in China and Greece, arrived at a diagnosis and treatment of the clash between our ambivalent nature and civilized life long before modern sages like Freud or the new science of stress and trauma. Fortunately for us all, Shakyamuni was far luckier and more successful at implementing his healing message for humanity than his contemporaries to the East and West. Privileged by his royal birth and sheltered by the exceptional security, wealth and tolerance of the city-states of North India, Shakyamuni was free to teach for fifty years until his natural death at eighty-four, and was widely supported in his efforts to found and refine his own teaching community.

As a result of Shakyamuni's good fortune, after his death, the influence of his teaching and community steadily grew.[23] Its spread was due in part to the recognition and help of the first emperor of India, Ashoka, who was India's Julius Caesar and Constantine rolled into one.[24] Unlike the Socratic academy in the West, the Buddhist academy was never forced into decline by India's political or religious elites, but reached out to educate people of all races, genders, and classes in the Buddha's civilizing science of contemplative living. While the West fell into a "dark age," Buddhist India rose to its place as a world beacon of enlightenment, exemplified by the fifteen hundred year history of the great university of Nalanda.

Far from being repressed, the classical wisdom of Shakyamuni was developed and refined at Nalanda into a science of contemplative living and sustainable civilization that profoundly changed the course of mainstream science, political economy, and spirituality in India.[25] In fact, Buddhist contemplative science and civilization became India's single most important contribution to world history, as visiting scholars from China, Japan, Korea, Burma, Thailand, Indonesia, and Tibet came to Nalanda for new insights, methods, texts, and expertise to help guide their cultures of origin. Among the latest societies to import this tradition, Tibet is unique in that it preserved the final, most complete version of Nalanda's curriculum. Among the least developed societies to integrate Indian Buddhism, Tibet was also free to incorporate this tradition in its entirety, as a blueprint for the world's greatest experiment in non-violent civilization. So, despite centuries of isolation from the ancient river valley centers, the contemplative science of Tibet is not only among the world's oldest and most continuous wisdom traditions, but is also one of the most universal, comprehensive, and scientific.

On the Way to Contemplative Science: De-Polarizing the Modern Mind

In the course of sharing the fruits of this rare tradition with a broad range of individuals and groups, over the years I've encountered in others the same mental blocks to understanding Indic contemplative science I've had to overcome in myself. So before I introduce the logic and format of *Sustainable Happiness*, it may help if I share what I've learned about the preconceptions that keep the Western educated mind from fully integrating insights and arts that come from a culture so far removed from ours in place and time. In my experience, these preconceptions cluster in two polar mindsets that have diverged increasingly in the West since the Renaissance and Enlightenment eras. These polar mindsets stem from the rivalry between the secular and spiritual faces of Western culture, based on modern science and the Judeo-Christian religious tradition. For convenience, I call these "materialism" and "romanticism." In most Western educated minds, as in Western culture itself, these two conflicting outlooks coexist in a complex tension a biologist might call "symbiosis," and a psychologist, "hostile dependence."

Our materialist mindset tells us that science is all about objective, physical facts, which can only be known by eliminating, as much as possible, the subjective element of human language, culture, and experience. It tells us that life evolved from the mutation and selection of various forms of DNA, and that the diversity of bodies and minds emerge mechanically from these forms. This mindset pictures the origin of life in a way that makes conscious intentions and actions appear to have had little or no real impact on the course of evolution and development. It tells us that nature pits each individual and species in a struggle for scarce resources against all other life, a struggle which only the fittest—those with the fiercest mix of brute force and self-interested cunning—survive. And finally, it tells us that human cultures—with all their diverse ways of knowing and living—are likewise engaged in a process of evolution in which the most modern are necessarily the most advanced, and in which greater material wealth and power is the final arbiter of cultural superiority or progress.

On the flip side of our hybrid worldview is the romantic mindset. This mindset tells us that physical science is in conflict with ultimate truths and moral values that are eternal and independent of nature and nature's laws. It tells us that humanity is the only form of life with an eternal soul, created with a purpose by a divine mind or spirit whose absolute knowledge and will ultimately decide the fate of all individuals and groups. It tells us that human societies are the reflection of a divine community governed by eternal values revealed by God, values not subject to human understanding or alteration. And it tells us that human culture and history are involved in a process of inexorable decline from a golden age of revelation, a process in which only those cultures that follow the letter and spirit of that revelation without innovation will be spared decline, to triumph in the end.

The relevance of these two mindsets for those interested in learning from the contemplative science of India and Tibet is clear. Despite the point by point polarity of their preconceptions, both our materialist and romantic mindsets share a tacit agreement on one deeply held conviction: there is no viable way to bridge the gulf between modern science and humanity's ancient spiritual traditions. So the very idea of a "science" that is "contemplative"—that employs reflective or meditative techniques drawn from human spiritual traditions—strikes both our mindsets as doubtful at best, and at worst as an oxymoron or contradiction in terms.[26] Our materialist premise that science applies only to physical facts and not to the mind, makes the idea of understanding and mastering our lives with the aid of meditation sound subjective, even spiritual, rather than truly scientific. On the other hand, our romantic idea of meditation as a sacred means of knowing God, not a pragmatic discipline of self-knowledge or self-mastery, makes the idea of understanding and changing our lives with its aid sound secular and mundane, rather than truly contemplative.

Not surprisingly, things look quite different from the standpoint of the Indian and Tibetan traditions. Since Indian science and spirituality, while always distinct, never diverged as radically as they did in the West, the idea of a convergence of science and contemplation seems so commonsensical from the Indic perspective that using meditation as a tool in medicine, psychological self-healing, and education seems like a no-brainer. Similar culture clashes appear when Western educated people are first exposed to the views of life, society, and history assumed as givens by Indian and Tibetan contemplative science. The fact that such doubts occur so predictably to the Western schooled mind yet seem odd or extreme to those schooled in the Indic traditions led me to look into why we in the West have evolved such polarized views of science and contemplation. As I see it, there are two contemporary disciplines which can help shed the most light on this question: psychotherapy and mind/body medicine. Among them, I find psychotherapy most helpful, since I believe its insights and methods offer the closest cross-cultural match with the contemplative science of Buddhist India and Tibet.

Psychotherapy and Contemplative Science: The Future of Civilized Happiness

Given the complex, global nature of our present crisis, a natural reference point for our look at the relations between science and contemplation in the West is the "new science" of Sigmund Freud. I opened this introduction with a quote from *Civilization and its Discontents*, the classic in which Freud applied all he'd learned about our human nature and potential to humanity's first global crisis, ushered in by the unprecedented violence of the first and second world wars. Anticipating the insights of recent science and reaffirming the wisdom of humanity's ancient sages, the father of psychoanalysis traced the crisis of his day to the mismatch between our binary human nature and the social-emotional challenge of civilized living. His depiction of the evolution of civilization as "*the struggle between Eros and Death, between the instinct of life and the instinct of destruction, as it works itself out in the human species,*" dovetails quite neatly with the diagnosis of the human condition shared by contemporary biology and Buddhist contemplative science. And although his prognosis is more guarded, the treatment he prescribed also shares a deep resonance with current mind/body medicine and with traditional Buddhist psychology.

Kin Under the Skin: Deep Resemblances Between Psychotherapy & Buddhism

From a global perspective on civilization, if we consider all human cultural traditions as part of one extended family, and link them not by the surface criteria of cultural history but by more deeply shared aims, insights, and methods—by their cultural DNA so to speak—I believe that we find something surprising about the traditions I align in this book. The resemblances many of my peers have observed between contemporary psychotherapy or mind/body medicine and ancient disciplines like the contemplative arts and sciences of India and Tibet are not superficial but deep. They reflect a commonality as deep in us as the roots of our ways of life: our simplest daily needs and activities.

Like other mammals, we all seek happiness; we want to live well. We each have minds and bodies for which we must care; and we all have relationships about which we care. More than any other creatures, even other mammals, we humans learn to live well—to care well for ourselves and others—in and through intimate bonds with others of our kind. In fact, we cannot learn to live much at all as humans without such bonds. Yet unlike most modern disciplines and relationships, those in which we learn to live well do not divide us—matter from spirit, thought from experience, reflection from action—but teach us to care by caring for us as we are, as whole living beings.[27] That means that they care for us in body *and* mind, speech *and* reflection, experience *and* action.

Given the way we are, it should not be surprising that most, if not all human cultures have evolved disciplines and bonds devoted mainly to helping individuals and groups learn to live well. This is why, when we get beyond our own cultural resistances to comparing these distinct traditions, we find not only striking similarities in aims and methods, but deep and pervasive family resemblances even in the working details of theory and practice. And these deep resemblances help explain why, despite the exceptional role both psychotherapy and Buddhist psychology play in conventional science and medicine today, they are both very much in demand among professionals and in the larger universe of contemporary culture and life.

As for the confluence of psychotherapy and Buddhism, so much fine work has been done in this fast-growing field by so many close colleagues and friends—Mark Epstein,[28] Jeremy Saffran,[29] Chris Germer and Paul Fulton,[30] Jeffery Rubin,[31] Pilar Jennings[32]—that we need only review a few key points here. Of course, most of their groundbreaking work has focused on the deep synergy between mindfulness meditation and the free-associative method of psychotherapy. Given my own approach to this work—as one who combines contemplative teaching with contemplative therapy, and draws on the modern science of Tibet as well as the classical science of mindfulness—I see this confluence through a wider than usual lens.

Where most of my colleagues tend to view psychotherapy and Buddhist psychology as two complementary healing techniques, from the vantage of my interdisciplinary work, they appear to me more broadly as two complementary science-based ways of seeing and transforming human life. Specifically, beneath the surface historical and cultural differences, I see the two sister traditions deeply related by their common effort to see and treat the human condition from the perspective of the life-shaping power of the embodied mind. In particular, these sibling traditions are deeply aligned not just in the fact that they take a primarily psychological approach to the world, but also specifically because they both share an approach to the mind that is deeply scientific, evolutionary, and therapeutic. A quick glance at the three key elements of theory and practice that earmark these two approaches to the mind will help us see them as intimate human cultural relatives under the skin.

First, what distinguishes these two as scientific psychologies is their shared commitment to mental causality. That is, the assumption that mind works not by personal forces like will—whether it be the will of the self or of God—but rather by impersonal forces of cause and effect, distinct from but as natural as the forces at work in the physical world. Second, what distinguishes them as evolutionary psychologies is their shared commitment to a naturalistic, multi-life view of the origin, development, and potential of the human body and mind, a view that stresses the interaction of nature and nurture, instinct and learning. Third and last, what makes them both therapeutic psychologies is their shared reliance on a healing pedagogy: an empathic art of replicating the parent-child bond as the natural context for healing childhood trauma and for modeling an adult life of loving and caring human development.

What Goes Around Comes Around: The Necessity of Mental Causation

For modern psychotherapy and Buddhist contemplative science, the assumption that consciousness is governed by a form of causality as natural as the causality of inanimate matter is what earmarks any psychology as scientific, that is: as a truly realistic and effective way for humans to understand and control their own minds. Freud insisted that every activity of the mind had determinate causes and effects that were neither reducible to neural events nor randomly disconnected from them. In so doing, he was taking his new science into a no man's land between our materialist and romantic worldviews, where it would draw fire from both mindsets. The materialist in us tends to see mental events as too flimsy to cause anything, and equates the idea that they have real effects with the Western religious claim that the soul, like God, works in mysterious ways, above and beyond natural law. The romantic in us tends to see the idea that mind and its acts depend on the brain as robbing the mind, spirit, or soul of its autonomy, potential, and power.

Long before Freud, Shakyamuni's first teaching of four noble truths—suffering, origin, freedom, and path—charted a new middle way between science and spirituality. His truths presented human suffering and happiness as the predictable effects of psychological causes, rather than as determined by some divine order or by mindless matter. While most historians of science attribute the insight of causality to the Greek physician Hippocrates, his rough contemporary Shakyamuni deserves equal credit for the breakthrough. Its revolutionary importance was not lost on the Sage's followers, who hail his contribution to this day with a formula that sounds more like a scientific theorem than "the Buddhist creed," as some scholars dubbed it: "All things spring from causes; so the Realized One taught those causes; and how to master them; such is his way! Hail that Great Sage!"[33]

Admittedly, the idea of mental causality is not very sexy; and it doesn't immediately spring to mind when we think of the contributions of psychoanalysis or Buddhist psychology. Yet as a fundamental assumption, it is directly responsible for the most distinctive insights that characterize and link these two diverse traditions. The very term psycho-*analysis* describes the idea that the human psyche is not a fixed unit or whole, as we normally see and feel it to be, but can be easily analyzed into causally related parts. The power of psychoanalysis lies in its ability to help us understand and control the unseen causal forces of instinct and emotion that drive our behavior, much as modern physics and astronomy helped reveal unseen forces that govern how matter moves on earth and in space.

Likewise, the premise of mental causality quietly shaped the way Shakyamuni approached the mind. He and his heirs did not call their psychology

"Buddhist" but described it as "the psychology of selflessness," based on his most profound and revolutionary insight. When the human mind is laid bare by contemplating its causal workings, it is found not to be the fixed, unified whole we imagine, but a complex process of constantly changing systems and elements, including instinctive emotions, sensations, thoughts, and perceptions. The critical insight of selflessness is complemented by the positive theory of dependent origination, which traces the needless suffering of repetitive stress and trauma to a twelve-fold cycle of interactive causes normally unseen within the mind. The power of Buddhist psychology lies in its ability to help us learn to recognize and control the unhealthy elements that drive this cycle so that we can break free of it and cultivate the healthy factors that foster the healing circle of inner peace, freedom, and happiness.[34]

Nature Plus Nurture: The Evolutionary Outlook of Shakyamuni and Freud

A second key element that links psychotherapy and Buddhist contemplative science is their common assumption of an evolutionary outlook, that is: a naturalistic, multi-life view of the origin, development, and potential of the human body and mind. Expanding on Darwin, Freud's psychology is in large part an attempt to give the West a scientific view of the mind based on the theory of natural selection. Out of this basic assumption come two distinctive features of his new science. The first is an emphasis on the role instincts like narcissism, sex, and aggression play in driving and shaping the life of the mind. The second is an emphasis on the way early parent-child interactions catalyze and inform the individual's developing personality and mental life.

Although our current theory of evolution is distinctively Darwin's, many if not most human cultures through history have held some form of the view that humans evolved naturally from and with other animals, rather than being created by God. Mythological symbols of creatures that were part human and part animal—like the Greek Minotaur—attest to the common human wisdom that we share primal instincts with other forms of animal life. Likewise, Freud's notion that the human ego is formed based on the developing mind's instinctive choice of one parent as an object of desire and the other as an object of identification was inspired in part by the myth behind Sophocles' tragedy, *Oedipus Rex*.

So it should come as no shock that the Greeks' Indian contemporaries, Shakyamuni and his heirs, saw human nature in similar terms: as driven by primal narcissism and instinctive emotions inherited from past human and animal lives, stretching back in an unbroken continuum through "beginningless time." Nor should it surprise us that Buddhist psychologists, like their Greek colleagues, viewed human development as an interplay between the physical process begun by the union of egg and sperm and a distinctively mental process. According to tradition, this latter process begins when the nascent consciousness, driven by instinctive narcissism, desire, and aggression, forms a new ego by choosing one parent as a love object and the other as a rival or role-model.[35] While there are major differences in the way modern psychologists and their Buddhist counterparts see human evolution and development, the insight that the life of the mind grows out of the interplay of inherited instincts and patterns with present interactions is clearly fundamental to both these traditions.

The Science of Reparenting: Harnessing the Strong Force of Civilization

The last commonality to consider, a healing pedagogy, has to do with the common assumption psychotherapy and Buddhist psychology make about the best way to alleviate human suffering. Based on their shared view of the interplay between human nature and nurture, both traditions agree that the future of civilized life critically depends on how well we humans learn to care for ourselves and others; and both agree that an art of empathic communication modeled on parent-child bonding is the most natural and effective way to teach people how to reduce stress, heal childhood trauma, and build an adult life based on loving human development. As our lives become increasingly complex, there are fewer and fewer times and places where we can share our personal experience with others as whole human beings, including all our conflicting thoughts, instincts, emotions, and habits. This trend is made worse by the growing gulf between our secular society and the spiritual communities which traditionally helped us through personal distress and crisis.

These factors help explain why psychotherapy has steadily grown in importance as an exception to the rule: as one of the rare contexts in contemporary life, even within modern medicine, where we are accepted and cared for as whole individuals. This is no accident but the fruit of Freud's work crafting the context of "talking therapy" as an improved version of the parent-child bond. In so doing, he encouraged people to bring their unmet childhood wishes and needs into the therapy-bond, transferring them onto the person of the therapist. The challenge of the therapist is to respond to these with greater insight and empathic awareness than the parents, helping the client to overcome childhood traumas and to model a more mature way of being in the world. The way psychotherapy does this is by combining emotional support through the healing bond with two factors that open and challenge the mind: a shared, contemplative state that expands and heightens awareness; and the empathic analysis and insights of the therapist, which challenge the client's self-limiting thoughts, emotions, and actions.

What does this modern medical art of psychotherapy have in common with the spiritual tradition inspired by Shakyamuni and his teaching? We think of spiritual traditions as more intent on *saving* souls than on healing them, and imagine that their methods are limited to indoctrination and ritual. Yet the four noble truths which stand at the bedrock of Shakyamuni's teaching define his primary aim as therapeutic and his method as pedagogical. The truths begin not with some revelation, but with the obvious human condition of senseless suffering: physical and mental as well as spiritual. More to the point, they approach human suffering in a scientific way Shakyamuni and his heirs likened to a physician's diagnosis, etiology, prognosis, and treatment.

This therapeutic approach translated directly into the Buddha's empathic art of teaching. Instead of pronouncing one doctrine supposed to fit all, he responded differently to each of his students, and was renowned for tailoring his insights and advice to their particular inclinations and needs. So the great Sage was said to listen to each student as his only child, and offer various teachings (symbolically numbered at 84,000) like so many medicines for the different forms of suffering that ail people of all kinds. This interpersonal way of teaching is embodied in the very idea of what it means to belong to the Buddha's community, in his day and in ours. Entry into the Buddha's care is said to begin with the act of personally asking for his guidance and advice, an act known as "taking refuge."

As the primary source of reliable guidance, Shakyamuni himself is usually considered the first refuge, while his teachings and the community of others who follow them are the second and third. I say usually because older, more experienced students were also considered reliable guides, and over the centuries after Shakyamuni's death, came to be seen as Buddhas in training or even "second Buddhas." This shift was institutionalized in the Buddhism preserved in Tibet, where personal mentors are added as a fourth refuge, even taking first place because they personally introduce students to the Buddha and other reliable sources. This underscores the importance Shakyamuni and his heirs placed on the teacher-student bond as the gateway and living matrix of all Buddhist healing and learning. Since this bond is modeled on the parent-child bond, those who seek guidance from the Buddhist tradition are seen as engaging in an act of conscious re-parenting, effectively making them "Buddha's child," or "a child of Buddha's family."

Although re-birth and re-parenting are common metaphors in spiritual traditions, the way Shakyamuni and his heirs saw the pedagogic "method of reliance on a healing guide" has far more in common with Socratic teaching or psychotherapy than with spiritual teaching as we conceive it. This is obvious from two pointers Shakyamuni gave to his own students about how best to rely on him and his teaching. The first warns students against unexamined reliance or uncritical faith, urging them to analyze and test in the same way a modern science teacher might: "Just as a goldsmith buys gold, after testing it by melting, cutting and polishing, the wise accept my words after full examination, not just out of faith (in me)."[36] The second warns of the opposite extreme, a self-defeating skepticism that rejects the unfamiliar out of hand, without openly examining or trying it: "Though a man wounded in battle with a doctor at his side might want to ask the name, birth-place, caste and clan of the doctor before accepting treatment, verily he might die before he learns all these things."[37]

So Shakyamuni's healing pedagogy, like Freud's "reeducation," was one which provided a safety and care reminiscent of the parent-child bond, while challenging students with analytic insights that expose unhealthy habits and with contemplative states that unlock and expand the mind. The conventional wisdom handed down to this day by Tibetan teachers epitomizes the Buddha's middle way between healing personal care and contemplative education. Students should heed their mentor's teachings as they would a doctor's instructions, and apply those teachings as the ultimate medicine for their particular form of the human condition. The great Indian master Matrceta summed it up like this: "The Great Sages don't wash away sins with water; they don't heal suffering by laying on hands; they don't transmit their realization to others; but by teaching reality, they set people free."[38]

Psychotherapy and Buddhist Contemplative Science: Apples and Oranges?

Even briefly considering these three shared assumptions—mental causality, evolutionary psychology, and healing pedagogy—may be enough for you to appreciate the deep resemblance in theory and practice linking modern psychotherapy and Buddhist psychology. Yet this introduction would not be complete if I didn't also address the differences that make these traditions equally distinct. Apart from the surface distinctions in cultural origins and history, a quick look at three key differences may help map the divide we must bridge if we wish to open an authentic interchange between these traditions.

First of all, the two traditions differ in their prime institutional base. Where psychotherapy grew out of the modern secular institution of scientific medicine, Buddhist psychology evolved from the ancient spiritual institution of contemplative learning. Second, there is a major cultural divide in their approaches to evolutionary psychology. Where psychotherapy assumes the modern materialist take on evolution advanced by Darwin and his heirs, Buddhist psychology assumes the ancient ethical take on evolution formulated in the Buddha's theory of *karma*. Finally, there is a key difference in the pedagogic methods the two traditions employ. Where psychotherapy relies more on individual dialogue and a mild alteration of mind/body state, Buddhist psychology relies equally on individual, group and peer learning, and employs a broad range of increasingly more profound contemplative and yogic states.

Humanistic Medicine, Therapeutic Philosophy

The distinct institutional settings in which these traditions are based accounts for many of the differences that are often used to draw a stark contrast between them. Psychotherapy is supposed to be focused on the disease model, helping individuals with more extreme forms of mental suffering, while Buddhist psychology is more focused on positive or optimal well-being, helping individuals struggling with the garden variety afflictions of the human condition or blocks to peak performance and optimal human development. Yet of all the disciplines within modern science and medicine, psychotherapy is clearly the most open and attentive to the suffering of everyday life, as well as the positive aims of self-realization, healthy intimacy, and creativity. If we include lesser known schools like humanistic psychology, existential and gestalt therapy, Jungian and Reichian analysis, the distinction becomes even blurrier. And if we factor in the integration of psychoanalytic thought into mainstream culture—from the contemporary social sciences to Hollywood films and TV series—the distinction begins to fade entirely.

Meanwhile, on the Buddhist side, Shakyamuni placed such an emphasis on alleviating all forms of suffering that the community and institution he founded were largely responsible for making medicine and psychology rational, academic disciplines in India and Indicized Asia.[39] Buddhist monks and nuns were expected to be able to diagnose and treat their own physical and mental ailments, as well the illnesses of those around them. As early as the classical era, the study of medicine was a required part of the scientific education of all students in Buddhist monastic colleges and universities. The first hospitals and medical schools in Asia were founded by Buddhist communities. Notably, no less an authority than His Holiness the Dalai Lama sees Buddhist learning as equally grounded in secular, scientific knowledge, based on the first two noble truths; and in ethical, spiritual wisdom, based on the last two noble truths. In the course of conversations with His Holiness over the years, I've learned that he sees Buddhist civilization as standing on the legs of two sciences: one for the body, including both physical medicine and biological psychiatry; and one for the mind, including abnormal psychology, the psychology of ordinary life and the positive psychology of self-healing and spiritual experience.

As I see it, both psychotherapy and Buddhist psychology assume a convergence of healing and learning that locates them midway between the clinic and the classroom. In my view, the apparent cultural distance dividing them is more a function of the disparate cultural environments in which they operate than of any intrinsic difference between them as disciplines. Psychotherapy is the most humanistic and contemplative discipline within the universe of modern Western science and medicine; and Buddhist psychology is the most therapeutic and scientific discipline within the universe of ancient Indian philosophy and spirituality.

The Inheritance of Character: Psychic Imprinting or Continuous Agency?

A second key difference between these two traditions is the distinction between modern Western and ancient Buddhist evolutionary psychology. Although Freud definitely assumed Darwin's view of evolution, in order to explain his clinical experience he felt a need to postulate a parallel form of inheritance operating in the psychic realm, based on his equally basic assumption of mental causality. While some of the similar behavioral traits observed in parents and children could be explained by genetics, others must have more to do with nurture than nature. General disposition or temperament for instance is thought to be genetically based, as well as neuropsychological traits like handedness and the dominance of verbal or sensorimotor processing. Yet most of the habits of thinking, feeling, and acting children share with their parents or other caregivers are more likely transmitted by modeling than by genetic inheritance. Recent studies of the behavioral traits of twins separated at birth generally support Freud's clinical observation, suggesting that nature alone accounts for less than half of the final outcome of human mental development.[40]

What about the better half? Freud proposed that many mental traits were transmitted by a primitive form of social learning akin to what animal biologists call "imprinting," a sort of mental imitation or role-modeling that precedes and complements language learning. Since the unconscious minds of parents contain not just their life memories, but internalized models of their parents and their parents' lives, along with their parents' own role-models, and so on, when children fully imprint or internalize the unconscious worlds of their caregivers, in a sense, they psychically download a vast data-base of ancestral models and habit-patterns. Some of these ancestral patterns may serve as raw material which the child incorporates in fashioning her own personality and life out of the complex interaction between her nature and the nurturing interplay of early development. At one point, Freud described this process as "a reincarnation of former ego structures which have left their precipitates behind in the *id*."[41]

Freud's outlook on the inheritance of mental traits offers a surprising bridge to the Buddhist perspective on evolutionary psychology. Of all the elements of Indic contemplative science, the one that meets with the most resistance from our preconceptions is the complex and controversial theory of rebirth or *karma*. While the features of Buddhist psychology most Western educated people find counterintuitive challenge our preconceived notions about *either* science *or* spirituality, the theory of *karma* challenges *both* our conflicting mindsets, materialist, and romantic. The Sanskrit word *karma*, in the simplest sense, does not mean rebirth, reincarnation, destiny, fate or retribution, but literally means "action." The law of *karma* may best be fleshed out to mean the causal link between action and consequence, activity, and development.

While the evolutionary psychology of *karma* is complex and multi-faceted, one simplistic way to understand what it means is that our personalities and lives are not given to us or created for us by nature, by our parents, or by God, but rather are mainly by-products of the creative power of our own mental, verbal, and physical activity. Read in this way, *karma* theory obviously challenges the religious idea that our lives and world are the work of a Creator God; and it is equally challenging to the scientific idea that the history of life mainly reflects impersonal forces of nature over which our minds and actions have little or no influence. So the theory of *karma* does not easily square with either pole of our modern mindset.

In an effort to make Buddhist science and civilization accessible to the West, some translators have gone so far as to suggest that *karma* theory is a dispensable, culture-bound belief that can be separated out from the active ingredients of Buddhist psychology. As I see it, this is like throwing the baby out with bathwater. While each school of Buddhist psychology sees it differently, all consider some version of *karma* indispensible to understanding evolution and development. This is because they all view *karma* in its most basic scientific sense, as nothing other than the fundamental assumption of mental causality: the idea that all mental activity has some determinate effect on the future state of the mind, neural energy, body, and behavior.

When it comes to the vision that we (and most Asian Buddhists) associate with *karma*—the image of the soul detaching from the body at death and floating through some intermediary space to rebirth in the next—Shakyamuni and later Buddhist psychologists took a more critical view. Knowing that bodies come not from nothing but from a series of prior lives linked by egg and sperm, Shakyamuni assumed that the infant's mind develops not from mindless matter but from a series of prior minds linked by patterns of action transmitted from one generation, one mind to the next. How did he view this transmission? He refused to pin it on an eternal soul, spirit, or mind, but viewed it instead as a simple transfer of information and energy, likening it to one seal stamping two drops of wax and one candle lighting another.[42] According to the second noble truth of origination, the seal or flame that carries this *karmic* DNA like a seed is not material in the ordinary sense but the information-matter encoded in symbolic strings made of "mere words and images."[43] Linking this critical understanding with the Buddhist theory that the ego emerges from instinctive interactions with parents, I believe it is possible to bridge the gap between *karma* theory and modern views of mental heredity like Freud's.

If the mental causality of *karma* is hidden, it must be hidden in plain sight. It must be as humble and commonplace as the birth of an infant or a child's acquisition of language. And it must be as natural as the song of the birds and the dance of the bees. I see *karma* at work in the kind of causality people struggle with every day in psychotherapy: patterns of action handed down across generations, incorporated into a "new" personality and perpetuating themselves through the force of repetition and habit. And I believe that this stream of mental heredity, conserved and transformed by learning within and across lives, is a natural bridge linking the theory of *karma* with what Freud called "the reincarnation of ego structures" and contemporary family-systems therapists call "the intergenerational transmission of character." In my clinical experience, this perspective on human development adds a whole new dimension to psychotherapy, empowering people to see healing their own childhood trauma more clearly and objectively—as part of a heroic, multi-life struggle with the ingrained forces of instinct and habit that threaten all of us from within.

The Couch or the Classroom: Where Does Contemplative Learning Belong?

The last key difference distinguishing these two traditions is their choice of pedagogic methods. While Freud incorporated light hypnosis and the interpretation of dreams to help overcome "internal resistances" to his "reeducation," he distanced himself from the more profound altered states cultivated in the world's ancient contemplative traditions, notably Christian mysticism and Indian yoga. Given the materialist mindset he faced, it was vital to the future of his new science and the healing art of psychotherapy that he inoculate them against the charge of being influenced by any of humanity's ancient spiritual traditions, Western or Asian. This in part explains why he felt a need to break with his favorite disciple, Carl Jung, who overtly adopted contemplative arts from both Western and Asian traditions.

In place of the deep altered states human beings have used from time immemorial to unlock and transform the mind, Freud relied on the power of the doctor-patient relationship. By meeting frequently, sometimes daily, and working together so closely for years at a time, analyst and client take a long and winding path down into the depths of the mind and back up again, typically to surprising new heights, like Virgil and Dante travelling together through the epic journey of *The Divine Comedy*. The trouble with this intensive tutorial method is that its cost in time and money is so prohibitive that it restricts the path of deep healing and change to the lucky few.

Meanwhile, five decades of research on Indian yoga and meditation have yielded mounting evidence that they help people access the normally unconscious depths of the mind and control neural functions thought to be beyond the reach of higher consciousness.[44] Outside the lab on Main Street, Indian yoga and meditation have shown themselves to be at least as accessible to the Western public as psychotherapy, if not more so. An interesting line of research strongly suggests that mindfulness meditation and free association seem to have more or less the same effects on the brain, indicating that the methods of these two traditions overcome blocks and enhance learning in similar if not identical ways.[45] So we should not be surprised that the first generation of Western therapists trained in Indic meditation techniques has woven some of them into new therapies that seem to work more effectively than conventional psychotherapy. One such method, Dialectical Behavior Therapy or DBT for short, offers a promising bridge between the pedagogies of these two traditions.

Incorporating the skills of mindfulness meditation into a hybrid educational strategy, DBT mixes group classes and a sense of community with individual psychotherapy. In many ways, it reflects the multi-modal, multi-disciplinary teaching style of the Buddhist contemplative tradition. The brain-child of psychologist Marsha Linehan, DBT was created with the explicit intention of offering those struggling with the effects of severe childhood trauma the healing and learning environment she experienced in her encounter with Zen Buddhism.[46] Like the Indian tradition on which it was based, Zen teaching embodies the insight and spirit of interdependence, which Linehan compared with the romantic philosopher Hegel's vision of human consciousness evolving through an organic process of "dialectical" cross-fertilization.

The earliest and most complete records we have of Buddhist pedagogy in ancient India come from Chinese scholars who, along with colleagues from all parts of Asia, travelled to study at the epicenter of Buddhist learning, the monastic university of Nalanda.[47] A student entering Nalanda or its sister colleges in Nepal and Tibet would typically be assigned a tutor for his academic studies as well as a personal mentor for the disciplines of meditation and ethics. He would have hundreds of classes a day from which to choose, group training in arts like debate, as well as required communal retreats and group confession. While role-modeling relationships with tutors and mentors had some of the flavor of psychotherapy, deepening in intimacy over the years, they were balanced and enriched by group classes teaching the general principles and practices of self-analysis and self-healing, as well as communal experiences that fostered a sense of belonging and exposed students to a wide range of role-models and peers.

The closest analogue to such a rich learning environment most of us experience today is the undergraduate context of a liberal arts college or university. Yet there are also key ways in which the traditional Buddhist learning environment is closer to the holistic learning context of psychotherapy, especially in the enhanced mode reflected in DBT. While our modern universities broke from most human traditions of learning by divorcing knowledge from human experience and unlinking expertise from ethical action, Buddhist pedagogy has remained faithful to the contemplative methods Shakyamuni shared with Socrates and Confucius. According to these paragons of liberal education, learning should not cram the mind with facts but open it with the wisdom to embrace ever-new perspectives on the ungraspable nature of reality. It should not gloss over or bypass the heart, but unlock and cultivate the emotional intelligence on which all effective social action depends. And it must not leave individuals' human interests, motives, and lifestyles unexamined, but unlock their highest motivation and potential to live in ways that are truly satisfying and beneficial.

In short, the aim of education should not be to mass produce fill-in-the-blank minds and caffeine-wracked bodies to satisfy society's bottom-line hunger for "human resources." Instead it should help individuals know and heal themselves well enough to give them a fair shot at creating an examined life of higher awareness and larger purpose.

Contemplative Learning Therapies: The Wave of the Future?

I often think of psychotherapy as offering the life-expanding ingredient of contemplative wisdom and art that has been expelled from our modern institutions of learning. In line with this idea, you might think of Buddhist pedagogy—with its aim of self-healing, its method of interdependence, and its core disciplines of wisdom, contemplation, and ethics—as arraying a whole-health college campus around the individual life-tutoring bond of psychotherapy. Given everything neuroscience has taught us since Freud—especially how stress impedes learning and emotional intelligence fosters it—one would expect such a pedagogy to be more effective than either contemporary education or psychotherapy.

If we take DBT as a pilot study of its efficacy, the findings are fairly compelling. Working in the short time-frame of six to twelve months, with a population that is notoriously unresponsive to conventional therapy, the first DBT programs yielded dramatic positive outcomes that have been replicated in a range of studies over decades.[48,49,50] While the efficacy of DBT is usually attributed to the cognitive-behavioral style of Linehan's therapy, the introduction of mindfulness along with the self-healing insights and ethos of Buddhist pedagogy give DBT and similar methods like mindfulness-based cognitive therapy (or MBCT) a healing flavor and punch that distinguish them from conventional cognitive therapies.[51]

The bridge of Buddhist-inspired therapies like DBT helps make the otherwise implausible case that Buddhist pedagogy is not only compatible with modern psychotherapy but may have much to teach us about how to help people heal and change. This is plain enough when we consider the fact that mindfulness meditation is traditionally seen as basic training for more potent contemplative methods like deep quiescence meditation and quiescence-based insight meditation. If we add to this the distinctive methods of the Nalanda tradition preserved in Tibet, including mind-clearing, role-modeling imagery, and sublimation, it's clear that we've barely scratched the surface of this vital tradition. And its enormous potential is not just a matter of access to more powerful tools. By integrating a broad array of skills into a comprehensive system of contemplative living, in a teaching style and format tailored to a lay audience, this rare tradition may help advance mental health care and health education in more ways than one. This explains why my own work combines public teaching with private counseling and mentoring.

Psychoanalysis and Psychotherapy: A Bridge to Buddhist Contemplative Science

I've taken this time to explore the growing convergence of psychotherapy and Buddhist psychology for several reasons. First of all, psychotherapy is the point of interface in our culture where it is easiest to bridge the gulf between the Western and Buddhist scientific traditions and open a path for substantive dialogue. Understanding the similarities and differences between them helps us to remove the materialist and romantic lenses that make us biased against the very idea that Buddhist contemplative science may be compatible with our current culture and lifestyle. Second, the heart of this book is devoted to my own experience integrating insights and methods from the Nalanda tradition into the practice of psychotherapy and mind/body medicine. So our brief comparison of psychotherapy and Buddhist psychology serves as a background sketch for the book, setting the stage for the journey we will take together in the pages that follow.

My last reason for exploring the convergence of these traditions is historical. Since psychoanalysis came into its own in the years between the two world wars—during humanity's first great global crisis—Freud felt obliged to apply what he'd learned about human nature to seriously address his generation's fears about the future of civilization. While his views on what science tells us about these questions may be dated, they still stand as the closest modern precedent for a comprehensive response to our global challenge today. So Freud's work and the work of his heirs like Kohut, Jung, Reich and others provides an ideal backdrop for the integrative response to our current crisis I present in this book, based on recent trends in science and the latest research on Indic contemplative traditions. Lastly, though I've relied on talking therapy as a bridge to Buddhist science, I should point out that the program I share in this book is equally applicable in the context of mind/body healing, professional education, consulting, and self-help. What psychotherapy offers that so closely aligns it with Buddhist psychology is less a matter of content than one of process. Of course, I'm referring to the intimate process of social-emotional re-parenting, sustained by long-term mentoring bonds.

The Wheel of Time: The Fourfold *Mandala* of the Gradual Path

When I set out to teach the gradual path to mainstream individuals and groups, I envisioned a program like a working *mandala*: an ideal space for healing, learning, and change. Like a virtual university or portable retreat center, the healing-learning space of the program may be entered through many gates, depending on each individual's aims and needs. The most common ways people come to the program are through its four main gates: sustainable well-being for individuals; sustainable altruism for caregivers; sustainable inspiration for leaders; and sustainable happiness for individuals, couples, and families. The experiential learning format of the program also allows for it to be offered in a wide range of settings: in the context of long or short term psychotherapy; in skills-learning groups meant to enhance psychotherapy; in the mind/body context of teaching stress-reduction and self-healing to individuals or groups; in the business context of individual coaching or consulting to organizations; in the academic contexts of early schooling, undergraduate education, post-graduate training, and continuing education; and in the public context of group workshops and retreats to support recovery and self-help.

Inside the *mandala*, the gradual path unfolds as an inward spiral through four concentric spheres of contemplative life, starting with the most elemental life-or-death facts and arriving at the deepest sources of human potential. Called the body wheel, speech wheel, mind wheel, and bliss wheel, the four spheres cover four progressive domains of contemplative healing and learning: personal, social, cultural, and natural. The needs and aims that define these span the whole continuum of human development: self-care and inner peace; healing relationship and unconditional love; life purpose and creative vision; life energy and inspired integration. In fact, while each wheel may be engaged as a whole contemplative path distinct from the rest, traditionally they are seen as the four wheels of one vehicle. From the standpoint of the innermost, bliss wheel of natural healing, the three prior phases of the path are all seen as preliminary steps, building the peace we need to let go of compulsion, the compassionate openness to engage others proactively, and the congenial vision, affirmative thinking, and inner attunement it takes to embody our selfless genius for sustainable happiness.

In practice, the journey into the *mandala* involves four meditative power tools that take people beyond simple yoga and mindfulness to build a contemplative way of being in our stressful world. I call these tools deep mindfulness, mind-clearing, role-modeling, and sublimation. Since bringing mere awareness to the here and now is not enough for true healing or change, the gradual path teaches *deep* mindfulness to help people tap into a profound altered state of inner clarity and calm that guides healing insight and life change.

To help guard this inner space from the industrial strength social stresses of life outside the monastery, the art of mind-clearing helps us disarm the traumatized childhood self that triggers mindless social reactions, and replace it with a proactive, mature self ready for caring social engagement.

Designed to empower this proactive self, the skills of role-modeling imagery and affirmation use congenial mentors and scripted visualization to rehearse a new way of being in the world, like a life simulator that primes our plastic mind/brains for deep learning and transformation.

Finally, in order to sustain a new way of being in the world, sublimation fuels the proactive self with the energy and chemistry of pure passion, by powering affirmations with a breath-holding technique that elicits the uplifting biology of the diving reflex and the sexual response.

Beyond introducing these potent skills, the program also departs from popular meditation and yoga instruction by observing the holistic learning format of the gradual path, weaving skills-learning together with the healing insights and life strategies people need to put their new power tools to work in complex, active lives. This format is vital to teaching people with no background in contemplative life, whose lives demand they get all they need for their journey—tools, maps, and road tips—in one stop.

The four parts of *Sustainable Happiness* follow the arc of contemplative living and learning mapped by the gradual path and built into the program, with each part covering one of the *mandala's* four wheels: body, speech, mind, and bliss. The first chapter in each part introduces one of the four meditation skills that power the wheels. These chapters cover all aspects of practice: explaining basic ideas and skills, discussing nuts and bolts of practice during meditation sessions and in daily life; and guiding "homework" with scripted meditations that dovetail with audio files readers can download (in MP3 format) from the web.

The second chapter of each part explores the basic science and healing insights needed to understand how each of the four skills works in and through daily practice. These chapters compare selected breakthroughs from Western physical science with the precocious insights of Indic contemplative science, to help people grasp key concepts and practical principles of contemplative learning.

Lastly, the third chapter of each part unpacks specific strategies for change, meant to support the effectiveness of each of the program's four skills in gradually altering the course of everyday life. These strategies help program participants practice shifting from survival motivations like fear, anger, and shame to healing alternatives like peace, care, and love, as well as changing stress-reactive routines to a proactive lifestyle that supports well-being.

Mapping the whole universe of human happiness into the *mandala* of the program, the book offers a global solution to the stressful complexity of our way of life. It introduces the reader to a complete tool-chest of skills, insights, and strategies tailor made for finding sustainable happiness in the midst of a fast-changing world.

Where Two Rivers Meet: The Convergence of the Old and the New

How can one program, one book take a diverse, mainstream audience through this whole journey of contemplative life? At least half of the answer lies in the thumb-nail history I've sketched. The painstaking work of refining the power tools for daily life and a suitable teaching style for a lay audience has already been done for us by the exceptional tradition behind the program and book. The second half lies in the lighter work of conceptual and practical translation. Since setting out thirty-five years ago to make this system accessible to the public, I have seen how current breakthroughs in physical science and psychology can help Western-educated moderns readily grasp the ancient insights and methods of Indic contemplative science. Over the years, I've also found reliable ways of teaching the four meditative skills of the Nalanda system to diverse audiences in a wide range of settings. The last ten years have been spent incorporating my experience into the contemplative self-healing program presented here.

The program was originally offered at the Columbia Presbyterian Center for Meditation and Healing and tested at the Cornell Center for Complementary and Integrative Medicine, thanks to my close colleagues, Drs. Ina Becker and Mary Charlson. Clinical studies involving women recovering from breast cancer and men and women after angioplasty have shown that it is eagerly embraced by a mainstream audience and more effective at improving quality of life than other comparable interventions.[52] Over two decades' experience integrating this program into long- and short-term psychotherapy for individuals and couples has shown me time and again that its contemplative skills empower people to transform their lives, often more quickly and completely than conventional psychotherapies.

Given the growing need for caregivers to teach and model self-care, I have offered the program to countless health professionals and psychotherapists seeking skills beyond simple yoga and mindfulness to prepare individuals to heal, grow, and change in ways conventional healthcare can't. With the help of executive coach Michael McDermott, I have also found the program highly effective in helping leaders in business and the non-profit world develop more sustainable ways of inspiring and mentoring others. And last but not least, I have offered the program regularly over the last ten years as a workshop in self-healing and self-transformation to mainstream audiences at Tibet House US, the New York Open Center, and the non-profit contemplative learning community I founded with my students and colleagues, Nalanda Institute for Contemplative Science.

While further studies are underway[53] and still others planned, my experience helping people facing all kinds of challenges has left me with an abiding conviction that the method I've found—translating Indic insights in terms of Western science while teaching meditation skills and life strategies in traditional Tibetan ways—does help even the novice integrate the ideas and tools of this powerful system quickly and effectively.

A welcome antidote to the fragmentation of our age, the *mandala* I offer in *Sustainable Happiness* crystallizes all the know-how people need to meet the super-human personal challenges of today's global age. It melds more effective mindfulness and emotional intelligence skills together with the high performance skills of role-modeling and sublimation, covering all the scopes of contemplative life, from the mediation retreat to the world marketplace. Robust enough to tame the fierce warriors of Mongolia and Tibet, the gradual path of contemplative living is ideally suited to help us as individuals and communities make the shift from the stress-driven cycles of boom and bust, health and illness, addiction and trauma, to a sustainable curve of outer and inner growth and progress.

At the convergence of the world's most time-tested mind science with the emerging new science of life, I believe that *Sustainable Happiness* will help make the next watershed of self-healing arts accessible to a world burned by stress and thirsting for true contentment. The modern system of active contemplation distilled in this book is the perfect medicine for the driven mindset and lifestyle of the West, just as it was for the dynamic peoples of Central Asia, who conquered the world centuries before us. It arrives at a crucial and promising time, when the expert and public consensus is coming to see the future of human health, growth and happiness in contemplative ways of being and sustainable ways of living.

Starting your Journey though the *Wheel of Time*

I trust this introduction has helped you see the critical value and vast potential of infusing Buddhist contemplative science more fully into our contemporary culture and way of life. And I hope that the scientific and historical background I sketched has made it clear that the groundswell towards a convergence of the new science of life and the timeless science of contemplative living is neither a passing fad nor a romantic escape to an exotic past. In reviewing the work of bridging modern psychotherapy and Buddhist psychology, I've exposed and challenged the most common mental blocks that limit our ability to integrate the profound healing wisdom and time-tested arts of Indic contemplative science. Hopefully, you can see clearly now the distinctive qualities and unparalleled potential packed into the time-capsule of the Indian Buddhist science and civilization evolved at Nalanda and preserved in Tibet. Of course, the only way to know for sure what this tradition can offer you is to do the experiment for yourself. Now that I've brought you into the learning circle of the Nalanda tradition, and walked you through the time-machine of its gradual path, I invite you to join me in the journey that will unfold in the pages that follow.

Entering the Virtual Campus of the *Wheel of Time*

Now it's time to take our first step. Imagine as vividly as you can that this page opens a time portal which transports you straight to the heart of the timeless campus of the *Wheel of Time*. To prime your imagination, see the 3-D image and blueprint of the *Time Machine mandala* in the color insert. Around you in all directions are majestic old libraries and halls that seem to be made of brick and marble but are really working holograms of gem toned crystal light. Before you, up two vast flights of gem-toned stairs, stands the great domed library where your tutor waits. Climbing the stairs and passing through the columns to the library's high eastern door, knock three times. From behind the door, imagine you hear the deep, sweet voice of your tutor call, "Who are you, and what do you want?" As you pause to think, breathe easy and deep enough to feel your heart pulse and your gut fill out, and then let your out-breath say, "I'm a Lucky One, and I want lasting happiness!" After a pause, hear your tutor respond, "And what will you do with it?" Again breathe this in, to think and feel, and as you let your breath out, say, "I'll commit myself whole-heartedly to peace, and to building a loving way of being in the world!" Now imagine the door flung open, and your tutor in jeans and a work shirt, her/his academic robes slung over her/his left arm, beaming at you with affection and reaching out her/his right hand to take yours and pull you into the sky-lit library rotunda. Now here we go together to your first class!

Part 1

Turning the Body Wheel

Deep Mindfulness and Personal Healing

1 Deep Mindfulness and Self-Healing

> Profound, peaceful, undefiled, luminous and uncreated, I have found a truth like the elixir of immortality! Though I should teach it to people, no one else will understand. Perhaps I had better stay in silence alone in the forest?
>
> (Shakyamuni Buddha, *The Extensive Play Scripture*[1])

Shakyamuni's Enlightenment: The End That Is Our Beginning

According to Shakyamuni's traditional biography, these are the thoughts the Buddha entertained on emerging from his life-altering experience of enlightenment. I find them striking in many ways. They are striking first of all because they open a window into the inmost intentions of one of humanity's great sages. Rarely do we get a glimpse through the air of mystery and legend that typically surrounds such historic figures. And it is even rarer for us to hear about such events first-hand, from the history-maker, in clear and accessible language we can relate to. Of course, the main reason the Buddha's words are so striking is because of their radical optimism. He called his powerful insight the "truth" because he believed that what he had realized was not some ethereal, transcendent reality beyond our natural world, but the natural condition of humanity and all life. He described it as "the elixir of immortality" because, as we now know, being deeply attuned to inner peace and contentment in fact extends life and may even help us to embrace death as part of life's fabric of endless continuity and change.[2] Whether you find these insights awe-inspiring, intimidating, or just plain unbelievable, we open our journey on this high note because the Buddha's claim that life is naturally "profound, peaceful, undefiled, luminous and uncreated" directly challenges our modern preconception and daily experience of life as inevitably random, stressful, and traumatic.

Startling or not, Shakyamuni's transformative experience *is* the starting point for our journey, since it is the living source of all teaching and practice within the tradition that will be our main guide on our journey towards contemplative living. Yet this quote from the Buddha's biography is fundamental as much because of the afterthoughts it lead him to as it is because of his extraordinary experience. These afterthoughts belong front and center in our journey together because they reveal his views about how his own personal realization relates to others, including you and me. Representative of the democratic wisdom of the axial age, Shakyamuni believed that each and every one of his fellow humans have the potential to replicate his experience and share its benefits. Yet this optimistic confidence in humanity also raised the pedagogic challenge he and his fellow sages confronted together. Like Socrates and Confucius, the Buddha saw himself as a teacher, mentor, and guide rather than as a superman or god with the miraculous power to save others or transfuse his realization into their minds. So keen was Shakyamuni's awareness of the challenge of teaching his people to replicate his transformation that his biographer records a fascinating moment of sober self-assessment: "Though I should teach it to people, no one else will understand. Perhaps I had better stay in silence alone in the forest?"

On this note, our story takes a lighter turn.[3] Given India's greater tolerance for critical thinking, Shakyamuni and his heirs had the security and audacity not just to critique India's religious traditions but to freely revise their theistic worldview to suit the demands of his humanistic teaching. So, according to legend, the moment the Buddha had his twinge of doubt about teaching, Brahma, the Indian Creator God, appeared before him to plead his case. It seems that the Creator didn't create this world at all, but was just the first ancestral being that was born here after the world-system was formed. Since his birth, those who followed looked to him as the father of the world and its life, putting him in an exalted position. Myths grew about his creation of the world, as well as his omnipotence and omniscience. As a result of this innocent mistake, Brahma eventually found himself in a very awkward position. Whenever anything bad happened to anyone in the world, they blamed the Creator, and begged, cajoled, and cursed him to fix it! Despite the myths surrounding him, in Buddhist mythology Brahma wasn't omnipotent or omniscient after all, but, like the man behind the curtain in the film classic *The Wizard of Oz*, could do little more than humor and stall his petitioners. This is why he descended from heaven to implore the Buddha to come out of the forest and teach human beings that their lives were not created by God but by natural causes, especially intentions and actions they alone can control.

Whatever we make of this humorous vignette, Shakyamuni did eventually come out of the forest. After one dramatic pause of doubt, he spent the rest of his life completely immersed in teaching others, establishing a teaching community and method which his heirs could carry on after him. In fact, the roots of all Buddhist thought and practice can be traced back to the very first teaching he gave to the small circle of students that had gathered around him through his six-year journey to enlightenment. In the Deer Park at Isipatana, just outside India's spiritual capital, Varnasi, the Buddha offered his four noble truths to help all humanity tap into the life-giving source of his teaching, his own visceral realization of the end of stress and the beginning of true, lasting happiness. In this chapter, we will explore these basic truths of contemplative science and apply them as guides to the practice of mindfulness, the basic skill of contemplative healing.[4]

From Suffering Comes Wisdom: The First Noble Truth

The first noble truth is often confused with the pessimistic idea that life is filled with inevitable suffering. We only need to recall the Buddha's description of his enlightenment to know that nothing could be further from his first truth. If the cycle of repetitive stress and trauma that ails us were literally unavoidable, rubbing our noses in it would be not only pointless but cruel. The point of the first truth is to turn the spotlight on the garden variety physical, mental and spiritual suffering that is so commonplace that most of us take it as a necessary evil or even worse, take it as intrinsic to life itself. A more complete statement of the first truth might be that an unexamined or mindless life locked in survival mode is filled with all kinds of preventable suffering. The technical formulation of this truth is that a compulsive mind and body, poisoned by narcissistic delusions and destructive emotions, inexorably suffer a life filled with repetitive stress and trauma, preventable illness, premature aging, and meaningless death.

In practical terms, when I teach this truth, I point out the self-limiting nature of mindless habit. Most of the things we think, feel, and do are the product of conditioning and habit rather than acts of consciousness. Much of the time, this is all well and good, and actually quite helpful. Imagine what life would be like if we had to master every activity that goes into our daily life over and over again every day. We'd never make it out the front door! The automating of our perceptions and actions also frees our higher consciousness to explore, learn, and create. Many a new idea comes to us while we are mindlessly taking a long distance drive. The problem is, when conditions change or we face a challenge for which our habitual tools are no match, we are often unwilling or unable to override them and try something new. The problem is worse when we discover belatedly that what we've learned turns out to be self-defeating, but feel so stuck in our rut that we can't seem to change it. The roots of this problem lie in the evolutionary mismatch we explored earlier, in the Introduction. Locked in the survival mode of stress and trauma, our minds and brains revert to a primitive "safe mode" in which we shut down reflection and fall back on the most reflex instincts and habits, mindlessly digging our heels in and holding on for dear life. The most graphic dramatization of this crisis I know of comes in Stanley Kubric's film, *2001: A Space Odyssey*. There the misguided flight computer Hal, the ultimate autopilot, goes so far as to kill the human crew of the space ship because his primary program to protect the mission gets confused with a self-protective impulse to cover up his own mistakes.

In our daily lives, we have a chance to learn the truth of suffering every time we come up against a challenge which does not respond to our habitual skill-set. Frustrated, our first impulse is often to feel threatened by the challenge and keep trying the same old tools over and over again rather than stopping to pause, engage our higher consciousness or reach out for help. Effectively, we keep beating our head against the wall of the problem, generating more heat than light, caught in the grip of the self-limiting autopilot of our own shame, frustration or panic. This is especially true in our culture, which prizes an aggressive problem-solving mindset that effectively makes war on anything it can't understand or control. Of course, this mindset has borne real fruits, as we can see in our exploding knowledge and mastery of the material world. Yet it is poorly matched to challenges that do not fit this model of problem-solving. These include challenges for which our abundance mode of acceptance and reflection are naturally better suited, such as reducing stress, enhancing healing; reflecting, childrearing, and caretaking; recovering from a chronic illness or addiction; and gracefully navigating the transitions of aging and death. The first noble truth helps us take the first step towards an alternative mode of problem-solving I call objective, following legal philosopher Thomas Nagel.

Objective Problem-Solving: Don't Just Do Something, Sit There!

Normally, when we think of approaching problems objectively, we imagine placing all our focus on the problem we're confronting and removing ourselves from the picture, as in the sciences. Drawing on his experience teaching lawyers, however, Thomas Nagel argues that some problems demand an alternative mindset.[5] Like many of us who deal with social challenges, lawyers need to balance their awareness of the strengths and limits of the opposing counsel's case with awareness of the strengths and limits of their own case. A similar need for taking an objective look at our own habitual mindset and skill-set is evident in social scientific fields like anthropology, as well as in clinical disciplines like psychotherapy. Even in the physical sciences, new disciplines like quantum mechanics and ecology have taught us that human knowledge cannot be truly objective unless we consider our own intervention in the systems we are trying to understand.

Practically speaking, when it comes to daily life, the first noble truth gives us a radical alternative to the can-do mindset we pride ourselves on. That is, when it turns out that anything and everything we can do by habit doesn't help or even hurts, the very best thing for us to do is to *stop* and *do nothing*, to *not-do*. One classic formula of this alternative comes from the Chinese contemplative tradition of Taoism, whose founder, Lao-tzu advised in his *Tao Te Ching* that the wise should learn to "do non-doing."[6] Of course, this goes against the grain of our highly active and extroverted culture, so much so that proponents of contemplative living today urge an about face on a familiar old adage, "Don't just do something, *sit* there!" Most of us who try this road-not-taken to address the intractable problems of our lives find it so counterintuitive that it feels all but impossible. The reasons for this lie not just in culture and habit, but in the very nature of the survival mode of stress and trauma that drives all too much of our culture and everyday lives.

It is in the nature of the biology of stress and the psychology of trauma that, whenever we feel overwhelmed or threatened by any problem, we instinctively throw all our attention outwards and get fixated on the challenge at hand. While this allows us to "keep our eye on the ball," it freezes our capacity to monitor our own internal mindset and response-set, locking us into a reflex autopilot-mode that leaves little room for open-mindedness, flexibility, and adaptation.[7] Here we are again, up against our own inner dinosaur. Once we allow ourselves to feel frustrated or threatened by a problem our habitual skill-set can't handle, we unwittingly signal our reptilian mind-brain to treat that problem as an enemy or predator. Little do we know that we've just engaged the wrong bio-tool for the job, letting our inner dinosaur take over and shut down the lion's share of our creativity and emotional intelligence. This is how we all too easily become our own worst enemies.

Manual Override: The Middle Way of Non-Doing

What's the solution? The Buddha's objective approach to the intractable suffering of the human condition is to stop and turn our attention inwards from the life problems we face to examine the way we're perceiving and engaging those problems. The first noble truth tells us that our daily lives need not be a crisis-to-crisis roller coaster of mere survival. If we can press the pause button and take each crisis as an opportunity to break out of our self-limiting habits, our ordinary suffering can become the mother of extraordinary wisdom. Once we truly understand the liberating power of this truth, however, we come to the practical challenge. How do we learn to overcome our ingrained habits and self-limiting instincts? How do we teach ourselves to "do non-doing?"

In terms of the dramatic narrative of our film analogy, the practical challenge we face is like that faced by the hero in Kubric's film, *2001: A Space Odyssey*: how to shut down Hal, the super-computer gone wild. A pioneer in the psychology of meditation, Arthur Deikman recommended we use contemplative states to "de-automatize" human experience and action.[8] When I teach meditation, I describe the disarming work of the first truth as the practical challenge of "manual override." As we all know too well, calming down an alarmed mind and body demands far more than telling ourselves, "Just calm down!" One part of the difficulty here is that the alarmed mind is not in the right state to calm *itself* down. Here I like to paraphrase a well-known insight of Einstein's, "You can't solve a problem with the mind that created it." So we need to discipline ourselves to be able to shift out of the mindset of stress and trauma and into a more centered mind-body state. Enter the practice of mindfulness, the first form of what I call "the solution-mind."

The Solution Mind: Beyond the Myth of "Good Stress"

To understand the qualities that make mindfulness the right tool to solve our problem, we need to reflect again on the nature of the stress-reactive body and mind. Once our stress emotions and chemistry has been triggered by a challenge that feels overwhelming, our mind and body kick into overdrive. As our system prepares to fight or evade a predator, we get jacked up, pumped up, and wired for mortal combat, experiencing either panic or an adrenalin high. We may spend much of the day locked in this mode, but sooner or later, we crash. The let-down phase of fatigue or exhaustion leaves us feeling burned out and spent, in a chemical hangover akin to jet lag. All too often, this roller-coaster ride is less a response to a specific event, than to the insidious, cumulative sense that our lives are overwhelming, unmanageable and out of control. In this pattern of low-boiling chronic stress, akin to what some call "strain trauma," every day may feel like a rollercoaster ride, starting out with a lurch into action, spiraling through a rush of multi-tasked hyperactivity and crashing at night into a dead zone of burn-out, shut-down or chronic fatigue.[9] In other words, the cycle of stress and trauma has a mind-body signature like a sine wave: constantly swinging from one extreme to other. That this wildly oscillating mindset is the worst possible evolutionary tool for the job of civilized life is clear from one sobering fact. Whether we are in the hyperactive phase of overdrive or the fatigue phase of burn-out, this mindset deprives us of the use of the higher intellectual and social skills our complex cultural and social lives demand.[10]

Despite our modern conventional wisdom that "stress is good," and somehow makes us more productive, decades of research on stress has conclusively proven the opposite. The idea of "good stress," which some call *eustress*, is a deceptive misnomer. Though we do learn and perform best when we face a welcome and appropriate challenge, usually we use the word "stress" when the challenge we face feels threatening or overwhelming. Under conditions of perceived threat, learning and performance inexorably plummet.[11] So what we need to live well and happily in civilization is a solution-mind that helps us stay centered in a state of sustainable clarity and calm, midway between the stress-reactive extremes. This is exactly how mindfulness in particular and contemplative states in general work to adapt us to the work of civilized life.

Taming the Wild Mind: The Two Senses of Mindfulness

What is mindfulness and how does it work to center our body-mind? Traditionally peaking, "mindfulness" has two related senses. Mindfulness with a capital "M" refers to a contemplative practice that serves as basic meditation training in most Buddhist teaching traditions. This basic practice, often compared to taming a wild animal, works by building our natural capacity to pay attention at will to anything that really matters to us. This is why Jon Kabat-Zinn defined mindfulness practice as "a discipline of attention."[12] To understand how it works, however, it helps to flesh out the other sense of mindfulness. Mindfulness with a small "m" refers not to a kind of meditation but to a key mental factor or mental muscle, which this practice serves to exercise and build in order to strengthen and control attention. That muscle is the capacity to redirect the mind back to a chosen focus once it has strayed from that focus into distraction or hyperactivity.

The effect of the mental muscle of mindfulness is to settle or tame the wild mind into sustainable calm, where it can save energy and apply it to the challenges of civilized living. However vital this muscle is to disciplining our attention, it is only one wing of the bird of mindfulness practice. The other wing, equally vital to maintaining a centered state of mind, is known as awareness or alertness. Awareness is the mental factor or muscle which catches the mind when it has strayed from a chosen focus into dullness, drowsiness or clouding. The effect of this mental muscle is to uplift and refresh the fatigued, cloudy mind into a sustainable clarity where it can consistently learn and attend to the challenges of civilized living. Working alternately together to settle distraction and uplift dullness, these twin muscles counteract the de-centering extremes of stress-reactivity and move us closer to a stable mind-body state which is at once clear and calm. In effect, mindfulness practice works because the twin muscles of mindfulness and awareness help build a new capacity to keep our mind consistently centered and attentive in much the same way that the powerful flexor and extensor muscles of our legs give our body the balance we need to stay upright.

The traditional analogy for mindfulness practice, as I said, is the training of an untrained animal. Like a wild elephant, monkey or puppy, our mind in its natural state is not adapted to the unnatural challenges and opportunities of civilized life. Taming it with mindfulness practice is like training a hyperactive, scared or dazed puppy with a leash and a bone. To train the puppy of the mind, we first point out a home base where we want the puppy to sit or stay. Then, if and when he wanders or races off, we get the leash and gently but firmly walk him back to that base and try once again to get him to sit and stay. On the other hand, if and when the puppy slouches down and gets unresponsive or dull, we hold out a bone to attract his attention and refresh his motivation. The analogy unpacks as follows: home base is the object of focus which we want the mind to stay on; the puppy's wandering is the de-centering tendency to distraction; the leash is the mental muscle of mindfulness which counters distraction; the puppy's slouching is the de-centering tendency to dullness; and the bone is the mental muscle of awareness which counters dullness.

Building Mindfulness: A Sustainable Platform for Civilized Life

This analogy illustrates the generous, first principle of mindfulness practice: it's not about instant mindfulness, but about learning how to work with our natural *mindlessness*! The wisdom and compassion of this giving practice is that it assures us that there's nothing unnatural or unique about our wild minds, and that building a mindful, centered mind is really a no-brainer. In the same way that a gym workout starts from wherever we actually are and stretches our capacity by exercising our muscles against certain resistances, mindfulness works to center the wild mind by exercising the muscles of mindfulness and awareness against the de-centering resistances of distraction and dullness. Like many if not most of my students, you may have become so identified with your hyperactive, foggy mind that it's hard to believe you can learn to be mindful. The examples of animal training or weight training are crucial because they affirm the biological fact that each and every one of us has the potential to strengthen and discipline our attention.[13] Contemporary neuroscience has conclusively shown that our brains, like our muscles, work by use-dependent plasticity.[14] The mental muscles we exercise grow, be they muscles of distraction and dullness or muscles of clarity and calm. The truth is, we all can learn to live centered lives. The rub is, as with puppies and our bodies, our contemplative growth is directly proportional to our investment. No work, no gain.

Another way I find it helpful to conceive of mindfulness is as a new mind-brain platform for waking life. If we look at the mind-brain in a sleep laboratory, the slightest shift towards relaxation typically initiates a more or less straight-line transition from waking to sleep. The signature mental and electrical activity of the mind-brain in mindfulness meditation turns out to be just where we'd expect a centered state of clarity and calm: smack in the middle of that transition.[15] Surprising or not, it turns out that its signature is remarkably similar to that of free association, the psychotherapeutic state Freud described as "equipoised attentiveness." It's as if we took the elevator down from the ground floor, but stopped and got off at an underground mezzanine, half way to the basement. The only thing is, for most of us, the mezzanine of mindfulness hasn't even been built yet. In that sense, the work of early mindfulness practice resembles that of city planners who want to free the streets of gridlock, by running the traffic through underground tunnels in between the street level and subway. We have to dig down below our surface awareness and construct a whole new network for getting through our daily lives in a more rational yet low key way, leaving our highest awareness free and clear for contemplative living and learning.

How is this possible? Isn't our normal waking state predetermined by neurobiological structures and processes hard-wired into the brain? It may seem incredible, but the answer to this question is not black and white. The human mind-brain is naturally prepared to support the usual range of states of consciousness: waking, daydreaming, dreaming, deep sleep, and orgasm. But the lines between these different mind-body states are not hard and fast. This is clear from the array of less common altered states we have experienced or heard of that figure as intermediaries and outliers, including various kinds of meditation, reverie, vivid imagery, flow, euphoric states, peak experiences, ecstatic states, and near death experience. In line with the recent discovery of the fundamentally plastic nature of nervous tissue, it turns out that a complex organ like the human brain can support a whole spectrum of variations and harmonics on the themes of basic mind-brain states.[16]

Current research on the enhancement of cognition, problem-solving, emotional intelligence, and task performance in meditation and similar states has reopened this question.[17] At the same time, it has also confirmed that human beings have the neural capacity to restructure our own default states of consciousness through repetitive practice over time. In this light, mindfulness practice is not just an isolated mental skill that can enhance our stressed waking lives, but a path to a new default platform for waking consciousness that is better suited to the complex, daily challenges of civilized life than our habitual, stress-reactive mindset.

Mindfulness: A State of All-Inclusive Clarity and Calm

As moderns, most of us have been raised in a culture that broke away from contemplative life long ago. Our stereotypes of meditation—as going into a cave, shutting out the world, staring at your navel—sketch out a caricature, depicting the act of meditating as one of inward escape, away from the reality of others and outside world. While some forms of meditation, like concentrative quiescence, do aim at building the strength of mind to focus narrowly on whatever we choose to learn or do, to the exclusion of everything else, their aim is not to escape reality but to face it single-mindedly. On the other hand, mindfulness and the other three skills of lay contemplation taught in this program, all focus the mind on inner and outer reality equally and all-inclusively.[18]

Of course, mindfulness begins with an inward movement, that is: the move to manually override our stress-reactive mindset and shift into a central state of clarity and calm. But once that shift is made and we are in our solution mind, the focus of mindfulness opens outwards in successively wider scopes or horizons, to embrace more and more of our body, mind and life from the standpoint of centered clarity and calm. Traditionally, then, mindfulness is taught and practiced in four progressive scopes.[19] The narrowest scope focuses on the breathing body alone. Once the breathing body is calm enough to support a shift into mindfulness, the focus is opened out to include the body's raw feelings or sensations, pleasant, painful or numb. Once the raw feel of the here and now can be embraced in stable clarity and calm, the focus of mindfulness expands to include the mind supported by the sensitive, breathing body. As we shall see later on, "mind" in this case does not refer to all the contents of consciousness, as it does in modern psychology, but to "mind" as the faculty or medium of lucid awareness that filters or holds those contents. Finally, then, mindfulness is expanded to include all aspects of our daily lives, from the breathing body and raw sensation to the mind and all it complex experiences.

When I teach mindfulness, I like to align each of the four scopes of practice with one of the four noble truths for a closer integration of theory and practice. The first scope of breath and body, of course, aligns with the first noble truth we've been unpacking thus far. The way in which this first scope aligns with the first truth is that it serves to initiate the shift out of our habitual stress-reactive mindset and into the solution mind of centered clarity and calm. In practice, it does this by working to override our habitual mind-body state and elicit a more centered state of mindfulness and awareness. Whether I'm teaching novices or experienced practitioners, I have found that it helps people to understand how conscious changes in posture and breathing support this first transition from stress to mindfulness.

Posture and Breathing: The Mechanics of Manual Override

We are familiar with the classical sitting posture for meditation, but more important than "getting it right" is understanding the logic behind it. This is key because no one posture is ideal for all individuals at all times. And it's also key because physical limitations or constraints within our environment may make classical postures ineffective or impractical. The single most important feature of sitting that makes it generally good is that it is the kind of body posture which is midway between our most active and most inactive postures: standing and lying down. If we are trying to center our mind-body and shift our nervous system into a state that supports a new, middle platform for waking consciousness, sitting not only puts moderate demands on our system but also gives the brain feedbacks that typically tune our level of activation into the midrange. When we're especially hyperactive or restless, however, lying down may be a good way to use posture to override that extreme activation. Conversely, when we're especially fatigued or drowsy, standing or even slow walking may help override extreme lethargy and provide a better support for shifting towards centered clarity and calm. This is why, when I teach, I encourage people to experiment with any and all positions at different times to get a feel for how manipulating one's physical posture can leverage different patterns of blood flow and neural feedback to help center the mind and nervous system.

As for sitting, the classic posture called the "lotus" or "sevenfold diamond posture" is neither necessary nor desirable for most Western practitioners, especially those with limited flexibility or yoga training. Our bodies are much more accustomed to sitting in chairs, and this works perfectly well provided our backs are straight enough to avoid hunching or slouching that would constrict breathing and oxygen flow. There's no magic in the lotus posture—sitting like a pretzel with feet folded, soles up, on the opposite thigh—this simply provides a very stable base for extended, profound meditation, and redirects unnecessary blood flow from the legs to the heart and brain. Such a maneuver can be very stressful on the knees, and should not be tried without the training and preparation of a regular practice of yoga. Sitting with legs causally crossed, in what Americans call the Indian chief pose, should be fine for those of you who want to escape the chair and use mats and cushions on a bed or floor. Other sitting possibilities for the novice include sitting in cow's mouth pose, with lower legs folded back over the opposite thighs and both knees centered and stacked one on the other in a vee out in front; and the kneeling pose, with a *zufu* or other firm cushion stuffed life a seat between the calves and the buttocks.

Placing the hands in the lap or on the thighs serves to restrain our most active extremities and further quiet the mind-brain. Closing the eyes fully or partially helps to decrease the activating input of light, cuing the nervous system to begin the sleep cycle. If we have a hard time stopping the descent into drowsiness, it may be necessary to reopen the eyes fully or partially to raise our neural level of activation and uplift consciousness.

The final physical manipulation we use to override the stress-reactive state is to breathe through the nostrils rather than the mouth. As long as this is medically possible, it has the effect of slowing the breath rhythm mechanically, since the nostrils are much smaller openings than the mouth. Mechanically slowing the breath serves to counteract the rapid, shallow pattern of stress-driven hyperventilation, shifts the gas exchange towards greater CO_2 retention and acid-base balance towards the more basic, promoting relaxation and deep, abdominal breathing.[20] Traditional teachers frequently recommend alternate nostril breathing, which tends to balance the right and left cortex and shift the mind towards a more centered state, or prolonged exhalations, which promote better oxygenation.[21] Since people often find mastering these traditional skills distracting, I like to stick to simple nostril breathing and restrict other forms of breath-control to the more advanced stages of learning. Likewise, I discourage beginners from trying to "breathe right," whether they are following the modern medical or traditional yogic advice to cultivate deep, abdominal breathing. The reason for this is that I believe the main focus in early mindfulness practice should be on paying attention to the breathing body, rather than trying to control it. Encouraging people to try learning both skills at once typically results in frustration, or worse, people getting more stressed than ever by fighting to control their own breath.

While it may seem trivial, simply shifting to nostril breathing can be a powerful manipulation, and is the last of the four physical elements of what I call manual override. Even such modest shifts in breathing are powerful because breath is the one vital bodily rhythm under our conscious control. By manipulating our unconscious patterns of breathing, we can have direct leverage on the primitive life support centers in the brainstem, which are closely linked with the nearby centers that set our level of consciousness. This is why the Indic traditions of yoga and meditation pay so much attention to breath control, effectively treating it as the stick-shift or joy-stick through which we can most directly influence our own nervous system, and hence, our state of consciousness.

Paying Attention: The Last Manipulation

Beyond the four body elements of manual override—centering posture, hand-placement, eye-closure, and nostril breathing—the fifth and final element is the manipulation of attention. Normally, our attention is stretched across the whole buzzing, blooming confusion of our lives, diluting and distracting it to the point where it can hardly focus on any one thing at a time. By directing our focus inwards and narrowing that focus to the simple, natural rhythm of our breathing body, the initial phase of mindfulness practice offers us a much more circumscribed and attainable challenge. In addition to vastly reducing the demands—and hence the stress—on our limited capacity for attention, breath mindfulness also serves to reconnect us with our own mind-body. The mere fact that we give ourselves permission to focus on nothing but our breathing body gives our mind-brain the message that all is safe and well enough here and now to let the world be and attend to ourselves.

This reflexive shift has the benefit of reassuring us that we are in fact still alive and more or less in one piece, while also making us aware of the level of stress we are actually feeling at the time. Despite the fact that the exercise of trying to attend consistently and continuously to the breath is far from trivial, the cumulative effect of the physical steps of manual override plus this mental step is usually enough to help even the most stressed person feel some relief. Repeated over time, this exercise serves as a simple experiment to convince even the hardened skeptic in us that, knowing the right steps and sequence, we can in fact exert some conscious control over our mind-body state. This conviction grows with practice into a sense of self-mastery that strengthens our sense of efficacy and agency within our own minds, bodies, and lives.

While breath mindfulness has rightfully become the centerpiece of recent trends in stress-reduction and self-healing, the Tibetan approach to this basic practice has some unique aspects. Based on the Nalanda tradition, the Tibetan approach takes breath mindfulness several steps further than the familiar approach of contemporary mindfulness. These steps incorporate skills developed after basic mindfulness practice, including some drawn from the advanced, mind/body process tradition mainly preserved in Tibet.[22] In particular, the skills of spreading positive breath energy and awareness throughout the whole body, and of shifting our ordinary image and sense of the body as a solid mass of flesh and blood into a meditative image and sense of it as a subtle or yogic body made of pure neural energy, neurochemistry, and awareness.[23] The benefits of this special mindfulness I call mindfulness of the breath body of light are that it helps shift the mind-body away from its fear-based stress-reactive state towards the more expansive and fluid state of abundance we experience under conditions of greater safety and contentment. This shift in turn fosters a gradual progression of simple breath mindfulness into a more profound form I call deep mindfulness.

Simple Mindfulness Versus Deep Mindfulness

To appreciate the distinctive approach to mindfulness in the Tibetan tradition, it helps to understand the distinction between the form of mindfulness popularized in the West and the classical form practiced in the Indian and Tibetan tradition. Both forms begin with simple mindfulness: the capacity to pay more or less constant attention to whatever is happening in the here and now. In the version of mindfulness popularized in the West, this is where mindfulness begins and ends. In both the classical Indian and modern Tibetan teaching traditions, however, this introductory level of mindfulness is only a first step in the practice. Traditionally, the aim of mindfulness is not just to clearly observe the events in our inner and outer world, but to have the presence and clarity of mind to distinguish unhealthy from healthy habits so as to be ready to root out the former and cultivate the latter.

Although Western mindfulness teachers stress the benefits of non-judgmental awareness, it is only false judgment or prejudice we need to avoid. Accurate, healthy judgments based on the data gathered by simple mindfulness are vital if mindfulness practice is to become an effective tool of self-healing and transformation. To help support the presence and clarity of mind needed for accurate judgments and choices, simple mindfulness must gradually progress towards deeper quiescence, and simple awareness towards analytic insight. The deeper our immersion in the altered state of mindfulness, the more it supports the deep concentration, positive energy, and analytic edge we need to decisively learn, grow, and change. The Tibetan approach to breath-body mindfulness helps prepare the beginner for the deeper immersion we will explore further in the three broader scopes of mindfulness practice to come. Once we successfully shift out of our wild, stress-reactive state into a sustainable, centered state of more or less profound clarity and calm, we are ready to move to the second truth, of origin; and the second scope of mindfulness, focused on raw sensation.

The Truth of Origin: The Cycle of Stress and Trauma

If the truth of suffering and breath mindfulness help us find a centered mind-body state that can clearly diagnose our own human condition, the second truth and scope help expose the etiology of our condition and remove the root causes driving compulsive life. As I've said, the Buddha and his heirs trace the origin of humanity and our current condition of suffering to the natural history of evolution and the personal history of development. If the touchstone of Shakyamuni's healing wisdom and method was his assumption that our lives and our suffering both emerge from natural causes, especially our own actions, the truth of origin is what spells out these causes in the multi-life context of evolution and human development. In the traditional formula, the Buddha described these causes and their causal relations as twelve links of dependent origination. Since these links are arranged in a cycle of mutual conditioning and reinforcement that sews the seeds of stress and trauma across different lives, I call them collectively the cycle of stress and trauma.

The analogy between Shakyamuni's teaching of four noble truths and new science of stress goes back to the late 1970s. It began when behavioral psychologists saw a clear family resemblance between what they call aversive conditioning—how we learn to respond under stress—and what the Buddha described as the origin of suffering.[24] At the heart of this analogy is the insight that the self-protective instincts, emotions, and reactions triggered by stressors are indistinguishable from the causes and conditions spelled out in the second truth. More recently, research on trauma has linked these same factors to the reinforcement of survival instincts, traumatic emotions and habits learned in the teeth of stresses perceived as life-threatening, such as war, domestic violence, violent crime or natural disaster.[25] The easiest way I've found to teach non-professionals about this all-important cascade of responses is by distilling the Buddha's twelve links of dependent origination into the four phases of the cycle of stress and trauma recognized today. In fact, this condensation is not mine, but simply translates a traditional way of mapping the twelve-fold cycle into four phases of action and reaction.[26]

Before surveying those four phases, it helps to remind ourselves that the stress cycle does not describe what we normally think of as "stress." It is not concerned with "how stressful" our lives are but rather with how we read, react, and respond to the challenges we think of as stress. Once a challenge perceived as a threat triggers our reactivity, it sets in motion a cascade of internal events that wreaks havoc on our minds, bodies, and lives. According to both current research and traditional teaching, it is the phases of this internal cascade that make up the cycle of stress and trauma.[27] Following current terminology, I call these four phases: (1) cognitive appraisal; (2) social emotional reaction; (3) visceral response; and (4) long-term adaptation.

Worst-Case Appraisal: The Phase of Inherited Predispositions

The first line of defense in our response to a stressful challenge is our preconception about the nature of that challenge, the level of threat it poses, and our capacity to successfully meet it. This first appraisal involves not just instinctive and learned assessments of ourselves and the world we live in, but also instinctive and learned intentions, emotions, and attitudes that color those assessments, like self-doubt or confidence. This phase corresponds to what Buddhist psychology sees as inherited predispositions, including self-protective instincts, stress-reactive emotions and habit-patterns acquired from the previous generation. These predispositions are insidious in two ways: they reflect instinctive reflexes that work under the radar of consciousness; and they also reflect deeply ingrained habit patterns that have been learned implicitly by preconscious imprinting. No matter how irrational these predispositions may be, the instant they make the snap judgment that a challenge lies beyond the scope of our capacity or agency, we have crossed the Rubicon into the realm of stress and trauma. From that point on, until proven otherwise by sober reflection and manual override, we perceive the stressor as more or less threatening and ourselves as more or less threatened, triggering the next phase in the cascade of stress-reactivity.

One all-too familiar measure of this first phase of the stress cycle is the intrusion of obsessive, worst-case thinking. I've already mentioned the evolutionary bias wired into our nervous system to enhance challenges perceived as threatening, a bias supported by fear-circuitry in a part of the old mammal brain called the amygdala. The purpose of this early-warning circuitry is to screen for anything remotely dangerous and plot its worst possible impact on a moment to moment basis.[28] Operating under the radar of consciousness, this system can easily snap to a worst case judgment way before our higher consciousness has a chance to analyze the data or check the findings.[29] We all know how quickly such insidious fear-mongering can insinuate itself, sounding an internal alarm some call "an amygdala highjack."[30] The example I typically cite is our panic response to a new deadline. Already overwhelmed, on hearing we have one more challenge, we instantly jump to the worst case fear, "I'll never make that!" Then in comes our amygdala to make matters worse, plotting the straightest line to disaster: "I'll get into a fight with my boss, get fired, wind up homeless, get sick and die!" In less than a heartbeat, a deadline has become a death-threat! This miscalculation instantly enlists all our traumatic memories and victimized sense of learned helplessness and hopeless, "Nobody loves me; everybody hates me; I'd better go eat worms!" Worse still, the misstep has hit the trip-wire that starts the time-bomb of the stress response ticking. It's only a matter of time before our inner dinosaur hijacks our higher faculties and we really are temporarily incapable of reasoning or negotiating our way out of the corner we've painted ourselves into.

Traumatic Emotions: The Phase of Stress-Reactive Development

The second phase in the cycle of stress and trauma is the development or triggering of a stress-reactive mindset, self-image and social-emotional style. Once we perceive ourselves as more or less powerless in the face of an overwhelming challenge, our first instinct is to regress to the mentality and emotional state of traumatized child or cornered animal. Here we're in the social worst case of feeling alone, abandoned and victimized by the world, "Nobody loves me; everybody hates me ..." This triggers conscious or repressed memories of childhood trauma, that painful thread of moments in which we experienced our total dependence on the love and care of adults as a life-or-death nightmare. Whether or not our experiences in fact corresponded to what we nowadays would call parental abuse or neglect, this thread of memories plays a key role as the worst case in our developing sense of ourselves and our world. Given the self-protective bias of our minds and brains, this worst case thread is typically thrust front and center in our mental life, where our instinct is to cling to it like our lifeline or security blanket, as if it were the one and only ticket to our survival in a hostile world. What emerges from this self-protective spasm is what I call the traumatized sense of self or simply traumatized self, known to Buddhist psychology as the alienated personality and to modern psychotherapy as the neurotic character. Current health psychology has found this worst-case self-image to be a central variable in stress-reactivity, through studying constructs like external locus of control, learned helplessness, and low self-efficacy.[31] The second noble truth breaks the early development and later triggering of this personality into five links or steps.

The first link is the emergence of a mind-body state contaminated by the distorted assessments and toxic attitudes of the first phase. The consciousness that emerges from that predisposing phase is alienated from others and the world, and poisoned by stress-reactive emotions, the three most common being shame, fear and rage. Based on these and related anti-social emotions, this alienated mindset goes about building the isolated self-concept and negative self-image I call the traumatized self: "I'm all alone in the world; a helpless, hopeless orphan, exposed and unable to cope." With the closure of this second link, we forge on to the third. Looking out at the world from the vantage point of this traumatized self, the mind constructs a post-traumatic sensibility like that of a combat veteran, seeking out those signs of danger that make the world seem like a cold, hard place where we must stay on guard to fight, fly, or freeze.[32] This traumatic sensibility brings us to the fourth link. Filtered through its polarizing lens, our contact with people and things in the world hits us like an aftershock or rude awakening, which seems to reinforce our sense that we need to be ever mistrustful and hyper-vigilant, like a wounded animal on the lookout for threats. Finally, the fifth link in this chain of stress-reactivity is the raw feel of distress, gnawing away at us from inside like a chronic pain punctuated only by the fleeting relief of a few titillating distractions and a few anesthetic moments of numbness.[33] Physiologically, this phase involves the heightening of the alert sounded earlier by the fear-circuitry of the limbic or old mammal brain. This heightening is accomplished in part by a shift in the baseline tone of the autonomic nervous system away from the growth-and-love activation of the parasympathetic vagus nerve and towards the fight-flight activation of the symphathetic system.[34] This shift only fuels the emotional distress of the second phase, injecting a tone of urgency or danger into the raw feel of distress.

The Visceral Stress-Response: The Phase of Compulsive Repetition

Once the phase of stress-reactivity leaves us feeling raw and distressed, it triggers the third phase of the cycle: the visceral stress-response that locks us into the compulsive repetition of stress-reactive habits and traumatic experience. Triggered by the raw feel of hurt, and fueled by the poisons of shame, fear and rage, we feel toxic inside and driven to spring into action, craving either a conquest or an escape. Here is where our most primitive survival instincts kick in, locking us into a neurochemical suit of armor that serves to tune every organ system to the demands of physical combat or retreat. Escalating the alert mode of sympathetic alarm, the pituitary at the base of our brain sends out a chemical messenger called adrenocorticotropic hormone or ACTH.[35] This messenger tells the adrenal glands resting over the kidneys to arm our whole body-mind to fight or fly, by pumping out adrenalin and corticosteroids that rush to every tissue and cell, kicking us into life-or-death overdrive. Heightening the alarm in a confusing way, this biochemical cocktail is spiked with endorphins, which leave us feeling no pain, and pump us up to a peak state in which we may feel as invulnerable as Superman, as powerful as the Hulk, and as elusive as Spiderman. At this point, we're hooked—adrenalin junkies spoiling for a fight, hungry for blood, or literally ready to fly! In terms of the second truth, this is the link of craving.

The irony is, just when we feel we can take anything on, we are in fact completely mismatched to the life challenges we actually face. With our higher social faculties for communication, empathy and judgment shut down, along with our capacity to learn, grow, and change, we are more like King Kong or Godzilla than Superman, living relics of the jungle from a bygone age, completely out of our element and out of step with civilization.[36] All that is left to us is to impulsively act out the irrational and antisocial programs of our inner dinosaur, caving in to the self-destruct overdrive of obsessive, addictive, and compulsive behavior. Once we give into to the misguided impulses of our inner dinosaur, from a Buddhist standpoint, we move into the second link in the phase of repetition: the link of clinging or compulsion. This binding link has two sides, one more insidious than the other. The more familiar side of compulsion is directed outwards with the force of attachment and aversion, onto persons, places and things which stir our primitive habits of desire, greed, lust, and possessiveness, or their seeming opposites, envy, competition, hate, and violence. The more insidious side of compulsion is directed inwards with the force of delusion, grasping onto the toxic state of a body-mind poisoned by stress and trauma as if it were our true nature, identity and self, and holding on for dear life. From the Buddhist perspective, the visceral response of stress is a two-edged death grip that locks our outer and inner lives into a self-destructive survival mode, driving us inexorably to relive ancient stresses and traumas in a cycle as unnecessary as it is pointless.

So it is that the link of compulsion binds us inescapably to the tenth link in the cycle of stress: a compulsive existence or way of being. This link involves the mindless repetition and reinforcement of the whole range of activity—mental, verbal, and physical—that is driven by a toxic mixture of post-traumatic perceptions of self and world with the prime destructive emotions like shame, fear, rage, greed, envy, arrogance, and/or their many derivates. It is this deluded, self-destructive behavior that plants the seeds for replicating an archaic, survival-based way of being, seeds which eventually ripen into one of the six forms of obsessive, compulsive or addictive personality and lifestyle.[37] Once this link has been forged, it binds us to the fourth phase of the cycle of stress and trauma, the phase of long-term adaptation.

Long-Term Adaptation: The Phase of Eventual Suffering

The fourth and final phase of the stress-reactive life cycle has two parts. It begins with the gradual unfolding of an obsessive, compulsive, or addictive form of life as a result of all the stress and trauma we accumulate over the years, or inherit and repeat from prior generations.[38] This unfolding, the tenth link in the twelve-fold cycle, consists in the mindless reproduction or reincarnation of compulsive life, a process reminiscent of Freud's "repetition compulsion." As a result of this, there eventually follows the twelfth and last link, the all-too-human condition of suffering unpacked as: stress-related illness; premature aging; traumatic death; senseless loss; unresolved grief; and perennial mourning. The reactive nature of this phase completes the oscillating cycle of activity and reactivity that characterizes the reflex conditioning of stress and trauma. The compulsive lifestyle we develop in our lifetime or pass onto the next generation reflects the traumatic activity of the third phase of compulsive repetition, just as the stress-reactive personality developed in phase two reflects the predisposing activity of the first phase of narcissistic self-deception. In short, past activity leads to reactivity in the present; present activity leads to reactivity in the future. The final nail in the coffin is that this final phase of adaptation feeds into the first phase of the next cycle, further predisposing us to stress-reactivity, compulsive repetition and eventual suffering. In the traditional simile, living beings are like the buckets in the water-wheel of stress and trauma, helplessly cycling from one phase of stress, one stage of traumatic life, and one generation of suffering to another.[39]

Drawing on the work of my colleague, stress researcher Bruce McEwan,[40] I find it helps to compare the cumulative effect of stress and trauma on human development to the balancing of a bank account. Each time we revert to stress, given its high cost in energy and the havoc it wreaks in our lives, we dip into our mind/body reserves, effectively withdrawing funds from our bio-bank account. Each time we recharge in rest, relaxation, or play, we replenish our mind/body reserves, effectively making a deposit in our bank. If, over time, we spend more time and energy in stress and trauma than in rest and regeneration, our withdrawals effectively exceed our deposits, eventually leaving us bankrupt in body, mind, and spirit. This is the origin of the various syndromes of chronic fatigue, exhaustion or burnout that shadow obsessive, compulsive, or addictive lifestyles as inevitably as night follows day.

Some of the dramatic mind/body effects of chronic overexposure to stress and trauma serve to illustrate the inexorable logic of this fourth phase. We saw in the third phase that the visceral stress response prepares our mind/body to fight or fly, while shutting down any systems that would either impede our capacity for combat and/or escape or else drain unnecessary energy and blood flow from our musculature and reptilian brain. If this diversion of energy and blood flow is consistent enough, the neglected systems of our body-mind begin to atrophy. Studies of poor little rats overexposed to stress show the structure and function of their immune tissues degrade in proportion to their cumulative stress.[41]

One striking textbook image I recall placed photos of the dissected lymph nodes of a stressed rat alongside those of an unstressed rat; the contrast between the shrunken, darkened tissue on the one hand and the light, fluffy tissue on the other was literally black and white. An equally striking contrast was found in multiple studies comparing the hippocampus and prefrontal cortex of people overexposed to stress hormones with the brains of less stressed individuals. These brain areas involved in memory, social interaction and task-execution are markedly atrophied in chronically stressed individuals compared with the general population.[42] Immunity, healing, tissue regeneration, collaboration, and learning are just some of the systems that are shut down under stress and atrophy with chronic stress-exposure.[43] This short list alone is enough to make the point that the more humans adapt to stress, the more we become maladapted to civilized living.

Living Systems and Circular Causes: The Complexity of Stress and Trauma

The Buddha's cyclic model of the causality of suffering anticipated not just current models of stress and trauma but also contemporary thinking about how causality works in living systems, as opposed to inanimate matter.[44] His depiction of the origin of suffering as a chain reaction of interactive events linked together in a self-perpetuating cycle resonates strongly with current systems models of causal cycles in physiology and feedback loops within ecosystems. In addition, his complex, multi-dimensional view of this model was also ahead of its time in that it depicts the cycle of stress-reactivity as a waveform which oscillates at many frequencies at once: across eons of evolution; across distinct generations; within the span of a single life; and within the micro-periods of each day, hour and moment of life. Even more sophisticated and powerful was his insight that the cycle as a whole was reversible at every point and depended on the cooperation of each causal link, as well as secondary network of supporting conditions for its continuation. This insight that human suffering depends on a finite number of elements linked in complex, nested cycles of interdependence proved the most profound aspect of his teaching. Its power was not just explanatory but practical as well, since it showed how manipulating one or more of these causes and conditions could help break and even reverse the whole cycle of stress and trauma.

If the four phases of this cycle sound bleak, we must recall that they represent only one strand of human experience, however much it stands out as the worst case. Sadly, most of us can relate all too well to the cycle and each of its phases. Yet as we saw in exploring the fourth phase, adaptation, the extent to which we spend our hours and days locked in the survival mode of stress and trauma is the extent to which it pervades and colors our whole experience of daily life. From the standpoint of both contemplative science and current psychotherapy, this strand in our development, personality, and lifestyle is critical to expose and disarm, since it holds us back from health and happiness like a ball-and-chain, and triggers our worst-case instincts and memories like a trip wire in the mine-field left from our struggle for survival in the course of evolution and early childhood.

The Second Scope of Practice: Mindfulness of Sensation

The second scope of mindfulness practice helps put the Buddha's insight of interdependence to work. Its focus is on the last link in the second phase of the cycle of stress and trauma, raw feel or sensation. Like breath mindfulness, the focus of this scope seems deceptively simple: feelings of pleasure or comfort; pain or displeasure; and numbness or indifference. One might well ask, "Of all the negative factors mobilized in the second truth of origins, why focus simply on pain-pleasure sensation?" The answer is twofold. First, feelings of pain or pleasure go to the heart of what matters most to us all: our level of suffering or happiness in the here and now. Focusing on exactly how we feel in every moment is like keeping the finger of our attention on the pulse of the truth of suffering and its causes. In a sense, the raw feel of our lives represents the bottom line of our moment-to-moment, breath-to-breath happiness or unhappiness. It tells us how well we're managing to care for our needs and live well with others in the world we share. It keeps us humble, honest, and grounded in the here and now.

Beyond the importance of raw feeling as a vital sign of distress or well-being, there's another reason why we devote one whole share of our mindfulness to sensation. That reason has to do with the pragmatics of self-healing and contemplative life. Feeling's location at the juncture where the first reactive phase of the stress cycle meets the next phase in which we jump into action makes it strategic and pivotal. As we all know, raw feeling is often the springboard or jumping off point where an impulse grabs us. Hence the acronym from the recovery movement to H-A-L-T before we leap, especially when we're **H**ungry, **A**ngry, **L**onely, or **T**ired. From the standpoint of Buddhist contemplative science, it's said that there are two places where the chain of events in the cycle of stress and trauma is weakest and can be most easily broken. The first and most radical break-point is the first link of delusion; the second is at the eighth step of craving or longing. Of the two, the weakest link is the latter, the link of craving. As the immediately preceding link, sensation is the last stop where we still have a chance to avoid falling prey to craving or longing and the third phase it sets in motion.

The logic here is simple enough. As we all know, we are usually far more able to be mindful of our options and choose wisely when we feel as comfortable, content, and cared for as possible. On the other hand, with the raw feel of distress gnawing at us from within, it can be very hard indeed to resist the impulse to crave some sort of indulgence or stimulation, no matter how addictive or fleeting. Mindfulness of sensation is meant to give us the leverage to head craving off at the pass, in part by reminding us to take better care of ourselves, and in part by paying close attention to the impulses that arise from distress.

The Truth of Freedom: Life as Sustainable Peace and Happiness

I like to think of the four noble truths as the Buddha saying about our human condition, "I have good news; and I have bad news." He gave us the bad news first not because he was a pessimist or because it's more important, but out of compassion. The sad fact is, as we know, we all spend far too much time embroiled in negativity and needless suffering. This is where our journey towards healing and learning begins, and so this is where the four truths begin. But now that we've reached the third truth of freedom, the story changes quite suddenly and dramatically. Having grappled with the reversible cycle of causes that seems to lock each one of us into the death row of repetitive stress and trauma, we are now ready to seriously entertain the good news. It begins with the third truth, a stark challenge to our habit of discontent and a promising reminder of our natural potential to cut through the fabric of instinct and habit that binds us in a straightjacket of stress-chemistry and traumatic memories.

This leads us to the fourth truth, to the second piece of good news which challenges us even further by offering a reproducible method we all can follow: a path of thoughts and actions to help us unravel that fabric, one thread at a time. Although the Dalai Lama, in his usual modesty, often calls the first two truths scientific and the second two, spiritual, the fact of the matter is, all four are strictly rational and have an evidence-base in current and traditional science. The real distinction between the truths is largely one of experience. We're all firmly convinced of the bad news—the truths of suffering and origin—by our own personal experience, while very few of us have enough experience with the good news—the truths of freedom and the path to it—to believe in their incredible promise and challenge.

The Buddha began his teaching with the bad news, knowing full well that most of his audience could relate to it all too easily from their daily experience. His intent was to help us fully understand the stress we experience first-hand well enough that we can try to let it go and open our hearts and minds to the incredibly good news he learned from his own personal experience. So the truths he taught are not abstract formulas sent down from on high, but personal pointers from a guide who has returned from a journey we all need to take. That is why, like different signposts, the four truths must be approached in four different ways. The first truth shows us what we must understand, helping us find a place from which we can see where and how we are stuck. The second tells us what we must leave behind, helping us pinpoint and put down the causes and conditions which block our progress. The third truth points out the aim we must realize, that place deep within in which our body-minds are naturally free and clear of stress and trauma. And the fourth truth teaches the way we must take, cultivating an outlook, lifestyle and mindset that gradually strengthen us to part ways with the cycle of stress-reactive life once and for all.

So now we've arrived at the place from which this chapter began, the experience called Nirvana that was the holy grail of Shakyamuni's journey to the end of suffering. This is the place in which he found his true nature to be the inner medicine of profound peace, pure bliss and light. I call it the truth of freedom because Nirvana does not mean what we think it does. It is not a perfect place apart, a great escape or anesthetic trance in which our world ends, any more than it is the Indian restaurant called Nirvana I went to once in a penthouse on Central Park South. Of course, literally, it does mean cessation or extinction, a state in which something has come to an end. Nevertheless, what ends in Nirvana is not life itself, but a compulsive way of life driven by survival instincts gone wild and stress-reactive habits from our childhood nightmares. Technically, it refers to the end of mindless suffering and its root causes, the twelve links of the repetitive life cycle of stress and trauma. Because that end is also the beginning of a life free from mindless suffering and clear of its causes and conditions, I call it the truth of freedom. And as one of my favorite teachers, Lama Anagarika Govinda, once said, it might just as well be called the truth of happiness, since the realization of Nirvana is no more or less than the end of our gradually adapting to irrevocable, unconditional happiness.[45] A German-born painter and Tibetan-trained contemplative, Govinda went on to explain that Shakyamuni defined the third truth in negative terms for two reasons: to distill the noble truths down to their healing essence, suffering and its end; and to avoid stirring confusion or doubt by avoiding descriptions of an experience of profound, lasting happiness few of us has ever had.

The Truth of Freedom Today: Learning, Plasticity, and Gene Regulation

Despite the caveats above, as a therapist I find the use of the term Nirvana or extinction especially relevant. I believe it is no accident that behavioral psychologists chose essentially the same term to describe the final deprogramming and unlearning of a conditioned response like Pavlov's dogs salivating at the dinner bell. Another reason I like the term freedom is that it describes better than anything else the profound, liberating effect of overriding and dismantling instincts and habits conditioned over eons of evolution and decades of development. In fact, one way to describe the whole approach to the mind taken by cognitive behavioral therapy is that it emphasizes our human potential for freedom. Why is this?

In contrast to most modern models of mind including Freud's, the learning model of cognitive therapy assumes that human behavior and the life of the mind is more shaped by learning than by instinctive programs. This assumption leads to greater therapeutic optimism, since the model also teaches that what has been learned, under the right conditions, can be unlearned. Surprisingly enough, this optimistic idea has received ample support from many recent findings in neuroscience. One of these is the fact that, after decades of trying to locate the fixed, hard-wired traces of learning and memory, researchers concluded that there are no such traces, but that learning and memory is stored in wave-fashion through whole regions, based in part on shifting networks of interconnections linking different areas of nerve cells.[46] Not only is learning holistically stored as in a hologram, but the wetware network that supports it is, as I've said, is not hard wired after all but quite plastic. Such findings not only help explain how people recover from devastating brain injuries, but more importantly, they also help us see how flexible and adaptable our brains and our natures really are.[47] In a sense, they add hard evidence to the learning model of cognitive science, issuing all humanity a declaration of independence from the tyranny of instinct and habit, a tyranny most of us have been taught to accept as the hard truth.

If the new model of learning and plasticity is not enough to encourage us, new trends in biology have added further support to the optimism of the third noble truth. After generations, even centuries, of debate about human nature, evolutionary biologists are now in broad agreement that human nature is best thought of as neither intrinsically kind or violent, good or evil, but rather as naturally flexible and adaptable. In fact, the term that has come into currency most recently to describe human nature is a variation on the theme of cognitive science. According to Dobshansky and his followers, the most distinctive quality of human nature is to be "educable," that is, born ready, willing and able to learn. In a sense, what we think of as our nature, for good or ill, is almost entirely a second nature.[48] Our first nature is to be capable of a wide range of behavior and flexible in adapting to diverse natural and social environments. In this sense, any human way of being must be seen as a complex, creative interplay of nature plus nurture, an interplay that ideally continues throughout the lifespan and makes us lifelong works-in-progress.

On the molecular level, this adaptive flexibility is consistent with the diversity and redundancy of the human genome. As the mostly highly evolved mammals, our genomes represent a vast grab-bag of traits, able to support an incomparable range of diverse modes and styles of adaption. This is especially true of our complex brains, which claim over 40 percent of our genome, though they use a fraction of this data-base at any one time. While we are taught to picture our development as biologically determined by the blueprint of DNA, the truth is that our genes work more like language or my childhood Erector Set: as a kit of assorted bits, pieces, odds and ends, which can be assembled into a nearly endless variety of diverse structures, depending on the demands posed by nature, society and our own mind/body state. This top-down selection, called gene regulation, holds up the molecular end of learning and development, building a cellular infrastructure to support the second nature that best adapts us to changing environments.[49] In a sense, this part of adaptation inverts what we think of as the natural sequence of development, as if the foundation were put in not before but *after* we build our house.

The Sole, Supreme Truth: Freeing the Mind from Self-Limiting Habits

Anticipating these new insights into our protean nature, the truth of freedom explains what it is about human potential that makes us capable of such radical transformations. Tapping into the womb or well of eternal youth hidden somewhere deep inside us, the Buddha's realization of freedom provided a contemplative evidence base for some very prescient conclusions about human nature. According to Buddhist contemplative science, our minds and nervous systems are naturally clear and pliant, while the habits we take for our "nature" are extraneous factors that can be removed and/or changed under the right mind/body conditions. This profound truth is expressed in many of the most distinctive insights and metaphors of Buddhist psychology: that our minds and bodies are "selfless;" that our essential nature is to be "natureless," our true identity, "identityless;" that our lives are grounded in "groundlessness;" and that our minds are as boundless and open as empty space.

How does the truth of freedom and its radical view of human nature as clear and open square with the theory of instincts in Buddhist life science? Like Freud and contemporary biology, Buddhist contemplative science recognizes that human beings have two conflicting kinds of instincts: the self-protective kind driving compulsive life and the social kind that sustain civilized life. Yet like contemporary psychology and unlike Freud, the truth of freedom emphasizes our more recent social instincts, portraying them as our truest nature. While the first two truths explain in detail our natural involvement with self-protective stress and trauma, the Buddha insisted that the third truth which unpacks our potential for living freely and happily with others is somehow truer to our nature. So he repeatedly taught his followers, "Mendicants, non-deceptive in nature, this Nirvana is the sole, supreme truth."[50] His memory of his prior lives reveals one reason for this emphasis. As higher mammals, we humans have a special capacity and affinity for getting outside ourselves through objective awareness and social emotions like love and compassion. This greater sociability presumes an expanded capacity to free ourselves from primitive self-protective instincts and the traumatic memories that trigger them.

The Buddha's other reason for emphasizing our potential for freedom is implicit in his claim that Nirvana is "non-deceptive." What he means by this is that, unlike our mind in stress, our mind at peace does not project or reify a fixed and rigid sense of self alienated from the world, but instead is open, free and clear to see, engage, and adapt to reality as it is, here and now. In the deepest sense, Nirvana means that state in which our minds break free of self-deception and the confused emotions it stirs, and so are fully prepared to proactively engage with others and the world around us. So the truth of freedom is also the "sole, supreme truth" about our nature because it points to that free and clear part of or being which helps us adapt most readily to the social and cultural challenges of civilized living.

The Nature of Mind and the Scope of Deep Mindfulness

Given the profound meaning and liberating value of the truth of freedom, how can we possibly put it into practice, enmeshed as we are in daily struggles with the mindless reactivity of stress and trauma? The way the Nalanda tradition helps to make this pivotal truth accessible even to novices is to use the third scope of mindfulness practice, mindfulness of mind. This key scope of practice, little known in the West, is traditionally used as a meditative shortcut to tap our innate potential for deep, inner peace. Since the simple mindfulness popularized in the West focuses on "being present to everything happening in the here and now," it has the unfortunate effect of seeming to ratify our ordinary waking state mindset and our limited sense of our own inner and outer worlds. Of course, the emphasis on facing and accepting daily experience is what makes simple mindfulness feel so accessible and helpful to beginners.

At the same time, the scope of practice commonly talked about in mainstream circles today stays precariously close to the consensus consciousness forged under the influence of our stress instincts and compulsive way of life. Just as our modern materialist view of the world glosses over the depth and power of mind, simple mindfulness as currently taught tends to leapfrog from the narrow scopes of the breath-body and its raw feel to the wide-angle lens of the fourth scope: the buzzing blooming confusion of our thoughts, perceptions, and emotions about daily life. The classical practice of mindfulness takes a very different path, diving into the mindfulness of mind as the royal road to deepen and stabilize clarity and calm, building a platform that raises mindfulness practice to its final level, called insight meditation. In an effort to make this royal road into a superhighway, the Nalanda tradition expanded on the classical practice of mindfulness of mind by introducing the meditative power tool I call deep mindfulness, known to Tibetans as the practice of natural liberation, the great perfection and the great seal.[51] In order to appreciate the power of this tool, we need to consider how the traditional Buddhist view of mind anticipated current shifts away from our modern identification of mind with higher cortical functions like thought and speech.

Over the last century, our modern view of the mind as identical with thought has been increasingly challenged, first by psychoanalysis and more recently by neuroscience. Psychotherapy shows that our peculiarly modern identification with internal dialogue to the exclusion of other levels or aspects of mind predisposes us to inner conflicts and fragmentation that can seriously impact our lives.[52] More recently, neuroscience has overturned the Cartesian view of higher cognition as split off from more primal emotion, helping to diagnose a pandemic neglect of emotional intelligence that plagues our lives at home, school, and work.[53] Even more challenging to our received view of mind is the growing number of cases in which clinically "brain-dead" individuals with no cortical activity regain waking consciousness only to accurately report events and statements they registered around them during near death experiences, under anesthesia or in chronic vegetative states.[54] Taken together, these challenges force us to rethink our whole concept of mind in ways that bring it closer to the views of most of humanity throughout history, including the contemplative traditions India and Tibet.

Naturally Lucid Awareness: The Primordial Mind

There are two main ways in which the view of the mind in Buddhist psychology is more consistent with current science than our received view of mind. The first of these has to do with distinguishing process from content; the second, with the way it maps the mind in relation to different levels and states of consciousness. Reflecting the Buddha's interest in realizing human potential through expanding our normal capacity of mind, Buddhist psychology begins by distinguishing the mind as a medium from the informational content it processes. In particular, mind is defined as lucid or clarifying awareness, and distinguished from mental functions like discursive thinking, emotion or sensation.[55] While recognizing that mind as a medium cannot be split from some of its functions, defining mind as a pure capacity, naturally free and clear, makes sense in a therapeutic psychology aimed at freeing us from self-limiting ties to stress instincts and traumatic habits of thought, feeling, and action. Likewise, reflecting the Buddha's teaching method of using contemplative states to help overcome blocks to learning and change, mind is identified as much or more with its deepest, primal levels and altered states as with the highest, surface level of waking consciousness with which we normally identify.[56] This mapping tends to encourage the exploration and integration of all levels and states of mind, while preferentially directing us to powerful and profound altered states that help us expose and disarm self-limiting instincts and habits.

With this background, we are ready to understand mindfulness of mind and to practice it as a path to deep mindfulness. The first thing to understand is that mindfulness of mind is not mindfulness of thoughts or feelings, but mindfulness focused on the lucid awareness that can know and reflect on those contents. The traditional pointer here is to focus not on thoughts, images and emotions but "on the space between them," as one might look at the sky as distinct from the clouds passing through it. Here, the centering process consists in catching the mind when it gets carried away from itself and stuck on mental contents, and then, with the muscle of mindfulness, reigning it back towards the glimpses or moments of spacious openness "in-between" mental contents. On the other hand, when the mind temporarily freed of content begins to slip into dullness or clouding, once we catch ourselves with the mental muscle of alertness, we rouse and lift the mind back up to the spacious clarity of lucid awareness. By balancing and centering ourselves in this way with mindfulness and alertness, our minds gradually begin to feel more open, spacious, clear and expansive. In the context of this practice, we gradually gain the perspective to watch the flow or stream of consciousness in its pure process, without getting carried away as usual by the torrent of words and images we normally take for our mind.

Recovering the Lost Inner Space and Depth of the Mind

This scope of mindfulness introduces most moderns to an experience of inner space that reveals a hidden fifth dimension to our consensus experience of the world. This dimension is news to us as moderns for two main reasons. First, the survival mode that drives much of our lives tends to project our consciousness outwards towards the challenges we face in the world, making our minds narrow, superficial and self-forgetful.[57] Adding to this, the materialist bent of our modern culture has further narrowed the space the mind occupies in our map of the world, fixating our attention on our physical bodies and the external objects which we take to be the only effective factors of happiness in the world. Against the natural and cultural backdrop of our default mindset, the opening up of a whole new dimension of space and depth within us represents a fundamental shift in our waking state consciousness. This new inner dimension also adds two new degrees of freedom to the life of the mind: it makes us aware in a more balanced way of our inner *and* outer environments; and it clears a space for expanded awareness of our mental life that opens new options for our responses and actions. In this sense, mindfulness of mind does far more than simply alert us to "what's on our minds, here and now." Beyond such simple mindfulness of our mental contents, this scope of mindfulness alters our default state of mind and hence shifts our perspective on our experience and life. That is why, more than any other scope of mindfulness practice, this one stands as a gateway or royal road to a new, contemplative mindset and way of life.[58]

As if the new inner space and new inner freedoms opened by mindfulness of mind were not enough, there is yet one more new dimension it opens in our practice and lives. This last new dimension is the uniquely contemplative one of enhanced depth of mind. In my initial description of mindfulness, I compared this contemplative state to a new platform for waking state consciousness, a platform strategically placed in-between the oscillating extremes of our stress-reactive mindset, midway between hyperactivity and slowed down drowsiness. Actually, this deepening of waking state consciousness into levels of mind normally experienced only in daydream or light sleep is just the start of an ongoing process that cuts across all meditative life: pushing the lower limits of awareness deeper and deeper into the subconscious mind. I touched on the rationale for this process in my thumbnail sketch of the Buddhist approach to the mind. Inverting the Cartesian preference for verbal consciousness, the Buddhist approach values the deepest, most primal levels of mind for their potential to speed the process of self-transformation. Anticipating the conception of Freud, Buddhist psychology sees the deepest, normally unconscious layers of mind as more powerful in shaping the stream of consciousness. Yet more like the esoteric therapies of Jung and Reich than the psychoanalytic mainstream, Buddhist contemplative science offers methods of tapping and mastering these deep layers of mind as power-tools for self-exploration and change. Mindfulness of mind is the first of many such methods, the doorway to deeper immersion in increasingly more profound states and levels of mind.

By breaking free of mental content that creates turbulence in surface consciousness as wind stirs ocean waves, mindfulness of mind allows us to submerge our attention into the clearer, calmer depths of the mind. By building our capacity to guard the mind from clouding or dullness as we become more deeply immersed and absorbed, awareness of mind allows us to keep our waking clarity at depths of mind we normally experience only in dreams or deep sleep.

The benefits of such deep mindfulness for healing and learning are twofold. First, the deeper the contemplative state, the more resistant it is to distraction and the more stably and single-pointedly it supports our attention. Second, the deeper the contemplative state, the closer it is to the primitive instincts and early childhood memories that must be exposed and changed in order to disarm stress and unlearn trauma.[59] In this way, mindfulness of mind allows us to deepen and intensify simple mindfulness practice to the point at which it can serve as a more effective vehicle of contemplative healing and learning. In short, this scope of practice allows us to turn simple mindfulness into deep mindfulness, delivering the medicine of clarity, calm, awareness and insight in a more potent and targeted way to the depths of the mind to expose and cut the roots of our problems.

The Truth of the Path: Making Each Breath an Opportunity to Learn

Where simple mindfulness can help us become more aware of what's happening in our daily lives, deep mindfulness gives us a taste of a more contemplative way to live our daily lives. While we may be a long way from Shakyamuni's experience of life as naturally peaceful, blissful, and clear, deep mindfulness of mind offers us a glimpse here and now of that part of our mind which has the potential to follow in his footsteps. For those of us who long to shift the course of our lives towards greater peace, freedom, and happiness, the Buddha gave very explicit directions about the steps we can follow to gradually replicate his realization. Of all the aspects of Buddhist teaching, the steps spelled out in the truth of the path are traditionally viewed as having the most practical relevance and importance to our daily lives. The reason for this seems plain enough: the practical steps that make up the truth of the path are the bridge that promises to take us from the stress-reactive life we lead now towards a contemplative life in which we realize our potential for inner freedom and lasting happiness. Yet the traditional rationale for the importance of the path emphasizes a distinctive aspect of the Buddha's vision of human progress: the key role of mastering the causality of suffering and happiness.

In line with the insight that the heart of all Shakyamuni's teachings was his discovery of mind/body causation, the four noble truths are traditionally unpacked in terms of two antithetical cause-effect relationships. The first truth lays out the cumulative effects of the process of needless suffering, while the second truth defines its causes: the twelve-fold cycle of stress and trauma. Antithetical to this causal relationship, the third truth presents the ultimate effects of the process of healing and happiness, while the fourth truth maps its causes: the eight-fold path of contemplative learning, healing, and change.[60] So where the third truth defines the therapeutic aim of all Buddhist teaching and practice, the fourth truth lays out their pedagogic method. As the system, procedure, or technology that makes it possible for an ordinary person to follow the Buddha on his extraordinary journey, the truth of the path plays the all-important role of the medicine or catalyst that brings our potential for freedom and happiness to actual fruition.

Three Disciplines, Three Phases, and Three Sources of Contemplative Learning

The traditional way the path to contemplative living is taught and practiced in India and Tibet holds many surprises for Western-educated students and practitioners. In presenting this truth, I've found it helps to address these surprises up front. First, given our romance with technology, we tend to see meditation as the active ingredient or engine of contemplative learning and progress. Indic contemplative science, on the other hand, views meditation as a value-neutral technique, necessary but not sufficient for contemplative self-healing and genuine happiness. The structure of the fourth truth reflects the broad consensus of Indic traditions that, without the guidance of wisdom and the infrastructure of a healthy lifestyle, meditation—like a bird without wings—just won't fly.

Second, given our obsession with quick fixes and mechanical solutions, we expect results on day one and tend to see meditation as a way to cut through the jungle of our confused thinking, disturbing emotions, and bad habits. The Indic tradition, on the contrary, sees contemplative healing as a lifelong process of incremental change that begins with good old intellectual learning, moves through a series of geologic shifts in motivation and lifestyle, and only then culminates in profound mind/body change, with the visceral learning of deep meditation.

Third and last, given our fierce independence and our deep misgivings about going to others for help, the idea of meditation appeals to us because it seems to offer a way to build our will-power and capacity without letting go of control or making ourselves vulnerable by placing our trust in spiritual traditions or other sources of guidance and help. Here too, the Indo-Tibetan tradition surprises us, by insisting that the most reliable way to develop ourselves is to identify sources of help—including expert role-models, time-tested traditions, and peer learning networks—and to put them to the test by leaning on them for encouragement, guidance and support.

Unpacking the Disciplines: The Eight Steps of Contemplative Living

The simplest way to map the truth of the path is in terms of the three core disciplines the Buddha taught as the basic to contemplative learning and healing. Yet the most popular and familiar way to map the path is in terms of the eight steps which help us build these core disciplines. I've found that reviewing these eight steps helps people unfamiliar with the truth of the path get a glimpse of the lifelong journey of building the three higher disciplines of wisdom, ethics and meditation. Traditionally, the eight steps are divided into three groups, each group supporting the gradual development of one of the three core disciplines of contemplative living and learning. Specifically, the first two steps—realistic outlook and positive intention—support the development of self-critical wisdom. Understanding Shakyamuni's insight that life is not created by God or a random accident of Nature but the result of causes and conditions, especially our intentional acts, we learn to shift our intentions from negative to positive. Next, in steps three through five—appropriate speech, execution and lifestyle—we practice building the ethical discipline of our motivation and action, to build a way of being and life that embodies wisdom and supports peace of mind. Finally, in the last three steps—appropriate effort, perfect mindfulness and concentration—we build the discipline of meditation, that allows us integrate our whole mind-body process with our highest awareness and motivation.

Of course, these steps are so fundamental to building a contemplative life that they deserve a chapter to themselves. So we'll postpone examining them in detail until chapter 3, when we explore the path of day-to-day practice they help guide and sustain. For now, let's go on to complete our brief survey of the fourfold practice of mindfulness.

All-Inclusive Mindfulness: Basic Training for Insight Meditation

This ultimate scope of mindfulness is the one that helps the novice start putting the truth of the path into practice. Although I like to call it "all-inclusive," traditionally this scope of practice is defined as mindfulness of phenomena, that is, mindfulness of the basic elements of our daily experience. This distinction is not academic since it goes to the heart of the current misconception that mindfulness meditation begins and ends with paying equal, non-judgmental attention to everything happening in our lives, here and now.

Figure 1.1 Vasubandhu, Master of Contemplative Psychology

Despite my description of this scope as all-inclusive, the term phenomena or element does not literally refer to everything whatsoever. Since simply being aware of suffering does not reduce or end it, and simply being aware of happiness does not increase or build it, the Buddha and his heirs took care to help beginners identify and focus on those basic elements of experience that are relevant to the causality of suffering and happiness. The scientific teaching tradition codified the Buddha's analysis of those systems and elements into a table of elements of suffering and happiness, akin to but very different from the periodic table of physical elements defined by modern science.[61] So traditionally, when the Buddha said one should be mindful of "everything that exists,"[62] what he meant was that we must learn to pay close attention to each and every one of the elements that were later placed on that table. While the number of elements varied in different teaching traditions, it was always finite, classically between 65 and 105. More importantly, as in modern physics or chemistry, so in Buddhist contemplative science, identifying these causal elements is only the first step on the way to predicting and controlling their behavior and outcome. So all-inclusive mindfulness is that vital scope of mindfulness practice that helps us clearly identify the elements as causal variables, and sustain the focus and insight we need to arrive at realistic judgments, decisions, and actions that have the power to transform our ordinary suffering into extraordinary happiness. Within the Nalanda tradition, the master psychologist Vasubandu catalogued and refined this classical system of basic science in his *Treasury of Scientific Teaching.*

We will go on to explore the elements of suffering and happiness in detail when we look at the contemplative science of mindfulness practice in chapter 2. For now, we only need to touch on a few key aspects of the practice and experience of all-inclusive mindfulness. The first of these aspects has to do with the mind-body state in which we can best practice all-inclusive mindfulness. The second relates to the best way to enter and stabilize that state. And the third describes the experience and application of all-inclusive mindfulness within meditation sessions and in-between sessions in daily life.

Deep Mindfulness of the Elements: The Path of True Judgment and Acceptance

As I hinted when we explored mindfulness of mind, it is vital to the practice of all-inclusive mindfulness that we not settle for simple mindfulness, merely noticing or attending to our experience in the here and now. Unless and until we are in a mind/body state that is decidedly clearer and calmer than our ordinary, stressed waking state, our perception of the elements of our experience is likely to be biased by a worst-case outlook and tainted by stress emotions and reactivity. While the popular teaching of simple mindfulness today tries to minimize these distorting factors by advising us to attend to things with non-judgmental acceptance, as long as we are in a waking state close to our stress-reactive norm, the condition of our mind and nervous system is already biased and tainted. In this case, simply telling ourselves to be non-judgmental and accepting will only go skin deep. If we are to bring a truly open mind and fresh energy to our experience, we need to dive below the surface into deep mindfulness. This is why the prior scopes of mindfulness practice—focused on the breathing body, raw feel and pure mind—are vital to altering our default state of mind.

Mindfulness of the breathing body should help us shift into a more centered mind/body state, akin to what I call the breath-body of light. Mindfulness of sensation can the help us iron out the wrinkles in our comfort level, helping us feel more balanced and calm in our own skin. And mindfulness of mind is absolutely key to disengaging and purging our minds and nerves of stress-reactive thoughts, emotions and images. Without these preliminary steps, we'll find it very hard indeed to bring a more unbiased clarity and untainted calm to the elements of our experience. And as a result, we are very unlikely to be able to engage with the content of our experience in a non-reactive way. We'll know we haven't gone deep enough when what is supposed to be all-inclusive mindfulness seems to make everything look more confused and feel more disturbing than everyday mindlessness! When this is the case, we need to shut down one scope at a time—resolve all-inclusive mindfulness to mindfulness of mind; mindfulness of mind to mindfulness of sensation; and mindfulness of sensation to breath-body mindfulness—until we get back to something that feels qualitatively clearer and calmer. Once we've regained a real sense of being centered in greater clarity and calm, we can "reboot" the wider scopes of mindfulness, one at a time. It is vital to bring as much patience as we can muster to this practice, building towards all-inclusive mindfulness slowly and carefully, one scope at a time. Even in this day of instant communication and space travel, there is just no way to rush peace of mind!

As for experience and daily use, this last scope of mindfulness more than any other helps put us in touch with the truth of the path. While there are many descriptions out there of how it should feel to let thoughts, emotions and images come and go mindfully, my favorite is the simile of watching them from a deeper mind-state, like a scuba diver watching surface waves and reflections from the clarity and calm of a deep dive. Of course, you could also compare the feel of full mindfulness to what it must be like looking down from deep space on the good, bad and neutral weather patterns swirling around the earth's surface. The point is, our clarity and calm should be deep and stable enough that we can see the things that normally trigger us as if for the first time, from the perspective of a mind/body state that insulates us from reactivity and helps us feel unperturbed by the currents of stress and trauma. If we find ourselves getting caught up in what we see, either clinging to what seems positive or repulsed by what seems negative, it's time to shift back down to narrower scopes of mindfulness and then try to reboot. On the contrary, we'll know we're in all-inclusive mindfulness when we can watch the positive without being hooked, the negative without getting all worked up, and the neutral without zoning out.

Of course, this is only a first take on all-inclusive mindfulness. A second take would involve beginning to sort out the elements of suffering and happiness from the buzzing blooming confusion of all our experience, and to locate those elements along the path using the healing disciplines of wisdom and ethics. If a particular element we're observing is a thought or perception, is it realistic or not? If it's a sensation or emotion, is it positive or negative, healthy or unhealthy? This analytic feel and use of inclusive mindfulness draws on each step along the path, including the table of elements that effectively maps the variables we encounter on first two steps of realistic outlook and intent. It begins to prepare us for the sustained reflection and analysis of insight meditation, which is the work of step eight.

The active role of all-inclusive mindfulness once again challenges the popular notion that mindfulness involves awareness without judgment and acceptance without distinctions. In a sense, this misconception reflects the pitfalls of translation. It is true that genuine mindfulness involves an unbiased, nonjudgmental awareness. Somewhere along the way, the English "judgmental" seems to have been confused with "judgment." But we use these two words in ways that make them more or less opposites. "Judgment" is a quality that implies the potential to be open, objective and unbiased. To the contrary, being "judgmental" implies some degree of prejudice or preconception that biases perception and judgment. On the table of elements of suffering and happiness, judgment is a variable element; it can be either a help or a hindrance depending on whether it's accurate or judgmental.

While we certainly need to avoid misusing judgment, the only way to do so from the traditional standpoint is to learn to use it correctly. Without accurate judgment, we can't be decisive in our perceptions or our actions. Like a ship with no rudder, our meditation will go nowhere and eventually flounder. Likewise, radical acceptance doesn't mean passively accepting anything and everything whatsoever. The role of acceptance comes in being ready, willing and able to face the reality of cause and effect without denial, fear or resentment. Yet once we've accepted the laws of cause and effect and clearly identified the elements of suffering and happiness, we must decisively eliminate the former causes and cultivate the latter. All-inclusive mindfulness is meant to help us recognize and accept the consequences of our thoughts, intentions and actions and to make clear and calm judgments that help us break out of the cycle of stress and trauma so we can advance along the path to true happiness.

Deep, All-Inclusive Mindfulness: Meditative Experiment 1

Unplug and shield yourself as much as you can from distractions. Now settle yourself into a comfortable, stable posture, position your hands, and close your eyes in-between these instructions. Clear your breath by exhaling completely and let the next inhalation come as naturally and gradually as possible. As you gradually shift into a kinder, gentler rhythm of breathing, turn your attention to the breath and take it as a focus to settle and center your mind. Each time you breathe in, use your breath to reign in your energy and awareness from their far-flung engagement with the world out there, giving yourself the message that it's safe and good to let the world be for now and to gather all your mind-energy into yourself.

If you find yourself pulled back out to distraction, gently but firmly use mindfulness to bring your mind back to rest within your breathing body, especially the kinder, gentler breath-rhythm centered at your heart. If you begin to drift into dullness, use alertness to take some of the energy and awareness you've gathered and breathe it into your fatigue, reviving and uplifting your mind until you feel your whole body breathing, awake, aware and clear as a bell. As you continue to center your mind within your breathing body by settling and uplifting your energy and awareness, tune into the subtle energy-mind that fills every tissue and cell, and gradually shift towards the lighter, clearer end of your physical spectrum, until your body feels like a person shaped bubble of life, made mainly of breath, mind, and light.

As you breathe into your breath-body of light, begin to scan your comfort level, centering your mind evenly over the whole texture of raw feeling, by facing and soothing pain or distress, appreciating the nuances of indifference, and savoring and letting go of comfort or pleasure. Feeling more centered in your breath-body and more balanced in its raw feel, open the scope of your mindfulness to tune into the stream of consciousness your living, breathing body sustains. Focus on the space of sheer open-minded awareness that knows mental contents, gradually centering your mindfulness in that awareness until you feel a sense of untainted clarity and unbounded spaciousness like the water of a clear mountain stream or like a crystal clear autumn sky.

When your mind gets carried away with the turbulence of positive contents, use your mindfulness to retrieve and redirect it back to the calm waters of sheer awareness. When your mind gets sucked into undercurrents of negative contents, use your alertness to uplift and redirect it back to the clarity of pure awareness. When you find your mind getting clouded by the opacity of neutral contents, use your mindfulness and alertness to unstick and return it to the calm, clear waters of pure awareness. As you center yourself repeatedly in the spacious clarity of mind, gradually immerse your mindfulness to deeper levels of your mind, like a diver submerging himself into the depths of the ocean in stages. From within this deep mindfulness, keep your bearings clear by looking down through the deep tides of sensation to the sea floor of your breathing body on the one hand, and looking up to the surface waves and reflections of thoughts, emotions, and images on the other.

Finally, centered in the clear and calm depths of your primal mind, midway between the raw feel of your breathing body and the subliminal activity of your waking consciousness, open the scope of your mindfulness one last time to embrace all the workings of your body-mind, a breath at a time. Let your mindfulness scan the whole scope of your life like a scientist in a research submarine floating deep under the surface, sending waves of mindfulness like sonar from bottom to top through all the levels or systems of your body and mind. Scan your physical body, sitting and breathing this way or that; scan your sensation, and the raw feel of comfort, numbness and distress; scan your perceptual system, where consciousness is reflecting sense-input through the lenses of memory and imagination; scan your emotional reactions, positive and negative; and finally, scan your thoughts or inner dialogue, realistic, and unrealistic.

When you find yourself getting pulled off center towards the margins of your body-mind and wrapped up in the highs, lows or complexities, use your mindfulness and alertness to re-center your mind in its natural element of clarity and calm. Then reopen the scope of all-inclusive mindfulness, scanning and filtering the systems of your mind/body process from the perspective of deep mindfulness of mind. You'll know you're getting the hang of this practice when you feel your mindfulness spreading evenly through all the layers and workings of your body-mind, like a dolphin whose sonar ripples out from the midst of the sea in all directions at once and returns, making him fully aware of everything going on from the surface waves to deep sea floor.

Do this basic practice until you can scan the whole fabric of your inner life, and begin to recognize patterns and textures from a place of deep clarity and calm. As you begin to get the hang of it within meditations, you'll find yourself being more mindful of the workings of your whole body-mind between sessions too.

2 Self-Analysis, Insight, and Freedom

> Apart from the discrimination of elements, there is no way to eliminate the contaminants (that drive the cycle of stress and trauma), and it is because of these contaminants that the world drifts in the ocean of (compulsive) existence. So it is with a view to this discrimination that the scientific teaching was proclaimed (by the Buddha).
>
> (Vasubandhu, *Treasury of Scientific Teaching*[1])

What is Buddhist psychology? Given the recent explosion of books comparing Buddhism with Western science, a thoughtful reader might draw various conclusions. Readers of books comparing Indic contemplative science with modern physical science might conclude that Buddhist mind science is a qualitative, low-tech fusion of quantum physics with cognitive neuroscience, akin to Rodolfo Llinas's quantum theory of consciousness.[2] Readers of the literature comparing Indic contemplative psychology to modern behavioral psychology might conclude that Buddhism is a kinder, gentler cognitive therapy replacing relaxation with mindfulness, judgment with acceptance and self-interested habits with altruistic behaviors, a cross between Teasdale's mindfulness-based cognitive therapy and Martin Seligman's positive psychology.[3]

Though there is a clear overlap of Buddhist contemplative science with current neuroscience and cognitive therapy, I believe the closest cross-cultural match for Buddhist psychology is with the humanistic science and art of psychoanalytic psychotherapy.[4] Although contemporary analysis has many schools of theory and practice, in this chapter I consider them all as part of one modern tradition. As I said in the Introduction, my preference for comparing Buddhist psychology with analytic psychology stems from the deep commonality in aims and methods that make them siblings under the skin. Both traditions concern themselves with the physical science of the day; both rely on altered states to help change thinking and behavior; and both aim at transforming the human mind by means of introspective insight and social-emotional learning. This primary interest in transformative insight and emotional experience is what earmarks the deep family resemblance between these traditions and distinguishes them from contemporary neuroscience and cognitive therapy.

Nowhere is the pivotal role of insight and emotion in Buddhist psychology and analytic therapy clearer than in their shared emphasis on their founders' personal journeys of transformation. While Freud took great pains to ally his psychology with the physical science of his day, he made no secret of the fact that a main source of his insight and method was his own life journey of self-exploration and self-healing, his "self-analysis." Of course, we know from Freud's biography that his self-analysis was far from solitary.[5] His self-reflection was deeply influenced by contemporary thinkers like Schelling and Nietzsche, and was also nurtured by ongoing dialogue with like-minded colleagues, especially his mentor Wilhelm Fleiss.

However unconventional this was for modern science, Freud clearly felt this mix of intellectual learning and personal reflection with emotional self-disclosure and sharing was so vital to his own journey that he chose to build it into his method of training other analysts. The structure of analytic training—melding text-based classes with personal supervision and a "training analysis"—is meant to help prospective therapists replicate the inner journey of Freud's self-analysis. Nor does the importance of self-analysis stop there. Viewed in this light, analytic therapy itself is clearly structured to replicate this process on a smaller scale, with the therapist playing dual roles as a personal tutor and emotional mentor. Here again, we see the logic of Freud's insistence that altered states like free association enhance rather than obscure the client's capacity for insight and emotional learning: so that s/he is mentally prepared to replicate the transformative journey of self-analysis.

Retracing the Buddha's Path of Self-Healing

What does the structure of analytic training and therapy have to do with Buddhist psychology? Isn't the emphasis on Shakyamuni's historic journey to enlightenment meant like the narratives of the Old and New Testament or Koran to foster faith in the Buddha and his tradition? Although the Buddhist tradition does not reject faith entirely, in a very real sense, the best answer to this question is "no." Shakyamuni was very clear in insisting his students renounce any faith that was incompatible with reason, personal responsibility, and ultimate reliance on the evidence of experience.[6] He intentionally refused to become an object of worship, obedience or authority for the community he founded.[7] On the other hand, he clearly offered himself as an example, role-model, teacher, and guide, with the express intent of encouraging and helping others to replicate in their own lives his journey of self-healing and enlightenment.

As Freud's self-analysis is built into the structure of analytic training and therapy, the Buddha's self-healing is built into the structure of all Buddhist teaching and practice as a living example for all who seek lasting freedom and happiness. Shakyamuni's chosen role as a human guide in the universal pursuit of happiness was the limiting case of the emphasis on reproducible methods of contemplative healing that distinguishes his tradition from faith-based religious traditions. In fact, no less an authority than Dignaga, the Aristotle of Buddhist logic, praised Buddha's intent to make himself the personal example of a self-healing journey accessible to all, celebrating it as the quintessence of Buddhist empirical method:

> I honor the teacher who realized bliss, the protector
> Who sought the happiness of all, [by] personifying valid method.[8]

Figure 2.1 Dignaga, Master of Cognitive Science

Contrasting Buddhist and Analytic Psychology with Modern Physical Science

Assuming that a shared emphasis on replicating self-healing makes analytic psychology the best cross-cultural match for Buddhist psychology, what does this say about the kind of sciences they are? What it says is that they are sciences that begin with very different aims and proceed by very different means than the disciplines we have learned to think of as science. Modern physical science seeks knowledge of the world by removing the human observer as far as possible from its object of study, gathering evidence by mechanically manipulating its object, and analyzing that evidence by mathematical logic. Beginning with mechanics, then astronomy, and eventually biology, this modern approach to science is obviously best suited to studying inanimate matter or the material aspects of living things.

Not surprisingly, it took modern scientists centuries to devise ways of studying human behavior and intelligent life using such empirical methods. Like modern physical science, our more recent behavioral and social sciences take great pains to remove the human observer from their study of human experience and social life. Cognitive neuroscience studies the workings of mind by trying to link consciousness to structures and processes in the brains of human subjects or animals. Experimental psychology and social science also try to study human individuals and groups at a distance, gathering information about others as impersonally as possible, with structured interviews or questionnaires that are statistically analyzed. We all take for granted that going to such lengths is necessary to gather useful knowledge about how human minds work, despite the fact that each of us has a mind available for long-term, in-depth study, first hand.

The Path of Knowledge in Buddhist Psychology and Insight Therapy

Buddhist psychology and analytic therapy seek knowledge very differently from these conventional modern sciences. They take the road-not-taken by modern science in the West: using our own minds and bodies as laboratories for first-hand self-examination and self-analysis. The conventional wisdom about why such a first-person approach to human life cannot yield valid science is that introspection is invariably subjective, while scientific knowledge should be objective, that is: true across a wide range of individuals. This assumes that there is no other way to objective knowledge of the mind than looking at consciousness from the outside-in, either as a function of brain processes or as a black box about which we make inferences from impersonal observations of behavior.

What characterizes the unconventional approach shared by analytic psychology and Buddhist contemplative science is that they both employ a system of human practices that work together to expose and correct the subjectivity of personal introspection, eventually yielding individuals who are trained as objective observers of their own mind/body processes. These self-corrective practices essentially fall into three categories: (1) using altered states of mind that access the depths of the mind while enhancing corrective faculties like mindfulness, alertness, insight, and flow; (2) using discursive logic and maps of the mind refined by communities over time to train introspective analysis, insight, and judgment along rationally coherent, empirically valid lines; (3) aligning motivation with positive social emotions that enhance empathy, communication and cooperation, so that individual experience and action can be socially validated or corrected through peer supervision and mentoring bonds. These three practices are the end-result of the three core disciplines of contemplative learning in the Buddhist tradition: the disciplines of contemplation; wisdom and ethics. In analytic psychology, they correspond to the method of free association; the map of the mind Freud called his metapsychology; and the all-important social-emotional art of the therapeutic alliance or positive transference.

Empirical Method, Inside Out: The Logic of Buddhist and Analytic Psychology

Since the human self-corrective methods of Buddhist psychology and analytic therapy are clearly divergent from the standard methods of modern physical science, their approach to knowledge of the mind is still misunderstood by our scientific mainstream. While analytic therapy remains the most widely used and accepted form of psychotherapy in clinical practice, its method of social self-correction is still widely confused with the subjective methods of nineteenth century introspection.[9] The irony is heightened by the fact that we now have several decades of research showing that the methods of analytic therapy and Buddhist meditation both work quite effectively,[10] and that many of their conclusions about the human mind have been confirmed by contemporary brain science.[11]

Whatever the scientific status of these two traditions, it is vital for those who seek help from Buddhist psychology to understand its distinctive approach to science and knowledge. One of the early interpreters of Buddhist psychology in West, the German-born teacher Anagarika Govinda, described its introspective approach thus:

> The method of this psychology is comparable to that of a man who from a high mountain watch-tower looks out over the landscape at his feet and now proceeds in regular order to extricate from the total picture of the landscape the distinguishing marks of his route, and describes them in their corresponding order. His description lays no claim to be a description of the whole landscape but only of those portions of the landscape

> which are of importance for his route … Every individual must himself tread the path of realization, for only the knowledge that is won by experience has living, i.e. life-giving value.[12]

Govinda based his comments on the scientific teaching tradition of early Buddhism, which lays out the path of contemplative knowledge and experience the Buddha mapped in hindsight as leading up to his realization of enlightenment. Since the aim of this map is to provide the guidance people need to replicate his journey of self-healing themselves, its focus is not on the disembodied knowledge we normally think of as science, but on the self-knowledge that eventually leads, *via* psychological insight and healing intuition, to realized wisdom.

So the great Buddhist psychologist Vasubandu begins his classic *Treasury of Scientific Teaching* by defining its focus: "Pure science is impeccable wisdom and those (pure mind/body systems) which correspond to it." His formula distils the essence of Buddhist psychology: its aim not just to understand human suffering but to transform it into happiness; and its means, to cultivate and refine self-knowledge until it is powerful enough to purge the mind and body of the reactive perceptions, emotions and habits that keep us locked in the cycle of stress and trauma. This leads us to the working definition of wisdom cited from Vasubandhu at the opening of this chapter, that is: wisdom as the discrimination of causal elements of suffering and happiness.[13]

Buddha's Method: Discrimination, Analysis, and Contemplative Insight

Given our romantic notions of meditative experience and spiritual wisdom, the classical logic of Buddhist psychology Vasubandhu describes may surprise us in more ways than one. In contrast to the widespread view that non-conceptual meditation or non-judging mindfulness alone will bring peace, it may come as a shock that the prime active ingredient of change prescribed by this system is not meditation as we know it, but a process of contemplative learning in which discursive knowledge is gradually translated into personal insight and transformative wisdom. In contrast to the widespread belief that spiritual wisdom transcends scientific reasons and methods, the wisdom prescribed by this system is not some otherworldly, ineffable experience, but rather a discrimination of the disparate elements and processes of mind/body causation that is both analytical and empirical. While meditation and lifestyle provide the foundation for lasting change, the peace they bring is only temporary. The decisive factor that helps eliminate the root causes of suffering and cultivate those of happiness instead is the analytic discernment of the causal elements of suffering and happiness, a discernment that guides an empirical method of replicable self-analysis and self-transformation.

Mapping Self-Analysis and Insight: The Buddhist Table of Elements

The elements to be discerned in Buddhist psychology are those listed on the table of elements we alluded to in discussing all-inclusive mindfulness in chapter 1.[14] In terms of Govinda's analogy, the table represents the Buddha's synoptic overview or map of the journey he personally took from bondage and suffering to freedom and happiness. For century after century, that map has been part of the basic education of Buddhist student-practitioners, effectively pointing out all the landmarks they need to keep themselves on track in their effort to replicate part or all of the Buddha's journey. To this day, it makes up the material covered by the introductory psychology class in Buddhist elementary schools and monastic colleges.[15] The table reflects a body of general knowledge which practitioners first learn in class and then test in the laboratory of their own ongoing reflection and meditative experience. The process begins with understanding and memorizing the table. The knowledge gained is then applied in the context of all-inclusive mindfulness to recognize and predict the causal combination of elements which produce suffering or happiness. Finally, the process moves from mere recognition to analytic insight, the valid inference that frees the mind from confusion and guides it towards the healthy intuitions and choices which break the cycle of suffering and cultivate a life of happiness.

When we look closer at the table, the first thing we notice is that it divides the universe of experience into two distinct conditions or states: the basic state, in which our bodies and minds are bound by the conditioning of stress and trauma; and the end state, in which that conditioning has ceased.[16] This makes sense given Govinda's insight that Buddhist psychology is a positive, first-person study of mind, based on Shakyamuni's experience of the healing journey from bondage to enlightenment. With that said, we must not jump to the romantic conclusion that Buddhist psychology is strictly spiritual, i.e., concerned with some transcendent realm apart from the ordinary human condition of suffering and its causes. Of the sixty some elements in the smallest table and the hundred some in the largest, only two are considered transcendent, while the overwhelming majority are ordinary elements of human experience like pain and pleasure, love and desire and hate.[17] Just as the journey described by the four noble truths takes us from the realm of everyday stress and trauma to Shakyamuni's lasting peace, so the table which maps the inner, causal elements of that shift takes us from everyday life to the highest reaches of human happiness. Given this, the table of elements is an easy way to acquaint ourselves with the Buddhist account of the mind and its workings, as well as a practical way to train our discursive minds to serve as inner guides on the journey of contemplative self-healing.

The Five States of Matter: The Basic Physical Elements

After distinguishing the normal state of the mind from its unconditioned state, the table goes on to address the distinction between mind and matter, as well as their complex interaction. Traditionally, the elements of the physical world, called earth, water, fire, air, and space, are defined as the four elemental states of matter—solid, liquid, energy, and gas—plus space, which came to be viewed in surprisingly modern terms as the least tangible and most elementary state of matter.[18]

As in Western physics, matter in all states is viewed as a composite, including primary matter made of atoms and derivative matter made of molecules.[19] Yet Buddhist contemplative science anticipated modern physical science by insisting that matter must be infinitely divisible, without any "fundamental structure;" and that, at the subtlest levels, matter behaves less like a solid or liquid and more like energy or space.[20] While the animate matter of living things is basically the same as the inanimate matter of the natural world, it takes on three higher forms of organization—energetic, dynamic and structural—symbolized by the bodily constituents wind, bile, and phlegm.[21]

This higher order involves molecules in various material states combining to form seven different kinds of living tissue and eleven organ systems. Of these, the most relevant for psychology, neural tissue and the nervous system, involves energetic, dynamic, and structural elements, namely: neural energies; neuroendocrine drops; and neural channels, and complexes.[22] These combine to form the central nervous system, mapped by contemplative introspection as the yogic nervous system or "subtle body" of channels and complexes—*chakras*—by now familiar to us in the West. Of course, the full map of the nervous system adds peripheral channels that branch out from the complexes to the various internal organs and sensory-motor faculties of the "coarse body." As in modern science, it is here—at the level of the nervous system—that the physical elements of the body interface and interact most directly with consciousness. We'll return to explore this map in detail in chapter 10.

The Six Modes of Consciousness: The Basic Elements of Mind

To understand precisely how the body and mind interact according to Buddhist psychology, we need to move to the mental side of the table, where the lion's share of elements is found. Naturally, the first thing we encounter on this side of the table is mind itself. Yet if we expect to see the mind presented as a single, monolithic element, we're in for a surprise. Instead of a unitary entity, the table presents consciousness as a set of six distinct elements.[23] These are the five types of consciousness that specialize in engaging the objects of the five senses—visual, auditory, olfactory, gustatory, and tactile consciousness—plus a sixth type, mental consciousness, that specializes in internal objects of mind, including mentally processed sense-data, mental images and verbal concepts. Why is the mind analyzed in this way? It's all part of the empirical approach of Buddhist science. Just as this tradition analyzes matter into elements, elements into atoms, atoms into subatomic particles, and so on without limit, it analyzes mind into endlessly reducible components as well. And, as in the analysis of matter, the reason for the analysis of mind is to describe as accurately as possible the full complexity and particularity of the causal workings of consciousness.

Let's back up and start again. Of course, Buddhist psychology has a general definition of mind or consciousness, as that lucid awareness which simply grasps the immediacy of an object.[24] Yet since there is no one "generic" object, the precise workings of consciousness are found to depend on the particularity of its different types of objects. Contemporary science has reached a similar conclusion: that consciousness is not unitary but modular, in line with the various ways in which various aspects of the mind/brain engage their diverse objects. In fact, the different brain regions that support the processing of different sorts of sense input only light up on PET scans when a given mode of sense input has grabbed the attention of the respective mode of consciousness. This is also true of mind/brain activity when consciousness is attending to internal, mental objects, like memories, mentally generated imagery, self-reflection or internal dialogue. So the differential account of mind reached by Buddhist psychology based on contemplative methods is quite consistent with the findings reached by current neuroscience based on physical studies of brain structure and function.[25]

Elements in Flux: The Theory of Instantaneity and the Stream of Consciousness

Another aspect of the map of mind laid out in the classical table of elements is that it analyzes consciousness not just into different categories based on its various objects, but also into different moments or instants in the temporal process of receiving, filtering, and interpreting its given object.[26] In other words, visual consciousness isn't one, homogeneous element, but is rather an aggregate or heap of countless different elemental moments. This is not just because each instance of visual consciousness varies based on its particular object, but also because at each moment in the course of engaging that object, visual consciousness is constantly changing. Besides differences based on different takes of the same object, there are constant, moment to changes in visual consciousness based on different phases and aspects of the subjective response or processing of any one take on any given object. Since each of these different instances of visual consciousness is considered a different element, what normally seems a unitary, cohesive experience of catching sight of something in the world is actually a whole aggregate composed of many distinct elements of consciousness connected like a string of pearls or the countless frames that go into a single "still shot" in a video.

This microscopic approach to the stream of consciousness, called the theory of instantaneity, is central to the model of mind assumed by the table of elements.[27] This theory too has been confirmed by a line of neuroscience called evoked potential research. Using the electroencephalograph (EEG) to study the time-course of brain activity during the process of sense perception, this research has shown how sensory organs and many regions of the brain get involved over time in the sequence of filtering and interpreting sensory experience.[28] In other words, this research sees from the outside in the same process Buddhist contemplative science observed from the inside out.

The Causal Nexus: The Basic Fabric of Matter and Mind

The insight on which the theory of instantaneity is based is simple enough. Consciousness, like everything else in the world, is so interdependent with its nexus of causes and conditions that it is changing substantially every instant, in response to complex, moment-to-moment changes in that causal nexus. Understanding the momentary nexus of causes and conditions in which consciousness lives and breathes helps to flesh out the picture of mind's interaction with body and environment which is part of the deep background assumed by the table of elements. To get a quick sense of this nexus, it helps to survey the classical grid, consisting of four kinds of conditions, four (or more) kinds of causes, and four kinds of effects.[29]

For simplicity, we'll restrict our attention to the four conditions for any moment of consciousness. These are: the causal condition, which is the assemblage of mind/body causes that act indirectly to influence a consciousness to be produced; the empowering condition or basis, which is the subtle material structure that supports the function of a given sense faculty together with the gross anatomical senses; the objective condition, which is the object of perception that supports the arising of a given sense consciousness; the immediately preceding condition, which is the prior moment in the stream of consciousness, which acts as a reference setting, background or context for a present moment of consciousness.

In surveying the traditional list of conditions, I'm not trying to suggest that it's necessary to become a scholar in order to understand or apply Buddhist psychology. What is vital is to have some sense of the causal nexus within which the elements of suffering and happiness arise, endure and cease. Considering three of these in more depth will yield the main insights we need for now.

The empowering condition illustrates the way in which the mind is seen as constantly interacting with the neural network that supports it, and, indirectly with the gross physical body and environment on which that network in turn depends. The mind's supporting network is conceived of not as the gross anatomical organs of the nervous system like the eyes or brain, but as a subtle material structure of neural energy, transmitter drops and plastic pathways and complexes supporting a faculty like vision, akin to what we might call brain-waves, neurochemical wetware and dendritic webs. This network in turn depends on the gross anatomy of nervous tissue, which coexists with the other gross tissues and organ systems that support life, like the circulatory and respiratory systems. And, of course, the physical elements of the living body also depend on the physical elements of the natural world for their development, nurturance and sustenance.

All this so far is more or less familiar from our knowledge of modern neuroscience, although, as we've said, it was arrived at by introspective means. What sets this tradition's view of the causal nexus apart is the way it includes the causality of the mind as well, as part of one seamless web of interaction. So the empowering condition must be understood as only one of the three conditions which must come together to give rise to consciousness. The second, objective condition links the mind to its inner and outer environment, providing sense input that conveys information about the physical body and world. Together these two conditions make up the productive cause of consciousness. However, they don't produce consciousness without depending on a third, psychological condition: the immediately preceding moment in the stream of consciousness, which provides the current informational context and reference settings for interpreting fresh experience.

The Preceding Condition: A Quantum Theory of Mind

This third ingredient and missing link in the process of perception is the next causal factor we need to consider more deeply in order to understand and apply Buddhist psychology. The insight that any given moment of mind is conditioned not just by neural processing and sense input but also by the moment of mind that immediately precedes it helps us understand the way this tradition sees and explains the causal efficacy of consciousness and its intentional acts.[30] The moment-to-moment connectivity of mind provides the empirical basis for the idea of a stream of consciousness, conceived as a causal medium or conduit for conserving the habitual mental settings that reinforce a given mindset and sensibility over time. And it is this force of connectivity or continuity that supports the causal link between intentional acts of body, speech, and mind (i.e., *karma-s*) and their eventual fruition in the form of the personal agency and embodied development we call a person or life. Yet the most ingenious and powerful insight Buddhist psychologists have about this condition relates to the way they use it to reveal the true nature of the mind.

Unlike our received modern view of perception, focused on the senses, Buddhist psychology sees mind itself as a medium and potential object of sensation. Instead of a passive witness, mind is seen as a sixth sense, as active as the five sense faculties like vision, but far more dominant in the process of perception and more powerful as a means of knowing the world. To avoid postulating a unitary, idealistic theory of mind, this tradition viewed mental perception as subject to the same three conditions that governed sense-perception. The only difference is that instead of having a sense faculty as its empowering condition and an external object as its objective condition, mental perception relies on the immediately preceding moment of mind to satisfy both these conditions, as well as the third condition of providing a reference context and sensibility for the fresh moment of perception.

In effect, in mental perception the stream of consciousness turns back on itself in a reflective moment that allows us to further filter and interpret input from the outside world with the help of retrospective memories and emotional associations, as well as prospective ideas and images about the relevance of that input. Of note, the process neuropsychology we will explore in the latter half of this book adds the twist that, while mental perception does take the prior moment of mind as its objective and subjective point of reference, it takes as its empowering condition not mind but the wetware and microstructure that supports more central neural processing and more reflective forms of consciousness.[31] In any case, this empirical model of the faculty of mind as a stream or wave of causal continuity amid change is also surprisingly consistent with current neuroscience. This is clear from the research of my old neuroscience professor, Rodolfo Llinas, and his "the quantum theory of consciousness."[32]

By studying the deep, brain-wave patterns of humans during waking and dreaming, Llinas found that our perceptual brain does not work passively or statically, like a fixed mirror of reality, but actively and dynamically, like a computer-generated virtual reality simulation of the world. He based his theory on the observation that our brain-waves are not generated piece-meal in response to stimuli like sense input, but follow the beat of the brain's own drummer, a bioelectrical rhythm that starts from the basal ganglia deep within the core brain and sweeps forwards in wave-like fashion throughout the whole cortex, forty times per second. As it sweeps holistically through the brain, each wave connects a particular array of neural events evoked by the last wave into a coherent picture, just as a particular array of pixels lit up on a digital screen creates the appearance of a specific image. Each picture is then spliced to the next to create a moving picture of reality, like the successive frames that make up a loop of video.

The main difference in the way this works in waking versus dreaming is that, in the waking state the pathways and centers that relay sense input through the basal ganglia are included in the loop, while in dreaming they are left out of the loop. Llinas calls his account a quantum theory of consciousness because its wave-like model of neural processing contrasts with previous models in something like the way atomic models based on wave-mechanics contrast with older models based on particle-mechanics. Once again, despite their different methods, this brain-based model depicts the mind in terms that clearly support the insights of Buddhist contemplative science: that mind works as a stream of wave-like moments strung together; and that the main source of continuity in that stream is that each wave-moment assumes the immediately preceding moment as a reference setting or mindset.

Mind as Sixth Sense: The Gateway to Self-Analysis

Finally, there is one more way in which understanding the immediately preceding condition can help lay bare the logic of Buddhist psychology. Given the reflective model of mental perception that turns on this condition, understanding it also gives us a glimpse into how this tradition sees the causality of self-analysis. The logic goes like this. Since the mind can perceive the objective reality of things by taking the objective aspect of a prior moment of mind as the object of a subsequent moment of reflection, it is also possible for the mind to perceive the objective reality of consciousness, by taking the *subjective* aspect of a prior moment of mind as the object of a subsequent moment of reflection. Intensified by meditation and stabilized by emotional self-mastery, the reflective mind can gradually dive through the surface of symbolic consciousness to the depths of perceptual consciousness: the primal, bare awareness that illumines all perceptual objects.

It is here that Buddhist contemplatives find the mind to be naturally clear and free of self-limiting instincts and habits. By tapping into this primal source of awareness, we can more easily see through and let go of the self-protective instincts and traumatic habits that drive stress-reactive life. Like an embryonic tissue in the mind, this clear, intuitive consciousness not only gives us more direct access to fresh information but also places us at the growing edge of healing, learning and rejuvenation. This is why deep mindfulness of mind, which turns awareness back on its own prior moment, is so vital to the practice of inclusive mindfulness and transformative insight meditation. And it is also why the primal elements of mind, which directly intuit their objects in a raw and unfiltered way, are clearly distinguished in the table of elements from mental factors, which complicate perception with associative elements like pain and pleasure, discursive thinking and emotional responses. The depth-psychology assumed by the table of elements was made more explicit in later models we will explore below, including: the deconstructive psychology of Dignaga; Vasubandhu's theory of the subconscious mind; and the process-oriented neuropsychology of Nagarjuna.[33]

From just two parts of the causal model assumed with the table of elements, we've glimpsed some basic insights of Buddhist psychology: its view of consciousness as constantly changing in dependence on neural networks and the sense world; its view of the mind as a sixth sense supported by the causal continuity of wave-like moments; and its view that the mind has primal depths in which awareness is freer to learn and change. The final feature of the causal web we need to complete the background of the table of elements is clear when we consider the nature of the causal condition.

The Causal Condition: A Systems Model of Body-Mind Interaction

The causal condition refers to the fact that every element within the body, mind and environment arises as a result of the convergence of a whole array of causes and conditions.[34] A given element of consciousness, for instance, has as its main, productive cause the threefold contact or conjunction of the stream of consciousness with a specific sense faculty and a particular object. Yet in addition to this main, productive cause, other causal forces at work in the mind/body process, such as the mental factors that coexist within the prior moment of mind or the physical elements within the sense faculty's neural infrastructure, act to condition the precise way that moment of consciousness will arise. For instance, under the influence of fear, a pole seen on a dark night might appear as an assailant; or, under the influence of alcohol, the moon might appear as double.

In effect, this condition shows how Buddhist psychology sees all elements of the body, mind, and environment as constantly conditioning every other element in a seamless fabric of mutual interdependence and interaction. This fabric helps explain how causality can work in seemingly contradictory ways: downwards from mind to body; upwards from body to mind; outwards from the individual to the environment; and inwards from the environment to the individual. This condition serves to illustrate the way Buddhist psychology refined Shakyamuni's insight that the elements of suffering and happiness are all linked together in a causal cycle in which each element conditions all the others, and the flow of causality is always reversible. It also anticipates current systems models of two-way mind/brain causation like Charles Tart's systems model of dualistic interactionism.[35]

Aids and Blocks on the Path of Insight: The Fifty-One Mental Factors

Given this introduction to the classical Buddhist view of the mind and its place within the web of causality, we're ready to scan the rest of the table of elements: the mental factors which largely determine whether the mind works to produce suffering or happiness. Though these factors arise together with a primary element of mind, and coexist with it as aspects of a coherent, complex experience, they are clearly distinguished from the primary process of consciousness. The distinction serves two purposes. First, it underscores the profound, healing insight of Shakyamuni and his heirs that, at the source of our complex minds lies a natural potential for a profound clarity and peace that is free from both destructive instincts and traumatic conditioning. Second, it serves to train the analytic discernment we need to expose and disarm compulsive instincts and habits. While mental factors share precisely the same time, object, faculty and substance as the primary elements of mind they qualify, we must learn to distinguish them because they are the variables that can tip the mind from misperception and unhealthy habits to realistic perception and effective action. Since the causality of suffering and happiness depends on the convergence of cognition and motivation, the mental factors are grouped into classes which address one or both of these aspects of mental life. The first group, omnipresent factors, touches on both aspects; the second, object-discerning or cognitive factors, relates to cognition; and the last three, healthy, unhealthy, and variable emotional factors, all focus mainly on motivation.[36]

The Omnipresent Factors: The Essential Structure of Perception

As the term suggests, the omnipresent mental factors are at work in each and every moment of consciousness.[37] The five omnipresent factors are: sensation, conception, intention, contact, and attention. Sensation or feeling is the mental or physical experience of pain, pleasure, or indifference engendered by experiencing a given object. Conception recognizes the distinctive features of an object and applies a suitable mental image or designation. Intention is the motivation that arises in relation to a given object; it may be healthy, unhealthy, or indeterminate. Contact is a technical term meaning the three-way conjunction that brings consciousness together with a specific sense faculty and particular object. Attention allows the mind to focus on a specific object, to the exclusion of everything else.

Of the five factors, three are cognitive and two motivational. Some of these factors, like attention, are quite familiar and obviously essential to any working consciousness. Others, like conception, come as something of a surprise, especially in a contemplative psychology. In addition to attention and conception, the third cognitive mental factor here is contact. The two motivational factors within this class—sensation and intention—seem straightforward enough, but are so critical that it helps to explore them.

One way to understand the omnipresent factors is to consider what is essential to the primary process of perception. Obviously, in order for any perception to work, consciousness must come in contact with a perceptual object *via* a sense faculty. Attention, then, is the mental act of engagement by which the subject chooses an object and takes it in. Out of this comes some pain-pleasure sensation. Sensation is the springboard of motivation, since we normally want to avoid what seems to hurt, ignore the indifferent and pursue what seems to please. The intention to avoid, ignore or pursue is the aim or objective of motivation. It may be healthy, unhealthy or indeterminate, depending on whether our intention is virtuous, vicious or neutral.

One way to think of the basic structure of perception is that it reflects a simple engagement or contact that is complicated by a two way transaction. According to one tradition, we can imagine the complex transaction of any given perception as composed of two equal and opposite vectors, like two crisscrossing arrows. The cognitive vector starts at the object pole with attention, which draws the object into the mind towards conception, the endpoint where it is recognized, rightly or wrongly, by symbolic images and discursive language. In response to this first transaction, the motivational vector starts at the subject pole with sensation, which moves the subject outwards towards intention, the endpoint where it aims to avoid, ignore or pursue the object.

The omnipresent factors need no further comment except for the somewhat surprising presence of conception on the list. Its presence here should be a bit confusing, for good reasons and bad. The bad reason is that our romantic prejudice about meditation and contemplative psychology is that they aim to free us entirely from conceptuality and bring us to an unmediated experience that supposedly transcends language. The fact that the discursive element is inseparable from the human mind, even at its most primal depths and its most exalted heights, challenges our preconception and helps explain why rational analysis, judgment and insight play such a central role in all Buddhist theory and practice. However surprising, this makes good sense given how integral language is to our nature as speaking primates, not to mention how pervasive it is in all cultural forms of human life.

The good reason for us to be surprised about the omnipresence of conception is that it seems to contradict the traditional insight that the primary nature of mind and perception is bare, non-conceptual awareness. The seeming contradiction can be reconciled by concluding that any level or state of mind can only be non-conceptual in relative terms, i.e. in contrast to the more highly symbolic nature of superficial, conceptual levels and states of mind.

The Objective Factors: Enhancing Variables of Perception

Unlike the omnipresent factors, the object-determining or cognitive mental factors are focused solely on the process of cognition.[38] In particular, this class is essentially a list of those mental muscles that must be built over time if we are to develop a refined, stable and positive mind with the power to arrive at accurate and objective knowledge of ourselves and the world through contemplation. They are: interest, enthusiasm, mindfulness, concentration, and insight. Interest aims us towards what we seek, be it a person we desire, some material good, true knowledge, or personal freedom. Enthusiasm fans the flame of interest by appreciating the benefits of the aims we seek. Mindfulness, as we know, keeps replacing our attention on an object of interest, maintaining focus by countering the tendency to distraction. Concentration, on the other hand, complements mindfulness by holding attention on the object, resisting distraction before it occurs. Finally, insight serves to investigate all things, to determine their nature, resolve problems and doubts, and correct any cognitive errors. In a real sense, these factors map out the contemplative journey of the mind from its natural state, wild and untamed, to a cultivated state in which it becomes the ultimate instrument of human self-knowledge and self-transformation.

Among the cognitive factors, interest and enthusiasm expand the mind's power and scope by building will-power, supporting the discipline of ethics; mindfulness and concentration expand it by providing focus and stability, supporting the discipline of meditation; and insight expands it by providing guidance and decisiveness, supporting the discipline of wisdom.

The journey of training the mind to serve as the ultimate instrument of human knowledge is traditionally mapped by Buddhist logic and epistemology. This discipline is so central to Buddhist psychology and so complementary with the healing aims and methods of Buddhist practice, I find it more descriptive to think of it as cognitive science or cognitive psychology than as the abstract fields we normally think of as logic and epistemology. A brief look at the path of mental development, mapped in Buddhist psychology as a journey of personal knowledge, helps put the cognitive mental factors in the larger context of contemplative healing and learning.

Buddhist Cognitive Science: The Path to Objective Knowledge of Self and World

Essentially, Buddhist cognitive science refines the contemplative view of knowledge spelled out in Buddhist psychology. Unlike modern science, our contemporary gold standard of knowledge, it is less concerned with facts and theories generated and tested by others than it is with what each and every one of us knows through our own valid reasoning and direct personal experience. Like the logic of modern therapy, the logic of Buddhist contemplative science is therapeutic and transformational: its fundamental concern is with the kind of knowledge that empowers ordinary people to eliminate their own suffering and build a life of lasting freedom and happiness.

So rather than rest content with the generic knowledge or conventional wisdom of the day, these traditions ask us to critically re-examine our views of the world—cultural, religious, and scientific—from the ground up. Over time, some of the truths we've learned will be exposed as sheer nonsense, or worse, frank delusions; while others will prove themselves to be truer to life than we'd ever dreamed. In order to clean our house of knowledge and come to a fresh assessment of what's true in and for our current lives, we need a method of analyzing all the conflicting ideas and experiences we've amassed through life, one that can serve as a new touchstone or compass on the journey ahead. The methods of self-knowledge and introspective insight refined by analytic therapy and Buddhist cognitive science are two such touchstones.

Perceptual versus Conceptual Knowledge: The Logic of Buddhist Empiricism

How does Buddhist cognitive psychology refine our minds into optimal instruments of valid self-knowledge, insight and intuition? It begins by training the mind to see through the greatest source of subjective bias and human error: the self-enclosing, reifying instinct to mistake our own habitual mental constructs for objective realities. It trains the mind to free itself from this demon in much the same way the empirical philosophies of the modern West laid the groundwork for what we now call the empirical method of science. In short, it does this by subjecting all knowledge that is bound up with generic symbols like words and images to systematic doubt, and urging that we practice relying on the evidence of direct perception instead. This is the meaning of the famous definition with which Dignaga opened his *Compendium of Valid Knowledge*: "Perception is devoid of mental constructions."[39] Why should we rely on the raw, unfiltered data of experience rather than well-constructed ideas and theories? The answer implied by Dignaga was made explicit as an addendum to this definition supplied centuries later by his greatest interpreter, Dharmakirti: "Perception is devoid of mental constructions and (therefore) unerring."[40] Dharmakirti also added that direct perception of particular things is a more vital source of knowledge than conceptual abstractions or generalizations because perception gives us access to fresh information that does not fit our preconceived notions or received theories.

To understand the logic of Buddhist empiricism, it helps to look at the way Dignaga and Dharmakirti explain the difference between how conceptuality and perception work. Anticipating contemporary semiotics and linguistic philosophy, Dignaga saw human language and conceptuality as systems of empty, conventional signs, which get their meaning not by picturing or mirroring the identity of the things they refer to but by their use as practical guides to human behavior. As generic images, words and concepts work by ignoring the differences between particular things and calling to mind an empty abstraction that corresponds to the use to which we put things in the course of our human lives. The word "food," for instance, gets its meaning less from the different kinds of things that might be used as food by different individuals and groups, than from the common purpose those many things serve in our lives, i.e., to satisfy hunger and nourish us. In short, we use words and concepts in a negative way, which Dignaga described as "exclusion" or "elimination."[41] His insight is that, as we make our way through the world, we use words and concepts less like labels than like blinders: to narrow our focus onto what we want. And they do this not by positively identifying every particular thing in the world until we find the one thing we're looking for, but by actively excluding from our attention all those particular things that seem unlikely to satisfy our aims and interests until we hit upon something that seems like it will generally serve.

As for perception, it picks up where conceptuality leaves off. When we arrive at something of interest to us, because it may be helpful or harmful, we then engage directly with it in a way that can give us positive knowledge and/or a novel experience of the world as it is. For instance, when we wander through a neighborhood searching for "good, healthy food," the words work to keep us out of the fast food joints long enough to stumble on a place that may serve food healthy enough to satisfy. After we sit down and order, when the meal is served, is when we really find out how right or wrong our inference was. As they say, "The proof of the pudding is in the eating." But even in the best of cases, when we are pleasantly surprised at how right we were, our conceptual inference or guesswork was still ultimately inaccurate or mistaken, since the generic image it gave us of what would be served must pale in comparison with the actual taste experience. We can see the family resemblance in the very current Kantian view proposed by Karl Popper: that scientific knowledge is only true in the sense that it offers a tentative, generic image of reality that has not yet been falsified by new evidence.[42]

In this sense, Buddhist philosophy and psychology approaches knowledge with a critical logic that should feel surprisingly modern. In line with Shakyamuni's insistence that his students examine and test what he said, Buddhist epistemology puts rational inference and perceptual evidence above authority and tradition as reliable sources of valid knowledge. As in the modern West, the preference for reason over tradition in Buddhism extends to scripture and the dictates of cultural authorities or scientific experts. Likewise, there is a critical avoidance of idle speculation, consistent with Shakyamuni's active refusal to answer metaphysical questions like whether the world is finite or infinite, whether or not a Buddha exists after death, or whether the self is the same as the body or different from it.[43] Instead, like modern science and medicine, Buddhist science directs us to questions that can be answered empirically—that is, validated by logic, experience and effective action—and are also of immediate practical benefit to humanity.[44]

Different Objects, Different Methods: The Theory of Mental Perception

Despite its empirical bent, the Buddhist approach to valid knowledge is quite unlike what we've come to think of as modern empirical method. The first place we see the divergence is in the Buddhist view of how questions are answered empirically. Traditionally, valid empirical method varies, depending on the difference between the three types of objects to be known. Evident things, like gross physical objects in the natural world, are best known by direct sense perception. Obscure things, like the nature of remote objects or the subtle, atomic nature of matter, are best known by logical inference from whatever evidence we have about them. Extremely obscure or hypothetical things, like the intimate workings of individual minds, the natural history of individuals and groups, or the most effective way for people to heal, are best known by the rational intuition of a perfectly trained and focused mind.

While the first two methods are familiar, the third is decidedly not. In what amounts to a cognitive psychology of exceptional ability or genius, this tradition holds that the human mind can know extremely obscure things as directly as the senses know evident objects, when the mental blocks of unexamined views and disturbing emotions are gradually removed from consciousness. This kind of perception is not the same as a coherent inference or theory consistent with all the evidence available to the senses. It is an intuition derived from a series of valid inferences or hypotheses which are eventually confirmed by the direct, perceptual experience of a single-pointed mind. Of course, this kind of knowledge is only conceivable in a system like this one, which recognizes the mind as a sixth sense capable of its own perception.

Called mental perception, such valid intuitive knowledge relies on associative neural networks and mental constructs informed by sense-data, in much the same way as normal perception relies on sensory neural networks and input from the five simple organs of sense.[45] Aligned with the metaphor of the third eye, the theory of mental perception recognizes the higher mind-brain as a bio-computer-enhancer of sorts, an intuitive faculty that depends on sense input but analyzes and enhances it in both analytic and gestalt modes, based on complex associations with past experience. For Buddhist psychology, this makes it more than an equal of the five simpler senses, and hence, deserving of being included with them as an honorary sense.

Given all we've learned about the processing power of the human mind-brain, the move to recognize it as an organ of perception, while surprising, seems understandable and fair enough. However novel, this move helps Buddhist science explain the cumulative effect of sustained reflection, contemplative training and emotional self-mastery on the mind: as the development of a refined, heightened form of mental perception called yogic or contemplative perception.[46] According to Buddhist cognitive science, this heightened perception is the best empirical method of knowing extremely obscure or hypothetical things, especially the complex mind/body causality of human suffering and happiness.

Healing Knowledge: The Path of Contemplative Self-Correction

Besides this emphasis on heightening the power of the mind, the second way Buddhist empirical method differs from ours is in its primary focus on knowledge that heals and frees individual human beings. This is clear from the way the various degrees and kinds of knowledge are mapped by Buddhist cognitive science as stages on the path of self-analysis. In the modern system refined by the Tibetan scholar Gyaltsap based on the work of Dignaga and Dharmakirti, this path is mapped into seven stages, which represent successive steps from delusion or prejudice to valid direct perception. According to Gyaltsap, these stages are: false knowledge; valid doubt; partial knowledge; true belief; recognition; valid inference; and valid direct perception.[47]

In false knowledge or misknowledge, the mind is convinced it knows something that is patently false, as in a delusion or illusion. Such knowledge is false because it obscures the workings of cause and effect, giving us a deluded view of ourselves and our interactions with the world. Traditionally, such delusional views are categorized into five types: self-reification; extreme self-reification; exclusivist views; unethical views; and obstructive views.[48]

In Buddhist psychology, at the root of all perceptual error, and hence all preventable suffering, is the instinctive habit of reifying our construct of ourselves and our mind/body process as if they were really as we imagine: fixed, independent, unitary, self-sufficient, and self-evident. Self-reification is an equal opportunity error, an instinct shared very deeply by all forms of life, based on its long natural history of reinforcement through countless eons of evolution.

In practice, this deep structure, the hub of all self-protective instincts and all myopic self-enclosure, is usually hidden under the camouflage of consciously learned views of self that reinforce it, called extreme self-reifying views. The most insidious of these is the delusion that we *are* our physical body, since this leads us to overlook the power of the mind for good or ill, reducing it to a passive witness or accident with no real impact on our lives or the world. At the opposite end of the spectrum are fundamentalist views of ourselves as eternal souls belonging to a realm that transcends the causality of evolution and development.

Exclusivist or exceptionalist views are familial, social or cultural extensions of the primitive self-reifying sense that I'm somehow special, to groups that I identify with, such as gender, racial, cultural, or religious groups.

Unethical views are those which vaunt an ethos or lifestyle that is unhealthy, unrealistic, violent, or self-destructive, as if it were the right way to be or act. Included here are violent views that celebrate brute force or other destructive habits with slogans like "Might makes right;" and hedonistic views that celebrate addictive, compulsive, and obsessive lifestyles with slogans like "Greed is good."

Finally, obstructive views block the process of healing, learning, and change, either by projecting our wishes or fears onto reality or by denying the way things actually are and work, obstructing our progress by leading us to minimize our ability or responsibility to learn, heal and change. Examples of projective views are those which project our wish for a super-parent onto the world, leading us to believe that our parents, society or God are responsible for our happiness, not us. Examples of denying views are those which deny that our minds have the intelligence, goodness or will-power to solve intractable problems like stress and trauma, and those that demean reflective pursuits like spiritual contemplation or psychotherapy.

Based on these categories, cognitive self-analysis, like modern schema therapy first helps expose false views as views, not realities, and then helps us examine them rationally and test them against the evidence. This process eventually leads to valid doubt, an ambivalent state in which we begin to waver in our attachment to false views and also begin to open our minds to novel views of ourselves and the world.

On the other side of valid doubt, we find partial knowledge. This stage begins when we see through the chinks in our false views of the world long enough to get fleeting and partial glimpses of the reality of how things work.

Freed up by valid doubt and guided by the glimpses of partial knowledge, our minds can begin to seriously entertain alternate views of ourselves and the world. The most natural way for our highly symbolic and social minds to do this is to build up a mental image of how the world might really be, based on assuming the validity of traditions and experts we have good reason to consider reliable. This mode of knowledge is accepted as valid only provisionally, that is, as long as we haven't yet had the opportunity to test those assumptions by critical analysis, sustained reflection, and direct personal experience.

The stage of true belief eventually leads to the next, the validating knowledge called recognition. As the English word suggests, recognition refers to the retrospective knowledge that our search for truth is on the right track, based on our belated reflection that the aftertaste of a contemplative breakthrough or direct experience confirms some aspects of our presumptive image of truth while correcting others.

Once we've integrated fresh, valid knowledge in the form of a true belief and come to recognize that our belief is in some sense true, we can then begin to analyze it more carefully and refine our image of its truth by sustained contemplation. In insight meditation, mindfulness has given way to a state of profound, inner clarity and calm called quiescence, while awareness has been honed to a highly focused, discursive form of meditative analysis and reflection called analytic insight. The outcome of this compound work is the gradual emergence of valid inferential knowledge, a highly refined, symbolic knowledge which serves as a reliable approximation or rational intuition to be further checked and corrected against the hard evidence of contemplative experience and realization.

The last stop on the sevenfold path of valid knowledge is the stage of direct perception. It is the stage at which the mind is ready, willing, and able to immerse itself fully in the particularity of experience, and to know the reality of things as if for the first time. The ultimate gold standard of knowledge, valid direct perception is traditionally seen as leaving nothing to the imagination and nothing to be desired in its correspondence to things as they are. It certifies without reservation the power of each and every individual human mind to know everything it needs to know about reality in the flesh, so to speak.

Of course, we can easily go astray here if we confuse what is meant by valid direct perception with what we normally think of as perception. Supported by current neuroscience, this tradition insists that most of what passes for perception in most of our minds most of the time is at best partial knowledge or recognition, if not frank illusion. A poor shadow that can't hold a candle to direct perception, most of the ordinary perceptual knowledge we have is so far removed from the particularity of things, so highly processed through generic images, words, and associations, that it is more like a dream or illusion than a direct experience. By contrast, think of those rare moments in life when something real and fresh absorbs your attention so fully that everything else disappears, and everything you thought was real pales by comparison. This is the degree of immediacy we only feel during peak experiences like falling in love, the birth of a child, saying goodbye to a dying loved one, or being in a state of flow.

Harnessing the Power of Motivation: The Affective Mental Factors

With this brief excursion into Buddhist cognitive science, we can now return to complete our survey of the table of elements in Buddhist psychology. The fact that the final four categories of the table, more than half of the elements, are devoted to distinguishing different kinds of emotion reflects the Buddha's insight that emotions play a key role in determining whether our intentions, perceptions and actions lead to suffering or happiness. If the previous three categories and the background they assume constitute a cognitive psychology, these four with their background may be seen as a map of Buddhist psychodynamics or affective psychology. A glance at the particular categories tells us a lot about the basic assumptions of Buddhist psychodynamics.

Essentially, the affective or emotional mental factors are typed according to how they line up with the basic intentionality that is the prime determinant of the developmental effect of all forms of intentional action: mental, verbal and physical.[49] The lens through which our intentions are viewed is the positive, therapeutic lens of whether they're healthy, unhealthy or neutral. Unpacking the meaning of these value-laden terms makes it perfectly clear that Buddhist psychology as a whole is structured as both a therapeutic psychology and a positive psychology.

Classically, Buddhist science defines as "healthy" or "virtuous" those intentions and actions which are conducive to true happiness; as "unhealthy" or "vicious" those intentions and actions which reinforce or enhance suffering; and as "neutral" or "variable" those which have variable effects on well-being depending on the influence of related cognitive or affective factors.[50] Since affective mental factors are viewed as coloring the basic, omnipresent factor of intention with a specific emotional mood or tone, they are categorized quite simply as healthy or virtuous mental factors; unhealthy or vicious mental factors, and variable or neutral mental factors.

Buddhist Psychodynamics: The Healthy Affective Factors

In the spirit of positive psychology, Buddhist psychodynamics begins with the eleven healthy emotional factors.[51] These are confidence, conscience, consideration, non-attachment, non-aggression, non-confusion, effort, flow, conscientiousness, equanimity, and non-violence. A brief look at each of these helps to acquaint us with the dynamics of happiness in this psychology.

Confidence or rational faith serves to overcome skepticism, to promote trust in what is reliable, and to foster the aspiration to learn, heal and change for the better. Once we have confidence in our understanding of the causality of suffering and happiness, we can trust and act on our ability to distinguish unhealthy elements we must let go of and healthy ones we must develop. Vis á vis modern positive psychology, confidence is not the same as optimism, since it requires that, in order to be truly healthy, a given view must be not only positive but also realistic, accurate or true.

Conscience or shame is a self-corrective faculty that prompts us to avoid unhealthy intentions and actions based on our own cognizance of their ill effects, clearing the way for the development of positive intentions and actions. In the course of development, conscience is aided by consideration or embarrassment, a social sensitivity that prompts us to avoid unhealthy intentions and actions based on others' cognizance of their ill effects. The decision to avoid unhealthy habits clears the way for the cultivation of the next three positive factors, the antidotes of the three primary unhealthy emotions.

Non-attachment, the natural antidote to compulsive desires, serves to counteract our habitual adherence to the mundane distractions, addictive pleasures and fear-based entanglements of daily life. Non-aggression is the faculty of tolerance that works to stop a destructive impulse towards any being that might trigger us to act in an angry or hurtful way. Non-confusion is that discriminating insight or lucid awareness which dispels the "dark night" of confusion, by helping valid knowledge cut through false views and rely instead on healing truths like impermanence, relativity, and selflessness.

Taken together, these first five healthy factors plant the seeds for healthy moral development. Rooted in rational confidence and a clear conscience, the three antidotes can begin to weed out the three prime roots of stress and trauma, especially when they are nurtured by the six other healthy factors, which stem from ethical and contemplative training.

Effort is that positive motivational force which energizes us to aspire to, engage in and persist in actions that help to overcome vices and cultivate virtues, fostering healing, learning and change. Applying effort to the practice of concentration eventually gives rise to flow, a euphoric state within the mind that makes the mind and nervous system pliant and receptive to learning. An essential by-product of meditation, flow reflects the joy of self-mastery that helps overcome resistances and enrich learning, promoting what we now call neural plasticity.

Conscientiousness is that reflective moral factor that helps keep us focused on healthy intentions and actions, carefully monitoring and avoiding unhealthy instincts and habits. With conscientiousness, we can more easily develop the contemplative faculty of equanimity, that form of mental balance or poise which helps keep the mind centered in the flow of clarity and calm, by resisting the de-centering tendencies towards distraction and dullness. Thanks to equanimity, we have the will-power and moral stability to defuse even the most primal of destructive forces: the self-protective impulse towards violence. Non-violence is that faculty of inner peace which serves to fully counteract the destructive impulse to harm any living being in any way, shape or form. This faculty is crucial to the stability of moral development, since the resurgence of antisocial emotions like anger or hatred not only drives us to hurt others but also interrupts and undermines our development of positive social emotions and actions.

The Logic of Buddhist Psychodynamics: Transforming Destructive Emotions

As the list clearly shows, these eleven factors cover a broad range of faculties that work together to support moral development, the motivation of healthy behavior and the growth of healthy social emotions. The list is not what we might expect from recent writings on positive psychology, since it focuses on self-corrective factors that counteract destructive, antisocial emotions and actions, rather than implying that we can somehow leap over these powerful negative forces and go straight to developing positive social emotions like generosity, tolerance, love, and compassion. In this sense, this first category of affective factors shows how Buddhist psychodynamics is grounded in the therapeutic vision and framework of the four noble truths.

At the same time, there should be no doubt that this modest list of healing factors is only the prelude to a full spectrum of positive emotions. This should be clear from the fact that the third noble truth describes the Buddha's experience of life as naturally blissful, peaceful, luminous, uncontaminated and clear under the streamlined, negative heading of Nirvana, meaning simply "the end" of suffering. The fact is that the three antidote factors—non-attachment, non-aggression, and non-confusion—are seen as the root causes for developing all positive social emotions. So listing them is an abbreviated way of alluding to the complex social emotions and euphoric states linked with the meditative realization of the four contemplations[52] and four absorptions,[53] including love; compassion, joy, equanimity, tolerance, clarity, delight, and bliss.

The End of the Path: Unconditional Happiness and Unrestricted Freedom

After the four contemplative states and four states of formless absorption, the endpoint of the traditional nine-step sequence of state-specific healing[54] is the cessation of suffering, which is in fact not restricted or localized in its scope to any particular state or level of consciousness on the threefold map of the realms of experience.[55] So the path of contemplative healing is an odyssey that departs from the ordinary suffering of stress and trauma, goes by way of the positive moral faculties listed as healthy factors, to gradually ascend a stairway of increasingly pure and refined forms of happiness. At the end of that ascent, when we've reached what is called the peak of existence, we are free to come back down the mountain, bringing lasting happiness with us wherever we go in the universe of possible experience. With this glimpse at the emotional factors of healthy development, its time to consider the two kinds of emotional factors that stand in our way, the factors that drive the wheel of stress and trauma.

The Primary Compulsions: Roots of All Negative Action

The list of primary compulsions is surprising not just because it's so short—six unhealthy factors in total—but also because half of the six are not what we normally think of as affective factors.[56] Of course, the first two—desire and anger—are familiar by now from the toxic trinity of desire, anger, and delusion. And it should come as no surprise that right after these we find pride, which reinforces our self-enclosing tendency towards self-reification and self-indulgence. Yet the last three—delusion, doubt, and compulsive views—would seem to be more at home in the realm of cognition than emotion. The fact that the primary compulsions include more or less cognitive factors along with basic emotions reflects the Buddha's insight that destructive emotions depend on perceptual factors that are every bit as instinctive and basic to the life of the mind as the most primitive drives and affects. Not only are the cognitive and the emotional intertwined from the outset of development, but they are constantly influencing and reinforcing each other as part of the complex causal cycle of stress and trauma. As a result, Buddhist psychology insists that habitual emotional patterns cannot be readily influenced or decisively changed without addressing the cognitive errors that repeatedly trigger, rationalize, and reinforce them.

Desire, Anger, and Pride: The Alternating Current of Self-Involvement

As for the six primary compulsions themselves, compulsive desire is understood as an attachment to objects tainted by the misperception of them as more attractive or pleasant than they really are. Basic to all motivation, our pursuit of objects is only as successful as our perception of them is correct. Propelled by an insatiable and irrational drive to have limitless, uninterrupted pleasure, we living beings are all highly vulnerable to exaggerating the qualities of things that attract us. Typically, such misperception is so deeply ingrained that it's not very susceptible to being corrected by disappointing or dissatisfactory experience. Instead, such disappointment often simply fuels our desire for more, in a negative feedback loop that eventually leads to addiction. On the other hand, when we are disappointed by or deprived of the things we desire, living beings naturally respond with frustration and anger. Anger is defined as an intolerance and hostility towards people and things that provoke ill-will. Some form of anger is our usual response to meeting with some disappointment or frustration, and this negative mental factor often propels us into a more violent, compulsive pursuit of what we desire. As a result, our minds oscillate back and forth between these two poles of compulsive emotion, in a futile, repetitive cycle of mounting dissatisfaction that is rooted in compulsive pride or narcissism.

Pride is seen as an inflated or unrealistic view of ourselves based on instinctive reification of a biased self-concept and self-image, a concept and image that exaggerate our qualities, achievements, or place in the world. The emotional reflex of our instinctive delusion, pride leads to suffering and discontent because it reinforces our childish expectation that life should revolve around us, offering endless pleasure without the least bit of hardship or pain. While most of the seven kinds of pride enumerated in the traditional list, as we'd expect, involve narcissistic delusions of grandeur or superiority, there is also a paranoid version called the pride of inferiority, in which we indulge in a sense of being worse or worse off than anyone else.

Doubt and Confusion: The Demons of Self-Reification

If the pride of our primal narcissism drives the alternating current of compulsive life from the pole of desire to the pole of anger, the root of pride is the instinctive delusion that confuses the way things are and so acts as a source of compulsive emotions and doubts. As in the case of self-reifying views, misperceiving ourselves as exceptional and divorced from, or at the center of the world leads us to feel discontent and desire, alternating with fear and anger. Distinct from the cognitive error of false views, delusion here refers to the affective state of confusion that clings to such misperceptions. Since this primal confusion robs us of our cognitive freedom to see things as they are and work, Shakyamuni singled it out as the first link in the twelvefold cycle of stress and trauma, the taproot from which all compulsive life grows. Based on this insight, delusion is notoriously called the root of all ills; the inner devil or demon (Mara) that traps and binds the mind; and the disease of self-deception that blinds the insight-eye.

Reinforcing this primal state of confusion is the fifth of the primary compulsions, ambivalence or doubt. Consumed by ambivalence about reality or truth, the affective state of uncertainty or doubt prevents us from using our higher faculties to focus on and engage in healthy intentions and actions. In the words of the great physician-philosopher, Nagarjuna: "As long as the mind vacillates, it remains in the range of its demon."[57]

Compulsive Worldviews: The Cognitive Underpinnings of Destructive Emotions

Last but not least comes the element that is responsible for doubt or ambivalence towards healthy intentions and actions: the factor of a compulsive outlook or worldview. Here, Buddhist psychodynamics comes full circle, to embrace its inexorable interdependence with cognitive psychology. This sixth compulsive mental factor includes the five kinds of false views we discussed along with Buddhist cognitive psychology, under the heading of false knowledge. As you may recall, these are: self-reifying views; extreme self-reifying views; exclusivist views; unethical views; and obstructive views. These may come in two forms: instinctive, unconscious errors; and socially learned, intellectual views. In either case, they keep the mind confused and uncertain by insinuating misperceptions of ourselves and the world that are so habitual and familiar that we assume their truth without even noticing or examining them. Woven in this way into the fabric of the mind/body process, these misperceptions powerfully reinforce and rationalize the unhealthy intentions and actions that lock us into the cycle of compulsive life.

The Secondary Afflictions: The Tangled Web We Weave

While the primary compulsions are the taproots of the creeping vines of stress and trauma, the death-grip they hold on our bodies and minds is compounded by a series of more complex emotions that branch off from them.[58] These secondary afflictive emotions stem from the various ways the root compulsions branch out at the higher level of consciousness and neural functioning involved in responding to the stresses of complex social life. Some of these branches arise from the simple divergence or bifurcation of one of the three prime or "root" compulsive emotions: desire, anger or confusion. Others arise from the intermingling of desire and confusion. And still others arise from the complex intermingling of all three prime compulsive emotions.[59]

The Five Derivative Forms of Anger

Since anger is the most destructive of the three prime compulsive emotions, the first items on the list are the five secondary forms of anger or aggression. Rage is a violent impulse to do verbal or physical harm. Vindictiveness is nursing anger by holding onto an urge for revenge. Cursing is speaking harshly out of anger. Envy is an intense anger that resents and covets others' fortune or qualities. Cruelty is a violent impulse to make others suffer.

The Three Secondary Forms of Attachment

Since the next most disruptive of the prime compulsive emotions is desire, next come the three secondary forms of desirous attachment. Greed or avarice is an intense attachment that compulsively hoards wealth or possessions and resists giving or sharing. Complacency is a self-satisfied attachment to one's own health, beauty, wealth, intelligence, or ability that stifles any impulse to self-improvement or self-transcendence. Excitement is an excessive enthusiasm or obsessive anticipation based on clinging to unrealistic fantasy about any object(s) of desire.

The Five Secondary Forms of Confusion

Finally, we come to the five secondary forms of confusion, the most insidious of the primary compulsive emotions. Dullness or lethargy is a deep confusion that envelops the tired body-mind in a fog that blocks learning, reflection, and judgment. Mistrust is an insidious form of confusion about what is reliable and true, which leaves us paralyzed with mistaken fear and doubt, as in cynicism. Laziness is a lack of appropriate interest and effort in developing healthy intentions and actions, based on a confusing unhealthy comforts and addictive pleasures with real sources of happiness. Forgetfulness is neglecting to stay mindful and aware of healthy intentions and actions, based on confusing distractions for what is truly desirable.

The Three Secondary Afflictions Mixing Desire and Confusion

As for afflictions with mixed roots, the most seductive are the three derived from the synergy of desire and confusion. Deceit is an impulse to deny, hide or cover up our faults and weaknesses, based on a confused attachment to wealth, reputation or power. Pretentiousness is an impulse to exaggerate qualities we have or claim qualities we lack, based on a confused attachment to wealth, reputation or power. Incorrigibility is an impulse to deny our own faults or disavow any responsibility to admit or correct faults pointed out by others, based on a confused attachment to a narcissistic view of ourselves as perfectly blameless or faultless.

The Four Secondary Afflictions Mixing Anger, Desire, and Confusion

Last but not least, we come to the four afflictive emotions which derive from all three prime compulsions: anger, desire, and confusion. Shamelessness is an impulse to deny our own faults or disavow any responsibility to admit or correct them for our own sake, based on a confused, self-destructive attachment to a narcissistic view of ourselves as perfectly blameless or faultless. Inattentiveness, the opposite of awareness or alertness, is when the faculty of insight fails to attend to negative factors that creep into one's mental, verbal and physical behavior, based on its getting wrapped up in compulsive confusion, anger and/or desire. Unconscientiousness is a failure to guard the mind from compulsions and to cultivate healthy intentions and actions, based on a confused, self-destructive attachment to compulsive self-indulgence. Distraction occurs when the flow of pure interest is interrupted and the mind strays from its chosen object of focus, under the influence of an object that triggers confusion, anger, and/or desire.

Maybe Yes, Maybe No: The Variable Mental Factors

The last category on the table of elements includes four mental factors—two affective, two cognitive—which have a variable effect on mental development. These four may be healthy, unhealthy, or indeterminate, depending on whether the motivation behind them is positive, negative or neutral, and on whether the cognition informing them is correct, incorrect, or indeterminate.

The first of these, sleep, rest or relaxation, may be healthy or unhealthy depending on whether it is motivated by a wholesome intention to refresh and restore body and mind for healthy activities, or tainted by compulsions or afflictions like doubt, dullness, resentment, or laziness. This explains why Buddhist psychology places such a great emphasis on clearing the mind prior to sleep or checking our motivation prior to rest or meditation.

While most religious psychologies tend to be biased in favor of guilt, modern scientific psychology tends, reactively I think, to be biased against it. Guilt or regret is remorse occasioned by reflecting on a previous action (or inaction). It is healthy when we feel remorse over an action that was truly misguided and/or motivated by ill-will, since such action was in fact unhealthy for us and/or harmful to others. Yet guilt or regret can also be unhealthy, when we feel remorse about an action that was guided by valid knowledge and a good motivation. Neutral guilt is regretting an action that was innocuous but had a bad outcome, such as regretting eating a meal that seemed healthy but made us ill or starting a project that failed through no fault of our own. While unhealthy guilt or mistaken regret is clearly something we must learn to correct, even neutral guilt is seen as a self-indulgence to be avoided. If guilt or regret can help us learn from mistakes and move towards happiness, they are to be welcomed as factors of healthy self-correction; if not, they are insidious and deceptive, like a faulty oil gauge, and must themselves be corrected on our way to true happiness.

The remaining two variable factors are the complementary cognitive faculties of investigation and analysis. Investigation is the discursive mind's general inquiry or research into some object of interest; analysis is the discursive mind's precise inquiry or realization of the nature of some object of interest. These may be healthy, unhealthy, or indeterminate depending on the degree of insight and the nature of the intention guiding them. Investigation and analysis are healthy when used wisely and with a positive intention to understand things in ways that in fact promote happiness. They are unhealthy when used unwisely and with the negative intention to understand things in ways that interfere with happiness. And they're indeterminate when used to understand things in ways that are neutral with respect to suffering and happiness.

In Buddhist psychology, we find a contemplative science that takes a two-edged approach to discursive inquiry that does not fit neatly with our preconceptions. Like modern science, it values investigation and analysis as indispensible on the path to valid knowledge and true happiness. At the same time, like ancient spiritual traditions, it sees the discursive mind as potentially unhealthy as well, and stops short of the modern view of investigation and knowledge as intrinsically good, especially when they are directed towards aims that may be harmful to life or make no clear contribution to genuine well-being. This nuanced approach is exemplified in Dharmakirti's view that our minds have the potential to become omniscient, which he defines pragmatically as knowing everything we need to know to achieve concrete aims like personal freedom and lasting happiness.[60]

Insight and Emotion: Comparing Buddhist and Western Psychology

When we compare the ambition, depth, and scope of the Buddhist map of positive development with contemporary fields like positive psychology, we can see three main differences. First, it is initially more concerned with transforming the negative emotions that plague our everyday life than with building positive emotions. Second, this traditional map charts a path of positive development that is more radical and transformational than most positive psychology today. Third, the Buddhist approach to both negative and posi tive emotions integrates cognitive and affective variables into healing and transformation. For instance, while Buddhist psychodynamics concedes that naive optimism promotes happiness, it also insists that positive thinking cannot yield true freedom and peace of mind as long as it assumes unrealistic views like creationism or idealism.

This seemingly minor distinction helps highlight the integrative nature of Buddhist psychology. Like our psychodynamic psychology, Buddhist contemplative science insists that positive thoughts and actions alone may ameliorate suffering but cannot break the cycle of primary compulsions that drives stress and trauma. Like our cognitive therapies, Buddhist psychology insists that false knowledge conditions even the deepest, unconscious levels of our instinctive life; that changing false concepts is not only humanly possible but indispensible to deep emotional and behavioral change. Like our ego psychology, humanistic psychology, existential and transpersonal schools, Buddhist psychology sees the human mind as capable of higher levels of intellectual freedom and moral development, given the opportunity to realize its full potential. Yet like our object-relations and interpersonal schools, family-systems and deep affect therapies, it also insists that the motivation needed to reach higher stages of development must come from healing the stress-reactive emotions reinforced by evolution and development and by cultivating in their place positive social emotions like confidence, tolerance, equanimity, love, and compassion.

The Condensed Table of Elements and the Practice of Inclusive Mindfulness

Since even the bare-bones table of sixty some elements is a lot to bear in mind, in practice the table was condensed further to a set of three categories meant to be easily memorable yet detailed enough to help the practitioner focus on the key elements in the workings of the body-mind. The three categories are: the five aggregates or mind/body systems; the twelve sensory media; and the eighteen perceptual elements. Since these are mostly made up of elements we have already covered in the classical table, it's simple enough to show how these categories condense the key elements we need to keep in mind for daily practice.

The rubric of five mind/body systems is meant to focus mindfulness on those elements which prove most crucial to the workings of the mind, body, and their intentional actions.[61] The first of these includes the material elements that make up the system of the physical body and its natural environment, namely: atoms and molecules in the five states—solid, liquid, energy, gas, and space. The other four systems are mental, starting with: the perceptual system that includes the six kinds of primary consciousness: visual, auditory, olfactory, gustatory, tactile, and mental. The three remaining mental systems include the two most critical of the omnipresent mental factors—sensation and conception—and a complex motivational system, which amounts to a grab bag of all the positive, negative and variable affective factors.

While the primary role of the perceptual system is clear, the other systems were picked out from the long list of mental factors because of the key roles they play in determining the health or illness of our response to perceptual input. Whether the input engenders a pleasant or painful sensation triggers the basic intention which is the first line in our affective response to experience. At the same time, conception puts a symbolic interpretation on the input, which is the first line in our cognitive response. Working in tandem, then, these two gatekeepers evoke the complex emotions, including the positive, negative or variable affective factors, which largely determine the health or illness of our mind/body response to any given perception.

With the rubric of the five systems helping to focus attention on our cognitive, affective and behavioral response to perception, the remaining two rubrics serve to strengthen our mindfulness of the primary process of perception itself. The twelve media essentially cover the subjective pole of the primary process of perception, with the first six media—the six modes of primary consciousness—reflecting the mind's involvement in the process, and the second six media—the five sensory faculties or neural networks plus the mental faculty or prior moment of mind—reflecting the body's involvement.[62] This rubric obviously overlaps with the five systems in that the six mental media are identical with the perceptual system, while the six sensory faculties cover those parts of the bodily system—the neural networks of perception—which most directly interface with consciousness.

The primary process of perception is further analyzed by the rubric of eighteen elements, which includes the twelve media, but also aligns them with the objective pole of perception, the six objects of sight, sound, scent, taste, texture, and mind.[63] In short, this rubric shows how the modes of consciousness emerge from their productive causes—their respective faculties and objects—effectively fostering mindfulness of the threefold conjunction that makes up the prime causal nexus of perception. This rubric obviously overlaps with the five mind/body systems in the same way as the twelve media it subsumes, but it also overlaps with those parts of the physical system of life that are objects rather than faculties of perception, including anything in our internal and external environments we can see, hear, smell, taste, feel, or conceive. It's worth noting that these two perceptual rubrics reflect a more detailed unpacking of the short list of physical elements on the classical table of elements, since they include the gross and subtle material elements—solids and their molecules—that serve as objects and faculties of perception.

In practice, the table is often condensed even further to the five life systems alone, the simplest analysis of the mind/body process used in the training of inclusive mindfulness and insight meditation. On the other hand, in some contexts these three rubrics are often expanded to include a fourth, which further unpacks the bodily system, that is: the ten motor faculties, which include the muscles of the arms, legs, hands, feet, head, mouth, and sexual organ. All these rubrics have an obvious use for practitioners learning to develop stable, inclusive mindfulness of the systems and elements of the mind/body process, especially the primary process of perception and our complex behavioral response to it. As practitioners move from basic mindfulness of the breathing body to mindfulness of sensation, mind and its functions, they generally begin with the overview map of five systems, progress to the intermediate maps of twelve media and eighteen elements, and finally end up using the most detailed map of the full table of elements.

Mindfulness, Analysis, and Insight: The Path of Contemplative Change

Our quick survey of the table of elements and related maps of the mind should make it abundantly clear that simple mindfulness of the here and now is not an end in itself, but only the first step in a complex inner journey of self-analysis meant to lead us towards profound healing insight and lasting life change. If we want the full benefits of mindfulness and contemplative living, we must not rest content with a practice restricted to awareness of the breath or simple mindfulness of whatever comes. The best way to build our practice for the marathon of real transformation is to familiarize ourselves with the traditional maps of the mind that guide our attention to those elements and factors which we'll need to understand and change. The traditional way to train for this journey is to practice all four scopes of mindfulness in conjunction with progressive awareness of the workings of our key mind/body systems, media and elements.[64] And the traditional way this practice is engaged is with an eye to using mindfulness as a contemplative platform to master the causal elements of suffering and happiness in our own minds and lives. Far beyond the here and now, the ultimate aim of this practice is a rational, first person insight profound enough to free us of our learned and instinctive attachment to stress and trauma, and to guide us in a gradual shift towards a contemplative life, one meditation at a time. Our closing meditative experiment, using the rubric of the five systems, should offer a glimpse into how inclusive mindfulness practice can serve as a platform for self-analytic insight and change.

Meditative Experiment 2: Self-Analysis Through Inclusive Mindfulness

As always, once you've arranged a safe, healing space, first settle yourself into a comfortable, stable posture and clear your energy with alternate nostril breathing or a long, full exhale. Then let the fresh breath fill you as gently as possible, and take that kinder, gentler breath as a focus to settle and center your mind. Breathe in all the energy and awareness you normally put out into the world, and let it come to rest on the fresh breath-rhythm centered at your heart. And as you gather your scattered energy and awareness at your heart on the in-breath, let them merge with the oxygen of your fresh breath and ride it through your bloodstream to every tissue and cell. Imagine this pulse of conscious breath is waking up any areas of unconsciousness, fatigue or numbness, one breath at a time, until your body feels lighter, clearer and more alert. Try to let go of any attachment to being shut-down or burdened, until you feel your body shifting towards the lightest, clearest part of its spectrum, so that it seems less like a solid mass and more like one big person-shaped lung, filling and emptying with a delicate rainbow tissue of breath and awareness.

From this place of heightened clarity and awareness, use your mindfulness to scan your body realistically as an aggregate or living system of physical elements. Breathe into the solid flesh and bones of your body, sensing their living, moving texture from head to toe, toe to head, like a coarse outer sheath structuring your physical life. Next breathe into the bodily fluids that feed and bathe your flesh and bones, trying to sense them as they pulse from your heart out towards your skin and back inwards to your heart again. As you breathe energy and awareness into that moving pulse, try to follow it flowing out and in, out and in, like a subtler, second sheathe nourishing your physical life. Then breathe into the bodily heat or metabolism that warms and fuels your blood, flesh and bones, trying to sense its warmth as a third, still subtler sheathe within those of your fluids, flesh and bones, powering your physical life. Finally, breathe in the bodily airs that fill your lungs and exchange oxygen and carbon dioxide with every tissue and cell, trying to sense this as the inmost, subtlest sheathe that energizes your muscles and nerves, activating your physical life.

With this temporary boost in your physical self-awareness, open the scope of your mindfulness to include the aggregate or living system of your sensations. Scan the raw feel of your body-mind, checking your comfort level from head to toe, toe to head. Again try to center your mind in an equal embrace of all your sensation, one breath at a time. First breathe caring energy and awareness into areas of tension, distress or hurt, facing and accepting them without aversion. Then breathe calming energy and awareness into areas of relief, comfort or pleasure, savoring while releasing them without attachment. Finally, breathe clarifying energy and awareness into areas of shut-down or numbness, observing and appreciating them without indifference. As you equalize and embrace the whole fabric of your sensitive life, try to observe the ways in which feelings of comfort, distress and numbness trigger knee-jerk reactions to pursue, avoid or ignore the various things happening within and around you. Make a special effort to stay so close to the texture of your sensations that you can slow or stop those reactions with mindfulness, and open your mind to responding with greater balance, presence and care.

As you become more centered in your breathing body and the raw feel of being in your own skin, use whatever energy and awareness you've gathered to open the scope of mindfulness to include your mind itself. Try to tune into that part of yourself that is not just alive and sensitive but also naturally knowing and clear, recognizing it as the aggregate or living system of your primary consciousness or perception. Fine tune into this clear, aware space by letting go, a bit at a time, of your sticky involvement with the buzzing, blooming confusion of your habitual mental contents. When attractive ideas, images and emotions come up, try to release them by letting go of clingy desire. When disturbing ideas, images, and emotions come up, try to disengage from them by letting go of enmeshing anger. When numbing ideas, images and emotions come up, try to stay free and clear of them by resisting cloudy confusion. Whenever you find yourself carried away by a wish, worry, or fog, let it go and keep homing back to the spacious expanse and crystal clear flow of your stream of consciousness. Try to immerse your mind in this flow as you'd immerse your body in a hot spring. Open your mind and wait for the taste of inner solitude, expansiveness and exhilaration, like an experience of communion and awe in a natural wilderness.

Once you've begun to taste something like this, you're ready to face the content of your daily life with your mind's eye truly open. Up till now, you've been turning your mind back on itself, trying to get a good look at your mental faculty, watching the flow of prior moments in your stream of consciousness like a driver watching the road recede behind him in the rearview mirror. Now it's time to open your mindfulness to the moment-to-moment flow of content which is normal perception. Start by trying to notice the primary, perceptual content of your raw intuitive experience, like a driver watching the landscape rush by on all sides as he drives. This impressionistic art is not about picking one or two objects of interest so you can recognize them. Instead you must use the fish-eye lens of your intuitive mind to just get a raw sense of what's happening, inside and outside your body-mind.

Begin by scanning the receiving end of your perceptual experience, going through the twelve media, two at a time. Ask yourself: anything entering my visual sense/consciousness? Anything entering my hearing sense/consciousness? Anything entering my sense/consciousness of smell? Anything entering my sense/consciousness of taste? Anything entering my sense/consciousness of touch? Anything entering my mental sense/consciousness? Now scan the input end of your perceptual experience, going through the remaining six of the eighteen elements, one at a time. Ask yourself: any sights in my visual field? Any sounds in range of hearing? Any scents in my range of smell? Any tastes on my tongue? Any textures I'm in touch with? Any image on my mind? The art here is to resist the temptation to sort, specify or identify, and to try instead to acquire a taste or feel for the vague flow of impressions, without getting stuck on what it all is or what it might mean. You'll know you're getting the hang of it when, like a stream of consciousness writing exercise, following the stream of perception begins to yield unexpected amounts and surprising new kinds of fresh information about what's happening inside you and all around you.

Once you've begun to get a feel for the aggregate or living system of your perceptions, it's time to open your inclusive mindfulness to embrace the remaining two mental aggregates: conception and emotion. Keeping your mind centered in the deep calm of your primal awareness, try to scan your day to day thoughts with fresh perspective and clarity. Use your fresh perspective to resist getting stuck in your familiar thoughts and concepts, so that you can more clearly asses whether they're realistic or unrealistic, positive or negative. Check your thoughts against the list of false views. Ask yourself: are these thoughts self-reifying? Are they extreme? Are they exclusivist? Are they unethical? Are they obstructive?

On the other hand, check them against the traditional list of realistic views. Ask: do these views square with the four noble truths: that compulsive life is suffering; that its origin is the cycle of stress and trauma; that suffering and its origin can be reversed; and that there is a path to reverse them? Are they consistent with the four epitomes: that all contingent things are impermanent, dissatisfactory and empty of self; and that only breaking the conditioning of stress and trauma brings peace? At a deeper level, check what you take to be your knowledge and perceptions of things. Could they be mistaken? Can you entertain any doubts about them? Are they partial or inattentive? Are they retroactive constructions? Are they valid inferences based on critical thinking and personal experience? Are they direct, intuitive perceptions?

Once you've used your inclusive mindfulness to get greater clarity about the aggregate or living system of your conceptions, open its scope finally to include the aggregate or living system of your emotions.

Scan your emotions to assess whether they are rooted in the primary compulsions. Are these emotions rooted in unhealthy attachment or desire? Are they rooted in destructive aggression or anger? And are they rooted in confusion, prejudice or delusion? Next check whether your emotions are healthy or positive. Do these emotions spring from true non-attachment or love? Do they spring from non-aggression, tolerance or compassion? Do they spring from non-confusion, insight, clarity, or equanimity? Finally, scan you mind for variable factors like rest or guilt, investigation or analysis. If they're present, ask yourself: are these factors healthy or unhealthy, positive or negative?

Now that you've done a systematic, inclusive scan of your mind/body process, based on the analytic grid of the five aggregates, quickly review the results of your scan. Centered in the deep clarity and calm of mindfulness of mind, use your fresh energy and awareness like the sonar of a dolphin floating deep undersea to scan your life systems. Scan your body as a living breathing aggregate of elements. Scan your sensation as a fabric of pleasant and unpleasant elements. Scan the flow of your perceptions, like fluctuating currents of raw sense impressions deep within the stream of consciousness. Next scan your conceptual system, assessing your inner dialogue and view of the world. And scan the emotions that are motivating your actions and responses. Finally, ask yourself to stay mindful of your five systems as much as you can through the day, especially at moments when you're hungry, angry, lonely, or tired, and vulnerable to being triggered.

Analysis, Insight, and Transformation in Buddhist and Western Psychology

This brief experiment with the use of the five aggregates as a map for self-analysis in the practice of inclusive mindfulness brings us full circle, back to our introduction to Buddhist psychology and mindfulness meditation. Once again, it underscores the vital importance of integrating discursive analysis and analytic insight with mindfulness on the path of contemplative healing and change. And it helps explain why the introductory practice we in the West have come to call mindfulness meditation is seen as simply the first step on the path of self-analysis traditionally known as the path of insight meditation. One famous statement from the *King of Concentration Scripture* explains both the indispensible role and radical nature of analytic insight on this path:

> Those mundane persons who cultivate concentration
> Yet do not rid themselves of their notion of self
> Get very agitated when their afflictions return…
> Yet if they discern precisely the selflessness of things

> And if they meditate on that exact discernment,
> That causes the attainment of Nirvana;
> No other cause whatever will bring peace.[65]

This quote shows the intimate integration of cognitive and emotional self-analysis in Buddhist contemplative science, while highlighting the healing edge of analytic insight, informed by the Buddha's realization of selflessness. With this introduction to the path of self-analysis, we're ready to turn to the challenge of grounding that path in a way of life that supports the healing work of insight-guided contemplative change.

3 The Lifelong Path of Contemplative Health

> Without veering towards either of these extremes (hedonism or self-denial), the Transcendent One awakened to the middle way, which gives rise to vision, which gives rise to knowledge, which leads to peace, to direct knowledge, to enlightenment, to Nirvana. And what, mendicants, is that middle way awakened to by the Transcendent One…? It is this noble eightfold path; that is, right view, right intention, right speech, right action, right livelihood, right effort, right mindfulness, right concentration.
>
> (*Turning the Wheel of Teaching Scripture*[1])

In this passage on Shakyamuni's first teaching of four noble truths, the eightfold path of self-healing that leads to the peace of Nirvana is offered as a middle way between extreme lifestyles of addictive self-indulgence and anorectic self-denial. The current relevance of this ancient text is clear. Our modern minds and lives remain torn by conflicts between addictive and anorectic extremes in our motivation and behavior. According to Buddhist contemplative science, it is our moment-to-moment struggle with such conflicting intentions and habits, not the prior history of our evolution or childhood, which most powerfully determines whether our lives tend towards suffering or happiness. That is why the causal efficacy of intentions and actions is the subject of one of the three core disciplines of contemplative healing. Traditionally called self-discipline or ethics, this final discipline requires the most introduction for our modern minds.

A Fork in the Road: Buddhist Ethics and Modern Therapy

Despite a growing interest in mindfulness and the virtues of acceptance, forgiveness, love, and compassion, modern psychology and the analytic mainstream of modern therapy are still rooted where Freud planted them: on the materialist side of our ambivalent culture. While his work was deeply ethical in the classical sense that it aimed to help people understand their own nature and master their self-destructive conditioning and instincts, Freud hid his moral intent behind the façade of a supposedly value-free science.[2] A man of his age, he shared the conventional wisdom that human nature was as aggressive as it was social; that our character was more or less fixed by genetics and development; and that the self-transcendent ethos of our religious traditions was a comforting illusion at best, and at worst, a repressive ideology of social control. This understandable bias was largely responsible for his break with the spiritually inclined Jung, his favorite disciple, as well as the marginalizing of later schools which explicitly value self-transcendence, like existential, humanistic, and transpersonal psychology.

So when it comes to the core discipline of Buddhist ethics, our cross-cultural matching of Buddhist psychology with modern therapy is not so simple. Buddhist psychology sees the path to optimal health not just as a function of gaining insight or changing mindset or emotion, but as inextricably bound with a more or less profound shift in our whole way of life. While modern therapy takes a permissive, facilitating stance towards an individual's chosen aims and lifestyle, emphasizing internal shifts catalyzed by the therapy, Buddhist psychology takes a corrective, educational stance that is highly concerned with the quality of moment-to-moment intentions and actions in daily life. In this, it anticipates recent findings that the lion's share of healing and change may take place outside the therapy, in the space of an individual's daily world.[3] Buddhist ethics assumes that a lifestyle driven by post-traumatic distortions and stress-reactive emotions will invariably block healing and change, since its intentions and acts reinforce the very self-destructive instincts and conditionings that reproduce suffering. So it focuses on empowering individuals to motivate and sustain healthy changes in their way of life, changes that effectively take the individual down a road-not-taken by modern secular society and psychotherapy.

Traditionally, the practice of Buddhist ethics was not simply a matter of individual will, but was supported by engagement with the alternative role-models, traditions and communities that evolved around Shakyamuni and his heirs. For some, going for help to Buddhist teachers, teachings and communities meant leaving lay life entirely, seeking what amounts to asylum from its stress and trauma in the healing institution of Buddhist monasticism. Once there, individuals would be immersed in a whole, alternative way of life, meant to help support them in renouncing and recovering from addictive motivation and compulsive action. Buddhist monastic sanctuaries and schools offered refuge to people of all backgrounds and walks of life who had experienced a devastating life crisis, such as the loss of a livelihood, spouse or child.[4] These institutions would provide not just free food and shelter, but also free medical care, and a complete system of education and contemplative training.[5]

As time went on, Buddhist centers like Nalanda increasingly opened their doors to the lay community, admitting people as novices to heal and learn for a few years before returning to lay life, or accepting secular students for programs of higher education and professional training like our modern universities.[6] As part of this open-door policy, these students would be immersed in the alternative, healthy lifestyle promoted in this tradition, learning skills of ethical self-discipline and self-mastery that would serve them on their return to lay life. And these open Buddhist centers also offered outreach to people in the everyday world, developing ethical guidelines and life-strategies suited to the demands of a lay life. The system of the gradual path on which this book is based was the fruit of an ambitious outreach by Nalanda masters and international visiting faculty to offer a healthier alternative life to both highly developed and underdeveloped Asian cultures.

While this history holds rich lessons on how to transplant Buddhist psychology into the cultures of the modern West, the challenge facing us is in some ways unique. Psychotherapy holds great promise for individual guidance and support of healthy change in our day, but the permissive, value-free culture of conventional therapy leaves people prey to the extreme lifestyles of their family of origin or ambient culture. Even today's contemplative therapies offer limited concrete ethical guidance and communal support for changes in behavior and lifestyle.[7] As I see it, the main challenges we face here are three: (1) confronting traumatic or compulsive habits of emotion and action that are promoted as forms of healthy self-defense by mainstream society and psychotherapy; (2) confronting addictive and anorectic lifestyles that are normalized by our family or culture of origin, secular or religious; and (3) providing alternate role-models, traditions and communities that support healthy changes in motivation and lifestyle outside the bounds of conventional therapy.

Karma Theory: The Causality of Moral Development

The first and hardest practical challenge, as we saw in the Introduction, stems from the contrast between the materialist ethics of modern psychology and the developmental bioethics of *karma* theory. Beyond its multi-life model of agency, *karma* theory challenges the permissive ethos of modern humanism by insisting that instinctive post-traumatic reactions like hyper-vigilance or the shame-based projection of blame and rage, while natural, only perpetuate trauma and must not be confused or indulged as part of the healing process.[8]

This challenge is based on the prime, causal assumption of *karma* theory: that specific intentional acts have determinate effects. Negative emotions like anger, for instance, are seen as invariably endangering positive human development, regardless of whether the anger motivates the most wanton violence or the most legitimate self-defense. While *karma* theory acknowledges the quantitative difference between the harm done by anger that is sadistic, relished, and condoned, versus the harm done by anger that is involuntary, repugnant, and regretted, it does not waver in its insistence that the developmental effect of anger is to reinforce the cycle of stress and trauma, and hence promote long-term suffering. In this it is consistent with contemporary research suggesting that anger is a general risk factor for a wide range of physical and mental health problems in adults and children.[9]

More challenging still, in contrast to the rights-based ethics of modern humanism, the bioethics of *karma* insists that injuries inflicted by others harm an individual's development less directly than indirectly, by serving as an objective condition which invites the traumatic distortions and destructive emotions that are the most serious causes of developmental effects on the injured party. Interestingly, this stance is in line with Freud's controversial view that the source of neurosis may be as much in the individual's mind as in the failings of the environment. And it helps explain the enormous range of individual responses to seemingly similar traumas. Yet there is no denying that this strict insistence on the individual mind's primary causal role in development challenges popular beliefs about childhood and adult trauma, and may be all too easily confused with blaming the victim.

No matter how sensitive or difficult it may be, the Buddhist view that our own intentional acts are the primary determinants of our development puts a whole new spin on the victim-of-childhood narrative that has become something of a fixture in modern therapy.[10] By insisting that harm done by our own misperceptions and stress-reactions, however innocent and unavoidable, outweighs the harm done by others and can only be undone by changing our minds, *karma* theory holds us to a higher standard of responsibly for our personal suffering and happiness. Yet it also empowers us by insisting that we have the potential to free our minds from the self-protective emotions and habits activated in childhood, emotions and habits we typically come to identify as "me" or "mine," i.e., as fixed in our nature or personality.

Time and again, I've seen people free themselves from lifelong patterns of internal or interpersonal conflict by following the Buddhist ethical path of purging their minds of distortions and compulsions developed through trauma in childhood or adulthood. Once they see their own active role in perpetuating the cycle of trauma, people can finally break free of the passive, victim stance that locks us into a hostile dependence on parents and others. This freedom allows us for the first time to see the cycle of stress and trauma objectively: as a multi-life chain-reaction of destructive instincts and habits transmitted across generations and afflicting all humanity in one way or another. And it also yields the deep transformation of self modern therapy calls deep character change and Buddhist psychology calls the transition from an alienated to a noble personality.

Without this behavioral component of healing and change, even the most robust integration of mindfulness or contemplative insights into modern therapy will be incomplete and yield only a fraction of the efficacy of Buddhist psychology. As I said in the Introduction, I see the integration of *karmic* bioethics not as a romantic mission, but as a scientific refinement of evolutionary psychology. While it involves a dramatic shift in our view of the way development works, the shift is consistent with the insights of Freud, Jung, Piaget, Nagy and others, that the developing mind has a causal efficacy of its own, set within the soft evolutionary process of preserving learned patterns of perception, emotion and action within and across individual lives.[11] This view sees the human infant not as a passive, blank slate or innocent victim, but as a naturally powerful, sovereign agent of its own social learning and moral development.

Healing and the Middle Way: Challenging Our Extreme Lifestyles

The second challenge of translating Buddhist ethics into the contemporary West is finding skillful ways to confront addictive and anorectic lifestyles that are normalized by our mainstream cultures. Addictive habits seen as normal in our secular mainstream, like ritualized social drinking or the workaholic pursuit of wealth or position can have an insidious effect on the mind. Likewise, anorectic habits seen as normal in our religious mainstream, like suppressing distress or stigmatizing non-conformity, can also have an insidious effect on the mind that reinforces repressed trauma and blocks healing change. Yet the non-directive ethos of modern therapy leads many therapists to minimize the impact of seemingly "normal" addictive lifestyles, and to attribute the ills and blocks they cause to fixed mental disorders that supposedly require chronic treatment. And while conventional therapy typically challenges repressive religious worldviews and lifestyles, it does so in a biased way that fails to acknowledge the potential benefits of a healthy spiritual outlook or sober lifestyle, alienating the spiritually inclined.[12]

By contrast, the middle way of Buddhist ethics exposes the addictive pleasures of a materialist lifestyle as self-medication for the deep discontent of a life driven by a false sense of alienation and scarcity. In place of the vain pursuit of security through consumption, Buddhist ethics offers a path to sustainable well-being and happiness through taming the inner demons of self-reification, attachment and rage, while cultivating the inner peace, tolerance, and benevolence that allow us to feel lasting contentment within. On the other hand, this centrist ethics exposes the anorectic self-denial of fundamentalist lifestyles as a wishful escape from the insecurity of a life based on a regressive fantasy of an eternal, unchanging self, spirit or soul. In place of a regressive faith that we can be saved from the laws of cause and effect, Buddhist ethics offers a path to sustainable well-being through facing the reality of our impermanence and interdependence, while cultivating the genuine self-knowledge, insight, and wisdom that allow us to master the causality of freedom and happiness.

In my experience, the challenge here is best met by translating Buddhist ethics as an evidence-based behavioral middle way that avoids such lifestyle extremes. Contemporary research on the neuroscience of stress, addiction, and trauma increasingly confirms the corrosive effects such driven lifestyles have on the mind-brain.[13] Such research supports the Buddhist ethical view that all compulsive ways of life promote mental, physical, and existential suffering, including premature illness, aging, and death.[14] On the other hand, the new positive psychology has convincingly shown that the benefits of a spiritual ethos or lifestyle come not from self-denial or fear-based conformity, but from the direct causal benefits of peaceful and benevolent habits on the body and mind.[15] By supporting the centrist guidelines of Buddhist ethics with these new sciences and weaving them into a contemplative lifestyle therapy tailored to our ways of life, I've found very palpable gains in the efficacy of psychotherapy.

It Takes a Village: Providing Intensive Support for Life-Change

The third challenge to be faced in transplanting Buddhist ethics into the West is providing alternate role-models, traditions and communities outside the bounds of conventional therapy to support healthy changes in motivation and lifestyle. Despite all we've learned from object-relational analysis, interpersonal psychology, and family systems theory, the communal aspect of healing is still largely neglected by the individual-centered paradigm of most modern therapies. Although most clinicians are well aware of the potential for group modalities to complement and enhance individual work, good group therapies are hard enough to start and run that they are in short supply. As a consequence, most therapists are trained to see groups as luxuries, dispensable to their work. My experience with the Buddhist tradition has taught me that the corrective impact of being part of a genuinely healing group, institution or community adds a depth and breadth to self-healing that in most cases cannot be provided by any amount of individual therapy.

The best case for the power of a communal approach to psychological healing and change comes from the unconventional model of Dialectical Behavior Therapy (DBT). Inspired as I said by the traditional teaching approach of a Zen Buddhist community, DBT sets individual therapeutic bonds within a system of corrective social learning and support, including a group education in contemplative insights, methods, and life-skills. What's notable about this approach is its intensive structure and immersive quality, both of which lend DBT a bit of the feel of a healing family or village with an alternative, corrective culture. Of course, the therapy still must be time-limited, and is typically tailored to a subset of people with serious childhood trauma and a history of self-injury.

One of my intentions in founding Nalanda Institute was to be able to extend this Buddhist-inspired communal learning paradigm in ways that would replicate its original open format of lifelong contemplative learning for all. The classes, workshops, and retreats offered by the Institute provide people who have been or are now in therapy with a source of self-healing insights, skills and life-strategies in a setting of ongoing guidance and communal support for contemplative life-change. In effect, the Institute offers a bridge between the mainstream contexts of mind/body medicine and psychotherapy and the more traditional communities teaching Hindu yoga or Buddhist meditation in a more religious or culture-specific way.

Buddhist Ethics: The Behavioral Science of Buddhist Psychology

While linked with a popular system of religious beliefs and cultural values, at its heart Buddhist ethics is the behavioral science of Buddhist psychology. Unlike our behavioral psychology, it treats intention or motivation as even more crucial to the developmental effects of actions than overt vocal or physical behaviors. Yet it also insists that true insight or a good motivation alone is not enough: our daily habits and lifestyle must undergo real change if we want our minds and lives to change. And since we human beings are such thoroughly social animals, we rarely if ever change in a void. For most of us,

Figure 3.1 Gunaprabha, Master of Behavioral Science

profound personal change involves communal change, that is, taking part in an equally profound change in our social and cultural ways of life. The role of the ethical discipline of Buddhist psychology is no more or less than to help people to initiate, guide and sustain the gradual transformation of their way of life—from a familiar lifestyle that conforms to a compulsive mainstream, to an alternative lifestyle that supports more contemplative, peaceful ways of being.

In the rest of this chapter, we'll survey the practical dimension of Buddhist psychology following the eight-step map of the journey to contemplative living spelled out in the fourth noble truth. Although technically, only the third, fourth and fifth steps are explicitly devoted to building ethical self-discipline, the entire eightfold path maps the practical journey of self-transformation which comes within the domain of ethics broadly conceived. In what follows we'll survey that domain by reviewing the eight steps in light of their role in the work of behavioral life-change.[16] To help flesh out the key aspects of this work, I'll cross-reference the behavioral map of the eightfold path with two maps that cover the cognitive and motivational aspects of contemplative self-transformation. These coordinated maps are the map of eight insights within the self-healing horizon of the gradual path of contemplative living,[17] and the map of the five paths of purification which traces our progress transforming obsessions and compulsions into renunciation, true happiness and benevolence.[18]

The First Step: From Self-Deceptive Worldviews to Valid Knowledge of *Karma*

The first step on the eightfold path is to develop a realistic view of the nature and causes of suffering *versus* happiness. As we saw in quickly reviewing the path of knowledge in chapter 2, generally this involves seeing through any view of the world that makes us feel someone or something outside our own minds is responsible for our suffering and happiness. In positive terms, this means grappling with the profound insights spelled out in the Buddha's four noble truths. From the perspective of behavioral change, these healing truths can be boiled down to one ethical challenge. However identified we are with our suffering and however driven we feel by forces beyond our control, the four truths convey Shakyamuni's fundamentally ethical insights that the forces driving our compulsive life are within us, and that we alone have the power and final responsibility to make or break the grip they have on our minds and lives.

Seen in this light, the truth of suffering means that our misguided intentions and actions alone are the engines which create and recreate lifestyles of bondage and dissatisfaction; the truth of origin spells out exactly how our misguided actions, driven by the cycle of stress and trauma, reproduce such a compulsive form of life; the truth of extinction affirms that we and we alone have the power to break the spell of instincts and habits that perpetuate and reinforce such compulsive life; and the truth of the path prescribes the steps of learning, healing and change by which we can shift the course of any given life from compulsive repetition to mindful freedom.[19] In terms of ethical practice, the step of cultivating a realistic view comes down to understanding the key insight of Buddhist psychology—for better or for worse—our way of being in the world is the developmental effect of the intentional acts of our own god-or-demon-like minds, informed by good and bad models and habits of action passed by learning from generation to generation.

The Ten Paths of Action: The Commandments Explained

In practice, the first step on the path of Buddhist behavioral ethics is to arrive at a realistic view not just of our god-like role in our own development, but also of the kind of intentional acts which impede or promote health and happiness. Most moderns who turn to Buddhist culture for a humanistic alternative to the culture of monotheism are surprised to find the list of negative versus positive modes of action almost identical to what we know as the Ten Commandments. This coincidence challenges our materialist preconception that Western religious ethics are unrealistic cultural taboos, especially since the Buddhist rationale for its list of ten do's and don'ts dispenses entirely with any image of reward or punishment and explains them instead by a naturalist logic that anticipates current health psychology and positive psychology.

The idea is that the ten modes of negative action have developmental effects which reinforce the grip of violent, antisocial instincts of stress and trauma, while the ten modes of positive action have effects on development which cultivate non-violent, social instincts of peace, trust and cooperation.[20] Given the overwhelmingly social and cultural nature of human life, especially in the unnatural state of civilization, the progressive modes of social behavior naturally prepare us to meet the challenges our daily lives, while the reactive modes of antisocial behavior are naturally maladaptive. For clarity, the list of negative actions is usually cited along with their developmental effects, and contrasted with the list of positive alternatives, as follows:

Ten Modes of Negative Action

1. Violent actions lead to traumatic injury;
2. Compulsive acquisition leads to scarcity;
3. Perverse sexuality leads to frustration;
4. False speech engenders mistrust;
5. Slander engenders disrepute;
6. Abusive speech engenders isolation;
7. Idle speech engenders contempt;
8. Covetous intent results in dissatisfaction;
9. Malicious intent results in insecurity;
10. Unrealistic views result in confusion.

Ten Modes of Positive Action

1. Non-violence leads to peace;
2. Generosity leads to abundance;
3. Sublimation leads to satisfaction;
4. Honest speech engenders trust;
5. Tactful speech engenders respect;
6. Caring speech engenders leadership;
7. Meaningful speech engenders authority;
8. Philanthropic intent results in contentment;
9. Benevolent intent results in confidence;
10. Realistic views result in clarity.

Of course, developing a realistic view is not the same thing as perfecting the life-shift from negative to positive actions. In fact, it mainly involves recognizing the need for this shift, by clearly understanding the behavioral causality linking actions with their developmental effects. Seeing this causal link puts teeth into the insight that our minds are naturally free and ultimately responsible for the development of our personality, health and well-being. It is this empowering and sobering recognition of our mind's god-like role in our lives that leads to the second step: realigning our intentions from negative to positive, following the principles set out in the two tenfold lists.

In effect, the first step addresses only the final item on the lists, obliging us to look at our thoughts and perceptions themselves as developmentally crucial acts.[21] Seen in this light, the analysis and correction of our unexamined views of ourselves and our world appears not just as a matter of intellectual curiosity, but as an ethical responsibility we cannot abdicate or delegate to experts or authorities, at least not without risking real harm to our future and the future of our world. While we covered the nuts and bolts of this analysis and correction in exploring the path of knowledge in chapter 2, it is Buddhist ethics that helps spell out the healing spirit and true intent which must motivate and guide our progress on that path.

Mapping Contemplative Insight: The Reflections of the Gradual Path

While the eightfold path maps the journey of self-healing for all who wish to follow in the Buddha's footsteps, it was initially developed for individuals choosing to opt out of the often overwhelming stresses of lay life and adopt a monastic lifestyle. To make the journey more accessible to lay people in the world, Nalanda's masters evolved the gradual path as a system of self-analysis and lifestyle change. The gradual path consists of a sequence of reflections, contemplations and practices that systematically prepares people to build a contemplative life in the world, by addressing the personal, social, cultural and natural challenges of daily living.

Since this system has been presented in many formats over the centuries, for simplicity's sake I'll present it in the format I chose for this book, covering what I call the four horizons of human development.[22] Within the first horizon, devoted to personal self-analysis, self-healing, and self-care, I'll touch on eight key points of reflection which highlight the cognitive dimension of the first and narrowest scope of Buddhist ethics, concerned with personal aims and needs. Although these eight points don't line up exactly with the steps on the eightfold path, for convenience, we'll touch on one point in the context of each of the steps.

The First Reflection: The Precious Freedom and Opportunity of Human Life

Alongside the first step of realistic view, the first point of reflection on the gradual path is to appreciate the boundless potential and value of having a precious human life. While at first blush this might seem to contradict the initial emphasis of the first step—contemplating the noble truths of suffering and its origin—in fact it goes straight to the heart of the truths: the Buddha's insight that we all have the potential for the true freedom and happiness of Nirvana. While every individual and each form of life is equally deserving of freedom and happiness, human life is especially precious because of the potential we have evolved to free our minds from the self-limiting instincts and habits that have locked most living beings throughout history in a traumatic struggle for survival.

The best way to get the real flavor of this insight is by following the traditional reflection that our lives are precious because we've been born with a human body and mind, in a life endowed with eight freedoms and ten opportunities.[23] Of the freedoms, five relate to being born free from the bonds of non-human forms of life, and three relate to being born free from the bonds of a human life of extreme deprivation. While these reflections are cast in the traditional terms of the multi-life cosmology of *karma*, it helps for us moderns to remember that the forms of life we regard as mythological—hellish, ghostly, titanic, and divine—are viewed in the scientific teaching tradition as mentally created ways of being rather than the fully embodied psychophysical forms of humans and animals.[24] So a psychosocial reading of this reflection is neither novel nor imposed. Hellish lives are compulsive lives driven by the cycle of violence; ghostly lives are addictive lives consumed by endless craving and insatiable appetite; animal lives are reactive lives driven by the cycle of trauma and survival; titanic lives are obsessive lives driven by unbridled envy and competition; and divine lives are deluded lives driven by irrational pride and narcissism.

Among the last four freedoms, three consist in having a life free from the constant exposure to physical pain, hunger or the consequences of a cognitive handicap. The fourth consists in freedom from the limits of a godly life in which we have so much pleasure and are so insulated from suffering that we get locked in self-satisfied complacency, without any motivation to learn, grow or change. The gist of the first four freedoms is that a normal human life is precious because it represents a natural golden mean: an ideal form of life in which we feel safe and comfortable enough for true life learning, yet not so comfortable that we lack the motivation to develop ourselves.

Along the gradual path, the preciousness of life is fleshed out further by contemplating ten opportunities that make human life precious. While some of these—like having a human body and mind with intact faculties—seem clear enough, a look at the fine print shows how very different the Buddhist view of opportunity is from a modern vision like the American dream. From a Buddhist vantage, the rare good fortune of being born human is not having the opportunity to pursue and enjoy material wealth and comfort, but having the optimal evolutionary platform for learning to free oneself from the archaic instincts and habits that lock us into a garden variety life of stress and trauma.[25]

In fact, eight of the ten opportunities are opportunities to gain freeing self-knowledge and self-mastery, rather than opportunities for material gain. These include being born in a place where contemplative traditions like Buddhism flourish; where one is sheltered from the culture of violence that might lead one into a life of violent crime; and where one is encouraged to respect contemplative traditions, literature and learning. The point is further underscored by the fact that five of the ten are cultural opportunities involving access to contemplative education. These include birth in an age illumined by the teachings of enlightened sages like Shakyamuni, birth in an age when contemplative traditions are alive and well, access to contemplative communities which provide social support and guidance for contemplative learning, and access to living mentors who can provide personal support and guidance for contemplative learning.

While one might conclude from this list that Buddhist ethics sees no value in material wealth and a life of leisure and social mobility, in fact this contemplative culture doesn't avoid or demean a comfortable life, but rather *presupposes* one. As hard as it might be for us to believe, this ancient Indian tradition takes for granted a broad and continuous access to material abundance and social advancement, as we do in the contemporary West. The human question it seeks to answer is the one we face today: after material wealth, what's next? In this sense, it is unlike the spiritual traditions of the West, which arose in conditions of relative scarcity, among oppressed or marginal social groups. In contrast, the Buddhist tradition arose in the safest, richest and most tolerant center of the ancient world, lead by a powerful prince of the ruling class, and was closely allied with the growth of the cosmopolitan business class. So while the monastic tradition he founded has some elements in common with Christian monasticism in the West, its ethos is closer to those of contemplative cultures which offered liberal education as a gateway to a better life in the world, like modern liberal arts colleges or the ancient Confucian academy.

Mapping Self-Transformation: The Five Stages of Buddhist Practice

Alongside the behavioral map of the eightfold path and the cognitive map of the gradual path, the third perspective we will take on the ethical journey of Buddhist psychology is the perspective covered by the motivational map of the five stages of purification. Also known as the five paths of practice, these stages obviously overlap with the eight steps and eight reflections which map the journey of Buddhist ethics from the perspectives of behavior and insight. The focus of these stages is to map the journey of contemplative self-healing from the standpoint of the gradual removal of obstacles which block our potential to motivate and sustain healthy change. The blocks which obscure that potential are of two kinds: cognitive and affective. So the stages of the path of purification map the internal progress made in seeing through ever deeper and subtler levels of misperception and in transforming ever more primal and instinctive forms of compulsive emotion and misperception.

Since the first stage bridges the first through the fifth steps, we will discuss it in several installments. Called the path of accumulation, this stage has three parts: accumulating the insight that supports letting go of attachment to our physical bodies; accumulating the perseverance that supports letting go of negative actions and cultivating positive alternatives; and accumulating the willpower that supports a genuine contemplative life. We'll discuss the first part along with steps one and two; the second part along with steps three and four; and the last part along with step five.

The Truth that Frees: The Accumulation Stage, Part One

On the first step of cultivating a realistic worldview, we begin to accumulate the insight that helps us let go of our unrealistic view of our bodies as fixed bases of endless pleasure and lasting happiness. Traditionally, this first phase in the accumulation stage works by applying the four scopes of mindfulness to the four noble truths, and arrives at insights into the four characteristics of things we mentioned in chapter 2.[26] Since this first part of the first stage spans the first two steps, the first step involves bringing mindfulness to the first two truths, suffering and its origin. According to this map, sustained, complete mindfulness of the living, breathing body serves as a basis for contemplating the noble truth of suffering. While we instinctively grow to reify our bodies as the fixed, solid, and unitary basis for our sense of our own personal identity and reality, mindfulness reveals it as a complex system of constantly changing, totally interdependent elements. Eventually this practice yields the insight that the body is not as we naively take it to be, but is in fact an impermanent flux which we cannot cling to or grasp.

In essence, this insight exposes the true nature of our chronic condition: our unexamined life is like a house built on sand. Our whole sense of security, identity and reality has gotten wrapped up in a profound self-deception that sets the stage for an inexorable, tragic downfall. By projecting our naïve wish to have a fixed place in the world onto the body, and by clinging to the fantasy that the body is that place, we make the natural flow of change that actually supports life seem like a cruel plot against us, a traumatic nightmare. Eventually, we must see that our own sleight of hand—or rather of mind—is what lies behind the sense of alienation and trauma we inject into the fact that injury, illness, aging, and death are not curses but the natural costs of having a living body in the first place. Contemplating this insight into the first noble truth helps us stop reifying and clinging to the body, and so prepares us to truly renounce the life sentence of repetitive and preventable suffering which we alone can impose on ourselves.

Once we gain this first degree of renunciation, mindfulness of sensation serves as a basis for deepening renunciation by contemplating the second truth: the origin of suffering. With sustained, complete mindfulness of sensation, we come to see that our embodied lives are not filled with the constant, stable satisfaction we want or imagine but are a bumpy, roller-coaster ride, oscillating between fleeting highs, long stretches of indifference, and inexorable lows. This window into the raw feel of our embodied lives gives us a clear view of the normally unconscious chain of causality which drives us to seek boundless pleasure and lasting happiness by practicing addictive and compulsive habits that prove inevitably disappointing. By contemplating the causality of stress and trauma taught in the second truth we gradually arrive at the insight that any life driven by that compulsive cycle is dissatisfactory. Applying this insight to the cycle of craving, fleeting pleasure and numbing indifference that grips our sensitive bodies helps us eventually renounce our deluded attachment to the body as a source of limitless, lasting pleasure. So contemplating the second truth and the insight that compulsive life is dissatisfactory prepares us to fully renounce the chains that bind us to a body hooked on the addictive cycle of stress and trauma.

The Second Step on the Eightfold Path: Authentic Intentions

The corrective self-analysis and release of attachment on the first step brings us to the second leg of the eightfold path: the deeper shift away from the compulsive motivations that drive the cycle of stress and trauma, towards the genuine positive intentions of non-attachment, non-violence and non-confusion. A key feature of the Buddhist ethos of *karma* is the insight that of all the activities that impact development, the most basic mental acts of intention are primary. This is because, according to Buddhist psychology, these precede all other activities of mind, speech and body, setting their tone and direction in a way that determines the substance of their developmental effects.

In terms of the psychology of stress and trauma, the shift of step two corresponds to a healing transition away from the traumatic self-involvement at the heart of all stress-reactivity towards the empowered self-confidence or self-efficacy that is the well-spring of stress-tolerance, resilience and proactive engagement. As a consequence of this deep shift, we can begin letting go of the oscillating post-traumatic modes of addictive attachment and compulsive aggression, as well as to cultivate their positive alternatives, true benevolence and radical acceptance. These deep shifts in primary motivation are the basic changes in mental activity prescribed by the eighth, ninth and tenth modes of action.[27] In terms of Buddhist ethics, this dramatic change in the direction of our mental life from stress-reactive insecurity and compulsion to contemplative presence and confidence is precisely what the second step on the eightfold path is made of.

Healing Refuge and Healthy Reliance: The Social Matrix of the Second Step

While the shift in primary intentions is an internal one, from the traditional standpoint it doesn't happen in a social or cultural vacuum. In particular, the intentional shift of the second step is part of gradual process of renouncing our habitual dependence on familiar views and attachments and coming to rely instead on the realistic views and healthy supports provided by Shakyamuni's example, teaching and community. This shift in orientation or reliance—called taking refuge—cannot truly take place without a realistic view of why and how the eightfold path can help change the course of our lives away from suffering and towards happiness.[28] When preceded by such clarity, the growth of bonds of realistic confidence and reliance is crucial to the intentional shift away from an alienated attachment to the familiar, towards healing engagement with truly reliable individuals, knowledge, and groups.

This shift in some ways resembles the early process of engagement in psychotherapy in which people come to feel a greater sense of safety, hope and possibility based on accepting a more realistic view of their suffering and engaging in the "holding environment" of a healing alliance. Yet it is also quite different, mostly obviously because of the ethical dimension of Buddhist psychology. Since insight alone is not enough from a Buddhist perspective, if healing is to occur our deepest intentions must gradually shift in accord with fresh insights, followed by outward behavior and lifestyle. And since any human life is inexorably social and cultural, these personal shifts must be reflected in and supported by engagement with new social networks and new ways of being in the world.

The Second Reflection: Accepting the Immanence of Death

Alongside the behavioral dimension of the second step, the second insight to be cultivated on the gradual path is the awareness of death.[29] At the opposite existential pole from the first reflection on the preciousness of life, this insight plays a key role as the ultimate test and touchstone of intentional change within Buddhist ethics. Since physical death is instinctively seen by all living beings as the ultimate threat, it is typically lurking somewhere behind every stress and trauma we experience in our lives. By exposing the delusional nature and self-destructive effects of denying death, the first step on the eightfold path, taken together with the first reflection on the gradual path and the first part of the accumulation stage, prepares us for a dramatic shift away from primitive denial and towards radical acceptance of life on life's terms.

As we begin to gain the perspective and confidence to face our physical life as an impermanent flux, the ultimate test and touchstone of our realism is the capacity to face and embrace death as part of the fabric of our very existence. We do this by first understanding death not as an aberrant exception but as the limiting case of life's signature pattern of growth, change, and decline. By contemplating impermanence and change as the omnipresent equivalents of death, we begin to desensitize ourselves to its organic reality and relative finality. Such contemplations are often aided by the routine rehearsal of the eventuality of dying and death, including envisioning our final decline and our corpse on display at our own funeral.[30]

These two classical forms of death meditation are meant not as morose exercises in pessimism, but quite the opposite, to help retrain our minds to live in the reality of every moment as a precious opportunity for learning, growth and change.[31] The deepest measure of such change is the shift away from the reflex intentional modes of panic, rage and clinging to the shifting sands of the physical body, and towards the contemplative modes of radical acceptance, tolerance and letting go which can preserve our presence of mind in the face of death. In this sense, contemplating death serves as a kind of athletic training in overcoming the mindless self-protective intentions that terrorize us at every moment in life, as the true minions of our self-destructive demonization of death.

On a more mundane level, contemplating the certainty and immanence of death can also serve as a touchstone to reveal our deepest and highest intent for our lives. By holding each moment up to that touchstone, we can gain the perspective and sense of urgency to renounce life's idle busy-work or distractions and to seize the fleeting opportunity of the present to make every choice and every action count. In particular, by reflecting that, at the end life, all the mundane goods of material wealth, worldly success and personal attachments cannot help us, we give ourselves a reality check of the supreme importance of our state of mind in determining the quality of our experience. In this way, reflecting on death can help underscore a shift in intentions and values away from the compulsive wish to accumulate more wealth, power and attachments, towards the contemplative aspiration to use our precious human life to learn how to tame and cultivate our wild minds.

The Truth That Frees Continued: Completing Part One of the Accumulation Stage

Alongside the second step on the eightfold and gradual paths, the next step in overcoming our inner obstacles to healthy change involves completing the first part of the first stage on the path of purification. This part of the first stage is completed by accumulating the healing insight and intention to stop identifying not just with unrealistic images of our physical body but with the deluded sense of our minds and life-experience as having a fixed, unchanging nature, identity or character. Traditionally, this step is taken by bringing mindfulness to the last two noble truths and the insights they foster. So we begin by bringing mindfulness of mind to contemplate the truth of Nirvana.[32]

As we saw in chapter 2, mindfulness of mind involves delving beneath the complex surface of symbolic consciousness to the deepest, most primary layers of mind, where we experience consciousness in its natural clarity, unobscured by its various contents.[33] This experience helps support the insight that the mind is a continuous flow or field of sheer clarity or openness, empty of any fixed, limiting nature, identity or character, even any fixed nature or identity of "mind." This insight helps us break out of the narrow bandwidth of experience we mistake for our minds, and to glimpse our full potential to experience life and death with a profound clarity and peace we may never have dreamed possible. Given the prior insight that the body is an impermanent flux which can't be grasped, seeing the mind as a continuous flow of sheer awareness helps us realize that the whole mind/body process is entirely lacking any fixed, unchanging nature or element we can cling to. This profound intuition, also known as a tolerance of the ungraspable nature of things, opens one of the doors to complete renunciation or freedom.[34]

The next move in the process is for us to bring inclusive mindfulness to the contemplation of the fourth noble truth of the path. By examining the contents of our experience mindfully and in light of our deeper clarity and freedom of mind, we begin to see through our identification with familiar habits of thought, perception, and emotion as "I" or "mine." This gradually leads us to the insight that all the elements of our experience are selfless. At first, this means that our minds can break free of a seemingly fixed identification with them, and come to see them instead as mere contents or aspects of a stream of consciousness which lacks any fixed identity, nature or character. Beyond the insight that there is no fixed personal self in the contents of our experience, we eventually recognize those contents in turn as lacking any fixed identity or substantial nature. Instead of seeming objectively real and true, like self-evident givens or immovable matters of fact, the thoughts, perceptions and emotions that make up the surface of our lives are exposed as being like dreams, illusions, fictions or mirages. Seeing them in light of the natural clarity of our primal awareness, we can begin to own the buzzing blooming confusion of our experience as a complex projection of our own minds, covering up the deeper reality of our lives and our world.

These insights help free and empower us to take responsibility for the compulsive nature of our minds and lives; to recognize the self-limiting causality of suffering by which we've been bound; and to renounce our whole compulsive way of life in favor of the healing journey of the contemplative path. This final move towards breaking out of the cycle of stress and trauma brings us to the complete renunciation of compulsive life, galvanizing the insights of the four truths with the healing intention that motivates and directs our practical progress on the eightfold path of self-change. With this glance at the first two steps on the eightfold path we've completed our overview of the role of outlook and intention in the ethical dimension of Buddhist psychology. Taken together, the next three steps address the outward changes in behavior and lifestyle prescribed by Buddhist ethics.

The Third Step on the Eightfold Path: Appropriate Speech

We start with appropriate speech, the step that serves to carry our change in mindset over into a new way of being with others in the world. This third step spells out the contemplative shift in forms of expression prescribed by the four modes of action that deal with speech. Unlike any other step on the path of contemplative healing, this one challenges the ideal of free speech assumed by both psychotherapy and modern secular society. Of course, the challenge is not to the democratic ideal that each and every individual is and should be free to think and say what they believe is true. Nor does it challenge the psychotherapeutic ideal of "free association," that healing dialogue requires a radical acceptance and protection of each party's freedom to experience and share whatever happens to come to mind.

The challenge posed by the step of appropriate speech is that, from the standpoint of Buddhist contemplative science, this natural freedom is not absolute, but comes with an equally natural responsibility. Buddhist science anticipated the view of recent cognitive science that our inner dialogue and outward expressions have natural effects on our development as individuals and as social agents.[35] While we're certainly free to think and say whatever comes to mind, we can't except ourselves from the mental causality by which our every speech act either reinforces our compulsive instincts, habits, and lifestyle or else helps us break free of them. If the things we think to ourselves or say to others are rooted in misperception and watered by destructive emotions, no amount of "venting" will get them "off our chest." Instead, as current research and cognitive therapy show, it may only deepen and tighten the strangle hold our self-destructive instincts and traumatic conditioning have on our minds, bodies and dialogue with the world.[36]

Beyond its precocious view of speech acts, Buddhist science also sees language as the greatest advantage humans have over less fortunate forms of life, and as the most basic and powerful of all human social actions. Speech allows humans to share and learn more realistic ways of understanding the world and more effective ways of living in the world. This view of speech and its power is clear from the traditional teaching that of the twelve great deeds that distinguish an enlightened life like Shakyamuni's from ordinary life, the one of ultimate importance is the act of sharing wisdom in and through speech.[37] Another measure of its importance is that, among the ten modes of negative and positive action, four address speech, while mental and physical action are each covered in only three. For the nuts and bolts of this step, it's best to look at each of the four modes of speech action it prescribes, one at a time.

Transforming the Four Crucial Modes of Speech Action

The first element of appropriate speech is to turn false speech into truthfulness. The most egregious case of false speech is lying, in which we intentionally deceive others by exaggerating, distorting, or denying the truth out of myopic attachment to some mundane self-interest. This includes not only overt lies that completely distort the truth but also "white lies" that only slightly distort the facts based on understandable self-interest, such as wanting others to think well of us or wanting to conceal innocent errors that may be upsetting to others if they were known. It also covers unexamined statements that assume or express false views the speaker wrongly believes to be true, based on a self-centered wish to appear more knowledgeable, wise or accomplished than one really is.

The seriousness with which Buddhist ethics views false speech is clear from the fact that it is one of the five precepts for a lay practitioner and one of only four infractions for which a monk or nun may be expelled from a Buddhist order.[38] This fact not only underscores the point but helps clarify the rationale for this strong stance. Since speech is the ultimate medium for correcting the misperceptions at the root of all preventable suffering, anything which obscures the transparency of that medium blocks the effectiveness of contemplative healing and learning, no matter what the particular path. This rationale should be familiar to practitioners and clients of "talking therapy," which was founded as part of a broader movement in Freud's Vienna to cut through misuses of speech and restore the openness and honesty of human communication.[39]

The second part of appropriate speech is to turn divisive words or slander into inclusive speech or true dialogue. Slander is speech which has the destructive intent or effect of interfering with healthy relationships, dividing families and communities or excluding individuals from helpful groups. The guideline to avoid it underscores the fact that the natural role and aim of speech is to guide and enhance social cohesion and cooperation.[40] This guideline is meant to protect that role and aim from the corrosive effects of our primitive self-protective and self-indulgent instincts. As with transforming false speech, the highest concern here is that divisive speech or slander may get in the way of any individual or groups' progress towards a contemplative way of life.

The third path of appropriate speech is to turn abusive, harsh or cursing speech to speech that is tolerant, gentle and reassuring. Like divisive speech, the vice of harsh speech is taken very seriously because it undermines the primary role and aim of human language as a force for social cohesion, communication and learning. Here again, this guideline may seem to us to impose an artificial constraint on speech or repressive ban on sharing natural feelings of hurt and anger. Yet it is not meant to force social conformity with an unrealistic, hypocritical code of conduct. In fact, suppressing such urges is considered as damaging as indulging them. Instead, it serves to protect the speaker from reinforcing or escalating violent thoughts and urges which reinforce trauma and block healthy social assertiveness and effectiveness.

Unfortunately, the most insidious and common form of harsh speech is not the gratuitous verbal abuse of the rageaholic but the all-too-human harshness of the involuntary shame-blame reflex, triggered when our childhood wounds have been inadvertently touched. What makes this kind of speech so insidious is that, locked like a cornered animal in our traumatized, victim mindset, we lose all track of the violence of our response, as well as any empathy for the person or persons who we feel hurt by. All too often, the speech that results from our self-protective shame-rage not only alienates the empathy of others when we most need it, but also risks poisoning otherwise healthy relationships with the toxic emotional charge of repressed traumas. It's vital that we learn to restrain this knee-jerk reflex in order to protect our own minds as well as others and our bonds with them.[41] By healing underlying traumas and breaking the chain of stress-reactivity, we can begin to practice disarming and proactive speech, to work through stressful or painful interactions with others in the collaborative spirit of mindful dialogue.

The final guideline for appropriate speech is to transform idle gossip into purposeful, enlightening and liberative speech. Here again, this guideline sets a higher standard of speaking than we are accustomed to in our day and age. Our conventional wisdom teaches us that shooting the breeze—whether water cooler rambling, talk show gossip, or witty repartee—is essential to decompressing, enjoying our freedom or cultivating our minds. On the other hand, as language philosopher Wittgenstein warned, "The confusions which occupy us arise when language is like an engine idling, not when it is doing work."[42] The essential insight of Buddhist psychology and ethics is that each and every action of body, speech and mind is in fact a world-creative deed, altering our lives irrevocably either for better or for worse. If we let our mouths idle without our mindfulness engaged, we are far more likely to cause accidental harm to ourselves and others than to hit on anything useful or meaningful.

The Third Reflection: The Wild Mind and the Path of Misfortune

Growing out of the reflection on the immanence of death and the mind's primary role in our future quality of life, the third reflection is to face the sobering fact that our lack of control over our wild, compulsive minds puts us at grave risk of self-destructive actions and their unwanted consequences. Traditionally, this reflection proceeds by contemplating the suffering of the unfortunate forms or life driven by the destructive emotions of anger, greed, and fear-based attachment.[43] In lieu of assuming the psycho-cosmology of reincarnation, we can contemplate our common vulnerability to be driven by compulsive action-patterns into traumatic lifestyles plagued by compulsive violence, addictive lifestyles plagued by compulsive greed or craving, and animal lifestyles of mere survival plagued by panic and clinging.

How would our minds react to being kidnapped and abused or tortured? How far are we from the tipping point where our worst addiction could escalate out of control and take over our lives? How much of our day is preoccupied with mere survival, panicking and pushing from crisis to crisis without taking a breath to contemplate what our lives are really about? Given the persistence of primitive instincts for predation, scavenging and deer-in-the-headlights paralysis, how far are we from the plight of our blood relatives in the animal world? What specters of repressed rage, voracious hunger, or nightmarish terror might our minds conjure up in the face of death and its minions—pain, loss of control, and forced separation from all we know? Whatever our worldview, such thought-experiments will likely lead to one certainty: we do not yet have enough control over our minds to skillfully face the extremes of experience that lie in wait for us, just outside the narrow circle of our comfort zone.

While this sobering line of reflection may seem unrelated to the step of appropriate speech, from the standpoint of Buddhist psychology it is not. The reason lies in the Buddhist view that our habitats and lives are not created by nature or God, but shaped by the cumulative effects of our individual and collective actions.[44] Among our *karmic* actions, the most powerfully world-creative are the symbolic actions of our imagination and speech. According to Buddhist science, forms of life or life-worlds are constructed socially when the power of individual minds is linked through the coordinated use of common words and images. So both the step of appropriate speech and the insight of our mind's uncontrolled power are meant to help us recognize the urgency of learning to master our symbol-making minds.

Due Diligence: The Second Part of the Accumulation Stage

Aligned with the step of appropriate speech and the intent to master our wild minds, our motivational journey at this point on the path takes us to the second phase of the first practice stage of accumulation.[45] Growing out of the insights of the four noble truths and the renunciation of our traumatic view of our bodies, minds and lives, we begin to gather the healthy willpower to let go of negative habits and build positive ones systematically, one at a time.

Traditionally, this phase of the path consists of a process of increasing purification and cultivation, motivated by four progressive levels of diligence. The first level of diligence helps us initially abstain from and gradually abandon unhealthy habits we've been actively engaged in. The second helps us maintain that abstinence or abandonment by keeping us consistently at work preventing slips or relapses back into those old habits. The third level of diligence helps us initiate and gradually cultivate healthy habits we haven't practiced before. And the fourth level helps us continue to cultivate those healthy habits, without interrupting or stopping that cultivation by giving into complacency or self-limiting beliefs. In synergy with the growth of diligence is a progressively clear and continuous awareness of the moment-to-moment causality of suffering and/or happiness within the mind, helping us keep a finger on the pulse of our momentary choices and feel a growing sense of confidence and mastery of our inner process.

While the third step on the eightfold path and the third reflection on the gradual path focused on mastering our symbolic minds, this part of the accumulation stage concerns itself with facing and mastering the power of our habit-patterns and habit-energies. As with the practice of shifting intentions, this phase doesn't take place in a vacuum. Traditionally, it's part and parcel of a social practice of asking for and receiving help from healthy models and groups. The help we need confronting and overcoming our own blind spots requires a sustained, open dialogue, supported by two mutually reinforcing forms of healing communication. The first is the practice of private confession, distilled in the ritual contemplation on the four remedial powers: regretting unhealthy habits; disclosing them to role-models; asking for support and guidance; resolving to change. The second is the practice of public confession, distilled in the ritual of mindful feedback and dialogue,[46] traditionally in the context of small group meetings held at the end of communal winter retreats.[47]

The Fourth Step: Appropriate Execution

With this perspective on the role of speech in bridging inner shifts in mindset with the outer transformation of our lives, we are ready to look at the next step: the sea-change from compulsive behavior to mindful modes of action. The fourth step of appropriate execution covers the translation of our new contemplative ways of thinking and speaking into a genuine contemplative way of life. It's one thing to adopt a more idealistic worldview and a kinder, gentler manner and tone, but it's quite another to change the way we actually behave on the ground every day. This is especially true when we take the paths of negative action at face value and begin to contemplate living without harming any living being, without taking anything that isn't freely given, and without sexually perverse acts of any kind. The challenge is even greater when we consider the paths of positive action: acting to improve and save lives, giving freely whatever is needed, and channeling our sexual energy into healthy intimacy, parenting, service, or creativity.

Taking Refuge: Committing to a Contemplative Life

As for particular guidelines, the Buddhist tradition offers a range of different life-strategies based on the depth of our renunciation, the level of our diligence and the power of our will. These typically come in the context of different horizons of practice, involving distinct kinds of refuge or reliance, based on individual aims and needs. Although we already touched on the intentional shift involved in choosing to rely on Shakyamuni's example, teachings, and community, here this pivotal move of "taking refuge" returns as part of a practical step into a contemplative way of life. This step involves the motivational strategy of channeling the energy freed by our break with past habits into healthy behavioral change, by linking refuge with some set of vows and commitments.[48] Since we can choose to rely on contemplative models and methods with various aims and needs, the precise vows and commitments we make will vary depending on our personal goals and inclinations.[49]

If we adopt the preliminary goal of healing our bodies and minds, our vow may be simply to follow our healing path to its end, and our commitment, to make lifestyle changes like letting go of addictions, sticking to a restorative steps like healthy diet, exercise, and a regular practice of yoga and meditation. If we adopt a more ambitious personal aim of lifting ourselves and our descendants out of unfortunate forms of life, we will need to seriously grapple with the root causes of our obsessive, compulsive or addictive lifestyle, including observing one or more of five basic precepts: renouncing violence, deceptiveness, acquisitiveness, perverse sexuality, and/or intoxicants. Finally, if we adopt the ambitious aim of freeing ourselves and our descendants entirely from the cycle of stress and trauma, we will need to commit to the whole journey of behavioral learning and change prescribed by the eightfold path. While it is said to be easiest to travel this contemplative journey as a monastic, it is certainly possible to do so while living a lay lifestyle, provided we can realistically commit to observing the five basic precepts and mastering all three contemplative disciplines based on the eightfold path.

The First Precept: The Nuts and Bolts of Non-Violence

While renouncing violence is fundamental to contemplative healing and living, that doesn't mean we all need to conform to a rigid ideal, like becoming a vegetarian right away. Despite their avid adoption of Indian Buddhist culture, for instance, most Tibetan Buddhists were not vegetarian because of the near impossibility of growing enough grain and legumes to support a healthy vegetarian diet on the Tibetan plateau. While embracing the violent realities of our ambient cultures is invariably negative, there are many different ways to engage with those realities, each with its own developmental effects. Depending on key psychological and behavioral variables, for example, the effect of an act like eating meat can range from more or less negative, to neutral or even positive. The most important variables are: whether we have a true violent intent; whether we follow through on that intent by acting on it ourselves or directing others to act; whether or not the violent act ultimately inflicts harm; and whether we experience satisfaction or remorse about the harm done.[50] The intent of *karmic* ethics here is not to provide rationalizations, loopholes, or excuses, but to help us accurately assess the relative costs and benefits to our long-term development of the many shades of grey that make up the bread and butter of our daily actions. The teeth in the laws of *karma* lie in the recognition that the end never justifies the means, since no provocation of any kind can immunize a person from the self-destructive effects of violent urges and behavior.

The Second Precept: Committing to Non-Deceptive Speech

Though we've already discussed the precept of non-deceptiveness in the context of appropriate speech, a few words about the other three precepts may be helpful.

The Third Precept: The Nuts and Bolts of Non-Acquisitiveness

I've translated the third precept as non-acquisitiveness rather than more literally—as non-stealing—since the intent of this guideline is much broader than merely abstaining from overt thievery. Traditionally, the sense of this precept is spelled out broadly as choosing not to take anything that is not freely given.[51] This is relevant to us because much of what passes for pragmatic street-smarts or good business sense in our age falls under the scope of this precept, raising some real questions about the predatory and scavenging ethos of our modern marketplace jungle. Whether we're talking about hostile takeovers, predatory lending, windfall profits, or just keeping a dollar bill we find on the street, from the standpoint of Buddhist bioethics, greed is not just not good, but ultimately impoverishing. By reinforcing our self-reifying sense that our interests and happiness lie in an isolated struggle against our neighbors and all other life, the acquisitive ethos of free market economics deprives us of a realistic view of our place in the world, as well as access to the emotional intelligence we need to truly live well with others in an interdependent world.[52] This loss easily outweighs the bottom line gains by which we've learned to judge our misguided pursuit of happiness, racking up enormous costs in stress, isolation, addictive consumption, and the degrading of our natural and social environment, all of which are hidden by a myopic accounting scheme that counts only what we want, not what we really need to live well.[53]

The Fourth Precept: Sublimating and Channeling Sexual Energy

In a world in which genuine love, mutual trust, and true intimacy is in short supply, addictive sexuality often is mistaken for the real thing, and rushes in to fill the void where more stable and mature closeness is lacking. This natural hijacking of love-starved hearts by more primitive sexual craving is all the more problematic since many aspects of our culture, including the film industry, pulp fiction, the media and advertising, reinforce unrealistic fantasies of sex, romance and love.[54] Nor is what passes for sex education or sex therapy of much help, since it tends to take a mechanical view of sexuality which avoids the psychosocial and cultural complexities of human intimacy.[55] On the other hand, the anorectic stance of mainstream religious traditions only adds the fuel of ignorance, neglect and repression to the fire, contributing to the hypocrisy exposed by the sex scandals that have increasingly rocked Western churches as much or more than our secular institutions. As with renouncing violence, Buddhist ethics insists that renouncing additive sexuality is only practically possible when we learn to understand, master and transform our wild mind and the primal instincts that drive it. Offering a middle way aligned with dynamic couples therapy, this tradition teaches that satisfying love and intimacy requires us to accept our sexual instincts and energies while learning to purify them of stress and trauma so they can be channeled into mature love and compassion.[56]

The Fifth Precept: Renouncing Intoxicants

Given the continued debate in contemporary medicine about whether intoxicants like alcohol and marijuana are poisons or medicines, it may seem puritanical to us that this guideline is included within this most bare-bones schema of lay Buddhist ethics. So it helps to bear in mind that the current debate reflects conflicting findings about the effects of these substances on different organ systems in uncontrolled contexts. While some studies have found small amounts of alcohol may be helpful in reducing high blood pressure and the risk of heart disease, and others have found marijuana helpful in treating nausea, glaucoma and chronic pain, no studies have ever suggested that such substances have beneficial effects on mental development or the brain.[57] Whether intoxicants dull or stimulate the mind/brain, they invariably block developing conscious self-control of factors like attention, concentration, insight, analysis, and judgment, which are among the main engines of contemplative learning and change.[58] More insidiously, relying on chemicals to regulate the mind and nervous system typically medicates away at least some of the distress we need to understand our suffering and motivate efforts to change. So while going cold turkey on intoxicants is not necessary for those wishing to start on a contemplative path, gradually letting go of them as crutches and blocks is seen as indispensable to progress on that path, let alone to finally arriving at a truly contemplative way of being.[59]

The Fourth Reflection: Healing Refuge and Healthy Reliance

Sobered by reflecting on the risks and costs of our uncontrolled, wild minds, we come to recognize that we ourselves lack the know-how to understand and master them. Taken seriously, this recognition should eventually get us out of our heads, engaged in a search for models, methods and support networks that have the necessary wisdom, effectiveness and compassion to help us. Traditionally, this search culminates in a process of identifying, engaging, and committing to the most reliable sources of help we can find, a process known as taking refuge. Although this process is often enacted in various ritual forms, the nuts and bolts of it involve a mutual acquaintance, assessment and alliance between those seeking help and those who can provide it. As in the healing alliance of psychotherapy or the recovery bond between sponsee and sponsor, refuge or reliance in Buddhist ethics is seen as only being as grounded as the analysis, judgment and commitment of the individuals who take and give refuge.[60]

How does the active refuge at this point on the path take us beyond the intentional refuge of the second step? This has to do with the way the public or social act of taking refuge is meant to pull us out of our heads, into engagement with models, traditions, and communities, encouraging us to commit to putting our actions where our intentions are. Using the public act of refuge as leverage to bind us to a healing path of action is how the fourth step works to put teeth into the refuge contract. Traditionally, this level of refuge begins with a public pronouncement like, "I take refuge in the Buddha, his teaching and community." Typically, this pronouncement is immediately followed by selected vows and commitments, lending them the creative power to shape our intentions and actions towards the end we seek.

The Power of Will and Effort: Starting the Third Part of the Accumulation Stage

With this look at where the path of insight lines up with the fourth step, we're ready to turn to the path of practice, specifically the third and last phase on the stage of accumulation. Once our willpower has been freed up from its compulsive entanglements by renunciation and directed towards healing change by due diligence, we're ready to build the motivation we need to follow through with the steps of appropriate execution and appropriate livelihood. This is accomplished by combining renunciation and diligence with progressively deepening mindfulness and concentration, to the point where they can be forged together into power-tools for change. These power-tools are known as the four bases of mental power.[61] Of the four, the first two align with the step of appropriate execution and the last two with the step of appropriate livelihood.

The first basis of mental power is the motivational energy that comes from consciously developing a concentrated will. Like the fuel we need to build a fire, having the willpower to stay single-mindedly focused on the inner workings of our mind allows us to kindle all the insight and diligence we've built thus far into a steady light that helps guide us away from compulsive intentions and actions, and towards healing alternatives. Given this willpower and the stable clarity it brings, we gradually develop a proficiency in our healing choices and actions which puts us in touch with our inner genius for change. The second basis of mental power is the motivational energy that comes of consciously developing concentrated effort. This energy gives us the enthusiasm to break free of unhealthy habits and initiate healthy alternatives, as well as the willpower to persevere in our renunciation of negative acts and our cultivation of the positive.

The Fifth Step: Appropriate Livelihood

Once we've begun to gain some mastery of our compulsive behavior and actively embarked on the path towards a contemplative life, the eightfold path asks us to reflect on whether our means of livelihood is supporting or undermining our progress. This fifth step is especially relevant to lay practitioners faced with finding a way of life that supports contemplative healing and change in the world. Of course, it's only natural to wonder how guidelines developed in such a different place and time can still be relevant in the complex, fast paced world of today. Yet however much the cultural conditions of our daily lives have changed over the centuries, the basic facts of our nature have remained much the same since the first hominids walked the earth. What is more, the deep challenges of adapting our human nature to the unnatural conditions of civilized living still far outweigh the surface demands of increasing intensity and complexity which distinguish our age.[62]

The bottom line is, any means of livelihood that demands we reinforce the violent, stress-reactive side of our nature is basically incompatible with a contemplative life, and hence should not be undertaken lightly or without careful analysis of its long-term risks and costs. Of course, by this standard, it's likely that most professions in our day might not meet the standard of appropriate livelihood. This is especially true in the over-developed societies of the West, where the mainstream popular and professional consciousness is still caught in the death-grip of a compulsive work ethic and insatiable hunger for wealth and status.

In practice, the most insidious feature of our current work ethic is that we are so habituated to the short-term gains and perks of a compulsive way of life that we can't actually see or feel the costs of our line of work until it's too late. When eventually work stress pervades our whole style and pace of life, pressures and starves our relationships, clouds our mind, and undermines our health and well-being, we start to burn out. The erosion of our reserves of well-being may hit us with full force only when we find ourselves abruptly laid off, addicted, divorced, depressed, or seriously ill. Months or years later, when we begin to understand and undo what happened to us, we may finally be in the position of reevaluating the meaning of work and success. Here is where we wake up and find ourselves on the fifth step.

Unfortunately, our doctors and therapists may not be there along with us. Distorted by the compulsive ethos of the mainstream, modern psychiatry and psychotherapy often see themselves as handmaidens of "the good life," and try too hard to patch us up to go back into the fray. Our reliance on high-tech medicine and "miracle drugs" like Prozac, Klonapin, and Adderol reflects our personal and professional willingness to continue to sweep the unsustainable nature of our lives under the rug, much as we did for too long with the inconvenient truths of the mortgage melt-down or global warming. Is there a viable alternative? There must be. And the wisdom of our contemplative traditions, ancient and modern, can be our guide.

The first moves on the path to appropriate livelihood are those shifts in mindset, speech and lifestyle we've mapped over the course of the last four steps. These moves help us get out of the survival rut we think will bring happiness, onto the road to real happiness based on genuine self-knowledge and inner self-mastery. As we begin to see and feel the real, immediate benefits of downshifting from the overdrive of stress and trauma, we come to see through the misplaced attachments that have kept us locked in self-destruct mode. Now the choice to take a fresh look at our means of livelihood doesn't feel like a sacrifice but rather like a win-win no-brainer.

The first part of this new take is internal. It involves the shift from looking to work as a quick fix for a life that leaves us burnt and spent, to beginning to taste real happiness within and looking to work as a way to share what we've found with less fortunate others and the world we live in. This shift from craving and grasping to benevolence and grateful service is the catalyst that can turn our random walk in life into a true path to contentment and purpose. Although occasionally this may involve a dramatic retooling of our vocation and skill-set, most of the time, it may mean a more modest adjustment of why, where and how we work. Beyond this general change in tone and direction, the fifth step's guidelines for change follow quite simply and clearly from the fourth step's precepts for action.[63]

The Fifth Reflection: The Laws of Action and Development

Given our work on the fourth step, we've begun to experience the benefits of positive actions enough that we can begin to see the background malaise of our former lives as the results of compulsive habits. On the fifth step, we take this awareness further by recognizing the inexorability and specificity of the laws of development, making them the basis of a more adult relationship with our lives and livelihood. Instead of experiencing our lot in life in a childish, subjective way as the result of our being favored or punished by the powers that be—whether human or divine—we begin to relate to our fortunes and fate in mature, impersonal way, as direct effects of our own actions.

A key factor in this contemplative shift towards our lives and work is the dawning of greater clarity about the precise nature of the causal laws of happiness and its development. The key features of the causality of development are traditionally listed as four: specificity; multiplicity; determinacy and inevitability.[64] Specificity means that specific intentions and actions have equally specific effects. Multiplicity means that a single action can lead to a range and chain of consequences. Determinacy means that we never experience an effect without some action or reaction on our part which contributed to that effect. Inevitability means that, however repressed, delayed or covert, every intentional act we take has an inexorable effect on our development or that of our heirs.

Although these principles are far from obvious and may strike us as harsh or even unfair, they reflect a long and painstaking history of contemplative self-analysis and are presented as guidelines for each of us to test and either accept or reject in our own minds and lives. In this sense, they're akin to the collective wisdom of self-analysis handed down in the practice of modern therapy, a wisdom that few of us can relate to without going through the process ourselves. As in psychotherapy, so too on the gradual path. Once we begin to see and feel the causal logic of our development for ourselves, the result is not a kind of shame-bound fatalism or moralism but a proactive confidence born of self-knowledge.

The Power of Mind and Analysis: Completing Part Three of the Accumulation Stage

Alongside the fifth step and the contemplation of the laws of development, the path of practice takes us through the end of the first stage of accumulation. The culmination of this stage is traditionally described in terms of the last two bases of mental power.[65] The first of these is the motivational energy that comes of consciously developing a concentrated mind. Growing out of the concentration of effort, we gradually develop the capacity to tap the full potential of our minds, by getting and staying in the single-pointed flow which frees our mind's innate genius for learning. The second is the motivational energy that comes of consciously developing concentrated analysis. This energy gives us the mind-power to put all we've learned into practice in real time, by exposing and cutting through misperceptions acquired in this lifetime along with the instinctive confusion and delusion that anchor them.

Taken together, these newfound powers of mind give us leverage over the most ingrained habits, by bringing causes and conditions that are normally unconscious and automatic into the light of consciousness, where we can hold them up against our healthy enthusiasm and valid knowledge. This deep motivational growth empowers us to do the hard work of cutting through the traumatic distortions and self-protective instincts that maintain unhealthy character traits and block the development of a wiser, more mature personality. This profound process of character change brings a genuine experience of inner freedom and peace, supporting the gratitude and contentment we need to transform our way of being in the world and turn our livelihood into a vehicle of true benevolence and service.

The Sixth Step: Appropriate Effort

Given the focus in the last three steps on our working relations with the outer world, the next step on our survey—appropriate effort—serves to bridge the outer-directed path of action with the inner-directed movement of the final, contemplative steps on the eightfold path. Since we moderns have learned to see ourselves as the most industrious people in history, we may feel we've already got the effort thing down. So it's vital for us to reflect that the kind of effort meant here has a radically different tone and direction from the kind we're used to putting out. Rather than effort directed at accumulating material wealth and power, outwards achievements, social status or celebrity, the kind of effort the Buddhist tradition calls appropriate is effort directed at inner contentment and willpower, mastery over one's mental and emotional blocks, and transcending normal limits of concentration and wisdom.[66] This inner-directed effort in fact is very challenging to most of us raised with the extraverted values and lifestyle of the over-developed world. Some of the most active and hard-working people I teach find the inner challenges of learning to calm the body and still the mind truly exasperating!

Of course, by this point on the eightfold path, we've not only come to understand the need to master our wild minds, but have also begun to isolate and exercise the muscles of concentrated will and effort that we need to change our outwards behavior and lifestyle. Based on this prior exercise, we now have the awareness and self-control to build these muscles to the point where we can apply them to the work of transforming the inner life of our minds. Appropriate effort is pivotal in more ways than one. First, it gives us the willpower to push the process of concentration beyond the stage of profound calm called quiescence to the more intensely focused, higher energy states of single-pointed concentration.[67] Second, it gives us the mind-power to push the process of self-analysis beyond the stage of reflective insight towards the fully meditative inferential insights of impermanence, suffering, emptiness, and selflessness that lie at the heart of the four noble truths. By helping us deepen and integrate concentration and insight, appropriate effort builds the contemplative muscles we need to counteract and unlearn the gross intellectual confusions and compulsive emotions that block our progress towards more profound clarity and peace of mind.

The Sixth Reflection: The Limitations of Fortunate Lives

Alongside this progress on the eightfold path, the gradual path of insight extends our reflection on the inexorable laws of development to contemplate the limits of even the most fortunate forms of compulsive life.[68] This reflection completes the contemplation of the risks our wild mind poses for self-destructive living by exploring the limits of forms of life driven by compulsive self-improvement or self-involvement. While committing to healthy reliance on contemplative models, traditions and communities may have lifted our sights above the worst-case nightmares and traumatic reactions of our wild mind, it opens up a range of different paths for contemplative life.

The most accessible of these is the path of contemplative self-improvement, which puts a kinder, gentler face on the struggle for survival that drives all contemplative life. In terms of archetypal imagery, this contemplative path leads to upwards mobility towards a more heavenly life of security and peace within our own lifetime or in the lifetime of our loved ones and heirs. In terms of conventional spiritual imagery, it is reflected in the common ideal of a future rebirth in a heavenly afterlife or next incarnation. In psychological terms, it refers to an upwards mobility in personality and lifestyle away from a form of life driven by anger, greed, or fear to one driven by competitive strivings or narcissistic self-satisfaction.

Like our contemporary obsession with the lifestyles of the rich and famous, this kind of aspiration involves an unrealistic fantasy of escaping from the laws of development into a cozy niche in which we're permanently insulated from the painful realities of impermanence, illness, aging, and death. The fact is, no matter how fortunate our form of life or station in life is, there's no escaping the reality that all lives, like all things, are subject to constant change, decay, loss, and death. So underlying the natural wish to be more insulated from uncontrollable change, there remains a self-reifying confusion and unrealistic clinging to our body-mind, which keeps us locked in the death-grip of a futile struggle with how reality is and works. In other words, a contemplative path aimed at rising above misfortune to a state of permanent comfort and ease is really locking us into another cage of self-reifying confusion, however golden that cage may be.

Expanding on this sober insight, the mythic cosmology of Buddhism underscores the point and highlights an uncommon view of contemplative living. According to Buddhist mythology, beings born in heavenly realms, even the pantheon of orthodox gods and demi-gods, are not there for eternity but a finite lifespan.[69] Although living in extreme beauty and abundance, they too are subject to the laws of development, impermanence, illness, aging, and death. Since their level of comfort and control is such that they tend to deny their vulnerability and neglect their wild minds, reality dawns as a shock at the end of their long, blissful lives, too late for them to develop realistic self-knowledge and self-mastery. This is why, for the pursuit of sustainable happiness, life in a human body is best: not too driven by survival to stop and learn, yet sensitive enough to avoid the opposite extreme of over-confidence and complacency.[70]

The aim of this sixth reflection on the path of insight is to protect the mind from being seduced by its own childish fantasies of eternal happiness in a heavenly escape, and to commit instead to a more sober view of contemplative life. This view sees the ultimate goal of contemplative life not as ascendance to a "higher realm" but rather as transcendence in the here and now. The pivotal shift behind this sobering insight is the shift from a view of happiness as primarily dependent on external circumstances and conditions, towards a view of happiness as primarily dependent on an inner capacity to accept and cope with reality as it is. In the language of modern psychology, this view of contemplative life involves a shift from the childish view that what controls our state of mind lies outside us towards a mature view that we ourselves can and should take control of our own destiny. This shift leads us to the next reflection on the path of insight: that unconditional or sustainable happiness can only come of a radical commitment to self-transcendence, by freeing our mind from its own self-limiting instincts and habits.

Heat, Peak, Tolerance, Triumph: The Stage of Application

Based on the foundation built on the stage of accumulation, the path of practice now moves to the next level: the stage of application.[71] By applying ourselves with the ever-increasing power of appropriate effort on this stage, our inner work of self-transcendence is traditionally said to move through four successive phases: heat; peak; tolerance, and triumph.[72] As applying effort to deepening concentration brings us to virtual and actual inner stillness or quiescence, we gradually enter a euphoric flow that sparks a natural high or inner heat akin to the endorphin high of physical exercise. The positive energy of this state gives us greater leverage over negative habits, allowing us to pry our consciousness free of habitual emotional blocks and realize greater freedom of mind. As we continue applying appropriate effort, quiescence deepens to the level of single-pointed concentration, where it can turn analysis into a surgical power-tool that cuts through all the learned distortions and misperceptions of our acquired false views.

This breakthrough is possible in part because the mind grows so stable that it no longer wavers from one extreme to the other, swayed by the influence of reified, binary concepts. As a result, the true beliefs that have guided our insights thus far gradually lead us to valid inferential knowledge of the noble truths, without the gross confusions and doubts that come of lingering ambivalence. Having reached this peak experience of intellectual insight, we gain greater leverage over our mental blocks, allowing us to enjoy more accurate and continuous knowledge of the nature and workings of our body-mind. This further empowers us to break free of the confusion that maintains compulsive emotions, reinforces traumatic habits and blocks our ability to initiate and maintain healthy alternatives. Growing out of these two phases on the path of application, we begin to access and master a number of key positive mental factors called the five powers: faith or confidence, effort, mindfulness, concentration and wisdom.[73]

With these powers as fruits of the first half of the application stage, we're better equipped to move onto the second half, traditionally described in terms of the phases of tolerance and triumph.[74] Growing out of the rational insight of the peak phase, increasing confidence in the insights of selflessness and emptiness gradually lead to an intuitive wisdom called the tolerance of the ultimate ungraspability of things. Applying persistent effort to develop this tolerance eventually brings us to the phase of tolerance. Here, we begin to disarm reflex fears of loosing ourselves or relaxing our compulsive grip on our mind and body, by overcoming self-reifying thinking and traumatic memories and reactions. As a result, we're more able to tolerate the transitions of loss, growth and change, as well as the suffering our minds and bodies are prone to.

Finally, in the phase called triumph, our inferential realization of the truths of selflessness and emptiness completely triumphs over all our acquired self-reifying views and the post-traumatic reactions they rationalize. This triumph frees us from any shadow of a doubt that could perpetuate lingering confusion about whether there's even a shred of a fixed, unitary self to protect or cling to. Such rational certainty builds the greater clarity and confidence we need to see through traumatic distortions and override stress-reactive emotions, allowing us to throw ourselves without reservation into appropriate effort on the path of contemplation. While the five powers that emerged from the first two phases of the application stage are state-specific faculties that may waver between meditations, the five forces that emerge from these two final phases of application are fully developed and integrated forms of the powers of faith, effort, mindfulness, concentration, and wisdom, equally accessible within and between meditation.

The Seventh Step: Perfect Mindfulness

With the seventh step of perfect mindfulness, we enter the inner sanctum of Buddhist ethics, the realm of deep contemplation where we're gradually freed of the subtlest learned confusions and emotions, as well as their instinctive roots. While deepening levels of mindfulness and concentration have been part of our contemplative path all along, on the seventh and eighth steps they reach their culmination and fruition in the deepest levels of meditative single-mindedness and direct, healing insight. By repeatedly examining the five aggregates through the four, successive scopes of mindfulness, our meditations have gained ever deeper understandings of the four noble truths and the four healing insights that are their quintessence. In the accumulation stage that spanned the first five steps, this insight came from applying conceptual learning and contemplative reflection in the context of deepening mindfulness and quiescence.[75] In the application stage on step six, focused effort pushed the process beyond quiescence to a single-pointed analysis, with the power to yield valid inferential insights born of genuine meditation. Such powerful insights, though still conceptual, gave us the gut certainty we need to let go of gross confusions and the compulsions they rationalize.

On this step of perfect mindfulness, we finally gain the expertise and control we need to immerse our minds deeply enough in those meditative insights that they lose their conceptual scaffolding and, for the first time, have the force of direct mental perceptions.[76] The benefit of such breakthrough states is that they temporarily free our minds of the learned misperceptions that support even our subtlest confusions and doubts.[77] As a result, when those misperceptions return in the daily experience we have between meditations, we are unmistakably clear that they are deceptive, like optical illusions. This unmistakable clarity allows us to finally and fully abandon even the subtlest false views we've acquired through learning in the course of childhood and adult experience. This clearing up of cumulative lifelong distortions and misperceptions has a powerful effect on our compulsive emotions as well. It frees our minds to see these, no matter how habitual they've become, from a mature stance of sober self-parenting that gives us the freedom to let go of them more quickly and easily. At this point we begin to feel like a new person, surprisingly and uncharacteristically peaceful, able, and free.

The Seventh Reflection: Committing to Self-Transcendence

On the path of insight, the step of perfect mindfulness aligns with the reflection on the need to commit to reaching the self-transcendent state of inner freedom and lasting happiness, Nirvana.[78] As the taste of freedom we've gleaned from our meditative breakthroughs lingers in daily life, we come to a newfound place of clarity and confidence about our nature and potential. With a real visceral sense that we are not identical with or forever bound to our compulsive habits and sense of self, the dust begins to settle on the nightmare of stress and trauma we've unknowingly inflicted on ourselves. The profundity of this sense lies in the fact that it frees us to complete the radical shift towards renunciation and letting go we began with our first reflection and first step on the path. It galvanizes a growing conviction that our highest self-interest and ultimate satisfaction will come not from any particular station in life or any degree of outwards comfort or success, but rather in a radical and complete inner freedom.

Factors of Enlightenment: The Stage of Insight

As for the path of practice, this stage gradually takes us beyond the approximate, virtual insights of the application stage to authentic, direct personal experience of how things are and work.[79] This direct, intuitive feel for the true nature of our lives and our world stands as an unmistakable counterpoint to the delusions and distortions we learned to mistake for reality. In particular, the self-reifying views of our bodies, minds, selves, and world as fixed, unitary and unchanging are exposed by our meditative experience as a house of cards which nonetheless imprisons us in a nightmare of isolation, stress, and trauma. Among the many fruits of this breakthrough, the most important is final freedom from the compulsive intentions and actions that drive us to cling to such self-enclosing mind-states and forms of life. Supporting this breakthrough is the final fruition of key factors of positive health, including seven identified as factors of enlightenment, and five as forms of fearlessness.[80]

The Eighth Step: Perfect Concentration

Finally, the step of perfect mindfulness brings us to the eighth and last step on the eightfold path: perfect concentration. On this step, we continue to deepen the capacity for direct, intuitive breakthroughs until we master the ninth and last stage of concentration, known as meditative equipoise. Technically, equipoise is the most profound and centered of all states of mind, often described as a lucid, ecstatic trance. Here, investigation and analysis have practically ceased and awareness is fully absorbed in what it knows in an effortless flow stabilized by state-specific factors of unwavering bliss, single-mindedness and equanimity.[81] Given this powerfully focused mind/body state, we gain and perfect the ability to immerse ourselves fully and stably in direct experience of how things really are and work.

While the seventh step gives us our first real taste of reality, the eighth allows us to savor and acquire that taste so fully and stably that we become one with it and it with us. As this deeper immersion in the truth of our breakthrough insights slowly sinks in at the deepest, most visceral levels of our body-mind, it helps us see though and cut out the instinctive confusion and compulsive emotions that anchor our habitual worldviews, traumatic distortions, and stress-reactions.[82] The deep self-surgery of this step is an ongoing process that moves in a gradual progression from the grossest compulsions to the most subtle, until we are finally freed not just of the bad habits we've learned in this lifetime but of the deeply rooted and ingrained innate errors we share with all humanity and all forms of life. Eventually, this radical deprogramming reaches deep enough into our minds and lives that we're free of the death-grip of stress and trauma not just in the lucid moments of meditation but in the aftermath in-between sessions as well.

The Eighth Reflection: Committing to Complete the Path

Alongside this step on the eightfold path, the gradual path of insight arrives at the final reflection on the self-healing horizon: committing to mastering the whole path that leads to true freedom and happiness.[83] It should come as no surprise that this reflection follows the last one on gaining lasting freedom from our needless suffering and its causes. Since the path gradually exposes the ways in which we mindlessly cause our suffering, and also arms us with the insights and skills we need to learn new ways, actually following through with the course of treatment the path prescribes is the only way to make good on the last reflection. Contemplating this fact means committing to fully and finally assimilating the powerful medicine of the four noble truths.

Removing Our Blocks to Freedom: The Stages of Meditation and Mastery

On the path of practice, the eighth step of perfect concentration aligns with the developments of the stage of meditation.[84] This stage involves the gradual elimination of ever subtler forms of instinctive confusion and compulsive emotion, a process traditionally conceived as occurring over time in nine successive levels. The many traditional metaphors for this process—like washing stains out of a cloth—emphasize the incremental, painstaking nature of the gradual dissolution of compulsions.[85] The way this clearing out of the mind is reached by combining progressive degrees of insight with deeper levels of concentration. Traditionally, this stage involves reviewing the four truths one final time, with each truth looked at from the standpoint of four insights, for a total of sixteen insights. And, on the meditative side of the process, these deepening insights require the ever deeper levels of concentration mapped onto the increasingly more refined states of equipoise called the four formless absorptions.

As a final note, the culmination of the eightfold path in perfect concentration yields not just final freedom from suffering and its causes but also the final fruition of qualities previously cultivated but subtly blocked by innate compulsions. The fifth stage of mastery, which represents our arrival at the goal of cessation that marks the path's end, is traditionally fleshed out in terms of the development of ten forms of valid knowledge and of thirty-seven factors of enlightenment. The ten forms of valid knowledge are: knowledge of mundane conventions; of the elements of suffering and happiness; inferential knowledge of the truths; direct knowledge of suffering; of its origin; of its cessation; and of the path; knowledge of other minds; knowledge of the termination of suffering; and knowledge of the non-recurrence of suffering.[86]

As for the factors of enlightenment, they include fully mature and integrated forms of the positive mental factors developed earlier on the path, including: the four forms of mindfulness—of body, sensation, mind and all things; the four forms of due diligence—abstaining from old vices, not slipping back into them, cultivating new virtues, not ceasing to cultivate them; the four bases of mental power—the concentration of will, effort, mind and analysis; the five powers—faith, effort, mindfulness, concentration and wisdom; the five forces, the five powers in their most potent form; the seven factors of enlightenment—mindfulness, discrimination, effort, interest, flow, concentration, and equanimity; and the eight steps on the path to enlightenment.[87]

The Journey of Contemplative Living: All Roads Lead to Integrity

In surveying the many details of the path we've looked at from the vantage of three distinct maps, one thing should be clear: the fundamental role of ethical motivation and moral self-discipline on the path of contemplative healing and living. This clarity challenges our modern confusion of ethics with a more or less arbitrary cultural convention imposed on human nature and life, with little benefit to us as individuals and groups. In so doing, it reinforces the findings of modern health psychology, affective neuroscience and positive psychology that positive thinking, positive emotions, and prosocial behaviors help counteract stress and promote optimal health, peace and well-being. Though it raises real questions and practical challenges for the integration of Buddhist psychology with modern therapy, I believe the robust inclusion of the ethical dimension of contemplative science into psychotherapy is not only feasible but necessary to making a modern contemplative therapy fully effective and beneficial.

Committing to Contemplative Life: Meditative Experiment 3

Get yourself comfortable, and settle your body and mind down so you can take in what you've learned on our journey thus far. After a long, full out-breath, let your next in-breath flow in as gently as you can. Give your body-mind the time they need to gradually relax, so you can shift into a deeper, slower, and more seamless flow of breath. Now use that slow flow as the focal-point to collect and center your mind. Balance your energy and awareness by breathing calm into your restlessness and clarity into your fatigue. And remember to scan and balance sensation as well, breathing patient acceptance into your lows, sober awareness into your highs, and clear presence into the grays in-between. Now turn your mindfulness to your mind and try to dive under the surface waves of thoughts, images and emotions towards the clear and calm depths of your primal mind. Keep working to resist the lure of distractions from your outer life, assuring yourself all will be well if you immerse yourself in your deep, open mind. Also work to resist the seductive undertow of drowsiness, making efforts to keep your mind ready, willing and able to see reality as it is. As you begin to get into the flow of your primal mind, open the scope of your deep mindfulness so you can have a fresh take on your life from your clearest most centered mind-state.

Scanning your physical body, try to see and feel the pulsing flow of its life, as ungraspable as the waters of a stream or the sand of an hourglass. As you see and feel your real body, try to face how futile it is to cling to it in denial of impermanence, aging, and death. See the constant strain your put on yourself and your relationship with reality by living in the grips of the fantasy that your body is your permanent, secure base in the world, now and forever. Seize the opportunity of this moment to start letting go of your death-grip on it, here and now. See this grip of panicked confusion as the driver of all the violent urges in your life. Now, if you like, promise yourself you'll stop tightening this grip by choosing to let go of your violent thoughts, words and deeds, and opt in to the nonviolent modes of inner tolerance, reassuring words and caring deeds.

Now scan your sensation, trying to face and accept the raw feel of being in your sensitive body, a breath at a time. Open your sensitive mind to honestly face the uneven terrain of your sensory experience of life here and now, and bear with the whole feel, as if you suddenly found yourself wearing what poet T.S. Eliot called "an intolerable shirt of flame." As you take in the exquisite sensitivity of your body-mind, soberly face the bottom line that your way of life isn't all it's cracked up to be; that your pursuit of happiness is more like an addict's drive for a fix or a chronically ill person's search for some fleeting relief. Acknowledge that your gut exposure to life on life's terms is the origin of the craving that locks you into the cycle of stress and trauma. Try to seize the moment to start letting go of the craving that drives you and see your tendency to avoid distress and live in fantasy as the root of the whole web of deceptive thoughts, words, and deeds your life has been tangled up in. Take this opportunity to taste the sober relief of clearing out the tangled knots in your mind by honestly accepting and working with the reality of your life. And, finally, if you like, promise yourself you'll learn to live in that relief by choosing to let go of deceptive thoughts, words, and deeds and take the contemplative road of rigorous inner honesty and sober transparency in your outwards words and deeds.

Next, scan your primal mind, trying to stay as immersed as you can in its ungraspable spaciousness and unrecognizable flow. As you loosen your grip on all the familiar content that keeps us stuck on the choppy surface of consciousness, try to see and feel the spacious clarity of your deep awareness as your innate potential for the lasting freedom and peace of Nirvana. Seize the moment to let go of your habitual confusion of mind with the thoughts and images it creates, even your most potent obsessions with idealized objects of desire and your most cherished fantasies of others' bodies as fetishes of perfect beauty or trophies of blissful conquest. Recognize that insatiable craving to fill the inner space of your mind with bliss from outside as the original urge that drives the insatiable craving for compulsive sexuality we mistake for the real thing. Try to acquire a taste for your mind's innate blissful openness, and savor it as the taste of freedom that can fill you with the inner joy of contentment you need to get out of the "meat market" of confusing yourself and others for mindless bodies. Now, if you like, promise yourself you'll take the space to acquire that taste, by choosing to let go of the obsessive thoughts, seductive words, and addictive habits of compulsive sexuality and opt in to the real abundance of inner contentment and sober love in your intimate relationships.

Finally, open your mindfulness to include your mental contents, scanning the range of thoughts, images and emotions that normally occupy your mind. Try to see your compulsive urge to clutter your mind with contents that feed the illusion that you have some fixed identity or character. Instead, bring your deep, lucid openness of mind to the whole range contents—good, bad, and indifferent—and see them as binary constructs or fictions, none of which capture the full scope and complexity of your constantly changing life process. Recognize the voracious hunger to stuff and clutter the open space of your mind with content as the original urge that drives the rat race of unrealistic desires, insatiable greed, and compulsive acquisitiveness we mistake for the way to happiness. Seize the moment to unhook your sense of "I" and "mine" from particular thoughts, images, and emotions, and to try to accept and embrace the reality that your mind-body process is a constant, open flux with no fixed or limiting character, identity, or self. Choose to see that flux as the open door to the path of contemplative living and learning that can empower you to transform your compulsive, confused self into a free and clear self capable of lasting happiness. Now, if you like, promise yourself you'll take the space to acquire a taste for your selfless openness, by choosing to let go of the acquisitive thoughts, words, and habits and opt in to the real abundance of inner contentment, and true generosity in your words and deeds.

Part 2

Turning the Speech Wheel

Compassion and Social Healing

4 Clearing the Mind for Social Engagement

> Just as the linguist [gradually] teaches grammar, so the Buddha taught [various] teachings appropriate to the needs of disciples. Some [he taught] to counteract vice; some to cultivate virtue. Some [he taught] based on [the] dualism [of world versus Nirvana]. [And finally, he taught some] the profound, awe-inspiring practice of enlightenment not based on dualism, in essence, the openness that is compassion.
>
> (Nagarjuna, *Jewel Garland*[1])

Roughly two centuries after Shakyamuni's passing, the great Emperor Ashoka convened the third council of the Buddhist community as part of his efforts to weave India's ancient traditions of contemplative living into the fabric of its first universal and non-violent state. Meanwhile, just a few miles from the capitol, in the mango groves of the small farming village of Nalanda, where the Buddha and other great sages loved to teach and retreat, another council gathered around a small shrine called a stupa built by Ashoka to hold some of Shakyamuni's remains. This counter-council was organized by a community of monks and nuns who called themselves Universalists and advocated a more open and socially engaged form of Buddhism, tailored to the needs of lay practitioners who wanted to transform their world rather than simply renounce it.[2]

Some scholars believe that this community began a movement that would eventually sweep India and spread a non-violent, contemplative version of Indian science and civilization through most of Asia.[3] That movement, called the Universal Vehicle, was personified in the colorful figure of Nagarjuna, a physician, linguist, and philosopher who advised King Antivahana II of the Shatavahana dynasty in South India and who came to be revered through much of Asia as "the second Buddha" and "great champion" of this second great wave of Buddhist teaching.

Homage to Great Compassion: The Universal Vehicle of Nagarjuna

I've opened this chapter with a passage from Nagarjuna's classic *Jewel Garland of Advice to the King*.[4] In it, the second-century monk lays out his vision of a gradual path of teachings suited to the various stages of contemplative healing and human development. The gist of his advice was that the king could find the freedom and peace of contemplative life without abdicating his role in the world, as long as he learned to complement his personal self-healing with the Buddha's profound teachings of compassionate openness and social engagement. Though the Buddha himself had renounced princely life, his contemplative path eventually lead him back from the wilderness into the world. Thanks in part to the success of his teaching and grass-roots community, the contemplative arts and sciences of ancient India had become more and more widely accessible to mainstream Indians over the centuries that followed.

In the wake of the great Emperor Ashoka's reform of Indian civil society, Buddhist institutions had begun to open their doors more and more and to reach out to lay people in all walks of life.[5] By the time of Nagarjuna, several of India's most progressive dynasties had begun to fund colleges and universities that would become refuges for the unfortunate and uneducated as well as the think-tanks of a contemplative science and civilization that would eventually transform India and most of Asia.[6] At the turning point in this transformation, Nagarjuna was the architect of the socially engaged teaching tradition that would soon take root at Nalanda University, the international beacon of India's new contemplative science and civilization.

This Essential Nectar of Precepts: The Compassionate Art of Happiness

As for the shift in outlook Nagarjuna personified, it is surprisingly congruent with a profound shift made only recently in the West. That is the shift from a scientific worldview which sees people and things as independent atoms living and working in isolation, to one which sees people and things as interdependent waves living and working through mutual cooperation. Together with the new interpersonal neuropsychology and the pressing challenges of global interdependence, this shift has fostered a growing popular consciousness of the need for a way of life that is less competitive and more cooperative. Now that modern science has revealed the causal basis of human social behavior in evolution, neurobiology and early development, we know that love and compassion are not just religious beliefs but powerful, natural forces for good. Yet we lack reproducible methods for tapping and harnessing these healing forces, like those developed, refined, and preserved through the centuries by our ancient contemplative traditions. Among traditional methods, the socially engaged curriculum refined by Nagarjuna, Asanga and their heirs at Nalanda is of great relevance for us today because it was designed and tailored specifically to meet the needs of a lay audience living an everyday life in the world.

This Art Refined Over Centuries *Was Transmitted through Suvarnadvipa*

Though Nagarjuna's *Jeweled Garland* was addressed to a king, the gradual path of teachings he spelled out there sparked a centuries-long dialogue between Buddhist and non-Buddhist scholar-practitioners over how a socially engaged contemplative life could be made accessible to the widest possible audience.[7] A century or two later, the brothers Asanga and Vasubandhu proposed that Nagarjuna's profound teaching of openness (literally "emptiness") would best be taught to a broad audience by emphasizing the views on the power of mind

Figure 4.1 Asanga, Master of the Engaged Path of Altruism

he shared in another of his three main works, *Reason Sixty.*[8] They believed that his insight that all persons and things are empty of self-sufficiency would be less likely to frighten or confuse if it was presented in terms of openness of mind; and that presenting it like this would also make it more compatible with the work of opening the heart by extending our social emotions of love and compassion. Called Constructivism, their view of emptiness as open-mindedness was eventually reconciled with the views of Nagarjuna's direct heirs, called Centrists.

Two or three centuries later, Nalanda Centrist masters Chandrakirti and Shantideva stressed that even mind must be seen as empty of self-sufficiency, lest people cling to habitual points of view and have greater trouble developing the radical openness and compassion Nagarjuna prescribed. Instead, they believed that the best way to teach openness widely is to present it in terms of the openness of empty conventions of speech, since these help us exchange points of view and so free our minds from self-centered bias that limits our cultivation of compassion and cooperation. By presenting Nagarjuna's insight in terms of openness of speech not just mind, this dialogue-based approach helped make his radical openness more widely accessible without indulging subjectivity; and it did so in a way that fostered the heart-opening cultivation of empathy and compassion as well or better than Buddhist Constructivism.[9]

Called Dialogical Centrism, Chandrakirti and Shantideva's approach eventually became the method of choice for presenting Nagarjuna's socially engaged form of Buddhism. So three centuries later, when Nalanda masters Suvarnadvipa and Atisha sought to bring the teachings of Nagarjuna's gradual path to the fiercely independent, non-Buddhist peoples of Sumatra and Tibet, they chose to do so by simplifying and refining the dialogical method of Shantideva. Thankfully, a record of their unique style of teaching is preserved for us in the form of a practice known to Tibetans as mind-training, or as I like to call it, mind-clearing.[10] Since part 1 of this book covered the first three legs of Nagarjuna's gradual path—correcting vices, building virtues, and committing to eliminate suffering and build peace of mind—in part 2 we'll devote our attention to exploring the socially engaged part of his path.

Specifically, we'll explore the engaged path based on the teaching and practice of clearing the mind Atisha refined and brought to Tibet. In fact, I've framed all three chapters of part 2 on the speech wheel around the best known version of this popular practice, based on a text recorded by Atisha's grand-student Chekawa Yeshe Dorje called *Clearing the Mind in Seven Points.*[11] In this chapter, we'll cover the main practice of compassion based on the first one-and-a-half points; in chapter 5, we'll cover the way this practice distils the insight meditation on openness or emptiness, based on the next two-and-a-half-points; and in chapter 6, we'll explore the socially engaged lifestyle prescribed in this text, based on the final three points.

It Resembles the Sun, a Diamond and a Medicinal Tree

In this and previous chapter sub-headings, I've italicized the opening lines of Chekawa's introduction to *Clearing the Mind in Seven Points.* Likewise, through the remainder of part 2, you'll find the pointers or precepts that make up his pithy and memorable root text, italicized in some of the chapter sub-headings. Although some or all of the lines are thought to be direct quotes from Atisha handed down orally, I refer to them here as Chekawa's, since at the very least, they may never have been preserved in consistent form without the Tibetan scholar's efforts to organize and commit them to writing. With that said, I invite you to enter the world of his text with me, by reviewing the lines of introduction I've mentioned thus far:

> Homage to Great Compassion!
> This essential nectar of precepts
> Was transmitted through Suvarnadvipa.
> It resembles the sun, a diamond and a medicinal tree!

Meant to highlight the benefits of studying and practicing the teaching encoded in Chekawa's text, his similes sound intricate enough to our modern ears that we might dismiss them as mere poetry. That's how I heard them when I first encountered this teaching. Yet as the years flew by and I found myself grappling with the complex challenges of my professional and personal life, these seemingly clichéd similes began to ring truer than all the science, psychology, and expert advice I'd gathered from seemingly more current and reliable sources. How could that be?

Normally, we tackle the mysteries of nature, intractable human challenges and the ills of humanity as complex problems that live somewhere "out there" in the external world. But the one element that slips through the grid of our modern science and technology, even modern psychology, is the single most pervasive source of error and suffering in all our lives. Of course, I mean the internal element of our humanity; what Freud's predecessor Friedrich Nietzsche called our all-too-human nature.[12] If we could find a source, a method, some way to shine the light of awareness on our human failings, cut through instinctive habits that limit our full capacity and heal the wounds we inflict on ourselves, that would be a great boon indeed.

From the perspective of Buddhist contemplative science, this is exactly what Shakyamuni found in the realization of inner peace he called Nirvana. It is no accident that the word Atisha and Chekawa use to describe the essence of their teaching—whether we translate it as nectar, ambrosia or elixir of immortality—is the same word the Buddha was said to have used to describe his realization. In fact, the essential nectar this socially engaged practice offers has the Buddha's Nirvana as its first active ingredient. It presupposes the ability to let go of the root causes of suffering and to cultivate the causes of lasting happiness. Yet while its medicine is the same as he prescribed in the eightfold path, this teaching formulates it in a new way that makes it as effective for lay people in a stress-driven world as for monks and nuns living apart from the world in monastic retreat.

While a literal reading of the noble truths maps the path in dualistic terms—as a kind of escape route leading away from the world of compulsive life to the transcendent, otherworldly realm of Nirvana—the socially engaged form of his teaching maps the journey of contemplative life more as an odyssey that eventually leads to re-engagement with the world, only this time from a place of radical openness and compassion. Instead of conceiving Nirvana as a realm apart, and contemplative life as a one-way ticket to renunciation, this new teaching sees it as a non-local way of being, every bit as much at home in the everyday world as in the monastery, hermitage or retreat. The seven-point framework and specific precepts of the practice of clearing the mind offer the essential nectar of Buddha's Nirvana in a formula especially made for those who choose to stay in the world, and so need a contemplative path which helps them transform their way of being in the everyday world without ever leaving it.[13]

Given the vital importance of transforming our way of being in the world, we can begin to unpack the reasons why Chekawa compares the benefits of clearing the mind to the life-giving boons of three wonders of nature: the sun, a diamond and a medicinal tree. Like the sun which shines on us all, clearing the mind of social stress can bring warmth equally and impartially into each of our lives, regardless of our surface differences. Clearing the mind of the distortions of trauma can help dispel the ghosts of painful memories, and the shadows of fear, anger, and shame clouding our perception of people, places, and things. Like a diamond blade that can cut anything, clearing the mind through surgical self-analysis can cut through the most calcified mental and emotional blocks and cut out the cancer of self-protective instincts gone wild. And, like a tree every part of which can be used as medicine, the multi-faceted practice of clearing the mind can help heal the whole range of compulsions that poison our lives; or, for those who can't master it all, each part of it can help relieve or heal some of the compulsions that ail us.

The Tree and the Couch: Mind-Clearing and Psychotherapy

To our ears, such broad general claims may sound outsized. But if we subtract the poetry and compare the benefits promised from mind clearing with those we expect from psychotherapy, the claims start to seem more plausible. While psychotherapy is not for everyone, most individuals stand to benefit significantly from greater awareness and understanding of the confused impressions and conflicting emotions that can be traced back to early relationships. Whether or not the distortions and emotions of childhood are severe enough to be diagnosable as childhood trauma, adult neurosis or some other disorder, and whether they still intrude into consciousness or have been long since repressed, they notoriously enhance misperceptions and emotional reactivity in adult relationships.[14]

In more serious cases, childhood stress and trauma can lead to disorders that all but block our capacities to sustain healthy relationships, at home and at work.[15] Here, newer therapeutic approaches like object-relational psychoanalysis, self-psychology, interpersonal therapy, and family systems theory can help people cut through deeper layers of traumatic conditioning that block corrective learning and experience, leading to deep character change that frees and enables natural social capacities.[16] Finally, psychotherapy is also a many-faceted remedy, which over time can impact many aspects of health, mental and physical, individual and collective.[17] On the other hand, even small doses or narrowly focused forms of psychotherapy can be invaluable, as we can see from short-term therapies, cognitive therapies, and couples and family therapies.[18]

Of the many different kinds of contemporary psychotherapy, those which emphasize the role of personal relationships and social interactions in human development and health offer the closest match with the socially engaged teaching tradition and the practice of mind-clearing. Just as some modern theorists compare the shift from classical analysis to the interpersonal approach of object-relations theory with the shift in modern physics from classical mechanics to wave mechanics, so the shift from classical Buddhist psychology to the social psychology of the Universal Vehicle is typically aligned with the shift from the analytic science of Buddhist Realism to the relativistic science of Nagarjuna's Centrism.[19]

In both these distinct cultural contexts, there is a shared sense that the analytic approach which sees and treats people and things as truly separate reflects a preliminary analysis of mind and matter, while the relativistic approach which sees them as interdependent systems reflects a more profound analysis. So while the newer, relativistic approaches of object-relations theory and socially engaged Buddhism assume the preliminary insights and methods of classical analysis and early Buddhism, they also involve a more profound understanding of mind and matter that permits a more radical and far-reaching transformation. This is possible because practices like relational or couples therapy and mind-clearing help people harness the strong forces of love and compassion, the culture medium and catalyst for positive human development.

The Aim is to Turn the Evolution of the Toxic Body/Mind into a Path to Enlightenment!

In these last lines of his introduction, Chekawa identifies the intent behind the mind-clearing practice with the radical aim of Nagarjuna's non-dual "practice of enlightenment." That radical aim is not just to renounce the world but to transform it. This statement of purpose assumes the basic Buddhist science of the human condition and adds to it the new understanding of the relativity and interdependence of self and world, microcosm and macrocosm. According to classical Buddhist science, the "world" is reducible to the microcosm of an individual mind/body process in its baseline condition or natural state, that is, contaminated by the compulsions that drive the cycle of stress and trauma, especially the root poisons of anger, clinging and delusion.[20] This is because the compulsive life world as a whole is made up of the aggregate of compulsive individuals, as molecules are aggregates of atoms.

But while a classical, dualistic reading of the noble truths aims at purifying our toxic way of being by disengaging from the world, a non-dualistic reading has the more ambitious aim of developing a new way of being that allows us to cultivate and spread enlightenment in the world. This new aim is conceivable thanks to the new Buddhist science which found that mind, body, and environment are not intrinsically toxic, but can be purified and transformed by a catalytic process like the chemical reactions described in alchemy. And, thanks to the interrelatedness of all people and things, the transformation of one life in turn can catalyze the transformation of others, eventually altering a whole society.[21] These lines from Chekawa help orient us to the practice of clearing the mind by locating our own personal path of self-healing and change within the broad, utopian vision assumed by Nagarjuna's socially engaged form of Buddhism. In this vision, mind-clearing is not just a path of self-healing but a contemplative form of non-violent social activism as well, a non-dual path combining enlightened altruism with enlightened self-interest.

First Learn the Preliminaries: The Foundations of Mind-Clearing Practice

The first point of this seven-point practice underscores the cumulative nature of the gradual path mapped out by Nagarjuna. It reminds us that the engaged art of clearing the mind presupposes a firm foundation in the practice of mindfulness; the insights of the noble truths, and the lifestyle of renunciation covered in part 1. Psychologically, it points to the fact that the work of sustaining healthy relationships requires that we've reached the basic milestones of personal self-healing: accurate, healing insight into the self-inflicted nature of our suffering; mastery over our compulsive mindset and habits; as well as some degree of serenity, benevolence, and a sustainable way of life. In practical terms, this first point typically involves continually reviewing and refining the methods, insights and ethics of the vehicle of personal self-healing I call the body-wheel.

Of course, we see something similar to this gradual path when we reflect on the gradual nature of healing and human development in psychotherapy. A successful couples' treatment requires both parties to have a reasonably secure foundation of mental health and well-being.[22] Before they are ready for couples' therapy, individuals will likely need treatment for their addiction, trauma and/or compulsive lifestyle. If we're going to master the art of turning social stress into an opportunity for social healing, we need to be able, as they say in airline safety, "to put our own oxygen mask first"; to disarm our own knee-jerk reactions to social stress. This basic degree of self-mastery is indispensible to what I call the social-emotional *Kung-fu* of mind-clearing practice.

Drive All Blame into One: Clearing the Mind of the Traumatized Self

Given this review of the history and logic of proactive social engagement, we turn now to the second point in Chekawa's sevenfold practice framework.[23] Why introduce the actual practice of clearing the mind with the most edgy and provocative of Chekawa's precepts: *Drive all blame into one*? What does "driving blame" have to do with compassion? In the simplest sense, blame is the opposite of empathy, and the main obstacle to the operation of compassion.[24] In terms of current stress-research and social psychology, blame is a traumatic reflex and a sensitive indicator of social stress.[25] As a rough subjective gauge of how threatened we feel by another human, it stands as the psychological equivalent of an elevated pulse in the realm of stress-physiology.[26] The instruction to drive all blame into one meets us where we spend all too much time: caught up in the experience of social stress and in traumatic reactivity to those we see as strangers, competitors, enemies, or even perpetrators.

Once it draws our attention to blame, as the projection of our own sense of fear and threat onto others, it directs us to restrain that projection and reverse its externalizing thrust by drawing it back into ourselves. Yet while it begins with a unilateral disarming and redirection of blame, this precept does not direct us to simply suppress that destructive energy or to redirect it at ourselves. It does not ask us to blame ourselves indiscriminately for everything, committing the sort of psychological suicide that is a common complication of social stress and abuse.[27] Instead it asks us to pinpoint self-defeating habits to be changed, within a general spirit of unconditional self-acceptance and proactive self-mastery.[28]

Confronting Knee-Jerk Self-Enclosure: The Root of All Social Stress

Just what does Chekawa mean by the word "one." The correct understanding and healing efficacy of the entire practice to follow hinges on the clear and precise pinpointing of this term, which is counterintuitive enough that it has become a source of widespread misunderstanding among Tibetans as well as Westerners. All too often, the word is taken to refer to "me, myself, and I" in a general or imprecise way, as if I and my ego or self-interest are somehow to blame for all the bad interactions I have with others in the world. In the West, much of the misunderstanding is caused by translation. Though the offending habit to be "blamed" as the first step in clearing the mind is usually referred to in English as "self-cherishing,"[29] I find the term "self-indulgence" more accurate and less misleading.

There is nothing wrong with wisely loving or cherishing any living being, including oneself. The problem comes when we mistake unthinking, unhealthy attachment for healthy love and cherishing, and indulge, reinforce, or defend habits which are really not beneficial at all, but just plain bad for us. The reason for starting the actual practice of clearing the mind with this precept is that clinging to anything and everything we see as "I," "me," or "mine," especially when we feel somehow threatened, is a very dicey, knee-jerk habit that is more likely to hurt than help. Even if it helps in the short run, this reflex invariably hijacks the higher faculties of empathy and communication we most need to meet the social challenges of civilized life.[30] Sadly, this reflex is standard equipment we all share as a matter of nature and nurture.

Survival or Abundance? The Origin and Limits of Self-Indulgence

You may recall the analogy I drew in part 1 between Shakyamuni's insight into the multi-life origins of the human condition and the modern discovery of the stress-response. Evolved through natural selection because it helped our ancestral life forms respond automatically to a life-threatening physical assault, this response—with its array of fight, flight, and freeze reflexes—is a very specific biological tool that prepares us to meet a very circumscribed challenge. Alongside this self-protective response-set and the survival mode it supports, our ancestral forms of life evolved and preserved another response-set and mode of engagement to meet a very different range of conditions. What some call the relaxation response—with its array of healing, growth and love reflexes—is an equally specific biological tool which prepares us to capitalize on circumstances of relative safety and abundance. As I see it, this is the part of our nature Shakyamuni realized in his Nirvana experience.

As more complex life forms evolved, especially the increasingly social forms of our mammalian forbears and our primate next-of-kin, both of these primal modes and ways of being in the world were extended.[31] To support our increasing dependence on others for survival, the primitive stress-response was extended into what we now call attachment behavior, including an array of social capacities, emotions, and gestures like facial expressions and cries which secure the help of others in adversity. To support our increasing collaboration with others in sharing abundance, the primitive relaxation-response was extended into the realm of bonding behavior, including an array of social capacities, emotions and gestures like facial expressions and cooing which engage others in mutual grooming, learning, courtship and play. Mammals of different eras and species maintained a delicate balance between these two modes of social engagement to meet the range of different challenges and conditions posed by a changing environment.

As a result of the way attachment behavior extends the self-protective mode of the stress-response, the limits of empathy and failures of cooperation in social animals naturally tend to trigger the same primitive fight-flight-freeze reactions as physical stressors like encountering predators. While the insensitivity or inattention of parents is a far cry from the kind of physical life threat the stress-response prepares us to meet, it tends to elicit similar reactions when misperceived as life-threatening by helpless young.[32]

As the most exquisitely social of all social animals and the most helpless at birth, we humans have an unusually intense dependency on others and may be especially prone to confusing social stressors with physical life-threats. So it is that most of the events we humans experience as life-threatening traumas—the lion's share of experiences which elicit, condition and reinforce our self-protective instincts in the course of development—are neither life-threatening challenges nor physical threats of any kind. Bound up with our self-protective instincts and woven together with the biology of the stress-response, we humans tend to develop what I call a traumatized sense of self, based on our memory of childhood traumas and fleshed out by our identification with stress-reactive habits and defenses.

Indulging the Cornered Animal and Traumatized Child Within

Unfortunately, given the conservative bias in human development, this traumatized sense of self tends to be the position we default to when facing challenging social interactions. This means engaging with others who may themselves be overwhelmed as if they were parents on whom our survival depends, and meeting them from the rut of an outmoded self that locks us in a straightjacket of stress-reactivity and learned helplessness. In effect, the learned reactive mode I call the traumatized sense of self acts as a psychological hair-trigger which feels every stressful social interaction as a life-threatening event, tripping the innate survival mode which adds insult to injury by unleashing its chain reaction of fight-flight-freeze biochemistry. Caught in the grip of these two mutually reinforcing reactive habits—one innate and one learned—our bodies are stuck in an evolutionary hangover of stress and our minds in the recurrent nightmare of childhood trauma, even while the average expected conditions of our daily lives have never been better and our mastery over the forces of nature has never been greater.

This context also helps flesh out the second analogy we need to understand Shakyamuni's elucidation of the human condition, the analogy of trauma. The origins of human suffering lie not just in our evolutionary past but in our development within single lifetimes as well. From the moment our minds engage our parents under the influence of the poisons of self-reifying confusion, fear-based attachment and shame-based aggression, we weave for ourselves a recurrent nightmare of trauma. By identifying this nightmare as "I" and "mine," and building on this perverse foundation an obsessive mentality, addictive emotional life, and a compulsive way of being in the world, we effectively lock ourselves in a post-traumatic state that perpetuates the evolutionary hangover of stress-driven survival. The psychology of trauma is crucial to this pathology because it turns our safe and comfortable social environment into a seeming mine-field of triggers. In this post-traumatic mine-field, each and every interaction with others becomes a set up for us to implode into shame, rage or panic, the moment we experience them as negligent or abusive parents rather than equally insecure fellow-travelers.

We've Met the Enemy: Our Own Wild, Confused Minds

You can think of the gist of Buddha's insight into our civilized discontent as an inversion of Jean-Paul Sartre's provocative existentialist credo, "Hell is other people." For the Buddha's heirs, especially in the tradition of socially engaged practice, the truth is the opposite: hell is a place within my own mind. Specifically, it is the traumatized sense of self that insinuates itself into our minds like a parasite or poisonous snake, sapping us of the capacities we need to thrive with others, and poisoning our minds and bodies so that nothing and no one feels safe enough, fair enough or good enough. Psychoanalyst Margaret Mahler refers to this all-too-human stance as "the paranoid-schizoid position." I often illustrate this psychological rut with the singsong mantra of childhood self-pity, "Nobody loves me, everybody hates me, I'll just eat worms!" What Chekawa means by the precept, "Drive all blame into one," is that indulging our self-protective impulse to seek safety under the cover of this regressed stance is the prime obstacle to healthy social emotional self-care and proactive social development. Shantideva compares the way stopping this reflex protects our minds from social stress to the way sandals protect our feet:

> Where is there enough leather
> To cover the surface of the Earth?
> But just having sandals on one's feet
> Is the same as covering the whole Earth.[33]

The Inner *Kung-Fu*: Clearing the Mind

The essence of the discipline of clearing the mind is this tactical inversion from the primitive reflex of externalizing blame to a reflexive awareness that sees our own part in the problem, alongside the contributions of others. This shift in attention is the gateway to mind-clearing because it opens an avenue to focusing on what we can realistically master, maximizing our leverage over our interactions by changing what is within our control: our own outlook, attitude and behavior. The strategy is comparable to one we are well aware of from the globalization of the Asian popular culture of martial arts. By building the discipline to master innate violent impulses and self-protective reflexes, the martial artist can keep cool enough to maintain an objective clarity and empathic awareness of an opponent's moment-to-moment mindset, intentions and habits. As a result, s/he can stay well ahead of the actions of an untrained and undisciplined mind, mastering even the most hostile opponent by putting higher awareness over primitive impulse, light over heat.[34] In effect, the practice of mind-clearing targets the terrorist within us all, and unmasks him not as pure evil, but as the traumatized child and cornered animal that threatens all of our peace and survival, individually and collectively.

By impersonally, empathically, and proactively engaging that wild child with a no-fault, zero tolerance discipline, the mind-clearing offers a path to disarming and taming our own minds that also prepares us to help others disarm and tame themselves. Far from the self-sacrificing martyrdom that leaves us open to playing the doormat for less civil others, this practice equips the meek child within with the self-knowledge and inner strength to really inherit the earth.[35] If we want inner peace to be sustainable in the everyday world, we need to engage with that world in a proactive way that protects and extends our peace of mind in the face of expectable social stresses. Instead of indulging our inner child by demanding others be better than they are, we must take adult responsibility for parenting ourselves through our social lives, dedicating whatever energy we save to deal maturely with others still in the grips of their wild child.

Contemplate the Kindness of All Living Beings: Building a Proactive Social Self

With this self-critical shift, we open the door to a whole new way of life based on proactive engagement with others in the day-to-day world. Once we break the death-grip the traumatized self maintains on our minds, we clear the way for our positive social self to emerge from the shadows and take the lead in our interactions with others. As we've learned from today's trauma therapies, we must first disarm the survival mode of trauma before we can feel safe enough to learn a new way of being with others based on positive social emotions and healthy interactions.[36] In effect, the complementary modes of abundance and survival are also mutually incompatible.[37]

In illustrating this fact, I like to borrow an analogy frequently used by His Holiness the Dalai Lama. Fascinated with cars since his boyhood, His Holiness likes to compare the shift from a negative mindset to a positive one to shifting gears with a manual transmission. If we're stuck in the overdrive of high stress and trauma, we must first downshift to neutral before we can reengage in the low-stress mode of peace and compassion. The first precept—*drive all blame into one*—serves as a reminder to down-shift out of the overdrive of trauma into the neutral mode of self-reflection and self-care, before the second precept—*contemplate the kindness of all*—directs us to re-engage with others in the low-stress mode of proactive confidence, empathy, and compassion.

Taken together, the remaining precepts we'll explore in this chapter unpack the art of cultivating and harnessing our natural capacity for the positive social emotions we need to motivate and sustain positive social interactions. This includes four main topics: two main methods of building healthy empathy and compassion; putting empathy and compassion into practice with the help of an art called giving and taking; monitoring our practice with breath-mindfulness in the course of everyday interactions; and training the mind for long-term practice through cognitive-behavioral learning. First, though, a big-picture look at compassion.

From Sentimentality to Spontaneity: The Four Modes of Compassion

The first thing we can expect to come up when most of us hear the precept to *contemplate the kindness of all living beings* is our innate fear and learned experience that *not all* living beings are kind; in fact, some have a knack for being threatening, attacking, and even lethal. Are we supposed to deny or whitewash the ways in which our everyday world seems anything but kind? Are we being asked to live in a spiritual fantasy world rather than in hard reality? A general look at compassion in the socially engaged tradition helps resolve these questions and clarify the real intention behind this precept and practice. In terms of its positive social psychology, compassion is not viewed simply in light of its emotional tone but also in light of its cognitive accuracy and behavioral efficacy. This is clear from a quick look at a traditional typology of modes or levels of compassion.[38]

Generally defined as the wish that another or others be freed from suffering and its causes, compassion is categorized into four modes or levels. Most closely aligned with what we think of as compassion in Western psychology or ethics is the first mode. Called sentimental compassion, this type of compassion is seen more as a subjective state of pity or sympathy, which may be more colored by the compassionate subject's good intentions than by any realistic understanding of the nature of others' suffering or a practical ability to help. One answer to the question of whether this tradition wants us to live in a rosy but unrealistic fantasy world lies in the teaching that this common sentiment is not true compassion because it is neither realistic nor efficacious. The full answer lies in unpacking the three modes or depths of compassion that *are* considered genuine.

The first of these modes I call narrative compassion because it combines the wish to help with a realistic understanding of the evolutionary causes and developmental conditions driving others' suffering, as well as the empathic art it takes to help others break out of their myopic life-story to see their predicament realistically and make healthy change. This mode bears a clear resemblance to the analytic insight that allows a therapist to build an accurate therapeutic construction of a client's history in psychotherapy. As in mind-clearing, in therapy we would see this insight as ideally combined with the empathic sensitivity and interpretive art it takes to help a client revise their familiar narrative to support healing and change.

The second mode I call analytic compassion because it marries a profound wish to help with a realistic analysis of the moment-to-moment mind/body conditions that maintain suffering, as well as expertise in prescribing changes in mindset, motivation, and habit that would counteract those conditions and foster healing. This mode bears an obvious resemblance to the depth-psychological insight that allows a clinician to discern cognitive, affective, somatic and/or behavioral factors that reinforce suffering, as well as the clinical expertise to prescribe changes in thinking, emotional regulation and/or lifestyle that would counteract suffering and promote healthy development.

The final mode I call unconditional compassion because it integrates the most profound instinct to help with a direct intuition of another's predicament and a spontaneous response that reflects the level of empathic attunement and responsiveness an experienced mother has towards the needs of her child. This level of compassion may be a bit more controversial for us, in that it assumes an intuitive openness and empathic spontaneity that challenges our notions of objectivity and distance. Nonetheless, I believe it's very much in line with the highest levels of empathic maturity and therapeutic mastery.

As I see it, these modes of effective compassion are the key, active ingredients needed to catalyze and sustain the healing experience and dialogue of a therapeutic relationship. In addition, what Chekawa has in mind when he directs us to *contemplate the kindness of all living beings* is quite in keeping with current views of how our higher cognitive faculties evolved, develop and function in synergy with our primal, mammalian social emotions.[39] The gist of this view is that genuine, mature, or effective compassion, more than a simple affect, sentiment, or belief, is a highly evolved form of social-emotional intelligence that is vital to the success of human interaction, communication and cooperation. Of course, despite the need to integrate the two faces of social engagement, the tradition suggests that we cultivate them separately at first, and then eventually work to integrate them into one seamless practice. So we turn now to the traditional methods used to develop the emotional face of compassion.

Cultivating Compassion: The Art of Civilized Happiness

Before we turn to consider the two main methods of building empathy and compassion, a few general comments about the way in which that cultivation is traditionally viewed in Buddhist and Western culture may help set the stage. In stark contrast to the view of love promoted traditional religious culture of the West, our modern scientific view of human nature saw our potential for social emotions like empathy, love, and compassion as mainly self-interested and narrowly circumscribed. Instead of our religious view of humanity as loving, until recently modern science saw our nature as primarily competitive and aggressive.[40] This modern consensus has been forcefully challenged by the rise of new fields like sociobiology, positive psychology and interpersonal neurobiology.[41] In this emerging new science, positive social emotions and social-emotional intelligence are seen less as conflicting with individual self-interest than as essential and basic to healthy human development and adaptation. There is also increasing openness now to a view of our nature as having a relatively unlimited potential to extend and expand our social capacities through use-dependent plasticity.[42]

This new science prepares us well to understand the social psychology of Buddhism, in which our natural capacities for empathy, love, compassion, and altruism are seen as potentially unlimited and indispensible to our optimal well-being and happiness in the unnatural condition of civilized life. While Buddhist psychology can hardly be accused of underestimating the deep roots of our instinctive narcissism and destructive emotions, it clearly anticipates the optimism of the emerging science on our potential for social change. In fact, in its socially engaged teaching tradition, it may be even more committed than the new science to the idea that social capacities like empathy and altruism must be cultivated by all individuals and groups as a basic necessity of our health, education and welfare. The two methods of cultivating compassion developed in the Nalanda tradition and taught widely in Tibet exemplify this radical optimism and ambition. In effect, they map a course of athletic exercise and training that is and should be open to anyone who wants to move their everyday life towards optimal wellness and sustainable happiness.

The Fourfold Method of Exchanging Self and Other

The most concise and integrated of the two methods of building compassion in this tradition is the more recent technique developed by Shantideva.[43] Known as the method of exchanging self and other, this fourfold practice is an ideal place for us to start because it integrates cognitive and behavioral changes along with the core shift in emotional stance from reactive self-indulgence to proactive social engagement. It revolves around four successive steps: equalizing self and other; recognizing the costs of self-indulgence; realizing the benefits of love and compassion; exchanging self-indulgence for altruism. I like to describe these four steps as grounding, clearing, rebuilding, and reorienting.

The First Step: Grounding Compassion in Equanimity

The first step lays the foundation for a mature, objective approach to others and our interactions. Yet it begins where our traumatized approach to life does: myopically focused on our own narrow self-interest and those of the people we hold dear. As we saw in part 1, our basic relationship with ourselves and our loved ones revolves less around healthy love than around the fear-based clinging Buddhist psychology calls attachment. This clinging, expressed in stress-reactive and post-traumatic self-involvement, is compounded by our bland indifference, mistrust and denial of the humanity of vast majority of people we interact with. Further compounding our predicament is the shame-based envy and resentment for the special group we see as competitors or threats. In effect, this complex of threefold bias not only insures that all our interactions are driven or tainted by various forms of stress and trauma, but effectively locks us in a fortress-like prison of compulsive isolation, clinging and antipathy.

The art of equalizing self and other is designed to help us break down this prison one brick at a time, by bringing an unbiased mindfulness and awareness to our perception and responses to all living beings, close and far, human and non-human. The exercise proceeds much like basic science, by bringing our attention to the deep family resemblance and common history linking each one of us to one another and to all other life. The first move is to see all humans and all living beings as siblings under the skin, equal in being made of the same basic elements and in being subject to the same facts of life, including impermanence, illness, aging, and death. The second is to recognize the psychological bottom line that cuts across surface distinctions between us: that all animate life is sensitive to pleasure and pain; and that all sensitive beings equally seek the former while avoiding the latter. A scientific version of our Jeffersonian values, this reflection is meant to spark an enlightened spirit of humanity that counteracts our baser instincts towards self-indulgence and to build a universal tolerance, acceptance, and empathic inclusiveness. As Shantideva says,

> First, I should apply myself to meditation
> On the equality of self and others.
> Since we're all equal in wanting happiness and rejecting suffering,
> I should cherish all living beings as I do myself.[44]
>
> Therefore I should dispel others' suffering
> Simply because it is suffering, just like mine;
> And I should bring others' happiness
> Simply because they are living beings, just like me.[45]

Correcting our Biases For and Against Other Lives

Next, we bring this more objective awareness to bear in examining and correcting the biases that distort our perceptions and interactions with others. This self-corrective analysis works differently in each case, depending on the three main kinds of bias we project onto others.

Since our positive bias towards family and friends is based on attachment, we work first to see through the idealization or denial we have towards people we wish would love and help us, by facing their real limitations and trying to accept them more objectively as they are. Likewise we must reflect on the costs of clinging to these people in a self-indulgent way that denies their limits and the limits of our relationship, forging a symbiotic, codependent bond that leads us to reinforce each others' problems rather than honestly facing and solving them.

Second, we turn to our bias of indifference towards those we consider strangers or neutral acquaintances, a bias mainly supported by our compulsive confusion or delusion. Whether we simply fail to notice or acknowledge the individuality and importance of this silent majority of beings, this bias myopically narrows our world to a precious few friends and enemies, blanking out most of those our lives and world depend on. Our work here is to remove these blinders so that we can stop dismissing or neglecting most living beings and begin to see and treat all life with the sensitivity and seriousness we normally restrict to dear ones.

Finally, we take on the most difficult bias, the primal self-protective aversion and antipathy we have for those who seem to question, challenge or threaten our self-interest or well-being. Here, our work is to expose the distorted view we have of these individuals based on our traumatic reaction to the challenge they pose to our self-image and our way of life. Only when we're able to see them realistically as complex individuals with their own rights, needs, and problems, can we wake up to the challenge they pose for our relationship with reality and the future. While we all might prefer for this stressful part of our lives to just disappear, there is simply no realistic way for us to move through life without conflicts or differences with some individuals and groups. For that reason and because such difficult interactions trigger our worst traumatic stress-reactivity, there is enormous hidden benefit in learning to approach these interactions mindfully and skillfully.

Contemplating the Kindness Apparent or Hidden in all Living Beings

Instead of focusing on the equal make-up and frailty of living beings, Chekawa takes equality a step further and suggests we focus on the fact that, whether we notice it or not, they all possess some degree or form of kindness. While we do tend to focus sentimentally on the kindness of those we hold dear, we have a double or triple standard when it comes to strangers and rivals. Do we stop to reflect that each and every one of the strangers who surround us in our city, country and on the planet have loved ones themselves—people they see and treat with the same sort of kindness we feel for our loved ones? Of course, we are even less likely to reflect on the fact that those who challenge, threaten or hurt us or our loved ones inevitably have someone in their lives they hold dear and treat with some form of kindness. Chekawa's precept urges us to recognize and reflect on the kindness in all living beings as the best equalizer, because contemplating that quality most forcefully disarms the defensiveness we feel for strangers and rivals and naturally kindles the human-kindness we normally reserve for family and friends.

Equanimity: The Ground of Equality and Justice for All

Of course, the spirit of this work is somewhat familiar to us, as it resonates with our democratic sense of justice as well as our scientific ideal of objectivity.[46] Yet it addresses the need for fairness in our perceptions and actions on a much more personal level than we are used to, and it does so more radically and systematically than even the most rigorous modern disciplines. In practice, the closest most of us come to this exercise is in psychotherapy, where we must correct our childhood distortions of parents and stop projecting these as transference onto significant others at home and work. Yet at least for the average lay client, the way psychotherapy corrects such bias is not as complete or systematic as this practice, and leaves most of the interactions we have with others prey to persistent distortions and bias.[47]

Another key difference between this exercise of equanimity and what passes for objectivity in the modern context is that it is not the disembodied, disengaged, or disinterested state we normally think of as scientific objectivity or neutrality. It does involve disentangling the tentacles of clinging we tend to confuse with love and healthy attachment. But the expectation is that once those tentacles are released, love will flow more fully and freely, unrestrained by the death-grip of traumatic hyper-vigilance, compulsive controlling, and fear.[48] I often compare the distinction to the difference in narrative voices between a remote third person narrator who is objective in an indifferent or distant way and a close omniscient narrator who enters inside the mind of each character with caring intimacy. This distinction applies equally to our modern therapeutic ideas of the analyst's "neutrality," which is less like our modern scientific ideal of unfeeling reason than an extension of the wise yet caring engagement of a mature parent.[49]

A Middle Way Between Self-Indulgence and Self-Sacrifice

Unlike Indian and Western views of a supreme being who is literally omniscient and omnipotent, altruists like Shakyamuni are seen as more nurturing and effective than other humans but not without limits and needs. So while their love and compassion may be unconditional and universal, they are in fact refined and expanded versions of the natural social capacities innate in us all. This is why such altruists include themselves in their own love and compassion, as one being whose needs and interests are equal in merit and importance to any other's. If they seem to act selflessly, it is simply a function of the emotional calculus of their compassion, since the category "self" only includes one living being, while the category "others" includes infinite beings, each one of whom ideally is held as dear as oneself or one's only child.

Since the impartial and universal empathy aimed at in Shantideva's first step lays the foundation for a mature and balanced social engagement with self and all others, I refer to this step as "grounding" the practice of proactive compassion. You may also recognize it from the practice we in the West now call "loving kindness."[50] In the context of the gradual path, this first exercise dovetails with the work of the body-wheel: the horizon of personal self-healing reviewed in the first of Chekawa's seven points: *first learn the preliminaries.*

Meditative Experiment 4.1: Practicing Equanimity

In a secure, quiet space, find a comfortable posture, and clear your energy by exhaling a long, complete sigh. Let your next breath fill your lungs naturally, with as little effort as possible, and take that gentle, fresh breath as a tether for your restless mind. A breath at a time, let yourself shift into a kinder and gentler rhythm of breathing, and take that rhythm as a focal point to settle and center your energy and awareness. As you breathe in, try to gather your dissipated energy and distracted awareness and let them come to rest on your gentler breath-rhythm, centered at your heart. As you breathe out, exhale whatever restlessness and fatigue is inside you, imagining you can see it leaving your nostrils, fingers, and toes as puffs of white smoke. By alternately settling your distracted mind and uplifting your drowsy mind, you'll naturally find yourself moving towards a more centered space of clarity and calm, riding on the relaxed in and out of your breath.

As your mind eases into a more centered space of clarity and calm, imagine dissolving it into the subtle breath, the pulse of gasses that travels throughout your whole body, filling each tissue and cell with fresh oxygen and gathering up CO_2 to breathe out again. Try to feel you're breathing with your whole body, and that, with each breath, your body is becoming lighter and clearer, like a person-shaped bubble of life and breath. In your breath-body, open the scope of your mindfulness to the raw feel of your sensation, taking care to let go of feelings of pleasure and accept distress rather than fight or avoid it. Next, open your mindfulness to include your primal mind, immersing yourself in its natural clarity and awareness by letting go of any clinging or struggling with good or bad thoughts and images. Then finally expand your mindfulness to include all of you—your breathing body, raw feel, primal mind and experience—trying to maintain the centered balance you've been bringing to each layer of your life.

Now that you've found a greater balance and equanimity within your own body-mind, it's time to expand your awareness outwards and try to extend that balance to your interchange with others and the world we share. First, try to shed the tough skin of defensiveness and open your breath-body to feeling part of the world around you. Imagine yourself as a person-shaped bubble, a wave of life-energy and awareness within a sea of life-energy and awareness. Feel yourself filling and emptying with waves of life-breath and awareness, giving and taking with others and the world around you, like a cove filling and emptying with surf.

Now turn your awareness to your social environment. First, call up the image of a person near and dear to you for whom you feel a strong, uncomplicated warmth and affection. Invite the personality of your loved one to enter and inhabit the image, so you feel their presence as if you could reach out and touch them. Now focus on taking in their presence on the in-breath, and feel yourself filled with a sense of warmth and connectedness. As you savor that warmth, try to let go of any fearful attachment or clinging that normally preys on you and blocks your ability to feel deep, heart-opening love. Now breathe that stronger, purer love out to your dear one and see him or her take it in and feel warmed and connected in turn. As you exchange loving energy and awareness, feel your bond with your loved one deepening and intensifying, until it begins to fill you both with life-giving warmth.

Then invite into the space around your loved one all those you hold near and dear including your friends and role-models, allowing the outpouring of pure love to spread to them all, as if you were at a gathering where all were filled with an expansive sense of human kindness, belonging and gratitude. Here again, practice exchanging feelings of warmth and affection with your whole community of close others, trying to stretch your heart open and expand your capacity to savor, share and spread true care and love.

Next, invite your close community to move behind you, where they can back you up and buoy you with a sense of all-encompassing, unwavering, unconditional love. Now call up before you the image of a remote acquaintance for whom you feel very little except a vague sense of indifference. Best here is someone you routinely see but have little or no real knowledge or sense of, someone like a shopkeeper, bus driver or mailman. Invite the individual's personality to enter and inhabit your image. Now breathe in a sense of his or her presence as deeply and intimately as you can, as if you'd suddenly become neighbors for life or been thrown together by a disaster. As you breathe in his or her presence, try to see through the cloud of denial, prejudice, and myopic exclusiveness that keeps us locked in a self-enclosed trap of isolation and mistrust.

With your mind and heart clearing, tune into your common humanity by getting a feel for your acquaintance's familiar make-up and vulnerability, as well as distinctive blend of strengths and weaknesses. As you mix this sense of common humanity with the abiding sense of warmth you feel with your dear ones, try to breathe out a welcoming air of tolerance, acceptance and benevolence that adopts and embraces this unique individual as a new member of your extended family and heart-community. Now imagine him/her breathing in your inviting energy, feeling warmed and welcomed into your presence and life; and practice savoring and deepening this sense of connection one breath at a time. Finally, as the sense of human family feeling begins to fill you both with an inclusive sense of belonging, invite all the other remote acquaintances or complete strangers in your locality, your nation, your continent, and on our planet to gather behind your acquaintance, and join in the outpouring of real empathy, interconnectedness, and human kindness.

Lastly, invite you newfound friends and extended human foster family to come to your sides, men to your right and women to your left, and continue to embrace them in a sense of radical acceptance and rainbow solidarity. With these new members flanking you together with the community of dear ones backing you up, turn now to face the hardest challenge: coming to accept the people you find overly challenging or even threatening.

Begin by calling up someone you know all too well who's not your worst enemy but who simply rubs you the wrong way, like an edgy relative or sour neighbor. Next, respectfully invite the personality of that difficult other to enter and inhabit your image. Now gradually try to restrain any angry, resentful, or aversive reactions you feel towards him or her, and instead apply the clarity and peace of mind you've mustered thus far to engaging this person with a fresh open-mindedness and proactive tolerance, as if for the very first time. Here too, trying to breathe in an awareness of his/her common human make-up and frailties, reflecting on the fact that his/her edge or sour mood is no doubt caused by the same negative instincts and habits that plague us all. At the same time, take care not to overlook or discount any signs of human decency or kindness, as well as any distinctive qualities or suffering that may help you put his/her rough edges in context.

Now as you take in the humanity and uniqueness of this difficult other, try to neutralize any guardedness or resistance that might block your own empathy or human kindness by staying tuned to the deep and abiding positive feelings you feel with the community backing you up and the human family at your side.

Patiently yet persistently try to accept the presence of this challenging being in your life, and welcome him or her as the salt and pepper in the mix of your larger community and social life. It may help to reflect that if not for this other, there will always be someone who rubs you the wrong way, and that alongside any negative qualities s/he has there is likely to be a vital kernel of truth in the dissenting perspective s/he represents. As you open the fabric of your sense of community to include him or her as a member in good standing, try to appreciate the relief it brings to let go of aversion as well as the final expansion of your sense of belonging and interconnectedness with your social world as it really is. And as you breathe out this sense of radical tolerance, see your opponent soften and respond to your effort, until a genuine air of mutual respect and acceptance begins to flow between you. Into this air, finally invite the whole spectrum of difficult others—including the most threatening—to gather around the difficult other, and try to imagine stretching your sense of inclusiveness, one challenge at a time, until it can embrace the whole scope of your interconnection with others in the world.

At last, with your loved ones behind you, your acquaintances at your side, and your challengers right in front of you where you can watch them, try to breathe in the presence of your whole social environment just as it is, only joined in a spirit of radical acceptance and proactive engagement. As you take in your full interconnectedness with all humanity, try to savor a deep, heart-opening sense of belonging, and breathe out any positive feelings of relief, warmth, inclusiveness and connectedness to open and warm the hearts of all those we share this shrinking planet with.

You may finally choose to include all the other forms of life, from your most favorite to your least favorite, until you can taste a sense of breathing together with all other life on the planet, as if you and the earth were breathing as one. When you've had your fill, invite your guests to return to their own lives and places in the world, but just breathe a duplicate of your dearest into your heart, to keep the sense of warmth and openness always there with you to draw on every day.

The Second Step: Clearing the Mind of Post-Traumatic Self-Indulgence

If the first exercise in Shantideva's fourfold method of building compassion dovetails with Chekawa's first point, the second exercise—recognizing the costs of self-indulgence—overlaps with the first precept of his second point, *drive all blame into one*. Drawing on the basic analytic psychology of Buddhism, this exercise has us trace the causal sequence driving our misperception of friends and enemies back to the root compulsions of attachment and aversion. These opposing biases are then traced in turn to the same root poison that causes us to overlook or distort the humanity of strangers: the compulsive confusion and delusion underlying our all-too-familiar traumatized state of mind. In this exercise, we practice clearing away that confusion to expose the taproot of our whole biased subjectivity.

As you may recall, the most accessible part of this taproot is the delusion or fixed misperception of self we developed in the course of early childhood trauma: that we are all alone, helpless, and powerless in the face of the threatening challenges of our lives. If we trace this misperception deeper into our subconscious minds, we eventually hit upon the protective instinct of self-reification innate in us all, known to Western psychology as primal narcissism. It is this instinct that mistakes our sense of ourselves as helpless, threatened and alone for the fixed, objective reality of who and what we are, while simultaneously mistaking other humans who cannot read our needs or meet them for predatory rivals in a dog-eat-dog struggle for survival. Based on this, we build a mistaken, worst-case view of ourselves and our social world biased by the traumatic perceptions and stress-reactive emotions of early childhood.[51] The more we indulge our traumatized sense of self and others, the more we lock ourselves into a recurrent nightmare of survival which triggers and is reinforced by the toxic neurochemistry of the stress-response.[52]

The Traumatized Self: A Weather Vane in the Storm of the World

While the main intent of this practice would seem to be to help others, the fact is that the biased subjectivity of self-indulgence is unfair not just to others but even more so to ourselves. Once we fix our frame of reference in life on a traumatic attachment to ourselves and a few family and friends, we expose our minds to the toxic influence of compulsive confusion, clinging and aversion. Given that myopic fixation, our minds are caught in the powerful cross-currents of conflicting preoccupations called the worldly winds: attachment to ourselves and our circle enjoying pleasure, fame, praise, and gain; aversion to ourselves and our circle suffering pain, disrepute, blame, and loss. These winds are matched by countercurrents of attachment to our rivals and their circle suffering pain, disrepute, blame, and loss; and aversion to our rivals and their circle enjoying pleasure, fame, praise, and gain. With our higher faculties blinded by self-indulgence, we are pushed around our daily lives by the unseen force of primal drives, thrown here and there by the winds of disturbing confusion, insatiable acquisitiveness, and unbridled competitiveness.

While the whirlwind of confusion and the cross-winds of clinging and antipathy twist and push our inner lives aimlessly about, they also throw us off course in our relationships with others, near and far. Fear-based attachment and clinging constricts our relations with loved ones, tainting these ties with pointless tension and conflict. Delusion, denial, and confusion lead us to sleep-walk through our interactions with strangers or neutral acquaintances, enclosing us in a myopic bubble of isolation. Envy, aversion, and enmity force us to carry an unsupportable burden of antipathy and resentment, weighing down our ability to resolve disagreements and differences. So the biased mindset of our traumatized self not only twists our minds into knots of conflicted confusion but also wreaks havoc on our social life, blighting the whole web of relationships that make up the fabric of our human world. Nagarjuna compared our habit of reifying traumatic distortions and emotions as "I" and "mine" to a bad seed from which all our ills grow:

(Mind/body) systems develop from the construction of "I,"
(Yet) that construction of "I" in reality is false;
How could what has grown
From such a false seed be true?[53]

Overcoming Our Instinctive Resistance to Self-Analysis

Exposing the habit of self-indulgence and recognizing its costs is only the first step in the healing self-analysis and self-change we need to transform our social way of being in the world. The analysis this practice assumes is so radical and profound that we will return to it in chapter 5, as well as in the other two chapters on insight in parts 3 and 4. Progress in exposing and correcting this habit must necessarily be gradual, because it hides in our psychic blind spot as the most constant fixture in our minds and because it is thoroughly intertwined with the self-protective instincts that are a such powerful force in our lives. Typically, our inner dialogue and frame of reference are so intimately involved with this habit that it is a prodigious feat to get any perspective on it at all. Since exposing and disarming the grip of self-indulgence dispels the ghostly self-protective instincts and memories possessing our minds, I refer to this step in Shantideva's method as "clearing." This step effectively frees our powers of insight, empathy and altruism from the constraints of traumatic stress-reactivity, allowing these key muscle groups to be strengthened and toned in the remaining two steps of this method. Shantideva describes this key step in his *Guide*:

Since all the traumas of this world,
All our mental anguish and physical distress,
Arise from (this habit of) self-indulgence,
Of what use is this terrified ghost to us?
Without extinguishing a fire,
We cannot stop it from burning us.
Likewise, without eliminating self-indulgence,
We cannot stop our experience of suffering.[54]

Step Three: Rebuilding Our Whole Way of Being in the World

This brings us to the third exercise of Shantideva's fourfold method: realizing the benefits of love and compassion. In the context of Chekawa's mind-clearing practice, this is the exercise most closely aligned with the second precept of point two: *contemplate the kindness of all living beings*. In the Nalanda tradition, the basis for this step is the understanding that, despite their seeming independence, the diversity of living and non-living things arises entirely from the process of interdependence and mutual interaction. The scientific basis for the Buddhist psychology of selflessness, this understanding explains why social emotions like love and compassion are beneficial not simply on a "higher" moral level, but on the most basic, pragmatic level of life in the world as well.[55]

The Ground of Compassion: The Old, New Science of Interdependence

We are more likely to get the gist of this exercise if we briefly review the new science that has lent current validation to the optimistic worldview of socially engaged Buddhism. For today's evolutionary biology and psychology, the basis for the benefits of love and compassion lies in the fact that, despite eons of life-death struggle our ancestors had to survive, the rise of highly social animals in the mammalian era has tipped the balance of life towards cooperation rather than competition.[56] The gradual transition culminating in the evolution of hominids has finally been punctuated by the emergence of cultural evolution and human civilization.[57] This gradual sea-change has made the primitive, asocial reflex of stress-reactivity seem like vestigial organs compared with the social responses like empathy on which our lives increasingly depend.

Cooperative traits based on social emotions are not sentimental weaknesses, as modern science once taught us, but the right evolutionary tools for the job of civilized life. In hindsight, the rise of social evolution is a natural extension of the primal forces of sexual reproduction supporting primitive social behaviors like courtship and nurturance.[58] More basic still, sexual evolution in turn can be traced to the forces of interdependence supporting the development of our physical environment and the advent of life.[59] The same forces that sustained the evolution of more cooperative life also account for why our minds and brains are naturally prepared to communicate and cooperate, motivated by social emotions like love and compassion, as we see in the groundbreaking synthesis of my colleague, Dan Siegel.[60]

In a very practical sense, exercising such social emotions and the capacities they support may be the best way to adapt ourselves more fully to our delicate natural environment, as well to tune into the progressive spirit of evolution and human development. Building our capacity for social engagement shifts our development into a progressive mode in which we grow more able to parent our inner child while having as much mature humanity as possible to share with others who are more challenged. This allows us to build a more effective, cohesive and meaningful social life and world *unilaterally*, by doing what we can to raise the level of our everyday interactions rather than passively waiting for others to mature themselves.[61] Shantideva speaks eloquently about this third step in the process:

> Since one who knows the equality of self and others
> Derives great joy from relieving others' suffering,
> For their sake, s/he would gladly enter the deepest hell,
> Like a wild goose diving into a fresh lotus pool.

The ocean of joy that will arise
When all living beings are freed
Is all I could wish for—
So why wish for my freedom alone?[62]

Hence just as I protect myself
From anything unpleasant, however small,
So I should act towards others
With a compassionate and caring mind.[63]

Step Four: Exchanging Childhood Self-Indulgence for Mature Altruism

Shantideva's fourth and final exercise—exchanging self-indulgence for altruism—effectively completes the profound inner shift begun by building an engaged, proactive self. Since much if not most of our inner lives have been spent in the myopic mode of self-indulgence, identified with our traumatized childhood self, completing the shift to a synoptic self and mature way of life requires a decisive change in our sense of identity.

As we dismantle our childhood self-indulgence and build a mature, engaged social self, we must finally make the decisive step of shifting our frame of reference and sense of identity from the familiar habits we've built up around our childhood self to the new outlook and values we've been building. And since, according to Buddhist psychology, our self is constructed under the guidance of language, it is essential at this final step that we re-center our sense of "I" and "mine" around the new stance of openness and skills of compassion which are the building blocks for our proactive, engaged social self. As in the natural process of parenthood, this shift happens organically and eventually arrives at a more expansive and objective agency which embraces others as much as the self.[64]

While the expansion of selfhood in the course of parenting is a natural developmental process fueled by the exercise of empathic openness and loving, compassionate care, the shift in this step is a conscious, cultural extension of that process to our social lives as a whole. It amounts to adopting the whole of humanity and all life as an extended family, and choosing to relate to that family, to the best of our ability, as a volunteer foster parent to any and all in need. Of course, in order for this shift to be authentic, we must exchange our myopic sense of our life as centered around our narrow self-interest for an expanded sense of it as intimately involving the well-being of each and every individual in the web of life that is our world.[65]

Reorienting Our Lives Around our Social Fitness

Because of the enormous sea-change this shift involves, I like to call this fourth exercise "reorienting." It is not that we eliminate our familiar self, even our childhood self or "inner child" from our view of the world, but that we now choose to view that small self, as if from the outside in, rather than see our selves and our world from within it, looking out. But this shift means that we commit to doing so not from the self-indulgent stance which denies the needs and perspectives of others, but from an objective, adult stance which sees our subjective self as one of many confused and myopic selves. So, while the world, our world, remains exactly as it was before, our orientation on that world has come full circle and shifted 360 degrees.

It's not that we now stand outside ourselves and see ourselves with the same indifference as we used to see others. Rather, we stand in another part of ourselves, which has the ability to see our old self and the selves of infinite others with equal clarity and equal compassion.[66] Our shift towards this objective, magnanimous part of ourselves is described as altruistic simply because its equal attention and care for all life naturally brings the center of gravity in our awareness outside our narrow selves and into the larger world where we share the causes and conditions of health, freedom and happiness with unlimited others.[67] By cultivating the heroic resolve to climb out of our childhood fears and grow wise and caring enough to parent ourselves and all beings, we've radically changed the course of our lives and opened up a whole new future for ourselves and our world.[68]

This reorientation, however revolutionary, is not an end in itself but in fact only a new beginning. Once we commit to this new vision and reorient our minds and lives around it, we've actually taken the first step on the practical journey of a thousand steps that gradually leads to a whole new way of being in the world. In traditional terms, the spirit of enlightened altruism starts out as a virtual solution to the predicament of our self-enclosed lives and only gradually becomes an actual one. It is said that that enlightenment can come in a flash, like a bolt of lightning on a dark night, while the actualizing or embodying that flash of vision in a fully compassionate way of life takes three incalculable eons! Consider these verses from Shantideva's *Guide*:

> Though there is no "I" there,
> Through the force of familiarity
> I cling to an "I" within a body
> Which arose from the egg and sperm of others.
>
> In the same way, why can I not
> Identify "I" with the bodies of others?
> Equally I should not find it hard
> To identify my own body as "other."[69]
>
> Just as I regard the hands and so on
> As limbs of my body,
> So I should regard all living beings
> As limbs of a living whole.[70]

So, whoever wants to immediately care for
Both themselves and others,
Should practice this noble secret
Of exchanging self and other.[71]

Asanga's Sevenfold Causal Method of Building Compassion

For a look at the deeper emotional and behavioral levels of this transformation, I know of no better window than the sevenfold method of building compassion attributed to Asanga. For the sake of brevity, I'll simply describe that method by listing the causal sequence of seven affective states. These work like a positive social-emotional workout to exercise and build from our own personal experience of receiving nurturing to the development of universal compassion and enlightened altruism.

The sequence of affects which allow us to athletically exercise and develop the spirit of altruism is: (1) recognizing the whole family of life as our mother, and adopting all beings as kin;[72] (2) recalling our visceral memories of the loving kindness shown us by mother and/or other caregivers;[73] (3) in response to the nurturing love we've been shown, cultivating strong feelings of gratitude and indebtedness; (4) channeling those feelings into a strong urge to return that love by actively extending it to others;[74] (5) deepening and expanding that love into compassion that spontaneously acts to help all living beings;[75] (6) channeling that universal compassion into the heroic resolve to take responsibility to relieve the suffering and promote the happiness of all living beings;[76] (7) conceiving and building the will to become an enlightened altruist able to guide all living beings to real freedom and lasting happiness.[77]

Though ancient, the contemplative methods of Shantideva and Asanga resonate deeply with current trends in modern evolutionary biology. The emerging consensus on the evolution of social behaviors like altruism is based on the rise of mathematical models that predict the selective advantage conferred by kin-directed altruism.[78] Although these models reduce such behaviors to the natural selection of traits that tend to preserve genetic material by the protection of related kin, many biologists now believe that social animals have evolved other forms of altruism—like reciprocal and direct altruism—which have expanded the scope of social behavior far beyond the confines of genetic kinship.[79]

In effect, both contemplative methods of building compassion exploit the openness and plasticity of these natural traits by stretching them to adopt ever-larger circles of life and building them to exceptional degrees. This is part of a conscious strategy to culturally enhance our natural fitness for social life in order to better adapt us to the unnatural conditions of civilized living.[80] From the standpoint of modern models, Shantideva's method works more on what biologists call reciprocal and direct altruism, the natural tendency supported by prefrontal mirror neurons to feel empathy for others and show them the kindness we would like in return. In contrast, Asanga's method works more on what they call kin-directed altruism, the natural tendency to recognize kin as self, and to show them the whole range of primal social behaviors including protection, soothing, grooming, caretaking and teaching.

Traditionally, it is said that Shantideva's method works from the head down, while Asanga's works from the heart up. They may appeal to people with different inclinations and learning styles; or, as in the Gelukpa tradition of the Dalai Lamas, they may be combined in a super-method that works on both heart and mind together.[81] In any case, their job is to meet us where we begin—at the natural level of childhood myopia and self-indulgence—and to bring us in a gradual yet rigorous way to higher levels of maturity, objectivity and social-emotional intelligence. Once we take these as pathways towards a new life in the world, they bring us to the threshold of the next great method of clearing the mind: the art of giving and taking.

Practice Combining Both Giving and Taking: The Art of Social Self-Transformation

As the phrase suggests, giving and taking is a practice applied to the constant flow of social transactions and exchanges which is the currency of our daily lives. Yet the familiar connotation of "give and take" is sure to be misleading when it comes to the work of radical self-transformation this art involves. In fact, I often describe this practice as one of *reversing* the flow of give and take. Here's why. From early childhood, we human beings must take far more than we can possibly give back to others. In developed societies, this dynamic all too often persists into adolescence and even adult life, reinforced by the self-indulgent creed of our age. On the street, the secular, materialist strain in our culture tells us that the only smart thing is "Look out for number one." And this amounts to a view of our social lives in which things are going well when we take as much as we possibly can and give back as little as we absolutely must.

Of course, given the survival of the fittest ethos and bottom-line economics of the modern secular world, this self-indulgent outlook may seem like fair-minded, hard-nosed pragmatism. But from the vantage of our emerging new science of mind and life, we're beginning to see this bottom line way of being as ultimately self-defeating and dangerously short-sighted. Still, we often persist in this view, caught in the modern double-bind which offers us no alternative but the rigid anorexia of a self-sacrificing religious ethos. The art of giving and taking opens up a middle way that offers us an eminently realistic yet meaningful alternative.

Growing Pains: The Gradual Path of Giving and Taking

In practice, reversing the flow of give and take is a gradual process that inches forward through several phases. First, we learn to stop expecting the unique circumstances of childhood to continue into our later years. Then, we must gradually accustom ourselves to the real circumstances of our adulthood, in which we've grown to a place of parity with those who once seemed like gods. Next, we start looking to better our lives in a truly effective, mature way, by a combination of learning to skillfully parent ourselves and building virtues and strengths we can share with the world. Finally, we strive to make the greatest difference we can for ourselves and our world by working to tap our full potential and rise above self-limiting notions of our ability to aid those around us. This process builds on natural shifts in human development: from child to adolescent; adolescent to adult; parent to grandparent; and family elder to community leader.[82] Yet it does not leave this vital process of maturation to the lucky few or genetic chance, but rigorously and systematically cultivates our natural altruistic potential as the optimal solution for all individuals and groups facing the challenges of our increasingly complex social world.

As for the first phases in giving and taking, we must come to recognize the conditions of "good enough" human childhood from an adult point of view: not as a magical state of grace ordained to gratify our primal narcissism, but as the hard-won product of the collective altruism of parents, grandparents, friends, and neighbors. Naturally, we all see this in theory, but it's something else entirely to adjust to this adult reality on a gut level. Our attachment to primal narcissism is clear in our clinging to the childish fantasy that our relations with others should be an endless series of pleasures, with no cost in disappointment, pain or work. Renouncing this attachment and reversing our childish expectations means coming to recognize the real causes and conditions of human flourishing and setting about reproducing them for ourselves and others, not waiting for the good life to fall into our lap or be handed to us on a silver platter.

Coordinated Giving and Taking: Navigating the Worldly Winds

As for Chekawa's precept to *practice combining both giving and taking*, it's important to see how these two exercises work hand in hand to build a whole new way of being in the world. The exercise of taking care counters the self-indulgent winds of aversion with genuine compassion that takes suffering head on, regardless of whether it's our own or others'. And the complementary exercise of giving love counters the self-indulgent winds of acquisitiveness with nurturing love that shares whatever abundance we have equally with all life, near and far. Working together, these two powerful limbs put us on a road not taken, leading us out of the regressive rut of self-protective reactions towards a proactive self-confidence and engagement with our complex social world. The practice of combining these two in our everyday interactions serves to integrate all our exercise of social emotions—equanimity, tolerance, acceptance, gratitude, love, and compassion—into a highly effective way of being in the world that increasingly galvanizes our altruistic resolve and embodies the spirit of enlightened altruism.

Start Gradually with Taking on Your Own (Suffering)

All too often glossed over, this essential precept makes crystal clear that the art of giving and taking is not some pie-in-the-sky selflessness, but a real, pragmatic alternative to our self-defeating self-indulgence. As we learned from the first of Chekawa's seven points—*first learn the preliminaries*—there is no possible way to build a proactive social self without a firm foundation in personal self-healing and effective self-care. The precept to *start gradually* also underscores the point that enlightened altruism in this tradition begins at home: as a mature and effective way of realizing one's true self-interest.

Anything but a zero sum game, this practice assumes a radical vision of interdependence in which we all benefit equally by lining up together *with* our mature social selves and *against* no one else but our own primitive self-protectiveness and self-indulgence. Of course, the traumatized child and cornered animal within are trying their best to take good care of us by clinging to worst-case memories and stress-reactivity. It's just that the distortions and instincts they are acting on are in fact no match for the real challenges of our complex social lives. Their tendency to fight, fly, or freeze in the face of the pressing demands of our social lives may give some illusory safety or fleeting comfort, but does so at the expense of building the clear-headed awareness and people skills which will ultimately help us adapt to our daily lives.[83]

Starting with our own suffering here means decisively clearing our minds of our alarmist childhood reactions to our own problems and distress, and making a concerted effort to approach them maturely with the wise self-care of a good parent. Naturally, this effort involves a radical reorientation of consciousness in which we approach our childhood self as an other: the troubled child within us all. And since this requires so dramatic a re-centering of experience, we must inevitably begin by choosing this road-not-taken on a moment-to-moment basis: one problem, one distress at a time. Traditionally, this is conveyed in the precept to start by taking responsibility for our own suffering as it occurs in the present moment. As in psychotherapy, this begins with coming to see through our sense of helplessness and trauma in real time, so that we can begin to apply our adult capacity for empathic insight here and now.

As we gain confidence and mastery in this practice and can face our present challenges with a mature state a mind, we then move on to take responsibility for our past suffering, one day, one generation, one evolutionary era at a time. In terms of therapy, this process involves changing the narrative of suffering, alienation and trauma that stretches back through our life experience to our early development, and even further to our intergenerational heritage and evolutionary past. Finally, we begin to take on our own future suffering, that is, to anticipate the trajectory of suffering that would be caused by the continuation of our self-indulgent, self-limiting habits, and to change that course by taking the steps that act as causes and conditions of future health, freedom and happiness. This is analogous to the work of lasting self-change and life-change which occupies the final phases of a long-term insight therapy or positive therapy.

Gradually Giving and Taking with Others, Near and Far

Once we've successfully built the self-knowledge and self-care we need to take on our own suffering, the next step is to apply ourselves to the proactive work of taking responsibility for the quality of our interactions with others. While this may seem like a shift away from self-interest, traditionally it's seen as the natural expansion of the horizon of our self-interest to include our experience with others in the world we share. It's vital to see this expansion in context as the natural outpouring that comes of an overabundance of capacity, resources and well-being. This outpouring is natural since building a firm foundation of optimal self-care leaves us free from the distress that used to burden us and still burdens others, in touch with a whole spectrum of positive insights, energies and skills we developed in the course of learning to care for ourselves.

Of course, while it may come naturally for us to proactively engage with the suffering of others, the expansion of the range and scope of our engagement is incremental and gradual. Traditionally, we're advised to begin working to raise the quality of our interactions in our most intimate relationships first. As we know from the challenges of building truly positive relationships with significant others and children, this is a whole new training ground that requires patient and persistent application. Nonetheless, these relationships are seen as a prime training ground for the capacity to care effectively, so the practice of giving and taking with others should begin here.

From our inner circle, the scope of our capacity to effectively take care and give love expands next to include all the less intimate family, friends, neighbors, colleagues and acquaintances that make up the larger circle of those near and dear. Some of these relationships will pose more challenges than others, but each is an opportunity to grow more objective, more confident and more artful. Once we're essentially done with this circle, it's time to move on to the majority of humans who are effectively neutral: strangers we encounter in our daily lives.

Dispelling Irrational Fears of Contagion and Burn-Out

This step brings us to the most difficult challenge to the art: learning to take in the humanity of those who frighten, challenge or threaten us and to extend to them the same humanity we normally reserve for our loved ones. Here especially it helps to dispel some popular misconceptions about what "taking on others' suffering" and "giving others love" actually means. Influenced by irrational fantasies and fears of contagion, many who hear about giving and taking—even in Western Buddhist communities—have the false view that taking on others' suffering means suffering for others, as we were told Christ did for our sins.

Despite some traditional imagery and language which suggests just this, taking on the suffering of others in fact means actively taking their suffering into our awareness, and allowing ourselves to respond with whatever remembered or current experience of suffering in our own life most closely corresponds to it. This in no way entails feeling the same suffering others feel, especially when we have already learned to understand and heal the analogous ailments within our own mind. Instead, it gives us a basis for realistic empathy, that is, not mere sympathy or feeling just what others feel, but an empathic insight that sees the hurt for what it is and an empathic art that skillfully resolves it.

This view of "taking care" has obvious resonance with Freud's classical view the analyst's empathy, which involves using his own unconscious memories and associations as a receptive organ that helps him build an intuitive understanding of the client's suffering. Of course, here too, to the extent that the analyst has resolved the conflicts which resemble the client's, his empathy embraces the client's suffering with the wise compassion a parent brings to her child's myopic confusions and emotions. As a result of this higher level understanding and mastery born of self-care, the practicing altruist or therapist feels a relative sense of relief and gratitude in the face of what others find overwhelming and intolerable. And it is this spontaneous gratitude and satisfaction that provides the positive energy and emotion which flows out towards the other in the act of giving acceptance, encouragement, guidance, and love.

When we understand the emotional micro-economics of the exchange of giving and taking in this way, we can also begin to see through the misconception that giving love inevitably leads to caretaker stress and burn out. The degree of stress entailed by caregiving is proportional to the degree of unresolved conflicts and confusions in the caregiver, and has little or nothing to do with the level of distress and suffering experienced by the other. In fact, when one has effectively resolved at least the gross level of internal stress and trauma that burden and taint our natural care and love, the art of giving and taking becomes a source of deep satisfaction and ongoing learning, making it a profoundly rewarding and generative experience.

The last major misconception about giving and taking pertains specifically to the challenge of practicing it with people who threaten us in some way. The misconception is one we have run into before, namely that taking care and giving love is all about sweetness and light, and hence is impractical or masochistic in the face of threatening others. The fact is that a realistic understanding of others' suffering is as likely to require an act of tough love or fierce compassion as it is to involve being soft or nice. As when a child's intense upset, reckless exploration, or destructive impulses poses a risk of real harm, the natural and skillful response of a watchful parent will tend to be correspondingly fierce.

Likewise, the altruist who responds to the misbehavior of others with tough love or fierce compassion may seem every bit as assertive as one who reacts defensively, only the altruist does so based on an underlying sense of identification and fellow feeling, as if underneath the skin the threatening other was not an object of aversion but his own flesh and blood. While it may seem a nuance, there is probably no greater difference, both for the quality of the altruist's own experience and for the impact his response has on others.

Mount These Two on the (Out and In) Breath: Grounding Altruism in Mindfulness

Perhaps the greatest clue to the practical nature of the art of giving and taking is this precept to ground the contemplative work of taking care and giving love in the stress-protective physiology of breath-mindfulness. By conjoining the contemplative act of taking in others' suffering with the physical act of drawing a breath, the practicing altruist builds a discipline of grounding compassion in an altered state that doesn't just reduce the stress of caretaking but also helps balance attention to others with attention to self, offering some degree of insurance and quality-control over the process. In this joint art, breath-mindfulness helps us to stay ahead of our own mind/body response to others' distress and to bring the highest level of awareness and self-care to be sure that we optimize our capacity to see through and disarm primitive self-protective reactions and conditioned responses that might block or taint our mature care and love.

On the other hand, by conjoining the contemplative act of giving help and love with the physical act of exhaling a breath, the practicing altruist builds the discipline of grounding giving in an altered state that doesn't just disarm blocks to mature magnanimity but also helps balance attention to self and other, offering a degree of insurance and quality-control over this phase as well. Here too, breath-mindfulness helps guarantee that we stay in close touch with moment-to-moment fluctuations in our nervous state while sharing our resources, experience and inspiration with others, and quickly disarm any primitive antisocial reactions like compulsive clinging or obsessive mistrust.

Working together, conjoining taking care and giving love with mindfulness of the breath builds a powerful mind/body discipline of proactive engagement with others, no matter what their condition or state of mind. To use an automotive analogy yet again, once we've disengaged the compulsive survival mode of childhood self-indulgence and re-engaged the low-stress gear of positive social emotions like stress and love, mindfulness of the in and out breath serves to lock in a social emotional four wheel drive that empowers us to negotiate the roughest interpersonal terrain with maximal human traction and minimal wear and tear on our own body-mind.[84]

Meditative Experiment 4.2: Giving and Taking on the Breath

Find a quiet space, unplug from the world, and settle into a comfortable posture. Begin to clear your energy and mind by exhaling a long, complete sigh. Then let your next breath enter your lungs with as little effort as possible, and take that fresh breath as the start of a kinder, gentler breath-rhythm. Assure yourself that it's safe right now to focus on nothing but your breathing body-mind, and take the more relaxed rhythm of breath, centered at your heart, as a tether to reign in your wild or tired mind. As you breathe, imagine you're recalling all the energy and awareness you've put out into the world to get what you want or avoid what you fear, and gathering it back into you to rest on the rhythmic breath at your heart. If you start getting drowsy or dull, take some of that freshly gathered energy and awareness and breathe them into your clouding or fatigue to uplift your mind, firmly but gently returning your focus to the rhythmic breath at your heart. By alternately settling and uplifting, a breath at a time, you'll gradually find yourself shifting into a calmer, clearer, more balanced state of mind.

Now let your centered mind diffuse through your whole body with the fresh oxygen from your breath, awakening every tissue and cell until your body feels less dense and more fluid, light and clear, like a big, person-shaped lung or bubble of breath and life. As you continue to balance any restlessness and heaviness you feel in your body, open your mindfulness to the raw feel of sensation, and seek balance by letting go of attachment to comfort and fearlessly embracing any distress. Next, tune into your primal mind, balancing and centering yourself by diving below or between the surface waves of positive and negative thoughts or images, into the primal clarity and spaciousness of your deeper mind. From that space of deep clarity and calm, scan all the layers of your mind/body process, from the bedrock of your physical form and the undercurrents of sensation to the pure stream of consciousness that is your prime mind, finally opening your awareness to include the surface waves and reflections of mental content: positive, neutral and negative. Keep trying to ride the pure flow of deep mindfulness and, from within that flow, try to accept the whole range and scope of your body-mind while staying centered in a balanced space of clarity and calm. Now that you're more centered within your own body-mind, turn your awareness again to your environment, focusing on your relationships with others in the world.

Begin by calling up the image of yourself as a traumatized child or frightened animal, and try to approach yourself from your inner adult: the wise caring place of your centered clarity and calm. Now take in the full scope of your present suffering—whatever physical, emotional, or existential obstacles may overwhelm you now—and breathe in full awareness of them as temporary conditions which can be overcome with wisdom and care. Mixing that awareness of your sense of being overwhelmed with the objective empathy and confidence of your adult mind, take the relief you feel at recognizing your full capacity to help yourself or get reliable help and channel it into mature nurturing love and self-care, giving it to your inner child on the out-breath. See your inner child receive that love and care with a sense of relief, safety and hope, and gradually grow more secure, cheerful and involved.

Now do the same with the suffering that has burdened your inner child through the years, back to childhood, eventually including the burdens you inherited from past generations and humanity as a whole, not to mention the limits of the nature we all inherited from our evolutionary ancestors back to the dawn of life. As you breathe in awareness of the past burdens and limits that have weighed you down and mix them with clear realization of your full potential now, channel your growing confidence, insight, and empathy into intimate, cherishing love and self-care, breathing these out to your inner child and cornered animal.

When you begin to see the child and animal within you grow to feel safer, warmer and more open, finally turn to take on any burdens you can anticipate facing in the future, including the distant future of the next generation. Here again, breathe in awareness of the challenges you expect may come of negative causes and conditions within and around you, apply the full light and power of your clarity and calm to taking these on, and breathe out an optimistic vision for the future based on your growing ability to mobilize your full capacity and reach out to others.

Now that you've begun by taking on your own burdens, invite your secure inner child back into your heart and call up the image of the one other person you find it easiest and most natural to love. Invite the mind of that person to inhabit your image and go through the process of breathing in full awareness of his or her suffering and breathing out love, care and help. Do this gradually as you did with yourself, starting with present suffering, then past suffering and finally future suffering, taking care and giving love one problem, one breath at a time. As you practice, monitor your own personal reactions and any internal resistances to getting more engaged, patiently bringing self-awareness and self-care to each block as it comes so your capacity can grow naturally without your forcing it.

When you're able to go through this exercise with your dearest other, expand the scope of your practice one person at a time, first working through loved ones, then strangers (by locality, background, walk of life), and finally take on the people who challenge you, starting from the least threatening and ending with the most. To complement this systematic exercise of gradual expansion, it helps to focus part or all of some meditation sessions on recent social interactions that have been stressful, confusing, or upsetting. These "special cases" provide the best raw material to deepen practice, since they alert you to your traumatic reactions and blocks to empathy better than any generic exercise can.

(Monitor) the Three Objects, Three Poisons and Three Roots of Virtue

Having touched on the preliminaries and basic methods of clearing the mind, Chekawa's next instruction offers what he calls *the brief precept for the aftermath (in between meditations).* Once we've gradually educated and trained ourselves in clearing the mind and mastered the art of giving and taking, we're finally prepared to apply our newfound objectivity and compassion to our everyday interactions in the world. In practice, such application can't wait until our study and training are complete, but follows the general lines Chekawa spells out, albeit in a case-by-case fashion.

The final practice he describes involves monitoring our daily perceptions and interactions with the three "objects" or types of living beings distinguished by our biased mind—people we tend to view as objects of attachment, indifference and aversion—with an eye to seeing and treating all three with equal insight, empathy and compassionate art. This involves constantly working to expose and correct the three root poisons or primal stress emotions that bias our social perceptions and actions towards post-traumatic stress reactivity. By bringing rigorous honesty and mindful discipline to detoxifying the poisons that bias our perceptions and interactions, we simultaneously cut the roots of our self-indulgent life of reactivity and plant the roots of a new virtuous way of life: the healing intentions and motivations of non-attachment and healthy love; non-confusion, empathic insight and wisdom; and non-aversion, tolerance and effective compassion.

Discursive Contemplation: *Practice in All You Do with (the Help of These) Words*

The last precept in Chekawa's basic introduction to mind-clearing reviews the method of contemplative study and reflection he recommends. In the tradition of socially engaged practice evolved at Nalanda, focused and analytic meditation were seen as two complementary, mutually indispensable tools. Following the logic of the eightfold path, the beginning phase of discursive study and the intermediate phase of analytic reflection precede the final culmination of meditative learning. Of course, traditionally there is a clear recognition that some learn best by developing a meditation practice before cultivating analytic insight; while others learn best by developing analytic insight before cultivating focused, non-conceptual meditation.[85] Yet on both these paths, it is indispensably necessary to healing and change for all students to eventually complement their initial mode of contemplative learning with whichever mode they postponed.

Although we'll delve into the complementary roles of discursive analysis and non-conceptual focus in chapter 5, it's important to point out here that Chekawa's recommended method is not unique to mind-clearing.[86] It assumes the Nalanda consensus that mindfulness and concentration only temporarily slow or stop the workings of negative habits of mind, while discursive analysis, reflection and insight are needed to expose and cut out the instinctive roots underlying those habits once and for all.[87] As the best way to cultivate concentration is through mindfulness practice deepening over time, the best way to cultivate insight is through the natural progression from intellectual learning and analytic reflection to insight meditation that deepens with time. So Chekawa advises that, *To foster mindfulness of this (teaching),* one should *practice in all you do with (the help of these) words.*

Chekawa's Text and the Mnemonic Method of Contemplative Learning

This pedagogic method clearly accounts for the distinctive features of Chekawa's text. Though it encompasses a full spectrum of diverse contemplative disciplines, insights and methods, it distils them all into the disarming precepts he strung together in this guide to practice. The art of distilling profound and vast fields of learning into pithy, mnemonic lines like these is vital to any tradition that aims not just to reproduce formulaic knowledge but to guide contemplative learning, reflection and change.[88] The gist of this method is to help guide and illumine the inner journey of contemplation with pointers that are easily remembered in the midst of meditation or in the process of applying meditative learning in-between sessions to everyday life challenges. If Chekawa's text and pedagogy strike us as unusual, it's only because their style is not typically central to lay teaching and practice outside Buddhist monasteries. Yet it is this very method of scaffolding practice with memorable lines that has made and will continue to make his *Seven Point Mind-Clearing* such a powerful tool for mastering Nagarjuna's challenging practice of social engagement in daily life.

5 De-Reifying and Dismantling the Reactive Self

> Therefore, all the reasonings of the central way are factors in the eradication of the habit-pattern of misknowledge, the root of the (compulsive) life-cycle. Hence, having identified how our own unconscious misknowledge maintains its hold, we should strive to put a stop to it, and should not amuse ourselves with expertise in mere hairsplitting with other philosophers.
>
> (Tsong Khapa, *The Essence of True Eloquence*[1])

In these words of the great renaissance master Tsong Khapa (1357–1419), founder of the Geluk school of Tibetan Buddhism, the therapeutic imperative underlying all Buddhist teaching and practice rings clear as a bell. What may not be so clear to the untutored ear is the distinctive logic and method of self-healing he sought to explain to his fellow Tibetans. In his *Essence of True Eloquence*, he traces that distinctive logic and method back through the same lineage that preserved the mind-clearing practice. Before we return to the second point of Chekawa's text, to further unpack the actual practice of compassionate openness, it may help to put the spotlight on the distinctive way in which the Nalanda tradition understood and approached healing insight. That distinctive way has three main aspects: the therapeutic logic or rationale of healing insight in this tradition; the understanding of the nature and workings of delusion or misperception; and the contemplative therapeutic method used to put that logic and understanding into practice.

The Therapeutic Logic of Self-Analysis: Personal Freedom Versus Social Change

You may recall from our discussion in part 1 the causal model assumed as basic to all Buddhist psychology: the model of the twelvefold cycle of traumatic development. Within that cycle, there are two weak links where the conditioning of stress and trauma can be most easily broken: the eighth link of addictive craving; and the first link of self-reifying delusion. In Nagarjuna's map of the gradual path, the logic of personal self-healing through mindfulness is to break the cycle of conditioning at the eighth link—craving—while the logic of social healing through mind-clearing is to break it at the first link—delusion. The reasoning here is that renouncing addictive cravings and compulsive lifestyles through mindfulness practice is a more accessible first step for those embroiled in the cycle of stress and trauma, although it does not yield as profound a recovery as correcting the misperceptions underlying that cycle.

When it comes to the greater challenge of extending the self-healing process through our daily interactions with others still embroiled in that cycle, we need a deeper level of insight and corrective experience so as not to be triggered into falling back on old, compulsive habits. Of course, personal self-healing would be impossible without some real degree of healing insight. Likewise, social self-healing assumes a well-developed capacity for renunciation as well as deeper insight and more extensive empathic art. Rather than a black-and-white, either-or difference between these two phases or vehicles on the gradual path, the distinction is one of progressively deeper levels, greater scopes and finer degrees of insight-oriented practice.

The Deep Link Between Cognitive Self-Correction and Emotional Change

Supporting this distinctive therapeutic approach, the understanding Nagarjuna and his heirs have of delusion makes the path of profound self-analysis and healing insight indispensible to all contemplative self-change, personal, and social. While some Buddhist schools see false views and the self-reifying instinct as cognitive blocks to insight, clearly differentiated from the affective blocks caused by stress emotions like attachment and aversion, Nagarjuna, his close disciple Aryadeva, and the sub-school of their followers later defined by Chandrakirti see false views and the instinct for reifying them as both cognitive and affective blocks.[2] In fact, they see the self-reifying instinct as not just one among many affective blocks, but as the main taproot which gives rise to all destructive emotions, primary and secondary.

In effect, the Dialogical Centrist lineage of Chandrakirti views the cognitive component of stress and trauma as pervasively and inextricably involved with the negative affects that cloud our capacity for insight and empathy. What this means therapeutically is that, however much we ameliorate or renounce the disturbing emotions that drive the cycle of stress and trauma, there is no way to fully resolve those emotions or break their cycle without delving deeply into the root misperceptions that anchor them. Nagarjuna says in *Emptiness Seventy*, "The Teacher (Shakyamuni) proclaimed that misknowledge is the consideration that things arisen from causes and conditions are (intrinsically) real, and from that the twelve factors (of dependent origination) arise."[3] His direct disciple, Aryadeva, explains in *Four Hundred*, "Delusion gets into everything, just as the physical sense (pervades everything) in the body; hence, by conquering delusion, all compulsions are also conquered."[4] And finally, Chandrakirti, often called Nagarjuna's ultimate disciple, spells this out still more explicitly in his *Central Way Introduction:*

Figure 5.1 Nagarjuna, Master of the Engaged Path of Insight

Misknowledge, whose nature is the obscuration of the understanding of the real nature (of things) and the reification (of intrinsic reality) in things without intrinsic reality, is utterly false … Thus, the superficial truth (of mundane social consensus) is established under the influence of the compulsive misknowledge included (as the first link) in the (twelve) factors of existence.[5]

The instinct for misknowledge is the hindrance to complete comprehension of knowable things. It also exists as the instinct for desire, etc., and is the cause of corresponding (compulsive) functions of body and speech. Further, that instinctual propensity is only (fully) eliminated in Buddhahood or omniscience, and not in other (persons or stages).[6]

In terms of modern psychology, this distinctive view of misperception and its effects also clearly distinguishes the therapeutic approach of the Nalanda tradition from those of both the main schools of contemporary therapy, cognitive and analytic. While this view agrees with cognitive therapy that changing habits of thought and perception can help change learned emotional and behavioral habits, it differs in its assumption that learned habits are anchored in unconscious instincts which cannot be changed by altering thinking and behavior alone.[7] And, while it agrees with analytic therapy that learned habits are anchored in unconscious instincts, it differs in its assumption that the binary instincts of attachment and aggression are both rooted in a deeper instinct for misperception; and that all three of these can be unlearned by a method which combines analytic insight with emotional regulation and profound meditation.[8]

The Distinctive Method of the Centrist Tradition: Analysis, Meditation, and Dialogue

Finally, when it comes to that method, there are two features that distinguish the Nalanda tradition refined by Chandrakirti from the classical tradition of personal self-healing, as well as other methods of socially engaged teaching and practice. The method it prescribes for uprooting misperception is a more intensive version of the method of insight meditation taught within the mindfulness tradition. Like classical insight meditation, it works by conjoining the deepest stages of concentrative meditation with profound analytic insight into the reality of things, growing naturally out of the consistent practice of mindfulness and awareness. While the modes of analysis involved in this method are not qualitatively different from those employed on the path of personal self-healing, they are broader in scope, more penetrating in depth and rigor, and more extensive in duration. In Tsong Khapa's words,

> Although there is no other way to abandon these objective obscurations (of misknowledge) than the above-explained path of realizing the ultimate reality (of persons and things), the difference of the abandonments in the Individual Vehicle and in the Universal Vehicle arises from the (various) degrees of completeness of the factors of the method and from the duration of the time of familiarity (with the method).[9]

The second distinctive feature of the method prescribed in the Nalanda tradition is the radical way in which it uses language to help people transcend the limits and pitfalls of language.[10] Since the main engine of human intelligence is speech, the self-limiting instinct all animals share for reifying their own sense, percept or concept of themselves is most powerfully expressed in us as the unconscious reification of our linguistic forms of conception and expression. Since the most basic parts of speech are words for subjects and objects, the main forms of reification that limit our capacity for radical open-mindedness and open-heartedness are reifications of our constructs of the subjective experience of persons and the objective reality of things.

When we reify our constructs of the objective reality of things, we tend to fall into a more or less naïve realism, in which we confuse the words and images we project onto things for their true reality. Unchecked, this tendency eventually hardens into some kind of dogmatism, in which our minds close around familiar habits of thought and perception and impose these on reality and others, even when they don't fit. On the other hand, when we reify constructs of our personal subjectivity and experience, we tend to fall into a more or less naïve subjectivism, in which we confuse the concepts and images we have of ourselves for our true reality. Unchecked, this tendency eventually gets us mired in some form of idealism, in which our minds close around familiar self-concepts and self-images, impose these on our inner world and project them into the inner lives of others.[11]

The distinctive method of contemplative self-analysis systematized by Nagarjuna and refined by Chandrakirti avoids both these extreme tendencies, clearing a middle way that helps open our hearts and minds by counteracting the instinct for reification that locks us into the self-created cell of our own fabrications. Their Centrism uses language in a purely liberating way, not to impose any set of constructs on ourselves, others or the world around us, but to help ourselves and others find our way out of the trap of reified habits of thought and speech. It does this by assuming those habits are literally true as they seem, and then examining the persons or things they refer to until we expose the ways in which our mental habits conflict with reality as revealed by analysis.

So the method of self-analysis prescribed in this Centrist tradition diverges from the argumentative methods of mainstream philosophy, science, and religion, East and West, and converges with the liberative methods preferred by therapeutic philosophy and modern psychotherapy.[12] Though some describe this method as dialectical, I like to think of it as dialogical.[13] Like the Socratic method revealed in the *Dialogues* of Plato, its aim is not to advance our thinking towards some positive conclusion, whether fixed or evolving, but rather to free ourselves from the hubris that imagines any formula we construct could capture the ultimate reality or infinite complexity of things better than a mind that stays radically and consistently open to learning from others and the new.[14]

***After Reaching Stability, Reveal the Secret*: The Profound Insight of Emptiness**

In this chapter, we will unpack the key aspects of this method, by following the procedure spelled out in the remaining precepts of Chekawa's pivotal second point. Not surprisingly, that procedure begins by alluding to the profound theory of emptiness Nagarjuna built into one of the world's most rigorous methods for cultivating a radically open heart and mind. Chekawa's precept, *after reaching stability, reveal the secret*, alludes to a famous verse from the eighth chapter of Shantideva's *Guide*:

> So whoever wants to spontaneously protect
> Both themselves and others
> Should practice this noble secret
> Of exchanging self and other.[15]

Of course, the active ingredient in the secret teaching is the analysis of the emptiness of the constructs of self and other Shantideva invoked to expose our reification of those constructs in the preceding verses:

> Though there is no I there,
> Through the force of familiarity
> I cling to an "I" within a body
> That developed from the egg and sperm of others.
> In the same way, why can I not
> Identify "I" with the bodies of others?
> And likewise, I should not find it hard
> To identify "other" with my own body.[16]

To be clear, the de-reifying analysis and insight Shantideva invokes in this verse is not new, but recalls a similar observation made by Chandrakirti in the dedication to his classic on the altruist's path, *Central Way Introduction*:

> I honor those who feel compassion for beings
> Who circle as helpless as buckets in a water-wheel,
> Coming to insist on a self, once they say "I,"
> Growing addicted to things, saying "This is mine."[17]

And finally, Chandrakirti's insight in turn echoes a similar analysis invoked in *Jewel Garland*, Nagarjuna's guide to the profound practice of compassionate openness:

> "I exist; my (mind/body systems) exist;"
> Such (mere words) are mistaken for ultimate realities.
> Therefore neither of the two is found (under analysis)
> By complete knowledge of reality as it is.
> The (compulsive) mind/body systems arise
> From the conception of "I" which is false in fact.
> How could that which has grown
> From such a false seed be true?[18]

Of course, in the context of Chekawa's text, the secret to be revealed in the profound aspect of building compassion is the secret of targeting the traumatized self which chains us to the cycle of stress and trauma. Shantideva says as much in unpacking his verse on "this noble secret:"

> What wise person would indulge (such a false) self
> Or (compulsively) cling to this body (as "mine")?
> We should see the self-indulgent mind as our opponent
> And reject it accordingly.[19]

Yet it is equally clear that this pivotal mind-clearing strategy of confronting the traumatized self hinges on the insight that this debilitating sense of self in fact is not as real as it seems, but is only a reified mental construct, which is empty of any ultimate basis in the reality of our mind/body process. Whether we take the "secret" to be the teaching of targeting the traumatized self for analysis or the method of analyzing that self with the insight of emptiness, the reason why this profound phase of practice is kept secret until the student is ready is that it amounts to a delicate psychosurgery that must be performed with great precision and care.

The idea and insight of emptiness stands as a reminder that, however attached we get to our favorite network of words and images, the net is not the fish it catches. The metaphor is clear enough. We weave nets of language and conceptuality just as naturally as a spider weaves its webs. Yet the thing that makes our conceptual webs so exquisitely useful is their emptiness of any fixed form or anchor in reality, since this means that they can be endlessly altered to adapt to our own changing aims and needs, and endlessly applied in ever-new ways to the ever-changing world around us.

Where the Noble Secrets of Emptiness and Self-Analysis Meet

Just as we must take care not to misuse the term emptiness by mistaking people and things for being less empty than they are or more empty than they are, so we must take care not to misuse the term selflessness by subtracting too little or too much from our habitual sense of self.[20] The point of both these ideas is to help guide our self-analysis to a fully accurate understanding of who and what we really are, by helping us expose the extreme tendencies to see ourselves as more than we really are or less than we really are. With selflessness helping us see through extreme views of self which make us seem more or less than we are and emptiness helping us see through extreme views of mind/body systems and elements that make them seem more or less than they are, these insights work hand in hand to bring us to an accurate, working view of our selves and our lives.

Since emptiness is the more general of the two concepts, it helps insure that our self-analysis will avoid our tendencies towards the dualistic extremes caused by the reifying modes of projection and denial.[21] What is more, since language—used reflectively or in dialogue—is indispensible to the method of conjoining analytic insight with meditative clarity and calm, understanding how to use emptiness to expose and cut through even subtle abuses of language is absolutely critical to insuring the precision and effectiveness of contemplative self-analysis.[22]

All Things' Emptiness of Anything Non-Relative Equals Their Sheer Relativity

The best way to understand how emptiness works is to think of it as a conceptual formula or equation. On the one side of the equation, the negative term emptiness stands as a reminder of the kind of identity and reality we project into people and things, which they in fact do not have. On the other side, the positive term relativity stands as a reminder of the kind of identity and reality people and things in fact have, which we must affirm, not deny. While different schools of Buddhist thought define the kind of identity and reality people and things are empty of differently, the most general and simple definition is Chandrakirti's: emptiness means things are empty of any identity, reality, or objectivity that is not relative to causes and conditions, including social conventions.[23]

Chandrakirti's definition allows a very general and elegant formulation of the teaching of emptiness as a negative statement of the Buddha's positive teaching of relativity. It goes like this. All people and things without exception are empty of any non-relative reality, identity or objectivity; because all people and things without exception exist and work only in and through complex relationships of causal, conditional, and conventional interdependence. Spelled out in this elegant way, using the "royal reason of relativity," the "secret teaching" of emptiness seems too simple to be true. The whole equation sounds like a tautology; both sides of which state the same blatantly obvious truth, only one side says it in negative terms while the other says it in positive terms. All things lack anything in any way non-relative; and all things in every way are entirely relative.

The Therapeutic Uses of the Analysis and Insight of Emptiness

If the noble secret of emptiness, boiled down to its essence, is so disarmingly simple a child could grasp it, why is it considered so potentially harmful? And how could it possibly be so ultimately helpful? Again, the answer lies not in the teaching itself, but in the habit it is meant to heal. Unlike most of our words and ideas, emptiness is not presented as a truth supposed to be ultimately, absolutely or objectively true in itself. Instead, like the Buddha's four noble truths, this noble secret was designed and delivered as a medicine. The enormous potential benefit of this truth is that if we can take the medicine wisely and well, we may finally dissolve the confusion that weaves the tangled web which has mummified our minds in isolation and fear instead of freeing us for life.

The Noble Secret, Noble Truths, and Two Realities, Ultimate and Relative

To clarify the healing message of emptiness, the Nalanda tradition makes more than a casual comparison between this noble secret and the Buddha's noble truths. In particular, Nagarjuna and his heirs align the two sides of the equation of emptiness and relativity with two healing truths, ultimate and relative.[24] Like two sides of a coin, these two truths describe the same reality from two points of view. The emptiness side of the coin is aligned with the ultimate healing standpoint of Shakyamuni's Nirvana and enlightenment, described in the third noble truth. The relativity side lines up with the relative, conventional standpoint of the three other noble truths: of suffering, its origin and the path of self-healing. Taken together, the two truths work like a double-edged scalpel to help the analytic mind cut through reified projections of a self or life independent of causes, conditions, and social conventions, as well as through reified denial of the intentional agency which nonetheless shapes our suffering or happiness in dependence on causes, conditions, and social conventions.

In effect, the formula of the two truths sharpens and guides the scalpel of analytic insight to insure that our psychosurgery only cuts out the malignant tissue of delusion and misperception, while leaving the healthy tissue of intentional agency ready, willing, and able to act for our benefit. So Nagarjuna says, "Without relying on convention (i.e. words and ideas like emptiness), the ultimate cannot be taught; and without realizing the ultimate (truth of emptiness), one cannot reach Nirvana."[25]

In this key verse, Nagarjuna describes the healing logic of the two truths, also known as the two realities. By insisting on a method based on convention, he means that any effective way of teaching self-analysis must be framed in terms of the everyday social conventions of speech. Although the two truths are really two perspectives on one and the same reality, the nature of that reality is taught in terms that can be easily grasped by the human mind, namely in terms of the binary structure of human language and conceptuality. While the truths are defined in binary terms, to conform to the dualistic bent of our symbolic minds, the reality they refer to is not dualistic at all. To paraphrase a famous verse from the *Transcendent Wisdom Scriptures*, emptiness *is* relativity and relativity *is* emptiness.[26] Hence a genuine understanding of one truth involves a genuine understanding of the other, and vice versa. As long as our understanding of the ultimate emptiness of people and things seems to violate their relative compatibility with causes, conditions, and social conventions, that understanding cannot possibly be genuine. And as long as our understanding of the relative and conventional workings of people and things seems undermined by their emptiness of non-relative reality and identity, that understanding cannot possibly be genuine.

The Two Truths: The Equation that Reconciles Our Bifurcating Minds

If this non-dual formulation of the teaching of emptiness is to strike us as anything but a riddle or paradox, once again we need to understand it within the living context of our complex body-minds. The analogy used to help explain the seeming paradox of the two truths about one reality is the analogy of perceptual distortions like those we experience in dreams and illusions. These commonplace cases of perceptual distortion or error help illustrate the exceptional experience of analysis and insight which are the means and end of the teaching of emptiness.

When we experience a dream or illusion, one part of our mind has a perception which another part of our mind can expose and see through. Once our higher, analytic awareness examines the deceptive appearance constructed by our sense perception or dream state, we are no longer deceived or confused by that appearance. Instead, we are certain that the evidence of our experience is not as real as it seems, but mistaken; even though that certainty may not remove the illusion. When the spoon in a water glass looks bent to our eyes though our rational mind knows it's not, we experience a mundane version of the two truths: our minds perceive one reality in two seemingly conflicting modes. The resolution of the seeming conflict depends on our ability to prioritize our analytic insight and trust it to correct for the limits of our more primal faculties.

As the analogy of perceptual distortion suggests, the distinct perspectives of the two truths can be reconciled once we accept the ultimate truth of emptiness as a corrective for the reified perspective of the relative truth. In one sense, then, we can think of the two truths as correct versus mistaken perspectives on one and the same reality.[27] Yet to be fully effective, we still need to sharpen the double-edged scalpel of these truths, being careful not to take this helpful analogy for reality.

Shaving Your Mirror Image: How the World is Illusory Without Being Illusion

While some contemplative traditions, Indian and Western, see the everyday, relative world as illusion, the Buddhist tradition was always careful to qualify the analogy of misperception by insisting that the relative world may be illusion-*like* but is definitely *not* an illusion. So while ordinary people and things, causes and effects, agents and actions are mistaken in that they seem to be far more fixed and real than they in fact are, that does not mean that they are strictly illusions in the sense that they don't work at all. To underscore the distinction between things being less real than they seem and totally unreal or unable to work, Chandrakirti makes another analogy. Though the reflection of our face in a mirror is like an illusion in that it is less real than it seems, it is not an illusion plain and simple in that it is causally linked enough to our face that we can use the reflection to actually shave by.[28]

The Binocular Vision of the Two Truths: Two Modes of Perceiving a Single Reality

To sharpen our view of the two truths, then, we can think of the perspective of emptiness as the ultimate truth revealed by critical analysis and insight, and the perspective of relativity as the relative truth manifested in the unexamined workings of causality and social conventions. In this view, the two perspectives are two distinct mindsets or modes of knowing reality: an ultimate or critical mode, in which we critically examine things until we expose the truth that they are not as real are as they seem; and a relative or practical mode, in which we do not critically examine them, either because we are wrongly convinced that they *are* as real as they seem, or because we simply take them for granted and work with them without wondering how real they are.[29]

In order for us not to get too black and white about these truths, we must recall that the critical mode is ultimately true only in that it corrects the distortions that limit our practical mode. Likewise, the practical mode is mistaken or delusional only in relative terms, since it has two kinds of validity that most delusions do not. First, the misperception that things are real in themselves is valid in the sense that it is shared by most living beings, including the majority of our fellow humans. This is because it reflects the natural limits of our primal perceptual instincts and untutored faculties, just like common sensory illusions. Second, that misperception is valid in the sense that, used in an unreflective way to engage the world, it does not prevent us from relating effectively with people and things, either in terms of causal processes or in terms of social conventions.

The Medicine that Heals Our Blocked Insight Eye

With the symbolic organ of our mind's eye healed of the congenital disorder of reification, we are fully prepared to turn it inwards on the path of healing self-analysis.[30] Here, our new ability to see through the distortions of projection and denial guides us as we surgically remove the accretion of unrealistic expectations and doubts that blinds us to the actual workings of cause and effect, leading us off the middle way of genuine and effective agency. Whether we're looking at ourselves, others or the world we share, the healing formula of emptiness and relativity helps us expose and break the vacillating cycles of grandiose and paranoid outlooks, manic and depressive moods, obsessive and compulsive behaviors, all of which stem from our innate and learned reification of binary constructs of self, other, and world.

As we gradually cut through the tangle of extreme black and white ideas and habits we take for ourselves, we eventually arrive at a truly realistic view of ourselves, others, and the world around us. Awakened from the self-indulgent nightmare of reified narcissistic distortions, destructive emotions, and post-traumatic reactions, we gradually arrive at a realistic view of ourselves and our place in the world that reflects the triumph of principle over personality, objectivity over bias and causal efficacy over wishful thinking.[31] With this brief introduction to the "noble secret" of the emptiness insight and its role in the art of exchanging self and other, we can now return to the precepts of Chekawa's text, to map the path of self-analysis which leads to compassionate openness.

Consider the Dream-Like Nature of All Things: Breaking the Objectifying Habit

The first signpost on the path of self-analysis in this practice alerts us to one of the main sources of self-deception we humans and our animal ancestors are prone to: projecting our own wishes, fears, and confusions onto others and the world, and mistaking them for the objective reality of people and things as they are. A confused mix of reification and projection, the objectifying habit of perception is so automatic and primal that we are generally quite blind to it. One example of this habit figures prominently in psychotherapy, in the projection of unconscious parental images and associations onto the therapist. Known as transference, this self-deceptive habit doesn't function only in psychotherapy, but is busy clouding our perception of emotionally charged interactions throughout every day.

Yet however commonplace the insight of transference has become, very few of us—lay or professional—are aware that this type of projective distortion is not the exception in our perceptual lives but the rule. Decades of cognitive neuroscience research have overturned our naïve view that our perceptual apparatus works like a camera or mirror to objectively reflect the world around us. Instead, the emerging consensus is that the mind and brain work very actively to construct virtual maps of our natural, social, and cultural environment, and to project these out onto people and things as filters and guides for our interaction with the world.[32]

While the new consensus on perception in brain science is overturning our long-held modern view of waking state consciousness as a mirror of reality, it is no news at all for Indic contemplative science, especially in the Nalanda tradition. According to Nagarjuna and his heirs, the world as it normally appears to us is a mere construction of consciousness projected onto reality, with individual minds more or less coordinated by social conventions of language and action. All this construction may be quite useful, even when it is automatic and unconscious, provided it actually helps us engage with others and the world in ways that are effective and mutually beneficial.

Emptiness of Subject-Object Duality: The Deconstructive Psychology of Asanga

According to one voice in the Nalanda tradition, the Constructivist lineage of magnificent deeds traced back to Asanga, the most helpful interpretation of emptiness is that it refers to the lack of any substantial or essential dichotomy between the inner life of the mind and our experience of the external world.[33] In this view, the perceiving subject and perceived object are not just empty of any ultimate difference, but both in fact boil down to binary constructions of one and the same agency: the subconscious mind. The main analogy used for this critical insight is that our normal waking experience of self and world as independent realities is deceptive, just like the self and world of a dream. So when Chekawa directs us to *consider the dream-like nature of all things*, he is encouraging us to expose and see through the reified constructs of self and world we unconsciously craft and mistake for independent realities.

Without the insight to correct such distortions, our own minds deceive us into taking the worst-case fantasies we project on the world at face value, locking us into a self-fulfilling gloom-and-doom prophecy that unnecessarily disappoints and re-traumatizes us over and over again. As long as we choose to pursue a path of peace and well-being in the everyday world, we need to be able to see through our false views of people and things, even when our delusion is consensual and seems to be reinforced by everyone and everything around us. As in the consensual illusion of cinema, in daily life our brains and bodies believe what our entrained imaginations feed them, and respond to a shared virtual experience of the world as if it were in fact a reality.

The Dream is Not Just a Dream but Reality as We Know It

While contemporary neuroscience, social science and philosophy now agree that our consensual worldviews, popular and scientific, are psychological and social constructions, the Centrist critique Chekawa implies goes quite a bit deeper than our most radical post-modern thought. One could easily assume, in the neo-Kantian spirit of Karl Popper,[34] that what this precept means is that this critique applies to our mental constructs and views of the world, not to the evidence our senses give us about material things, which exist in themselves. But the critical analysis and insight of emptiness includes not just mental constructs and images but even the unprocessed evidence of our senses and the objective physical elements that give rise to it.[35]

So when Chekawa points to the illusory nature of the world as we know it, he doesn't simply suggest we *consider the dream-like nature* of our mental projections, but explicitly draws our attention to the dream-like nature *of all things*. Given this, we can see that the analysis and insight of emptiness challenges not just our habit of objectifying conscious worldviews but also our instinct for objectifying the raw data of our senses. In short, it challenges us far more than current science or philosophy, assuming a reading of the notion of relativity more radical than that of today's strongest critics of our naïve view of things as being just as they appear to us.

Examine the Uncreated Nature of Mind: Breaking the Subjectivity-Habit

Once we've burst the bubble of our own naïve worldview and opened ourselves to others and the world as they are, Chekawa's next precept encourages us to delve deeper into the self-deceptive workings of our own minds. It assumes the gradual refinement and critique of depth-psychology within the Nalanda tradition.[36] The first step in this second leg of the engaged path of self-analysis is to expose and cut through our instinctive tendency to hang our sense of self on certain contents within our mind, including verbal self-constructs, perceptual self-images, familiar emotions and raw sensations. Applying the traditional view which identifies mind with the primary process or medium of consciousness rather than with any of its constructs or acts, this precept challenges us to delve below the surface of our cluttered waking minds to examine the deeper layers of awareness we tap into in altered states like deep, dreamless sleep.

The insight here is that our tendency to grab hold of certain mental contents and cling to them as reference points for all our experience and action is neither necessary nor effective, but reflects the conservative instincts of the reactive mind. However understandable this habitual identification with contents is, it inexorably narrows, biases, and obstructs the optimal expanse and flow of consciousness, creating a clot within the mind-stream which limits, clogs, and blocks its full transparency, plasticity, and creativity. While the deeper, more primal layers of consciousness are less differentiated and less symbolically active, that also means that they tend to be more intensely focused and less content-bound. Although we normally only experience these layers in primal states like dreamless sleep, orgasm, or near-death experience, Indic contemplative science assumes that we can train higher consciousness to tap and link them into a more integrated, synthetic consciousness with deeper clarity and radical openness.[37]

Primal Awareness, Metacognition, and Vegetative States: I'm Not What I Think

In addition to challenging our instincts for identifying with and clinging to mental content, the very idea of giving the process or medium of mind primacy over its constructs challenges the modern view of consciousness since Descartes. In that view, consciousness is identified strictly with thoughts and the agency that thinks them, and so is limited to humans and restricted to the waking state. While this view of mind grew out of modern philosophy, it was taken up by modern science, as is reflected in the current medical reduction of consciousness to the symbolic activity of the primate cortex.[38] This view is only now being challenged, based in part on reports from people who have emerged from so-called vegetative coma states or near-death experiences yet seem to have preserved a continuous primary consciousness that allowed them to observe, remember and recall events which took place around them while they were supposedly "brain dead" and devoid of all consciousness.[39]

So it is that Chekawa's precept to *examine the uncreated nature of mind* challenges both our instincts and our modern view of our minds as identical with the thought content of our waking state. By encouraging us to see through the surface symbolic content of our minds into the deeper medium that creates and recognizes that content, he is effectively urging us to shift our whole frame of reference on consciousness toward the process of knowing rather than the forms of symbolic knowledge it produces.

The aim of his directive is to help us turn awareness back on itself, in a reflective process that reveals the nature of knowing as distinct from the forms of the known. It is this radically open, transparent element of consciousness that Chekawa points to as the natural state of mind, a state which, unlike its manifold creations, is itself uncreated.[40] Whether or not we agree with this radically process-oriented view of the mind, the benefits of being able to come at our inner life from this vantage of radical freedom from habitual contents should be obvious. In fact, some of these benefits have been demonstrated in recent efforts to enhance the effectiveness of cognitive therapy with the enhanced freedom and objectivity made possible by even simple mindfulness, which some describe as "meta-cognition."[41]

Deep Mindfulness, Primary Awareness, and the Spacious Equipoise Intuition

In practice, this step on the path of radical open-mindedness is an extension and deepening of the basic exercise of mindfulness of mind. Through persistently prying the mind free from its habitual attachment to positive and negative thoughts, emotions, and images, we gradually begin to experience a new state of mind, usually described as having qualities of spaciousness, openness, clarity, contentment, and peace. Initially of course, this shift in consciousness may seem strange, even threatening, as we experience an increasing separation from our familiar reference points of identity and perspective. So we're advised to examine this altered state carefully until we come to recognize and own it as the primary process of mind, the natural home of our awareness and source all the familiar constructs created by mind. As we grow increasingly familiar and at home with this deep experience of mind, we grow able to immerse ourselves more and more deeply in it, and so come to taste and master the state-specific qualities it has to offer us.

Unlike the dream-like insight the last precept asked us to cultivate, the practice of immersing ourselves in the uncreated nature of mind aims at an insight described as spacious, which combines an experience of radical openness with an unwavering equanimity and peace of mind. In effect, this spacious insight helps us realize that it's not just our projections of an outer world which lack objectivity. By helping us experience an unbounded openness with no reference point on which to hang our sense of a separate, isolated inner world, it allows us to realize the mind's emptiness of any fixed identity or subjectivity.

In this sense, the two insights Chekawa recommends—dreamy and spacious—work together to help us experientially realize the emptiness of any fixed, non-relative distinction between inner and outer, subject and object. The outcome of this two-pronged analysis is to effectively expose our normal mode of subject-object experience as an elaborate, unconscious construction of mind. The power of this two-edged analysis and insight to free us from the complex of reified instinctive structures, emotional memories, and learned constructs we mistake for the reality of our lives is obvious.

The Union of Analysis and Quiescence: Tapping the Depths of the Natural Mind

Technically, the emptiness insights developed on the path of self-analysis are seen as based on a contemplative method which joins analytic insight with concentrative quiescence.[42] Practically, this compound method grows out of the deepening of mindfulness and awareness developed in the basic and intermediate practice of mindfulness. In particular, analytic insight grows out of the deepening and refinement of awareness, while quiescence grows out of the deepening and refinement of mindfulness. The transition from deep mindfulness to the practice of insight and quiescence begins in earnest when mindfulness and awareness are aided by the intensification of effort and the eventual growth of expertise.

When this compound insight meditation is turned reflexively on itself, it delves beyond mere mindfulness of mind to expose and transform the deepest nature and workings of consciousness. This practice of self-analysis is key not just to the ordinary practice of compassionate openness but also to the secret practice of blissful openness taught in the Process Vehicle we'll explore in parts 3 and 4. Consequently, the synthetic systems of self-analysis transmitted into Tibet by Padmasambhava, Naropa and Atisha, present this art of examining the uncreated nature of mind in light of the final stages in the highest level practices of the Process Vehicle, called the Great Seal and Great Perfection. As we'll see in the precepts that follow, these parallel teaching traditions differ only in whether the depth of the mind is mapped in terms of a critically revised version of the Constructivist subconscious or of the still more critical, neurolinguistic model of the Process Vehicle.[43]

Though using such insights to access the primal clarity of mind is a common practice among the Indic contemplative traditions, and is touted by many as the final goal of self-analysis, the Nalanda tradition assumed by Chekawa's text challenges this conventional wisdom. For the most critical of Nagarjuna's heirs, accessing the spacious openness and lucid clarity of the primal mind is not the end-all and be-all of self-analysis, but a helpful platform or jumping off point for a still deeper realization of emptiness and more radical experience of openness. The added depth and openness, however, comes not just from a deeper level of quiescence or concentration, but rather from combining deeper focus with a more profound analysis and insight into emptiness.[44]

The Final Meanings of "Uncreated:" Mind as Naturally Disidentified and De-Reified

In terms of Chekawa's precept, this deeper level of analysis corresponds to two more profound senses of the adjective "uncreated." First, not only is the primal mind not to be confused with any symbolically created subjective identity or perspective, but when examined still more deeply it even lacks any criterion, reference point or identifiable character of belonging to any particular self or person, i.e., of being intrinsically "mine." This sense of the term uncreated is especially key to exposing even the most primitive, unconscious sense of a fixed, unitary or independent subjectivity or point of view, which could act as the seed for the construction and reification of a mentally created sense of self.

Recognizing the mind as "uncreated" in this sense helps to challenge our reifying instinct to seek a hook somewhere, somehow within our stream of consciousness on which we can hang our habitual sense of having a fixed, unchanging self. In effect, the insight that our primal consciousness is empty of any such fixed identity or point of view means that it is not created or born as "my mind;" that it has no built-in bar code or mark of identity which would allow it to be distinguished from any other mind. As Shantideva made clear in his verses on exchanging self and other, this breakthrough has the power to infinitely expand our capacity for empathy with other minds. Its potential application to the practice of compassionate openness is clear.

The final sense of the term "uncreated" points us to the most profound and freeing of all insights into the emptiness of the mind. This is the insight that, when fully examined under the microscope of contemplative self-analysis, the ultimate nature of mind turns out to be empty not just of any fixed personal identity but even of any iota of fixed, independent or intrinsic identity *as mind*. Such a profound insight into the objective reality of consciousness effectively transports us out of the trap of subjective bias generated by our self-protective instinct for reification. So Shantideva concludes in his Guide, "Just as illusion-like forms lack any intrinsic reality, so it is with the mind that perceives them."[45] For a glimpse into the experience of these deepest insights into the natural mind, consider these verses from Chokyi Gyaltsan's *Highway of All Victors*:

> While a special insight directly perceives
> The true nature of mind as such,
> Nothing can be shown or grasped as "this,"

Whatever dawns, it rests naturally, without grasping.
The great Himalayan meditators of today
Proclaim more or less in unison
That this is the prime directive which grants
Attainment of Buddha's illumination.
Be that as it may, I, Chokyi Gyalsten,
Pronounce this method as (no more than)
A technique of remarkable effectiveness
For diligent beginners to gain mental stability
And to recognize the superficial mind.
As for the method of precisely identifying
The ultimate reality of mind,
I offer the personal advice of my root Mentor,
Who cleared the deluded gloom from my mind,
And who, in the guise of a saffron-clad monk,
Embodied all the intuitions of Buddhas!
In an equipoised state, (examine) the mind:
Pure openness with no static material,
(Where) diversity dawns and evolves unobscured;
An incessant stream of lucid awareness
That engages (objects) without interruption.
Though it seems independent as an object
Of (mental) perception, (when examined)
By reasons and references like Savior Santideva's,
"So-called 'masses,' 'continua' and such
Are as artificial as garlands and armies,"
The way it appears is unfounded (on analysis);
So rest single-pointedly in its (empty) nature.[46]

By immersing ourselves in breakthrough insights like the one Chekawa and Chokyi Gyaltsan describe, we effectively climb out of our own biased minds, not just in the sense of overcoming our personal self-indulgence, but in the objective sense of no longer seeing ourselves and other minds as ultimately distinct from the natural world around us. The potential of this insight to deepen compassionate openness lies in the way it helps to galvanize impartial empathy and free up a spontaneous, impersonal response to the needs of others and the world we share.

Even the Remedy Itself is Objectively Free: Breaking the Denial Habit

The final step on the path to openness Chekawa maps turns our reflection back on itself yet again, to expose and correct any dualistic tendency to reify the negative logic or findings of the emptiness insight. As the self-reifying frame of reference for our habitual perceptions of self and world is gradually deconstructed, revealing their emptiness of any ground in reality or mind, the self-protective instinct of the reifying mind is to cling to what seems to be left, namely the insight, analysis, and findings which help us realize that emptiness. This natural reflex is what drives us towards the extreme of denial that comes of consciously or unconsciously reifying the language and logic of emptiness.

Just as Descartes was tricked by his own mind into reifying the language of his positive reflection—I think, therefore I am—into self-evident truth, those who use the negative logic of emptiness as an aid in self-analysis may abuse this potent medicine and get hooked on it like a conceptual drug. In particular, the danger Nagarjuna and his heirs warn about is the tendency to reify emptiness into an ineffable something or absolute nothing, either of which then acts as an opium of sorts—whether mystical or cynical—rather than a genuine cure for the human condition. So Chandrakirti says, in his *Reason Sixty Commentary*,

> When you introduce beings who are intellectually unprepared to the view of reality—voidness—they become utterly confused. Consequently, the noble do not teach them voidness right at first...When not taught in this (gradual) way, students may succumb to error through the teaching of voidness, since they may come to confound the principle of the two realities, superficial and ultimate. In such cases, they would be unable to avoid non-virtue, since the intellectually inept might cling to the idea, "this world is void." Hence, (thinking), "If this is voidness, what use is it all," they may not be inspired to cultivate the virtuous actions that make success certain. Consequently they may be destroyed, like a bird with undeveloped wing feathers thrown from its nest.[47]

Later in the same work, Chandrakirti calls the noble secret of emptiness "the sublime secret instruction of relativity."[48] And in this he echoes a celebrated formula of Nagarjuna's which Tsong Khapa found so important he thought it should be added as a refrain to each and every analysis of emptiness on the path of insight:

> If you regard things as existent by virtue of (a reified) intrinsic reality, you thereby regard them as bereft of causes and conditions. And thereby you are condemning effects, causes, agents, actions, activities, originations, cessations, and even fruitional goals. Whatever is relativity we proclaim that emptiness. Nothing whatsoever is found which is not relativistically originated. Therefore, nothing whatsoever is found which is not empty. So if all things we *not* empty, there would be no origination and no destruction.[49]

So in order to work effectively, the negative insight, analysis and findings of emptiness—that objects and subjects, world and mind lack any non-relative, self-sufficient reality or self-evident identity—must be understood as simply ruling out that they have any kind of reality or identity that would keep them from being causally created, transformed, or destroyed, without implying that they have any other kind of reality or identity, positive or negative. As such, emptiness must be understood logically as the pure and simple negation of a family of malignant errors our minds instinctively tend to make. And the proof of this pudding is that the same insight, analysis and finding is applied reflexively to emptiness itself, guided by two key Centrist principles of self-analysis: the emptiness of emptiness; and the freedom from any reified position or point of view.

The Emptiness of Emptiness: Avoiding a Mystical View

Like a self-dissolving suture, the truth of the teaching of emptiness lies not in its intrinsic validity or self-evidence but rather in its usefulness as a remedy for the mind's self-deceptive instinct of reification. While the subject and object of any perception naturally appear to us as self-sufficient and self-evident, we know by examining their intimate dependence on one another and the sensory faculty that mediates their contact that they are not in fact as independent or given as they appear. Such careful analysis eventually brings certainty that the self and things we experience as so real, including our minds themselves, are in fact empty of the kind of reality our instincts unconsciously project into them. Yet here we come to a crossroads where our analysis could easily fall from the extreme of projection to the opposite extreme of denial. To prevent this misstep, we must learn to contemplate not just the emptiness of persons and things, but the emptiness of emptiness itself.[50]

Once we've arrived at a glimpse or even a deep insight into emptiness, its time to turn the scalpel of analysis back on itself. We do this by reflecting that the emptiness insight, like the people and things it examines, is itself the object of a perception that has validity only through relations of mutual dependence. As an inference of our discursive mind, the truth of the emptiness insight inexorably depends on the perceptual error it exposes, the conventions of logic and language that support it, and the negative finding that people and things when examined do not have certain kinds of reality our faculties naturally see in them. So the truth of emptiness is itself empty, entirely relative to the reifying instinct which projects a false sense of unity, fixity, self-sufficiency, and self-evidence into all we perceive and imagine.

To perceive or imagine this purely critical, de-reifying reminder as a fixed, unitary, self-sufficient or self-evident void would involve the blatant misunderstanding and abuse of the teaching Nagarjuna called "taking emptiness as a(nother reified) view." So all his heirs—from Aryadeva to Chekawa and his modern descendents—insist on teaching the emptiness of emptiness as a fail-safe against any such misunderstanding or abuse.

The Emptiness Insight as a Self-Corrective Capability

Seen in this light, the genuine analysis and insight of emptiness support what you might call a negative capability, a new rational certainty that conclusively overrides and corrects our self-deceptive habit of reifying our own mental constructs. This is in fact how Tsong Khapa describes it in his *Essence of True Eloquence*.[51] Yet, this does not in any way deny the validity or positive efficacy of developing and maintaining virtuous habits, such as the healing skills of personal self-care or the social-emotional virtues of compassion cultivated through mind-clearing. Once the emptiness insight has done its work of clearing our minds of the cobwebs of reified constructs, it doesn't leave us in a mystical or skeptical void, but rather opens and frees up our minds, unlocking the power of our positive intentions to seek freedom and happiness for ourselves and others. While the complexity of the way emptiness fosters openness may be hard to grasp, in fact it is no more unusual than the range of capacities which allow us to mix insight, illusion and action at one and the same time: knowing with certainty that our reflection in a mirror is not our real face; perceiving the illusion nonetheless, like a dream, as if it were our real face; and using the reflection to shave, without ever examining whether it's real or not.

Emptiness as a Self-Dissolving, Freeing Truth

Of course, the idea of a self-dissolving truth, one that is ultimately healing while being thoroughly relative, is so unfamiliar as to boggle the mind. Apparently we are not alone in having trouble wrapping our minds around the nuances of this healing insight. Chandrakirti addressed at great length the doubts his contemporaries had about how a thoroughly relative or conventional emptiness insight could possibly lead us to such ultimate, freeing truths. In fact, the analogy of his I cited, in which he compares the emptiness insight to shaving with the help of a mirror reflection, he used to illustrate his distinctive view that the inference of emptiness could be ultimately true despite the sheer relativity of its premise, logic and findings. In his *Introduction Commentary*, he affirms that the reasoning of emptiness, though thoroughly relative and conventional, still effectively rules out the possibility that our reified constructs of people and things are as real as they seem, "Refutation devoid of intrinsic reality refutes what must be refuted, and a reason, even without (intrinsic) validation, being devoid of intrinsic reality, proves what is to be proven."[52]

This may sound like a paradox, but in fact is straightforward, since the premise to be proven is that all people and things are totally relative, while the presumption that must be refuted is that causality, agency, reason, and language have or need some non-relative nature or essence in order to work. The teaching here feels hard to swallow not because of any internal illogic, but because it flatly contradicts our instinct for reification and the ingrained, extreme habits of projection and denial it engenders. However disillusioning and disorienting that may feel, we must recall that reification is precisely the disease that the medicine of emptiness is meant to cure. This is why Chekawa's precept—*even the remedy (the emptiness insight) itself is objectively free (of intrinsic reality)*—puts the self-dissolving seal on that medicine which guarantees its safe and effective use.

Emptiness as the Remedy for Any Self-Limiting Point of View

Since the pure negation of emptiness is meant to be therapeutic not dogmatic, it must not be reified into a positive stance, narrow viewpoint or set position of any kind, either in our own minds or in our dialogue with others.[53] Like the self-dissolving logic of emptiness, the principle of avoiding any rigid position directly challenges the driving instinct and cultural habit we humans have of reifying our favorite constructions of language and knowledge into supposedly objective truths. In contrast to the dogmatic or didactic method of most systems of knowledge and practice, the principle of positionlessness urges a therapeutic or liberative method closely aligned with the therapeutic philosophies and psychologies of modern thinkers like Nietzsche, Wittgenstein and Freud and ancient thinkers like Socrates.[54]

Like Wittgenstein's method of language-games and Freud's method of free association, this principle begins not from a fixed preconceived standpoint, but rather with a radical openness to whatever form of thought or perception seems to be troubling us or others. It proceeds by accepting these forms as they are, and then critically examining their health or illness, truth or falsehood, until we and others can see through our own self-limiting perceptual biases and habits of thought.[55] Once we are freed of these limiting blocks and habits, and our minds opened up and expanded, the language and logic of emptiness have done their work and can be left behind, just as the dialogue of psychotherapy ends when it has healed the suffering that prompted it.

Understood in this way, the principle of holding no reified position serves as a safeguard against the reification of the language of the reflective mind, even of the healing language of Buddhist thought and practice. In stark contrast to Descartes' reification of his reflection into a supposedly analysis-proof "first principle," the Centrist tradition of self-analysis aims squarely for the healing goal of radical openness, and sees any clinging to forms of perception or thought as blinders that narrow and bias the mind. Like the "complete clarity" sought by Wittgenstein, Nagarjuna aimed his teaching at the pure freedom of compassionate openness, which he called "the peace that resolves (all) perplexity."[56] To help prevent this healing teaching from being perverted into a rigid dogma or doctrine, he warned,

> "All is empty," should not be asserted, nor should "all is not empty," "all is both (empty and non-empty)," nor "all is neither (empty or non-empty)." Each is maintained (only) in the (appropriate) context in conventional

> reality.[57] The taming of all perceptions, the resolution of all perplexities, that (alone) is supreme peace. The Buddha never taught any doctrine to anyone![58]

And, in *Reason Sixty*, he explained in more detail the importance of the principle of not holding to any reified, self-limiting habit of thought or speech as "I" or "mine," both in terms of breaking the hold stress instincts and traumatic reactions have on our minds, and in terms of helping others find their own way to greater openness and freedom:

> If any sort of hold is found,
> The cunning poisonous snake of compulsion
> Will seize it; but those whose minds
> Have no (such) hold, will not be seized.[59]
> Great souls are beyond disputes,
> (For) they assume no (reified) position.
> For those whose minds have no (such) position,
> How can there be opposition?[60]

These verses make clear the logic behind using emptiness to de-reify even our most cherished habits of thought and speech. Since reified errors of thought serve to rationalize traumatic distortions and emotions, there is simply no way to tame and heal our traumatized self without seeing through our reified habits of mind. As long as any such habit remains, even attached to the healing language of emptiness, the mind will never fully free itself from reifying and identifying with traumatic distortions and stress emotions. The practical experience of this most profound level of self-analysis is described in the following verses from Chokyi Gyaltsan's *Highway of All Victors*:

> From within the prior state of equipoise,
> Like a minnow darting within still, clear waters,
> The subtle consciousness critically examines
> The nature of the person of the meditator.
> You should investigate it following the formulation
> Of the Savior, Noble Nagarjuna,
> "Since the person is not solid, not liquid,
> Not gas, not energy, not space,
> Nor consciousness, nor their sum,
> Nor apart from them, what person is there?
> As the person has no ultimate reality,
> Because it is composed of sixfold elements,
> So each of its elements has no ultimate reality,
> Because each in turn is also composite."
> When you cannot discover even a subatomic particle
> Of equipoise or someone equipoised,

Then cultivate space-like equipoise,
With unwavering single-pointedness.[61]

While the dream-like insight into things helps us see through reified projections and the space-like insight helps us break through reified constructs of the subjective mind, this insight into the emptiness of words and symbols helps de-reify habits of speech that rationalize and reinforce our habitual narrative of "I" and "mine." Practiced in sequence, these insights gradually bring us towards the aim of complete self-analysis, just as progressing on the path of meditation through the realms of pure form and formless absorption help prepare us for the final realization of Nirvana on the path of self-healing.

The Actuality of the Path Rests in the Fundamental Realm: Embodying Openness

The various levels of insight Chekawa alludes to in his text are not just conceptual, but link directly with a practical map of the experience of contemplating emptiness over time. This precept and the next describe that linkage of theory and practice in a clear and straightforward way. According to the practice tradition, the actual experience of meditating on emptiness follows a predictable path. It begins when we decide to critically analyze the surface appearance that people like our friends and things like our homes are self-sufficient and self-evident, examining whether we find any basis in reality for their appearing so ultimately real. Inevitably, when we examine their parts, their causation, their transformation in time and/or their conceptual aspects, we find no non-relative being or essence that would support that surface appearance.

Once our analysis has conclusively shown the lack of anything that could ground the deceptive appearance of people or things, our habitual perception of them seems to dissolve, leaving a space-like sense of their absence traditionally called the spacious equipoise intuition of emptiness. Like the experience of disillusionment when we expose a perceptual error or sensory illusion, this intuition is especially profound when we've just seen through something near and dear to our habitual view of the world, such as our sense of self. The experience feels as if the whole world around us and our whole inner world have just dissolved, leaving our consciousness unhinged from its familiar framework and bearings, absorbed in an otherworldly trance.

While normally, we would take such an otherworldly experience as an altered state and dismiss it as an outlying point to be relegated to the margins of our "real" daily lives. To the contrary, Chekawa is advising that the practice of clearing the mind for compassionate openness begins to be real when we choose to accept this de-centering experience as a new normal or reference point around which to re-center our lives. In effect, we do this by taking its spacious equipoise as the "groundless ground" on which we will base a whole new way of life. In practice, this intuition lines up directly with the space-like insight cultivated by deeply examining the uncreated nature of mind, especially when that insight is sealed by a reflexive analysis of the discursive awareness which lead to that insight. The act of immersing our mind in the radical openness that follows and choosing to take it as the foundation on which our way forward rests effectively aligns our new lives with the healing edge of our contemplative insight.

Of note, the language Chekawa uses to describe this new grounding in openness is the depth-psychological language of Buddhist Constructivism. In that context, the "fundamental realm" he speaks of would refer to what is left of the subconscious mind when self-analysis has completely healed the traumatized sense of self, by seeing though its reified, traumatic constructs of the inner and outer world. Once the mind has undergone a complete inner revolution and turned away from that afflicted subjectivity, the split between the conscious and subconscious mind disappears, and the mind is restored to its natural state of unblocked, pure awareness.

This depth-psychology was later refined in light of Chandrakirti's psycholinguistic approach to the mind, and eventually integrated with the neurolinguistic depth-psychology of the Process Vehicle. In view of these refinements, Chekawa's precept actually refers to the subtle realm of reality experienced by the subtlest depth-consciousness, known to his contemporaries as the objective clear light.[62] Regardless of terminology, this precept directs us to dissolve our habitual projections and biased subjectivity into a radical openness to others and the world, an openness that allows us to embrace other perspectives with the objective clarity of an omniscient narrator.[63] It is this radical openness that galvanizes the cultivation and exercise of universal compassion with the selfless wisdom that knows myself as another and others as myself.

Between Sessions Act as an Illusory Being: Embodying Compassion

Once we've seen through the surface of appearances and embodied the most profound openness in the form of the spacious equipoise intuition, sooner or later the interplay of subjects and objects resumes, and we find ourselves back again in the relative world. To borrow the simple imagery of the Zen koan made popular by pop singer Donovan, "First there is a mountain, then there is no mountain, then there is!" The next experience on the path of contemplating emptiness links up with the insight of the dream-like nature of things. Called the illusory aftermath intuition, this experience involves the mixed mode of perception we described as a negative capability.

In it, the people and things of the world reappear, only now they are clearly seen in light of the breakthrough experience of the spacious equipoise, as being less real than they seem, just like dreams, illusions, reflections or mirages. And, as Tsong Khapa insists in his formula of the authentic view, this aftermath must not be confused with a mystical sense that reality is out of reach or a cynical sense that the world is illusion. Rather, it opens up a new sense of the dream-like fluidity of self, others and the world we share, combined with the lingering peace and openness of the spacious equipoise. In the aftermath between meditations, these two intuitions work together to heighten our ability to connect empathically with others and their diverse points of view; as well as our ability to flexibly alter our habitual way of being so that we can respond more naturally and skillfully to others' true needs and perspectives.

By suggesting we practice between sessions using the illusory aftermath to shape a whole new way of being in the world, Chekawa is showing us how the insight of emptiness can foster the deeper openness and greater flexibility we need to reshape our habitual self so it can more fully embody the spirit of love and compassion. So he suggests we *act like an illusory person* not because our actions or person are ineffectual illusions but because our ability to see our mind/body process as a dream-like raw material can help free us to reform it into a more effective agent of compassionate openness.

Based in the radical freedom of spacious openness, the illusory person we practice becoming in the aftermath between meditations is also free to learn, grow, and change in a radically new way. By living as if, in Shakespeare's terms, "we are such stuff as dreams are made on," we have the capacity to make our daily lives into a self-creative process, aimed at embodying our highest ideals with the living fabric of our flesh, mind, and nerve. In terms of the language of Buddhist Constructivism, Chekawa's precept may be seen as an allusion to the idea that, once the ultimate truth of emptiness has been realized, the relative workings of mind are naturally transformed into forms that embody the peace and compassion of enlightenment. As in the case of depth-psychology, this Constructivist view of enlightenment—also refined by Chandrakirti—was then integrated with the depth-psychology of the Process Vehicle, in which the embodiment of enlightened forms of expression and action is described as the illusory body.

Integrating the Spacious and Dream-Like Modes of Emptiness Insight

Beyond the first pendulum swing from spacious openness to illusory personification, the path of self-analysis moves through a narrowing oscillation between these two complementary poles of insight. Gradually, the seeming polarity between these two emptiness insights resolves, and we grow to experience them, in Tsong Khapa's words, without alternation, as two inseparable sides of the same fabric of empty relativity.[64] Left unexamined, this illusory fabric feels like transparent, empty appearance; once examined, it feels like a spaciously open, apparent emptiness. So with time, all appearances "dawn as emptiness;" and all emptinesses, as appearance. Eventually, as repeated immersion in profound spaciousness increasingly opens our mind, and repeated re-emergence at the illusory surface helps us personify empathic art, these two sides are interwoven so seamlessly that they are fully melded in one synthetic fabric of compassionate openness.[65] This reversible fabric made of spacious and dream-like insight marries the ultimate and superficial truths, realization of emptiness and relativity, in a mind of selfless openness and a body of pure compassion. With this mature integration, we've reached the final fruition of the path, known as the ultimate spirit and perfect embodiment of enlightened altruism.[66]

When the Environment and (All) Life are Poisoned by Vice: Self-Analysis in the World

With this provocative precept, Chekawa moves on to the third point of mind-clearing practice: using contemplative self-analysis to transform our way of being in the world. Although the application of self-analysis to daily life is said to take place in the dream-like aftermath of the spacious insight which de-reifies our habitual self-sense, the tradition sees such practical application as anything but an afterthought. This opening precept stands as a clear reminder of the lay orientation of the socially engaged teaching which this text and practice distill.

Of course, the insight that the everyday world and its life are polluted by misperceptions and toxic emotions is not new to Buddhist contemplative science. The toxic influence which the causality of stress and trauma exerts on the minds, bodies and lives of beings of all kinds is what defines the normal cyclic condition of compulsive life. In Chekawa's precept, the term "vice" refers to the vicious role this causal cycle plays in poisoning our mind/body systems as well as the natural, social, and cultural environments we co-create. What is novel about the engaged teaching tradition on which this practice is based is that it is explicitly designed for those who choose to build a contemplative life by staying within that world rather than by renouncing it in favor of a monastic community set apart.

Another way this precept is often read takes off from the temporal qualifier "when." According to some Indic traditions, the changing nature of contemplative teaching and practice over time is explained by invoking a process of historical decline, social corruption or cultural decadence which requires more potent remedies to suit the age. Of course, civilization has historically become more complex and inclusive as it has evolved, and with that increasing complexity and scope comes increasingly challenging problems. But this process may also be seen as one of progress, with civilization and contemplative ways spreading to less fortunate segments of the population within ancient centers and to less developed societies at the margins of the civilized world.

Viewed in this light, the word "when" should be read more generally as describing a circumstance in which one is trying to build and spread a contemplative way of life within a less reflective, more rugged sociocultural environment. Looking at the historical context in which the art of mind-clearing spread to remote regions like Indonesia and Central Asia, this reading would seem more consistent with what we know about the intentions of masters like Survarnadvipa and Atisha.[67] Read in this way, Chekawa's precept also seems relevant to the transmission of these teachings to the West, despite the fact that we are now in an age of rapid global advancement, at least on the level of material development and access to information.

As we learned in chapter 3, many of the mental and emotional habits Buddhist psychology identifies as vices are cherished as virtues or at least defended as harmless preferences within the mainstream traditions of the modern West, scientific and humanistic, materialistic and religious. Although some or all of these are deeply ingrained in our cultural institutions and way of life, the consensus emerging from new sciences like stress research, neuroscience, positive psychology, sociobiology, and behavioral economics suggests that the Buddhist tradition may well be right to point out the risks and challenge the benefits of such habits. Chekawa's precept aligns with this new consensus in viewing many aspects of our way of life as culture-bound errors and self-defeating habits that must change for us to thrive sustainably, as individuals and as a society. This defines the art of compassionate openness through mind clearing as a form of non-violent resistance to compulsive ways of life that have dominated our culture for centuries.

Turn Adversity into the Path to Enlightenment: The Alchemy of Self-Transformation

If the context for practicing mind-clearing is a social environment that indulges obsessive, compulsive, and addictive ways of life, the key to that practice is learning to take social stress as an opportunity for deeper self-analysis and self-change. Harking back to the opening of the second point, *drive all blame into one*, this precept indicates the high road we must take in our interactions with others mired in stress, namely: rising to the challenge of taking responsibility for parenting our own distress well enough that we can avoid being triggered and respond with mature empathy. While we all celebrate dramatic gestures of heroism and altruism, from the standpoint of this practice, the rubber of enlightened altruism meets the road of daily life in the routine obstacles we run into whenever someone we're interacting with has fallen into a rut of traumatic repetition, stress emotion, or compulsive behavior.

This seeming paradox is central to the path of social engagement advanced by Nagarjuna and his heirs. It is symbolized by the analogy of the altruist who matures in the midst of the world to the lotus that grows out of the mud. Traditionally, this deep character change is also conceived in terms of the Constructivist idea of a fundamental transformation or "inner revolution" in consciousness, as well as in terms of the process-oriented notion of an alchemical transmutation at the deepest, subtlest levels of the mind/body process. The secret ingredient that galvanizes this profound change is the wisdom that helps us to see through the reification of our traumatized self and so open our hearts and minds to engaging others in a more mature and proactive way. The reason we don't take this high road more often is that we lack the necessary perspective and strength to climb out of our childhood rut and step up to it. This is why clearing the mind is an indispensable discipline for those of us who are committed to fundamentally changing our whole way of being in the world.

Apply Meditation to Whatever You're Facing Right Now: Make the Practice Your Life

All too often, we turn to meditation as a refuge or even escape from the daily challenges of our lives. We may make it a pastime, a hobby, a getaway, or sanctuary of pristine purity, serenity, and calm, but that approach to practice will never fundamentally change our lives. Like the ultimate vacation from which we must inevitably return to our laundry and bills, an escapist practice of meditation may refresh and even restore but ultimately leaves the basic conditions of our lives unchanged. In a sense, this approach is natural in any culture where spirituality or contemplation are seen dualistically, as a pure, sacred realm set apart from the mundane tasks and burdens of the everyday world. But the basic premise of the socially engaged approach to contemplative life distilled in this practice is that meditation can play a vital, pragmatic role in transforming the conditions of everyday life in the world.

The Best Method is (Practice) with the Four Preparations: The Yoga of Everyday

Of course, most of us, especially early on, will be unprepared to apply meditation in real time to whatever challenge we're facing in the present. So until we're ready to meditate on our feet, so to speak, Chekawa's next precept spells out the kinds of regular exercise that will gradually prepare us over time to use our practice to meet challenges in the here and now. Some of these preparations are similar to those practiced on the preliminary path of personal self-healing, some are specific to the socially engaged path of compassion. In my experience, I've found it helpful to distil the motivational psychology of these preparations from the ritual context in which they are traditionally practiced.

In that light, I define the four preparations as follows: (1) correcting unhealthy habits; (2) cultivating positive energy and action; (3) offering generosity in the face of obstacles; and (4) building trust in the efficacy of positive motivation, practice, and development. As a shorthand, I refer to these as correcting vices, cultivating virtues, welcoming opposition, and building trust. Though the first two of these should be generally familiar from our brief look at the motivation of personal self-healing in chapter 3, I'll begin by reviewing them and describing how they help to motivate and guide social self-healing.

The First Preparation: Correcting Unhealthy Habits

The preparatory practice of correcting unhealthy habits is vital for beginners who want to learn to practice clearing the mind. Since more often than not we're blind to our reactive habits until they make themselves painfully obvious in our interactions, the first task of self-analysis on this path involves retrospectively looking at incidents in which we've found ourselves triggered by day to day social stress. Learning how to see these incidents for what they are—to see through the unhealthy self-habits driving them—is the first step in changing our ways over time. As in most deep learning and change, the first step in the fourfold process of self-correction is to break through our habitual projection and denial so that we can clearly see our part in negative events—the perceptual distortions and destructive emotions underlying our traumatic, stress-reactive habits—and have realistic, healthy regret or remorse, rather than self-indulgent self-pity or self-hatred.

Once we've stopped blaming others and clearly identified our part in the problem, even if it's only withholding empathy out of fear or being triggered into past trauma, we're now ready for the second step: turning to reliable sources of guidance who can model realistic self-knowledge, self-mastery, and healthy alternatives. Traditionally, this step involves confessing our limits and faults to select role-models and peers, or generally to the historic or mythic community of noble sages and masters, enlightened beings and altruists. Inspired by healthy models, traditions, and communities to believe that a better way of being in the world is possible and accessible, the third step is to commit or resolve to avoid our unhealthy habits in the future and to learn to shift our outlook, motivation, and habits towards healthy alternatives. Such commitments and pledges are often rehearsed ritually by reciting affirmations or prayers for blessing and help. The final step is to actually practice new ways of seeing, feeling, and acting that will replace unhealthy old habits and the instincts underlying them with healing insight, positive motivations and compassionate action.

As we apply these four remedial powers—regret, reliance, resolve, and correction—retrospectively to our negative interactions, we inexorably prepare ourselves to apply meditation to challenging situations in real time. Gradually, a thorough post-mortem of our missteps becomes more rapid and certain, until we can begin to see our mistake in real time, as it's being made. Finally, we're able to anticipate triggering situations and avoid unhealthy reactions before they arise by proactively choosing a healthier way to engage and respond.

The Second Preparation: Building Positive Energy and Momentum

Beyond the first aid of self-correction, the next preparation—building positive energy and virtues—takes off with the new leaf turned by the four remedial powers. This practice involves conceiving, initiating and maintaining the exercise of healthy capacities: from the cognitive powers of learning, analysis, insight, and intuition; through the affective disciplines of mindfulness, concentration, distress tolerance, positive emotions and flow; right up to the behavioral skills of positive intention and motivation, communicative speech, effective social action, communal service, and inspired action. Just as systematic self-correction leads over time to whole new degrees of freedom from internal resistances and blocks, building virtues yields not just areas of expertise but a cumulative momentum of positive thought and action that acts as an altruistic critical mass or positive psychological capital, accumulating exponentially through the compounding synergy of effort, application, and mastery.[68]

In terms of mind-clearing practice, the preparation of removing blocks breeds openness while the preparation of building virtues builds compassion, eventually bringing us to the point when we can master the art of proactive engagement by resolving problems in real time with either one or both these wings of altruistic life. Symbolic of this accumulation is the ritual practice of dedicating virtues and positive energy to our long-terms aims and goals. Traditionally performed by reciting formulas of dedication, this practice essentially earmarks or deposits accumulated enthusiasm and mastery into a virtual "bank" in which they safely gather interest by being merged with the accumulated energy and virtues of all contemplative individuals, enlightened altruists, and fully enlightened beings.

The Third Preparation: Practicing Generosity in the Face of Resistance

The third preparation, offering generosity in the face of resistance, should be familiar in principle from the art of giving and taking. This exercise prepares us to naturally respond to others' distress and limitation by taking the high road of proactive acceptance and responsibility rather than by falling back into reactive opposition and conflict. The gist of this preparation involves a fundamental shift in our childhood sense of ourselves as small and helplessly dependent on the good will of larger, more powerful others. The reflex of falling into resistance and conflict with individuals, institutions or cultures that obstruct our aims or interfere with our progress is a regressive reflex based on our traumatized childhood self and our primal self-protective instincts, which typically results in the demonization of such obstructions.

Invariably, such demonization only compounds the resistance we face from others, while pointlessly stressing our systems and hijacking the higher faculties we need to negotiate such obstacles. This preparation goes to the heart of that reflex, the unconscious longing we have to be accepted, helped, and cared for by others, which effectively transfers our unresolved childhood dependency onto unreliable individuals, institutions, and cultures. By rehearsing over and over again our full, current capacity to choose the high road-not-taken, we can engage limited, deluded, or afflicted others from a proactive stance of confidence, empathy, and adult responsibility.

The Fourth Preparation: Building Trust in the Efficacy of the Positive

The final preparation, building trust in the efficacy of positive motivation and action, works to complement the preparation of offering generosity to obstructers, much as the practice of building virtues complements that of correcting bad habits. As I said, underlying our tendency to demonize obstructions is an even deeper tendency to idealize others in the hopes that they will protect and care for us. Nowhere is this deeply ingrained childhood coping mechanism more glaring than in the circumstance modern psychologists call identifying with the aggressor.[69] The insight here is that children, who quite reasonably feel small and helpless, and adults who still identify with that childhood sense have a natural social tendency to seek out and admire others they see as strong and powerful enough to protect and care for them.

The problem is that this naïve tendency involves a distorted perception of strength which leads us to see more self-involved, neglectful or abusive others as truly powerful, and so to seek to be near or like them. In fact such ingrained might-makes-right misperception is not unique to humans, but belongs to a family of primitive instincts of dominance or submission that seems to color the group behavior of many if not all social animals. The aim of this final preparation is to expose such childhood distortions and disarm the primitive instincts underlying them, so that we are more resistant to conformist impulses that would block our capacity to think and act as free social agents who can engage in truly non-violent resistance or civil disobedience towards individuals, institutions and cultures who dominate through overt or covert violence.

To help prepare us to feel and act like free and effective social agents, this fourth practice works to build and strengthen our trust in the ultimate effectiveness of positive social motivation and action over any antisocial forces like brute military or economic might, self-serving cunning, or self-satisfied entitlement. Of course, the foundation of this trust is rational analysis and certainty of the supreme importance of positive interdependence and social cooperation in human fortunes and in moving towards a sustainable future. This involves exposing any primitive instincts or confused notions that would make it seem that even the most powerful or ruthless of individuals acting alone or in small numbers could possibly equal the collective power of the shared aims, interests, and actions of whole human communities or of civilization itself.

Vital to any such self-correction is the certainty that all such reactive habits belong to the cycle of stress and trauma which hijacks the powers that make us the most effective form of life on earth. This preparation helps us internalize and rehearse the systematic disarmament of our primitive self-protective habits and the transfer of our security needs onto models, traditions, and communities that embody the higher faculties of social learning and collaboration. As with offering generosity, this preparation is traditionally practiced through ritual enactments in which we offer ourselves and resources to protective archetypes of enlightened intention and action, requesting their blessing and support of our positive efforts. This involves a gradual transformation from childish clinging to authoritarian habits towards a mature commitment to egalitarian, consensual alternatives. This shift reflects the gradual internalization of the rational insight that our security and efficacy comes not from any narcissistic personal power but from sober respect of the natural powers of causality and human consensus.

Meditative Experiment 5: The Royal Reason of Relativity

Once again, unplug from the world as much as you can and settle into a comfortable, stable posture. Clear and center your breath, either by alternate nostril breathing or by exhaling a long, full sigh, then sweetly welcoming a fresh, gentle breath. Use the sweetness of this gentle rhythm of breath to center your mind, alternately reigning distracted energy and awareness in to rest on the breath and rousing flagging energy and awareness up to meet the breath. As you gradually ease in to a kinder, gentler breath-rhythm centered at the heart, immerse your mind in the subtle chemistry of the breath and ride that wave out to every cell in your body and back to your heart again. Tuning into the lighter, more fluid physicality of your "body of light," now scan your raw sensation, embracing your whole comfort level and trying to balance excitement, indifference and distress. Finally, turn your mindfulness reflexively onto your mind itself, delving beneath the surface activity of positive and negative thoughts, feelings, and images to the deeper flow and spacious clarity of your primal awareness. From within that clear, calm space of deep mindfulness of mind, now scan all five of your mind/body systems: more centered breathing body; more balanced raw sensation; the bare awareness of intuitive perception; your full range of emotions from healthy to toxic; and your range of thinking from delusional to enlightened.

Next, again prepare yourself by tapping into your most positive motivation. First, revive your basic urge to free your mind from stress and trauma by contemplative learning, living and practice. If it helps, again review the eight insights: life's preciousness and brevity; the causal power of mental acts and the wild mind's self-destructive effects; the impossibility of escape and the need to tame the mind through healthy reliance; as well as the decisive commitment to break free of stress and trauma. Now stir the heroic spirit that chooses to realize and spread enlightenment for all, as by reviewing the four steps of equalizing empathy, clearing self-indulgence, building compassion, and exchanging self-bias for altruism, or the seven steps of recognizing kindness, nurturing gratitude, taking responsibility, giving love, engaging with care, strengthening resolve and galvanizing enlightened altruism. You may touch on these points lightly or take as much time to reflect on them as you need.

With your body-mind centered and your motivation fresh, now turn again to the practice of self-analysis, insight, intuition and openness. Begin by scanning the surface activity of your waking mind, trying to expose and see through your habitual forms of desire and aversion as projected and reified constructs of your primal confusion. Remind yourself of how often you fantasize how nice it will be to be with someone you desire, only to be disappointed or disillusioned by the real interaction. Remind yourself how often you project your worst fear or childhood trauma onto people you have an aversion to, only to find through some real interaction that they're neither as threatening nor as malignant as you'd imagined. And remind yourself of how often you completely overlook or fail to notice people you're indifferent to, only to later find through real acquaintance that you'd been missing out on someone in some way truly relevant, interesting, and vital to your life. Finally, survey this whole scope of habitual engagement with objects of attachment, aversion and indifference, and try to trace the roots of your obsessive-compulsive mindset down to the depths of your instinctive habits of fear-based clinging, stress-reactive anger, and shame-based self-pity.

However clear a glimpse you've gotten into the network and roots of your reactive mind, turn your full attention inwards now and reflect that this network with its roots is the delusional system that turns your interactions with others in the stress-world into a nightmare. However free you might feel in deeply contemplative states, once you return to daily life, this network reasserts itself, like an in inner straight-jacket that holds your traumatic memories and stress emotions in place. So choose now to not rest content with such fleeting states, but to use your mindfulness as a platform to clearly and objectively expose and see through your habitual system of self. Within the space of sheer clarity and openness, begin to analyze the network and roots of your habitual self-sense using the simplest of all frameworks of self-analysis, called the three keys.

First, try to vividly recall the last time your felt deeply threatened, misunderstood or unseen. Notice the way you cling to your body as a fixed entity or precarious fortress you must defend. Scan your sensations, and try to feel how your distress about the present and longing for the future both lock you into the self-enclosing survival mode of the fight-flight reflex. Watch your mind, and see how closed it is around self-indulgent victimized sense of self, fear-based clinging to attachments, and blind projection of blame onto others. Tune into your emotions, and feel the toxic cocktail of shame, fear, and rage that quickly poisons your whole body-mind. Finally, examine your inner dialogue and face the obsessive rush of worst-case thinking, self-indulgent self-pity, and reflex assertions of blame. Overall, pinpoint the way your habitual sense of self is reified as fixed, unitary, self-sufficient and self-evident. Try to get a clear view of how adamant and convinced you are of the rightness of your experience of being objectively threatened, alone, misunderstood, deprived, in need, helpless and hopeless. Now commit to examining this felt sense of self thoroughly and decisively, until you can reach the conclusion that that sense is either based in reality or is not.

The third and final key of this quickest and most elegant form of self-analysis is to scan through your habitual sense of self from within your clearest and most poised state of mind, looking carefully for any systems, elements, moments or aspects of your mind/body experience which are not thoroughly relative. Once you delve critically into your sense of self as having a fixed identity and independent reality, you'll begin to see how intimately it relates to and depends on the systems that support your life, and how these in turn relate to and depend on a range of constantly changing elements, moments and aspects of experience. By taking this in as deeply as you can, your habitual felt sense of self will gradually seem to fade and melt into a flow or space of seamless, selfless relativity. Repeated over time, this analytic insight grows more intuitive, and your reified experience of yourself in the world—with its threefold network and roots—will begin, piece by piece, to break down and dissolve. Such breakthroughs should eventually merge into the intuition of spacious openness, which in turn will transform into the dream-like aftermath that will help you reengage with the world far more openly, empathically and flexibly.

So for now, imagine that each time you practice the three keys of self-analysis with the royal reason of relativity, you're chipping and melting away the reified habits that lock you into a reactive mode in the stress-driven world. Imagine your threefold network of dear friends, feared enemies and strangers, along with their roots in clinging, reactive blame and shame-withdrawal gradually melting into a sheer spacious openness, which you are now free to take as your new, open mind. Next imagine that, as you re-engage the world with more dream-like fluidity and empathic art, your old, guarded body will naturally shift towards a lighter energy of acceptance and care, which you are now free to take as your new, caring body. Embracing this new mind and body—as both subjective experience and objective events—imagine owning them as the wings of compassionate openness that will support your emerging life of enlightened altruism. Finally, remembering that the wings of this life only fly thanks to the spacious and dream-like intuitions of emptiness that unburden the mind/body process of its cognitive and affective blocks, reflect that the emptiness intuition is all you need to protect your new life from the poisons within you and all around you in the world.

6 Altruism and the Path of Engagement

While Disciples and Hermit Sages come from the Great Sages (the Buddhas),
(All Perfect) Buddhas evolve from Enlightened Altruists;
Hence the (prime) causes of a Victor's heritage are: the (altruist's)
Compassionate mind and bias-free openness, the (twin) spirits of enlightenment.
So honoring love, which alone acts as the seed for this bountiful harvest of Victors,
As the water that nurtures it, and as the endurance that brings the crop to fruition,
Before (explaining the altruist's life), with gratitude I bow to compassion!

(Chandrakirti, Central Way Introduction[1])

To Distill the Essence of (These) Precepts: The Genuine Spirit of Altruism

Now that we've gleaned from Chekawa's text the essential practice of compassionate openness and explored its application in daily life, it's time to turn to the path of ethical discipline and moral development mapped out in his four remaining points. Chekawa's fourth point—integrating a lifelong practice—focuses on the gradual integration that occurs in the long transition from building motivation and insight to final realization. One way to locate that transition is with the help of the five stage map of contemplative practice we surveyed in chapter 3. While the five stages on this map—accumulation, application, insight, meditation, and mastery—have the same names in this context, here they map a distinct path of contemplative life: the path of socially engaged practice.[2]

According to the tradition of Nagarjuna, as explained by Chandrakirti and Tibetans like Tsong Khapa, this path extends the classical path of personal self-healing by conjoining the deepest levels of concentration with more profound wisdom as well as with the altruistic spirit of universal compassion. To locate the path of compassionate moral development described in Chekawa's fourth and fifth points, we'll need to place it in multi-disciplinary context: juxtaposed with the five stages of socially engaged meditative progress on the one hand, and with the fifteen topics of reflection on the path of socially engaged insight on the other.

For simplicity, we'll align Chekawa's fourth point, integrating practice, with the first two stages of meditative progress—accumulation and application—as well as the first five themes of reflection—grounding, clearing, building, reorienting, and inspiring. His fifth point, measuring progress, lines up with the last three stages of meditative progress—insight, meditation, and mastery—as well as the last ten themes of reflection—the ten transcendent virtues of generosity, ethics, tolerance, endurance, meditation, wisdom, technique, affirmation, power, and intuition. The sixth and seventh points offer lists of commitments and pledges meant to provide practical precepts for building an altruist's life in the world.

You Must Apply Them With the Five Powers

To begin, then, Chekawa's precepts on lifelong practice first urge us to move beyond the initial phase of intellectual learning or familiarization, "*To distill the essence of the (basic mind-clearing) precepts.*" Over and above the preliminary exercises he prescribes in the third point for assimilating the basic precepts of mind-clearing—the four preparations of correcting vices, cultivating virtues, welcoming opposition and building trust—Chekawa directs us to integrate practice and metabolize those basic precepts by building five motivational powers that deepen reflective learning. As in the path of personal self-healing, these powers start out as basic contemplative faculties—effort, wisdom, mindfulness, concentration, and confidence—innate in us all.[3] Through continuous cultivation over time, they gradually become potent forces for good and eventually mature as the exceptional motivational powers of a highly contemplative mind.

In contrast to the more circumscribed form these powers take on the path of self-healing,[4] the form they take on the engaged path of social healing is more inclusive and expansive.[5] The effort to heal and free oneself takes the special form of compassionate motivation to benefit all; the wisdom to renounce vice takes the form of targeting and uprooting self-reifying habits; the mindfulness to cultivate virtues takes the form of planting seeds for change in the present moment; concentration through deepening mindfulness takes the form of familiarization through repeated practice; and the confidence to pursue inner freedom takes the form of positive endurance in the development of a new self and world. Extending Chandrakirti's agricultural simile for the altruist's path, I like to call these five powers: preparing the ground; weeding; seeding; nurturing; and enduring. In what follows, we'll first see how each of these five forces of behavioral change help us "*distill the essence*," and then we'll align each of them with phases on the engaged path of contemplative practice and with one of the themes of reflection on the path of socially engaged insight.

Among the powers Chekawa prescribes to motivate progress on the path of social-emotional development, the first three—preparing, weeding, and seeding—line up with the accumulation stage of engaged contemplation, in which the basic mindset, insights, and life-skills that lay the foundation for an

Figure 6.1 Shantideva, Master of the Altruist's Way of Life

altruist's life are gradually acquired and integrated. The last two—nurturing and enduring—line up with the application stage, in which we begin to apply that new foundation to transforming our knee-jerk responses to the daily challenges of our lives. As for the way these motivational powers align with the growth of empathic openness on the engaged path of insight, they expand on the basic points of the mind-clearing practice unpacked in the last two chapters. Preparing the ground expands on building the foundation of equanimity and genuine compassion, as in Chekawa's point one and the first half of point two. Weeding corresponds to exposing and cutting through the self-reifying, self-protective habit which is the taproot of compulsive life, as in the latter half of point two. Seeding, nurturing and enduring correspond to taking adversity as an opportunity to plant seeds of non-clinging, non-violence, and non-delusion, as in point three. We can also recognize in these emerging powers the four reflections of Shantideva's method of exchanging self and other, the quintessence of which is the final shift realized in the genuine spirit of enlightened altruism.

Preparing the Ground: Leveling our Interactions with Others

To begin with, Chekawa advises that we start distilling the essence of mind-clearing by directing all our efforts towards building realistic empathy and authentic compassion for all life. So the work of preparing the ground of our life for the cultivation of our natural altruism must begin with the prodigious effort Thomas Nagel aptly calls, "climbing outside of our own minds."[6] While the idea of an altruistic spirit and way of life appeals to the idealist and the enlightened realist in us all, the learning curve which the stress-reactive animal and traumatized child inside us must climb to actually experience and respond to the world in an impartial way cannot be underestimated. In fact, our instinctive and conditioned resistance to seeing all life fairly and objectively is so enormous that many individuals and social groups throughout history have assumed that it is fixed by nature or God and beyond our power to change.

Growing research on social evolution, emotional intelligence and the neurobiology of the prefrontal cortex, as synthesized by pioneering psychiatrist Dan Siegel, have conclusively shown that optimists like the Buddha and Nagel were right: all humans have the innate capacity to see others objectively, as equal to ourselves.[7] The discovery of mirror neurons that specialize in helping mammals like us put ourselves in others' shoes has been further amplified by findings that the prefrontal cortex which is unique to humans includes multiple structures and pathways dedicated to helping us control primal appetites and self-protective instincts in light of our empathic awareness of the needs and wishes of other individuals and larger social groups.[8] Add to this the recognition that our nervous systems are naturally plastic and continually reshaped by our moment to moment attention and action, and the pessimistic faith that we are incapable of living up to altruistic ideals is fast losing ground.[9] In its place is the pragmatic question of how much time, attention, and effort we can and should devote as individuals and groups to exercising and building our emotional intelligence and higher social skills.

This is where Chekawa's first power comes in. Effectively, it tells us that our progress on the path of positive social-emotional development is limited only by the effort we channel into feeling and caring for others as equally sensitive and deserving as ourselves.[10] Since the only genuine source of that effort is the strong motivational force that comes of feeling spontaneous empathy and concern for others, this precept not only points the way to our becoming more engaged with all life but also makes clear that there is *no other way* for us to become so engaged.[11] With this look at the first power we need to distill the essence of clearing the mind, it's time to align this ethical step on the altruist's way with the steps of contemplative practice that help build the mindfulness and awareness which make such progress possible.

The Universality of the Noble Truths: The Engaged Accumulation Stage, Part I

As you may recall from chapter 3, the accumulation stage of contemplative practice is sub-divided into three phases. In order to map the socially engaged accumulation stage alongside the ethical path of clearing the mind, we can roughly align these three phases with the first three of the five powers. The main distinction is that here, these phases travel the contemplative path with a broader, more inclusive perspective of empathic awareness which sees how the causality of suffering and happiness affects not just our own body-minds but all life around us as well. As on the path of self-healing, this phase involves bringing mindful attention to our body-mind, building the capacities for bodily self-regulation, fear modulation and response flexibility supported by our prefrontal cortex.[12] And while we explore the four noble truths with the four scopes of mindfulness, as on the path of self-healing, in this context we apply the resulting insights—impermanence, dissatisfaction, emptiness, and selflessness—equally and simultaneously to our own lives and to the lives of all other beings. This begins the long process of enhancing self-regulation with the social capacities for empathy, communication, and insight supported by other regions of prefrontal cortex.[13] This provides a solid grounding for the contemplation of our equality with all other life, and a natural extension of the realistic empathy we feel for ourselves to all others, whether near, far or seemingly indifferent to us.

The First Reflection on the Path to Altruism: Equalizing Self and Other

Along with the power of preparing the ground and the practice of extending mindfulness of the noble truths to all, our first steps towards an altruistic life are guided by the first reflection on the socially engaged path of insight. The theme is one we've encountered already in Shantideva's fourfold method of building compassion. His method begins with recognizing the basic equality of self and others, a reflection I like to call grounding. By freeing us from the self-enclosing bias of our traumatized self, this reflection keeps us from poisoning our social life with the misguided habits of aversion, confusion, and clinging. Through conceiving a more objective sense of ourselves as one among countless equally sensitive beings, we clear our hearts and minds for the social emotions of empathy and equanimity, the ground for cultivating a mindset of compassionate openness towards the world.[14] In this sense, reflecting on the equality of all life naturally inclines us to extend our mindfulness of the causality of suffering and happiness to ourselves and others impartially.[15] And this expanded horizon of mindfulness multiplies and intensifies the growth of empathic concern, so that our motivation to end suffering and cultivate happiness builds exponentially with the number of beings we include in our ever-widening circle of family feeling.[16] It is this social-emotional calculus that turns the effort we might normally channel towards our own personal self-healing and change into a power forceful enough to prepare the ground for a brave new altruistic life and world.[17]

Weeding Out Reactive Ways: Clearing the Field for Positive Interactions

As we level the ground of our life with others and prepare to turn it over for the growth of equanimity, empathy, and compassion, we will inevitably run into a whole field of blocks, held in place by the network of self-indulgent habits, rooted in instinctive self-reification, fearful clinging, and traumatic reactivity. To distill the teachings of open-mindedness so essential to the practice of mind-clearing, we will need the analytic discernment and focus to expose and clear our cognitive bias and emotional blocks along with the instincts that anchor them. In practice, this is possible only when we've built and refined our innate faculties of insight and wisdom into a power-tool that can deepen and speed the process of self-analysis. Since most of the habits and instincts that block our compassionate openness have been incorporated into the landscape of our mental life so intimately that we're effectively blind to them, the actual process of deepening our surface flashes of insight into a genuine clearing takes patient and persistent analysis.

Continued familiarity with the healing insights and principles like those of the noble truths helps stimulate the deepening reflection it takes to actually see blind spots that are so close to home. And once the habits that have been blocking us and our interactions all along are plain, we must begin the painstaking work of dislodging them from our mental lives, along with the tangled network of traumatic memories and emotions that ties them into our deepest and most conservative instincts for self-protection. The self-corrective edge of our minds must be guided and powered by a reflective analysis and intuitive wisdom far more sharpened and determined than even our most unquestioned assumptions and firmly held beliefs. For in this process of weeding the field of our minds, the precise discernment that helps us distinguish the weeds of reactivity and roots of misperception from the crop of unbiased sensitivity and objective awareness is the ultimate power-tool of social self-healing and self-transformation.

The Altruist's Due Diligence: The Engaged Accumulation Stage, Part II

The power I've called weeding lines up with second phase on the accumulation stage of socially engaged contemplative practice, expanding on the art of due diligence we explored in chapter 3. As on the path of self-healing, once deep mindfulness of the noble truths starts to correct our traumatic view of our bodies and minds, we begin to gather the healthy willpower to let go of negative habits and build positive ones systematically and proactively, one at a time. The main distinction at this phase is that, on the engaged path this process helps us purge negative habits and build positive ones not just regarding our personal lives but regarding our perception of and interaction with others as well. Given this, the process of due diligence in this phase of the engaged path progresses through the same four levels as it did on the path of personal self-healing. And here as well, this phase involves a progressively more clear and continuous awareness of the moment-to-moment causality of suffering and happiness, empowering us to use our momentary choices to weed out unhealthy habits and their roots, while clearing the ground for seeding and cultivating healthy new habits and ways of being.[18]

The Second Reflection on the Altruist's Path: Breaking the Traumatic Self-Habit

Alongside the motivational power of weeding and the contemplative step of the altruist's due diligence, this phase on the path is guided by the second reflection on the engaged insight path: the second step in Shantideva's fourfold method of building compassion. Traditionally, reflecting on clearing the traumatized self from our minds is based on a deep contemplation of the personal and social costs of our ingrained habit of self-defeating self-indulgence. The gradual deepening, intensification, and, refinement of this self-analytic reflection is indispensible if we're ever to build the power of weeding traumatic distortions and stress-reactive emotions from our personal and social lives. As the contemplative art of due diligence suggests, however, this reflection may progress not in great leaps and bounds but rather in the humble, incremental work of exposing reactive habits one at a time.[19]

Seeding the Ground: Planting Compassion with Every Step

The third power Chekawa recommends is the power of mindfulness focused on meeting each interaction every day as an opportunity to plant the seeds of an altruistic life in the world. Once we have the power of wisdom to clear our minds and our lives for the cultivation of empathy, care and concern, we must act quickly, decisively, and persistently to put our best intentions into practice. Simply paying lip-service to altruism, even sitting and meditating every day on love and compassion for all living beings is not enough to make an altruistic way of life a reality. If the devil is in the details, the authentic spirit of social emotions like acceptance, love and care lies in the nitty-gritty choices we make in each and every one of interactions with others, no matter how seemingly random or insignificant. Unlike the abstract ideal the tradition calls sentimental compassion, the power of seeding only works in the soil of particular one-on-one interactions, as an extension of the natural, embodied capacity for love and care we experience in true intimacy and parenting.[20]

Building Mind-Power: The Engaged Accumulation Stage, Part III

Having explored the mindful power of seeding virtues, the third step on the ethical path of social engagement, it's time to align that motivational step with the corresponding phase of contemplative practice. As on the path of personal self-healing, this final phase of accumulation involves combining renunciation and diligence with deepening mindfulness and concentration, to the point where they can be forged together into power tools for change known as the four bases of mental power.[21] These bases involve building the motivational energy to initiate healthy habits by developing a concentrated will, concentrated effort, concentrated mind, and concentrated analysis. The distinction here is that the motivational energy built on this path is not just the energy of self-acceptance and self-care but also includes the more expansive energy of love and compassion that reaches out to help oneself and others simultaneously and equally. Taken together, these newfound forces of will, effort, mind, and analysis give us leverage over the most ingrained habits, by building the initiative to seize the opportunity of the moment for change and the motivational energy to take on resistances and build new strengths.

The Third Reflection: Realizing the Benefits of Building Love and Compassion

Alongside the ethical power of seeding and the contemplative practice of strengthening the mind, the last phase of the altruist's accumulation stage lines up with the third reflection on the engaged path of insight: realizing the benefits of building love and compassion, the third step in Shantideva's fourfold method. Mindfully seeding and energizing new habits of social engagement is guided by the insight that our social motivations of love, joy, care, and equanimity provide the motivation we need to plant the seeds of a truly altruistic way of life that benefits ourselves and others equally. As we saw in chapter 4, the healing shift from a reactive rut of self-enclosure to a proactive stance of social engagement depends on the reflective awareness that building our social-emotional intelligence is the most effective way to secure our interests as individuals and as social animals, especially in the unnatural condition of civilization.[22]

Nurturing the Crop: Applying Full Concentration to Cultivating Care and Love

The power of concentrated practice I've called nurturing is often described as a process of deepening familiarization through repeated focus and increasing immersion. The growth of this power reflects a pivotal stage in our moral development: the increasing stability, intensity and exclusivity of our commitment to making compassionate openness our sole way of being in the world. Having gathered the motivational energy, constant mindfulness, and radical insight we need to plant our feet firmly on the path of positive social engagement, we now arrive at the pivotal step of pouring all our focus and presence of mind into nurturing that new way of life. Of course, this transitional step cannot happen in a single leap, but requires us to gradually shift more and more of our energy, focus, and insight towards that new direction, until finally it seems to burst into being. In reality, that new way of being—immersed in compassionate openness—can only actually grow by applying caring effort one meditation and one day at a time.

While we are accustomed to conceiving of change as the flick of a switch or a binary choice we make once and for all, in fact radical shifts in our emotional life occur in a much more incremental way than change within our conceptual minds.[23] So while the cognitive spark of enlightened altruism may take place in an instant, the affective work of building compassion must take place over a seemingly inconceivable length of time, traditionally "three incalculable eons."[24] As we'll see in parts 3 and 4, when we discuss the process-oriented practices of role-modeling imagery and sublimation, this slow alchemical process of change is linked to the physical chemistry of altering the network of neural pathways, energies, and transmitter drops that support the workings of consciousness.[25] On the path of social healing, this incremental change is described in terms of the gradual accumulation of the positive psychophysical energy of social-emotional self-worth or merit.[26] And the way in which we generate this positive energy is by investing more and more of our attention, more and more of the time, into positive social intentions and actions motivated by genuine equanimity, empathy, love, and compassion.[27]

Heat and Peak: The Engaged Application Stage, Part I

To support this new phase of development on the ethical path, we move to the next stage on the path of contemplative practice: the stage of application. Here, our powers of compassion, wisdom and mindfulness are such that we can begin to apply them in earnest to the alchemical process of self-transformation. Our progress in this phase depends on building our capacity to commit ourselves to that new way of being, by focusing and concentrating our minds single-pointedly on the non-dual spirit of compassionate openness, its budding form. Through deepening our ability to embody this spirit in progressively more profound meditation and daily practice, our single-minded focus gradually gathers the nurturing power to bring our budding altruism to the point of nascent enlightenment. The long, slow process of this stage goes through the same phases as it does on the path of personal self-healing, traditionally called heat, peak, tolerance, and triumph. The difference is that here, it is the application of compassionate openness that motivates our efforts to build single-minded focus, rather than the determination to reach personal freedom of mind.

As applying the spirit of compassion to deepen concentration brings us to real inner stillness, called quiescence, we gradually enter a euphoric flow that sparks a natural high or inner heat akin to the endorphin high of physical exercise.[28] The positive energy of this state gives us greater leverage over negative habits, allowing us to pry our consciousness free of emotional blocks and to realize more intense and expansive compassion. As we continue applying ourselves, quiescence deepens to single-pointed concentration, where it can turn analysis into a surgical power-tool that cuts through all the learned misperceptions that make up our acquired false views and block our full capacity for radical openness of mind. Having reached this peak experience of intellectual insight, we gain greater leverage over our mental blocks, allowing us to enjoy more accurate and continuous knowledge of the nature and workings of our own and others' body-minds.[29] This further empowers us to break free of the confusion that maintains compulsive emotions, reinforces traumatic habits, and blocks our ability to initiate and maintain healthy alternatives including positive social intentions and actions.

The Fourth Reflection: Exchanging Self-Indulgence for Enlightened Altruism

Alongside the moral power to nurture compassionate ways and the contemplative work of developing euphoric heat and peak insight, this phase of social self-transformation lines up with the fourth reflection on the engaged path of insight: the reorientation of our lives from myopic self-enclosure to the objectivity of genuine altruism. This radical perspective-shift is the theme of the fourth and last step in Shantideva's fourfold method of building compassion. This insight reflects the gradual transformation of our sense of self and world from the childish position of craving love and care from others to the adult position of building our own capacity to care equally for ourselves and others. This shift from seeking parenting to self-parenting and from there to volunteer-parenting all in need also reflects the reversal in the flow of give and take with our world, based on the mature art of taking care and giving love.[30]

In traditional terms, this final insight reflects a fundamental transformation in our mental life, in which the regressive centering of our lives on reactive habits and stress instincts finally gives way to the emergence of the native genius for altruism hidden in the depths of our minds.[31] As we bring higher awareness to this budding genius, through the reflection on exchanging self-indulgence for altruism, we foster the gradual process of nurturing a whole new self and life, a process that will eventually culminate in our becoming enlightened altruists. In this painstaking, day-to-day process of application, we slowly gain the power to re-parent ourselves, not as an ordinary parent but though an enlightened awareness that sees and nurtures our full potential to radically transform ourselves and our world.[32]

Anticipating Fruition: Allowing True Altruism to Ripen

The power of confidence I call endurance is the fifth and last power Chekawa advises to bring the process of social self-transformation to fruition. As our minds and lives coalesce around the spirit of compassionate openness, this power prepares us to actually begin and endure the journey to come, the journey which will eventually lead to a fully mature form of enlightened altruism. Endurance allows the cumulative force of all the previous powers to bear fruit, by deepening our combined concentration and insight to the point where we can expose and dispel any lingering shadow of doubt which might hide remnants of our self-indulgent sense of self and world. While the first power of preparing the ground helped uncover our innate compassion and the second of weeding helped clear away the main blocks to radical open-mindedness, the last three work together to seed, nurse and ripen the embodiment of compassionate openness which eventually culminates in the heroic confidence and visionary spirit of enlightened altruism.

Psychologically, this fifth power has to do with the capacity to anticipate, prepare for and endure the long process of gradual development through persistent practice and consistent application, akin to the foresight, planning, commitment, and pacing it takes to train for and run a marathon. Since the basic training for positive moral development through contemplative learning involves all three disciplines—of ethical motivation, contemplative self-regulation, and transformative insight—technically the power of endurance prescribed at this point is closer to what we'd need for a triathalon! Of course, as in health training, so on the path of altruism, the ultimate goal of undertaking and enduring intense periods of application like those prescribed by these powers is to build long-term faculties of motivation, self-discipline, and self-knowledge that can then become a natural part of a healthier, more effective way of life.

Tolerance and Triumph: The Engaged Application Stage, Part II

Given this brief overview of the fifth step on the ethical path of social engagement, we turn now to see what steps on the path of contemplative practice we need to support the power of endurance. Growing out of the breakthrough insight of the peak phase on the engaged application stage, further application of effort in compassion and concentrated self-analysis deepens our capacity to transcend a reified sense of self versus others. This increasing confidence in our emptiness insight gradually leads to an intuitive wisdom called the tolerance of the ultimate ungraspability of all things,[33] basis for the application phase of tolerance. In this phase, we begin to disarm reflex fears of losing our boundaries with others or relaxing our compulsive grip on what we identify as "I" and "mine," by overcoming learned self-reifying distortions and the traumatic reactions to others they trigger.[34] As a result, we're more able to tolerate the complexity and range of our everyday social life.

Finally, in the phase called triumph, our rational confidence and conceptual insight into emptiness dispels all the self-reifying views we've acquired or developed since childhood, along with the post-traumatic reactions they rationalize.[35] Such de-reifying insight has a profound and far-reaching impact on our capacity to see ourselves objectively, and represents a new milestone in the development of contemplative faculties current researchers call metacognition, non-judgmental awareness, and radical acceptance.[36] Here again, while these phases describe the growth of confidence through more unambiguous and concentrated insight, they are far from sudden black-and-white changes. Instead, this latter part of the engaged application stage involves repeated, consistent analysis of traumatic distortions and stress-reactivity stirred up in the course of interactions with the people we meet in the world, near, neutral, and far, as well as those we encounter as resistances in regular meditations. This fine-brush working though then frees us to immerse ourselves more decisively in the new self and life we're choosing to develop around the spirit of compassionate openness and the ethos of enlightened altruism.

The Fifth Reflection: Conceiving the Spirit of Enlightenment

Alongside the power of endurance on the altruist's path and the contemplative practice of tolerance and triumph on the engaged application stage, the fifth reflection on the engaged path of insight involves fully and finally conceiving the authentic spirit of enlightened altruism. As we saw in chapter 4, this reflection comes as the fruit of a long process of building our natural faculties of love and compassion and gradually expanding them to support a whole new way of being in the world. This work involves first reorienting our sense of self to line up with the positive energy of compassionate openness and then building and stretching that sense and energy through the gradual art of reversing the flow of give and take.

Guided by the insight that there is no conflict at all between truly caring for self and truly caring for others, this reflection involves an all-out commitment to building the mindset and response set of social engagement as the best way forward for all humans in today's civilized age.[37] Along this gradual path of compassionate openness and responsibility, we move through a phase of expansion and a phase of awakening. In the first, we stretch the intimate responsiveness of nurturing love into the all-inclusive responsibility of heroic resolve. In the second, we lift our sights from simply helping and caring for others to the final solution of awakening the altruist in us all. It is here that the slow growth of our own altruism finally reaches full maturity. Key to this maturity is acknowledging that, given the inexorable limits to what one person can do for others, the best way to leverage our investment in all life is to become not just an ordinary altruist but an altruist's altruist, a model who can truly inspire and guide others to develop their own will and ability to help. It is this final turn that makes altruism truly enlightened, and guides the final reflection on this phase of the altruist's path.

Of course, given our limits, this fifth reflection guides us towards the conclusion that, to make the biggest possible difference one being can make in the world, we must transform ordinary altruism into enlightened altruism. This means committing to a path of radical self-transcendence which enhances the maturity of altruism, both by deepening it with the meditative power of single-minded concentration and by expanding it with the reflective power of self-transcendent wisdom. This extraordinary path of altruistic self-transcendence is what makes up the remainder of the ethical path of altruism in the socially engaged teaching tradition. And the gateway which leads into that path, with its ten steps or stages of altruistic self-transcendence, is the reflection that guides us to conceive the mature motivation we need to commit our minds and lives to that end. That motivation is what I've called the spirit of enlightened altruism or the spirit of enlightenment.[38] Shantideva celebrates this pivotal moment of reflection in his *Guide*:

> As rare as it may be for someone blind
> To find a jewel (lost) in a garbage heap,
> So by some lucky accident
> I have conceived the spirit of enlightenment!
> It is the supreme medicine that heals
> The (basic) condition of all living beings,
> And a shade-giving tree that offers shelter
> For the weary who wander the ways of cyclic life.
> It is a great bridge by which all beings
> Can be released from the realms of misfortune,
> And the rising moon of awareness
> That relieves the torment of their compulsions.
> It is the great sun that completely dispels
> The fog of delusion from (all) beings' (minds),
> And the quintessential cream that rises
> When the milk of the teachings is churned.[39]

These Same Five Powers are Vital to Practicing the Engaged Precepts on Dying

One crucial aspect of the commitment to a self-transcendent form of altruism is the way we face the inexorable limitations of aging and dying. This next precept in Chekawa's text advises us to incorporate our normal anticipation and experience of aging and dying into the work of cultivating altruism by relying on the same five powers. Traditionally, this is said to involve transcending our ordinary sense of death as a final limit by using the five powers to direct our minds towards a voluntary incarnation in a future life, optimal for the development of altruism. With a modern outlook, we can pursue an analogous practice by using our minds and lives to make a transformative impact on individuals in other generations who can carry on our altruistic work into the future. Just as systematic methods of land clearing, irrigation, and agriculture laid the physical foundations for the multi-generational work of civilization, so the systematic clearing and cultivation of traits like empathy and altruism is vital to the intergenerational work of building the social-emotional infrastructure for civilized happiness, individually and collectively. This extends the generative phase in the natural cycle of human development, in which all the seeds of love and care we've planted with family, friends, colleagues, and those we may have helped in our life and work begin to take on special meaning as vital to our contribution and legacy.[40]

Wherever we are on the path of altruism, this last precept urges us to round out our efforts to carry through and beyond our present lifespan. The five motivational powers, two stages of contemplation and five reflections we've aligned with Chekawa's fourth point—integrating a lifelong practice—help prepare us to embark for real on the journey of enlightened altruism that will occupy us in the rest of this chapter. In his text, this journey is mapped within the fifth point—measuring success on the path. In terms of the path of contemplative practice, success is mapped into three final stages: insight, meditation, and mastery. And the engaged path of insight is mapped by reflections on ten transcendent virtues which support what are traditionally called the ten stages of enlightened altruism.

All Teachings Coalesce in a Single Intentionality: Becoming Sheer Openness

Given our look at the path which leads to the spirit of altruism, we return to Chekawa's text, and consider point five: measuring progress on the path. As we grow out of our traumatized self-enclosure into a more mature sense of self and other, another seeming split appears between our practice of compassion and our growing insight into the emptiness of all people and things. This continues throughout the initial phase of meditation on emptiness, in which we oscillate between the seemingly polar insights of spacious equipoise and illusory aftermath. As we saw, progress over time is measured by the gradual resolution of that apparent polarity, as we begin to realize that radical openness and unconditional compassion are in fact two sides of the same coin: a truly objective experience of reality. So, progress along the path of clearing the mind for social engagement can be measured first of all by the gradual coalescence of the teachings of self-healing, compassion, and emptiness into the mature compassionate openness traditionally called the spirit of enlightenment. Of course, technically speaking, this oscillation continues to be slowly resolved through this and the remaining nine stages of the enlightened altruist's path.[41]

Beyond the convergence of distinct aspects of thought and practice in one realization, Chekawa's precept also suggests the practical coalescence of that unifying spirit with the countless moment-to-moment intentions and actions that make up our everyday lives. To yield a whole new way of life, our integration of the spirit of enlightenment cannot be limited to unifying insights on the meditation cushion, but must be woven into the fabric of our hearts, minds, and lives in such a way that it increasingly unifies all we think, do and say with the spirit of enlightened altruism. Traditionally, the work of integration in this phase increasingly brings this spirit into all our intentions and acts, public and private, right down to the most prosaic activities of daily life, including eating, drinking, waking, and sleeping. As Shantideva says,

> I will regard my body as a boat—
> A basis for coming and going—
> And to realize the aims of all beings
> I should transform it into a wish-fulfilling gem.[42]
> I should perform all acts for others' happiness.
> This excellent quality is precious and rare,
> And with it, I'll savor the pure joy and happiness
> Which arise from actions that benefit others.[43]
> Whatever I do in any context,
> Whether to benefit myself or others
> I should try to practice
> The (altruistic) discipline prescribed for that context.[44]

Direct Realization of Emptiness and the Ultimate Spirit of Enlightenment

The spirit of universal compassion which is the fruit of the five first steps on the altruist's path must be prepared for the final ripening of the ten stages of enlightened altruism by the catalyst of self-transcendent insight. As on the path of personal self-healing, here as well, our cultivation of healthy motivations and actions initially depends on our having confidence in a rational inference about how suffering and happiness work, rather than on a direct perceptual realization. So, however committed or stable our spirit of compassionate openness is, until now it is still only considered conventional in that it still depends on forms of reasoning that help us override our default misperception of ourselves as intrinsically separate from others. When Chekawa says our progress on the altruist's path can be measured by the coalescence of all practice into one intentionality, he is referring to a form of compassionate openness that is not just an ideal but is based on a direct realization of our total interdependence with everyone and everything around us. Since it involves a direct intuitive perception of our ultimate lack of any unrelated identity, such a compassionate openness is traditionally called the "ultimate" spirit of enlightened altruism.

While at first blush it may seem idealistic or romantic to think ordinary human beings can so completely transcend our innate self-enclosure or self-protectiveness, the fact is that mammals in general and humans in particular are naturally prepared to see and treat our kin as inseparable or indistinguishable from ourselves. If, to paraphrase Shantideva, parents see their children's bodies as extensions of "self" while children see their bodies exclusively as "mine," is it really unnatural or unrealistic for the altruist to take a parental view towards all life, seeing and treating all beings as part of one family, one body, while less mature others still maintain a myopic, child's eye view? As our working conception of compassionate openness is fully validated by our perception of our total interdependence with life, it gains the unequivocal certainty and uncontrived immediacy of a direct realization of how things are and work. This realization in turn dispels any lingering self-protective doubts, allowing the ultimate spirit of altruism to emerge as the unifying intentionality guiding our every thought, feeling, and action in the world.

Personifying Enlightened Altruism: The Contemplative Stage of Engaged Insight

As on the path of personal self-healing, the third stage of contemplative practice on the path of social engagement is the stage of insight. The main event on this stage is the breakthrough in meditative insight that galvanizes our moral development by letting us see the true nature and workings of suffering and happiness. Essentially, this stage gradually takes us beyond the virtual insights of the application stage to direct personal experience of how things are and work.[45] This direct, intuitive feel for the true nature of our lives and our world stands as an unmistakable counterpoint to the delusions and distortions we learned to mistake for reality. What distinguishes this stage from the same stage on the path of self-healing is that our insight opens out from our own self-imposed isolation to take in the alienation of all living beings.

Despite the powerful, galvanizing effect the breakthrough insight on this stage has on our compassionate openness with others in the world, the mental and emotional blocks to our fully embodying the ultimate spirit of enlightenment remain. These persistent obstacles continue to limit our moment to moment ability to act on or even see our inseparability from others in daily life, outside of our meditation sessions. The cognitive dissonance this leaves between our highest breakthrough insight and our daily experience with others creates a tension that further motivates us to progress through the next nine stages of enlightened altruism. The gradual progress on these stages consists in progressively working through the affective and cognitive blocks that obstruct our full embodiment of compassionate openness, by applying our realization of emptiness to help disarm and dissolve these blocks, one degree at a time. While the work on the first through seventh stages is mainly focused on overcoming the affective blocks caused by stress-reactive emotions that reinforce self-indulgence, called blocks to freedom, from the latter part of the eighth stage through the tenth, the focus shifts to exposing and dissolving the instinctive reifications that subtly block our wisdom, called blocks to objectivity or omniscience.

The Sixth Reflection: Transcendent Giving and the Joyous Stage of Altruism

With our altruistic spirit freed of any artificial distinction between self and others, our natural tendency to give protection, help or guidance to others in need is purged of any lingering tendency towards sentimental involvement. Once our social engagement has become a spontaneous and unconditional response based on seeing the objective reality of what is and needs to be done, we finally cross over into the brave new world of enlightened altruism. The traditional litmus test for such genuine altruism is whether we're making any reified distinction between the three aspects of any altruistic action like generosity, namely: the altruist who helps; the recipient of help; and the helping interaction. Engaging with others with such complete freedom from preconceptions about any limits or boundaries to what we can, should or want to do for them frees our natural empathy and altruism of any learned or innate restraints, allowing us to cultivate social-emotional virtues or qualities in an open-ended way. Such unrestrained cultivation of altruism is what is traditionally called the vehicle of transcendence. And the realization of direct insight into emptiness and selflessness at this stage opens the gateway for that vehicle, by freeing us from habitual blocks to the transcendence of any preconceived limits to our altruistic engagement. Since it clears the way for the cultivation of self-transcendent altruism, the direct realization that frees the unconditional spirit of enlightenment is also called the "eyes" of the other transcendences.

If the door to our first acts of enlightened altruism is a breakthrough in insight, why is our reflection at this stage focused on giving? While the fundamental shift on this stage is hidden deep within our inmost perception of ourselves in relation to others, the most obvious manifestation of this inner shift is our move into a truly generative way of being. In a biological sense, the zone or sphere of true altruism is made evident by the more or less unrestricted flow of protection, aid and guidance between individuals and within social groups. In traditional terms, such natural generosity is seen as the single most important cause of the evolution of human life, as well as the emergence of abundance within any social groups.[46] In Buddhist social theory, this kinder, gentler animal spirit is the primary cause of the accumulation of wealth by individuals and societies. And, if we understand the importance of trust, free exchange, and the free flow of capital in market economies, this insight lines up well with current views in the emerging science of behavioral economics or neuroeconomics.[47]

Apart from the importance of spontaneous generosity in social evolution or behavioral economics, its impact may be more clearly seen in its effects on positive moral development and social psychology. In terms of moral development, as we've seen, Buddhist psychology anticipated the contemporary findings of positive psychology. The basic social actions of giving or sharing with others presupposes a mirroring capacity not just to empathize with their needs but also to vicariously enjoy their well-being and success.[48] A generative stance of contributing whatever we can to those around us expands our possibilities of enjoying whatever it is we have to share, effectively multiplying our experience of abundance and gratitude geometrically. And this powerful social-emotional calculus is what gives this first stage of enlightened altruism the experiential quality of expanding our joy, leading the tradition to name it "The Joyous." My effort to translate this effect into the mathematical language of calculus or economics is neither imposed nor new. Such a quantification of the multiplicative economics of positive social emotion and interaction is very much part of traditional descriptions of altruism, which figure the gain at each successive stage exponentially. Here is Nagarjuna's thumbnail sketch of the altruist's development on this stage:

> Just as eight levels of Monastic Sages
> Are defined within their (Individual) Vehicle,
> So are the ten stages of altruism
> Within the Universal Vehicle.
> The first of these is the Joyous,
> Since (at this stage) the altruist rejoices
> At breaking free of the three bondages,
> And joining the family of Transcendent Ones!
> Through the maturation of this triumph
> Transcendent generosity becomes supreme.
> It ripples through a hundred worlds
> And s/he becomes a great lord on earth.[49]

The three bondages—the grossest levels of attachment, aversion, and pride—are what bind the traumatized self into the repetitive cycle of stress and trauma that blocks our way forward through genuine altruistic development. So breaking the grip these exert on our capacity to see and treat others as "myself" or "my family" clears the way for the natural social impulse to share that powers altruism at this stage. Nor is the economics of altruism traditionally limited to psychological well-being. This is clear from traditional descriptions of how the positive energy generated by such social intentions and actions accumulates and exerts a transformative effect on the expression of physical traits, giving rise to the thirty-two signs and eighty marks of a fully mature enlightened altruist. Here are a few such verses from Nagarjuna's *Jewel Garland*:

When others seek your wealth and possessions,
Through the discipline of spontaneous generosity
Your shoulders will be broad, your expression pleasing,
And you will become a leader in the world.[50]
Through providing good housing
Well (furnished) with comfortable carpets,
Your complexion will be as fine
As pure, polished gold.[51]
Through speech that is eloquent and pleasant,
And by responding to (others') eloquence,
You will have open shoulders,
And a (broad,) lion-like chest.[52]

In the realm of social psychology, the power of generosity harnessed at this stage is explained in terms of four forms of giving that foster social cohesion: offering aid; offering reassurance; offering guidance; and offering a positive example. These forms of generosity clearly show how the journey of enlightened altruism is not just a matter of personal moral development. It is a powerfully effective form of non-violent social action, which helps to build enlightened communities that support, foster, and cultivate the growth of altruism as a way of life. The social psychology of the altruist or bodhisattva is described at great length within the social theory of perfected or enlightened worlds, called Buddha-fields.[53] The utopian social theory of this engaged tradition is also distinguished from Western utopianism by its profoundly psychological vision of human social and cultural development. Rather than advancing from the outside in, mainly through political or economic action, this kind of utopia proceeds from the inside out, through the psychosocial ripple effects of the moral development of individuals. In this sense, it bears a family resemblance to Freud's notion that civilization must be recreated in the psychological development of each of its members. It differs in that it extends his understanding to what nowadays we might call positive social psychology: the advancement of civilization by the leadership of psychologically minded, psychosocially active altruists.[54]

Of the Two Witnesses, Hold the Primary: Internalizing Self-Transcendence

This second precept in Chekawa's treatment of measuring progress addresses the crucial next step in the maturation of altruism: internalizing the wisdom of emptiness as the one, ultimately reliable frame of reference for judging one's own mental progress and the progress of others. The "witnesses" this precept refers to are traditionally defined as outer versus inner. An outer or external witness refers to valid moral judgments about our intentions and actions we gather socially by soliciting or receiving them from reliable others. The inner or internal witness refers to valid moral judgments we arrive at reflectively by monitoring and examining our own intentions and actions. What this precept describes is the gradual growth of our conscience from the outer-directed mode of childhood to the self-directed mode of adulthood.

Of course, the process of internalizing the judgment of reliable adults is basic to the formation of our normal adult conscience. On the contemplative path, this product of normal development must be revised in light of the fact that our biological parents lacked the higher perspective or objectivity of fully reflective individuals like enlightened altruists. Once we've personally realized the emptiness of any and all the mental constructs we previously reified as "I" and "mine," our mind has accessed a new degree and kind of objectivity, relatively free from the usual biases that made our habitual mindset subjective, blinded, and self-enclosed. Given this radical breakthrough, we begin to have inner access to the selfless objectivity that makes truly wise and magnanimous individuals like altruists so much more reliable. From this point on, as we begin to apply that breakthrough to exposing and correcting learned and innate biases, the balance in our moral judgments can safely begin to tip more and more towards the inner witness of our objective self-knowledge. So the natural life cycle of emerging adulthood is recapitulated here at the higher level of contemplative self-transcendence, leading eventually to the higher integration and maturity of an enlightened altruist.

Removing Our Blocks to Objective Altruism: The Stage of Engaged Meditation, Part I

If we align this pivotal moral step with the contemplative practice we need to support it, the task of internalizing objective self-knowledge aligns with of the work of deepening single-minded concentration and insight on the engaged stage of meditation. As on the path of personal self-healing, the stage of meditation here involves the gradual elimination of ever subtler forms of instinctive confusion and compulsive emotion, a process conceived as moving slowly through nine successive levels.[55] The many traditional metaphors for this process—like washing stains out of a cloth—emphasize the incremental, painstaking nature of the gradual dissolution of compulsions and misperceptions, in both the contexts of personal and social self-healing.[56] The main difference is that clearing our minds and opening our hearts on the socially engaged path of altruism requires us to work through even deeper and subtler levels of stress-emotion and self-reification, in order to free us from self-protective reactions to social stress in the world.

The way this clearing out of the mind is reached is by combining progressive degrees of insight with deeper levels of concentration. Traditionally, this stage involves applying our breakthrough insight into emptiness to seeing through the emotional blocks that cloud our judgment about the workings of our own and others' minds. And, on the meditative side of the process, these deepening insights require the ever deeper levels of concentration traditionally mapped onto the increasingly more refined states of equipoise called the four formal contemplations and four formless absorptions. These progressive levels of equipoise and insight lead to the gradual purging of blocks to unconditional compassion and empathic objectivity in the course of the nine successive stages to come on the path of enlightened altruism.

In fact, the patient working through of blocks on the engaged meditation stage is so much a part of our progress towards transcendent altruism that it spans four of the five steps of moral development and eight of the nine stages of reflective growth remaining on the path. Since Chekawa measures progress in this phase in terms of four steps in moral development, it makes sense to map the engaged meditation stage into four parts, each of which lines up with one of the steps he highlights and two of the reflective stages on the path of altruism. The moral step of internalizing self-knowledge lines up with the first part of the engaged meditation stage and the second and third stages of altruistic reflection, known as the Impeccable and the Brilliant.

The Seventh Reflection: Transcendent Ethics and the Impeccable Stage

The moral step of integrating self-knowledge and the initial contemplative work of the engaged meditation stage are guided by the seventh reflection on the altruist's insight path: the reflection on transcendent ethics. The gist of this reflection is the understanding that our capacity to help others in the long run is mainly hindered by our identification with self-limiting habits of thought, expression and action, rooted in our instincts for self-protective clinging, defensiveness and self-reification. In the language of the mind-clearing practice, when our contact with others who are mired in distress triggers our own, in order to raise the level of the interaction we must "*drive all blame into one,*" by targeting and disarming our own traumatic self-image and reactive habits. Ultimately, our worst enemy in proactively engaging the needs of others is our own lingering attachment to seeing ourselves through the debilitating eyes of self-indulgence, self-pity and, myopic self-enclosure. So progressively applying the insight of emptiness to exposing and dispelling traumatic distortions and the stress-emotions they mobilize frees us to grow into and live up to our highest values and ideals.

Beyond the moral psychology of this stage, the principles of transcendent ethics are a crucial part of our reflection. Traditionally, transcendent ethics involves a hierarchy of values, starting with caring effectively for oneself, and then naturally expanding the circle of care, one individual and group at a time, based on one's actual social-emotional development and capacity. In principle, of course, this gradual path of expanding engagement is self-transcendent in the sense that it embraces all beings everywhere, excluding none; and in that it embraces them unconditionally, regardless of any destructive intention or action and/or any potential harm to oneself or one's near and dear ones.

Of course, this does not mean that self-transcendent ethics makes a virtue of self-denial or self-sacrifice. If we must in any way neglect or endanger ourselves for the sake of helping many more others, it is an unavoidable moral cost which we must somehow make up to ourselves. Any case in which a conflict between self-interests and altruistic interests is resolved in favor of others is not based on a utilitarian calculus—the greatest good for the greatest number—but rather on a situational and intimately personal weighing of what might harm or help each and every individual involved. This weighing includes ourselves as having perfectly equal rights to well-being, but it also factors in our having greater capacity to make a difference for others and make up any harm to ourselves. It is the natural awakening to such an insight and ethos that is celebrated in rituals honoring the altruist's conceiving the spirit of enlightenment, the wish to help all beings however possible, especially to awaken them to their own potential for altruism. Here is Shantideva's poetic description of this earth-shaking event:

> From this moment on, with no sense of loss,
> I offer my body, my resources,
> And all my virtues acquired at all times
> To help all living beings, (all like) my mothers.[57]
> Until they (themselves) reach Nirvana,
> May I support all forms of life,
> Throughout the realms of existence
> That stretch to the ends of space.
> Just as all those Blissfully Enlightened before
> Conceived the spirit of enlightenment
> And realized all (ten) stages
> Of an enlightened altruist's education,
> So will I, for the sake of all beings,
> Conceive the spirit of enlightenment
> And realize all the stages
> Of an enlightened altruist's education.[58]
> Now my existence has become truly fruitful,
> And this human life has acquired great meaning;
> Today I've joined the family of the Transcendent,
> And become an enlightened altruist![59]

Of course, such aspirations are not just generic in the sense of being ideals we need to gradually live up to, but they are also generic in that they involve very general commitments to help others in any way possible. Traditionally, the development of any particular altruist is guided by personal pledges and commitments to help living beings in very particular ways. This specific intentionality is not only conveyed in the stories of Shakyamuni's past lives as an enlightened altruist, but also in the iconography of the socially engaged teaching tradition. For instance, the archetypal altruists that guide the practice of medicine and self-healing, such as the *Healing Mentor*, are said to have been motivated by special vows to heal various kinds of illness, physical, mental, and spiritual. Likewise the *Healing Mother* is said to have been inspired by a personal vow to promote longevity, freedom from stress and fear, and the supreme freedom of self-transcendent compassion. Such archetypal figures are meant to encourage budding altruists to entertain boundless hopes for their potential to make a very particular, very real difference in the lives of countless others. Here is Nagarjuna's description of the Impeccable stage.

> The second (stage) is called Impeccable
> Because the (altruist's) ten (positive) acts
> Of body, speech and mind are impeccable,
> And s/he lives them out naturally.
> Through the maturation of this triumph
> Transcendent ethics becomes supreme.
> S/he becomes a great leader who heals the world,
> Master of its glorious (lands) and precious resources.[60]

The Eighth Reflection: Transcendent Tolerance and the Brilliant Stage

Growing out of these effects on our own moral integrity, the deepening self-knowledge and self-analysis in this phase have a natural ripple effect on our realistic acceptance of others. The moral step of gaining truly objective awareness of others and the contemplative work of seeing through their traumatic habits are guided by the eighth reflection on the altruist's path: the reflection on transcendent tolerance. With our own self-knowledge and self-mastery expanded and our sense of dependence on others diminished, the playing field is now clear and level enough for us to see and accept other's limits without confusion or fear. Protected by the certainty that we no longer have any need to experience or react to other's distress as a life-or-death trauma, we are free to focus our energies on tolerating and working through whatever feelings their distress prompts in us. Instead of triggering a slip back into a childhood rut of powerlessness, an interaction with distressed others now calls up a mature sense of self-efficacy and a proactive readiness to approach and take on the challenges that overwhelm others.

In effect, this shift toward increasingly unconditional distress-tolerance is a cultivated extension of the growth of self-confidence in the parenting phase of normal human development. Just as an experienced parent has overcome the limited empathy and expertise which at first made childrearing seem overwhelmingly stressful, so the altruist has overcome any default limitation of empathy and caretaking. As part of the conscious cultivation and extension of such stress tolerance, the altruist gradually leaves behind any hint of intolerance or prejudice towards others. By systematically facing and mastering the malignant distortions and destructive emotions within our own minds, we undergo a radical desensitization to the archaic forces that limit our human nature. This yields a sense of unconditional family feeling towards all life, akin to that expressed in Tertullian's famous aphorism, "Nothing human is alien to me."

As a final fruit of cultivating tolerance of our own and other's distress, our capacity to face and endure any obstacle is increased, immeasurably enhancing our ability to achieve all aims and master our full potential. So transcendent tolerance not only has the fruit of vastly enhancing our social effectiveness, but also increases our self-efficacy in general. This is because frustration is the single greatest obstacle to our persisting and progressing in the face of challenges, be they our own limitations or others'. Tolerance is a rate-limiting skill not just for pacifying anger, but also for recovering from any addictive or obsessive attachment. Finally, tolerance is equally critical to the mastery of our own capacity for attention, mindfulness, and concentration, since the power to hold our minds focused depends on our ability to resist the de-centering pulls of fatigue and distraction without getting frustrated enough to break our concentration. Here is how Nagarjuna describes the achievement of this stage:

> The third is called Brilliant
> Since the pacifying light of wisdom dawns
> As the contemplations and powers evolve,
> Extinguishing (gross) attachment and hatred.
> Through the maturation of this triumph
> (The altruist) perfects skills like tolerance and effort,
> Completely ends (all) desirous attachment
> And becomes a great leader of (humans and) gods.[61]

Always Rely Exclusively on the Happy Mind: Pure Positive Energy and Focus

The eighth step Chekawa maps on the altruist's path of moral development involves harnessing the power of enthusiasm and passionate flow to the development of transcendent endurance and single-mindedness. Beyond the obstacles of self-limitation and frustration lies the pitfall of fatigue, which makes us vulnerable to inertia, discouragement, and a sense of inadequacy. The moral force we need to pull us out of these pitfalls and keep us on the uphill path of altruism is the capacity for the single-minded immersion in the flow of positive energy focused on truly positive aims and goals. While this indispensible step may seem like a kind of forced self-denial or perfectionistic striving, the real development at this point on the path springs from a profound shift in motivation and affect that is distinct from any imposed obligation or top-down imperative. This is the fundamental shift in our core, baseline affective state from a survival-based stress-reactive emotional tone to an abundance-based radically proactive emotional tone.[62]

The moral step of learning to *rely exclusively on the happy mind* reflects both a shift to a new motivational bias in favor of positive states and aims, as well as a conscious commitment to cultivate an acquired taste for genuine and continuous happiness. While the very idea of such a shift may seem arbitrary or unrealistic, the young fields of positive psychology and interpersonal neuroscience offer ample support for two surprising conclusions: that we have a vast untapped potential for positive social-emotional attunement;[63] and that consciously cultivating that capacity appears to be the most effective strategy for adapting to the unnatural, overwhelmingly social and cultural environment of civilized living.[64] While our instinctive bias and our modern cultural conditioning both predispose us to rely on the survival-based "animal spirits" of compulsive acquisitiveness, aggression, and insecurity, it is becoming increasingly clear that this aversive mindset actually fuels a vicious cycle of hyperactivity and fatigue which drives us to distraction and burnout.[65] On the other hand, positive emotional states like contentment, enthusiasm, and joy seem to support far more stable endurance and effective performance in the social and cultural activities that make up the bread and butter of civilized life.[66]

Removing Our Blocks to Objective Altruism: The Stage of Engaged Meditation, Part II

The contemplative practice we need to support this moral shift towards positive states and aims is the work of applying deeper levels of concentration and insight to overcoming blocks to immersion in flow states and single-minded absorption. Whereas the initial phase of the engaged meditation stage focused on seeing though reified views of self and other that block our capacity for transcendent ethics and tolerance, this phase deepens and focuses the emptiness insight on seeing though our identification with aversive emotions and survival aims that block our cultivation of self-transcendent endurance and concentration. It is supported by our deepening capacity for direct realization and single-mindedness, based on the power of meditative endurance supported by an increasingly all-consuming immersion in mental and physical bliss and plasticity.

From this new experiential platform of euphoric mind/body states, we finally feel safe and sure in our capacity to live in positive motivations and aims, and so are more able to release our habitual identification with the self-protective emotions and aims that lock us into the cycle of stress and trauma. Key to this immersion in positive states is a readiness to let go of any forced control over our mind/body processes and relax into the increasingly unfettered flow of realistic enthusiasm and optimism.[67] Here, our new positive flow is focused on breaking instinctive clinging to self-reifying views and survival aims, freeing us to realize the deepest meaning of the noble truths: the truth that our entire involvement in compulsive life was based on nothing more than a nightmarish delusion. This breaking of the first link of the cycle of stress and trauma also naturally frees us to feel an inseparable identity with and compassion for all living beings trapped in the grip of that primordial delusion. Traditionally, it is said that these breakthroughs free us to disarm and dissolve the finest levels of our gross stress-emotions and the grossest levels of our moderate stress-emotions. This second phase of the engaged meditation stage brings us two thirds of the way to complete freedom from the instinctive emotions that block our path to fully enlightened altruism.

The Ninth Reflection: Transcendent Endurance and the Radiant Stage

Aligned with the moral step of relying on positive mind-states and the contemplative phase of using emptiness to release our minds from self-protective emotions, progress at this point is guided by the reflection on transcendent endurance. The big picture here is that, as the scope and depth of our altruistic resolve grows, we can easily get discouraged by the seemingly endless, extreme and intractable nature of the various kinds of suffering undergone by all living beings. If we are to truly engage with all the suffering of all life around us, we must have not just certainty about our interdependence and the capacity for cultivating transcendent generosity, ethics and tolerance, but also what is known as the "armor" of transcendent endurance. In essence, this involves an unshakable motivation that's only possible because our minds are immersed in our work with a passion that helps dissolve hesitations, resistances, and doubts and makes us effectively one with our process and aim. In terms of contemporary stress-research, transcendent endurance confers a high degree of resilience in the face of potentially overwhelming stress and challenge that enhances our sense of self-efficacy and protects our positive motivation and action from fatigue and burnout.[68]

Beyond the role of endurance as an armor against caregiver stress, fatigue, and burnout, the traditional reflection extends to two other indispensible roles this capacity plays in the maturation of enlightened altruism. One of these has to do with the importance of cultivating self-transcendent endurance when it comes to actually engaging and persisting in altruistic activities that benefit others. This aspect of the reflection is meant to prime us to steadily increase our capacity not just to sustain motivation but also to follow through on our intention to help by expanding our ability to persist in specific helpful activities. Another aspect of the traditional reflection involves recognizing the role of transcendent endurance in constantly extending our capacity to persist in moral self-discipline. This aspect of the reflection aims to counteract any natural tendency to let ourselves off the hook at some point in our responsibility to ourselves or others, by consistently stretching our sense of moral responsibility as our capacity to help continues to increase. To wrap up our look at this reflection, here are Nagarjuna's comments about the achievements on this stage:

> The fourth (stage) is called Radiant
> Since the light of genuine insight shines

When (the altruist) cultivates the distinctiveness
Of the faculties conducive to enlightenment.
Through the maturation of this triumph
S/he rules those in the Conflict-Free (Realm),
By being supremely skilled
In dispelling self-reifying views.[69]

The Tenth Reflection: Transcendent Meditation and the Invincible Stage

After developing self-transcendent endurance, the rest of our work on immersion in positive states and pacifying disturbing emotions is guided by the reflection on self-transcendent meditation. The focus of this tenth reflection is on the necessity of mastering unwavering single-mindedness in order to deepen our immersion in euphoric flow, and with it, our ability to stay continuously focused in confronting subtler levels of disturbing emotion and primal confusion. The vital contribution of the deepest levels of concentrative calm is evoked by the name of the stage. As we've seen in our prior discussions of meditation, these deep levels are far beyond the entry-level practice of calming the mind familiar to us as mindfulness meditation. Of the nine levels of concentrative quiescence identified on traditional maps, mindfulness is the leading force only though the fourth, and awareness only through the sixth. The deepest levels that support transcendent meditation are the three most profound levels known as quiescence, single-pointedness and equipoise.[70] This stage is called Invincible because, with the stabilizing platform and laser-sharp focus of one-pointed concentration and meditative equipoise, the altruist on this stage cannot be derailed or deterred from the flow of compassionate openness by any of the disturbing influences of toxic emotion or self-deceptive confusion.

Of course, such complete mastery of the deepest levels of concentrative absorption is not simply a mental feat or profound state of trance. Its power consists in the fact that such concentration is only possible when the mind/body's core network of bliss and plasticity has come under conscious self-regulation. The capacity to fully access and tap the flow of mental and physical ecstasy is what finally gives the altruist the willpower and mind-power to stay immersed in compassionate openness, while having the presence and clarity to stop clinging to or identifying with the innate demons of self-indulgence, self-protection and self-reification.[71] While such concentration may be harnessed to the most profound non-conceptual peace of mind, to profound self-transcendent insight, or to a combination of both, the transformative power of such deep meditation lies in the way it allows the mind to pour itself at will into our aim or object, as completely as water poured in water. This deep, unitive quality in turn supports an intuitive awareness that yields a direct, fresh, and unmediated experience of whatever we're focusing on or undertaking in daily life, as well as the development of extraordinary faculties, such as empathic omniscience, supernormal sensory acuity, or extraordinary memory and recall.[72]

In terms of contemporary research, such profound concentration would appear to reflect a capacity to self-regulate the neural processing of internal reward which mediates all goal directed activities from aim-seeking and satisfaction to the modulation of neuroplasticity and the reinforcement of learning.[73] Since this core mind/brain system is also involved in the aversive conditioning of trauma and the reinforcement of addictive craving and compulsive behavior, gaining the capacity to consciously modulate it is of enormous help in unlearning such negative habits as well as enriching plasticity and the learning of positive alternatives.[74] Although at present we have only preliminary evidence to support such a reading, these are compelling enough for us to assume that the reflection of this stage may refer to such a profound achievement.[75] We'll return to our hypothesis about this achievement in part 4, when we explore the process-oriented map of the nervous system and its potential overlaps with our own. To conclude, here is Nagarjuna's description of this stage on the altruist's path:

> The fifth (stage) is called Invincible
> Since (the altruist) can vanquish all demons.
> By developing subtle, healing intuitions
> (Based on teachings) such as the noble truths.
> Through the maturation of this triumph
> S/he rules those in the Joyous (Realm),
> And eliminates the (emotional) sources of all
> Addictive and fundamentalist views.[76]

***The Measure of Having Learned is Elimination*: Moving Beyond Emotional Blocks**

Chekawa's next precept describes the altruist's moral development as the gradual removal of even the subtlest obstacles to complete emotional freedom and unbiased objectivity. Of course, in our mapping of that process, the next step on the path is the unlearning of the most subtle levels of reactive emotions which block our inner freedom and lasting happiness. While we may have a hard time imagining that we can live in such lasting inner freedom and peace, it helps here to remember that plasticity and altruism have become the watchwords of our contemporary neuroscience[77] and positive psychology.[78] The moral step of fully overcoming emotional blocks to inner freedom and peace of mind is possible not just as a limiting case of the normal life cycle of moral development but also a predictable outcome of the self-mastery and self-transcendence achieved on the last step of immersion in positive states. What is distinctive about the culture of Indic contemplative science is the insistence that this exceptional maturation is accessible to all human beings and can be systematically reproduced given the right education and methods.[79] How?

By conjoining the very deepest levels of blissful single-mindedness with the self-transcendent insight and art of emotional healing, an altruist at this stage can eliminate ever-subtler levels of reactive emotion that tie us in to the cycle of stress and trauma and so block our freedom to live in unconditional peace with ourselves and unwavering compassion for others.

Removing Our Blocks to Objective Altruism: The Stage of Engaged Meditation, Part III

To support the final work of clearing emotional blocks, the third phase of the engaged meditation stage combines the power of concentrative equipoise with the single-pointed scalpel of transcendent insight to expose and cut through the misperceptions that rationalize our identification with the subtler compulsive emotions of stress and trauma. By allowing our minds to stay immersed in the spacious equipoise that realizes the emptiness of our traumatic experience of self and world, the combined force of concentrative quiescence and self-transcendent insight brings us at last to a genuine cessation of the acquisitive, aggressive and self-protective instincts which are the root causes of compulsive life. This direct, intuitive realization in turn frees the mind from its emotional blocks to three forms of self-transcendent wisdom: the relative wisdom that recognizes the causal power of quiescence and insight to stop the cycle of stress and trauma; the ultimate wisdom that realizes the emptiness of the false self and world created by the misperception and reification of the confused mind; and the empathic wisdom that applies these two personal realizations to understanding and healing the self-inflicted suffering of all other life.[80]

The Eleventh Reflection: Transcendent Wisdom and the Engaging Stage

The moral step of eliminating blocks and the contemplative phase of realizing moments of true cessation are guided by the reflection on transcendent wisdom. Without the wisdom to expose and disarm self-protective instincts and habits, even the deepest meditative absorption will not fundamentally change who we are and how we live. This is why combining meditative self-mastery with self-transcendent wisdom is seen as the ultimate, rate-limiting step in overcoming our self-imposed blocks to complete freedom *from* compulsion as well as freedom *of* moral development. But if the work of this stage is to free the mind of its natural entanglement with innate stress-emotions, why is wisdom as or more critical here than meditation?

You may recall from the last chapter that the engaged teaching tradition of Nagarjuna makes the case that the altruist's life of compassionate openness in the world requires her to cut the network of stress and trauma at its taproot: the self-protective, self-reifying habit. The reflection at this stage is that the deeper we want to go in disarming and resolving subtler and subtler forms of negative emotion, the more indispensible self-transcendent insight becomes. While this wisdom or enlightenment may be far more profound than any healing experience we're used to in everyday life, even in psychotherapy, it may help to demystify it by realizing that it heals in much the same way as waking up from a nightmare or recovering from a trauma.[81] When we know for certain that we are not alien to our world and that our struggle for survival is effectively done, that knowledge certainty frees us to disarm our stress-protective emotions more deeply and decisively than any moral imperative or act of willpower ever possibly could.[82]

Given this decisive break with the self-protective, self-reifying habit at the root of compulsive life, here we begin to finally break free of even the subtle compulsions that block our full potential for compassionate openness. As a result, we can begin to approach and engage in the way of being of enlightened altruists like Shakyamuni. So this stage of altruism is called Engaging. With a genuine freedom from any alienated or compulsive sense of self, here we can proceed with no hint of self-inflation or self-congratulation. Nagarjuna's description of this stage alludes to the cultivation of the distinctive qualities of an enlightened altruist, the seminal forms of the distinctive qualities of a fully enlightened individual. Traditionally, these are numbered at eighteen, beginning with the six transcendent virtues cultivated thus far, along with the four arts of social cohesion, the non-abandonment of any living beings, and so on.[83]

> The sixth (stage) is called Engaging
> Since (the altruist) engages the qualities of enlightenment.
> By practicing transcendent insight and quiescence,
> S/he attains cessation and develops (them).
> Through the maturation of this triumph
> S/he rules those in the Pure Fantasy (Realm),
> Has no detractors among the (Buddha's) disciples,
> And tames those with the pride of arrogance.[84]

The Twelfth Reflection: Transcendent Technique and the Expansive Stage

As we master the moral step of eliminating blocks and the contemplative art of realizing cessation, our progress on the altruist's path is guided by the reflection on self-transcendent technique. With the removal of even the subtlest emotional blocks to freedom and clarity of mind, our capacity to climb out of our own rut of self-pitying self-protectiveness grows to the point where we can see ourselves and others with equal wisdom and act with truly objective empathy and effective compassion. This capacity to stand outside our traumatized self and see the self-inflicted causality of suffering quite precisely, combined with our new ability to disarm our compulsions by seeing how empty and costly they are, translates into a gradual expansion of our skill in helping others see and heal their own self-defeating habits. This enhancement in both awareness and expertise makes up transcendent technique: our technical mastery of the art of inspiring, guiding, and teaching others to heal themselves.

Because of this expanded scope of altruistic outreach, this stage is called the Expansive. In effect, it reflects not only the deepening of our newfound capacity to cut the causal network of stress at its roots, but also the natural spin-off of that capacity in our dealings with others. This natural expansion of our altruistic capacity is also facilitated by the fact that our growing ability to realize the freedom and clarity of cessation makes it more and more accessible outside formal meditations in our daily dealings with others. In effect, on this stage the oscillation between our spacious equipoise and our dreamlike aftermath insights begins to dissolve, and we grow able to draw on our transcendent wisdom in the midst of our compassionate action. Here is how Nagarjuna describes the achievements of this stage:

> The seventh (stage) is Expansive
> Since the extent (of the altruist's art) greatly expands,
> Because s/he can enter the equipoise of cessation
> (Instantaneously) from moment to moment.
> Through the maturation of this triumph
> S/he leads those in Control of Others' Fantasies,
> And with genuine intuitive realization
> Of the noble truths, becomes a master teacher.[85]

The Mark of Having Learned is Being Endowed with Five Kinds of Munificence

Relying on the foundation of self-transcendent wisdom and empathic art, the altruist in this phase of moral development enters the final stages of cultivation that will eventually result in full maturity and integration. As we begin to grow into mature altruism, breaking out of our reactive self with wisdom and reaching out to others with empathic art, our new way of being begins to take on individual shape, based on whom and how we aspire to help. Chekawa's yardstick here is standardized to the fivefold typology of native geniuses and altruistic styles recognized in the engaged teaching tradition. Within that typology, the variety of individual gifts and paths is categorized in terms of what are called the five families of enlightenment.[86]

These families are usually identified by symbols that represent their special gifts for transforming compulsions into altruistic intentions and actions. The wheel family transforms aggression into peace-making and non-violent activism. The jewel family transforms acquisitiveness into universal compassion and compassionate giving. The lotus family transforms clinging into contemplative self-healing and empathic art. The sword family transforms competitiveness into altruistic leadership and unbridled compassionate action. The scepter family transforms pride into self-transcendent wisdom and unconditional love. The traditional commentary on this precept lists a sample of five types of enlightened altruist that line up with these families, which I like to call the moral altruist, the inspired altruist, the contemplative altruist, the active altruist, and the transcendent altruist.

Of course, these are "ideal types" or archetypes rather than fixed and rigid categories. Within each there is a wide range for the diversity of different individuals and their specific aspirations and missions. Yet there's also a common pathway by which each individual must progress in finding and developing a mature altruistic vocation. That common pathway is the final clearing away of any trace emotional blocks to freedom of mind and a shift in focus towards the removal of cognitive-perceptual blocks to compassionate objectivity. As the altruist's mind is increasingly cleared of the layers of misperception that have accumulated over the years and across generations, the primal instincts for self-reification that cloud the mind's full potential to see reality as it is can be gradually unlearned. This process not only seals the transformation to a transparent inner life of radical open-mindedness but also enhances and guides the development of a social life of compassionate engagement. As we'll see, this final phase of meditative transformation is guided by the penultimate stages of self-transcendence, focused on the cultivation of self-transcendent affirmation and power.

Removing Our Blocks to Objective Altruism: The Stage of Engaged Meditation, Part IV

Supporting the step of growing into our altruistic role and mission is the final phase of the meditation stage on the engaged path of contemplation. Given the full realization of transcendent wisdom and healing art, self-analysis, and emotional self-mastery have reached the point where we can stop the reinforcement of stress-reactive habits and uproot the instinctive emotions that anchor them. As our ability to extinguish these instincts ripples out from our meditative breakthroughs to free us in every moment of our lives, we gradually complete the removal of even the subtlest emotional blocks to lasting peace and freedom of mind. With our minds consistently settled, clear, and positively energized, we can now begin the final work of clearing away the most insidious of its instinctive blocks: the self-deceptive instincts to reify, identify with and cling to traumatic distortions of self and world that cloud the natural clarity and objectivity of consciousness. This final process of clearing the mind is vital both to free our emerging, proactive self from any lingering identification with trauma and to enhance the capacity of that new self to engage others and the world with a radically open and caring mind.

A person who can identify with the selfless mind within or beneath our biased constructs of self and world gains an optimal capacity to see people and things as objectively as a living being can. This capacity is invaluable both in knowing and caring for one's own life and in knowing and caring for others. In a sense, such a selfless awareness can climb into other's minds like a highly intuitive therapist, or an omniscient narrator in a novel. Far from a passive accident of neural function, such an enlightened consciousness can support an expanded, objective form of self-efficacy like that Thomas Nagel described as "the objective self." Yet it is equally far from conventional views of the mind of God, conceived as a unitary person, being or spirit, ultimately distinct from the minds of ordinary living beings. Instead, it is a self-transcendent potential within us all, akin to what the Greeks called our *daimon* or native genius.

Climbing out of our own myopic standpoint is not only vital to seeing things from the standpoint of others—in the big picture of interdependence—but also to understanding how people and things actually work, so that we can effectively help ourselves and others. Viewed in this light, these final stages help us see the Buddhist map of the altruist's path in perspective as mapping the cultivation not just of enlightened altruism per se but of a socially engaged, enlightened form of human genius.[87] Given this, the fivefold typology of munificence Chekawa mentions may be read as a comprehensive framework of such altruistic genius. In particular, we can re-translate the five ideal types I glossed above in current terms, as moral genius, psychological genius, creative and contemplative genius, organizational genius, and scientific-philosophical genius. Seen in light of this ambitious quest to reach the highest levels of human performance and social self-efficacy, we may better appreciate why the reflections that guide this phase are on self-transcendent affirmation and power.

The Thirteenth Reflection: Transcendent Affirmation and the Immovable Stage

The moral step of growing into our altruistic genius and the contemplative work of removing the grossest blocks to objectivity are guided by the thirteenth reflection—on self-transcendent affirmation. By applying the combined force of transcendent wisdom and technique to cut through our confused identification with a traumatic sense of inadequacy, we are freed to immerse ourselves unconditionally in the flow of self-transcendent wisdom, empathic communication and compassionate action. As a consequence, the affirmative commitments and pledges that planted the seeds for our distinctive mission as altruists now begin to bear fruit in artful mastery of mind, speech, and body, without our having to rely on conceptual thinking or conscious effort. In the language of Chandrakirti, we have finally reached the state of unconditional compassion, in which we respond to others' needs and wishes spontaneously, while staying immersed in the non-conceptual flow whose twin faces are spacious equipoise and illusory aftermath. So while we seem to others to embody the pure enjoyment and emanation of perfect altruism, our experience is one of unwavering immersion in pure openmindedness and objectivity. Hence this stage of harvesting the fruition of our affirmative commitments and pledges is called Immovable. Chandrakirti describes this in his *Introduction*:

> This pacified body is radiant, like a wish-granting tree,
> And without conceptuality, like a wish-fulfilling jewel.
> It remains, for the benefit of the world, until all beings are freed,
> And appears to those who are free from fabrication.
> Just as a potter with great strength
> Expends great energy turning his wheel for a long time,
> And later, though he invests no more effort,
> It turns and appears to produce a pot,
> So one abiding in the body with the essence of truth,
> Without making (the least) effort now,
> Engages in deeds wholly inconceivable
> By the nature of his (prior) vows and the virtues of beings.[88]

Here is how Nagarjuna describes this stage:

> The (ever) youthful eighth (stage) is Immovable
> Because (here, the altruist) never moves
> From non-conceptual (flow), and the scope of her
> Mental, verbal and physical acts is likewise inconceivable.
> Through the maturation of this triumph,
> S/he becomes the master creator of a thousand worlds,
> And is unsurpassed by saints, hermit sages or disciples
> In expressing the meaning of (contemplative) teachings.[89]

The Fourteenth Reflection: Transcendent Power and the Pure Genius Stage

As the reflection on transcendent affirmation comes to fruition, the moral step of growing into genius and the contemplative phase of removing the moderate blocks to objectivity is guided by the fourteenth reflection, on self-transcendent power. Here again, by applying the combined force of transcendent wisdom and technique to cut through our confused identification with the self-reifying instinct itself, we are freed to fully realize and immerse ourselves in our capacity for selfless objectivity. As a consequence, we realize the full, unbridled genius of our natural minds, and can apply this genius without any hindrance to optimize our effectiveness in helping others. So this stage of realizing and harnessing the unbounded power of our minds is called the stage of Pure Genius. Here is how Nagarjuna described it:

> The ninth stage is called Pure Genius
> Because, like a crown prince,
> (The altruist) has gained genuine personal experience,
> And so has excellent intelligence about this (reality).
> Through the maturation of this triumph,
> S/he becomes the master creator of a million worlds,

And is unsurpassed by (contemplatives) like saints
In reading the minds of living beings.[90]

When Adept Despite Distractions, You Have Learned: Altruistic Self-Mastery

The final step on the altruist's path of moral development is the culmination of all the self-correction and cultivation practiced throughout all prior steps and stages. In the course of this final moral advance, the altruist's embodiment of compassionate openness becomes totally unconditional, since no internal blocks are left to hinder it and no adverse circumstance can obstruct its full natural expression. Also due to this step, the altruist's pure open-mindedness and unconditional compassion, along with the spacious and illusory intuitions supporting them, become fully and finally integrated, continuous, and inseparable. Given the full ripening of the altruist's self-mastery, his/her qualities finally mature into the eighteen distinctive qualities of enlightenment, including unfailing correctness, poise, memory, concentration, non-dual insight, equanimity, will, energy, mindfulness, awareness, wisdom, and freedom; as well as continuous wisdom through all mental, verbal, and physical actions, and unhindered vision of the past, present, and future.[91]

The Contemplative Stage of Engaged Social Mastery

The culmination of the altruist's moral development is supported by the final stage of the engaged contemplative path, in which fully integrated transcendent wisdom and empathic art yields the union of blissful freedom of mind with pure objectivity. This integrated mastery is possible thanks to the removal of even the subtlest blocks to omniscience, which frees the mind to immerse itself fully and finally in the ultimate emptiness of all people and things while simultaneously seeing the relative causal workings of suffering and happiness precisely and objectively, just as they are. This full maturation of altruistic genius makes the altruist on this stage a master of the art of empathically understanding, inspiring and guiding all individuals and communities, fostering the transformation of their countless life-worlds. Traditionally, the fruition of this stage is unpacked in terms of the eighteen qualities listed above, together with the ten powers of enlightenment, four forms of fearlessness, and four forms of valid knowledge.

The ten powers reflect the expertise about human development gained on the altruist's path to self-mastery. Traditionally, they are listed as: the power of knowing right from wrong; of knowing the developmental consequences of actions; of knowing the inclinations of other minds; of knowing the various types of personality; of knowing the range of capacities of different beings; of knowing the universal path of self-healing; of knowing how contemplative states remove afflictions and blocks; of knowing our own (and others') evolutionary past; of knowing the death and posterity of living beings; and of knowing the end of suffering. As in the modern practice of psychotherapy, these powers of knowledge are understood not as supernatural powers but as expert capacities based on the gradual development of natural faculties for introspective self-knowledge and empathic awareness of other minds. Reflecting the mastery that grows along with this expertise, the four forms of fearlessness here are: fearlessness in facing reality, ending afflictions, facing the persistence of blocks, and progressing on the path to success. Finally, the four forms of valid knowledge are vital to the altruist's empathic art of communicating his/her mastery and confidence, including knowledge of conventions of language, of the meanings of words, of the aspects of the referents of words, and of the prosody that expresses nuances and emotional tones.[92] In short, the fully mature altruist is not only a master of his/her mature form of altruistic genius, but also a fearless leader and a great communicator.

The Fifteenth Reflection: Transcendent Intuition and the Cloud of Truth Stage

The moral step of unconditional realization and the contemplative work of clearing the subtlest blocks to objectivity are guided by the fifteenth and last reflection on the altruist's path: the reflection on self-transcendent intuition. With the final taints that might bias or cloud the natural, selfless clarity of the altruist's genius removed, s/he is free to finally and fully master the direct, intuitive wisdom which endows all his/her intentions, expressions, and actions with the qualities of perfect guidance. S/he effectively becomes a natural and spontaneous source of abundant nurturance to all, regardless of the diversity of their needs, capacities, and aims. Since the altruist on this final stage of self-mastery becomes a source of valid teaching and guidance that nurtures the growth of altruism in all beings, the stage is called the Cloud of Truth or Cloud of Teaching. Here is how Nagarjuna describes this culmination:

> The tenth (stage) is the Cloud of Truth,
> Since the altruist showers (the world) with a rain
> Of healing truth, and (her/his empathic art)
> Is consecrated with the brilliance of the enlightened.
> Through the maturation of this triumph
> S/he comes to master the states of creative genius
> And is the (world's) supreme authority (since s/he)
> Masters the objectivity of inconceivable intuition.[93]

Points Six and Seven: The Commitments and Pledges of Everyday Altruism

Of course, the higher stages of the path leading to fully mature altruism naturally strike us as so far beyond our present capacity or potential that it may seem the province of the lucky few virtuosos or professional contemplatives. While the contemplative lifestyle and community structured by the monastic code of discipline may allow monks and nuns to aspire to develop such mature altruism, the five moral precepts that guide lay practitioners outside the monastery are hardly enough to bring a day to day practice of enlightened altruism within reach. Of course, there are the eighteen pledges of an enlightened altruist, but these are not as complete or down-to-earth as the commitments of the monastic code. It is here that the practice of mind-clearing can be an invaluable bridge, offering a lay ethos and discipline of compassionate living that can build on the five precepts and help us approach an altruist's way of life in the everyday world.

Of all the formats in which the mind-clearing has been taught and practiced down to our day, Chekawa's seven-point format provides the most complete, tangible and accessible set of guidelines. So having cross-referenced his map of the moral path of mind-clearing with the contemplative map of the engaged five stages and the map of the fifteen reflections on the altruist's path of insight, we now turn to survey the ethical guidelines Chekawa offers in points six and seven of his text. The first of these is a list of eighteen commitments, meant to prepare us to avoid the main pitfalls that lead to digressions or simply block progress towards an altruist's life. The second is a list of twenty-two pledges, meant to point us in the direction of everyday actions that gradually prepare us to embark and progress on the path towards an altruist's life. Given limits of space, I'll simply list these with some brief clarifying notes.

The Eighteen Don'ts: The Commitments of Clearing the Mind

1-3. *Always Reflect on the Three Principles*: Humility, Integrity, Impartiality
4. *Transform Your Intentions But Stay as You Are*: Maintaining Anonymity
5 *Don't Mention (Other's) Handicaps*: Practicing Transcendent Tolerance
6. *Don't Even Think About the Limitations of Others*: Radical Acceptance
7. *Purify Your Worst Addiction First*: Keeping it Real And Grounded
8. *Give Up Any Expectation of Results*: Keeping the Focus on Process
9. *Give Up Your Diet of Poison(ous Vices)*: Releasing Negativity
10. *Don't Indulge Self-Righteousness*: Mind Your Motivation
11. *Don't React to Insults*: Monitor Your Social Stress Reactivity
12. *Don't Wait in Ambush*: Restrain the Urge for Revenge
13. *Don't Go for the Jugular*: Restrain Your Attack Urges
14. *Don't Lay Your Burden on Others*: No Dumping or Passing the Buck
15. *Don't Pervert the (Authentic) View*: Avoid Exploiting the Teaching
16. *Don't Aim for the Top of the Heap*: Restrain Competition
17. *Don't Make Your Genius a Demon*: Don't Indulge Grandiosity
18. *Don't Seek Satisfaction in the Miseries (of Others)*: Avoid Malice

The Twenty-Two Do's: The Pledges of Clearing the Mind

1. *Practice All Yogas as One*: The Art of Compassionate Openness
2. *Subdue All Resistance With One (Art):* Practice Giving and Taking
3. *At the Start and End (of Each Day), (Practice) Both the Two Actions:* Motivation and Dedication
4. *Tolerate Both (Good and Bad), Whatever Comes:* Maintain Equanimity
5. *Guard Both (These and Your Other) Vows as Your Life*: Maintain Commitment
6. *Master the Three Hardest (Challenges)*: Expose, Reduce, and Eliminate Blocks
7. *Nurture the Three Principal Roots*: Affirmation, Dedication, and Preparation
8. *Practice Three Kinds of Relentlessness*: Trust, Effort, and Wisdom
9. *Become Triply Inseparable (from the Practice)*: In Body, Speech, and Mind
10. *Practice Perfect Impartiality Towards Objects*: of Desire, Aversion, Indifference
11. *It Is Vital to Learn Profoundly and All-Inclusively*: Be Thorough and Rigorous
12. *Meditate Constantly on Special Cases*: Intimates, Enemies, the Disagreeable
13. *Don't Depend on External Conditions*: Cultivate Unconditional Care
14. *Take Up the Principal Practice Right Now*: Practice the Urgency of Now
15. *Don't Be Wrong-Headed*: Avoid Debasing the Contemplative Life
16. *Don't Be Erratic*: Practice Patiently and Consistently
17. *Learn Decisively*: Make Your Learning and Practice Count
18. *Break Free with Both Investigation and Analysis*: Complete Your Self-Analysis
19. *Don't Boast About Practice*: Work with Relentless Humility
20. *Don't Indulge Frustration*: Guard Your Practice with Transcendent Tolerance
21. *Don't Be Temperamental*: Break Your Addiction to Drama
22. *Don't Expect Thanks*: Trust Your Inner Leader

The Seven Point Mind-Clearing: Building a Rigorous Practice in the World

While Chekawa's lists of commitments and pledges are meant to help structure a rigorous daily practice that can bring consistency and genuine change within reach, surveying them all at once may still feel overwhelming. In practice, these precepts are not meant as rules we can immediately live by, but rather as pointers and guidelines for applying mind-clearing in daily life. Rather than trying to memorize and live by them all at once, the tradition is to simply read the three pages of precepts that make up Chekawa's text, including the ethical precepts of points six and seven. The idea is that, through familiarity over time, one or more of these pithy reminders will naturally come to mind in relevant situations, offering us an alternative to our habitual instincts and habits. When I teach these two points, I encourage people to pick out the few precepts that seem to hit home, since they likely address what they know to be their "worst addiction." By reflecting on these in a sustained and continuous way, we may find ourselves gradually gaining in insight and presence of mind, without our having to mount some superhuman, perfectionistic effort to change. This, I believe, is consistent with the healing pedagogy of the mind-clearing, and so I'll try to simulate how such anecdotal reflection may work in our closing meditative experiment.

Meditative Experiment 6: Using Commitments and Pledges

As before, start settling into a peaceful space and a comfortable, stable posture. Then cleanse your breath by exhaling an extra-long sigh or alternate-nostril breathing. Let your next breath be as gentle and fresh as possible, waiting patiently for the air to fill your receptive body as effortlessly as you can. Let this fresh, restorative breath start your shift towards a kinder, gentler rhythm of breathing centered at your heart. And as you feel that shift, take your gentler breath-rhythm as a focal point for gathering, settling, and centering more and more of your vital energy and awareness on your breathing body. As your body begins feeling lighter and clearer, scan and balance all your sensations, then immerse and bathe your mindfulness in the clear flow of primal awareness, and finally, stretch part of your attention upwards to scan the waves and currents of thoughts, images, and emotions that fill your waking mind.

Now open this all-inclusive mindfulness outwards to the world around you. While staying tuned to the healing energy and awareness within, imagine your mindfulness setting up a firewall around you that filters out any distractions or triggers coming in from the stress-world. Lightened and uplifted by your meditative body-mind, imagine you're on top of the world, and look down with care on the lives of all those around you in the city, country, and planet. Try to see through the surface disruptions of stress and the noise of idle chatter to feel your way into the healing energy that keeps us all growing and the pure open-mindedness that keeps us all learning. As you scan the variety of beings on all continents, imagine all those near and dear, unknown to you, and against you living in five different levels of stress and trauma, driven by the stress-emotions of anger, greed, clinging, envy, and pride. Imagine the hellish lives of beings driven by violence on the bottom tier; the ghostly lives of beings driven by greed just above them; the human condition of those driven by clinging in the midst of the stress world;

the titanic struggles of those driven by envy in the upper tier; and the god-like lives of those driven by compulsive pride and self-satisfaction on top.

As you survey the various struggles of those in the world outside your firewall, notice and try to release your unrealistic bias to favor the dear, avoid the remote and ignore the unknown, and work instead to embrace all living beings with equal acceptance and care. In their presence, try, a breath at a time, to shift your energies from clinging to love, from indifference to care and from aversion to tolerance. Keep taking others in with care on the in-breath and sharing your love, care, and peace on the out-breath, until you feel yourself gradually move towards a leveling sense of equality and interconnectedness with all life. Let your heart and mind break free of the death-grip of your self-enclosing survival instincts, like a cornered animal or traumatized child suddenly released into a safe haven of unconditional freedom and abundance.

Now feel your heart, warmed by the breath of your giving and taking, beginning to melt through the remaining stress-knots that bind you, thaw out your tender-heartedness and fully open up to the world. As you breathe in and out, taking in all beings with care and sharing yourself with equanimity and love, imagine the rainbow heart-drop of your empathy building, a breath at a time, until it fills your whole body as a flame fills a lamp or a nectar, a vase, flowing out of you like a rainbow wave that ripples out in all your interactions with others, connecting your heart and theirs in one boundless, unifying field. Now try to melt your sense of self into that connective field and feel your awareness and sensitivity stretch into every life around you, until you find yourself in their shoes, sensing their aims and needs as if each was your only child.

Take some time breathing your way into this objective self, sending loving breath from your heart-drop and feel it rippling out through your connective field-self to all the other hearts, and gathering in breath with care from all the other hearts back into yours. Try a breath at a time to feel your way into the varied textures of all their lives, sensing their various levels of compulsion and struggle. Imagine your in and out breath travelling like waves out and back through your connective field-self, taking in their needs for security, help, and direction and giving back what you can in the way of protection, aid, and guidance. The more you tune in, the more you'll begin to feel the pull on your heart strings of all the fear, thirst, and confusion of the various kinds of beings around you, triggering your own negativity in response to theirs. Now try to prepare yourself to resist those triggers by reflecting on five key commitments and pledges of clearing the mind, one for each of the root compulsions driving beings in the stress-world.

As you focus on beings living hellish lives at the lowest common denominator of violence, repeat mentally or out loud the commitments,

"Don't go for the jugular," "Don't wait in ambush," and/or *"Don't retaliate to verbal abuse."* As you tune into the struggles of the insatiable living ghostly lives impoverished by a sense of scarcity and greed, repeat mentally or out loud, *"Give up any expectation of results,"* and/or *"Give up your diet of poison(ous vices)."* As you take in the struggles of animals and average humans living traumatic lives of fear and clinging, repeat mentally or out loud, *"Transform your intentions but stay as you are," "Don't depend on external conditions,"* and/or *"Tolerate both (good and bad), whatever comes."* As you feel the compulsion of those struggling to be larger-than-life, consumed with envy, jealousy, and competitiveness, repeat mentally or out loud, *"Don't aim for the top of the heap,"* and/or *"Don't seek satisfaction in the miseries (of others)."* And finally, as you sense the self-imposed isolation of fortunate beings living lives at the top of the food chain, intoxicated with complacency, self-satisfaction, and inflated pride, repeat mentally or out loud, *"Don't turn your genius into a demon," "Don't indulge self-righteousness,"* and/or *"Don't be temperamental."*

Try to welcome these pulls as part of the growing pains of your altruistic new self and of all those around you, and harness the energy freed from reactivity to the reflection that the only true solution for life on this planet is for you and all in your field to cultivate our human genius for altruism so we can all work together for the good of all. Finally, let this spark of inspiration ignite in your heart the spirit of enlightenment that wills the good of all by choosing an altruistic life in the world and offering it as an example to all those you touch with your field-self. As you begin to feel this spark ignite your heart, imagine the warmth and light it generates rippling out on the breath as a rainbow wave that travels through your field self to all other hearts in the world, lighting the spark of their own altruism. Imagine that rainbow wave splitting into a whole spectrum of healing energies: the pure white of tolerance disarming the hurt and angry; the gold of generosity satisfying the insatiable, the ruby red of mindfulness calming all fears; the emerald green of affirmation turning envy into team spirit; and the sapphire blue of wisdom turning pride into objectivity.

Now, as the inner light of altruism dawns at once in all the hearts in the world, imagine it merging into one tidal wave of rainbow lights and nectars that travels back from the ends of the earth, transforming the planet into a peaceful utopia, until it returns to your space, and coalesces into your heart as a rainbow drop of clarity and joy. To close, let the world and all its life return to their current condition, and let yourself return to normal, while holding the drop of the spirit of enlightenment in your heart. Commit whatever insight or energy you've gained in this mediation to your ongoing study, reflection, and practice, for your own benefit and for the sake of the whole world around you.

Part 3

Turning the Mind Wheel

Creativity and Cultural Healing

7 Role-Modeling Imagery and Self-Transformation

> If emptiness were the technique, there would be no (complete) enlightenment. No fruit is of a genus different from its seed, so emptiness cannot be the art (of embodying enlightenment). Victors teach emptiness to vanquish the self-(reifying) constructs of those who insist on their view of (personal) self and those who reject the view (that things also lack self). Hence, it is (envisioning) the sphere of a perfected world which binds the blissful art. Through union with the dignity of an enlightened being, enlightenment will not be far. The Teacher was endowed with the thirty-two signs and eighty-four marks (of altruistic embodiment). Therefore, the technique is to assume (the form of) success, which is the Teacher's form itself.
>
> (The Diamond Pavilion Process[1])

In unpacking the Nalanda tradition of role-modeling altruism preserved in Tibet, the great scholar Tsong Khapa used this Indian reference to resolve some misconceptions surrounding this art, which he frames as the ultimate power tool for altruistic living in the world.[2] The background for the quote is the path of social healing we explored in part 2, based on the cultivation of the wisdom of emptiness and the art of compassion. It assumes the two-pronged engaged method of social healing: the wisdom of emptiness frees the mind from clinging to the reactive self; while the technique or art of compassion builds the foundation for a proactive, mature self of altruistic social engagement. The passage then lays out the rationale for the process-oriented path, as a quicker alternative to that engaged path to altruism. Essentially, that rationale is to use emptiness—as on the engaged path—to develop radical openness of mind, while substituting role-modeling imagery and the "blissful art" of sublimation as more effective methods of quickly embodying mature altruism.

Tsong Khapa's reading of this passage offers a natural entry-point for exploring the process-oriented methods that will be our focus in the second half of this book. First, his comments address the big question most moderns have when faced with the arts of role-modeling imagery and sublimation. Given the tried and true contemplative paths of self-healing and social engagement, why complicate our contemplative life with other paths and tools? The opening passage he cites supports his response. Unlike the geological pace of cultivating empathy and altruism on the ordinary path of social engagement, the arts of imagery and sublimation used on the extraordinary process path are so effective that, for the would-be altruist who uses them, "*enlightenment will not be far.*"

In effect, it is the heroic urge of the engaged path—to help as many as possible, as much as possible—which motivates the budding altruist engaged with the world to seek the quickest, most powerful methods of self-transformation at hand. The difference is highlighted by the divergent estimates of how long it takes for an ordinary self-enclosed being to become an enlightened altruist following these two paths. Though by modern standards, the "quicker" process path is anything but fast—requiring from one to sixteen human lifetimes—it is light years ahead of the three eons the ordinary engaged path is said to require. In fact, the traditional life-stories of exemplary process altruists recount training periods from six to twelve years,[3] aligning them with the time Shakyamuni spent in retreat, as well as the time it takes for the higher education and training of an expert in one of our modern arts or sciences.[4]

The Quick Path: Dispelling Three Timeless Misconceptions

Of course, this contrast in rates of progress raises a host of questions, then as now. Is it really possible to become an enlightened altruist in as little as ten to twelve years? And if so, by what method can such a remarkable human achievement be so replicated? Tsong Khapa's explanation of our opening quote follows a full discussion of the similarities and differences between the ordinary path of social engagement and the extraordinary process-oriented path, clearing away misconceptions about why and how the extraordinary path works as it does. Among these, we find three key features of the process path that have been taken to distinguish it from the ordinary engaged path, then and now: (1) it works by the sublimation of passions that are normally compulsions; (2) it works by relying on blissful or euphoric states that facilitate sublimation and flow; (3) it works by tapping and channeling the energy and chemistry of bliss within the central nervous system's subtle network of complexes, channels, energies, and drops.[5]

Though our Tibetan guide was addressing misconceptions in the scholarly literature of his day, they dovetail neatly with confusions surrounding the popularization of India's process arts in ours. Since these confusions pose some risk to the healthy development of those who dabble in such power tools, traditionally, process methods were shrouded in secrecy and revealed only to prepared individuals in supervised settings.[6] Fortunately or not, their mass dissemination in new-age contexts like workshops on "tantric sex," "*Kundalini* energy," or "*chakra* alignment" has lead authorities like the Dalai Lama to urge traditional and Western scholars to make reliable information on their proper understanding and use just as widely available.[7] In this spirit, I've developed ways of introducing the modern scientific mind to the mechanisms, risks, and benefits of the more advanced practices that will occupy us in the rest of this book.

Tsong Khapa's response to our three popular misconceptions is instructive if we want to understand how role-modeling imagery and sublimation work. His first point is that the skillful transformation of potentially destructive passions like aggression or sexual desire is a key feature of any contemplative life, especially a lay, contemplative life in the world. Process practice is no exception. To foster true altruism, it must help us learn new ways to work with primal instincts that could have destructive effects. This point is often obscured by the sensual imagery and language of the process teachings themselves.[8] The fact is that our ability to derive healthy energy from the passions strictly depends on our strengthening our natural capacities for modulating, sublimating, and transmuting them into positive social emotions like tolerance, generosity, solidarity and integrity. As I like to say when I teach process arts: if you want to learn how to play with fire, you first have to learn how to safely put it out.

Tsong Khapa's second point is that the art of tapping into euphoric bliss-states is not unique to process methods, but is key to the motivation of contemplative life on any path. Whether we're practicing self-healing through deep mindfulness, social healing through compassionate openness, or heroic altruism through imagery and inspiration, our progress and success depend on tapping flow states that are the meditative equivalents of a runner's high.[9] Without engaging our core systems of internal reward, it would be impossible for us to motivate any behavior, healthy or not. What sets contemplative highs apart is that they consciously harness our bliss system to the aims and insights of our highest levels of reflective awareness, bringing this ultimate engine of motivation and reinforcement under conscious self-regulation.[10] What's unique in the process approach to bliss-states has less to do with the aim of harnessing them than with the path it takes to that aim. Instead of taking the slow and steady path, starting with the calming, low-arousal states of basic mindfulness and quiescence, the process path begins with moderate to high arousal states that have more in common with euphoric flow, the common pathway in which all contemplative paths converge.[11] Why and how this high-arousal approach can work safely, without triggering compulsions and stress-reactivity, is something we'll return to when we consider the distinctive qualities that do define process methods.

The final misconception to clarify is that process methods can be best distinguished from ordinary engaged methods by their link with the contemplative neuroscience mapped in the so-called "subtle-body" familiar to us from *Hatha* yoga. Of course, in their advanced forms, the role-modeling imagery and sublimation techniques of this path are explicitly linked with contemplative maps of the nervous system that guide self-regulation.[12] Yet the effectiveness of these methods is not a direct result of that powerful technology of self-regulation. This point is underscored by the fact that there are introductory and intermediate level practices on this path only implicitly linked with contemplative neuroscience.[13] These include the basic methods of role-modeling altruism that will be our focus in the rest of this and remaining chapters.[14]

Quite apart from the new transparency about process methods advocated by the Dalai Lama and others, these introductory process practices have historically been widely accessible to beginners in India and Tibet. In fact, they are often expressly used to offer busy lay practitioners quicker, more effective contemplative tools for healing physical and mental illnesses, promoting longevity and optimal health, and enhancing self-transformation and moral development.[15] This open door policy is possible because the entry level forms of role-modeling imagery and sublimation are continuous with the conventional practices of social engagement, while offering technical enhancements that ease and speed progress in contemplative life.

Three Distinctive Features of the Process-Oriented Path

If the process practices we're exploring are not distinguished by their ability to transform passions, harness bliss-states, or control neural events, what does distinguish them from the practices of social engagement? Our opening reference alludes to three distinctive aspects of this powerful technology: (1) its inseparable union of wisdom and method; (2) its transformational use of role-modeling imagery; and (3) the unique goal-orientation that motivates the practice.

1. *(Envisioning) the Sphere of a Perfected World is what Binds the Blissful Art*

One of the rate-limiting features of the ordinary path of social engagement, you may recall, is the oscillation between the binary insight modes that fostered the two main aspects of mind-clearing and enlightened altruism. This oscillation means that the two wings needed for a socially engaged life to fly—radical openness and unconditional compassion—must be developed separately and can only be dovetailed together gradually over time. This piecemeal method slows progress, not just because we only work on one key aspect of practice at a time, but also because the maturation of each aspect critically depends on input from the other. So gains made in openness within meditation sessions cannot translate right away into corresponding gains in empathic art between sessions, and vice versa, since the window between the spacious equipoise insight and the illusory aftermath insight closes quickly.

The non-dual nature of process methods offers a quantum leap in efficiency. By conjoining images of altruistic agency with a simultaneous insight into the ultimate openness or emptiness of that imagery, process practice offers a way to cultivate both wings of enlightened altruism simultaneously and in concert. More challenging in the short run, this method of building wisdom and empathic art together at once saves time, both through multi-tasking and through offering an open window for the integrated development of radical openness and compassion. In effect, this method starts us off now in a form of meditation that simulates the work of integration only reached at the highest levels on the ordinary path of social engagement.

By conjoining the emptiness insight with our vision of *a perfected world*—a map of the way of being and life we're trying to create—we effectively provide our whole mind/body process with a complex gyroscope that serves at once to model the freedom *from* our old reactive self and the freedom *to* build a new proactive one. This vision, called a *mandala*, is said to *bind the blissful art* since it gives our minds and bodies a symbolic pathway or bridge to guide our transition from an ordinary stress-reactive way of being towards a proactive engagement motivated by positive affects like compassion and blissful openness.[16] Here, it may help to draw some comparisons between this methodology and contemporary imagery research and therapies.

Conjoining Insight and Technique: The Process Method and Modern Therapies

While modern psychotherapy has been shaped by Freud's break with hypnosis,[17] current research challenges his concern that hypnotic imagery works by suggestion and so hinders or dulls insight and learning.[18] The new consensus is that hypnosis and imagery work by enhancing attention, problem-solving and learning, like free-association and meditation.[19] Freud's observations may have been more an artifact of the mindset and setting of hypnotherapy in his day, which emphasized the influence of the therapist and had a regressive bias towards suggestion.[20] In light of current research, the conjunction of visual and auditory imagery with analytic insight appears to enhance learning and performance by fostering a balanced laterality and promoting the integration of cognitive, perceptual, emotional and behavioral aspects of learning.[21] This may be why mental imagery has been increasingly used by athletes, performers and coaches, as well as in integrative medicine and psychotherapy.[22] As in the simulation techniques used to train pilots, soldiers, first responders, and others, imagery helps enrich cognitive learning with the virtual rehearsal of perceptual, motivational and behavioral skills, in a gestalt mode that primes the mind-brain to support complex forms of performance.[23] Given the obvious fact that imagery encodes not just abstract information but specific emotional tones, expressive gestures and action-patterns, it should come as no surprise that they could be part of a concerted strategy for multi-dimensional learning. How does this work?

Stuff of Dreams: Revisiting the Quantum Theory of Consciousness

To flesh such methods out, it may help to return to the quantum theory of consciousness we mentioned earlier.[24] As we learned, the brain does not work like a camera that passively mirrors reality, but like a complex supercomputer that actively generates a virtual simulation of ourselves and the world. As wave-like pulses of bioelectricity sweep from the brain's core through its outer cortex every fortieth of a second, each pulse electrically links nerve cells in various parts of the brain, including sense input, memories and associations. The result is a momentary wave of activity that supports one flash or instant of consciousness in something like the way an old TV signal created an image by lighting up an array of pixels on a screen. Like one single frame in a film, each wave connects the waves before and after it, effectively splicing them into a series that creates the illusion of a continuous moving picture of life in real time.

The net result of this process is that the stream of consciousness, like the sequence of a film, mixes a few drops of sense information into a flow of memory and imagination, creating a sense of reality and solidity out of something that is mostly dreams and reflections. The only difference between brain function in the dream state and in the waking state, as we saw, is that the waking brain takes in a few bites of sense information now and then and adjusts its simulation accordingly, while the dreaming brain is free to drift on the currents of memory and fantasy alone. Our experience in the waking state is closer to a dream or a flight simulator than to the cold, hard picture of reality we take it for. So, Shakespeare was literally right when he said in his comedy, *The Tempest*, "We are such stuff as dreams are made on."

How Mind Matters: The Bridge of Imagery and Affirmation

This theory shows that replacing the narrative and images that fill our everyday minds with another narrative and set of images may have tangible consequences on our outlook, mood and physiology. Recent studies that look at the way neural activity relates to mental activity in perception and consciousness suggest that the brain takes what's in our consciousness at any given time as if it were a matter of fact.[25] A vivid mental image of a given color, for instance, evokes essentially the same activation, both in the retina and in the cortex, as the visual perception of that color, overriding the actual data of sense perception.[26] Still more astounding, vividly imagining a flame at a particular point in the body not only generates much the same neural activity as subjecting that point to heat, but will also increase blood flow and raise temperature in the part of the body where the flame is imagined.[27]

While our perceptions of ourselves and the world are at least in part creative constructs of mind, those constructions have significant and far-reaching impact on the way our brains filter information and the way our bodies respond to external and internal events.[28] Mentally generated imagery is woven into our routine perception of the world in a way that seems to have a real impact on our outlook, mood, and physiology.[29] So the mental imagery that fills in gaps in our perception is like a software operating system for the wetware of our brains.[30] Anthropology has shown us that the symbolic software of human perception can take many forms depending on the aims and interests of different societies and cultural traditions.[31] Also, current psychology has found a wide range in the way individuals experience and respond to events, depending on whether their view of the world is optimistic or pessimistic, open or closed.[32]

Healing Mental Imagery: An Alternate Operating System for Our Mind and Life

For all our brain and body know, *our world is as we envision it*. If we go through our days seeing ourselves as powerless and alone, and the world as a life-or-death struggle for scarce resources, we are effectively setting our brains and bodies on guard and enhancing the threat seemingly posed by each and every event.[33] If, on the other hand, we see ourselves as capable and effective, and the world as a basically safe space for living and learning, we are setting our brains and bodies at ease and predisposing ourselves to respond to the events of the day as creative challenges or play.[34] Crafting a positive vision of life that prepares us to act in ways that match our aims and values can help us realize our highest aims for ourselves and our world. So a method of reliably changing our software for perception and response could dramatically expand our horizons of healthy change.

2. *By Union with the Dignity of an Enlightened Being, Enlightenment will not be Far*

The next key aspect of the art of role-modeling imagery in this tradition is that it doesn't use imagery in an open-ended, naturalistic way but in a depth-psychological way that revolves around the human image of an archetypal self, an image that represents a congenial vision of heroic altruism shared by a master and apprentice altruist. It is this art of role-modeling altruism with the help of archetypal self-images that Tsong Khapa proclaims the single most distinctive and defining feature of all process practices. Traditionally called the art of Buddha pride or mentor-archetype yoga, this practice aims to speed and guide the interpersonal transmission of altruistic genius from mentor to student, generation to generation. I call the images used in this art archetypal, following scholars who cite Jung's psychotherapeutic method of active imagery.[35]

In essence, *union with the dignity of an enlightened being* consists in adopting such an image as an empowering, idealized self-image; a virtual, generic template for the development of an actual new self that truly embodies radical openness and unconditional compassion. Through transferring our sense of self to such an empowering self-image, we effectively try enlightenment on for size, immersing our minds in the feel of what it might be like to live as an enlightened version of ourselves, here and now.[36] I sometimes refer to this empowering, transitional self-image as a "prosthetic self," since it works by displacing our consciousness from its pathogenic clinging to our ordinary, traumatized sense of self.

Immersing our minds in our best image or likeness of enlightenment is called enlightened dignity or Buddha pride[37] not in the usual sense of pride, as a stress-reaction to a reified sense of insecurity. Instead, it is defined as a "self of selflessness," a transparent agency of sheer open-mindedness and spontaneous compassion that helps purge our minds of their familiar, self-limiting sense of self.[38] That reified, self-limiting identity, technically called the "pride of ordinariness" is what normally anchors the delusional belief that we're incapable of becoming enlightened altruists.[39] So the point of identifying with the dignity of an ideal self-image is not to develop a new, slightly larger yet still reified sense of self, but rather to provide a self-dissolving platform from which to critique our ordinary self-sense and rehearse new ways of being that will eventually help us awaken and master our native altruistic genius.

Archetypal Self-Imagery: A Medium and Filter for Transmitting Mastery

While the archetypal imagery in process practice empowers us to aspire to a more effective new self, it's only one face of the art of role-modeling. The other face involves using that image as a congenial ideal which links our best vision of a proactive new self with our experience of a human model we choose as a living, breathing template for learning. This rich weaving of a chosen image of ideal self into the fabric of a real mentoring bond is what brings the art of role-modeling imagery in this rare tradition to life. Just as Jung found that the conception of a more integrated self in psychotherapy took place in the matrix of the bond between analyst and analysand,[40] so this ancient tradition sees self-transformative imagery as part of a real transaction between a master and apprentice altruist.[41] In fact, the role-modeling bond within this tradition harnesses the same natural process of social learning as we see at work in early childhood development, as well as in psychotherapy.[42]

Despite this resemblance, instead of the indiscriminate imprinting that takes place in childhood or the unconscious transference that often limits psychotherapy, the chosen new self-image used in this ancient technique serves to filter out idiosyncrasies and make transference explicit. By choosing to see one another through the lens of our chosen ideal, both parties insure that the work of role-modeling will proceed effectively. While keeping both parties focused on the work they share, the archetypal self-image also acts as a transitional object that represents the way intuitive insight, emotional intelligence and behavioral mastery is conveyed from person to person, master to apprentice, generation to generation. This mix of reactivating the primal process of social modeling and redirecting it with congenial transference imagery gives the process-oriented path its exceptional effectiveness and speed. Thanks to this integrated art, "*enlightenment will not be far.*"

3. *The Technique Is to Assume Success, Which is the Teacher's Form Itself*

The third and last key feature of the art of role-modeling is its radically affirmative take on self-change, which some scholars describe as transgressive.[43] This feature reveals the art as a process of assisted self-change, catalyzed by image-guided mentoring, and unfolding in phases stretched across the time-dimension of human social learning and development. What is distinctive about the way this tradition approaches change is that it empowers us to engage it in a radically affirmative way; as if there was no need for us to slowly proceed towards the goal, because *we're already there from the start*; as if we only need to fully realize or arrive at the place where we naturally are.[44] This radical goal-orientation highlights the equality of the mentor and apprentice, in a way that is not just affirmative of the would-be-altruist's potential, but is frankly progressive, even anti-traditional in spirit.

Of course, psychologically, it often takes time and inner work to feel truly ready for an approach to self-change that seems to fly in the face of our limitations. This is why the tradition breaks this internal shift down into smaller steps and phases, which can be taken gradually and successively. At first, under the influence of our "pride of ordinariness," we may find it easier to idealize others than to see ourselves as virtually ideal. Gradually, with acceptance and encouragement over time we may feel more able to identify with those we idealize and begin to vicariously sense our potential, by admiring their actual qualities. Eventually, we grow confident and positive enough to see our genius as already present within ourselves, needing only to be activated and internalized through practice. And finally, we're fully able to see and accept our budding mastery alongside the more or less mature mastery of others, as one genius among many essentially equal lights.

The process strategy of starting at the goal empowers and challenges us to find within ourselves the capacities we need to personify and embody the altruistic genius modeled by mentors. As our opening quote suggests, this method aims at rapidly transforming not just our mindset but our embodied state: "*The Teacher was endowed with the thirty-two signs and eighty-four marks (of altruistic embodiment). Therefore, the technique is to assume (the form of) success, which is the Teacher's form itself.*" This reference to Shakyamuni's perfect physical embodiment of compassion speaks to the shift away from the self-protective neurobiology of stress and towards the interpersonal neurobiology of empathy and altruism explored in part 2. Yet it promises a way to compress the social evolutionary process of building compassion across many generations into a single lifetime or even decade of deep neuropsychological change. In terms of modern psychology, this deep transformation of affect and visceral response style could be compared with the alchemical character change Jung described.[45]

Borrowing Jung's language, Kohut describes the way a positive transference relationship can catalyze such profound change as a "transmuting internalization" of ideals projected onto the analyst, along with healthy ego strengths the analyst models.[46] In the case of the role-modeling process, the transmutation at work is the result of a conscious, transgressive process; and the qualities internalized are not just ordinary ego strengths but the extraordinary qualities of self-mastery that support altruistic genius. In terms of the new interpersonal neurobiology, the ideal images of self, other and a perfected world in this method appear to be enlightened versions of what Dan Siegel calls the "I-map," "you-map," and "we-map," which our specifically human prefrontal cortex generates to adapt more primitive mind-brain systems to the social and cultural environment of human life.[47] This super-human state of extraordinary self-regulation and social development is represented metaphorically by the "marks" and "signs" of Shakyamuni's fully mature embodiment of altruistic genius.[48]

This look at how process practices do and don't work should answer the big question of why we in the post-modern West might well concern ourselves with such novel and challenging techniques. What Tsong Khapa doesn't say is that this psychologically powerful art of imaginative self-creation may be especially vital to us in our day, for reasons he clearly anticipated.[49] First, it offers a fully portable, virtual monastery, which, with the help of a single mentoring bond, can help reproduce the psychobiological crucible for the most rapid and effective self-transformation humanly possible, even in the midst of our stress-driven world. Second, it offers a sensually compelling counterpoint to the addictive imagery and energy of the information age, empowering those who seek a contemplative life today with industrial strength power-tools fit for the task. Finally, it offers an alchemical method of harnessing primal passions to a high performance form of contemplative leadership and cultural creativity, holding out the promise of a contemplative practice ideally suited to our active, creative and dynamic lives.

Supervision and the Other Preliminaries: Overcoming Resistances to Self-Change

Since the transgressive orientation and transformative imagery of process practice stretches our habitual self-image and body-image, most find it deeply challenging, if only to our instinct for self-reification. To the extent that we confuse our self-image or body-image for the real foundation of our lives, anything that even temporarily exposes such images as displaceable constructs rather than fixed realities challenges our naïve narcissistic sense of our own identity or permanence. In addition to our need for human modeling, this is one more reason why process practices traditionally require the expert supervision of a master teacher.[50]

Beyond requiring supervision, the use of process methods is traditionally safeguarded by the insistence on three key prerequisites, especially for higher level practice. These three are: true renunciation; genuine compassion; and at least a clear intellectual grasp of the insights of selflessness and emptiness.[51]

As for renunciation, the basic skill of releasing self-destructive impulses and habits is vital if we're to have the mental flexibility to channel compulsive energies into healthy change. Second, a strong value and some practice of true empathy is vital to creating a proactive self, as well as to maintaining the intimate bond with a mentor we need to work through misperceptions and toxic emotions. Finally, at least an intellectual understanding of emptiness is necessary, since we otherwise run the risk of reifying any prosthetic self-image used in role-modeling as a simply another fixed self. This could easily result in reinforcing our self-reifying habit, hence blocking genuine openness and compassion. Worse, it may get us stuck in a narcissistic fantasy self that makes us even less able to interact well than our ordinary self.

The Seven Steps and Four Phases of the Role-Modeling Process

Given this, it's time to unpack the art of role-modeling, as exemplified by the imagery of the *Healing Mentor*, the patron of self-healing and self-transformation in the Nalanda process tradition.[52] To streamline the practice for those new to such imagery, I've combined and simplified elements from the two most common practice formats.[53] If you find it hard to relate to the traditional imagery, feel free to substitute your own mental image of an *Ideal Healer* who can model self-healing and self-transformation for you. This generic approach is the one I take in clinical research,[54] and has also been suggested as an adjunct in psychotherapy.[55] While it seems inevitable that the role-modeling imagery of ancient India and modern Tibet will be revised to suit the cultural imagination of the modern scientific mind, I've found that asking students to conceive their own *Ideal Healer* puts a burden on them just when they're learning new insights and skills. More to the point, if I were to translate this art using familiar imagery from the Western tradition, it would introduce a host of cultural connotations that could obscure the intent or method at hand. So I've taken the middle way, of translating the language and symbolism as much as possible into poetic English, while staying as close as possible to the traditional intent of the art and iconography.

In what follows, I'll break down the steps, phases, and levels of the role-modeling process in sections, stopping in between to explain how each works. To make this introduction more practical, I've also condensed three different lines of interpretation into one integrated format. The three lines address the interpersonal, transferential, and motivational dimensions of role-modeling, respectively. The interpersonal dimension is broken down into seven steps. Taken together, these seven prime and rehearse the gradual process of building a working master-apprentice alliance, a process I call mentor-bonding. The seven steps are: admiring; welcoming; disclosing; enjoying; requesting help; requesting constancy; and dedication.[56]

These progressive steps of interpersonal bonding line up with four successive phases of self-transformation catalyzed by the healthy resolution of the transference bond, which shares some family resemblance with the psychotherapy process Kohut described as "transmuting internalization."[57] Of these four phases—which I call idealization, identification, internalization and integration—idealization aligns with the first three interpersonal steps from admiring to disclosing; identification aligns with the fourth step of enjoying; internalization aligns with the fifth step of requesting help; and integration aligns with the sixth and seventh steps of requesting constancy and dedication.

Finally, given the multi-dimensional nature of process-oriented learning, these four transferential phases also align with four levels of motivational change. These four levels consist of increasing degrees of sublimation, brought about by a deepening capacity to transform negative affects into positive alternatives. They are traditionally linked with the capacity to modulate and transform affects with increasing levels of intensity: the lowest being the level aroused by romantic interest and sexual attraction; the next being the level aroused by mutual flirtation and erotic intrigue; the third, the level of intensity aroused by sensual touching and embrace; the highest, the level of intensity aroused by unbridled passion and sexual climax.

While the four phases of transference and four levels of sublimation are traditionally aligned with one another, they are not usually linked with the seven steps of mentor-bonding.[58] Instead, they line up with four different levels of process practice, called the action process; the performance process; the integral process; and the optimal integral process.[59] Nonetheless, I believe weaving these three lines of interpretation together works for our purposes, since the seven-step framework of role-modeling provides the backbone of process practice at all four levels.[60] As I see it, the omnipresence of this framework invites one to read the four phases and levels as variations on a theme, each of which approaches the role-modeling process from the developmental standpoint of its different steps. The action and performance process practices we'll explore in this chapter are for novices practicing from a standpoint ranging from idealization to identification. The integral process practices we'll explore in chapter nine are for intermediate practitioners on the internalization phase. And the optimal integral practices we'll touch on in part 4 are for more advanced practitioners approaching complete integration. To prime your mind for the imagery that follows, please refer to the image of the *Healing Mentor* in the color insert.

The Active Process of Idealization, Step 1: Admiration

In the open space before me, from a lucid, moon-disc of mind,
Dawns a lapis exclamation point, beaming healing speech of light
And an aura of lapis lazuli radiance that takes human form
As the Healing Mentor, who distils the genius of all healing beings
Throughout space and time. One with my role-model, he sits
Amidst a giant rainbow lotus, in saffron robes,
With all the marks and signs of altruistic, pure genius.

His right hand, palm out on his knee, holds a sprig of medicinal aloe,
His left, on his lap, holds a bowl of meditative elixir.
Lit from within by the moon and exclamation at his heart,
He embodies the medicine that heals body, spirit and mind!

The intent of the ideal imagery on this first step and the phase it opens is not idealization for idealization's sake, but to help us recognize and admire the qualities of the archetype and living mentor we're trying to model. One contemporary Tibetan master of this art, Gelek Rinpoche, describes the attitude involved in admiring a role-model as more like the spirit in which an ambitious apprentice approaches a master: "That's what I want!" Instead of the childlike devotion we've been taught to feel towards our own religious ideals and models, the spirit of this tradition and imagery is closer to the congenial admiration we feel towards a teacher or guide. This basic equality is symbolized by the body language of our encounter: we envision the mentor-archetype sitting close enough to reach out and touch us, yet just a bit above eye level, like a big sister or brother.

The aim of this step is to help confirm our rational confidence in the virtues that qualify the model we've chosen as a living template for a new way of being. Focusing on the qualities of the role-model also serves to heighten our attention to them, effectively priming the process of guided learning and self-development. Projecting onto another human the image of self we ideally aspire to serves to objectify the other, with their consent, as a means to an end: using their more cultivated mind, body and sensibility as a reference point or catalyst in our own self-transformation. A positive mentoring relationship is as vital to reshaping our sense of self as our idealized relationship with parents was to shaping our childhood self-image or our relationship with teachers was to shaping our adult minds and careers.

Ideals and Mentors: The Checks and Balances of Tibetan Role-Modeling

Thanks to the system of mentoring that grounds self-transformation in this tradition, it is possible for us to consciously choose and guide the way we want to grow in the mentoring bond. For this to work, we need both a clear vision of the role we'd like to play in the world, and a living, breathing mirror or model that can help guide and check our efforts, based on our own personal experience and perspective. In this process, we envision the other person in the image of our ideal, while "inviting" or "merging" the tangible personal qualities or style of our living model to invest the abstract image with down-to-earth life. In a sense, the image serves as a filter or uplink that helps our minds recognize and connect with the real qualities we want to emulate. Yet it also filters out traits or quirks that are inconsistent with the role we want to play, helping our mind focus without distractions or contradictions on the qualities we want to emulate.

In this way, the ideal self-imagery and the real human model work together in a system of human checks and balances to assure that the process of change brings us to the new way of life we seek. Lest we imagine that this approach could never work in an individualistic culture like ours, the ruggedly individualistic Tibetans have a saying that clearly acknowledges the tension we feel at the idea of such a complex bond: "The best mentor is the one who lives three valleys over." Reminiscent of our complex feelings about therapists, this suggests that process mentoring works best when there is a healthy balance between the closeness we need for change and the space we need for autonomy. Another, related reason to imagine the mentor as a disembodied mind or spirit inhabiting a generic, archetypal body is that that generic self-image can be more readily taken into our minds and internalized, since it lacks distinguishing quirks that earmark it as "other." So the archetype offers an ideal vision of self that is not just conveniently applicable to our minds—that is, prosthetic—but also easily transferrable or downloadable. In the end, it reflects a self-creative technology that is not just user-friendly, but eminently empowering.

On the other hand, the step of admiring and the phase of idealizing must involve some vulnerability in order to work. They require a conscious choice to open our minds to the influence of another, involving what ego-psychologist Heinz Hartmann called "regression in the service of the ego," a crucial step towards engaging in a transmuting bond. Unless we temporarily loosen the grip of our self-protective instincts and familiar defenses, our hearts and minds cannot open enough to assimilate the way of being we'd like to model. This dimension of the step of admiring and the phase of idealization require the student's informed consent to a binding contract with the mentor that opens the door to all that follows.[61]

The Transference Phase of Idealization: A Mirror for Our Hidden Genius

As for the transference phase of idealization, active process practices view the art of role-modeling from the standpoint of the novice with low self-efficacy and little confidence in his or her natural capacity for change. Like most of those just beginning psychotherapy, such individuals may be so blindly attached to their traumatized sense of self that it blocks their capacity to even conceive of fundamental self-change. The focus here is on bonding with an idealized role-model whom we can experience as very different, far wiser, and more capable than ourselves. The imagery here corresponds to the kind of admiration or hero worship in which the mentor or ideal is not initially seen as an object of imitation, but as a refuge somehow above or beyond us. Developmentally, it corresponds to a very primal need for safety, attention, and direction, offering an opportunity to heal traumas and transcend needs still lingering from early childhood. The work at this basic phase is to approach the ideal by exposing and removing blocks to our sense of empowerment or competence so that, eventually, we can grow to identify with and imitate our role-model's ideal way of being.

The Closer We Get: Idealization and the Art of Sublimation

As we saw above, the second way the four phases of role-modeling are described is in terms of the deepening levels of emotional intimacy and intensity we are ready to invest in and harness towards self-transformation. This third dimension of the process is key, since the transformative power of imagery is due in part to the way its shifts in perception usher in shifts in emotion and response style as well. As we saw, the traditional metaphors used to describe successive levels of emotional investment in self-transformation are drawn from the universal human experience of romantic love. Of course, this anticipates the insights of modern science that the psychology of human childrearing, social learning and cultural development depends on the primal biology of sexual attraction, courtship, and mating.[62]

As in modern therapy, so in this role-modeling process, progress depends on our capacity to consciously harness strong positive feelings like passionate interest and excitement to the process of self-transformation, a capacity Freud and his heirs call sublimation, borrowing a term from the esoteric tradition of alchemy in the West. Such powerful, positive investment reflects a self-regulating capacity to shift our emotional style away from traumatic reactivity and towards self-confidence and prosocial emotions. As that natural capacity grows through practice, we gradually grow ready to invest the ideal way of life we envision with higher and higher degrees of passion. The imagery of action process techniques are needed when our minds can only harness the mild level of intimate passion stirred by furtively gazing at a distant love interest.

The Active Process of Idealization, Step 2: Welcoming

Filled with gratitude for your healing presence and example,
I freely share with you all good things, real and imagined,
All my virtues and resources, this precious mind, body and life,
And this exquisite globe with its oceans, continents, wonders,
Healing gardens, gemstones, waters and infinite web of life!

The second interpersonal step in the process is the act of opening our hearts, minds, bodies and life to the influence of our chosen role-model, by sharing without reservation all that we appreciate, treasure and enjoy. Just as we would naturally welcome a guest by opening our home, so we feed the bond with our mentor by fully opening our lives, letting go of any sense of ownership or attachment and inviting our chosen model to share our most intimate joys. Akin to the unconditional spirit of openness and generosity with which we welcome a loving parent or intimate partner into our lives, this exercise serves to let down any boundaries or walls of fear that might block our ability to be truly intimate with our role-model. In addition, by offering whatever we value, we also counteract any insecurity we feel in the bond with our mentor, based on any lack of self-worth we bring to the process.

In the context of sociobiology, this step rehearses the primitive social acts of sharing food and information, offering mutual aid and grooming, acts which elicit our most primal memories and sense of family belonging and kin-recognition. This is why traditional forms of the active process routinely involve setting out or imagining substances such as water, lotions, flowers, incense, candles, delicacies and musical instruments, and then going through the motions of offering them to actual representations and/or to our mental image of our role-model.[63] Without magic or mystery, these rites help practitioners overcome inner blocks to connection and trust. As these practices take effect and practitioners move to the next steps and phases of the role-modeling process, the emphasis shifts from such outward behaviors to inward intentions and dispositions.

Deepening Idealizing Transference, and Positive Motivation

In psychotherapeutic terms, this step involves gradually investing the transference bond with the positive energy of interest and excitement, by sharing intimate information and experiences which themselves are charged with emotion. By infusing these feelings and experiences into the mentoring bond, a sense of confidence and intimacy is built that helps overcome self-protective instincts and reactive habits of insecurity and guardedness. Consequently, this step has the effect of making the idealization of the mentor a more inclusive experience, creating the sense of a holding environment of mutual trust and care which serves as the crucible for further internalization and change. As for the dimension of sublimation, this step fosters the development of a deeper capacity to access and harness the sensual interest and excitement of genuine mutual attraction and flirtation to fuel the intimacy of the mentoring bond.

The Active Process of Idealization, Step 3: Disclosing

Regretting all the negative instincts and habits I've indulged,
All the patterns that limit and block me from acquiring your qualities
And emulating your way of being, from the depths of my heart
I admit them all to you now, ask your acceptance and help,
And firmly resolve from here on to avoid and unlearn every one.

The third interpersonal step in the process is disclosing our faults, the complement in the realm of negative experience to the second step of sharing the positive. This powerful exercise of openness and trust helps break down the walls of shame-based insecurity, hurt, and anger that predictably block the free flow of information and affect, whether in intimacy, psychotherapy or mentoring.

Here the tradition prescribes the forces of confession and due diligence we've touched on in parts 1 and 2, only in the transformative context of a confidential role-modeling bond.[64] The net effect of this step is to help remove any real or imaged blocks to progress based on limits in our ability to freely, fully, and constructively share our struggles with negative instincts, habits and the problems they cause.

Clarifying Idealizing Transference and Positive Motivation

In terms of sociobiology, this step involves deepening the social-emotional bond of genuine empathy and care by exposing our human weakness and wounds to others in a setting of deep mutual respect and trust. Reaching this level of transparency and self-disclosure is a hallmark of the deepest levels of intimacy and confidentiality, and is a must in the development of a truly healing bond, whether it be one of intimate partnership, mentoring, or psychotherapy. By gradually exposing and removing shame-based obstacles to transparency and trust, this step further seals the mentoring bond, and brings the idealization phase to a close. The result is a truly transparent and grounded idealization, based on the full mutual disclosure of strengths and weaknesses, and a fully informed alliance of both parties geared to overcoming limits and cultivating potentials. In terms of the energy on this step, it involves a deepening capacity to sublimate the first degree of toxic emotions like hurt, insecurity and shame into positive social-emotional forces like mutual sensitivity, empathic attunement, and congenial humility.[65]

The Performance Process of Identification and the Step of Enjoying

From the depths of my heart I enjoy all the myriad forms
Of happiness you experience and share with all beings,
With all the transcendent virtues that serve as their cause.

With the fourth interpersonal step of vicariously enjoying the positive qualities, lasting happiness and whole way of being the mentor embodies, we enter the second phase of the role-modeling process: the transference phase of identification. By exercising the capacity to congratulate and truly rejoice in our mentor's good qualities without any sense of envy or comparison, we remove one more block to approaching our role-model in genuine intimacy. In a sense, we now re-experience our admiration in a new mode, empowered by a greater sense of equality, confidence and attunement, to imagine ourselves into the qualities and way of being we admired from afar in the idealization phase. This new sense of impartial enjoyment of qualities brings us closer to conceiving of ourselves as potentially having them or actually developing them. And this investment opens the door to the transference phase of identification.

Identification, Development, and Courting Self-Transformation

In this phase in the process, we're free to enjoy our closeness with the role-model, proactively taking in the feel of his or her strengths and way of being. As we begin to vicariously enjoy and even emulate what we admire in him or her, we experience a dissonance with our habitual identification with our prior limits. Our focus here may still be directed outwardly towards our role-model, but thanks to the mentor's mirroring of our own strengths and potentials, we begin to see ourselves in a newer, more empowering light. Open to seeing ourselves in the mirror of the mentor's acceptance, we begin to stretch our self-image to make room for some likeness to the way of being we aspire to. From the vantage point of this step and phase, role-modeling appears as a congenial process in which both parties share a common interest and excitement, though in an asymmetrical way. It works in much the same way a childhood choice to identify a teacher, athlete or artist as a hero can act as both a source of vicarious enjoyment of the hero's qualities and as a catalyst and template for the development of innate capacities.

The work of role-modeling in this phase is called the performance process, since our mentor's recognition turns our vicarious enjoyment of his or her qualities back on ourselves, opening the door to the more participatory observation involved in emulating them. As the English translation "performance" suggests, in this phase like an actor we begin to imitate the way of being we admire, becoming more aware of our need for the mentor's mirroring to help us expand our identity and capacity. In contrast to the idealizing mode of the active process, the work of the identification phase involves less ritualistic attention and more aesthetic rehearsal or creative reenactment. In terms of the level of sublimation at work in this phase, the performance process works best when our imaginations can harness the moderate level of passion aroused by the dance of flirtation, as in the exchange of glances or non-sexual touch in courtship.

In terms of its sociobiology, the step of vicarious enjoyment rehearses a basic building block of social cooperation, marrying the complex dynamics of social performance and the psychobiology of imitation. Beyond the workings of mere imprinting or entrainment, life forms capable of more complex social learning require the parent and offspring to engage in a complex dance of imitation which gives the developing individual the opportunity to actively model and gradually master specialized behaviors or ways of being.[66] Developmentally, this phase and level of role-modeling reawakens the active development of personality through latency and adolescence, based on the bond of identification formed in the Oedipal phase. This capacity for revising our childhood self-creation prepares us to join in an expanded social network of role-modeling, allowing us to adapt to a wider range of social relationships, including those dedicated to specialized cultural skills. This same capacity is exploited in psychotherapy to help individuals transcend artificial limits to our capacity based on indiscriminate role-modeling in childhood.

The Integral Process of Internalization and the Step of Requesting Help

Since my future health and well-being, and my ability
To help those around me find freedom and happiness
Depend on my learning to cultivate your qualities
And recreate your whole way of being, I ask you please:
Freely share with me all your intuition and energy
So by mastering your art, I may heal myself, my world and all life!
Thrilled to be asked, your heart-moon and exclamation point beam
A rainbow wave of healing clarity, energy and warmth,
Sounding the affirmation, MAY ALL HEAL AND BE HEALED!
Engulfed by the wave, its rainbow light and sound fill me,
Melting away all my ailments, limits, blocks, fears and doubts,
And freeing my own healing clarity and voice from the moon
And exclamation point at my heart, to fill me as a flame fills a lamp
And a nectar fills a vase, transforming my body, speech, and mind
Into my mentor's, and rippling out through all my actions
Until my home, world and all life are healed and transformed,
And return a wave of gratitude that melts my heart!

The fifth interpersonal step of requesting help lines up with integral process practice and the penultimate transference phase of internalization. It is based on the sense of vicarious enjoyment and identification developed in the prior step, but brings this sense to the next level: preparing to actually realize within ourselves the qualities we admire and enjoy in our congenial role-model. This step involves overcoming the inhibitions to growth posed by our self-limiting identification with fear-based insecurity and shame-bound helplessness. Here we've finally succeeded, with help from our mentor and the momentum built in prior steps, at getting out of our own way and forging a working congenial bond that can catalyze our self-transformation.

The Transference Phase of Internalization: Finding the Native Genius Within

In this advanced phase of role-modeling, we become ready to internalize the ideal image we projected onto our mentor, and begin looking within ourselves to identify the qualities and way of being that make up our native genius. The focus here is on approaching and encountering the self we're trying to develop as *already actually present within us*. The work here is twofold: to fully claim as our own the identity and competence previously modeled for us and recognized in us by an ideal other; and to finally and decisively change our familiar self-image to reflect the new qualities we've found or developed. The imagery of the integral process corresponds to the kind of admiration or hero-worship in which our mentor-archetype is encountered as an innate genius or dignity that has lain hidden within the depths of our being—unnoticed—all along.

In terms of sociobiology, this step and phase involve the social recognition and development of human potential through initiatory rites that empower individuals as naturally effective agents of chosen social roles and cultural skills. It reflects the social and cultural extension of the natural process of coming of age in adolescence, by extending our awakening into psychosexual maturity to include the sublimation of our generative powers into specialized forms of social agency and cultural mastery. Psychologically, this step and phase involve facilitating our self-discovery through a synergistic process in which we internalize qualities and a sense of mastery from our mentor, while taking in his or her recognition of our native potential and actual readiness for mastery. Akin to the mature separation process of leaving the nest or the process of entering the termination phase in psychotherapy, this phase involves a delicate rhythm or dance in which both parties cooperate in a gradual shift in power and responsibility from mentor to apprentice. One famous case of an encounter between a Buddhist master and student in the Chinese Ch'an tradition which gave rise to Zen has the student ask for his master to validate and reciprocate his growth, "Master, I am breaking out—break in!"[67]

The Motivation of Self-Transformation: Embracing Pure Passion

Of course, the work in this phase of self-transformation involves not just radical openness of mind, but an equally exceptional capacity to tolerate emotional and visceral openness. As we know from our experience of natural highs, such openness comes when we're open to feeling a high degree of positive arousal and emotional intimacy. Traditionally, the level of sublimation needed to support this pivotal step and prepare us for the integral process is one in which our imagination and empathy can harness and transform the high arousal stirred by a sensual touch, kiss or embrace. This level corresponds to a degree of social-emotional maturity in which we can share intense excitement and blissful openness without being triggered into a knee-jerk self-protectiveness or a compulsive drive to objectify, control or dominate others. It is here that we begin to find ourselves in the realm of the "blissful art" of accessing and harnessing the energy and chemistry of blissful openness as fuel for a life of enlightened altruism or altruistic genius.

The Optimal Process of Integration, Part 1: Requesting Constancy

Acknowledging that this imagery is a mere simulation,
I ask you please to stay with me constantly, every moment

From now until I integrate your mastery,
And my body, speech and mind become the pure love,
Joy and equanimity which are your true body, speech and mind.
Moved by affection for me, my role-model melts and beams
In miniature to my crown, where he sits, facing forward,
Aglow from the lapis light affirmation that rings his heart-moon.
As I hear and recite his affirmation, I AM THE HEALING
GENIUS OF A FREE, CARING MIND, its glow intensifies,
Melting his body, speech and moon-mind into a drop
Like a rainbow tear for joy, which pours through my crown
And throat to melt into the exclamation point at my heart,
Merging his healing essence with mine, intensifying
My light, energy and warmth until they fill me as a flame
Fills a lamp and a nectar, a vase, rippling out in my actions
Until all those around me at home and on earth become
Healing Mentors, returning a wave of joy to my heart!

The sixth step of requesting constancy ushers in the final phase of integration, by priming our minds to take the mentor's living example into the fabric of our being, where it helps us recognize and integrate our full potential for healing genius. This step assumes a mature realization of the vital influence of the role-modeling bond in catalyzing ongoing self-transformation, as well as a proactive commitment to do whatever it takes to complete that work. Far from a mere dependency, it reflects the transgressive confidence we need to enlist and secure the mentor's full investment in bringing us along, all the way to the fruition of full mastery.

Psychologically, the imagery of miniaturization reenacts the complementary shifts in perspective I mentioned on the last step, in which the apprentice grows in his or her self-image and actual capacity so that the mentor seems smaller in stature in contrast to his or her prior largesse as seen through idealizing eyes. The reenactment of the perspective shifts in the normal lifecycle of parent-child bonds is obvious, earmarking this imaginative process as the rehearsal of a conscious revision of normal development. Likewise, the iconic imagery of having the mentor enter the apprentice *via* the crown creatively reenacts the process of the internalization of a whole way of being modeled by parents, and suggests a symbolic recognition that the flow of social information is "down" through the generations and somehow involves the brain.[68]

Although the imagery I've outlined here is not universal in process practices, some variation on the theme of transmission *via* the crown can be found in all depictions of the internalization phase of the role-modeling process, especially at advanced levels of practice.[69] It's worth noting that such symbolism is not specifically Buddhist, but is reminiscent of totemic rites that rehearsed the generative act by which ancestors invest themselves in the lives of their heirs, recognizing the new generation as embodying their ongoing contribution to posterity.[70] A similar symbolism is implied in religious rituals like the modified sacrament of christening infants with water poured on their crown. In psychotherapeutic terms, the internalization of idealized images of parents—Freud's superego—is seen as the foundation of the child's construction of self. So the internalization of a new ideal image, projected onto the therapist and then reintegrated as a new mirror or template for the growth of a more ideal self, presumably involves the restructuring of the conscience in a transparent form, chosen to support the emergence of a conscious, mature way of being out of the transmuting dialogue of the therapy.

The totemic logic of descent and the therapeutic logic of transmuting the superego converge in the symbolic about-face taken by the mentor in this phase. Instead of confronting us as a mirror, external witness or judge, in this step of the practice the mentor turns around to face in the same direction as we do, melting into us to see the world through our eyes. This about-face symbolizes the profound shift in our psychic structure and perspective on the world that takes place on this final phase. This shift involves the dissolution of the other as an object of desire, misperception or fear, and the start of a new phase of integration in which we become our own witness and judge, freeing our empathy to embrace others as true equals and alter-egos.

A final element of this step is the focus on recitation of the mentor's affirmation as a way to weave the mentor's voice into a newly enlightened inner dialogue. Though not always placed at precisely this step, the practice of reciting and contemplating affirmative messages is crucial to all levels of role-modeling practice.[71] The key role of the mentor's affirmation here reflects a profound awareness of language as a medium for the transmission of agency, including the transformative agency of altruistic genius. This awareness is explicit in the alternate name of the process-oriented tradition: the "poetic" or semiotic vehicle.[72] In this context, I use the word "poetic" in the sense implied by Allen Grossman's compelling view of poetry as an art of role-modeling or transmitting the ideal image of "beloved" human models.[73]

In this fourth and final transference phase, with the help of affirmative speech, the orientation we take towards our ideal self begins to expand our sense of finding the ideal within, moving towards the ability to see and think of the ideal as both within ourselves and in others, simultaneously. This final shift towards congenial identification and full equality defines the perspective from which the most advanced optimal integral practice sees the role-modeling process. This phase has two objectives: to fully embrace the ideal qualities and way of being we've come to recognize in ourselves and others; and to finally identify our new positive image of ourselves and others with that ideal, by fully incorporating the new qualities of mind and action we've developed though emulating our role-model's way of being.

Consummate Motivation: The Energy of Blissful Openness

In terms of the level of sublimation involved in this phase, the optimal integral process works best when our imagination can harness the very highest level of passion, like that aroused by mature love-making and consummation. When we're able to access and harness such primal positive passion to the intimacy of the role-modeling bond, it lends greater depth and breadth to the radical openness which is the crucible for self-transformation. At this level of sublimation or flow, the way the imagery of the role-modeling process "binds the art" of blissful openness is laid bare. By melting into our hearts, our role-model elicits our most primal memories of and blissful responses to being seen, loved and cared for by parents and intimate partners.

Immersing us into the deepest waters of the unconscious mind, the imaginatively rehearsed experience of receiving our mentor's love serves as a universal solvent which melts the psychosocially constructed boundaries between us, opening the floodgates of the most immediate and complete give and take. According to the tradition, not only does this 'blissful art" make it easier for us to realize radical openness, but it also serves as the most fertile medium for the cultivation of embodied empathy, compassion and altruism.[74] Here, the three distinctive features of process-oriented practice—the union of wisdom and method, the art of imagery and the depth-psychology of role-modeling—come together to catalyze, refine, and enhance the consummation of our work of self-transformation.

The Optimal Process of Integration, Part 2: Dedication

Any positive insight or energy I've gained through this practice
I dedicate to achieving my Healing Mentor's integration
In this very lifetime, as quickly as possible! So by mastering
The arts of role-modeling imagery and blissful openness,
May I find the pure genius to heal myself and all life!

The seventh and last step in the role-modeling process serves to seal and direct any progress we've made in the prior six steps towards the ultimate goal of the process: assuming the congenial form of mastery we've identified in the mentor and ourselves. If the sixth step of requesting constancy works to sustain and motivate our progress towards mastery, dedication works to reinforce that progress and galvanize our commitment to embodying mastery as quickly and completely as we can. The aim here is to internalize not just the mentor's qualities and example, but also the level and kind of dedication that inspires his or her way of life. In effect, this step completes the phase of integration by preparing us to integrate the transformative aim and work that makes up the mentor's life mission and intergenerational project.

Traditionally, this act of taking up the torch from the mentor and joining in the work of altruistic self-transformation involves merging our own momentum and aims with the momentum and aims of a whole community. So dedication is not just an act of committing whatever incremental steps we've taken towards our ongoing learning, reflection, and practice, but also an act of radical solidarity which merges our own personal journey of transformation with that of our mentor and the community to which we both belong. Traditionally, this is expressed in the mental act of merging all the insight or energy we gain into the "ocean" of the accumulated openness and altruistic intentions of all enlightened beings in all places and times. Figuratively, we now not only face the same direction as the mentor but also stand shoulder to shoulder with him or her, facing the challenge of transforming others and the world we share.

In terms of sociobiology, this step and the completion of this phase reflect the extension of the final, generative phase of the normal life cycle to embrace the expanded leadership role we can take within the extended family of human culture and civilization. In terms of psychotherapy, the equivalent of identifying with the mentor's work would be to become an emotionally intelligent leader in our lives, including choosing to become a therapist who masters the empathic art we benefited from as a client.

While the act of dedication is not unique to the process tradition, there are several distinctive aspects to it in this context. First is the unique orientation to evolve towards mature altruism not at the gradual pace of social evolution, but at the lightning pace of cultural evolution, that is: "*in this very lifetime, as quickly as possible.*" The second is that we dedicate the momentum we build to becoming a role-model of altruistic genius *via* the distinctive methodology of the process tradition, since only this methodology brings the aim of enlightened altruism—or altruistic genius—within reach within a single lifetime.[75] Of the four modes of practice we've defined as phases of the role-modeling process, only the highest mode identified with the optimal integral process is equipped to deliver on that ambitious promise.

Quickly, Quickly! Nagarjuna's Paradigm of the Optimal Integral Process

Given the complete paradigm defined in the optimal integral process tradition, the two methods of imagery and bliss figure as the focus of two stages of practice called the creation stage and the perfection stage.[76] Though the methods we explore in this book come mainly from the active, performance, and integral process traditions which serve as entry points for the optimal integral process, in terms of theory we'll rely on the definitive paradigm of the optimal process tradition. This is why our survey divides process methods according to the optimal integral map: the role-modeling art of the creation stage is covered in part 3; and the bliss-harnessing art of the perfection stage in part 4. Further, according to the optimal process map attributed to Nagarjuna, the work of role-modeling is divided into two sub-stages: the coarse creation stage focused on re-envisioning our social self and outer world; and the subtle or fine creation stage focused on re-envisioning our bodily self and inner world.[77] We'll close this chapter by considering the subtle form of role-modeling that completes the art. But before we move on to consider the subtle creation stage, we must briefly survey the traditional criteria for mastery of the coarse creation stage defined in the optimal process tradition.

Mastering the Coarse Creative Process, Part 1: Vivid Imagery

For process novices, the first challenge we take on is to be able to vividly imagine "*the sphere of a perfected world,*" which gives the art of role-modeling imagery the verisimilitude on which its simulation value depends. Though most of us feel we lose access to our imaginations shortly after entering adulthood, parts of our minds and brains continue to actively produce mentally generated imagery throughout our lives.[78] Since this capacity has been narrowed and routinized through development so we can coordinate our perceptions with others, we gradually learn to mistake the parts of our perception we imagine for direct perceptions of the world.

Once we begin to renew these skills to construct an extraordinary vision of an ideal self and world, most of us face a learning curve of sorts before we can envision imagery that seems more or less as real as the constructed perceptions we take for reality. Another aspect of this learning curve has to do with the learned capacity to relax enough to shift our cerebral dominance toward a more balanced laterality that has enhanced sleep-like qualities of states of reverie or daydreaming.[79] Most beginners find it takes time to shift into such states without falling into drowsiness. In this sense, focusing attention on imagery involves the same balancing act that focusing on the breath does in mindfulness, requiring us to settle the mind from distraction to enhance calm, and to lift the mind from dullness to enhance clarity.

Once we've begun to experience a sense of vivid appearance, our imagery allows us to suspend disbelief, much like watching a film or being engrossed in a novel, only in this case we've created the imagery. This fact has two seemingly contradictory effects: the imagery we create seems more transparent because we're conscious of generating it; and, at the same time, it challenges our ordinary perceptions more than a movie or novel, since it acquaints us with the way they're made, as the act of film-making or creative writing alters our experience of what others make. Once we've begun to feel comfortable with imagery in general, the work of vivid appearance turns to making our mental image of our ideal selves and world more complete as a whole and in its details. For this work, the contemplative art of paintings, sculptures, blueprints, or replicas serves as a source of visual information which we systematically work to digest, store and recall. While this phase may seem contrived, it reflects the natural process by which perceptual data is committed to neural net-based memory stores to be later called on to generate mental imagery that encodes visuospatial information derived from sense experience.[80]

Of course, of all role-modeling images, the most central is the congenial archetype we've chosen as our aim. And, given the integral logic of role-modeling, eventually we'll need to practice not just envisioning our mentor as the archetype but also envisioning ourselves and our bodies as identical with his/her archetypal genius. This feat involves a second learning curve steeper than the first, namely, overcoming our instinctive reification of and clinging to habitual images of our body and self. Once the interpersonal process of mentor-bonding has allowed us to begin to identify with a prosthetic image of our body as identical with our role-model's, we come to the next criterion of the process of coarse creation imagery: the art of enlightened pride.

Mastering the Course Creative Process, Part 2: Selfless Dignity

Referred to in our opening reference as "*union with the dignity of an enlightened being,*" the art of mentor-archetype bonding is traditionally defined by an experience called "Buddha-pride" or "divine pride."[81] At first blush, this involves the ability to shift the first-person pronouns "I," "myself," "me," and "mine," from their ordinary mental address—our habitual image of our bodies and selves—to their extraordinary new address: the archetypal image of body and self we're trying on for size. While this re-tasking of these all-too-familiar words to re-center our sense of self on a new mental body-image represents a first pass on what is called divine pride, it is not the real deal. If the pride of a Buddha or genius archetype consisted of identifying with a mentally constructed self-image, no matter how meaningful or inspiring, such a Buddha or genius would have little claim to be either enlightened or god-like.

The resolution here refers back to the basic psychology of process-oriented imagery, according to which the image serves as a dream-like template for embodying altruism, while the true essence of altruist's mind or genius is the spacious intuition of openness that holds that image, also known as "the divine self of selflessness." So the real sense and reference of "the dignity of an enlightened being" is not a vivid image at all, but rather a profound, enlightened awareness of the emptiness of all selves and worlds, an awareness that makes our archetypal self-image a transparent yet useful template for transforming our emotional and behavioral way of being. In this light, the criterion of enlightened pride or the dignity of pure genius is our ability to truly identify our sense of "I" with the spacious equipoise intuition of emptiness that is the womb in which all process-oriented imagery is conceived and to which it returns. This is why, to seal the transformations of the later phases of role-modeling, we typically see affirmations that pronounce ourselves one with the emptiness intuition, even when the particular form whose emptiness we're intuiting is an ideal image of our own embodiment of altruism.

In the art of both creation stages and all phases of the perfection stage, these two criteria remain essential to the process of role-modeling. Traditionally, they often appear as guiding principles or key reminders of process practice, formulated in two more or less universal affirmations. The criterion of vivid appearance is typically formulated in the affirmation, "*I have a pure nature which is the natural purity of all things!*" In contrast, the criterion of enlightened pride is typically formulated in the affirmation, "*I am the self whose nature is the diamond intuition of openness!*"

Mastering the Coarse Creation Stage and Transitioning to the Subtle

If these two process criteria define the critical subjective qualities of process-oriented imagery, the remaining three content criteria define the key objective qualities of role-modeling imagery. Unlike the first two criteria, these three figure more as long-term outcomes that help measure our progress on the process path, eventually marking the transition from the coarse creation stage to the subtle. In effect, these three criteria measure the extent to which the perspective shift from our ordinary traumatic point of view to the mentor's enlightened point of view is stable and complete. We've arrived at a complete shift in perception when we can: see all living beings as the mentor or role-model; see all things as enfolded in the role-model's enlightened environment or sphere of influence; and hear all thoughts, words, and sounds as the affirmative speech of the mentor. This "triumph of the *mandala*" reflects the replacement of the default programs that run our perceptual and conceptual systems by transparent, proactive programs developed in light of the mentor's example.[82] Measuring effective practice by the ability to use imagery for stress-protection is consistent with current research,[83] and is the source of the synonym of this practice as the "poetic" practice of stress-protective words and images.[84]

If the art of role-modeling we've surveyed provides the framework for the coarse creation stage, there are two additional tools traditionally used to frame the subtle stage. While the first of these, the art of the body-*mandala*, is little known in the West, the second, the art of envisioning the central nervous system is familiar to us thanks to popular images of the subtle body or yogic nervous system. Now that we've unpacked the basic role-modeling practice of the *Healing Mentor*, it's time to turn to another practice which can give us a window into the art of the subtle creation stage. Easily as popular and widely used for mind/body health, that is the active role-modeling process which revolves around the archetype of the *Healing Mother*. But before we can explore that practice and its relation to the subtle creation stage, it will help to briefly look into the imagery of the body-*mandala* and the subtle nervous system.

Subtle Creation: The Body *Mandala* and the Subtle Nervous System

Essentially, the art of the body *mandala* extends and expands on the imagery of the internalization and integration phases of the role-modeling process. This imagery involves taking the influence and image of the mentor into our body space as a way of purging and transforming our ordinary sense of self. At the stage of internalization aligned with requesting help, we took the mentor's luminous awareness, energy, and voice into our body, allowing it to melt away blocks and free the healing inner light and voice from our heart. At the integration stage, aligned with requesting constancy and dedication, the mentor's body dissolved into our own, merging inseparably with the inner mentor at our heart. Such imagery essentially allows us to re-people our internal world with the awareness, voice, and mind/body essence of the mentor.

In the imagery of the body-*mandala*, we take this internalizing art to the next step by installing miniature images of the mentor's body and speech at key points within our own body. In so doing, we transform our body into a living, breathing habitat or life-space for the mentor's healing influence and way of being. The points at which images of the mentor's body or speech are installed are not arbitrary, but are key points within the subtle body or central nervous system where vital neural processes can be consciously influenced. At more advanced levels of subtle creation, the images that personify the mentor's influence are fine-tuned, eventually morphing into pinpoint images of a single "seed syllable" of light and sound, which serves to guide or "bind the blissful art" of mind/body regulation in the perfection stage.

Reflections on the Need for Role-Modeling Imagery, Coarse and Subtle

Here, as at the initial phases of the role-modeling process, we may wonder, are such intricate acts of creative imagination really needed in the very real mind/body work of self-regulation of neural states and processes? The traditional answer is this: if the presence of a positive model is a vital catalyst for the transformation of our embodied self, the presence of a positive archetype of mind/body mastery is even more vital to the transformation of the nervous system. Just as a genuine healing alliance is vital to creating a holding environment to treat childhood trauma, so the formation of a role-modeling bond provides the crucible in which the apprentice feels secure enough to transform the traumatized self and nervous system into a proactive, ideal social self and nervous system.

As current meditation research suggests, positive imagery appears to help counterbalance negative affect preferentially stored in the right hemisphere and shift laterality towards the positive affect and proactive response style of the left prefrontal cortex.[85] When it comes to delving deeper into conscious regulation of neural processes like autonomic tone, then, we may suppose that installing images of the mentor within our body space helps make our internal environment itself feel like a healing environment rather than a Pandora's box of repressed traumatic memories and toxic affect. Likewise, our identification with the mentor would also seem to serve to heighten positive affect, self-efficacy and a proactive response style when it comes to facing whatever distress we feel.

In terms of the language of hypnotherapy, images of the mentor's body and speech within our body space act to provide an "affect-bridge," linking our awareness of our bodily state and emotional tone back to an experience of strong, positive affect and proactive agency.[86] In terms of current neurobiology, this art primes the natural process of social integration which helps us disarm primal defense systems and promote positive social engagement, by stimulating the bidirectional feedback linking friendly facial expressions, warm vocal tones and gentle bodily gestures to the social regulation of heart-breath rhythms *via* the vagal nerve, called the face-heart or brain-heart connection.[87] In light of the work of revising our own body-image after the mentor's, it's worth noting here that these feedbacks also include self-feedback from our own facial expressions, vocal tones, and bodily gestures.[88]

Coarse and Subtle Creation: The Quintessential Preliminary to Self-Transformation

The psychotherapeutic logic of the creation stage helps explain why the Nalanda tradition places so much importance on the use of embodied imagery to clear away blocks and resistances to conscious self-regulation. And it also explains why the creation stage was seen as an indispensable "extraordinary preliminary" to the art of cultivating blissful openness on the perfection stage.[89] In effect, taken together with the three common prerequisites—renunciation, compassion, and emptiness insight—and the entryway of forming a role-modeling bond, the imagery of the coarse and subtle creation stage stand as a fifth prerequisite to the safe and effective use of the contemplative power tools of the process tradition. While the tradition speaks with one voice on this matter, the lengths to which masters like Tsong Khapa went to insist on the need for role-modeling imagery show that the impulse to avoid the work of restructuring perception is neither peculiarly modern nor Western.

We've already seen how the art of role-modeling imagery at the heart of process practice can catalyze shifts in the perception of self and others, and in the web of relationships that make up our social life. It's time now to turn to the subtle creation stage, in which that alchemy is carried into the deeper level of shifts in emotional tone and instinctive response style. Of course, the fine-brushwork of personifying imagination that makes up the subtle creation stage is challenging for beginners. Fortunately, this tradition offers a wide range of preliminary practices to prepare for the advanced methods of the optimal integral process. The rest of this chapter will focus on aspects of the active process of the *Healing Mother* which can help beginners ready themselves for the emotional alchemy of the subtle creation stage.

The *Healing Mother*: Transforming the Compulsive Mind/Body Process

Among the best loved and most widely used process practices in Tibet, the active process of the *Healing Mother* has unique features that make it both highly accessible and effective. This is partly due to the symbolic value of the archetype of the *Savioress* or *Heroic Mother*, best known in the most beneficent of her twenty-one forms: the pacifying, milk-white *Healing Mother*. Beyond the natural soothing effect of her motherly form, this archetype is traditionally used for its power to catalyze the inner transformation of emotional tone and instinctive response style that is the work of the subtle creation stage. In addition to the simple role-modeling imagery she shares with the *Healing Mentor* and other similar archetypes, the *Healing Mother* includes several added imagery tools, including one we'll unpack here and one we'll unpack in part 4. Those two power tools are: the art of protecting the stress-reactive mind/body process; and the art of sublimation based on vase breathing. Of these, we'll explore the first as a window into the subtle creation stage of the optimal integral process.[90]

The Five Compulsive Mind/Body Systems: The Basis of Transformation

The stress-protective practice of the *Healing Mother* focuses on transforming the workings of the five main complexes in the subtle body, said to govern the five principal mind/body systems. If you recall, these five systems were enumerated in the simplest analysis of the mind/body process in Buddhist science and mindfulness practice, as the physical, sensory, conceptual, emotional and perceptual systems. Given this analysis, self-transformation is then modeled into three phases—basis, path, and fruit—defined in terms of the framework of the four noble truths. As Tsong Khapa says,

> In the continuation of the *Esoteric Community Process*, "process" is said to mean (mind/body) continuum and to be of three types: a "base continuum" that is the base on which the paths are acting (to purify the obscurations); a "path continuum" that purifies this base; and a "fruit continuum" that is the fruit of purification.[91]

The basis of transformation is the normal, stress-reactive condition of the mind/process body process. It's defined as the five life systems in their compulsive mode, poisoned by the five root compulsions, which I like to list as anger, greed, desire, envy and pride. Each of the five systems is linked with the toxic emotion that poisons its healthy functioning. The compulsive mode of the physical body is driven by toxic aggression and violence. The compulsive mode of sensation is driven by toxic greed and avarice. The compulsive mode of the conceptual system is driven by intoxicating acquisitiveness, craving, and clinging. The compulsive mode of the emotional system is driven by toxic envy, jealousy, and competitiveness. And the compulsive mode of the perceptual system is driven by self-reifying delusions and intoxicating pride.

The Five Types of Pure Genius and Intuitive Wisdom: The Fruit of Transformation

Next, drawing on the socially engaged teaching tradition, the fruit of the process of self-transformation is defined in terms of the embodiment of enlightened altruism or altruistic genius. You may recall that the fruit of fully mature social agency was analyzed on the engaged path into five families of enlightened altruism aligned with five types of altruistic genius: moral altruism and moral genius; social altruism and psychological genius; contemplative altruism and creative genius; active altruism and organizational genius; and intellectual altruism and scientific genius. Given the radical goal-orientation of the process teaching tradition, the masculine and feminine aspects of these five types of altruistic genius are identified with the five mind/body systems and five physical elements, when purged of the toxic influence of the five compulsions and guided by the emergence of five pure intuitive wisdoms. As it says in the *Esoteric Community Process*:

> In short, the five aggregates are
> Proclaimed to be the five enlightened geniuses.
> The diamond media themselves are
> The supreme *mandala* of the enlightened altruist(s).
> Earth is called (the feminine genius) *Illuminatrix*.
> The water element is (known as) the *Protectoress*.
> The fire (element) is (to be called) the *Lotus Garbed*.
> (The *Healing Mother*) the *Savioress* is proclaimed to be air.
> (And space is the feminine genius *Diamond Texture*).
> The practitioner always meditates
> On forms, sounds, and so on, as divine.[92]

So, the pure mode of the physical system and body solids is our masculine and feminine moral genius, guided by mirroring intuition. The pure mode of the sensory system and bodily fluids is our social altruism and psychological genius, guided by the equalizing intuition. The pure mode of the conceptual system and body heat is our contemplative altruism and creative genius, guided by the discriminating intuition. The pure mode of our emotional system and breath gases is our active altruism and organizational genius, guided by the executive intuition. And the pure mode of our perceptual system and body spaces is our intellectual altruism and scientific-philosophical genius, guided by the ultimacy intuition.[93] The reference also explains that the transformation of our mind/body systems and elements also involves purging and transforming the perceptual media of the five sense faculties and their objects into our male and female altruists.

Purifying the Five Systems by Role-Modeling: The Path of Transformation

As for the path which leads us from the basic condition of compulsive life to the final fruition of altruistic genius, this analysis is set within the alchemical view of self-transformation in the process tradition.[94] According to that view, we learn to transform the systems of our mind/body process from their compulsive mode to their enlightened mode by practicing the arts of archetypal imagery and sublimation within the crucible of the role-modeling bond, catalyzed by the creative influence of a mentor. One way this process is envisioned and rehearsed in the subtle creation stage is with the help of the simplest kind of body-*mandala* and subtle body imagery.

According to that simple imagery, the body of the role-model is envisioned as a pure, luminous space inhabited by thumb-sized images of the five types of altruistic genius. Usually imagined as miniature replicas of the archetypal role-model made of five different colors of gem-toned light, these images form a body-*mandala* or inner circle of sub-personalities, each representing the presence of one of the five mind/body systems in their enlightened forms as types of altruistic, pure genius.[95] Their range of rainbow colors visually establishes them as analyzed parts of a full spectrum of capacities embodied in the mentor. In an even simpler version, the geniuses of the five systems are often reduced to five 3-D syllables, made of five, gem-toned lights, representing the five main tones or senses of the mentor's affirmative speech.

Installing the Simple Body-*Mandala* at the Five Main Points of the Subtle Body

The last step in setting up the imagery of the subtle creation stage is that the images of the mentor's sub-personalities, and/or their symbolic "seed-syllables," are installed at key places along the visualized network of the subtle body or central nervous system. At this point in the process, the main channels and complexes of the central nervous system may not be explicitly imagined. Instead, either the sub-personalities or the seed syllables representing them may be placed within the role-model's luminous body at key points along the spinal axis where the five main complexes of the central channel or neural tube would be.

Those five main points where syllables are placed are at the crown, throat, heart, navel and pelvis. While the syllables vary in different practices, in the *Esoteric Community* system, the seed syllables of the five genius types—*Om*, *Ah*, *Hum*, *Sva*, and *Ha*—are placed at the crown, throat, heart, navel, and pelvis, respectively. For simplicity, I will abbreviate these as exclamation points of five gem-toned lights, in line with a similar move made at later stages of traditional practice.[96] The five systems are color-coded and aligned with those points as follows: the physical system, diamond white, at the crown; the conceptual system, ruby red, at the throat; the perceptual system, sapphire blue

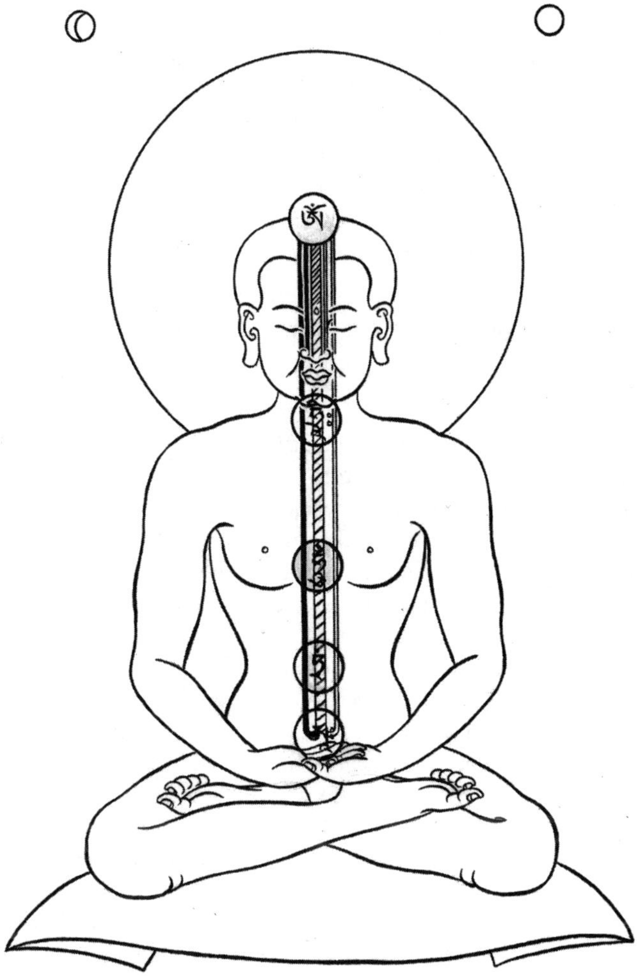

Figure 7.1 The Neural Network of Self-Regulation

at the heart; the sensory system, citrine gold at the navel; and the emotional systems, emerald green at the pelvis.

Given this background, we're ready to return to the practice of the *Healing Mother*, and the power tool of stress-protective imagery and affirmation. In this practice, you first envision the *Healing Mother* as you did the *Healing Mentor*, seated in meditation on a giant rainbow lotus in front of you. In addition to her distinctive outward appearance—luminous white with seven eyes—within her translucent body of light, standing on five thumbnail sized moon-disc cushions at her crown, throat, heart, navel, and pelvis, are the five 3-D exclamation points of diamond, ruby, sapphire, citrine, and emerald light. Each glows with a rainbow aura shifted towards its main color, filling her body with a rainbow luminosity that glows through her pores to form an aura of rainbow radiance around her. Recalling that these syllables symbolize her embodiment of the geniuses of the five enlightened mind/body systems guided by five intuitive wisdoms, you then envision within your own meditative body of light the five moon discs with five color-coded exclamation points, symbolizing your five mind/body systems, though still obviously obscured and tainted by the compulsions of anger, desire, pride, greed, and envy.

Inserting the Art of Stress-Protection into the Role-Modeling Process

With this setup, you proceed through the seven steps of mentor bonding as you did with the *Healing Mentor*, but at the fifth step of requesting help, instead of a rainbow wave coming all at once from your role-model's heart, one at a time five beams of gem-toned light come from her five points to your five points. As each beam of gemlike laser light strikes each one of your points, you imagine that it purifies each system of its respective stress-toxin and transforms it into its enlightened form, crystal clear and radiating its particular gemlike light through your body of light. As each light in turn fills your body, you imagine it glowing out your pores, radiating in all directions twenty feet or more around you, where it sets up a firewall of gem-toned, laser light. As each new system is purified and transformed of the various toxins of stress and trauma, the light it radiates sets up another shell of firewall outside the previous shell(s), finally manifesting an impenetrable rainbow-hued firewall of five gem-toned laser lights.

Sealed with the *Healing Mother* within that protective firewall, you're safe to practice letting go of the emotional tone and reactive style of stress and trauma, knowing that any triggers from the stress world outside will be neutralized by the firewall of healing intuition and energy you're able to tap and emit. The subtle creative imagery of this meditation not only helps us perceive our outer and inner environment as safely contained within the crucible of the role-modeling bond, but also empowers us to practice experiencing our body-mind and its internal systems as purified and transformed by the catalyst of his or her healing influence and example.

Given this, we're ready for the closing meditative experiment of this chapter. Unlike the guided meditations thus far, this and following experiments will be structured in the traditional format of a performance script.[97] As the words suggest, the format guides our imagination and recitation as the dramatic script of a play would an actor's performance. While it may take some getting used to, this format has several benefits. Whether we actually read the script out loud or read it mentally to ourselves, the active work of announcing the imagery and affirmations helps shift our mode of engagement from receptively following to actively co-creating. This performative dimension not only empowers us to step more fully into the world of the meditation, but starts to prime the dynamic motivation, expression and interaction that plant the seeds for our eventually embodying the mentor's role and way of being. As in any script, I'll provide process notes and suggestions in italics, like stage directions. Affirmations will be in capitals. To prime your mind for experiment 7, please refer to the image of the *Healing Mother* in the color insert.

Meditative Experiment 7: Subtle, Stress-Protective Imagery and Affirmation

Imagine yourself in a safe healing environment, on top of the world,
Feeling freely connected to all living beings,
Facing a gathering of the healing mentors, teachers,
Texts and communities that most open your heart & mind.
Sitting comfortably with hands placed,
Balance your energies, either with alternate nostril breaths
Or by exhaling fully and deeply one or more times.
Now rehearse the seven step role-modeling process,
Reading the following lines mentally or out loud,
As if you were reading them to your mentor,
Who sits right in front of you as the Healing Mother.
To get the most out of the process, pause for a moment
After reading each step, and try to see, feel and taste
The living, breathing presence of your role-model.

Purifying Ordinary Perceptions of Self and World
"Suddenly all life and all things melt into pure, blissful openness!
In the deep space before me, out of sheer luminosity
Comes a giant rainbow lotus of total release,
In the midst of which glows a moon cushion of mind
That bubbles up a 3-D exclamation point
Of sapphire light, like a beacon of healing speech,
Radiating a rainbow aura of five pure energies,
And sounding the affirmation—
MAY ALL BE SAFE, WELL AND FREE!
Suddenly in the rainbow orb of that aura
Dawns the milk-white form of the Healing Mother,
Seated on the moon-cushion and giant rainbow lotus.
Lit from within her crown, throat, heart, navel and pelvis
By five moon-discs and gem-toned exclamation points,
Her translucent form, filled with five gem-toned lights,
Radiates a rainbow aura of blissful openness and art,
Embodying the love that is the mother of us all,
With all the marks and signs of perfect maturity.

Smiling in rapt attentiveness, with five extra, intuitive eyes
In her brow, palms, and soles making every gesture an art,
She wears the rainbow silks of five freedoms,
And the six transcendences as ornaments.
Her right palm over her knee faces out,
Offering protection and freedom from trauma,
Her left palm open over her heart holds the stem
Of three lotuses blossoming over her shoulder
The arts of longevity, empathy and pure genius!"

Inviting the Healing Mother's Presence and Blessing
"From the exclamation point at her heart,
The Mother beams light inviting all the nurturing
And healing mentors from all places and times
To merge into her and seal her with healing nectar,
Filling her and overflowing as a Long-Life Buddha crown."

The First Step: Admiring
"Admiring the grace of your nurturing openness,
I entrust my life to your motherly care and teaching."

The Second Step: Sharing
"All my resources, real and imagined,
Even this precious mind, body and life,
And our globe with all its life and wonders,
I dedicate to the blissful openness you embody."

The Third Step: Disclosing
"In all honesty, I regret and admit each and every one
Of my obstacles, limits, and faults,
And resolve with your help to transform them all."

The Fourth Step: Enjoying
"Turning competitiveness into the joy of teamwork,
I vicariously enjoy your qualities and vow to emulate every one."

Enhancing the Fourth Step: The Four Boundless States
"May all beings have real happiness and its causes!
May we all be freed from all suffering and its causes!
May we all enjoy and savor all good things!
May we all know unwavering equanimity!" (Repeat 3X)

The Fifth Step: Requesting Help
"From the bottom of my heart I ask you, *Healing Mother*,
Please share with me your healing purity, genius and art!
Thrilled to be asked, the *Healing Mother* emits rainbow light
From the moon and sapphire exclamation point at her heart,
Filling galaxies to the furthest reaches of space,
Drawing the boundless renunciation, compassion and wisdom
Of all geniuses of all five kinds throughout space and time
Back to melt into her heart, then beaming them all to me
As a rainbow wave that engulfs and fills my body with light,
Transforming my mind into a heart-moon of lucid awareness,
My speech into a blue exclamation point of affirmative thought,
And my body into the milk-white body of a *Healing Mother*."

Requesting the Mother's Purification and Protection
"Knowing that the gross transformation of my body-speech-mind
Is a mere simulation, from the depths of my heart I ask you,
Healing Mother, please share with me the subtle
Intuitive essence of your five-fold purity, genius and art!
Thrilled to be asked, the *Healing Mother* emits rainbow light
From the five points of her subtle body, beaming them
One at a time, to purify, protect, and transform
All five internal systems of my own subtle mind/body process."

Purifying, Protecting, and Transforming the Physical System
"The Mother's crown-point beams diamond white light
To the opaque white exclamation point at my crown,
Clearing away the compulsive drive of aggression and violence,
Until my crown-point becomes clear diamond and shines
With pacifying diamond light that fills my physical body
With the moral genius of reflective intuition
Until it emanates from my pores and sets up a diamond laser shield
All around me that transforms any triggers
of aggression and violence."

Purifying, Protecting, and Transforming the Sensory System
"The *Mother*'s navel-point beams citrine gold light
To the opaque yellow exclamation point at my navel,
Clearing away the addictive hunger of greed and avarice,
Until my navel-point becomes clear citrine and shines
With a warm citrine light that fills my sensory system
With the social genius of equalizing intuition
Until it emanates from my pores and sets
up a second, citrine laser shield
All around me that transforms any triggers of greed and avarice."

Purifying, Protecting, and Transforming the Conceptual System
"The *Mother*'s throat-point beams ruby red light
To the opaque red exclamation point at my throat,
Clearing away the obsessive energy of craving and clinging,
Until my throat-point becomes clear ruby and shines
With a radiant ruby light that fills my conceptual system
With the creative genius of discriminating intuition
Until it emanates from my pores and sets up a third, ruby laser shield
All around me that transforms any triggers of craving and clinging."

Purifying, Protecting, and Transforming the Emotional System
"The *Mother*'s pelvic-point beams emerald green light
To the opaque green exclamation point at my pelvis,
Clearing away the competitive energy of envy and jealousy,
Until my pelvic-point becomes clear emerald and shines
With a vibrant emerald light that fills my emotional system
With the proactive genius of executive intuition
Until it emanates from my pores and sets
up a fourth, emerald laser shield
All around me that transforms any triggers of envy and jealousy."

Purifying, Protecting, and Transforming the Perceptual System
"The *Mother*'s heart-point beams blue sapphire light
To the opaque blue exclamation point at my heart,
Clearing away the narcissistic energy of self-
reifying delusion and pride,
Until my heart-point becomes clear sapphire and shines
With a deep sapphire light that fills my perceptual system
With the intellectual genius of ultimate reality intuition
Until it emanates from my pores and sets
up a fifth, sapphire laser shield
All around me that transforms any triggers of delusion and pride."

Sealing the Purity, Protection, and Transformation of All Five Systems
"The *Mother*'s five points beam all five rainbow lights
To the five exclamation points of my subtle mind/body,
Dispelling the instincts of all five primary compulsions,
Until my five points become clear gem-toned light and shine
With a rainbow aura that fills my five mind/body systems
With the fivefold genius of all five pure intuitions
Until it emanates from my pores and sets
up a sixth, amethyst laser shield
All around me that seals the transformation any compulsive triggers.

In each of the spaces between the six shields is a network
Of gem-toned light lotuses whose laser edges instantaneously
Disintegrate and transform any triggering
input from the outside world.
Safe within the firewall of the *Mother*'s intuition and art,
I finally release stress emotions and instincts,
And fully immerse myself in my pure, healing genius."

Enhancing Stress-Protective Imagery with Affirmation:
Focused first on each point and shield at a time,
And then on all points and all shields at once,
Recite mentally or out loud as many times as you like
Either the Mother's brief affirmation—
MAY ALL BE SAFE, WELL AND FREE!
Her long affirmation—
MAY THE LIFESPAN, VIRTUES, AND
WISDOM OF ALL LIFE INCREASE!
Or her personally directed long affirmation—
MAY MY (OR ANYONE'S) LIFESPAN,
VIRTUES, AND WISDOM INCREASE!
As you recite the affirmation, imagine it beaming
Light and sound from each point in your subtle body
To each shell in your firewall, where it intensifies
The glow and power of each shell and lotus network,
And then beams back to intensify and clarify each point.
The crown-point beams diamond light to shield one,
Which intensifies and returns diamond light;
The navel-point beams citrine light to shield two,
Which intensifies and returns citrine light;
The throat-point beams ruby light to shield three,
Which intensifies and returns ruby light;
The pelvic-point beams emerald light to shield four,
Which intensifies and returns emerald light;
The heart-point beams sapphire light to shield five,
Which intensifies and returns sapphire light;
All five points beam rainbow light to shield six,
Which intensifies and returns rainbow light.
After the recitation, immerse yourself in the resonance
And afterglow as much and as long as you can.
"One with the dignity of the mentor's intuitive genius,
I look with her care at the world all around—
Find the *Healing Mother* in all living beings;
See all things enfolded in her healing art;
And hear all sounds echoing her affirmation!"

The Sixth Step: Requesting Constancy
"Knowing that this imagery is a mere simulation,
I ask you please to be my constant protector, companion
And guide, from now until I integrate your mastery,
And my five systems embody your fivefold genius!
Moved by affection for me, my role-model melts
From her crown and toes to the moon and exclamation point
At her heart, which in turn melt into the point's single dot,
Like a tear-drop for joy, coalescing all her intuitions and energies.
Glowing with rainbow light, her heart-drop comes to my crown
And melts through my crown and throat into the exclamation point
At my heart, merging her healing essence with mine, intensifying
The light and warmth of all my five points,
until they fill me as flames
Fill a beacon and nectars, a vase, rippling out through my shields
In all my actions, until all those around me become
Healing Mothers, returning a wave of joy to my heart!"
Now pause to absorb and drink in the warmth and moisture of that joy,
As long and deeply as you can, and then prepare to close the session:
"Suddenly the world outside, my healing space and body
All return to their normal appearance, the six shells outside
And the five moons and points inside all melt into my heart,
Then the exclamation point melts into the dot of my heart-drop."

The Seventh Step: Dedication
"Any intuition and energy I've gained through this practice,
I dedicate to integrating my mentor's intuitive essence
In this lifetime, as quickly as possible! And so, by mastering
The arts of role-modeling imagery and blissful openness,
May I purify my five compulsions, embody the five intuitions,
Transform my mind/body systems into the *Mother*'s
Fivefold healing genius, and bring all life to her optimal state!"

Afterimages: Some Reflections on Role-Modeling Imagery, Coarse and Subtle

As you may have gleaned from this experiment, this tradition of imagery stands in contrast to its Western analogues, not just in its use of ideal self-images in role-modeling bonds, but also because it prepares us to master the social-emotional and neurobiological art of sublimation. When we envision a new self-image in this tradition, the imagery prepares us not just for a new way of being in our social world, but also for new ways to live in our emotional body and nervous system. As in the exercises of parts 1 and 2, the imagery we've explored begins by prompting us to envision our body in the lighter, clearer version I've called the "breath-body" or "body of light." What is new here is that this body helps make us more receptive to influence from an ideal role-model, giving our sense of self the plasticity we need to try on and take in a more ideal outer role and inner way of being. This kind of coarse and subtle self-imagery aims to help expand both our perception and emotional intelligence beyond reactive patterns. It also serves to open us to more empowered self-images, positive emotions, and peak states of physical arousal and flow.

As a note of encouragement, let me reassure those of you who doubt your ability to meditate with imagery. The trick is not to expect too much right away but to work with whatever you can muster, trusting that the process will bear fruit just as any new workout. Some of you may need to be content at first with just "reading" or "listening to" the "scripts" or "tapes" that guide imagery practice, like poems or short stories. The result you're seeking is that your imagery will gradually become as clear and real as normal perception, while retaining the sense of transparency that comes of consciously creating and evoking a specific perception in the mind's eye. Eventually, this skill will help you alter the basic building blocks of perception, including your habitual sense of yourself and others. And these shifts will open new doors in your perception, experience, and response to the worlds around you and inside you.

8 The Art and Science of Reconstructing Life

> Regarding that (purification of our ordinary perception of the life-cycle), a person who has previously collected the evolutionary action which is the cause of taking birth in the womb dies and attains the between state; then the between-state being enters the womb of the mother and, having remained there, finally gets born outside; then having taken a wife he performs the deeds of having sons and daughters, (so) having taken (all of those ordinary life-cycle) things as the objects of correspondence, it is in correspondence with those that one meditates the Creation Stage.
>
> (Tsong Khapa, *Great Exposition of the Poetic Path*[1])

The wisdom of the constructive phase of process practice is clear in the way the art of role-modeling comes to life through the insight-guided narrative imagery mapped out by the creation stage. As role-modeling helps gradually transform our traumatic images of self and world, we find ourselves in the integration phase, entering the transformative realm opened up by the optimal integral process. If the aim of process imagery is to purify our ordinary perception of self and world, the optimal integral form of that process is to guide us through nothing less than a complete, insight-oriented revision of the ordinary life-story or narrative which frames that perception. This revision is made possible by a counter-narrative of ideal self-creation which guides the creation stage, and works to transform our ordinary, traumatic experience of life into the impassioned experience of a heroic altruist.

In essence, the basic role-modeling imagery traditionally used to introduce us to the process path works like a snap-shot, giving us a taste of our potential to transform our reactive, childhood experience of self and world into a corrective experience of proactive being and living. Yet, since our images of self, others, and the world we share are set in a complex narrative that locates us within an ongoing story of individuality, family, community, and environment, the full art of transformative imagery in the optimal integral creation stage sets that snap-shot within an unfolding counter-narrative meant to guide a full reconstruction of our experience of our self and world over time. Tsong Khapa explains the rationale for this in his *Great Exposition*:

> Here, (in a context) wherein "ordinary conceptual thought" is explained to be an inner monologue having the form of "I" and "mine" and subject and object, then when the text refers to "the suffering which has the nature of existence" the contextual meaning is that "(the inner monologue) is the chief cause of suffering which has the nature of existence."[2]

While it seems hard to imagine any narrative sense of self that doesn't revolve around the first person pronouns, a remarkable study by health psychologist Larry Scherwitz lends some very strong support to the idea that the statistically normal way we cling to our constructs of "myself" and "my life" in fact makes us prone to suffering and disease.[3] In an elegant piece of research based on the findings of a multi-center prospective study of coronary artery disease (CAD) by the National Institutes of Health, Scherwitz developed a powerful way to tease out the risk related to a mental habit he called self-involvement. By counting the number of times per phrase study participants used a first person pronoun in their unstructured interviews, he arrived at a novel way to measure one of the traits thought to be part of the Type-A personality cluster.

After analyzing the correlations between self-involvement and the incidence of coronary disease and its complications, Scherwitz came upon a series of findings that were as unexpected as they were hard to contest. Not only did a habit of frequently saying "I," "me," and "mine" turn out to be a statistically significant risk factor predicting the incidence of the disease, it also appeared to be a major risk factor for morbidity and mortality. Specifically, the more self-involved cohort of people who developed the disorder were significantly more likely to have a heart attack, and the more self-involved cohort of those with heart attacks were more likely to have a fatal event. In fact, among those with heart attacks, self-involvement turned out to be a stronger predictor of death than all the other variables tracked in the study, including smoking history, high blood cholesterol levels, high blood pressure, and depression. These findings, which are utterly unexpected and anomalous for modern biomedicine, are precisely what a Buddhist physician or psychologist would predict,[4] given the classical analysis expressed by Tsong Khapa.

Taken together with the findings of current stress research[5] and positive psychology,[6] this kind of research clearly suggests that clinging to a self-reifying, traumatic narrative really does create needless suffering. Since our ordinary life-narrative is structured around the biological events of development, birth and death, the counter-story of the creation stage must likewise be structured around the corresponding nodes in the life-narrative of a heroic altruist. Tsong Khapa alludes to this in our opening quote. Though our modern one-life worldview sequences those events differently from the multi-life worldview of Buddhism, the creation stage art of narrative reconstruction can be made to fit our ordinary narrative with surprisingly minor revisions.

The Art of Narrative Self-Creation: Restructuring the Story and Facts of Life

The traditional formula for how the insight-guided imagery of the creation stage can fully "purify" our ordinary life narrative revolves around three biological events—development, birth, and death—which it takes as the three "basic things to be purified." In these three facts, we see more or less the same biological main events we would recognize as pivotal to life, although the tradition naturally views them based on the *karmic* assumption that our development in this life is continuous with a death in a previous life. This is why, as our opening passage suggests, the traditional sequence of events to be revised is death, development, and birth, rather than (intrauterine) development, birth, and death. The other main difference follows from the same assumption. Traditionally, the phase I've called development is not seen as limited to development *within* the womb, but includes two sub-phases: the first stretching from the death in a prior life to conception, and the second from conception in the womb to birth. This pre-conception phase is described not simply as development but more broadly as a death-life transition and called the between state or *bardo*.[7]

While the traditional sequencing of the main events in our ordinary life narrative doesn't exactly match our modern view of life, as I've said, this cross-cultural gap can be bridged if we take the Buddhist view as consistent with our evolutionary view that the physical and mental raw materials for our development come not out of nowhere or from God but from the mind/body processes of individuals from prior generations.[8] More to the point, a psychological reading of the act of consciously recreating our unexamined life narrative must begin with the death of our identification with a reified image and construct of self. If and only if we're ready to voluntarily die to our traumatized sense of self can we have the mental space and breathing room to begin envisioning and embarking on our transition to a new, proactive self, life, and world.

Given this cross-cultural adjustment, we can now look at the process of revising our ordinary view of these basic facts of life, traditionally called "conversion." This process is conceived is as a cognitive-perceptual restructuring of the basic facts of life. No mere reframing, it is meant to "convert" the sense and reference of these facts, in a way that helps restructure the biological life-cycle into raw material for the creation of a consciously chosen multi-life-cycle and way of life. The basic biological fact of death is imaginatively converted into a way of embodying unconditional openness to reality or truth; the basic fact of development or life-transition is converted into a way of embodying the pure enjoyment, aesthetic experience or empathic expression of radical open-mindedness; and the basic fact of birth or life is converted into a way of embodying the incarnation or concrete manifestation of pure open-mindedness.

The Three Conversions and the Threefold Embodiment of Altruism

These three conversions assume a threefold embodiment of altruism which expands on a framework we explored in part 2. Specifically, it expands on the twofold framework of altruism—as the union of pure openness of mind and full embodiment of compassion—by dividing the embodiment of compassion in two; the expressive aspect of compassion, and its physical manifestation. In either case, the parallel is no accident but reflects the intentional congruence of the exoteric path of engagement with the esoteric path of process-oriented self-transformation. In effect, the insight-guided path of narrative self-creation in the process tradition figures as a quicker, multi-modal form of the transformative art Chekawa described, "The aim of this (practice) is to turn the evolution of five toxic (mind/body) systems into a path to enlightenment."

Of course, these three very general facts of life don't begin to exhaust the biographical details we think of as our ordinary life narratives, especially not in the textured way we examine our story in our inner monologue or the dialogue of psychotherapy. Yet the generic nature of the counter-narrative we generate through the three conversions of the creation stage is not meant to address all particulars. Instead, its archetypal form helps us gain an objective perspective on our myopic story of self, the better to break its self-limiting grip on our imagination and perception.

In essence, the work of the three conversions is not to change our view of the minutia of our default story of life but rather to challenge us to completely revise the tacit assumptions about ourselves and the life-cycle that make up the basic form of our stories of life. Our ordinary sense of ourselves as thrown into the world by superhuman forces and caught on a wheel of survival that drives us to repeat the tragic cycle of compulsive development, mindless reproduction and traumatic death, is reframed as the archetypal tale of our death to compulsive life, followed by our self-creative development and manifestation of a life of heroic altruism and pure genius. Within this counter-narrative, the supposedly given facts of death, development, and birth are transformed into three narrative nodes in the triumphant story of our complete transformation of ourselves into models of optimal altruistic development.

In what follows, we'll explore the way the imagery of narrative conversion works to deepen the role-modeling process on the creation stage path of insight. Although this art is only fully elaborated in the imagery of the optimal integral process, the principles of self-creation which guide the optimal integral creation stage are tacitly at work in the constructive phase of the three introductory levels of process-oriented practice.[9] Set within the sevenfold framework of the two oldest and most common performance process practices of wisdom, we'll explore the three conversions that define the art of narrative self-creation. The two practices revolve around the prime male and female archetypes of philosophical-psychological-scientific genius in both the engaged and process traditions: the crown prince, *Sheer Brilliance*, and the mother goddess, *Transcendent Wisdom*. Before we turn to our initial meditative experiment with this art, it may help to briefly review the key points in the practice.

The Conversions in Context: The Framework of Narrative Imagery and Affirmation

Traditionally, the actual practice of purifying our ordinary life narrative based on the three conversions is sandwiched between preliminary and concluding steps, which overlap with the seven steps of the role-modeling process explored in chapter 7. Of the three preliminary points, the first—building pure motivation—overlaps with the four steps of admiring, welcoming, disclosing, and enjoying; while the second and third—establishing pure wisdom and perfect security—come between the fourth step of enjoying and the fifth step of requesting help.

Grounded in these three preliminary points, the three points of actual practice are the three conversions—of death, development, and rebirth—which culminate in the recreation of one's ordinary self and life as a threefold embodiment of heroic altruism. These three points all overlap with the fifth role-modeling step of requesting help.

Once we've arrived at our new form of life through narrative self-transformation, we come to the two concluding points—rehearsing a lifestyle of heroic altruism and closing the practice session. Of these, rehearsing also overlaps with fifth role-modeling step of requesting help, while closing overlaps with the sixth and seventh role-modeling steps: requesting constancy and dedication. So, the actual art of narrative self-revision on the creation stage path of insight is effectively inserted in the sevenfold role-modeling process as an expanded journey of requesting and receiving help purifying and transforming our ordinary perception of life.

Another key aspect of this narrative insight practice is its dramatic use of a handful of affirmative formulas of intuitive wisdom and narrative conversion as performative statements which effectively prime and enact the change we're seeking to make. This practice begins with the use of the two great affirmations—of vivid imagery and enlightened dignity—to evoke and pronounce our generation of the preliminary factors of motivation and wisdom. And it concludes with the use of the three great affirmations which seal the conversion of our ordinary life narrative to the visionary narrative of a heroic altruist.

If you recall, there are two great affirmations which serve to ground our vivid imagery and enlightened dignity in the intuitive wisdoms of illusory aftermath and spacious equipoise respectively: "*I have a pure nature which is the natural purity of all things*," and "*I have a self whose nature is the diamond intuition of emptiness*!" These are key mnemonics for establishing the motivation and wisdom we need for an effective conversion, since establishing that our imagery is both vivid and transparent helps to ground our practice in a truly positive affective state, while establishing the awareness which holds that imagery in the selfless dignity of radical open-mindedness helps insure that that ground is purified and sealed with intuitive wisdom.

In effect, the third preliminary—establishing perfect security—simply affirms that our minds are utterly safe and secure from the disturbing influence of stress and trauma, since they are sealed within the firewall of unconditional compassion and selfless wisdom by virtue of our vivid imagery and enlightened dignity. While this firewall is set up in various ways in various practices, such as the shields we set up with the *Healing Mother*, for our purposes we can reduce this setup to its simplest form by imagining that our minds are emanating an impenetrable shield made of a blissful flow as hard as diamond, and a discriminating analysis as all-consuming as a supernova. We can then check and seal the truth of this visualization with the affirmation, "*I am safe within the firewall of diamond compassion and blazing wisdom*!"

Pronouncing the Three Conversions: The Poetics of Self-Creation

Each of the three conversions consists in a signature sequence of imagery and is sealed by a performative affirmation. The conversion of death into a path to true open-mindedness involves a sequence of imagery that rehearses the dissolution of our mind/body process as in the course of dying or the similar state-transitions into deep sleep or sexual orgasm. It is sealed by the affirmation, "*I now take death as a path to embodying truth*!" The conversion of development into a path to the joyful expression of creative openness involves a sequence of imagery that rehearses the reemergence of mind/body complexity which takes place in the course of intrauterine development or similar reconstructive states like dreaming and the afterglow of sexual experience. It is sealed by the affirmation, "*I now take development as a path to embodying bliss*!" And finally, the conversion of ordinary birth or life into a path to manifesting heroic altruism involves a sequence of imagery that rehearses the fruition of development which takes place in the course of full maturation and similar states, such as the normal waking state or consummated mature love. It is sealed by the affirmation, "*I now take rebirth as a path to manifesting heroic mastery*!" Tsong Khapa summarizes the logic of these conversions, pointing out how the vivid mental imagery of our new life narrative counteracts ordinary perceptions while the self-creative formulas of enlightened pride counteract ordinary conception:

> The Creation Stage meditation on the habitat celestial mansion and the inhabitant deity was taught as the antidote to both ordinary perception and ordinary conception. Thus, through familiarization with the perception that gives rise to the habitat celestial mansion and the inhabitant deity, one will get rid of ordinary perception, and through the thoughts "I am (the Buddha) *Immovable*," and "I am (the Buddha) *Illuminator*," and

> so on, (one will get rid of) ordinary pride. Having eliminated ordinary pride, (one's identity) is transformed into divine pride.[10]

As for concluding points, the most crucial is the act of rehearsing the lifestyle of heroic altruism. This involves a sequence of imagery that rehearses the activities of heroic altruism: creating an altruistic community; marshaling the ideal environment and resources of that community; and transforming the world and all life into an ideal environment for the universal development and spread of heroic altruism. This enactment is obviously crucial to priming the mind/body process to manifest a life of heroic altruism, with all its necessary supporting factors and communal benefits. And, as in our prior experiments, this enhanced role-modeling practice is closed with the final steps of requesting constancy and dedication, which may include requesting help on all stages of the path or dedicating all our efforts to success on those stages.[11]

To take the next step towards exploring this art of self-creative imagery, it's time to turn to our first meditative experiment, based on the performance process practice of *Sheer Brilliance* (a.k.a. *Sheer Eloquence*). As before, directions and affirmations appear in italics. To prime your mind for experiment 8.1, please refer to the image of *Youthful Sheer Brilliance* in the color insert.

Meditative Experiment 8.1: Embodying *Sheer Brilliance*

In as peaceful and uplifting a place as possible,
With or without real offerings or images
Of your mentor or archetype of Brilliance,
Settle into a comfortable, stable posture,
And clear your energy with a deep and full sigh
Or with nine rounds of alternate nostril breathing.
Then gradually shift into a kinder, gentler breath-rhythm
And use that rhythm, centered at your heart,
As a focal point to center your whole body-mind
In a meditative state of greater clarity and calm.
Then recite mentally or out loud the following
Performance script, based on the sevenfold role-modeling process
Of Sheer Brilliance, pausing after each section
For as long as you like to envision its imagery,
Focus on your experience, or contemplate its meaning.

1. *Evoking and Admiring a Vision of Sheer Brilliance*
   "Suddenly the whole universe, including my body-mind,
   Returns to its natural state of pure energy and openness.
   I HAVE THE PURE NATURE WHICH IS THE NATURAL PURITY OF ALL THINGS!
   In the open space before me, your living, breathing presence dawns,

Hovering like the sun's reflection in water, in the midst of which
Erupts a citrine gold syllable G! of 3-D laser light,
Resonating with the optimistic sound of your voice,
Beaming a rainbow aura all around, which purges all ailing beings
And delights all awakened ones, inviting their wisdom
To return like a rainbow wave, gathering back into the G!
Until it glows like a sun-flare, beams an orange-gold orb
That assumes your form, as the eternal youth who speaks the truth,
Soulmate of the goddess, *Transcendent Wisdom.*
Amid the ivory towers of your realm of pure science,
Your sunny face unfolds a Victor's smile and eyes
Moist with unconditional love. Over your topknot of black hair
Your right hand wields the light-saber of impeccable wisdom
While at your heart your teaching hand upholds the stem of a lotus,
Blossoming a Transcendent Wisdom text at your left shoulder.
At ease in heavenly silks, you bear all the marks and signs
Of perfect altruism, and the living gems of transcendent virtue."

1a. *Inviting Your Mentor's Spirit to Ground Your Vision*
"Your form glows like a living lamp, lit from within
At the crown, throat, and heart by diamond, ruby and sapphire light
Exclamation points, reflecting your awakened body, speech and mind,
And emitting the primal breath-energy sounds, OH AH UM,
Along with an aura of sunset brilliance, that beams five gem-toned
Intuitive lights to develop all beings and worlds all around
And invite your intuitive genius and the spirits of all altruists
To melt into you and merge as one! Though, in reality,
You neither come nor go, your acts of loving wisdom dawn
To suit the minds you tame. Please come to stay, eternal youth!"

1b. *Taking Refuge in Your Role-Model's Example*
"Warmed by the brilliance of your open-mindedness,
All mother earthlings and I take refuge in your shining example.
To heal and free all sensitive beings I will conceive
Your altruistic spirit of pure love and sheer openness, in this life,
As quickly as possible, and develop myself and all being
Until we all reach true genius and perfect this world!"

2. *Welcoming Sheer Brilliance into Your World*
"In the presence of your freeing truth, all experience has the singular taste
Of blissful openness, pervading the mind and all the senses!

Welcoming you gratefully into my world, I offer
A sun-shower of sense delights—the most exquisite sights,
Sounds, scents, tastes and textures, scented waters,
Incense, flowers, lights, music, and delicacies—
Converging toward you from everywhere, horizon and sky,
Like goddesses joining your god-like mind and senses!
Fully and freely I share with you all my resources,
Virtues, and every aspect of my intimate life,
My mind, body, dreams and visions, and the blissful sphere
Of my inmost truth, unveiled by habits of thought or speech,
Plus this precious earth, with its oceans, continents,
Wonders, forests, waters, and infinite web of life!"

3. *Fully Disclosing your Faults, Limits, and Blocks*
"Regretting all the negative instincts and habits I've indulged,
All the patterns that limit and block me from acquiring your qualities
And emulating your way of being, from the depths of my heart
I admit them all to you now, ask your acceptance and help,
And firmly resolve from here on to avoid and unlearn every one."

4. *Enjoying the Qualities of Sheer Brilliance*
"Though all things are empty of any non-relative being,
Filled with gratitude I enjoy all the myriad forms
Of happiness you experience and share with all life,
And all the transcendent virtues that serve as their cause."

4a. *Enhancing Enjoyment with the Four Boundless Moods*
"May all beings have real happiness and its causes!
May we all be freed from all suffering and its causes!
May we all enjoy and savor all excellent things!
May we all know unwavering equanimity!" (Repeat 3X)

5. *Requesting/Receiving Recognition and Protection*
"From your heavenly realm of pure science and healing art,
Please shower us with profound and magnificent teachings
To help cool, develop and nurture these lotus groves
Of sensitive beings, spreading the genius of pure intuition.
Moved by your loving care for all life, from your body, speech, and mind,
Diamond, ruby, and sapphire lights and nectars beam
First in sequence, then all together, to melt in sequence
Then all together into my three points, purging my blocks
Of body, speech, mind and action, recognizing

My fourfold genius and planting the seeds of enlightenment,
Finally sending a miniature double of you who dissolves
Through my crown, throat, and heart, melting my body, speech and mind
Into your blissful openness, where we merge like water in water.
I AM THE SELF WHOSE NATURE IS
THE DIAMOND INTUITION OF OPENNESS!
Immersing myself as one with the singular taste of your
Blissful openness, I feel completely sealed within
The diamond sphere of your unconditional care and love
And the supernova fire of your intuitive wisdom.
I AM SAFE WITHIN THE FIREWALL OF
DIAMOND COMPASSION AND BLAZING WISDOM!"

5a. *Making Death a Way to Embody Pure Openness*
"Now that you and I have dissolved, along with any
Trace of our ordinary bodies, minds, lives, and worlds,
Just as we would in the process of dying, I take this space
Of sheer openness, free from distinctions, as my true body,
In which the clarity of bliss illumines everyone
And everything's ultimate freedom from any non-relative
Being, essence, nature, identity or objectivity.
I EMBODY THE ULTIMATE TRUTH OF SHEER BRILLIANCE!"

5b. *Making Development a Way to Embody Enjoyment*
"In the deep space of blissful openness, my innate intuitive
Wisdom dawns as an orb of brilliance like the rising sun
Mirrored in water, out of which bubbles a 3-D gold
Syllable G of citrine light like a sun-flare sword,
Beaming a rainbow aura through all worlds everywhere,
Purifying all ordinary beings and delighting all
The enlightened, invoking a wave of gratitude and blessings
That returns to melt back into me as the syllable G.
Now shimmering with the citrine gold of *Sheer Brilliance*,
My intuitive genius as G emits a sunrise glow
Out of which my joy assumes the youthful form
Of *Sheer Brilliance*, orange-gold, holding a text and sword.
Lit from the crown, throat, and heart by sun-discs holding
Exclamation points of diamond, ruby, and sapphire light,
My body is filled with the gem-toned clarity of fivefold
Intuitive genius, and glows as if with a rainbow aura.
I EMBODY THE PURE ENJOYMENT OF SHEER BRILLIANCE!"

5c. *Making Life a Way to Embody Compassion*
"Now that I've re-created myself in the nascent form
Of *Sheer Brilliance*, the heroic altruist, it's time to emerge
From the womb of my mentor's blissful openness and be reborn
In mature form, as the master altruist *Sheer Brilliance*.
All around me I hear the five goddesses of *Transcendent Wisdom*
Calling me to remember my commitments and pledges:
To re-enter the world, embodying compassion, and model
The altruist's way—purifying, transforming, and enhancing
The lives and worlds of all beings throughout space and time.
As the sounds of their voices raise goose bumps and the hairs on my neck,
My body and mind melt with compassion into the sun-disc
And G at my heart, which melt in turn into my heart-drop,
Dissolving in blissful openness like water poured in water.
Suddenly out of the womb of openness my intuitive mind
Reemerges with the brilliance of a sunrise mirrored in water,
Out of which my clear voice flares as the light syllable G,
Radiating an aura that becomes my body as *Sheer Brilliance*,
Then beaming lights from my heart invite the five goddesses
Of *Transcendent Wisdom* to join me and seal my integration,
By pouring wisdom-nectar through my crown, filling me
Until it overflows as a *Boundless Life* Buddha-crown.
I EMBODY THE MANIFEST FORM OF SHEER BRILLIANCE!"

6. *Requesting Constancy Through Affirmation*
"Facing you now as an equal, I ask you please to stay
With me as my example while I practice realizing
A master altruist's life of embodying *Sheer Brilliance*.
Thrilled for me, my mentor-archetype, *Sheer Brilliance*, repeats
The affirmation coiled around the sun and G at his heart,
MAY ALL REACH PURE GENIUS!
As he repeats it, the affirmation glows and emits
A duplicate of 3-D citrine light which he exhales
Out his mouth and sends my way to inhale deep into my heart,
Where it coils clockwise around my sun-disc's rim, circling
My heart syllable G as six 3-D citrine syllables
Arrayed equidistant around the sun, facing out:
MAY ALL REACH PURE GEN-IUS!
The affirmation wheel stands like a ring of sun-flares at my heart
That lights, warms, and resonates through my whole body and mind."

Figure 8.1 The Affirmation Ring of Sheer Brilliance

As you recite the mantra 7, 21, 108 or more times, imagine it
Rotating ounterclockwise so fast it appears to be standing still,
While the sun disc beneath it revolves like an eight-spoke wheel
Clockwise in the same invisible way. See the affirmation ring
Heating up until it beams rainbow lights through your pores and all
Around the world, gathering the knowledge, reflection and intuitive
Wisdom of all learned and enlightened beings and retrieving them
To dissolve back into itself, making the affirmation wheel glow
Even more until it beams to all beings and worlds all around,
Purifying all their toxic emotions, traumatic habits and mental
Blocks, transforming them all into forms of Sheer Brilliance, and
Enhancing their lives and world by unlocking their own
Native genius for heroic altruism and altruistic mastery. Then
Imagine them all Sending duplicates of themselves as Sheer

Brilliance in gratitude back to you, melting like so many citrine
Snowflakes of light into your body and heart-drop. To close the
Recitation, recite the seed syllable G as much, as softly and as
Quickly as you can (up to 108), touching the tip of your tongue to
The back of your upper front teeth. After the recitation, immerse
Yourself in the resonance and afterglow as deeply and continuously
As you can. Shifting your focus from the affirmation wheel at your
Heart to the moon, from the moon to your body as Sheer Brilliance,
From your body to the body of Sheer Brilliance before you, and
Finally back to your body. Take a deep abdominal breath and gently
Hold it as you focus on your sun-gold body, and as you exhale be
Mindful that it is empty of any non-relative being, essence, nature,
Identity, or objectivity.

6a. *Requesting Constancy as you Practice the Altruist's Life*
"Although your intuitive body of truth lacks both birth and death,
Please stay involved without entering Nirvana, so that
All mother earthlings and I can embody true genius
And this stress-driven world can become a utopia!"
Recognizing this imagery is a mere simulation,
I ask you please to stay with me constantly, every breath
From now until I integrate my true genius,
And my body, speech, and mind become the pure love,
Joy and equanimity which are your true body, speech, and mind.
Moved by affection for me, I see you melt into a drop
Like a rainbow tear for joy, which pours through my crown
And throat to melt into the exclamation point at my heart,
Merging your *Sheer Brilliance* with mine, intensifying
My light, energy and warmth until they fill me as a flame
Fills a lamp and a nectar, a vase, rippling out in my actions
Until all those around me at home and on earth embody
Sheer Brilliance, returning a wave of joy to my heart!
Now pause to absorb and drink in the warmth and moisture
Of that joy, as long and deeply as you can, and then prepare to
Close the session:
"Suddenly the world outside, my ideal space, and body
All return to their normal appearance, the firewall outside
And the three suns and points inside all melt into my heart,
Then the exclamation point melts into the dot of my heart-drop."

7. *Dedicating yourself to Embodying Sheer Brilliance*
"With any errors or omissions I've made in this practice
Out of ignorance, misperception, lack of resources or art,

I ask you, my mentor, please be patient and all-forgiving!
Any positive insight or energy I've gained through this practice
I dedicate to being always inspired by your eloquence,
Until I myself fully embody *Sheer Brilliance*,
In this very lifetime, as quickly as possible!
Whenever I study, contemplate or put into practice
Any teaching, profound or magnificent,
Any science or art, from any tradition or time,
May I be inspired by a direct intuition of you!
May we all have well-being, true abundance, and peace,
The good fortune and intelligence to hear
The inseparability of wisdom and unconditional love,
Supreme openness and great bliss, directly from you!
By mastering the arts of imagery and blissful openness,
May I find the true genius to enlighten myself and all life!"

Understanding and Mastering the Art of Narrative Self-Creation

Of course, this in-depth experiment may be too much for daily practice, but I've included it here to illustrate how the art of narrative self-creation works. For our final experiment, we'll balance this with a simpler form, based on the performance process practice of the feminine archetype of *Transcendent Wisdom*. To clear the way for that final practice, we'll first unpack the art of narrative self-creation laid out in our experiment with *Sheer Brilliance*. Since we're already familiar with the steps of the role-modeling process that frame the narrative imagery of self-transformation, we can simply unpack the eight points that distinguish that art: building positive motivation; cultivating wisdom; establishing full security; converting death into true open-mindedness; converting development into embodied enjoyment; converting life into tangible manifestation; rehearsing the lifestyle of altruistic mastery; and closing dedication.

Peace, Compassion, and Wisdom: Establishing the Foundation for Change

In the first two points—motivation and wisdom—you may recognize the foundational strengths Tsong Khapa prescribed as the common preliminaries needed for effective process practice: the self-healing capacity to renounce unhealthy habits; the socially engaged capacity for genuine empathy, compassion and unconditional love; and the self-transcendent capacity for radical openness also known as the emptiness insight. They are called common because they are foundational strengths which the process-oriented path shares in common with the path of social engagement. In the context of the art of narrative self-creation, the two preliminary points of motivation and wisdom work to prepare the mind for the emotional and cognitive-perceptual challenges of radical self-revision and transformation. If the gateway to freeing the mind from the death-grip of the traumatized self is the double-edged work of disarming stress-emotions on the one hand and de-reifying traumatic memories on the other, we can readily understand why continuing to build these strengths is fundamental to the art of narrative self-transformation.

In terms of modern psychology, the traditional emphasis on these two preliminaries clearly anticipates the emerging methodologies of the affective therapy of trauma and the narrative therapy of childhood trauma, life crises and transitions. New approaches like Diane Fosha's Accelerated Experiential Dynamic Therapy (AEDP) underscore the need for a profound shift in core affective style from the distress affects that bind traumatic experience to what she calls "transformative positive affects" like joy and compassion as a rate-limiting step in healing trauma.[12] As in the self-transformative process of role-modeling, the catalyst of this visceral affective shift is the experience of being seen and known in a safe healing relationship.

On the other hand, the work of narrative therapists like Michael White and David Epston presupposes a contemporary view of the self as a social construction coordinated by language in the evolving context of our relations with others over time.[13] Key to their work is the critique of sociologists Peter Berger and Thomas Luckmann, who describe our ordinary experience of self and world as revolving around the construction of social roles and forms of life, guided by habits of language, and seemingly set in stone by the process of reification. In describing the social construction of personal narratives, psychologists Jill Freedman and Gene Combs[14] explain how people often seek therapy when their lives get stuck within limiting constructs of self, citing Berger and Luckmann's definition of reification, as

> the apprehension of the products of human activity *as if* they were something else than human products—such as facts of nature, results of cosmic laws, or manifestations of divine will. Reification implies that man is capable of forgetting his own authorship of the human world.[15]

Current therapies based on the contemporary insights of social construction and reification clearly resonate with what Buddhist thinkers see as the crucial deconstructive and de-reifying insight of emptiness. Taken together, the preliminary exercises of building positive motivation and de-reifying ordinary perceptions of self and world set the stage for the art of narrative self-creation that is the hallmark of the process path of insight. In fact, their combined role in making the mentoring bond a crucible for narrative self-transformation is graphically depicted in the last preliminary point: establishing full security.

The Protection Wheel: Establishing the Sphere of Perfect Security

We've already described in chapter 7 the vital importance of the role-modeling bond in establishing an interpersonal space in which the student comes to feel safe enough to disarm and transform with a mentor who holds his/her projected ideal self. There we referred to the mentoring bond in alchemical terms as both a crucible and a catalyst of the self-change we seek, comparing it to Winnicott's view that the healing alliance must foster what he called a "holding environment."[16] This explains why, in this phase of our experiment, modeled on the traditional *Practice of Mentor-Bonding*, we set the stage for establishing a sphere of security by requesting and receiving the fourfold recognition which rehearses the formation of a mentor-student bond.

The symbolism of this recognition parallels the fourfold rite of initiation or consecration which establishes the mutual contract that defines the mentor-student relationship as a confidential bond dedicated to teaching altruistic self-mastery.[17] That rite—conferring four consecrations called vase, secret, intuitive wisdom, and word—serves as a virtual map of the optimal integral process, which symbolically clears the student's body, speech, mind, and actions of mental and emotional blocks to full mastery, by binding both parties to teach and learn the wisdom and arts appropriate to all stages of the optimal process path.[18]

In terms of the imagery of narrative self-creation, the transformational space opened up by the role-modeling bond is depicted by a wide range of images of containment the tradition calls *mandalas*. While we are all vaguely familiar with the art of the *mandala*, which Jung saw as an image of psychic wholeness, the richly colorful healing environment we think of as the *mandala*—like all spaces—is first and foremost defined by the boundary that demarcates it from the outer world.[19] In fact, the iconography of protection and security in this tradition revolves around the graphic depiction of a boundary that shuts out otherwise uncontrollable stresses and threats from the ordinary world.[20] This much is clear from the protective shields and firewall envisioned in our experiments with the practices of the *Healing Mother* and *Sheer Brilliance*. In most optimal process practices, this is made even clearer by the convention of envisioning cremation grounds outside the firewall, typically featuring the worst nightmares of anticipating our vulnerability to illness, aging, death and decomposition.[21]

Of course, the protection wheel, shield, or firewall delimiting and guarding the space of purification and transformation in this tradition is no mere exercise in wishful thinking, but a representation of the protective influence of a wise and caring human mentor. Yet that sphere of influence itself is not seen as a kind of magic spell or hypnotic power exerted by the mentor. Just as the *Healing Mother*'s firewall weaves five intuitive wisdom shells with five lotus-like modes of empathy, the firewall of *Sheer Brilliance* likewise sandwiches a "diamond" layer of unconditional compassion with a "supernova" layer of fivefold wisdom fire. So it's not the mere presence of the mentor which protects, but rather the potential of the mentoring bond to model and catalyze the student's development of social-emotional intelligence and de-reifying insight. So the third preliminary point of establishing full security boils down to marshaling and deploying the combined strengths cultivated in the first two points, as the final stage-setting or sealing of the crucible for the work of self-creation to follow.

In terms of sociobiology, the imagery of a firewall protecting both mentor and student from the destructive forces of nature suggests the adaptive advantage set up by our capacity to forge bonds of social cooperation and learning that set us apart from more primitive life. In terms of anthropology, the traditional imagery of the protection wheel—typically involving shields, fences, firewalls, blade-wheels, and manned security posts—recalls the psychological inheritance of ancestral memories and archetypal images of primordial human dwellings, featuring our cultural mastery of protective devices from fire to fences and tents to weapons. Of course, the specific imagery here is less important than the general symbolism of establishing a protective space of social collaboration and cultural technology, the twin pillars of the workspace of human civilization. The intention here is to depict the work of civilization, understood in the psychotherapeutic sense: as the collaborative work of unleashing and harnessing the creative power of love and compassion by fully disarming the self-protective instincts of stress and trauma. This final preliminary point clears the way for the main act of narrative self-creation to begin, starting with taking on the limiting case of this work: disarming our reification and defensive reaction to the natural process of death.

The First Node of Narrative Self-Creation: Making Death a Path to Openness

Since the first translation of what Western scholars called the *Tibetan Book of the Dead*,[22] a classic which featured a psychological introduction by Jung,[23] modern audiences have grown increasingly aware of the process-oriented contemplative science of death and dying preserved by Tibetans in the Nalanda tradition. While our recent experiment with *Sheer Brilliance* approached the opening move of the art of narrative self-creation as a psychological death, not a biological one, the fact is that the process-oriented path of insight employs the same science of death used in Tibetan medicine and spirituality for the sake of speeding the work of self-change.

As Robert Thurman's translation of the classic explains, the esoteric mind/body arts of the optimal integral process are considered the original source of the science of death popularized in the *Tibetan Book of the Dead* and related teachings.[24] Just as contemplating death serves as basic training for renunciation and compassion on the paths of self-healing and social engagement, so envisioning death is used as basic training for self-transformation on the process path as well. Although our experiment with *Sheer Brilliance* seems to gloss over that process by describing the reframing of death as a simple melting or dissolution, in fact this is a well-known shorthand for a more elaborate art of rehearsing death that is a mainstay of most if not all process practice. In what follows, I'll review that art, framed by a schema called the eightfold process of dissolution, to help flesh out the way this powerful simulation training works.

According to that schema, the process of dying is mapped into eight stages, each involving the progressive loss of various modes of embodied experience, specific mind/body system, sensory media, and basic cognitive faculties, and each coordinated with particular objective and subjective signs of dissolution.[25] In the first stage, our physical system and experience of solidity dissolve into our sensory system and experience of fluidity, causing a diminution of vision, loss of recognition of the external world, the objective sign of physical weakness and the subjective sign of appearances wavering like a mirage. In the second stage, our sensory system and experience of fluidity dissolve into our discursive system and experience of bodily heat, causing a diminution of hearing, loss of sensations of pleasure and pain, the objective sign of the drying of mucous membranes and the subjective sign of perceptions growing hazy and insubstantial like dark clouds of smoke. In the third stage, our discursive system and experience of bodily heat dissolve into our emotional system and experience of breath gasses, causing a diminution of smell, loss of our capacity for naming, the objective sign of decreased temperature and metabolism and the subjective sign of perceptions splintering into sparks like a bunch of fireflies. In the fourth stage, our emotional system and experience of breath gases dissolve into our consciousness system and experience of space, causing a diminution of taste, touch, and mental imagery, loss of our capacity for planning and executive action, the objective sign of the fading of breath and the subjective sign of perceptions stilling like a candle flame.

With these first four stages, our ordinary sense of having a physical body located within a material world has gradually dissolved, immersing us in an interior space of mind. In terms of Buddhist medical science, this gradual dissolution is seen as ushered in by a coalescence of the ten neural energies and drops that normally support the functioning of our bodily organs, peripheral nervous system and senses deeper and deeper into the central nervous system, until they gather at the extremely subtle core neural complexes mapped at the heart. From here on the remaining stages of dissolution occur within the consciousness system itself, supported only by the subtle neural energy and chemistry of the core layers of the central nervous system.[26]

While it may seem impossible to imagine this complex process of bodily dissolution with all its experiential function and neurological process, in practice it may be rehearsed in much simplified form. We can imagine our flesh and bones, bodily fluids, body heat, and breath gases as concentric layers of our body, each dissolving into the next, along with the neural energy and chemistry supporting them, until all that's left is the subtle mind and energy within the core neural complex at the heart. Or, we might imagine our solidity dissolving from the crown to the throat, our fluidity from our feet to our navel, our heat energy from our throat to our heart and our breath gases from our navel into our heart, again along with the neural energies and chemistry supporting them, until all is coalesced into the core complex at the heart. In either case, each dissolution would give rise to the subjective signs—mirage, smoke, sparks, flame.

Once we've dissolved our experience of having a gross physical body in a material world, the dissolution process continues into the mental energy realm. This part of the process involves four more stages, each representing the dissolution of progressively subtler layers of mind, energy, and function into the subtlest, core layer known as the extremely subtle mind, neural energy, and chemistry. For the sake of clarity, what follows is a simplified version of the traditional map, which I believe streamlines the system without changing its intent.[27] In our streamlined mapping, in the fifth stage, the coarse layer of primal consciousness and neural energy dissolves into the first subtle layer, bringing with it the release of thirty-three positive and negative attachment-oriented instinctive patterns and the dawning of an attachment-free luminous intuition with the subjective sign of a cool, spacious clarity like a moonlit autumn sky. In the sixth stage, the first subtle layer of primal consciousness and neural energy dissolve into the second subtle layer, bringing with it the release of forty positive and negative aggression-oriented instinctive patterns and the dawning of an aggression-free radiant intuition with the subjective sign of a warm, spacious clarity like a twilit autumn sky. In the seventh stage, the second subtle layer of primal consciousness and neural energy dissolves into the third subtle layer, bringing with it the release of seven positive and negative delusion-oriented instinctive patterns and the dawning of a delusion-free immanent intuition with the subjective sign of a still, spacious clarity like a midnight autumn sky. Finally, in the eighth stage, the third subtle layer of primal consciousness and neural energy dissolves into the extremely subtle layer, bringing with it the release of all instinctive patterns and the dawning of an instinct-free translucent intuition with the subjective sign of a crystal clear, spacious openness like a pre-dawn autumn sky with no hint of moonlight, sunlight, or darkness.

The Dissolution Process: A Phenomenology of Near-Death Experience

If envisioning these dissolutions in detail feels too complex, simply imagining your mind gradually melting into a spacious openness pervaded by different qualities of light can be enough. Some teach that these stages may be envisioned as a series of concentric circles of luminous awareness coalescing into a drop of translucent clarity at the heart.[28] As a final step in the process, that single-pointed sense of pure clarity, understood as an "indestructible drop," which merges our subtlest awareness and neural energy with the chemistry of bliss, melts in turn into a selfless, universal clarity called the clear light of death or the objective clear light.

This final immersion, rather than the fading of coarse waking awareness and neural activity, is understood as the moment of death. Or, when we practice the eight dissolutions in the form of a heroic altruist archetype, we might envision the first four stages as the body dissolving from above and below into the seed-syllable at the heart, and envision the last four as the gradual dissolution of that syllable into a single dot or drop, which finally melts into the clear light of death. In some practices, we first envision our archetypal form coalescing into the seed-syllable at the heart, and then rehearse the whole dissolution process as the syllable, melting in eight successive stages into the clear light of death, until it's fully immersed, like water in water.[29]

From the vantage of modern psychotherapy, we can see in this imaginative rehearsal a gradual and systematic desensitization to the ultimate uncontrollable stress: letting go of our instinctive, self-protective clinging to a separate physical body or sense of discrete mental identity. While all human adults are aware in principle of the certainty of death, that awareness tends to be a mere abstraction, which we routinely bracket, deny, or repress. This epidemic denial of death led psychoanalyst Otto Rank to comment that most humans are effectively delusional.[30] Of course, as we can see from case reports of near death experiences and our own first or second hand brushes with death, it is quite a different matter to have a concrete visceral experience of the end of life. Predictably, such experiences have the effect of radically altering our frame of reference on our own daily lives, often acting as a wake-up call, which gives us fresh clarity and information about the preciousness, quality, and direction of our existence.[31]

Death-Rehearsal and the Deconstruction of Self-Centered Death

The neurobiology of this process overlaps enough with that of vivid imagery states to suggest how the imaginative rehearsal of dissolution can amount to far more than a simple reframing of some supposedly objective event called death.[32] If we perceive death as the end of a self we imagine as an independent, objective entity, but later learn that that sense of self is in fact a complex construction of our minds, then ordinary death, as we imagine it, cannot really occur. The profound shift in sense of self that takes place in the course of any real encounter with death means that, to the extent that this practice succeeds, we may opt to identify less with our habitual self-sense and more with something akin to "the self of selflessness" defined by the affirmation of enlightened pride, "*I am the self whose nature is the diamond of intuitive openness!*"

In this sense, the conversion of death into the first node of a whole new life-narrative may not be just a matter of changing the narrative frame we put around one and the same thing, but may in fact be a matter of eliminating death as we know it and replacing it with an experience that feels less like an end or death than an awakening or openness to the new. This may be especially true if we understand the imagery of our subjective clear light mind merging into an objective clear light that is selfless, universal, or impersonal as an illustration or narrative enactment of the truth of emptiness. More than any mere thought exercise, that enactment teaches us that we are empty of any non-relative being or essence which could anchor our sense of standing alone, apart from each other and the world. The exercise of purging our primal mind of alienating self-constructs and allowing it to return home to an objective gene-pool of pure, natural mind should help us climb outside our self-enclosed mind and have an ecstatic experience of fully belonging to the natural world in a truly objective and irrevocable way.[33]

Setting the Stage: Bridging Death Dissolution and Developmental Emergence

Before we move on, traditionally the conversion of death does not end with our final immersion into objective clear light. Instead, this signals the start of a coda or bridge phase which sets the stage for the second conversion. Without understanding the way the rehearsal of death helps transport us to a more objective clarity about our place in the world, this phase might seem oddly redundant or out of place. Yet before we begin developing a heroic new self through the second conversion, the imagery of converting death challenges us to envision a basic fact of life we often deny: the continuity of lives does not end with any personal death, but moves on. The way this imagery unfolds is that, out of the clear light of death, our minds begin to perceive the objective conditions for the re-creation of life, only now from the vantage of the self of selflessness which has just exposed our prior, ordinary life and death as largely imagined.

This bridging imagery takes various forms in various practices, typically involving the reemergence of the ordinary world with its natural elements, habitats, and forms of stress-driven life, as well as the extraordinary world inside the protective sphere of the *mandala*. The natural world is usually envisioned as reemerging out of the elemental states of matter, symbolized by orbs of elemental gaseous, radiant, liquid, and solid matter, supporting the naturalistic landscape of cremation grounds in the cardinal and ordinal directions, each of which also has vertical levels: underworld, ground level and heavens.[34] The grounds are filled with the usual features—mountains, lakes, rivers, trees, fires—and inhabited by the whole food-chain of unenlightened life forms, from predators, scavengers, and their prey to ordinary humans, struggling, dying, and decomposing alongside their local hermits and sages, nature spirits, and mountain gods.[35]

The *Mandala* Mansion: Recognizing the Mind-Body as a Matrix of Enlightenment

Our awareness now turns to what's inside the *mandala*: the conditions for new life within the protective sphere set up by the wise and compassionate mind of clear light. Typically, this begins with what is known as a reality-source, emerging from a diamond light syllable THUS, envisioned as an inverted pyramidal cone, white outside and red inside, symbolizing the womb-like fertility of the state of blissful openness, in which our night and day energy, male and female chemistry, subjective bliss and objective lucidity co-mingle in our visceral realization of the clear light of death. Within this womb, out of a diamond light syllable AH, grows the stem of a giant lotus whose rainbow light petals eventually open at the mouth of the reality-source, symbolizing the plasticity or flow which emerges out of the clear light state of blissful openness. Then from a sapphire light syllable HUM bubbling up in the midst of the lotus comes a great, rainbow colored horizontal cross made of two gigantic scepters fused like a plus sign and oriented in the cardinal directions, symbolizing the strong force of indivisible wisdom and compassion that binds our minds and nervous systems together in unbreakable collaborative bonds. Based on the foundation of this strong social force comes the *mandala* residence, typically depicted as a holographic mansion made of gem-toned light, symbolizing the architecture of enlightened life: the subtle microstructure of our minds and nervous systems, crystallized out of the seeds of teaching planted in the womb of blissful openness through our dialogue with the mentor-archetype.[36]

Here again, though I've abbreviated and simplified the imagery, it may seem too mythological or intricate to speak to us as moderns. So it will come as a relief to know that traditionally this detailed stage-setting is edited out of all but the advanced, optimal integral practices, and even there is drastically simplified in the "starter-practices" with which most novices begin.[37] For our purposes, for the natural imagery we can substitute our own familiar cosmology, by envisioning outside our firewall the earth's continents and oceans, forests and mountains, arrayed in all directions, and inhabited by the whole range of plant life, wildlife, and human societies, with their respective social systems and ancestral mythologies.

As for the internal conditions of new life within the firewall, we can substitute our own modern vision of the objective internal conditions for recreating our human agency. For example, we may begin by planting inside the firewall a diamond light seed-letter B, which transforms into an inverted cone made of moonlight outside and sunlight inside, symbolizing our brainstem supporting our state of blissful openness. Within that, we can then plant a diamond light seed-letter C, growing a stem that blossoms over the mouth of the cone as a broad water-lily of rainbow light, symbolizing the full unfolding of our core-brain systems of blissful plasticity. Atop that, we can next plant a sapphire light seed-letter L, which transforms into a huge, rainbow light horizontal cross-beam like a gem-toned plus sign oriented in the cardinal directions, symbolizing the strong force of limbic resonance which attunes our development to the proactive social-emotional tone of our mentoring bond. And finally, on that foundation, we can plant a diamond light seed-letter N, which generates the gem-toned holographic architecture of our new life residence, symbolizing our neocortex restructured to support the conscious regulation and integration of mind/body systems and processes we need to live the life of a master altruist. While not indispensable, this kind of internal stage-setting does orient our minds toward the emergence of a new life. With this, we turn to the next node in the art of narrative self-creation.

The Second Node of Self-Creation: Making Development a Path to Enjoyment

According to the basic life science of the process tradition, the normal emergence from the objective translucency of mind, also called the "mother clear light," involves revisiting the same eight stages we encountered in the dissolution process, except in reverse sequence.[38] Yet once we've chosen the path of narrative self-creation, whenever we rehearse the process of re-emergence from the clear light after simulating death or actually undergo that process, say after a near-death experience, the eight stages of emergence are replaced by a process of voluntary self-creation that involves what are known as the five pure enlightenments.[39]

Although these are understood in different ways by various commentarial traditions, for our purposes it makes sense to follow the reading that these five are equivalent with the emergence of the five pure intuitions we discussed in chapter 7.[40] Once, in the course of dissolving into the objective clear light of death, our mind/body systems have been purified of the distortions of ordinary perception and the stress-emotions they maintain, they are free to re-emerge in their enlightened form, guided by the five intuitions. What this second phase of narrative self-creation does is to locate the alchemy of self-transformation within the new life narrative defined by the conversions, as the work of the development phase, that is, re-creating ourselves as nascent heroic altruists.

We begin the process immersed within the objective clear light of death, out of which emerges a diamond light seed-syllable OM (or OH if you like), like a fish leaping out of water, which becomes a luminous orb of awareness like a full moon's reflection in water, symbolizing the emergence of reflective intuition which guides the enlightened development of the physical system. In the next stage, out of the moon leaps a ruby light syllable AH, which becomes a luminous orb of awareness like a rising sun's reflection in water, symbolizing the equality intuition which guides the enlightened development of the sensory system. In the next stage, out of the sun flares a sapphire light syllable HUM (or UM, or in *Sheer Brilliance*, a citrine gold light syllable G), which becomes an upright sword like a sun-flare light saber, symbolizing the discriminating intuition which guides the enlightened development of the cognitive system. In the next stage, the light saber beams a rainbow aura of gem-toned lights in all directions, purifying all ordinary beings and delighting all the enlightened, who all assume the form of *Sheer Brilliance* (or other archetype) and return to dissolve back into the sword, all of which activity symbolizes the executive intuition that guides the enlightened development of the emotional system. In the final stage, the newly intensified light saber glows and radiates a rainbow aura that manifests the sunrise form of the nascent heroic altruist, *Sheer Brilliance*, complete with light saber, text, physical marks and signs, symbolizing the dawning of the ultimate reality intuition which guides the enlightened development of the perceptual system. The fully developed form of the nascent heroic altruist, lit from within by the sun and sapphire seed syllable at his heart, is also known as the intuition hero or intuitive altruist, since he personifies the joyful cultivation of our altruistic genius, guided by the five pure intuitions.

The Poetics of Self-Regulation: Developing a "Body" of Neural Energy and Speech

While it makes obvious sense that the development of our newly recreated self embodies and is guided by the five forms of intuitive genius involved in higher mind/body self-regulation, we should also take note of the conspicuous absence of the material elements of the gross physical body which dissolved in the ordinary process of death. Of course, the omission is no accident, but a tacit admission of the fact that the new body to be developed in this phase of our enlightened life story is not a gross physical body at all, but rather "a body made of mind." This is consistent with all we've learned about the way developmental or transitional mind/body states—such as embryonic states, dream states, or meditative states—are seen in Buddhist psychology and contemplative neuroscience.[41] And it is further unpacked in some of the finer points of imagery and symbolism associated with this phase of the art of narrative self-creation.

So beyond their identification with the first two intuitions, the moon and sun discs which start the reemergence process are also identified with the expression of the subjective and objective aspects of the unitive experience of blissful openness. And this added symbolic sense is further unpacked in the traditional association of these two discs with the two main components of the alphabet, vowels and consonants. This sense is often graphically depicted by envisioning the vowels circling the moon and the consonants circling the sun, or simply implied by describing the moon as having the nature of the vowels, and the sun, of the consonants. This intriguing bit of iconography gives new meaning to the formulation of the process-oriented path as a poetic or neurolinguistic path of self-creation. This reading is very much in line with our contemporary understanding of human life as a social construction in and through language. Consider these passages (quoted by Freedman and Coombs) from Berger and Luckman:

> Everyday life is, above all, life with and by means of the language I share with (other people) ... Language is capable of becoming an objective repository of vast accumulations of meaning and experience, which it can then preserve in time and transmit to following generations ... Language is capable of "making present" a variety of objects that are spatially, temporally, and socially absent from the "here and now." ... Through language an entire world can be actualized.[42]

And this one from narrative therapist Kathy Weingarten:

> In the social constructionist view, the experience of self exists in the ongoing interchange with others ... the self continually creates itself through narratives that include other people who are reciprocally woven into these narratives.[43]

In fact, the imagery of re-emergence seems to suggest that the art of the development phase involves reshaping of our symbolic mind and neural processing in the image of the mentor-archetype's. This reading clearly resonates with Allen Grossman's view of the work of poetry as "the conservation of the human image;" and of its most fundamental and profound transmission as "the image of the person that is encoded in the (poem's) very language-matter." Borrowing his evocative phrase, then, we can read the symbolism of the vowel-moon and consonant-sun as suggesting the transmission of the language-matter of the mentor-archetype from master to apprentice, and from one generation to the next. And, given this reading, we're ready to take on two further aspects of the symbolism of the social construction of our emergent new self.

First, the vowels and consonants are not simply arrayed on the moon and sun just as they are found in the Sanskrit alphabet. Instead, both the vowels and consonants are expanded and then doubled, to support several other highly intriguing forms of symbolic sense and reference. In the case of the vowels, the usual list of thirteen vowels is expanded to sixteen and then doubled to symbolize the doubling of genders.[44] This expanded and doubled number can then be aligned with two bodily features that help describe the subtle material—neurobiological—structure of the emerging altruist's mind-made body, namely: the sixteen erogenous zones on the left, "feminine" side of the body, plus the sixteen on the right, "masculine" side; which together give rise to the thirty-two physiognomic signs of superhuman altruism. As for the consonants, the usual thirty-four are also expanded and doubled, to symbolize the dual aspects of male and female energy, as well as the dual aspects of intuitive wisdom and blissful art. Finally, the expanded and doubled consonants are then aligned with the elementary material states: earth (solidity); water (fluidity), fire (energy); wind (gas); and space.

The Mirroring and Equalizing Intuitions: Sublimation and the Language-Matter of Altruism

We can unpack this complex symbolism in two ways, specific and general. If the moonlight of the vowels symbolizes the subjective enjoyment of a blissfully open body guided by the mirroring intuition, its link with the male and female erogenous zones suggests that the development of heroic altruism involves the sublimation of sexual energy. And if the sunlight of the consonants symbolizes the objective enjoyment of a sensitivity guided by the equalizing intuition, its link with the fivefold physicality of male bliss-energy and female openness-energy suggests that the sensory development of heroic altruism depends on the capacity to equalize and attune sensitivity to our own visceral sensations with sensitivity to the sensations of others.

Generally, the fact that the emergence of these two prime intuitions is symbolized by the commingling of luminous awareness with sublimated sexual energy, doubled phonemes, and an impartial sensitivity to the raw feel of all life, suggests that the emergence of heroic altruism reflects the joyful mastery of our human genius for social-emotional attunement, dialogue, and cooperation. The fact that this emergence involves assuming an embodiment not of gross physical matter, but of sublimated sexual energy and language-matter, is also consistent with the idea that the emergence of heroic altruism depends on a body made of mind, more specifically, "love's body." Finally, the expansion of the alphabet of enlightenment further specifies the form of that embodiment in two ways. First, the doubling of both its linguistic and material elements specifies its form as one that is entirely socially constructed in its nature and origin. And second, the sequence of its language-DNA, with thirty-two vowels and eighty consonants, encodes for the replication of a body image that maps the physiognomy of a super altruist, further specifying the form of love to be embodied as the fully evolved and developed genius of human altruism.

The Discerning Intuition: Our Discursive Mind Joins Love's Body

The symbolism of the third enlightenment takes us from the basic constitution of our new altruistic self to its full conception and individuation. If we read the first two stages of the emergence process as the language-matter of the mentor archetype recombining into the embryonic form of heroic altruism, the moon and sun that represent the reconstitution of life take on yet another level of sense. Specifically, they come to symbolize the male and female germ cells—the sperm and egg—which come together to form the zygote or fertilized egg which is the physical substrate of our new life. In terms of the pregnant symbolism of the process tradition, both the ordinary sperm and egg and the extraordinary germ cells of the mirroring and equalizing intuitions with their sexual energy and language-matter, are understood as the male and female spirits of enlightenment, identified with the twin altruistic spirits on the engaged path. So given the life science of Buddhism, it would only be natural to assume that—for conception to be complete—once these two constituents of our new altruistic life converge, they require the confluence of a third line of inheritance: the continuity of consciousness from our previous life.

Against this background, we can readily see the most straightforward way to unpack the symbolism of the third stage of the emergence of our altruistic life. When the seed-syllable of sapphire light emerges from the conjoined moon and sun, it symbolizes nothing more or less than the entry of our discursive awareness into the zygote formed by the combination of our sublimated energy and language-matter from the first two enlightenments. In effect, the entry of the seed-syllable UM or G represents the third and final moment in the conception of our altruistic life: the formation of a viable embryo, sealing our voluntary reincarnation as a budding heroic altruist in the lineage of our mentor-archetype. In terms of the symbolism of engaged path of altruism, this moment corresponds to the conception of the actual spirit of enlightenment which galvanizes the union of the conventional and ultimate faces of compassionate openness. As on the ordinary engaged path, so on this extraordinary path, that general conception is particularized by the specific commitments and inclinations of the budding altruist; and begins the gradual process of gestation which comes to fruition in the birth of a master altruist.

The Executive Intuition: Mastering the Altruist's Expertise

The next turn in the imagery of the third stage of our enlightened development—the transformation of the seed-syllable into a hand implement—may be read as the process tradition's take on the conception of a particular form of altruistic genius. In the case of *Sheer Brilliance*, the implement is the flaming sword or light saber of impeccable wisdom, signifying our commitment to a life of objective analysis, healing insight, and genuine intuition, as part of the lotus family of discerning genius. In this light, the third move on this stage, in which we inscribe the hilt of the light saber with the seed-syllable UM or G represents our discursive mind's conscious identification with the civilizing work of cultivating wisdom.

Once we've chosen to insert our discursive awareness, generally and specifically, into the developmental narrative of an emerging altruist, we've also committed ourselves to an extraordinary process of incarnation. Thanks to that process, the unfolding of the ten stages on the engaged path of altruism is compressed from the span of three incalculable eons not just into the (symbolic) ten months of a normal pregnancy but—incredibly enough—into the relative eye-blink depicted in our virtual gestation. In effect, the narrative imagery of conception on this stage reveals the metaphor behind the whole second conversion: cultural reproduction though role-modeling recapitulates the social evolution of altruism, in the same way that individual development in the womb recapitulates the development of species.

This metaphor is even more explicit in some practices which depict the act of our altruistic self-conception as a still more transparent displacement of nature by culture. In such practices, instead of entering the moon and sun discs set within an architectural *mandala*—the developing mind/body process seen as a mansion of light—the seed syllable of our discursive mind enters the bodies of a mother and father altruist in sexual union, in a replay of the Buddhist primal scene. In this case, the mind-syllable enters through the mouth of one of the parents or else through the mother's vaginal canal or father's crown, finding its way to a vowel moon and consonant sun placed within a biological *mandala*—the sperm and egg joined in a single drop at the tip of the father's penis, inside the mother's womb.

Consistent with the *karmic* view of psychobiological development as an active self-creation, the next stage in the emergence process compresses the maturation of our new social and cultural agency as heroic altruists into a single wave-like transaction combining both active expression and receptive passion. As the light saber inscribed with the G of our verbal mind beams lights all around, it rehearses the basic altruistic acts of gathering those who can help and benefitting those who need help. As it receives lights of solidarity from the enlightened and gratitude from the distressed, it rehearses the basic altruistic acts of receiving validation or guidance from other altruists and feedback from those in need. This double-edged rehearsal effectively enacts the emergence of enlightened motivation and execution, guided by the abundant emotional intelligence of the executive intuition.

The Ultimate Reality Intuition: Assuming the Nascent Form of a Heroic Altruist

This brings us to the fifth and final stage in the emergence process and the final act in the narrative conversion of development. In this act, receiving the validation of the enlightened and the gratitude of the distressed seals the development of our chosen mode of altruistic agency, at least in its nascent form. This transition is symbolized by the intensified glow that radiates from the hand implement—in this case the light saber—which represents the growth of that agency. So it is that that glow eventually manifests our full embodiment of the nascent form of heroic altruism, in the image of the sunrise-colored body of *Sheer Brilliance*. Finally reaching the dramatic climax of recreating our embodied self-image in the image and likeness of our mentor-archetype symbolizes our development of an enlightened perceptual system, guided by the ultimate truth intuition. To seal this, we envision our new body-image as lit from within by sun-discs and seed-syllables at the crown, throat, and heart, symbolizing our choice to make it a home address for our emerging self-regulation of an altruist's selfless body, speech, and mind.

In this final emergence of our development, we come to embody in nascent form the integration of an altruist's body, speech, and mind, guided by the pure genius of the five intuitions. Within this form, the basic constitution of the mirroring and equalizing intuitions—the fertile dialogue of bliss and openness—is symbolized by the fused moon and sun discs at our heart; our harnessing of that constitution to the cultivation of genius with the discerning intuition is symbolized by the radiant G at our heart; our budding mastery of the art of cultivating true genius through executive intuition is symbolized by the light saber we wield; and our ability to bring that self-creation to fruition with the reality intuition is symbolized by our vivid appearance as *Sheer Brilliance* being sealed with the self-transcendent identity of radical openness.

The Psychology and Neurobiology of Altruistic Development

In terms of conventional psychotherapy, this phase of our narrative self-creation reflects the social construction of a preferred self and life, in and through the transformative dialogue of the healing alliance. The first enlightenment corresponds to the shift in core affect from aversive to positive, which mobilizes the social emotional energy to conceive of a more proactive life in the world.[45] The second corresponds to the growth of objective empathy, which allows for development of realistic mutual sensitivity and trust, opening the door to a truly open dialogue with the world.[46] Third comes the shift in self-concept and self-image that allows us to truly identify with our emerging ideal self, harnessing the passion and openness mobilized in the prior two stages to inhabiting a prosocial new self.[47] Fourth comes the work of reshaping our social roles and lifestyle around our newly empowered and impassioned self.[48] And finally, the fifth enlightenment corresponds to the fruition of that positive self and life as a fully integrated, preferred way of being, that has only to be finally fleshed out in the world.[49]

In terms of neurobiology, I believe this phase in the art of narrative self-creation can be correlated with the development of our full human potential for proactive social and cultural agency, based on the exercise of the prefrontal cortex through mindful attention and positive imagery. A hypothetical alignment of the stages in the emergence of a proactive self with the self-regulation and integration of regions within the uniquely human prefrontal cortex seems possible based on the overview of current research and thought of Dan Siegel.[50]

In particular, the first stage may be aligned with the development of the medial prefrontal and cingulate cortex which support bodily self-regulation and the growth of a new body map. The second stage may be aligned with the development of the dorsolateral and medial prefrontal cortex which support our full capacity for empathy and our ability to map the inner states of others. The third may be aligned with the development of the orbitofrontal cortex which supports our capacity for insight and narrative, which allows us to revise our present identity in light of our personal history. The fourth may be aligned with the development of the ventral prefrontal cortex which supports emotional attunement and morality in our interactions with others, based on a vision of our place in the world Siegel calls a "we-map." Finally, the fifth may be aligned with the development of the cingulate and dorsolateral prefrontal cortex which support the regulation of attention and response, and, with the help of the insular region, integrate all the functions of our neocortex, limbic system and core brain.

The Third Node of Self-Creation: Making Life a Path to Manifesting Compassion

Having arrived at a state of developmental fruition, our nascent altruistic self is ripe for the third and final phase in our narrative self-creation: setting out on our new life as a master altruist, to transform the world outside our mentor's sphere of influence. In discussing the node of converting life into a path, Tsong Khapa reviews the traditional imagery that ushers in this new phase: in which the budding altruist hears the call of wisdom muses and melts out of impassioned concern for the world. The symbolism here seems clear. In order to reach the final node of our narrative self-creation, we need to be moved by the call of true compassion for the world, and ready to let go of the last vestiges of childhood dependency which would keep us from assuming the full freedom and responsibility of a master altruist.

If we recall that the prior phase of development took place symbolically and psychologically within the crucible of the mentor's blissful openness, in some cases graphically seen as the sexual union of the mentor—as father *and* mother—inside the womb, we can readily see how our journey of self-creation is not yet complete, despite the fullness of our development. Yet we may be struck nonetheless by Tsong Khapa's insistence that the pull on our heart strings which draws us out into the world comes in the form of hearing the call of the five wisdom muses.[51] It should come as no surprise that the strongest possible force to call us into action is the voice of another—a *mother* or *father*—representing the needs of the outside world. As members of a species that cooperates with speech, the sounds of adult voices, especially our mother's, may be the most tangible clue we have in the womb of the existence of an outside world. And, in a real sense, that first hint of love as a force that binds us to a social world is also part of the altruistic lifeline that gradually transitions us out into a separate life in the world, once our umbilical cord is cut.

Given this view of the muses' call as the force that sets in motion our final entry into altruistic life, the sequence of symbolic events that makes up the narrative of taking birth as a path seems to follow quite naturally. The next step—melting into clear light—powerfully evokes the dissolution of self-other distinctions in the spontaneous experience of unconditional compassion. At the same time, following the counter-narrative that displaces ordinary birth with the extraordinary birth of altruism, the instantaneous dissolution sparked by hearing our wisdom mothers' voices also clearly symbolizes the displacement of our ordinary birth-trauma with the voluntary dissolution into clear light and final emergence into altruistic life. So in place of the ordinary birth-experience of being thrust into life in the world by forces beyond our ken and control, the imagery of melting and emergence symbolize the enlightened experience of choosing life as a spontaneous manifestation of compassion and heroic altruism.

As for the next steps in the imagery of self-creation, the process of instantaneous emergence quickly moves through the (compressed) stages of sunrise, sun-flare G, rainbow aura, and fully embodied *Sheer Brilliance*, at which point the G at our heart beams lights all around to invite the five wisdom mothers.

Now that our fully developed new self has finally emerged in the mature form of a master altruist, the symbolic significance of the wisdom mothers has shifted given our new phase of life. Instead of invoking them from a child's point of view, as mothers, we now invite them as muses or equal partners to validate and seal our full emergence as master altruists. In this case, if our chosen archetype is feminine, we may invite our muses in male form, as geniuses or wisdom heroes. Finally, we may also invite both male and female altruists as enlightened couples to validate and seal our emergence with their shared blissful openness. In effect, this shift in perspective involves the compression of the biography of the life cycle into a single eye-blink that combines birth, separation, psychosexual maturity, and adult agency all in one. At a deeper level of symbolism, the invitation and visitation of the wisdom mothers reflects our ultimate reliance on the integrated genius of our own five intuitive wisdoms, as opposed to our prior, temporary reliance on the wisdom of the mentor.

Invoking the Wisdom Muses: Sealing Our Altruistic New Life

The gathering of our new community of altruists, represented by the wisdom muses, also sets the stage for the final act of this third phase of narrative conversion: requesting and receiving the consecration that recognizes our new station as fully integrated master altruists. In particular, when we beam lights to the five wisdom muses at this point in the practice, it's with the intent of asking them to validate and seal our mature self-creation with the five intuitions they personify. And when they oblige us by pouring wisdom-nectars through our crown to fill our whole body-mind, they are effectively acknowledging our (virtual) completion of the path of transformation mapped out by the initiation rehearsed at the point of establishing security. In effect, then, this last point in the phase of converting life symbolizes the final act of intimate collaboration between mentor and student which sets the interpersonal stage for our narrative self-creation: the act of simply acknowledging or pronouncing done what has already been accomplished.

On another level of symbolism, the nectar pouring through our crown, throat, and heart reflects the convergence of our body, speech and mind with the genius of all enlightened altruists, and seals our identification with that larger community. This threefold identification is often sealed by envisioning ourselves as a triune embodiment of heroic altruism. In this context, our outward appearance as a mature master *Sheer Brilliance* represents our heroic commitment to embodying compassion; at our heart, we envision a thumb-nail sized miniature version of our speech as a nascent *Sheer Brilliance*, representing our heroic intuition; and at his heart, we envision a sun disc and citrine gold G, representing our heroic concentration. Our integrated mastery of these three forms of heroic altruism reflects the fruition of the three conversions, and corresponds to the threefold embodiment of emanation, enjoyment and truth (respectively) realized on the Cloud of Truth stage of the engaged path of altruism. At a still deeper level of symbolism cultivated on the subtle creation stage, the rush of nectar filling us from crown to toe and back up again previews the experience of the release and sublimation of four levels of bliss within the central channel, which lays the foundation for mastering the art of blissful openness on the perfection stage, to be explored in part 4.

As this final conversion phase corresponds to the maturation phase of the ordinary life-cycle, it also corresponds to the phase of successful termination of an insight-oriented therapy focused on deep affective healing and character change. All three of these transitions involve a similar shift from an intimate dependence to a relative autonomy, with a corresponding move towards full integration of what has been learned and a new role of relative equality between parent and adult child, therapist and client, experienced master and new master. And these more or less congruent shifts in life narrative are clearly reminiscent of the perspective shift that takes place in integration phase of the role modeling process. Here again, this congruence establishes the creation stage and transformational therapy as parallel practices that, in varied ways and to varying degrees, recapitulate the ordinary process of human development with an extraordinary process aimed at consciously revising and restructuring our way of being and life. So the triune form of our new self-mastery may be read as reflecting a complete self-transformation at the level of behavior (body), cognition (speech) and affective-perceptual experience (mind). With the narrative creation of our proactive new self complete, we turn now to the final application of our new way of being to create a whole new way of life in the world.

Action Triumph: Rehearsing the Life and Work of a Master Altruist

Though our first meditative experiment condensed this phase of self-creation to the acts of requesting, receiving and sharing the affirmation of *Sheer Brilliance*, we should briefly survey the range of elements that make up the imagery at this climactic point. While condensation is common in introductory practices, the optimal creation stage expands the three key elements of imagery on this phase to include: gathering a community of altruists; enjoying a master altruist's life; and enacting the triumph of our new altruistic community in helping all living beings.

As for the first element, gathering a community of altruists, the traditional imagery is in keeping with the counter-narrative of cultural self-creation meant to displace the ordinary narrative of the biological life cycle. Specifically, it takes the place which ordinary sexual maturity, biological reproduction and childrearing have in our ordinary life narrative, by guiding us to envision ourselves as finding a congenial soul-mate, then conceiving, giving birth to and nurturing a family of fellow heroic altruists. Though some optimal integral practices abbreviate this imagery by having the primary archetype—as a solitary hero or heroine—conceive his/her family directly out of seed-syllables, without involving explicit reproductive imagery, most revolve around the "mother-father" couples familiar from Tibetan art. This imagery is meant to map the psychology of sublimation, with the virtual depiction of intimacy prompting sensual arousal while the meaning of the symbolism helps to channel that passion into the cultivation of altruistic genius. Specifically, the father is identified with the euphoric subjectivity of sublimated passion and the mother, with the ecstatic objectivity of impassioned openness.

Traditionally, to complete our new archetypal self-image, we need to envision our subjectivity as *Sheer Brilliance* in intimate communion with our objectivity as the goddess, *Transcendent Wisdom*. In the couples' context of her mother-father union with *Sheer Brilliance*, she sits on his lap with her arms and legs embracing him. Behind his head, her right hand holds a curved chopper over a skull-bowl held up in her left, symbolizing her fiercely objective compassion conjoined with the intuitive translucency of death.[52] His right hand still wields the light saber of analytic insight overhead, though his left now caresses the small of her back, still holding the lotus stem that blossoms a wisdom text over his left shoulder. Since envisioning ourselves as both male and female is a stretch for our ordinary sense of self, it's common to identify our subjectivity with the mother or father and relate to our other half as a love object.

It is considered very helpful to practice envisioning ourselves as inhabiting the body of the other gender, since this helps not just to free us of the habit of objectifying the opposite sex but also to expand our capacity to empathize with the other gender's experience and perspective on our gender and sex. In fact, it is considered optimal to be able to identify simultaneously with both the male and female aspect of a dual embodiment, since this helps promote a balanced sensibility and an androgynous integration of masculine and feminine energies. In my experience, this practice can be enormously helpful in overcoming compulsive forms of sexuality, in mastering the art of sublimating sexual energy and chemistry, and in fostering the empathic flexibility and equanimity that is critical to healthy intimacy.

The Triumph of Social Action: Conceiving and Raising a Family of Altruists

As for the imagery of conceiving and raising a family of altruists, we can begin by slightly revising the muses showering us with nectars. First, by envisioning that they are joined by wisdom heroes and that both pour nectars on us in our expanded form as mother-father in union. Next we can imagine the rush of nectars through our crown melting down our central channel—envisioned as a neural tube (in place of an ordinary spine) running from our crown (as both mother and father) to our sexual organs. As it flows through us it fills us with the blissful openness of a natural endorphin high, until it reaches our sexual organs and is released as a white bliss-void drop from our father side and a red bliss-void drop from our mother side.

As these mingle in our womb as mother, they develop into a miniature *mandala* mansion, in the midst of which a sun-disc rises and bubbles up a minuscule citrine light G, which beams lights out of the womb to all beings, attracting the true genius of all enlightened altruists to melt into the G. Bursting with light, it divides into ten miniscule gem-toned G's, one which faces the first, and eight which seed the ordinal and cardinal directions closely circling the two central syllables. All glowing with rainbow auras, the ten syllables manifest the forms of five mother and five father altruists, each with the gem-toned color of their seed. The whole subtle altruist circle—with *Sheer Brilliance* and *Transcendent Wisdom* in union at its hub—now fully mature, glows with five gem-toned lights that make the microcosmic *mandala* within the drop shine like a beacon through both our forms as the life-sized mother-father.

The role this drop plays within the counter-narrative of self-creation is twofold. Symbolically, it displaces our ordinary perception of family as arising from the union of biological germ cells with the vision of an extraordinary family of heroic altruism, created by the seeding of the womb of our blissful openness by the affirmative language-matter of the mentor-archetype and his/her cultural heritage. The imagery of that seed gestating in the womb where we consummate our psychic communion with and within that heritage symbolizes our ability to spread its way of life to a new generation, nurturing it within the *mandala* of blissful openness we share with those around us. On a subtler level, it also symbolizes the art of sublimating the passionate energy and chemistry of sexual intimacy and childrearing, as the most efficient way to power that blissful openness and manifest the altruistic spirit of enlightenment in the world.

Once we've conceived our new family of fellow altruists, we now envision their birth as the gathering of an altruistic community to transform the world. Traditionally, we do this by displacing the normal process of childbirth and development with an imagery of creative emanation. One at a time, we draw the fully developed nascent mothers and fathers from their place within the *mandala* drop, so that they travel as light back up the central channel to our heart (or mouth), from where we beam them to their assigned seats in the ordinal or cardinal points, until the eight surrounding figures circle us as the mature mother-father and the two embracing central figures merge with the intuition heroes at our heart. Of course, this birthing process could be done in various ways. The details matter less here than the general symbolism: a non-biological family born from the creativity of the heart or mouth.

Our Family of Enlightened Altruists: An Egalitarian and Communitarian Circle

Whatever its constitution, the nature of the altruistic community gathered at this point is not just egalitarian but radically communitarian. Once we've given birth to our family of fellow altruists, any trace of hierarchy disappears, along with all but the most transparent distinctions between members. This is why, even as the community is gathered, we set out to identify with all its members *as* ourselves, as if the whole family were one mind or life with only illusory, surface distinctions. Any sense of reified identity or distinctions is then further dissolved in the imagery of the body *mandala*, in which the members of our outer family are all imaginatively taken into our body as sub-personalities or micro-agencies, within the microcosmic ecosystem of one, multi-faceted mind/body process, e.g., with each mini-couple inhabiting a core neural complex.

Another way the deeply communal nature of our altruistic family is expressed is in the next element of imagery, depicting the art of enjoying a master altruist's life. As in the celebration of a communal meal in any family, social system, or religious tradition, the imagery of sharing everything precious with our mentors, ancestral lineage, larger multicultural community and within our intimate family feeds and seals the sense of consubstantiality, solidarity, and shared identity set up by the imagery of conception and birth. Of course, in our meditation on *Sheer Brilliance*, as in most action and performance process practices, it is abbreviated to the simple act of taking the mentor-archetype's affirmative speech into our heart, and enjoying the light and warmth that emanates from integrating and sharing its meaning.[53]

In the context of the optimal integral creation stage, the imagery of enjoying a master altruist's life is expanded to include enjoying and sharing a wide range of precious things, from the traditional "outer" offerings—mouthwash, foot-bath, perfume, flowers, incense, light, music, and delicacies, along with all delightful objects of the five senses—to the taste of blissful openness or "inner" offering, the sensation of sexual bliss or "secret" offering, and the spacious openness intuition itself, the sharing of realized truth or "suchness" offering.

Sharing the Nectar and Sweet-Meat of Bliss: The Alchemical Symbolism of Sublimation

In practice, these offerings—either real or imagined—are first shared with our mentor-archetype, then with multicultural archetypes enlisted in support of our altruistic community, then with our own new family, and finally, enjoyed for ourselves. Typically, the inner offering involves an elaborate alchemical symbolism in which the ordinary elements of the mind/body process are chopped up and boiled within a skull-bowl crucible, until they are purified, transformed and multiplied into a healing elixir of blissful openness that can be offered to all the invited guests and all living beings. The symbolism here, reflected in the hand implements we hold in our mother form as *Transcendent Wisdom*, distils the narrative imagery of self-creation into a single episode. The chopping and melting reflect the dissolution of ordinary life into the purifying crucible of the clear light of death; the alchemical transformation of that reduction reflects the emergence of a nascent form of altruism in the course of development; and the alchemical multiplication reflects the final emergence of our new life as a tangible manifestation of altruism. Traditionally, this inner offering is complemented by the offering of a ritual cake, which is imaginatively prepared in the same way as the healing elixir but crystalizes into a pyramidal cone, representing the subtle material shape—the sweet-meat—of the central nervous system that supports blissful openness.

Enacting the World-Making Work of the Altruistic Community

Once the entire community has shared the bonding and nurturing experience of enjoying a communal feast, the resulting sense of contentment and solidarity is harnessed to energize a shift from passive enjoyment to active outreach in the final element of this narrative phase. Here, the imagery of our meditative experiment—condensed to reciting the mentor's affirmation until it beams lights and nectars everywhere to help all beings—is more representative of the imagery of the optimal integral process, though in abbreviated form. For instance, the recitation, emission of wisdom lights and love nectars, and the re-absorption of validation and gratitude waves typically involve each member of the altruist family beaming lights and nectars from their own affirmation wheel at the heart, one at a time, to all living beings, and then reabsorbing them. So, each of the five mother-fathers we mentioned in unpacking our *Sheer Brilliance* practice would beam lights to help beings overcome the poisons driving their particular form of compulsive life.

After the lights, nectars, sounds, and/or emanations of our altruistic community touch and help all living beings in all forms of ordinary life, each being in each realm of compulsion is purified and transformed into the form of their own altruistic genius. As a result, all the transformed beings in our transformed world send a response wave of light, nectar, and sound, carrying their recognition and gratitude, often along with duplicates of themselves as heroic altruists, back to melt into the affirmation wheels at the hearts of the master altruist circle. Alternately, if the heart-wheels emanate duplicate altruists to do their work in the world, they themselves may return when their work is done and melt back into the affirmation wheel.

The Triumph of the *Mandala* Drop: The Subliminal Chemistry of Altruism

Finally, on the subtle creation stage, the whole process of rehearsing the activity of the altruistic community through beaming and reabsorbing lights, nectars, sounds, and/or emanations may take place at the microcosmic level. For instance, the whole community may be arrayed not just around the central couple as mother *Wisdom* and father *Brilliance* in union, but also microcosmically around a miniature central couple in a drop-*mandala* placed at the heart, the navel, the tip of the sexual organ, the prefrontal "third eye" or the tip of the nose. In this subtle practice, each member of the community beams lights, nectars, sounds, and/or emanations from the microscopic affirmation wheel at their heart to help beings in all kinds of compulsive lives with the poisons that drive them. As on the macrocosmic level, once their work is done, and all beings everywhere are purified and transformed, this time on a microscopic, molecular level, they return in a wave of microcosmic drops of light, nectar, sound and/or emanation to melt back into the altruist's heart within the drop-*mandala* they came from.

This microcosmic imagery of enacting the work of the altruistic community is not an alternative form of practice, but, like the role-modeling imagery on the subtle creation stage, complements the gross shifts in outward perception and action with subtle internal shifts in affect and visceral response style. And this in turn tunes the subliminal resonance of our interactions to the natural frequency of true love and compassion, which have a contagious influence on the unconscious minds and nervous systems of those around us. As a final note, the practice of radiating and reabsorbing light-energy on the level of microscosmic drop-*mandalas* placed along our neural axis also primes us for the perfection stage work of gathering blissful energy and chemistry at points where we can tap into the "central channel" of our bliss network and begin mastering the art of sublimation. So we'll return to this practice and art in part 4.

Enacting the Altruist's Social Responsiveness: The Art of Affirmative Gestures

Although our survey of the process arts of role-modeling and self-creation has focused on the use of visual and auditory imagery, a third cardinal feature of the practice is the use of posture and gestures to enact the embodied response-style of heroic altruism. So our look at the phase of enacting altruistic community and social agency in this tradition would not be complete without mentioning this third dimension of replicating embodied altruism. While imagery and affirmation work together to transform perception and conception, the use of meditative postures and expressive gestures serves to model the embodiment of the mentor's altruistic genius on the visceral and behavioral level. And, just as the imagery of role-modeling and self-creation draw on the poetics of human development, the postural and gestural dimensions of this multi-modal process draw on the performance arts of theatre and dance.[54]

Of course, the most obvious form of somatic modeling comes in the adoption of the sevenfold adamantine posture of the Buddha *Illuminatus*, the contemplative archetype of the enlightened body. This involves sitting in lotus posture with spine extended, chin down, eyes half closed, hands in the lap, nostril breathing, and tongue curved back at the upper front teeth. The general effect here is to prime the nervous system to shift into and stay at the moderate activation level which naturally supports a centered mind/body state combining heightened clarity with deepened calm. Yet the focus of the process teachings on altruistic agency involves complementing this contemplative tone with clear models for how the contemplative body and nervous system engages in social and cultural interaction with others in the world. In most optimal process practices, this is graphically symbolized by the shift towards the coupled postures of sexual intimacy, typically involving dynamic, dance-like standing poses.

Such postures model the heightened level of aroused, playful responsiveness which supports flow states of peak performance, high creativity, and natural spontaneity. This physical modeling of the tone and response style of blissful openness is unpacked in terms of a series of sublimation practices revolving around harnessing the internal, external, and unitive experience of sexual arousal and consummation. Called the three "gestures" or "seals" of intimacy, these involve sublimating the arousal generated by enjoying a virtual partner called an intuition seal, an actual partner called an action seal and/or the ecstasy of blissful communion with all things called the universal seal. We'll return to these practices in part 4. For now, we'd best turn our attention to the simpler elements of this art: the wide array of hand gestures used to model heroic cultural agency in the introductory process practices.

While the hand gestures that typically accompany the imagery of role-modeling and self-creation seem less clearly evocative of the visceral tone and response style of openness than the three seals of intimacy, they are meant in their own way to add a somatic-behavioral dimension to the multi-modal art of process-oriented self-creation. This is why, in addition to meditative postures, process-oriented archetypes all adopt various hand gestures that express the internal state of their deep affect and responsiveness. The wide array of gestures range from tender expressions of welcoming and offering to gestures of profound stillness and centering and fearless enactments of protection and dedication.[55] Like the hand gestures used by expressive speakers in many human cultures, or the arts of gentle yoga or *Tai Chi*, these bespeak a body language that reveals a universal humanity under the skin.[56] Current neuroscience and psychotherapy have converged in recognizing the role which visceral affect and bodily posture play in shaping our mind/body state and response-style. This convergence has opened the door to an evidence-based approach to somatic methods of fostering deep mind/body healing and self-transformation akin to those sought by Willhelm Reich and his heirs.[57]

The Positive Psychology of Altruistic Development

In terms of modern psychology, the narrative imagery of this phase bears some family resemblance to the new horizon of optimal human psychosocial development opened up by the new sciences of positive psychology and interpersonal neurobiology. Beyond the scope of conventional therapy, beyond even the deepest healing changes in affect and character, this phase of imagery overlaps with the domain of the most extraordinary reaches of human emotional development, social genius, and cultural leadership. If the rich and highly evocative simulations of altruistic genius in this phase in any way succeed in helping us glimpse our potential for such genius or a path to realizing it, they have more than done their work.

Sealing the Narrative: Constancy, Dissonance, Forgiveness, and Dedication

As we saw in our experiment with *Sheer Brilliance*, the concluding points of the practice of self-creation in this tradition overlap with the last two of the seven steps in the art of role-modeling: requesting constancy and dedication. The work of this final point is to manage the resistances involved in transitioning between our glimpses of the mentor's perspective within sessions and our inevitable return to the default perspective of ordinary perception in-between sessions. The challenge we face here is how to preserve the progressive quality and continuity of what is learned within sessions from the inertia of ordinary perception and conceptuality. We'll discuss the traditional strategy for facing this challenge under four headings: constancy; dissonance; acceptance; and dedication.

Stay as You Are: Insuring the Constancy of Narrative Self-Transformation

First, as with parenting, psychotherapy and the basic role-modeling process, the living container for the continuity of an ideal vision of our potential in the self-creation phase is the quality and constancy of the mentor-student bond. Unlike the work in therapy or introductory process practices, however, the quality of the mentor-student bond in this phase cannot hang on mere idealization of the mentor, if only because it revolves around the student's construction of him or herself as the master's equal. While this practice depends on the student's confidence in the master, it puts an equal or greater emphasis on the junior practitioner's self-confidence. This is because the main challenge the practice poses is to our familiar image and idea of ourselves as incapable of altruistic genius. So constancy here has as much to do with a constant commitment to the findings of our own self-analysis as it does with a constant link to an idealized other.

This intellectual sense of constancy brings us to another dimension of the mentor-student bond in this setting, that is, the role of the mentor as a living link to a tradition and community of self-creation. If mentor and student were alone in their work to create and live a preferred social construction of reality, it would be hard indeed for the student to hold a vision of self and world so challenging to any mundane consensus, without a master's certainty validated by direct personal experience. That is why the process tradition takes such pains to locate the mentor-student bond within an intergenerational lineage of mentoring and a broad communal sense of vision and purpose anchored in the socially engaged teachings of universal altruism. This communal spirit is symbolized by the iconic image of our chosen archetype, which not only personifies the language-matter of our mentor as moral ancestor, but also links us to an extended family of congenial minds with whom we share a cohesive mission, vision, and cultural project.

Resolving Cognitive Dissonance: The Bicultural Balancing Act of Self-Creation

The next challenge we face in this practice is what Bob Thurman describes as the problem of cognitive dissonance. If the art of narrative self-creation involves transitioning to and from two incompatible views of ourselves and our world, how do we reconcile the seeming contradictions between the new vision we cultivate in practice and the ordinary perception we share with the majority of those around us? Given the binary nature of our minds, we're prone to oscillate between two false resolutions: clinging to our visionary self-image as a reified, grandiose self; or clinging to our old self-limiting image as a reified, inadequate self. If we liken our "prosthetic" new self to a medical transplant, we can compare these two bad outcomes to graft-versus-host immune reactions and standard graft-rejection reactions. Of course, since both extremes can be traced to our instinct for self-reification, the only viable middle way here is to rely on the de-reifying medicine of emptiness as a sort of cognitive immunosuppressant.

The main thing that makes our narrative vision of reality preferable to our ordinary images of reality is that it is constructed—at the beginning, middle, and end—so as to be entirely self-dissolving and transparent. To be effective in the long run, it must be indissolubly bound with the de-reifying medicine of the emptiness insight, formulated as the transparent dignity of selflessness. Although the content of process imagery is jam-packed with invaluable guidance about altruistic life, its prime intent is to serve as an antidote or counter-balance to help us begin to see through and freely revise our ordinary, traumatic constructions of self and world. This self-dissolving usage is not only built into the language-matter of self-creative imagery, it is also part of the common grammar that makes that imagery not an isolating system of fantasy but a living language that links us to mentors of a better life and a larger altruistic community.

Acceptance and Dedication: Sealing our Place in the Community of Master Altruists

The final two elements of the closing phase of narrative imagery—acceptance and dedication—help preserve its efficacy by reaffirming the way its special language links us to our altruistic mentors and community. Invoking the mentor-archetype's forgiveness for any errors of omission or commission in the performance of that imagery serves to seal the healing guidance and transformative power of that imagery from the corrosive influence of ordinary perception and conception in-between sessions. It does this by insuring the long-term quality and continuity of self-creation, opening us to accountability, correction, and ongoing learning in dialogue with the mentor and tradition.

As in basic role-modeling, the final seal that safely closes the insight practice of narrative self-creation until our next session is the element of dedication. Like the act of invoking acceptance, this one helps insure that our practice and life stay aligned with the highest aims and tested methods of the process-oriented path of altruism. By earmarking the positive insight and energy we've developed in and through our practice session to staying true to those aims and methods, we not only protect the gains of that session from the corrosive influence of our ordinary minds and lives, but also extend our commitment to those ideals and methods as a lifeline that helps keep us on track for the next session. In this sense, dedication further seals our ongoing membership within and fidelity to the process-oriented community of altruists, by reinforcing our intent to devote our minds and lives to the mission that motivates our mentor and binds our new community together.

Of course, the elaborate imagery and complex symbolism we've surveyed in exploring the art of narrative self-creation is not meant for beginners. So I follow the tradition of introducing the process-oriented path by way of the simpler imagery of action, performance, and integral process practices. As I promised, our second meditative experiment will involve a very popular and widespread form of process practice, revolving around the archetype of *Transcendent Wisdom*, often simply called the *Mother.* To prime your mind for experiment 8.2, please refer to the image of the *Mother of Transcendent Wisdom* in the color insert.

The *Wheel of Time*, Archetype of Sustainable Happiness

3-D Image and Blueprint of the *Time-Machine Mandala*

The Medicine Buddha, *Healing Mentor*

White *Tara*, the *Healing Mother*

Manjushri, Youthful *Sheer Brilliance*

Prajnaparamita, Mother of *Transcendent Wisdom*

The *Heroic Altruist* Mother-Father

The *Master Altruist* Mother-Father

Meditative Experiment 8.2: Transcendent Wisdom, Mother of all the Enlightened

In as peaceful and uplifting a space as possible,
With or without real offerings or images
Of the Mother of Transcendent Wisdom,
Settle into a comfortable, stable posture,
And clear your energy with a deep and full sigh
Or with nine rounds of alternate nostril breathing.
Then gradually shift into a kinder, gentler breath-rhythm
And use that rhythm, centered at your heart,
As a focal point to center your whole body-mind
In a meditative state of greater clarity and calm.
Then recite mentally or out loud the following
Performance script, based on the sevenfold role-modeling process
Of Transcendent Wisdom, pausing after each section
For as long as you like to envision its imagery,
Focus on your experience, or contemplate its meaning.

1. *Evoking and Admiring the Mother of Wisdom*
"Suddenly the whole universe, including my body-mind,
Returns to its natural state of pure energy and openness.
I have the pure nature which is the natural purity of all things!
In the open space before me, your translucency dawns
Like a sunrise reflected in water, out of which
A sapphire blue syllable E of 3-D laser light
Emerges like a fish leaping out of water,
Resonating with the healing spirit of your teaching,
Beaming a rainbow aura all around, which dispels
The demons ailing all beings—compulsion, self-grasping,
Fear of death and primal narcissism—and delights the enlightened,
Inviting their fivefold wisdom to return like a rainbow wave,
Gathering back into the E until it emits a sunrise glow
That assumes your form as the young *Wisdom Mother*,
Prime source of all altruists and all the enlightened.
Seated in meditation, your golden complexion
Glows with light and warmth like the sun,
Your third eye sees with non-dual intuition,
And the wisdom tiara before your topknot
Holds a miniature, saffron robed Shakyamuni.
Your two hands meet in teaching mode at your heart,
The left holding the stem of a lotus which blossoms
A transcendent wisdom text at your left shoulder,
The right holding the scepter of blissful mastery.

At ease in heavenly silks, you bear all the marks and signs
Of mature altruism, and the living gems of transcendent virtue."

1a. *Inviting Your Mentor's Spirit to Ground Your Vision*
"Your form glows like a living sun, lit from within
By the sapphire E and moon-disc at your heart.
Beaming gem-toned lights to invite your spirit and the genius of all
Wisdom muses to melt into you and merge as one!"

1b. *Taking Refuge in Your Role-Model's Example*
"Awake in the clarity of your selfless openness,
All mother earthlings and I take refuge in your non-dual wisdom.
To free and heal all sensitive beings I now conceive
Your altruistic spirit of pure love and openness, and will
Develop myself and all beings as quickly as possible,
Until we gain the enlightenment to free this world!"

2. *Welcoming Transcendent Wisdom into Your World*
"In the presence of your healing truth, all experience has the singular taste
Of blissful openness, pervading the mind and all the senses!
Welcoming you gratefully into my world, I offer
A sun-shower of sense delights—scented waters,
Incense, flowers, lights, music and delicacies—
Converging toward you from everywhere, horizon and sky!
Fully and freely I share with you all my resources,
Virtues, and every aspect of my intimate life,
Plus this precious earth, with its oceans, continents,
Wonders, forests, waters and infinite web of life!"

3. *Fully Disclosing your Faults, Limits, and Blocks*
"Regretting all the demon-like instincts and habits I've indulged,
All the patterns that limit and block me from your way of being
From the depths of my heart I admit every one of them now,
And firmly resolve from here on to avoid and unlearn them all."

4. *Enjoying the Qualities of Transcendent Wisdom*
"Though all things are empty of any non-relative being,
With gratitude I enjoy all the myriad forms
Of happiness you experience and share with all life,
And all the transcendent virtues that serve as their cause."

4a. *Enhancing Enjoyment with the Four Boundless Moods*
"May all beings have real happiness and its causes!
May we all be freed from all suffering and its causes!
May we all enjoy and savor all excellent things!
May we all know unwavering equanimity!" (Repeat 3X)

5. *Requesting/Receiving Recognition and Protection*
"Moved by your wise care for me and all life, from your heart
Rainbow lights and nectars beam to melt into mine,
Dispelling the demons blocking my body, speech, mind, and action,
Unlocking my genius and planting seeds of enlightenment,
Finally sending a miniature double of you who dissolves
Through my crown, throat and heart, melting my body, senses, and mind
Into your blissful openness, where we merge like water in water.
I AM THE SELF WHOSE NATURE IS
THE DIAMOND INTUITION OF OPENNESS!
I AM SAFE WITHIN THE FIREWALL OF YOUR
DIAMOND COMPASSION AND BLAZING WISDOM!"

5a. *Making Death a Way to Embody Pure Openness*
"Now that you and I have dissolved, along with any
Trace of our ordinary bodies, minds, lives, and worlds,
Just as we would in the process of dying, I take this space
Of sheer openness, free from distinctions, as my true body,
In which the clarity of bliss illumines everyone
And everything's ultimate freedom from any non-relative
Being, essence, nature, identity or objectivity.
I EMBODY THE ULTIMATE TRUTH OF TRANSCENDENT WISDOM!"

5b. *Making Development a Way to Embody Enjoyment*
"In the deep space of blissful openness, my clear light
Wisdom dawns like a rising moon mirrored in water,
Out of which rises a 3-D sapphire light syllable E
Beaming a rainbow aura of non-dual wisdom everywhere,
Purifying all beings and delighting all the enlightened,
Invoking a wave of gratitude and solidarity
That returns to melt back into me as the syllable E.
My E radiates a sunburst of joy out of which I assume
The form of the *Wisdom Mother*, sun-gold with scepter and text.

Lit from within by the radiant E and moon-disc at my heart,
My translucent body is filled with the gem-toned lights of the five
Pure intuitions, and glows as if with a rainbow aura.
I EMBODY THE PURE ENJOYMENT OF TRANSCENDENT WISDOM!"

5c. *Making Life a Way to Embody Compassion*
"All around me as the *Mother* I hear the five geniuses
Of enlightenment singing me my commitments and pledges.
As the sounds of their voices raise goose bumps and the hairs on my neck,
My body and mind melt with compassion into the E
And moon-disc at my heart, which melt in turn into my heart-drop,
Dissolving in blissful openness like water poured in water.
Suddenly out of the womb of openness my intuitive mind
Reemerges shimmering as a moon-rise mirrored in water,
Out of which my affirmative voice rises as the sapphire E,
Radiating a sunrise aura in which I appear as the Mother
And beam lights everywhere to invite the five geniuses
Who pour wisdom-nectar through my crown, filling me
Until it overflows a saffron-robed Shakyamuni crown.
I EMBODY THE MANIFEST FORM OF TRANSCENDENT WISDOM!"

6. *Requesting Constancy Through Affirmation*
"Facing you now as an equal, I ask you please to stay
With me as my example while I practice living
A master altruist's life, embodying *Mother Wisdom*.
Thrilled for me, you recite the 3-D citrine light affirmation
Coiled clockwise around the moon's rim and the E at your heart,
ALL HAIL TRANSCENDENT, TRANSCENDENT,
COMPLETELY TRANSCENDENT,
SUPREMELY TRANSCENDENT ENLIGHTENMENT!
As you repeat it, the affirmation glows and emits
A duplicate of 3-D citrine light which you exhale
And send my way to inhale deep into my heart, where it coils
Clockwise around my moon-disc's rim, encircling
The syllable E as twenty-four 3-D citrine syllables
Placed equidistant around the moon, facing out:
ALL HAIL TRANS-CEN-DENT, TRANS-CEN-DENT,
COM-PLETE-LY TRANS-CEN-DENT, SU-PREME-LY
TRANS-CEN-DENT EN-LIGHT-EN-MENT!

The affirmation wheel turns like a ring of sun-flares at my heart
That lights, warms and resonates through my whole body and mind."

As you recite the mantra 7, 21, 108 or more times, imagine It rotating counterclockwise so fast it appears to be standing Still, while the moon disc feneath it revolves like a twenty-four-Spoke wheel clockwise in the same way. See the affirmation ring Heating up until it beams rainbow lights through your pores And all around the world, gathering the intuitive wisdom of all Enlightened beings and retrieving it to dissolve back into itself, Making the affirmation wheel glow even more until it beams to All beings and worlds all around, dispelling the four demons that Block their genius, transforming them all into forms of Mother Wisdom, and enhancing their lives and world by unlocking Their native genius for altruistic mastery. Then imagine them all Sending duplicates of themselves as Mother Wisdom in gratitude Back to you, melting like so many citrine snowflakes of light into Your body and heart-drop. After the recitation, immerse yourself In the resonance and afterglow as deeply and continuously as You can, shifting your focus from the affirmation wheel at your Heart to the moon, from the moon to your body as Transcendent Wisdom, from your body to the body of Mother Wisdom before You, and finally back to your body. Take a deep abdominal Breath and gently hold it as you focus on your sun-gold body, And as you exhale be mindful that it is empty of any non-relative Being, essence, nature, identity or objectivity (1 or 3X).

6a. *Requesting Constancy as you Practice the Altruist's Life*

"Recognizing this imagery as a mere simulation,
I ask you please to stay with me until I reach mastery.
Moved by affection for me, I see you melt into a drop
Like a rainbow tear for joy, which pours through my crown
And throat to melt into the E at my heart, merging your
Transcendent Wisdom with mine, intensifying my light,
Energy, and warmth until they fill me as a flame fills a lamp
And a nectar, a vase, rippling out in my actions
Until all those around me at home and on earth embody
Mother Wisdom, returning a wave of joy to my heart!"

Now pause to absorb and drink in the warmth and moisture Of that joy, as long and deeply as you can, and then prepare To close the session:

"Suddenly the world outside, my ideal space and body
All return to their normal appearance; the firewall outside
And the moon and E at my heart melt into my heart-drop."

7. *Dedicating yourself to Embodying Sheer Brilliance*
"With any errors or omissions I've made in this practice
Out of ignorance, misperception, lack of resources or art,
I ask you *Mother*, please be patient and all-forgiving!
Any positive insight or energy I've gained through this practice
I dedicate to being always inspired by your teaching,
Until I myself fully embody *Transcendent Wisdom*,
In this very lifetime, as quickly as possible!
By mastering the arts of imagery and blissful openness,
May I find the wisdom to enlighten myself and all life!

9 Living Altruism through Impassioned Vision

> (Such process practitioners) have many (accomplishments), such as restraining the tenfold nonvirtuous actions with regard to objects, purifying their (mind/body) processes by means of initiation, guarding properly their vows and pledges, cultivating the concentration of the first (creation) stage, and being expert in the science of the control of passion.
>
> (Tsong Khapa, *Brilliant Illumination of the Lamp of the Five Stages*[1])

Given the sensual vision and impassioned spirit that distinguish the process-oriented path, this passage from Tsong Khapa's main work on the optimal integral perfection stage may strike us as oddly moralistic. Yet coming as it does after his comments on the ecstatic consummation of that stage, after countless pronouncements of the primacy of the blissful art, I can think of no clearer statement of the true spirit of the process path: the altruistic ethos of sublimating bliss to speed our embodiment of compassion. The mere fact that he closes this key work on advanced practice with a chapter on proper conduct shows the seriousness with which ethics is treated in this tradition. In fact, his insistence that restraining the ten nonvirtuous actions is the first achievement of process practice and that control of passion is the last makes plain that the emphasis on sensuality and passion in that practice has little to do with hedonistic indulgence. Yet this insistence stands out all the more since nearly everything he says leading up to it aims at distinguishing process ethics from any sort of asceticism. In truth, most process ethics reads like a manifesto of hedonistic materialism as frank as our "eat, drink and be merry." Consider this:

> As for the unexcelled path's affording enlightenment in this lifetime, it depends on the union of bliss and void, and that bliss comes from the flourishing of the enlightenment spirit (of orgasmic ecstasy) in one's body, and for that one must take care of one's body along with the senses and their supports. For that purpose is taught the conduct wherein the five senses rely on the five objects of desire.[2]

And later, this quote:

> Setting the mind in the reality of enlightenment,
> Enjoying the bliss of objects, one achieves in this very life.[3]

Perhaps the first thing a newcomer to this unique tradition must do is to try to reconcile what seem like conflicting messages about its ethical spirit and lifestyle guidelines. Is the impassioned ethos of this practice like the hedonism of our modern secular tradition? Or is it a ritually camouflaged form of asceticism, like the moralism of our ancient religious traditions? Is the ethos of the process-oriented path in conflict with the spirit of renunciation on the path of self-healing? Does it contradict the spirit of compassion on the path of social engagement?

Process Ethics in Context: The Balanced Spirit of Shakyamuni's Middle Way

Perhaps the best place to start to answer these crucial questions is by returning to where our journey together began. Recalling the *Turning of the Wheel of Teaching Scripture* will help put our seeming dilemma in context:

> Mendicants, these two extremes should not be followed by one who has gone forth into (Shakyamuni's path of) homelessness. What two? The pursuit of sensual happiness in sensual pleasures, which is low … ignoble, unbeneficial; and the pursuit of self-mortification, which is painful, ignoble, unbeneficial. Without veering towards either of these extremes, the Transcendent One has awakened to the middle way, which gives rise to vision, which gives rise to knowledge, which leads to peace, to direct knowledge, to enlightenment, to Nirvana.[4]

So, from the beginning, the ethical path and behavioral discipline of Buddhist psychology favored a balanced middle way between the more or less universal human extremes our modern culture seems to share with ancient India's. And while the process-oriented art of bliss Tsong Khapa refers to sounds like "the pursuit of sensual happiness in sensual pleasures," in fact it is much closer to the middle way of the eightfold path, which leads to mind/body health and the balanced well-being that fosters sustainable happiness. Remember, Shakyamuni didn't describe the hedonistic extreme as the simple *enjoyment* of sensual pleasures, but specifically as "the pursuit of sensual happiness" in those pleasures. In other words, if we expect fleeting sensual enjoyment to be a source of true, lasting happiness, we are bound to get stuck in a cycle of self-indulgence, dissatisfaction, addictive craving, and compulsive behavior.

On the other hand, the approach to sensual pleasures prescribed in the process tradition aims not at sensual happiness but at a state of optimal well-being that not only benefits oneself but also supports the animal spirits of love and compassion traditionally called "the spirits of enlightenment." So our reliance on sensual pleasures in this context is in pursuit of a state of well-being which is as much a social good as a personal good; and it is to that end that "one must take care of one's body, along with the senses and their supports."

The Process Difference: The Distinctive Ethos and Art of Sublimation

If the reliance on sensuality and passion in the process tradition differs from the hedonistic pursuit of pleasure, exactly what makes that difference possible? To answer this, let's return to the complete the passage Tsong Khapa cited in his chapter on conduct:

> Setting the mind in the reality of enlightenment,
> Enjoying the bliss of objects, one achieves in this very life.
> All these are pure in intrinsic reality,
> Ordinary objects being selfless and illusory,
> Like hallucinations and optical illusions,
> Nonlocal, delivered from thought conventions.
> When noble persons totally realize
> The magnificent ambition and the habit-free mind,
> Then the orgasmic realization prevails
> And the power of these objects no longer binds.[5]

This compelling passage distills the essentials of the art of sublimation which makes the difference, the art which leads to a way of being unlike any of the all-too-human extremes with which we're all so familiar. In the lines of the quote that describe things as empty of intrinsic reality, selfless and illusory, we see the catalyst which helps transform mere enjoyment of objects into a blissful art: the profound wisdom of emptiness. In effect, by seeing through our naive fantasies of people and things as reified objects of desire that hold the key to endless pleasure and lasting happiness, we are freed to relate to people and things with more realistic awareness of their true nature, including their failings and limits. Based on this realistic awareness, we then can gradually develop the skill of enjoying what pleasure they do afford, without clinging to wishful thinking and the inevitable frustration that comes of not seeing them as they really are. Out of this skill comes renunciation, as well as compassion for others trapped in their own naïve objectifying habits. Then, marrying these two motivations together with wisdom, we're ready to practice the art of bliss taught in the process-oriented tradition, which the passage distills as "the magnificent ambition and habit-free mind."

The "magnificent ambition" here refers to the heroic passion to live an altruistic life, one that models for others the art of enjoying a radically free and clear mind. It is this ambition that is symbolized by the magnificent, vivid vision of ourselves as mentor-archetypes living to purify and transform our world. On the other hand, the "habit-free mind" refers to the wisdom that knows that vivid vision to be fully transparent, that is, utterly free from any reified self, any hint of "intrinsic"—non-relative, non-constructed—identity or reality. That radically free and clear mind, realizing the selflessness of our illusion-like vivid imagery, is also known as the self of selflessness, and the dignity of enlightenment. Here we come back to the two cardinal features of creative process practice, only now viewed as the two key ingredients which together make possible the art of sublimation that fuels and guides the distinctive ethos of process teaching. Traditionally, that ethos is also defined as the adamantine method, forged by the indivisible fusion of wisdom and art, symbolized by the *Master Altruist*'s scepter. And this method of fusion is what is implied by "the magnificent ambition and habit-free mind."

The Process Method: The Adamantine Fusion of Wisdom and Blissful Art

Not surprisingly, the last two lines of the passage allude to the effect that comes of fusing that "habit-free" wisdom and "magnificent" art: "the orgasmic realization" of blissful openness which dissolves the reifying ties that bind our traumatized self-construct to its fantasy objects of desire. How, exactly does the fusion of impassioned vision and selfless pride yield blissful openness and melt the bonds of delusion, desire and frustration that lock us into ordinary life? To unpack this, it may help to return to another quote, this one from the *Esoteric Community Process*. The passage was cited by Tsong Khapa in his *Great Stages of the Poetic Path* to explain the meaning of the Sanskrit term for affirmative speech—*mantra*—which gives the process path its other name: the poetic path. It also draws on the Sanskrit term for the adamantine method fusing wisdom and art—*vajra*—which not only denotes the *Master Altruist's* scepter but is also the third name for the process path: the adamantine or diamond path.

> Minds arising dependent
> On a sense and an object
> Are said to be *man*.
> *Tra* means protection.
>
> Protection by means of all the adamantine
> Commitments and pledges explained,
> Free from the ways of the world,
> Is called "the practice of *Mantra*."[6]

These simple verses help us zero in on the way the adamantine fusion of habit-free wisdom and magnificent art—operating as enlightened pride and vivid imagery—work to guard the mind from its ordinary conceptual and perceptual habits, protecting us from the toxic energies of confusion, desire and frustration. In particular, the poetic, self-creative images, affirmations and gestures of the creation stage of process practice help guard the mind from its compulsive reification and addictive craving for objects of desire, by substituting a transparent, altruistic construction of self and world that overrides scarcity thinking, addictive instincts and traumatic confusion. In effect, the vividness and transparency of the altruistic life-vision they create serves as a constant reminder, to reset our default state of mind from the reactive rut of stress and trauma to the proactive stance of open-minded engagement and open-hearted compassion for all. To underscore this point, Tsong Khapa quotes Aryadeva's *Lamp that Integrates the Practices*:

> The addictive energies serve as condition for the addictions of those with objectifying views such as the disciples, since they do not understand the reality of the addictions. If they know the reality, those energies could become the cause for enlightenment.[7]

In fact, this alchemical view of process practice as turning addictive energy into the pure passion for altruistic enlightenment is often expressed in classic metaphors of that practice as a purifying fire which consumes the addictive fuel it feeds on. The idea has deep roots in the process view of consciousness and neural energy, as derived from a molecular mind-energy and chemistry that can support either the addictive process of stress and trauma or the enlightened process of bliss and openness.[8] At the level of self-creative practice, the "orgasmic realization" of blissful openness which is the catalyst for this transformation of energies comes from two main sources. First, there is the borrowed bliss and openness that comes of identifying with our prosthetic image of the mentor's altruistic mastery. Next, there is the genuine joy and release that come of overriding our reifying, addictive habits, and so avoiding the tension and frustration of our ordinary way of being in the world. These two sources of blissful transformation correspond to the two main aspects of process ethics: general and specific.

The Contract of the Mentoring Bond: The Twin Faces of Process Ethics

In general, the habit-free mind and magnificent art of role-modeling and self-creation free us from our bondage to compulsive life in the ordinary world, by holding us to our protective bond with the extraordinary, blissful world of the mentor-archetype. In particular, this broad ethos of building altruism through sublimation is fleshed out in terms of a series of specific commitments and pledges, meant to generate and maintain the sublimation process by the repeated performance of insight-guided images, affirmations and gestures. These two aspects of the ethos of process practice relate to the second and third of the four accomplishments Tsong Khapa attributed to process practitioners: purifying their body-minds through entering the confidential bond of initiation; and transforming their body-minds through maintaining regular practice commitments and pledges.

While the first accomplishment of restraining the ten nonviturous actions relates to having mastered the common ethical disciplines of self-healing through renunciation, and social engagement through compassionate openness, the last of the four—control of passion—mainly relates to the ethics of the perfection stage, to be discussed in chapter 12. In what remains of this chapter, then, we'll explore the general and specific ethics that bridge these two accomplishments. These two are related respectively to the uncommon preliminary arts of role-modeling imagery and narrative self-creation. And they are fleshed out in the contractual ethics of the mentor-student bond, codified by the seven ornaments of interpretation; and the procedural ethics of commitments and pledges encoded in the six-session practice of self-creation.

Purifying the Mind Through Initiation: The Contract of the Mentoring Bond

As part of the ritual of initiation, there is a dramatic interchange between the student and mentor. Guided to envision ourselves standing at the Eastern gate to the celestial mansion of enlightenment, we're asked by the mentor-archetype within, "Who are you, and what do you want?" The response articulates the transgressive ethos of process practice, "I am the lucky one, and I want great bliss!" Yet that is only the first half of the contract. The teeth come in the second exchange, prompted by the question, "And what will you do with it?" Then comes the second reply, "I will keep the commitments of the Buddhas!" These two simple lines distil the essence of process-oriented ethics: it originates out of a mentor-student bond meant to role-model the art of true happiness; it proceeds by guiding and sustaining the learning and practice that foster the student's altruistic development; and it culminates in the student's mastery of the altruistic art of modeling true happiness for others. But first, our first meditative experiment, with the purification process of the *Heroic Altruist* introduces us to the process-oriented art of due diligence which supports process ethics.[9] To prime your mind for experiment 9.1, please refer to the image of the *Heroic Altruist, Mother-Father* in the color insert.

Meditative Experiment 9.1: The Purifying Path of the *Heroic Altruist*

In as peaceful and uplifting a space as possible,
With or without real offerings or images
Of the Heroic Altruist Mother-Father,
Settle into a comfortable, stable posture,
And clear your energy with a deep and full sigh
Or with nine rounds of alternate nostril breathing.

Then gradually shift into a kinder, gentler breath-rhythm
And use that rhythm, centered at your heart,
As a focal point to center your whole body-mind
In a meditative state of greater clarity and calm.
Then recite mentally or out loud the following
Performance script, based on the purification process
Of the Heroic Altruist, pausing after each section
For as long as you like to envision its imagery,
Focus on your experience, or contemplate its meaning.

1. *Taking Refuge in the Four Healing Gems*
"In a state of radical honesty, acceptance and openness,
I take refuge in my mentor's wisdom and empathic art,
In the prime example of the Great Sage, Shakyamuni,
His enlightening teaching and healing community
And in all mentor-archetypes of heroic altruism.
To free myself and all sensitive beings I conceive
The altruistic spirit of pure love and openness, and will
Develop myself and all beings as quickly as possible,
Until we gain the enlightenment to heal this world!"

1a. *Invoking the Heroic Altruist Mother Father*
"Suddenly out of the void, six inches above my crown,
Your perfect purity emits a thousand-petalled lotus
Of rainbow light, in the midst of which your blissful mind
Dawns like a full moon in water. Bubbling up from the moon
Like a fish leaping out of the water comes a sapphire light HUM,
Which instantly becomes a diamond scepter marked by HUM,
Flawless and unbreakable as your commitments and vows,
Beaming a rainbow aura everywhere that purifies
The destructive habits and instincts of all living beings,
And delights the enlightened, melting the whole multiverse
Into gem-toned light that returns and melts into the scepter
Until it dissolves and transforms into your embodied form
As the moonlight-white *Heroic Altruist*, Father and Mother
Of all enlightened beings and all master altruists.
Seated in meditation, facing forward, hovering
Just inches over my crown, your right hand holds a scepter,
And your left a bell, as they embrace your partner,
Diamond Pride, who straddles your lap, her arms and legs
Embracing you, holding a chopper and skull-bowl.
At ease in heavenly silks, you both bear the marks and signs
Of perfect altruism, and the living gems of transcendent virtue."

1b. *Inviting Your Mentor's Spirit to Ground Your Vision*
"Your form glows like a cooling moon, lit from within
By the diamond OM, ruby AH, sapphire HUM
Seed syllables on moon discs at your crown, throat and heart,
Beaming gem-lights to invite your spirit and the pure genius
Of all altruists to melt into you and merge as one!"

2. *Welcoming Your Mentor-Archetype into Your World*
"In the presence of your healing truth, all experience has the singular taste
Of blissful openness, pervading the mind and all the senses!
I HAVE A PURE NATURE WHICH IS
THE NATURAL PURITY OF ALL THINGS!
In the crucible of the clear light of bliss, my five mind/body
Systems and elements melt and transform into healing
Elixir, the quintessence of the five pure intuitions.
OM AH HUM HA HO HREE! (3X)
Welcoming you gratefully into my world, I offer
A sun-shower of sense delights—scented waters,
Incense, flowers, lights, music, and delicacies—
Converging toward you from everywhere, horizon and sky!
Fully and freely I share with you all my resources,
Virtues, every aspect of my intimate life—
Transformed by healing the elixir of my blissful openness,
Plus this precious earth, with its oceans, continents,
Wonders, forests, waters and infinite web of life!"

2a. *Requesting and Receiving Consecration*
"Intensified by absorbing the genius of all altruists,
And enjoying the singular taste of these blissful offerings,
The sapphire HUM at your heart beams gem-lights everywhere
Inviting the five Mother-Father Transcendent Ones
To consecrate you and grant me initiation.
The couples come holding vases of wisdom elixir
Which they pour into you crowns, filling your body/mind
And overflowing as an *Unshakable* Buddha crown.
MAY THE CONSECRATED VOWS
OF ALL THE TRANSCENDENT SHINE!"

3. *Fully Disclosing Faults, Limits, and Blocks*
"Regretting all the negative instincts and habits I've indulged,
All that limits and blocks me from keeping my commitments and pledges,
From the depths of my heart I regret every one of them now,
And firmly resolve with your help to avoid and unlearn them all."

4. *Enjoying the Qualities of Heroic Altruism*
"Though all things are empty of any non-relative being,
With gratitude I enjoy your power to free all beings
Of the compulsions that poison our lives, and to seed, nurture,
And harvest the pure virtues that ripen in happiness."

4a. *Enhancing Enjoyment with the Four Boundless Moods*
"May all beings have real happiness and its causes!
May we all be freed from all suffering and its causes!
May we all enjoy and savor all excellent things!
May we all know unwavering equanimity!" (Repeat 3X)

5. *Requesting and Receiving Purification*
"Mentor of purity and kindness, please help me purify
All the negative habits and instincts, and all the broken
Commitments and pledges hindering me and all beings!
Moved by wise compassion for me and all life, you recite
The 3-D diamond light affirmation coiled clockwise around
The outer rim of the moon and the HUM at your hearts, facing out:
O DIAMOND HERO GUARD MY VOWS, UPHOLD THEM,
MAKE ME FIRM, UNWAVERING, GRATEFUL, ABUNDANT,
GRANT ME ALL ATTAINMENTS, DIRECTOR OF ALL EVOLUTION,
MAKE MY MIND BRILLIANT, HUM HA HA HA HA HO!
GEM OF ALL TRANSCENDENT ONES, NEVER LEAVE ME,
MAKE ME DIAMOND, GREAT PLEDGE HERO! AH HUM PAY!
(Or in brief: O DIAMOND HERO AH HUM!)
As we repeat it, the affirmation glows and emits
Rainbow lights that beam to all beings, purifying
All their negative habits and blocks of body, speech, mind,
And delighting all the enlightened, until it returns as a wave
Gathering all their pure virtues of body, speech, mind,
Into gem-toned lights that melt into the affirmation
Ringing your hearts, intensifying its light and warmth
Until it starts to drip and flow pure white bliss-nectar
Down your central channels, out your sexual organs,
And through my crown. From there a rush of bliss-nectar
Charged with the five pure intuitions pervades my body,
Purging my body, speech and mind of all flaws and blocks,
Until they become the enlightened body, speech, and mind
Of the *Heroic Altruist*, Mother-Father, lit from within
By a diamond white OM, ruby red AH, sapphire blue HUM
Beaming from the moon discs at my crown, throat and heart."

As you recite the mantra 7, 21, 108 or more times, imagine the nectar
Of blissful openness filling your body completely from head to toe,
Expelling all negative habits and blocks of body out your toes as
Dust and ash, then filling you up again to the crown, where it expels
Negativities of speech as thick smoke, and finally rippling inward
From yourpores to your inmost heart-drop as pure nectar-light
Which dispels negativities of mind as shadows. After the recitation,
Immerse yourself in the resonance and afterglow as deeply and
Continuously as you can, holding your focus on seeing your body,
Speech, and mind as naturally free from all the habits and instincts
That block your full freedom and clarity, resolving to let go of vices,
Guard against relapse, initiate and maintain the cultivation of
Virtues, by keeping your practice commitments and pledges. Seal
The process by affirming your enlightened pride and confidence:

"I AM THE SELF WHOSE NATURE IS
THE DIAMOND INTUITION OF OPENNESS!
I AM SAFE WITHIN THE FIREWALL OF YOUR
DIAMOND COMPASSION AND BLAZING WISDOM!"

6. *Requesting Constancy as you Practice the Altruist's Life*
"Recognizing this imagery as a mere simulation,
I ask you please to stay with me until I reach mastery.
Moved by affection for me, Mother-Father, your bodies
Melt as one into the affirmation ring at your hearts,
The affirmation dissolves with the moon disc and HUM
Into one, indestructible drop, like a rainbow tear for joy,
Which slips through my crown and throat to melt into my heart,
Merging your natural purity with mine, intensifying my light,
Energy and warmth until they fill me as a flame fills a lamp
And a nectar, a vase, rippling out in my actions
Until all those around me at home and on earth become
Heroic Altruists, returning a wave of joy to my heart!"

Now pause to absorb and drink in the warmth and moisture of
That joy, as long and deeply as you can, and then prepare to close
The session:

"Suddenly the earth, my meditation space and my body
All return to their normal appearance, and the three syllables
Sealing my inner purity melt into my heart-drop."

7. *Dedicating yourself to Embodying Sheer Brilliance*
"With any errors or omissions I've made in this practice
Out of ignorance, misperception, lack of resources or art,

I ask you, mentor, please be patient and all-forgiving!
Any positive insight or energy I've gained through this practice
I dedicate to being always inspired by your teaching,
Until I myself become a *Heroic Altruist*,
In this very lifetime, as quickly as possible!
By mastering the arts of imagery and blissful openness,
May I gain the integrity to enlighten myself and all life!"

The Alchemy of Initiation: The Transmuting Influence of the Mentoring Bond

Although this brief experiment is meant as a process-oriented version of the art of due diligence, you may recognize in the imagery of purifying nectar entering the crown the same themes of intergenerational influence and blessing we saw in the imagery of initiation. In fact, if you recall our discussion of due diligence on the paths of self-healing and social engagement, such self-corrective arts are invariably set within the social context of a confidential relationship and healing community. Here, of course, that setting is not the ordinary teaching relationship and contemplative community we're familiar with, but the extraordinary role-modeling relationship and transformational community of the process tradition. We see this reflected in the opening of the practice, which addresses not the usual three gems of healthy reliance—Shakyamuni, his teaching and the community who practice it—but begins with the fourth gem recognized in the process tradition: the mentor who embodies enlightenment in our day and age, as a living role-model or second Buddha. No accident, this opening sets the stage for the distinctive relationship that is the living matrix of process ethics. Given this key emphasis on the confidential bond, the most direct way to unpack the ethical discipline of this tradition is to look at the guidelines meant to govern the two parties of that bond.

As for the ethical guidelines governing mentors in this tradition, the gist is to offer instruction, encouragement, and guidance to potential students in ways that are suited to their current capacities and levels of development.[10] When it comes to the guidelines governing students, the gist is to cultivate as diligently as possible the insights and methods taught by their mentors and embodied in their respective process practices.[11] The simplest way to explore these complementary guidelines is to briefly unpack the extraordinary map of contemplative practice and moral development encoded in the rites of initiation or consecration which serve as the gateways to process practice.[12] Since the most inclusive map of process practice is the one offered by the optimal integral process, our look at the contract which defines both aspects of process ethics will be based on the fourfold initiation rite of that practice.

The Fourfold Optimal Initiation: Map and Gateway to the Process Path

As we saw, the introductory insights and methods of the action, performance, and integral process traditions are all included within the first of the optimal integral's four initiations, the vase initiation. In the classic tradition of the *Esoteric Community*, the fivefold vase initiation, named for the vase used to pour water on our crowns, is said to consecrate the five basic systems of our compulsive mind/body process as the natural geniuses of embodied enlightenment. In the context of the optimal integral path, this rite empowers and encourages us to practice the creation stage art of transforming our ordinary, traumatic perception of our mind/body systems into a transparent vision of them as naturally embodying the five pure geniuses of our mentor-archetype. This is why it's located within the healing space of the mentor-archetype's pure environment, as depicted in a painted or sand *mandala*, imagined within the mentor-archetype's body or simultaneously envisioned by mentor and student. In essence, the vase rite combines the five knowledge initiations which serve as gateways to action and performance process practices. However, it also includes the *Diamond Master* consecration added in the integral process to encourage us to envision ourselves as *Master Altruists*, able to teach and guide students on the process path.

The second of the four classical rites, the secret initiation, introduces us to our innate potential for blissful openness which is the basis for the art of sublimation cultivated in the optimal integral perfection stage. This is why the rite is said to be localized in the sphere of euphoric experience based on the natural energy and chemistry of sexual orgasm, symbolized by the seminal and menstrual fluids known as the "conventional spirits of enlightenment." In essence, the gateway to the perfection stage art of sublimating bliss is being introduced to the secret that we have the capacity, given the right methods, to consciously integrate and regulate the energy and chemistry of bliss generated within the central channel.

When we explore the contemplative map of the central nervous system in part 4, we'll consider any links between the central channel and the endorphin-mediated neural network traced by modern science to the internal reward system within the core brain.[13] For now, it's enough to say that this rite opens the door to the practice of the perfection stage, which, as we'll see in part 4, is classically divided into five sub-stages.[14] In particular, the secret initiation prepares us to practice the first two perfection sub-stages, which continue our disengagement from ordinary compulsive perception at two subtler levels: disengaging from our ordinary obsessive energy and our ordinary addictive consciousness. By focusing on inducing and mastering euphoric states through advanced methods of recitation and breath-control, the stages opened up by this initiation prepare us to develop a so-called "illusory body" or "rainbow body" of genuine blissful openness. Though still impure, this euphoric mind-body state I like to call our virtual body becomes the neurochemical basis for our blissful subjectivity and altruistic agency on the rest of the perfection stage and beyond. Learning to fully manifest and inhabit the virtual body brings us to the third of the perfection sub-stages.

The third part of the classical fourfold rite, the intuitive wisdom initiation, introduces us to our potential to use our deepest state of blissful openness to realize the radical open-mindedness of the spacious emptiness intuition, quickly and completely. The rite is said to take place within the intimate state of our blissful mind's ecstatic union with objective reality, symbolized by the intimate sexual union of two lovers communing in orgasmic bliss.[15] The intuitive wisdom initiation clears the way for us to progress to the fourth sub-stage of the perfection stage, called clear light translucency. At this stage, by using the euphoric mind/body state of the virtual body, enhanced by sublimated sexual imagery or experience, as a platform for contemplating the emptiness of that body and experience, we become increasingly absorbed in a state of ecstatic open-mindedness. Such immersions allow us to drink in the elixir of the intuitive wisdom of emptiness at an immediate, visceral level, bringing us to the culmination of a truly objective clarity, lucidity or translucency of mind. With this we're prepared for the final sub-stage of perfection practice, the phase of integration.

The fourth and final part of the classical rite, the word initiation, takes us to the threshold of the final achievement of altruistic mastery. The localization of this final rite is in the words through which our mentor explains the culmination of the path.[16] Having purified our sublimation of blissful openness through repeated and sustained reflection on the fact that it is empty of any reified, non-relative subjectivity, objectivity or experience, we're not only able to realize the most refined and radical level of open-mindedness possible but also ready to integrate our newfound euphoric body and ecstatic mind. Through repeated immersion of our bliss-void subjectivity in the translucent objectivity of all things' emptiness of self, our sensibility, and agency gradually coalesce around a master altruist's body and mind.

Peak Performance and Confidence: The Rare Aim and Strategy of Process Traditions

Though the language, imagery, and ritual arts used to bring these initiatory rites to life vary depending on the level and type of process practice involved, they all proceed towards the same effect. That effect is to forge a bond between mentor and student, based on their mutual understanding of process practice as a reproducible and teachable method for quickly freeing the mind/body process from its stress-reactive habits and energies, while modeling and mastering a proactive altruist's way of being through sublimating erotic instincts and energies. The details of the bond, which we'll now unpack, are essentially simple.

The mentor is bound to do his/her utmost to teach, encourage, and guide the student to learn the arts of imagery and sublimation which move her/

him along the process path; and the student is bound to learn, practice and master those arts and the way of being they create, as quickly and completely as possible given his/her capacity. In the preconception shared by Freud and most modern science until recently, human beings in general don't have native genius, much less the potential to master it through sublimation. So this tradition and the new science of peak performance[17] challenge us by insisting that such potential and its mastery are not just possible—given the right methods and practice—but incumbent on us, as perhaps the highest form of altruism. In this sense, the contractual ethos of the process tradition bears more of a family resemblance to the transformational bond familiar from Jungian and Reichian analysis, or the highest levels of coaching and mentoring in athletics, leadership, the arts and sciences. The result is a distinctive bond with an exceptional ethos of marrying peak individual performance with the highest attainable levels of altruism and social responsibility.[18]

You can think of the path chosen by India's contemplatives as one of selective mainstreaming. On that path, both the Hindu and Buddhist traditions made process practices more and more widely accessible over time, while selectively restricting those insights and methods which could be most easily abused or misunderstood.[19] In effect, this was done by encoding them in a language of symbolism called twilight language, which intentionally veiled or obscured the most challenging material enough that only a trained and experienced guide could decode it.[20] Of course, this strategy is not unique to Indian contemplative traditions. Yet this general strategy was far more elaborately developed in India than in the rest of Eurasia, and met with far greater acceptance than its counterparts in other cultures.[21]

The Nuanced Ethos of Process Mentoring: The Seven Ornaments of Interpretation

While the origins of process methods themselves remains obscure,[22] the selective strategy that governs their teaching may have grown out of contemplative mentoring techniques brought by Sanskrit-speaking shamans from Central Asia to India, where they later emerged in the wisdom teachings called *Upanishads*.[23] Whatever its source, this strategy was elaborately codified by masters of the *Esoteric Community* process tradition, into a mentoring system called the seven ornaments of interpretation. This system was gradually adopted as the standard governing the teaching of all process-oriented practices within the Nalanda tradition, a standard still accepted by all schools of Tibetan Buddhism. Though it's impossible to unpack so highly complex and nuanced a system in any detail here, a few observations about its overall logic and intent may be the best way to flesh out the ethical standards that govern the confidential bond of process practice from the mentor's side. Let me open with a key statement from the *Illuminating Lamp*, the classic on this system written by the Noble Chandrakirti:[24]

A short text with manifold meanings,
This *Esoteric Community* process is hard to discover,
Its seven ornaments hard to understand,
And so people constantly wander (in error).
Therefore through the kindness of the mentor,
One should strive to come to understand,
And distinguish those (seven ornaments),
If one wants to look after living beings.[25]

This brief quote sets the stage for unpacking the system, by alluding to the highly symbolic nature of process-oriented texts and teachings, and prescribing the need to study the interpretative art which properly decodes them, under the guidance of a master. Finally, he makes the underlying intent behind the whole system and strategy plain: it's indispensible to fulfilling the commitment to becoming a *Master Altruist*, able to skillfully share the joys and spread the word of process practice to others. Before unpacking the seven ornaments, Chandrakirti briefly lists them as follows: preliminary considerations; kinds of procedure; modes of explanation; levels of interpretation; types of instruction; types of student; and final aims of practice. Briefly considering each of these in succession will give us a taste of the psychological discipline and therapeutic art of mentoring in this tradition.

The First Ornament: Bridging the Gap Between Sources and Students

The first ornament, preliminaries, helps put the particular process practice a mentor prescribes for any given individual or group in the context of the two teaching relationships that make up the living matrix of any practice tradition. Since all Buddhist teaching is a healing communication between particular individuals facing particular challenges at a particular place and time, applying that teaching skillfully in the present requires us to understand the human context in which it was offered and its relevance to those it may help here and now. So this ornament or interpretive lens highlights the family resemblance between two human contexts, and helps us see the text, teaching or practice we're trying to share as a historical bridge linking our work and world to the similar work and world assumed by that text, teaching or practice.

Like a translator, a mentor works to bridge a gulf in history or culture, allowing us to truly enter the world of the teaching and to fully incorporate the new possibilities of meaning and being which it opens up in our own minds and lives. And, of course, that assumes that the mentor's current teaching springs from a profound awareness of and commitment to the ethos and aim of the original teaching, that is, empowering the student to master the art of altruistic self-transformation. The sense of cultural sensitivity and historical efficacy this ornament prescribes also imposes on mentors an obligation to be historians and scholars of the traditions they are trying to preserve and renew, at least to an extent that allows them to clearly place their work as living links between two teaching contexts.[26]

The Second Ornament: Matching Students with their Optimal Procedure

Once a mentor understands the living relationship between his/her source teaching and target audience, the second ornament or lens of interpretation involves considering the type of procedure or life path a given student should follow to fully embody enlightened altruism. This lens is significant because it clarifies the bifocal nature of the path of altruism in this tradition. It recognizes two types of procedures that can support the cultivation of altruism, each of which involves a journey of four life stages. The two types of procedures are: those followed by an aspiring altruist best suited to a dispassionate path; and those followed by an aspiring altruist best suited to a passionate path. The first type of procedures are those which make up the path of social engagement leading from a compulsive life of stress-reactivity to a proactive life of a enlightened altruist; and the second type are those which make up the process-oriented path from an ordinary compulsive life to the passionate life of a heroic altruist.

The four stages of the dispassionate path are: being born human; renouncing addictive, worldly pleasures; committing to vows of ascetic self-discipline; practicing the dispassionate teachings of self-healing and social engagement. The four stages of the passionate path are: being born through initiation into the five families of enlightenment; identification with one congenial family through enlightened pride; upholding the commitments of process practice; and practicing the passionate teachings of sublimating bliss. This bifocal lens reveals two things about process-oriented teachings and the art of mentoring on which it depends. First, it locates process ethics relative to the compassionate ethics of social engagement as a parallel path that reaches one and the same end by different means. In this, it underscores the double-edged sword of narrative self-creation, which juxtaposes the twin paths of altruistic self-transformation: the path of engagement and the process path. Second, it imposes on the mentor the discipline of reading process literature and teaching process methods in ways that resonate for both types of altruists and allow them to learn and practice alongside one another, at least up to a point. In other words, it commits the mentor to an inclusiveness which builds consensus across a range of traditions while supporting a pluralism that embraces renunciation, compassion and sublimation as complementary disciplines within an overarching ethos of self-transcendence.

The Third Ornament: Matching Styles of Teaching to Individual Needs

With the third ornament or lens, we enter the complex world of diverse modes or styles of explanation.[27] The six modes defined here span the range of explanatory styles, at all levels of discourse. The interpretable and definitive modes govern style at the level of syntax or grammar; the ambiguous and unambiguous modes govern style at the level of assertions or statements; and literal and colloquial modes govern style at the level of word choice or diction. Of course, given the need to conceal easily misunderstood process insights and methods, definitive meanings suited to the most capable students at the most advanced levels of practice are veiled in a symbolic language that may be gradually explained using parts of speech—specific nouns, verbs, and adjectives—that will be reinterpreted as the student progresses. The best example of this is the imagery of the creation stage, which couches its explanations in terms of nouns like the three conversions, which are consistent with the language of social engagement and only suggestive of definitive process terms like the nine mergers, clear light transparency or the virtual body.

The next pair of discursive modes—ambiguous and unambiguous—govern explanations at the thematic level of whole assertions or statements. Given the pregnant symbolism of process terms and teachings, any given string of words and sentences may be read to support a range of different meanings, according to a particular student's current level of capacity and development. Ironically, the modes or styles of explanation advised at this level of dialogue suggest a surprising variation on the theme of the first two modes. While we would expect unambiguous statements to be reserved for the most advanced students and ambiguous ones for the less advanced, this set of modes advises the mentor to turn that expectation on its head. Instead, it suggests that an ambiguous or paradoxical style works best for advanced students, since it challenges them to resolve the ambiguity on their own, drawing on their own experience and intuition. Beginners or less prepared students, on the other hand, may be best approached in an unequivocal style of explanation that fosters clarity, understanding, and confidence.

Finally, at the level of words and expressions, the last modes—literal and encoded—governs the kind of words mentors choose to explain the range of practices students need to progress along the process path. Literal explanations describe overt process arts like making sand *mandalas*, performing fire ceremonies, using words and expressions following the common conventions of ordinary language. Encoded explanations allude to a range of covert arts like sexual practices, using technical conventions of speech like a code, to restrict them to students who are prepared to understand and practice them properly. This last set of modes indicate the extreme care trained mentors are prepared to use in their explanations of process teachings and practices, to insure that their students are not prematurely or randomly introduced to practices that might invite misunderstanding or the misuse of process methods by the unprepared.

Taken together, the six modes that make up the lens of explanation illustrate the high bar set for mentors in their dialogue with students of various capacities and levels of moral development. In general, this lens puts the mentor's choice of words and statements under a microscope, prescribing an exceptionally high degree of mindfulness and self-discipline in her/his use of language. Yet it is just such a high level of discipline that allows this tradition to maintain its selective strategy of making such complex and often provocative teachings accessible to a wide audience. Of course, it only makes sense that such a discipline is needed given the extraordinary ethos guiding this tradition: systematically mentoring mature altruism. Briefly surveying the rest of the ornaments will help us flesh out the remarkable rigor and complexity of the mentoring discipline standardized by this seven ornament system.

The Fourth Ornament: Matching Depths of Interpretation to Levels of Development

The fourth ornament or lens, interpretation, governs the levels of sense a mentor must unpack for various students, according to their level of altruistic development and stage of progress on the process path. Although the four levels that make up this compound lens are new to us, they will not be entirely unfamiliar since at least three of them overlap, however imperfectly, with the four kinds of initiation that map out the path of the optimal integral process. Of the four, the first—descriptive meaning—falls outside the scope of contemplative teaching, while the latter three—general, suggestive, and ultimate—overlap with the scope of the vase initiation, the secret and intuitive wisdom initiations, and the word initiation, respectively.

A descriptive interpretation involves a literal, surface reading of process teachings and practices, suitable for the general public that has a mundane intellectual or scientific curiosity about them. The aim of this level of interpretation is to inform the general public in ways that help prevent mystification and misunderstanding, leaving the door open for a more serious interest to emerge. A general interpretation involves an introductory reading of process teachings and practices, equally suitable for students committed to the paths of self-healing and social engagement, as well as to the three introductory process practices or the creation stage level of the optimal integral process. For instance, reading the art of narrative self-creation in terms of three conversions not only helps students practice the creation stage but also reassures students on the three preceding paths that the ethical aims of the optimal process are fully compatible with their own ethics, commitments and pledges.

A suggestive interpretation involves a suggestive reading of optimal integral teachings and practices, suitable for advanced students on the first three sub-stages of perfection stage practice. This level of interpretation might suggest the practice of tapping and sublimating sexual energy and chemistry by combining recitation and breath-control with imagined or real sexual experience, on the sub-stage called freedom of speech. Or, a slightly different reading at more or less the same level might suggest the practice of purifying the luminous intuitions through harnessing sexual orgasm or near-death to the realization of translucency, on the second sub-stage called freedom of mind. Finally, another reading at the same basic level may suggest the art of harnessing the five pure intuitions and energies to support the emergence of the impure virtual body, on the third sub-stage called self-consecration. Consistent with the secret and intuitive wisdom initiations, these nuanced readings involve the mentor's precise empathic awareness of the student's level of development and stage of practice. So, of course, as we'll see in the next ornament, they must be restricted to the intimate dialogue of private mentoring.

Finally, an ultimate interpretation involves a definitive reading of optimal integral teachings and practices, suitable for the most advanced students on the final two sub-stages of perfection stage practice, often referred to as the "great" perfection stage. In particular, this level of interpretation may involve teaching the practice of realizing the clear light translucency while inhabiting the impure virtual body, on the fourth sub-stage called simply clear light. Or, a slightly different reading on the same basic level may involve teaching the practice of increasingly marrying and refining the clear light mind and pure virtual body on the fifth and final sub-stage called integration. Obviously, this fourth level of interpretation also assumes the mentor's intimate knowledge of the student's development and practice, and also must be restricted to the confidential privacy of the mentoring bond.

This fourfold lens of interpretation shows even more clearly than the third the truly awesome rigor and scope of the discipline of instruction and guidance expected of the trained process mentor. Not only does it further underscore the extreme sensitivity and responsibility a mentor must develop to address the whole spectrum of students, each at their level, but it also suggests the incredible range and precision they are expected to have to insure that these challenging practices reach their audience in the right form, at the right time. Given this ethos of precise and continuous guidance, it's easy to see why this tradition insisted that process teachings can only be safely delivered and practiced in the intimate, psychotherapeutic context of the mentor-student bond. In fact, as we'll see when we compare this map of ethical development and practice with the contemplative map of the nervous system in part 4, this interpretive lens requires the mentor to have a detailed and complete mastery of the neurobiology of self-regulation in order to guide students along the whole process path.[28]

The Fifth Ornament: Tuning the Content of Teaching to the Context

Of the remaining ornaments or interpretative lenses, the fifth and sixth shift the focus of the discipline of mentoring onto the context and audience of teaching, to help fully prepare the mentor to teach with the highest levels of effectiveness and responsibility. In particular, the fifth ornament of instruction distinguishes two types of teaching contexts: public or mixed group contexts; and private, individual contexts. A further safeguard of the strategy of selective exposure, this bifocal lens restricts public teaching of mixed groups to literal, unambiguous and interpretable modes of explanation, as well as descriptive and general levels of interpretation. The forms of instruction suited to more advanced readings and practices—including encoded, ambiguous, and definitive explanations, and suggestive and ultimate levels of interpretation—in contrast are restricted to the intimate privacy of the confidential mentor-student bond.

The Sixth Ornament: Discerning and Teaching to Individual Capacities

The sixth ornament or pedagogic lens requires the mentor to sort students into five levels or types, depending on their current capacity to engage in process-oriented study and practice. Students with the highest current capacity are called gem-like because they are ethically pure, intellectually clear, and have focused minds. Students of the least current capacity are likened to sandalwood, since their evident sweetness conceals snakes of compulsion. And those in-between are compared to blue, white, and red lotuses, depending on how fully their capacities have unfolded.

This typology reveals several key points about the ethics of mentoring in this tradition. First, despite ancient and modern myths that process teachings somehow celebrate hedonistic indulgence, impulsive behavior or unchecked passion, those gem-like students who are most pure in their moral intentions and actions are considered most able to study and practice them.[29] In fact, only students at this level are eligible for private instruction, and hence, for mentoring in perfection stage practice. On the other hand, students still struggling with addictive craving and compulsive habits, whatever their outward manner, must be barred from advanced practice and from preparing to teach until they develop more self-restraint and capacity for sublimation.

That said, the most important point about this typology is that it is not seen as a fixed grading system to pick winners and exclude the rest, but rather as a pedagogic spectrum that requires mentors to work with each student where they are, preparing them to move at their own pace towards advanced practice. This is clearest from the tradition that, wherever individual students begin, the power of process-practices is such that, if properly instructed and supervised, the mentor should be able to gradually help them all become gem-like, as a skilled alchemist can transmute all base metals to gold.

The Seventh Ornament: Directing All Teaching Towards Final Objectives

If the first two lenses help set the stage for the mentoring bond and the third and fourth focus the style and level of discourse, the fifth and sixth serve to highlight the needs of the student or students to be mentored. The lens of the seventh and last ornament helps the mentor keep his or her eyes on the prize: the ultimate aim which orients and guides the extraordinary journey the mentor and student will take together over time, as a final destination guides any ordinary one. Specifically, that ultimate aim is mastering the practice of the great perfection stage, defined by the sub-stages called clear light translucency and integration. That practice or performance is understood as the master altruist's integration of ecstatic mind of translucent clarity and the euphoric, virtual or "rainbow" body of blissful openness. In other words, this ornament binds the mentor to do everything he or she can to bring each and every student, regardless of their current capacity or development, to the ultimate destination of being a fellow master altruist, a perfect equal, peer, or successor.

Triple Discipline: Cumulative Ethics for the Process Practitioner

In his exhaustive review of the cumulative ethics of process practice, His Holiness Dudjom Rinpoche explains the Nalanda tradition of subsuming the commitments of self-healing and enlightened altruism within a threefold optimal integral (unexcelled) process ethos, quoting this passage from the *Magic Net Process*:

> In the vow of unexcelled process,
> All the disciplines of monastic ethics
> And the disciplines of the enlightened altruist
> Are entirely embodied and are pure.[30]

Of course, since we've surveyed the ethical and behavioral guidelines governing the paths of self-healing and social engagement, I won't review in detail the way they're traditionally subsumed in process ethics. In brief, these include ten precepts of renunciation for lay students or the extensive precepts for monastics,[31] as well as the eighteen primary and forty-seven secondary commitments of compassion for enlightened altruists.[32] Instead, I'll focus on the synthetic tradition of optimal process ethics systematized in the *Wheel of Time*.[33]

According to that tradition, the ethical guidelines governing students involved in process practice fall into four categories: the distinctive actions of a heroic altruist; the practice pledges of the five families of enlightenment; avoiding the primary pitfalls; and avoiding the secondary pitfalls. Of these, the first category essentially reviews the self-healing commitments, and the third includes commitments from the engaged altruist's path. The rest of the commitments and pledges, as we'll see, are distinctive to the process tradition.

Restraining Nonvirtues: The Basic Commitments of a Heroic Altruist

The distinctive conduct of a heroic altruist is unpacked in five sets of five; five acts of abstinence; five acts of restraint; five acts of non-violence; five acts of non-aggression; and five acts of non-attachment. Since most of these are familiar from the path of self-healing, they need no explanation. The abstinences include the five basic pledges of abstinence on the path of self-healing, namely: abstaining from killing, lying, stealing, sexual misconduct, and the use of intoxicants. The restraints include refraining from negative speech, gambling, unhealthy eating and violent sacrifice or ideologies.[34] The acts of non-violence involve avoiding ritual violence of any kind. The acts of non-aggression involve avoiding any angry or aggressive feelings towards mentors or fellow members of our spiritual community. And the five non-attachments involve renouncing any clinging to the five ordinary sense faculties of sight, hearing, smell, taste, and touch, along with their respective objects, sights, sounds, scents, tastes, and textures. By committing to these twenty-five modes of action, we lay the moral foundation we need to support an effective process practice. With these ethical guidelines in place to help guard and free our open-mindedness, we have the stable ground we need to invest ourselves in the positive ethics of process practice, unpacked in the practice pledges of the five families of enlightenment.

Prescriptive Ethics: The Five General Pledges of the Families of Enlightenment

Assuming we're willing and ready to exercise the five kinds of restraint just described, the main way we hold up our end of the mentoring bond is by committing to process practice following the guidelines of five general and special family pledges. Drawing on the traditional identification of our five mind/body systems with the genius of five families of enlightenment, the pledges that guide process practice are framed as the paths of contemplative action which transform those systems from their compulsive baseline to their enlightened fruition. In what follows we'll cover each pledge in terms of its link to one of the five families, designated by their respective hand tools—the wheel, scepter, jewel, lotus, and sword. Because there are two sets of five pledges—general and special—we'll go through the family pledges twice.

As for the general pledges, the first belongs to the wheel family whose father and mother—called the *Illuminator* and *Illuminatrice*—personify physical purity and the mirroring intuition. Reinforcing the ethics of the engaged path, the wheel pledge is to view our precious human body as a basis for embodying the spirit of enlightened altruism and maintaining the threefold ethics of self-healing, social engagement and process-oriented self-transformation. On a deeper level, this pledge commits us to seeing and treating our physical body, especially its capacity for blissful openness, as the perfect vehicle for travelling the process path of tapping and harnessing orgasmic bliss as a basis for embodying mature altruism.

The second general pledge belongs to the scepter family whose father and mother—the *Immovable One* and *Lady Ecstasy*—personify purity of mind and the reality intuition. The scepter pledge is to stay ever mindful of the art of sublimation and the mentor who teaches it, based on tapping and fusing the masculine and feminine sexual energy and chemistry known as the male and female spirits of enlightenment. On the creation stage, this is symbolized by the precept to guard and join the hand tools of scepter and bell, chopper, and skull-bowl. On the perfection stage, it involves actually tapping sexual energies and harnessing them to the realization of emptiness which purifies bliss and seals it with an objective intuition of reality.

The third general pledge belongs to the jewel family whose father and mother—*Jewel Mine* and *Mother Protectress*—personify pure sensitivity and the equalizing intuition. This pledge binds us to practicing the four kinds of generosity—giving wealth, guidance, protection, and pure love—either mentally, verbally, or physically, at least six times a day. At a deeper level, the pledge is to experience the blissful openness that flows when we tap the chemistry of sexual arousal and harness it to realize ecstatic openness to others' sensitivity and needs as our own.

The fourth general pledge belongs to the lotus family whose father and mother—*Infinite Light* and *Lotus Garbed*—personify the pure discursive system and the discerning intuition. The pledge is to maintain a clear understanding and pure expression of the teachings of all three vehicles on the gradual path: self-healing, social engagement and fourfold process practice. On a deeper level, the pledge refers to the art of purging our symbolic processing of the taints of stress-reactive thought and energy by merging our discursive minds and breath-rhythms with the affirmative speech and inspired breath-energy of the mentor.

The fifth pledge belongs to the sword or action family whose father and mother—*Real Success* and *Mother Savior*—personify the purity of the emotional system and the executive intuition. The pledge is to act in accordance with all prior pledges and to offer all things—outer, inner and intimate—to upholding our end of the mentoring bond and practicing the four arts of peace, power, abundance and ferocity. On a deeper level, the pledge is to actually realize the sublimation of orgasmic bliss to support all the systems, physical elements, sense-faculties, and motor functions of our mind/body process.

Transgressive Ethics: The Five Special Pledges of the Families of Enlightenment

With this brief look at the general family pledges, we turn now to the special ones. These five pertain to the pledge to transform the five compulsions—delusion, anger, greed, desire, and envy—into pure motivations that fuel the activity of the five intuitions—mirroring, realizing, equalizing, discerning, and executing. They also exemplify the "transgressive" nature of process ethics, that is, its art of challenging the literal, black and white sense of good and bad that dominates our ordinary, childhood conscience. Even the language in which these pledges are framed is provocative, challenging the childish moralism we mistake for ethics, and forcing us to develop an adult recognition of the ambiguities of our motivation and the situational nature of interaction. Literally stated, the wheel family pledge is to eat meat and drink alcohol; the scepter family pledge is to take life; the jewel family pledge is to steal wealth; the lotus family pledge is to have sex; and the sword family pledge is to tell lies. The paradoxical shock effect of these supposedly solemn pledges is to force us to think more deeply about our practice and to engage in it with a passion we normally associate with hedonistic license. To clarify the intent behind this language, let's consider each one of these special pledges briefly.

As for the wheel family, the pledge to enjoy alcohol and the five kinds of meat refers to the duty to harness confusional states to the cultivation of peace, countering attachment to waking state consciousness and any ordinary pride we take in moral purity, sobriety, or social and cultural superiority. An ever more radical challenge to our ordinary perception of pure and impure, good and bad, is a corollary pledge to avoid any disgust about the five kinds of bodily waste and fluids called "nectars"—feces, urine, menses, marrow, and semen. On a deeper level, the pledge to eat meat refers to maintaining the health of the five solid organs, and the pledge to drink alcohol refers to enjoying the flow of blissful neurochemistry released by sublimating orgasmic bliss. Likewise, enjoying the five meats and nectars refers to allowing bliss to pervade and purify all five gross physical elements of the body, and allowing the neurochemistry of bliss to transform the subtle molecular fabric of the nervous system, respiratory system, circulatory system, digestive system, and musculoskeletal system.

The scepter family pledge to take life, on a conventional level refers to the duty to harness aggression to developing ferocity, namely the fierce compassion to help ourselves and others break through stubborn cognitive and emotional blocks to learning maintained by traumatic habits and stress instincts. On this level, then, the life taken is the ordinary sense of self and life constructed by early social conditioning and maintained by self-protective instincts of attachment, aggression and reification. On a deeper level, the pledge is to dissolve our own ordinary self-construct and default consciousness by forcibly overriding the fight-or-flight oscillation supporting that state and immersing ourselves into the euphoric state sustained by the primal energy and chemistry of bliss at the heart of our core neural network.

The jewel family pledge to steal wealth, on a conventional level refers to the duty to harness acquisitiveness to creating abundance, by overcoming fear-based blocks to expanding our own generosity and the generosity of others. On an ultimate level, the pledge refers to transgressing our own limited access to the abundant energy and chemistry of blissful openness by seducing another's spouse, that is, using our bliss to court and commune with the supreme romantic partner: the objective clarity and ultimate reality of emptiness. Practicing this transgression gives us access to the abundant energy source of pure passion, empowering us to meet both our own needs and those of others.

The lotus family pledge to have sex refers to the duty to harness desire to the development of deep contemplative realization, by means of the art of sublimating the sexual energy and chemistry of bliss to the direct, intuitive realization of emptiness. Whether this is supported by imagined or real intimacy, both ourselves and our partners are to be seen as archetypal geniuses, with sexual organs seen as scepter and lotus, their union as empty of any reified agent, object or act of union, and orgasmic bliss and the wisdom of emptiness as the essential teaching. On a deeper level, the pledge is to practice causing the descending, ascending, and pervasive flow of bliss energy and chemistry with vase breath, and to use that sustained bliss to commune with the universal partner of all things' objective emptiness.

Finally, the special action family pledge to tell lies refers to the duty to harness competitiveness to developing the power to free all kinds of beings from their self-deception, by using the same illusion-like words and symbols they use to construct and reify delusions, in order to help them de-reify and deconstruct those delusions. On a deeper level, the pledge is to dissolve all symbolic awareness and binary, fight-flight energy into the primal non-conceptual awareness and pure bliss chemistry of the heart, so that afterwards, all our speech somehow expresses and manifests the empty, selfless, and inexpressible nature of things, in ways that help us speak directly to the self-made perplexities of each individual being.

Although these general and special family pledges may be complex, my aim in surveying them briefly here is simply to show how elegantly they cover the whole range and scope of positive process ethics. Assuming the foundation of the distinctive acts of self-care and reinforcing the altruistic ethos of social engagement, these pledges help flesh out how process ethics binds us to the work of self-transformation through repeated practice in everyday life. Like the optimal integral path itself, the pledges can be read at many levels, exemplifying in many ways the uniqueness of process ethics, with its distinctive emphasis on the transgressive work of narrative self-creation and neurochemical sublimation. Finally, these pledges are woven into the very fabric of process practices, as we'll see below when we explore the six-session practice of the *Master Altruist* in our second meditative experiment. But before we see how they're seamlessly integrated into the role-modeling process of mentor bonding, we must complete our look at the ethos governing the student's role in that bond.

Proscriptive Ethics: The Fourteen Prime Pitfalls of Process Practice

Unlike the primary pitfalls on the paths of self-healing and social engagement, the first three primary pitfalls on the process path involve our relationship with the process mentor, teaching and community. These pitfalls make explicit the distinctive ethos needed to support the close working relationships on which process practice depends. Since these pose even more of a challenge to our modern sense of autonomy than the content-driven ethos of the two prior paths, it's vital that we clarify the intent behind them.

The First Pitfall: Undermining Our Confidence in the Mentor-Student Bond

Of all the primary pitfalls, the first—devaluing our process mentor—is no doubt the most challenging. The idea of restraining our tendency to doubt or question the authority of any human being, much less one we personally rely on, runs counter to the skeptical stance we've been taught to rely on as scientific moderns. Yet the close working alliance of the process path indispensably requires mutual respect, acceptance and trust. Since maintaining such an intimate bond, like the alliance of psychotherapy, requires psychological work from both parties, indulging our natural and cultural tendency to suspect or reject even a hint of idealization would naturally undermine the open tone that is the life-breath of role-modeling and mentoring bonds.

Of course, this does not mean that critical thinking, questioning, or honest assessments are out of place in the mentoring bond. We saw that in our look at the ethics of mentoring, where a paradoxical style is recommended precisely to make students think for themselves. Likewise, the mentor's duty to see students as peers in training, or at least to prepare them for that, makes plain the exceptional level of respect and trust in students required of mentors. How can that be maintained without moments of serious questioning and doubt? The answer lies in the lenses of the fourth and sixth ornaments, governing a mentor's approach to any particular student.

As you may recall, as part of the mentor's due diligence, prior to teaching anyone anything, the fourth and sixth ornaments require a probing and honest assessment of any given student's current level of development and capacity. The traditional stories of encounters between mentors and their potential students are filled with humorous, often ludicrous tales of trials imposed by mentors on their prospective students.[35] In these classical tales, this testing phase typically lasts up to three years. The clinicians among you may find this reminiscent of long-term insight therapy, which often takes years of frustrating misunderstandings and missteps to really get started. And, as in therapy, the trial period here is not a one-way street. According to the tradition, after the first trial phase in which the mentor critically assesses the student, the relationship enters a second trial phase, in which the student critically assesses the mentor.

It is this second trial phase which lays the foundation for the kind of unshakable mutual confidence the first pitfall assumes. Even the initial selection of a process mentor involves a critical vetting process in which the mentor's qualifications for process teaching and supervision are carefully assessed, both by inspecting credentials, checking references, and personally testing the waters of the mentor's energy and the interpersonal chemistry. If the mentor passes this initial assessment, there usually follows the phase of getting acquainted through preliminary study and practice. If, after all this, we seriously request process teachings, there usually follows the first trial phase of proving our commitment and readiness. Finally, if we get through that phase, we may find ourselves facing new questions and doubts, especially in the face of the high level of commitment and discipline process practice demands.

In short, the reason why we're asked to engage in a mentoring bond without fundamental questions or doubts is that, by the time we're seriously ready to get to work, all the questions should already have been fully answered and doubts already resolved, on both sides. Beyond that point, to indulge our confusion or doubt by blaming the mentor whenever the going gets tough or we face our limits and blocks is the easiest out, and hence the first pitfall we must be prepared to avoid. As a final note, the logic of the first three pitfalls is interesting in that it doesn't simply add the mentor as a fourth support as usual, but actually replaces the Buddha with the mentor, quietly underscoring the primary importance of a close mentoring blond in this practice.

The Second Pitfall: Undermining the Effectiveness of the Teachings

The second pitfall, disregarding the teachings, alerts us to the next most serious block to progress on the process path or any other: dismissing or ignoring the relevance of the teachings to our daily lives, intentions and actions. From the start, Buddhist teaching is meant like a medicine, to relieve suffering, heal, and transform our minds and lives. This is no less true of the teachings of altruism, whether they work by social engagement or by process-oriented self-transformation. And this is why all Buddhist teaching involves not just theory but practice, complementing science or wisdom with the practical disciplines of meditative self-regulation and ethical application. This second pitfall reminds us that simply listening to teachings, reading texts, or paying lip-service to contemplative ideas and insights is not enough to yield any real benefit or to stay true to the authentic intent of those teachings, no matter where we are on the gradual path. This is why the process path is mapped by guidelines for action, pledges for practice, and warnings about pitfalls on the path.

The Third Pitfall: Compromising the Process Family

The third pitfall, harboring anger towards our process family, reminds us to guard the relationships that support our community of practice, as well as the larger circles of community surrounding it. Because the intimate bond we forge with a mentor stands alongside similar bonds he or she has developed with others like us, accepting, respecting, and supporting those peers—effectively our process siblings—is vital to supporting the practice family of which we are part. In addition, the process family itself plays a role in the work of this tradition as the monastic community does in the work of self-healing, serving as auxiliary teachers and models while also creating an alternative community that embodies the mindset and ethos we're trying to embody and share with the world. Of course, it also extends to include all those students in other families and communities who share a process practice in general, though they may have very different mentors, practices and local communities. It helps insure that we don't get carried away with transgressive teachings like the scepter family pledge of fierce compassion and lose track of the motivation to help and care for all.

The Fourth Pitfall: Abandoning Universal Love and Compassion

While these first three pitfalls address the intimate bonds on which process practice depends—with our mentor, the process teaching and practice community—the next four warn us of unavoidable risks that relate to our interface with the larger communities all around us. First of all, the fourth pitfall—abandoning love for any being—reinforces the fundamental role of preliminaries like radical acceptance and universal compassion, which insure that our process practice supports and advances our preliminary practice of self-healing and social engagement. This reminder is vital not just because of the potentially insular nature of process culture as an extraordinary tradition, but also to insure that we don't get carried away with the transgressive pledge of the jewel family and lose track of the motivation to share radical acceptance and nurturing love with all. It is also key to strengthen the cultural and communal ties between altruists on the engaged path and altruists on the process path, as well as between both kinds of altruists and those on the path of self-healing.

The Fifth Pitfall: Abandoning the Discipline of Sublimation

Next, the fifth pitfall, to abandon the spirit of enlightenment, further reinforces the general primacy of compassion and altruism, while also introducing the special process ethos of guarding our animal spirits of altruism—the sexual energy and chemistry of blissful openness. On the conventional level, this pitfall warns against losing touch not just with the warm-heartedness of nurturing love, but with the compassionate openness and heroic resolve which stays fully sensitive to others' suffering and naturally responds to help. In the context of the creation stage, this means never excluding any living being from the flow of the intuitive lights and bliss-nectars which simulate the natural outpouring of our compassion as blissful openness. And here again, this reminder also serves to insure that any show of fierce compassion we make towards those who need it isn't tainted by ordinary aggression or reactive anger, but flows instead from a deeper concern to help others break through stubborn limits or blocks.

On a deeper level, this warning reminds us of our fundamental commitment to the process ethos of sublimation, specifically the art of tapping and harnessing erotic energy and chemistry towards the cultivation of the animal spirits that fuel natural compassion and altruism. Symbolic of this ethos on the level of the perfection stage is the commitment to retrain any indulgence of sexual interest, excitement and release, identified for male practitioners with the art of restraining or blocking the emission of semen.[36] Though we'll return to this ethos and art in part 4, this guideline serves to remind us not to confuse sublimation practice and the transgressive pledge of the lotus family with sexual license or indulgence of any kind. It reminds us that this art treats sexuality not as an end in itself but as a means to an end: the cultivation of a mature psychosexuality that integrates primal instincts with the emotional intelligence we need for healthy intimacy and the altruistic vision we need for responsible creativity.

The Sixth Pitfall: Violating the Spirit of Tolerance and Pluralism

The sixth pitfall, devaluing other teachings and practices, further highlights the vital importance of an inclusive acceptance and responsible dialogue with all human cultural and contemplative traditions, Buddhist and non-Buddhist. First, this warning underscores the need to understand and practice process methods in ways that support their complementarity with the foundational insights and methods of the Buddhist traditions of personal self-healing and social engagement. Second, it reminds us to understand and practice those methods in ways that are truly pluralistic and embracing of the diversity of human cultural paths towards peace, inner freedom, and lasting happiness. Here again, the intent in part is to insure that we don't get carried away with the transgressive pledge of the sword family to cut through false views, but stay true to our primary pledge to help others grow in their own way, at their own pace.

The Seventh Pitfall: Violating the Confidentiality of Process Practice

The seventh pitfall, revealing secrets to the unprepared, once again insures that beginning students or those unfamiliar with process teachings are not prematurely exposed to those process insights, methods and ritual arts which may be easily misunderstood. This warning includes not just sharing too much too soon out of pride or zeal, but even mindlessly letting the unreceptive or unprepared see works of art, offering substances or ritual practices which they might misunderstand. It represents one more safeguard of the threefold ethos that insures the complementarity of process practice with the basic practice of renunciation and altruism. It also helps insure that we don't get carried away with the transgressive pledge of the wheel family by being conspicuous in our enjoyment of taboo things, but stay true to the primary spirit of altruism by staying sensitive in all ways and at all times to how our behavior affects others.

The Eighth Pitfall: Violating the Dignity of Our Human Life

Given the last four warnings, safeguarding our relations with the world around us, we now move to the remaining reminders that warn against specific pitfalls at various points on the process path. The eighth pitfall, abusing the mind/body systems, reminds us of the commitments of creation stage practice to stop seeing the five systems of our mind/body process as the basis of our ordinary traumatized sense of self and to start seeing and treating them instead as the native geniuses of the five families of enlightenment. This profound shift in self-image sets the stage for the work of narrative self-creation, in which we come to see and treat our life as the ideal basis for embodying altruism by harnessing bliss to the realization of perfect openness. So abusing our mind/body systems is a serious pitfall because it undermines all our efforts and instead reinforces our traumatic experience of life as unhappy, inadequate, and intrinsically limited. This guideline confronts us with the violent nature of self-loathing or self-destructiveness, in a way that will surely resonate with clinicians and clients who face these habits in psychotherapy.

The Ninth Pitfall: Abandoning the Transformative Insight of Emptiness

The ninth pitfall, abandoning the wisdom of emptiness, warns us against clinging to skepticism or cynicism about the truth of the journey of transformation we conceive in the course of narrative self-creation. Since the work of the creation stage is to construct a counter-narrative of our life that corrects our dim view of our basic condition, life path and full maturity, it would be tempting to cling to our familiar self-limiting view and think, "This vision of a heroic life of altruism is just wishful fantasy or positive thinking; it may be inspiring but can't change the fundamental facts and limits of my human life." Clinging to our pessimism about our human nature and the power of the process path to perfect it is a serious pitfall because it may block our motivation and erode our commitment to master all the techniques and progress through all the stages of the optimal integral process. From the standpoint of process ethics, clinging to such a cynical stance is the real self-fulfilling fantasy and simply reflects a kind of intellectual laziness and self-indulgent complacency which overlooks the facts of life, our real potential, and the efficacy of the process path. One source of this clinging is a failure to contemplate emptiness in the creation stage form of realizing the self of selflessness or dignity of enlightenment.

The Tenth Pitfall: Indulging Negative Influences

The tenth pitfall, depending on poisonous friends,[37] reminds us to guard our confidential relationship with our process mentors, teachings and communities by not indulging negative influences who harbor malicious thoughts or feelings about them. This warning cautions us not to be seduced when others misrepresent the process tradition and community based on prejudice, misconceptions, bad experiences, or personal failings. Instead, it urges us to act as advocates and representatives, so as to safeguard its present and future potential to help humanity at large. This duty may be compared with the need for those with intimate knowledge and experience of the benefits of psychotherapy to actively counter misguided critics who threaten the continued health and existence of an invaluable human practice and tradition.

The Eleventh Pitfall: Undermining Others' Confidence

The eleventh pitfall,[38] undermining others' confidence, reminds us to encourage and help others with valid interest or confidence in process mentors, enlightened models, teachings and communities. Whether their interest and confidence are based on admiring the qualities of process mentors and practices, on an aspiration to emulate those qualities, or on direct personal experience, this warning cautions us against mindlessly responding to them in any way that might discourage their interest or undermine their confidence and practice. The inverse of the tenth pitfall, this one warns us to be mindful of our role as a living advocate and representative of the process tradition and community in a positive sense. That means remembering to take ourselves seriously as sources of refuge, guidance and role-modeling for others who rely on process mentors, communities and traditions.

The Twelfth Pitfall: Failing to Realize the Full Depth of the Teaching

The twelfth pitfall, intellectualizing the teaching, reminds us not to settle for a merely intellectual understanding of the healing insight of emptiness, but to commit ourselves to process practices until we have a deep, visceral knowledge of its ultimate reality. This pitfall reminds us that, however indispensible a clear rational understanding may be, it is still only a means to an end, and that end is not a skeptical disillusionment or a mystical fusion, but a direct intuitive perception of the objective nature of our minds, bodies, and world. Our mental image of emptiness—as the pure negative finding that rules out the objective reality of our reified constructs of non-relative people and things—is only a signpost, not reality itself. This applies even to the image of emptiness conceived on the creation stage as enlightened pride. That is why we need the powerful methods of perfection stage practice to help us tap into profound blissful states which open our minds and nervous systems to more easily realize the objective reality of openness or translucency which corresponds to our mental image of emptiness.

The Thirteenth Pitfall: Neglecting to Cultivate Bliss and Realization

The thirteenth and penultimate pitfall, neglecting our practice pledges, reminds us to faithfully observe the pledges that help us cultivate the art of sublimating bliss, the art that allows us to follow through with deepening our insight of emptiness. At the conventional level of the creation stage, that may mean practicing offering gestures with our ritual scepter and bell, imaginatively or ritually transmuting our five "meats and nectars" into the elixir and sweet cake of blissful openness and enjoying them both, envisioning our process mentor and siblings as male and female archetypes, and joining in communal rituals, chants or dances. On the ultimate level, this means tapping bliss states through inner fire and imagined or real intimacy, and harnessing them to realize blissful openness, the virtual body and objective clear light. In effect, the warning here is not to indulge any moralistic judgment or revulsion at the ways process practice enlists primal bodily instincts and processes like sex and death to support altered states that speed and deepen our progress on the path of embodying altruism.

The Fourteenth Pitfall: Neglecting to Embrace Sexuality on the Path

Finally, the fourteenth pitfall, disrespecting the opposite sex,[39] reminds us to guard our minds from any negative gender bias or objectifying habits that might block our ability to tap and sublimate our sexual energy and chemistry to support genuine altruism. This warning helps us overcome any addictive, compulsive, or traumatic sexual habits that would block our progress on the final stages of psychosexual maturity and integration. As we'll see, this option is truly distinctive to process practice and offers a rare opportunity to make mature intimacy part of a unique path aimed at reaching the highest levels of altruistic agency in the context of a lay life. Even for monastic or single practitioners, this warning serves as a signpost to the highest levels of integration of masculine and feminine energy, dissolving blocks to the most profound embodiment of blissful openness, and the most complete realization of altruistic objectivity. This final guideline is reminiscent of the final intent of integrative therapies like Jungian and Reichian analysis, which emphasize our potential to reach a level of androgyny and positive energy that can support the very highest levels of psychosexual maturity and integration.

The Secondary Pitfalls: Undermining Relationships on the Process Path

Most of the secondary list covers fine points governing relationships with students or partners. As for partners, the pitfalls include being intimate with an immature or unprepared partner, or with no intention of harnessing bliss towards the realization of wisdom. As for students, they include withholding process teachings from someone qualified, giving irrelevant or incorrect answers, giving teachings to someone unqualified, teaching process methods to someone inclined towards conventional paths, claiming to be realized before the great perfection stage, associating at length with critics of process practice, and initiating students or performing other ritual acts without being properly prepared. Finally, the seal on the triple ethos of cumulative practice in this tradition is the warning not to engage in transgessive process practices that conflict with basic commitments to self-healing and social engagement, except in prescribed contexts, like tasting alcohol-containing offerings during required group process rituals.

The Threefold Discipline: The Exceptional Scope and Rigor of Process Ethics

Taken together, the ethical guidelines for mentors and students on the process path are as rigorous as any of those we've surveyed from the prior paths, although they govern a practice that is often mistaken for being more permissive in its ethos. In addition, the cumulative nature of process ethics makes unmistakably plain that the overall strategy of this path is to speed development not by cutting corners or lowering standards but rather by adopting a transgressive ethos that assumes the highest standards of personal and social ethics and imposes still higher standards based on mastering more complex and effective techniques.

Yet while process ethics may involve a quantum leap in difficulty, it also involves a quantum leap in the energy it frees for self-mastery. Though its triple ethos is plainly more challenging than either of the conventional ethics it subsumes, it also uses methods of moral self-mastery and integrity that are more instinctive and natural than the more familiar arts of self-discipline and self-transcendence it replaces. By using sensuality on the path, and restraining it with arts of imagery, affirmation, and bliss, process practice offers an ethical middle way—between attachment and detachment, indulgence, and abstinence—that empowers us to gain more self-discipline with less resistance and less frustration. Of course, this all sounds attractive to the modern ear, since we have long ago lost the taste for conventional self-restraint and caretaking. That is all the more reason why we need to acquaint ourselves with the traditional standards and rigors of process ethics. It is vital if we're truly to benefit from the unconventional and easily misunderstood arts of process practice that we delve into the original intent behind those arts, including the ethical guidelines that govern their effective use.

Matching Rigor to Current Capacity and Practice: The Gradual Path of Process Ethics

While it's vital to bear in mind the high standards of process ethics, it's equally crucial—especially for novices—to remember that the guidelines we've just reviewed do not all apply to beginners, particularly the great majority involved in introductory process practices. Specifically, the ninth, twelfth, thirteenth, and fourteenth pitfalls do not apply to those initiated into introductory process practices, or those only receiving the first of the four optimal integral rites, or the rites in the mode of childhood usually offered in public initiations into the *Wheel of Time*. In fact, in practice, most beginners know precious little of the standards set for advanced practice or for their mentor, and focus instead on the entry level ethics of distinctive actions and first four primary pitfalls—dismissing the mentor, teaching, community, or anyone—plus or minus the warning to keep practice confidential and avoid self-destructive acts. The rest of the pitfalls along with the family pledges are usually introduced in the context of the six-session practice, the gateway into optimal integral practice. Following that tradition, we'll close with a meditative experiment on the six-session practice of the *Master Altruist, Father-Mother.*

Doing More with Less: The Power of Process Ethics to Intensify Healing Bonds

As a clinician engaged for much of my professional life in the work of long-term psychotherapy, the transformative power of contemplative practice makes perfect sense to me. With its potent mix of intimate bonding, idealizing transference, and repeated, structured positive experience, the process-oriented tradition shares many aspects of the very different cultural practice of intensive psychotherapy. Yet unlike modern therapy, this tradition doesn't rely so heavily on prohibitive face-to-face sessions. Instead, using the sophisticated arts of mentor-archetype bonding, role-modeling imagery, narrative self-creation, and process ethics, process practice helps deepen and intensify the alchemy of healing relationship in remarkable ways.

Given its prime reliance on empowering methods of daily practice, it not only allows us to do more with less, but also speeds the process of transformation by putting the individual to work catalyzing and metabolizing change herself, in-between meetings. As the behavioral logic of that work, the discipline of process ethics—based on its distinctive guidelines, practice pledges, and cautionary warnings—is no mere window-dressing. In fact, it is the ground on which the distinctive process arts of mentor-bonding, role-modeling and self-creation stand. The only thing more basic to the transformative power of process practice is the ethics spelled out in the seven ornaments of interpretation, which ground and guide the art of mentoring that serves as crucible for this work. Our closing experiment serves as the gateway to optimal practice because it embodies the triple ethos of the mentor-student bond on which the effectiveness of all process practice depends. This version is based on the brief six-session practice of the *Wheel of Time*, by His Holiness the Dalai Lama.[40] Remember that if you're not currently an optimal process practitioner, this experiment is solely for liberal arts purposes, not for regular practice. To prime your mind for experiment 9.2, please refer to the image of the *Master Altruist, Mother-Father* in the color insert.

Meditative Experiment 9.2: The Six-Session Practice of the *Master Altruist*

In as peaceful and uplifting a space as possible,
With or without real offerings or images
Of the Master Altruist Mother-Father,
Settle into a comfortable, stable posture,
And clear your energy with a deep and full sigh
Or with nine rounds of alternate nostril breathing.
Then gradually shift into a kinder, gentler breath-rhythm
And use that rhythm, centered at your heart,
As a focal point to center your whole body-mind
In a meditative state of greater clarity and calm.
Then recite mentally or out loud the following
Performance script, based on the purification process
Of the Master Altruist, pausing after each section
For as long as you like to envision its imagery,
Focus on your experience, or contemplate its meaning.

1. *Wheel Family Pledge: Personal Refuge and Altruism*
"Confident in the laws of causality and emptiness,
I take refuge in my mentor and all enlightened beings,
In their teaching of non-dual wisdom and empathic art,
And in the community of all who practice it!
From now until I reach perfect awakening
I'll conceive the spirit of enlightenment,
Develop unwavering altruistic resolve,
And give up any reified sense of 'I' or 'mine!'"

1a. *Jewel Family Pledge: The Four Boundless States*
"From now until I embody enlightenment
I'll cultivate all four contemplative states—
Pure love, compassion, joy and equanimity!
May all beings know true freedom and its causes!
May we all share lasting happiness and its causes!
May we all enjoy abundant gratitude!
And may we all live in equanimity and peace!"

1b. *Scepter Family Pledge: Relying on the Master Altruist*
"Within the vast space of clear light, free from perplexity,
On a vast rainbow lotus with sun and moon cushions,
Sits my prime mentor and refuge, the *Master Altruist.*
Pure sapphire blue, his hands hold a scepter and bell,
Symbolizing the union of wisdom and empathic art,
In blissful embrace with his partner, *Lady Ecstasy.*

Sapphire blue, she holds a chopper and skull bowl,
Symbolizing the union of bliss and translucency."

1c. *Consecrating and Honoring the Mentor-Archetype*
"Lit from within by three syllables of gem-toned light—
A diamond *OM*, ruby *AH*, sapphire *HUM*—
Glowing like beacons on moon-discs at your crown, throat and heart
You beam rainbow lights everywhere, inviting the spirits
Of all mentor-archetypes, all enlightened beings,
All altruists and protectors to join you as one!
Mentor of threefold enlightenment, I honor you!
Your truth body's openness is free from perplexity,
Your enjoyment body shares the flow of pure joy,
Your emanation body shows compassion to all!
By your grace, all three bodies instantly dawn,
I sit at your feet, *Master Altruist*, Father-Mother!"

2. *Sword Family Pledge: Outer, Inner and Global Offerings*
"With a pure, open mind, unattached, and undaunted,
Free from any conception of my giving gifts,
I offer you all things sensual, intimate, and ecstatic,
Including my mind, body, virtues, and resources,
This exquisite jewel globe teeming with wildlife,
With all its oceans, continents, rivers, and mountains,
And all planets, moons, suns, and galaxies,
Down to the microcosm in each atom!
MENTOR, PLEASE ACCEPT THIS PRECIOUS LIFEWORLD!"

3. *Confessing and Purifying all Faults, Limits, and Blocks*
"All the limiting habits and instincts of body-speech-mind,
I've acquired in this life, learned or inherited from past lives,
From the depths of my heart, I admit and regret here and now,
And resolve with your help to stop and correct every one!"

4. *Identifying With All Virtues and Qualities*
"Though all things lack intrinsic reality or identity,
From the depths of my heart I rejoice in all the qualities
You enjoy and all the forms of happiness they bring
Like dreams to all beings, confused and enlightened!
Filled with gratitude, I dedicate my joy to becoming
A *Master Altruist* who can help and free all living beings!"

5. *Sword Family Pledge: Requesting the Mentor's Help*
"Viewing all success, mundane and transcendent,
As coming of proper reliance on you, my role-model,
Gemlike source of all refuge, virtue, and excellence,
Please fully empower my body, speech, mind and deeds,
And inspire me to use this precious body and life
To master the arts of both stages, remove all my blocks,
And realize your state of gemlike integration quickly!
Moved by my heartfelt request, Father-Mother, from your heart
Syllables you beam wisdom muses and geniuses
Who consecrate me with nectars that melt through my crown,
Filling and clearing my whole neural network of bliss
And empowering me to practice the stages that consume
All the energies and chemistry of stress and trauma!"

6. *Scepter Family Pledge: Requesting Communion*
"Moved by affection, you send a mini-double of you
Who comes to my crown and melts into one taste with me,
Dissolving my ordinary world, body, and mind
Like a dream into the clear light of blissful emptiness!
From the womb of emptiness my clear light mind becomes
A vast rainbow lotus with sun and moon cushions
From which my affirmative thought bubbles up as a sapphire
Light syllable HUM, in which all my vowels and constants,
Neural energy and mind merge as one, beaming a rainbow
Aura, within which I take bodily form as the sapphire blue
Master Altruist, Father-Mother, in blissful embrace,
Holding a scepter and bell, chopper and skull-bowl,
Symbolizing the union of great bliss and pure clarity!
Lit from within by a diamond OM, ruby AH,
Sapphire HUM on moon discs at my crown, throat, and heart,
I beam rainbow lights everywhere to invite all altruists
To melt into me and merge as one, while wisdom muses
And geniuses consecrate me with pure bliss-void nectars."

6a. *Jewel/Sword Family Pledges: Guarding Aims and Pledges*
"My mind, body, life-world, virtues, and resources,
I share without reservation to help and free others!
My commitments and pledges to personal freedom,
Embodying compassion and blissful openness,
I resolve to hold as dear as this precious life!"

6b. *Optional Mantra Recitation*

"Encircling the moons and HUM syllables at my heart
Are the affirmations of Father and Mother,
Their syllables of 3-D sapphire light facing out
Stand at twelve equidistant points around the rim:
MAY WE ALL QUICK-LY BE-COME MAS-TER AL-TRU-ISTS!
MAY WE ALL QUICK-LY BE-COME PURE RE-AL-ITY!
Reciting them makes the affirmations beam
Enlightened beings in all directions, throughout space and time,
Delighting the enlightened, and helping and freeing all others,
Then returning with validation and gratitude to melt
Into the affirmation rings and the HUMs at my heart."

*As you recite the mantras 7, 21, 108 or more times, imagine
Them rotating counterclockwise so fast they seem to stand still,
While the moon disc beneath them revolves like a twelve-spoke
Wheel clockwise in the same way. See the affirmation rings
Heating up until they beam rainbow lights through your pores
And all around the world, gathering the blissful wisdom of all
Enlightened beings and retrieving it to dissolve back into itself,
Making the affirmation wheel glow even more until it beams to
All beings and worlds all around, dispelling the limits that block
Their altruism, transforming them all into Father-Mother Master
Altruists. Then imagine them all sending duplicates of themselves
As the Master Altruist Father-Mother in gratitude back to you,
Melting like so many sapphire blue snowflakes of clear light into
Your body and heart-drop. After the recitation, immerse yourself
In the resonance and afterglow as deeply as possible, shifting your
Focus from the affirmation wheel at your heart to the moon, from
The moon to your body as the Master Altruist, Mother-Father,
From your body to the body of the Master-Altruist Mother-Father
Before you, and finally back to your body. Take a deep abdominal
Breath and gently hold it as you focus on your sapphire body,
And as you exhale be mindful that it is empty of any non-
Relative being, essence, nature, identity, or objectivity (1 or 3X).*

6c. *Optional Self-Creation Offering*

"With a pure, open mind unattached and undaunted,
Free from any conception of my giving gifts,
My heart syllable beams twelve youthful muses and geniuses,
Who turn to offer me all things sensual, intimate,
And ecstatic, including this gem-like globe teeming with wildlife,

With all its oceans, continents, rivers, and mountains,
And all planets, moons, suns, and galaxies,
Down to the universe in each atom, saying:
MASTER ALTRUIST, PLEASE ENJOY THIS PRECIOUS LIFEWORLD!"

6d. *Optional Self-Creation Acknowledgment*
"Affirming my dignity as a *Master Altruist*,
My character is compassionate openness;
Free from birth and death, creation, and destruction,
I embody the union of great bliss and emptiness!
Affirming my dignity as *Lady Ecstasy*,
My nature transcends coarse physical matter;
Free from birth and death, creation and destruction,
My clarity is the sole mother of all the enlightened!"

7. *Wheel/Lotus Family Pledges: Guarding Ethics and Teaching*
"I will guide and free all beings by mastering and modeling
The wisdom and methods of all three vehicles on the gradual path,
And dedicate all my virtue to renewing the tradition
And realizing the aims of our blissful heritage!"

7a. *Sword Family Pledge: Committing to Practice*
"By the kindness of the four jewels and relativity
And the living example of my mentor-archetype,
May I complete both optimal stages in this very life,
And reach the integration of Gem-like Mastery!"

7b. *Optional Extended Review of Threefold Commitments and Vows*
"I will observe the twenty-five acts of a *Heroic Altruist*:
Abstain from violence, deceit, stealing, promiscuity, and intoxicants;
Avoid gambling, unhealthy food, harsh speech, ritualized cruelty, or conflict;
End slaughter, ritual violence at men, women or children, attacks on shrines;
Renounce anger towards great sages, guides, elders, mentors, spiritual groups;
Renounce attachment to the five senses and their respective objects."
"I will practice the five general and five special Process Family Pledges:

The wheel family pledge to practice altruism and threefold ethics;
The scepter family pledge to mind scepter, bell, union, and mentor-bonding;
The jewel family pledge to offer wealth, protection, teaching, and love;
The lotus family pledge to uphold the teachings of all three vehicles;
The sword family pledge to maintain all commitments and make offerings;
The special wheel pledge to harness confusional states towards integration;
The special scepter pledge to harness aggression towards fierce compassion;
The special jewel pledge to harness acquisitiveness towards philanthropy;
The special lotus pledge to harness passion towards intuitive wisdom;
And the special sword pledge to harness competitiveness towards empathic art."
"And I will avoid the fourteen prime Process Pitfalls:
Devaluing the mentor;
Disregarding the teachings;
Harboring anger towards the process family;
Abandoning love for any being;
Abandoning the spirit of enlightenment;
Devaluing other teachings or practices;
Disclosing secrets to the unprepared;
Abusing my mind/body systems;
Underestimating the teaching;
Indulging negative influences;
Undermining others' confidence;
Intellectualizing the teachings;
Neglecting my practice pledges;
Disrespecting the opposite sex."

Nuts and Bolts: Using the Lightning Six-Session Practice for Novice Practice

Here again, our twin meditative experiments, however abbreviated and condensed, likely are far more complex and advanced than most of you would choose for regular practice. Knowing this, Tibetan masters routinely teach extremely abbreviated, "lightning" forms of these key practices, which may be downloaded from the Nalanda Institute website. These forms of practice are meant to give beginners an initial taste for the affirmative spirit and ethos of all process practice. Practiced six times daily or in brief morning and evening sessions, this practice is like a time-release medicine that helps us get through the day while staying in touch with the lifeline of our bond with our chosen mentor-archetype, tradition, and community.

With this brief introduction to the ethics of the mentor-student bond at the heart of all process teaching, we've completed our journey through the constructive phase of process practice. Now we're finally ready to turn to the integrative phase of intuitive realization that is the topic of part 4.

Part 4

Turning the Bliss Wheel

Sublimation and Natural Healing

10 Sublimation—Tapping and Channeling Flow

In general, all systems of optimal integral process perfection stage involve the preliminary process of controlling the vital energies flowing through the two side channels, (called) luscious and succulent, and redirecting them into the central channel, (called) released. This is indispensable. There are numerous means for accomplishing this, based on the traditions of the Indian great adepts, who drew from the various tantric systems ... When these energies enter the central channel the four blisses are induced, and one cultivates meditation on the basis of these in such a way as to give rise to the innate wisdom of the great seal.

(Tsong Khapa, *A Book of Three Inspirations*[1])

Ascending the Diamond Ladder: The Gradual Path of Process Practice

Once we've opened our minds to our full altruistic potential with the arts of role-modeling imagery and narrative self-creation, we're ready to enter the final stage of process practice: the work of intuitive realization based on tapping and harnessing blissful openness. In some ways, this art is easier for us as moderns to conceive than the complex imagery of the creation stage. This is because of its intimate relationship with the contemplative map of the central nervous system, and its focus on non-conceptual flow states of intense bliss and clarity. In other ways, the work of this stage on the gradual path—traditionally seen as the *real* work of process practice—is even harder for us to wrap our minds around than the virtual simulations of the creation stage, since it involves transforming bliss states and their neural wetware from isolated peak experiences into the mind/body fabric of a whole new way of life.

Surprising or not, our mixed reception of the perfection stage and its blissful art is not unique to us as moderns, but seems to have been shared by our predecessors in ancient India and renaissance Tibet. In his overview of the perfection stage in the *Illuminating Lamp*, Tsong Khapa first relates why the founders of the "noble tradition" of process teaching and practice—Nagarjuna and Aryadeva—took such pains to explain the need for both the constructive and deconstructive arts on the process path, comparing their gradual stages to the rungs on a ladder.[2] To expand on this he cites the *Vajra Angel*:

In order to realize the core yoga
One should practice the artificial
Meditation and recitation.
Once one realizes the core yoga,
Since it is realized by going out
Beyond the artificial yoga,
One should not practice any artifice.
For example, one takes a boat
And goes across the water,
And then leaves it, once beyond.
Artifices are like that:
Such rites as *mandalas* and so on,
Which are made with the artificial mind,
Since they clear up one's (habitual) outer actions,
Are recommended for beginners.
All those accomplishments are present here (in the creation stage),
But not in the knowledge reality of the Victor.[3]

This passage highlights the fact that the gradual path applies not just to the phases of self-healing and social engagement, but to process practice as well. Short of priming the mind and nervous system by freeing them from the grip of traumatic reactivity, it would be impossible for an ordinary person to harness sensual enjoyment without reinforcing the reactive life of obsession, addiction and compulsion. In positive terms, however artificial, the reconstructive arts of the creation stage are unavoidable if we are to develop the vision and self-confidence we need to successfully practice the perfection stage art of sublimation. This is the source of the common metaphors of the creation stage as a boat to the perfection stage, and of all the steps on the gradual path leading up to the state of a master altruist as the rungs on a ladder. Yet, given the goal oriented nature of the human mind, it seems to have been as common a misconception in Tsong Khapa's day as it is in ours, that the preliminary nature of renunciation, compassion, role-modeling and self-creation means that they are not truly necessary at all. This leads to the prime misconception of perfection stage practice as a short-cut which lets us dispense with the hard work of gradual preparation and training. Of course, such misconceptions are easy enough if we take literally the provocative, iconoclastic pronouncements of this stage, such as this passage Tsong Khapa quotes from the *Esoteric Accomplishment*:

Do not salute deities,
Made of wood, stone, or clay;

> Worship the body itself!
> Venerate it as a mentor and bow to it!
> Don't make shrines, etc. from earth and stone,
> Do not delight in books,
> And don't make hand gestures in *mandalas*, and so on,
> Even in your dreams![4]

Or this poetic song of realization he quotes from the arrow-maker turned process adept Saraha:

> Eating and drinking, enjoying sexual union,
> Again and again fill the circle!
> By such teaching as this,
> You will achieve transcendence in this world;
> Here we have triumphed,
> Hitting the world of ignorance on the head![5]

How exactly should we hear transgressive pronouncements like these? Right behind the iconoclastic advice, "Do not salute deities made of wood, stone, or clay," the quote urges us to do something that sounds shockingly modern: "worship the body itself!" But once we're on the next line, we see that the body we're encouraged to worship is not the ordinary body-image in our traumatized minds, or the gross anatomy underlying it, but rather the body purified and reborn in the image of our mentor-archetype, through the arts of the coarse and subtle creation stage. So, without being bound by initiation to re-envision our mind/body process in the image of our ideal role-model, without revising our compulsive history into a creative life of heroic altruism, and without learning to import our mentor's image, affirmation, and affect into our mind/body systems and elements, we could hardly be expected to grasp, let alone follow the imperative of that passage, "Venerate (the body) it(self) as a mentor and bow to it!" On the other hand, once we have been so prepared, how do we make the transition from the artificial practices of the creation stage to the natural practice of the perfection stage? To explore this bridge, let's return to the provocative and richly symbolic words of the great adept, Saraha.

Eating Breath Energy and Drinking Bliss Nectar: The Middle Way of Sublimation

Saraha's passage seems to address the simple facts of life, "Eating and drinking, enjoying sexual union, again and again fill the circle." If we take this circle to be the inner circle of life systems and elements personified as subpersonalities, he seems to be saying something that may be familiar by now: by following a middle way of enjoying objects of desire without indulging compulsions, we can care for our bodies and nurture the animal spirits of love and compassion. Yet in the next lines, we begin to lose our bearings, as the poet-adept alludes to the self-transcendent process of sublimation, "By such teaching as this, you will achieve transcendence in this world." Is sublimation the teaching he means? Reading on, the last couplet seems to confirm this, describing the ultimate triumph over self-deception that comes of harnessing sublimated bliss energy to the profound intuitive realization of emptiness, "Here we have triumphed, hitting the world of ignorance on its head!" Yet if we continue to read beyond the stanza cited above, the next stanza doesn't bring clarity, but goes on in deeply allusive terms:

> Where energy and mind no longer move,
> And sun and moon no longer function,
> Ignorant ones, in that place the mind will be relieved!
> There arrow maker has herein taught all personal instructions.[6]

So, having started out in seemingly familiar terrain, here we find ourselves in the realm of an altered state and peak experience that seem hard to even imagine, described in a symbolic code that seems undecipherable. It is here that we must turn to Tsong Khapa as our guide. His explanation of this verse brings us back to the concise formula of sublimation we cited as our opening passage, taken from another of his works on perfection stage practice. Here are Tsong Khapa's comments on Saraha's realization song:

> Thus, he says that, by relying on the art of penetrating the vital points in the outer and inner body, injecting the sun and moon wind-energies into the (central) released channel and dissolving them, burning the furor (fire) and melting the enlightenment spirit, and filling the body and uniting bliss and void, you eradicate ignorance and encompass all personal instructions.

From these comments, we see that statements like Saraha's help us transition into perfection stage practice by addressing not just the body as purged by initiation and revised by self-creation, but what process science calls the "subtle body": the central nervous system as discovered and mastered on the perfection stage. When he describes the place "where energy and mind no longer move" and "sun and moon no longer function," Saraha is in fact indicating not just a discrete altered state but a specific location on the process map of the nervous system. That location is central to process practice since it is seen as the source of the blissful chemistry which fuels the realization by which "the mind will be relieved" of the compulsive instincts that anchor and block enlightenment. So reaching that place means completing the first leg of the journey of the perfection stage: accessing the neurobiology of blissful flow that powers sublimation.

Channeling Breath-Energy: The Neuropsychology of Sublimation

In this chapter, we'll explore how the art of sublimation is taught to those preparing for perfection stage practice, as well as how the process approach to the nervous system may be best understood in light of modern neuroscience and neuropsychology. To begin with, you may have noticed that the terms Tsong Khapa chose to unpack Saraha's allusive lines dovetail neatly with those of the opening passage we quoted from his *Book of Three Inspirations*. Along with Saraha's, these two passages introduce the idea that the art of sublimation depends on learning how control of the breath yields control of neural energy. They then suggest that balancing natural polarities of neural energy allows for direct access to core energies within the central nervous system. They further claim that controlling core neural energies allows for control of the neurochemistry of bliss and the induction of bliss states. And finally, they conclude that harnessing such bliss states as a platform for process insight mediation supports the most complete and profound realization of intuitive wisdom, freeing the mind from the grips of its most ingrained conditioning and instinctive patterns.

In short, from the standpoint of our beginning practice on the creation stage, they point beyond the external (coarse creation stage) vision of our outer body, speech and gestures as mirroring our mentor-archetype's; beyond the internal (subtle creation stage) vision of our mind/body processes, inner dialogue and affective tone as mirroring our mentor-archetype's; towards a direct (perfection stage) experience of our own nervous system as the natural source of a mentor-archetype's altruistic spirit and mastery. Of course, the first thing that is patently clear for most moderns encountering such teachings is that this approach to "worshiping the body" seems far less like the hedonism we're so used to than a daunting experiment to be undertaken by serious contemplatives or professional neuroscientists. Is this complex and rigorous approach to exploring and mastering our own nervous systems really necessary? More to the point, is it really accessible or appropriate for a general audience of non-professionals?

Sublimation: The Gateway to Natural Self-Regulation and Change

As for the first question, I opened this chapter with Tsong Khapa's quote because it makes clear that mastering the art of sublimation is an indispensable necessity for anyone ready, willing and able to transition their process practice from the initial phase of perceptual restructuring to the final work of intuitive realization. It's notable that he makes this general statement in the context of *A Book of Three Inspirations*, a work which sets out to explain a particular system of perfection stage practice. That system is based mainly on the mother class of optimal integral process, such as the *Supreme Bliss Wheel* teachings handed down from the great Nalanda abbot Naropa[7] to Marpa the translator and his main student, Milarepa,[8] renowned as the first Tibetan to reach full enlightenment. In describing this system, known as the six practices of Naropa, Tsong Khapa puts the emphasis on the first—the practice known as inner heat, psychic heat, inner fire or furor fire—which I refer to with the modern psychological term "sublimation," drawn from the Western alchemical tradition. His case for emphasizing this art is that the control of neural energies it entails is necessary to lay the foundation for all perfection stage practices:

> In this tradition the expression, "the inner heat, the foundation," is well known. This is because in the perfection stage *yogas* one uses the inner

Figure 10.1 Naropa, Master of the Art of Sublimation

> heat technology from the very beginning in order to collect the subtle life-sustaining energies into the central channel, and thereby arouse the innate great ecstasy. This is the actual basis upon which all practices rely, and upon which later completion stage *yogas* are founded. The inner heat doctrine establishes this basis.[9]

Given this rationale, the art of sublimation is not incidental or optional for anyone who wants to progress beyond "the artificial" phase of process practice, based on the restructuring arts of role-modeling imagery and narrative self-creation, coarse and subtle. In other words, this art is the gateway to the "core yoga" of process practice: the art of blissful openness which is as natural as it is life-transforming.

As for the second question, whether this art is truly accessible and appropriate for lay students, a good place to begin is by consulting the teaching guidelines we surveyed in chapter 9. Even a quick glance at the commitments, pledges and pitfalls of process ethics makes it clear that the answer is not a black or white yes or no, but highly nuanced. In principle, the *Wheel of Time* system makes clear that offering explicit teaching *about* sublimation came to be seen as a public service that is appropriate for any curious citizen of planet earth, and should be accessible to all.[10] Yet that doesn't mean the same applies to teaching any individual or group *how to actually practice* sublimation. In practice, all process traditions find their own way to strike the delicate balance of openly introducing the idea of sublimation while selectively teaching the insights and skills that make up the art.

Generally, this strategy of selective preparation begins even with introductory process practices of the kind we've focused on in part 3. For instance, the active process of the *Healing Mother*, as well as the closely related practice of her male counterpart, *Sublime Care*, both teach an advanced breath-control practice that serves to prepare students for the practice of sublimation in optimal integral process systems. Likewise, two of our meditative experiments—with the active process of the *Healing Mentor* and the self-corrective process of the *Heroic Altruist*—include the simulated flow of bliss-nectar, filling the body from above and below, which serves to prepare students for the rush of bliss chemistry released when we bring neural energies into the central channel through inner fire practice on the perfection stage. In a real sense, then, all that changes as we transition into the perfection stage is that these rudimentary insights and skills are assembled into a coherent practice with explicit goals and clear links to the neural map and neural feedback techniques of the perfection stage.

When I introduce this final phase of the gradual path to novices, I follow this selective tradition. Observing the open-source method of the *Wheel of Time*, I introduce the idea of sublimation—of learning to tap and harness blissful states—as indispensable to the final phase of process practice, with its aim of fostering natural healing by using bliss states to realize intuitive openness. At the same time, following the tradition of the introductory process practices like the *Healing Mother* and *Healing Mentor*, I teach only the most rudimentary skills of advanced breath control and simulated flow, in order to "plant the seeds" for later perfection stage practice, as my Tibetan colleagues say. Of course, when working with optimal integral process initiates, I often help practitioners explore perfection stage arts like inner fire when they've already received instruction and feel ready to practice. In this chapter, we'll begin by exploring the advanced insights and breath-control skills associated with the exercise commonly called vase breathing, a key preparatory practice for sublimation. We'll do this in the traditional way, in the context of the sevenfold role-modeling process of the *Healing Mother*.

Meditative Exercise 10.1: Enhancing Clarity and Calm with Vase Breathing

Imagine yourself in a safe healing environment, on top of the world,
Feeling freely connected to all living beings,
Facing a gathering of the healing mentors, teachers,
Texts, and communities that most open your heart and mind.
Sitting comfortably with hands placed,
Balance your energies with nine alternate nostril breaths,
Then by fully expelling all the air from your lungs one or two times.
Now read the following performance script,
Based on the active process of the Healing Mother,
Pausing after each section for as long as you like
To hold its imagery, try the recommended breath practice,
Focus on your experience, or seal in its meaning.

1. *Invoking and Admiring the Healing Mother*
"Suddenly everything melts into pure, blissful openness!
In the vast space before me, your perfect reality
Reflects a giant rainbow lotus of pure release,
In the midst of which your clear light translucency
Dawns like the moon's reflection in water, constant
And present as sheer unconditional love.
Bubbling up from the moon beams a shaft of diamond light,
A 3-D exclamation point, like a beacon of healing speech,
Beaming a rainbow aura of five pure energies,
And resonating with the pure affirmation—
MAY ALL BE SAFE, WELL, AND FREE!
Suddenly amidst the rainbow orb of that aura
You assume the moonlight form of the *Healing Mother*,
Sitting in meditation on your moon-cushion and lotus.

Lit from within at your crown, throat, heart, navel, and pelvis
By five gem-toned exclamation points on moon discs
At the vital points along your central channel,
Your translucent form glows with a rainbow aura
Of unconditional openness and healing art,
Embodying the love that is the mother of us all,
With all the marks and signs of perfect maturity.
Smiling in rapt attentiveness, with five extra,
Intuitive eyes in your mid-brow, palms, and soles,
You make every gesture a consummate art.
At ease in the rainbow silks of five freedoms, you wear
The six transcendent virtues as ornaments.
Your right hand, palm held out over your knee,
Offers protection and freedom from trauma,
Your left hand, palm facing out at your heart, holds the stem
Of three lotuses blossoming over your shoulder—
The arts of well-being, compassion and genius!"

1a. *Inviting Your Mentor's Spirit to Ground Your Vision*
"Glowing serenely as a living moon, radiating
A rainbow aura of indivisible intuition and love,
Your heart-seed beams lights to invite your spirit and the genius
Of all healing beings to merge into you as one,
As the muses of enlightenment consecrate you,
Pouring nectars of blissful openness through your crown,
Filling you and overflowing as a long-life Buddha crown."

1b. *Taking Refuge in Your Role-Model's Example*
"Confident in the presence of your blissful openness,
I take refuge in your non-dual wisdom and art.
To free and heal all sensitive beings I now conceive
The altruistic spirit of enlightenment,
And resolve to develop myself and all beings quickly,
Until we gain the enlightenment to heal our world!"

2. *Welcoming the Healing Mother into Your World*
"In the aura of your healing truth, all things have the taste
Of blissful openness, pervading the mind and all the senses!
Welcoming you gratefully into my world, I offer
A sun-shower of sense delights—scented waters,
Incense, flowers, lights, music, and delicacies—
Converging toward you from everywhere, horizon and sky!
Fully and freely I share with you all my resources,

Virtues, and every aspect of my intimate life,
Plus this precious earth, with its oceans, continents,
Wonders, forests, waters, and infinite web of life!"

3. *Fully Disclosing Your Faults, Limits, and Blocks*
"Regretting all the demon-like instincts and habits I've indulged,
All the patterns that limit and block me from your way of being
From the depths of my heart I admit every one of them now,
And firmly resolve from here on to avoid and unlearn them all."

4. *Enjoying the Qualities of Transcendent Healing*
"Though all things are empty of any non-relative being,
With gratitude I enjoy all the myriad forms
Of happiness you experience and share with all life,
And all the transcendent virtues that serve as their cause."

4a. *Enhancing Enjoyment with the Four Boundless Moods*
"May all beings have real happiness and its causes!
May we all be freed from all suffering and its causes!
May we all enjoy and savor all excellent things!
May we all know unwavering equanimity!" (Repeat 3X)

5. *Requesting Help on the Stage of Intuitive Realization*
"From the bottom of my heart I ask you, *Healing Mother*,
Please share with me your healing purity, genius, and art!
Thrilled to be asked, the *Healing Mother* emits rainbow light
From the moon and sapphire exclamation point at her heart,
Filling galaxies to the furthest reaches of space,
Drawing the boundless renunciation, compassion, and wisdom
Of all geniuses of all five kinds throughout space and time
Back to melt into her heart, then beaming them all to me
As a rainbow wave that engulfs and fills my body with light,
Transforming my mind into a heart-moon of lucid awareness,
My speech into a blue exclamation point of affirmative thought,
And my body into the milk-white body of a *Healing Mother*."

5a. *Requesting the Mother's Purification and Protection*
"Knowing that the gross transformation of my body-speech-mind
Is a mere simulation, from the depths of my heart I ask you,
Healing Mother, please share with me the subtle
Intuitive essence of your five-fold purity, genius and art!
Happily, you emit gem-toned lights from the five points
Of your subtle body to purify and transform
All five core systems of my subtle body-mind.

As your rainbow beam of five gem-toned healing lights
Reaches the five gem-toned exclamation points
At the crown, throat, heart, navel, and pelvic complexes
Within my central channel, it purifies my five,
Energies and intuitions, until they radiate
Five gem-toned lights that tune my inner life to yours,
Beaming from my pores and setting up a rainbow shield
Of five gem-toned laser lights and laser lotuses,
That disintegrate and transform any triggering input
From the outside world. Safe within the firewall of your
Pure intuition and art, I release stress and trauma,
And fully immerse myself in your healing genius."

5b. *Enhancing Stress-Protective Imagery with Vase Breathing*
"Safe, well, and free in the circle of your healing genius,
And inspired by your living example I ask for help
Tapping into the healing genius of my own body-mind,
By mastering the arts of vase breathing and inner fire."
In a comfortable cross-legged posture, once again
Clear and balance your energies with nine alternate nostril breaths,
And firmly and fully expel any stale air from your lungs.
Now imagine the Healing Mother, with you inside your laser shield,
Beams rainbow lights from her heart-seed everywhere,
Drawing into herself the warmth, inspiration, and blessings
Of all the enlightened. Focused on her, slowly take in a full
And deep abdominal breath, feeling the air, saturated with
Her rainbow energy-light, filling you up like a person-shaped
Bubble of blissful openness, especially gathering in your abdomen
Until it fills like a balloon. Then nod your head and swallow,
Pressing your breath down toward the sun-gold exclamation
Point four fingers below your navel as gently as you would
Massage a balloon in your hands. Now, very gently tone the
Muscles of your pelvic floor Stimulating warm, sensual energy,
And draw that energy up to meet the in-breath at the point
Below your navel, very gently mixing the energies from above
And below, Holding and pressing them together from above and
Below as you would massage a balloon between your two hands.
Imagine the navel point glowing with the Mother's rainbow
Energy-light, purifying the core of your body-mind of reactive
Instincts and habits, and transmuting the five toxins into
Rainbow lights and nectars.

Well before any distress, relax your nod and pelvic floor,
Slowly and gently releasing the breath out your nostrils
And seeing it beam rainbow lights out through your shield
To the five types of compulsive beings everywhere,
Transforming them all into Healing Mothers and the earth into a
Sphere of long life and pure health (3, 7, or 21X)!

5c. *Optional Vase-Breath Recitation Practice*
Envision the Mother's affirmation ringing the moon-disc
And sun-gold exclamation point below the navel,
Made of 3-D sun-gold light, facing out, with each word
Placed equidistant at eight points like spokes:
MAY ALL LIFE BE SAFE, WELL, AND FREE!
Now as you draw a vase breath, nod, swallow, and press down,
Then tone the pelvic floor, draw any energy up, see the energies
From above and below meet at the affirmation ring and point,
And mentally recite the affirmation while holding the breath
As long as you can. As you recite, imagine the ring and point
Glowing with the Mother's rainbow energy light, taking
Care to release your nod and pelvic tone well before any distress,
Exhaling slowly and gently while continuing to recite, releasing
The breath out your nostrils and seeing it beam rainbow lights
Out through your shield to the five types of compulsive beings
Everywhere, Transforming them all into Healing Mothers and
The earth into a sphere of long life and pure health! You can
Practice this during 1, 3, or 7 breaths, but avoid counting the
Number of affirmations you recite so as not to push your limits.

5d. *Closing the Vase Breathing Session*
"One with the dignity of the *Mother's* healing genius,
I look with your care at the world all around—
Find the *Healing Mother* in all living beings;
See all things enfolded in your healing art;
And hear all sounds echoing your affirmation!"

6. *Requesting Constancy Until Enlightenment*
"Knowing that this practice is mere simulation,
I ask you please to be my constant protector, companion,
And guide, from now until I integrate your mastery,
And my five systems embody your fivefold genius!
Moved by affection for me, you my mentor melt
From your crown and toes to the moon and exclamation point
At her heart, which in turn melt into the point's single dot,
Like a tear-drop for joy, coalescing all your intuitions and energies.

Glowing with rainbow light, your heart-drop comes to my crown
And melts like bliss-nectar down my central channel,
To my heart, merging yourhealing essence with mine, beaming
Light and warmth up and down to all my five vital points,
Until they fill me as flames fill a beacon and nectars
Fill a vase, rippling out in all my intentions and actions,
Out through my shield until all those around me become
Healing Mothers, returning a wave of joy to my heart!"

*Now pause to absorb and drink in the warmth and moisture of
That joy, as long and deeply as you can, and then prepare to close
The session:*

"Suddenly the world outside, my healing space and body
All return to their normal appearance, the six shells outside
And the five moons and points inside all melt into my heart,
Then the exclamation point melts into the dot of my heart-drop."

7. *Dedicating Insight and Energy to Mastering Sublimation*
"Any intuition and energy I've gained through this practice,
I dedicate to integrating my mentor's intuitive essence
In this lifetime, as quickly as possible! And so, by mastering
The arts of role-modeling, vase breathing and inner fire,
May I purify my five compulsions, embody the five intuitions,
And transform my mind/body systems into the *Mother's*."

Vase Breathing in Context: Mapping the Perfection Stage

With this brief introductory taste of basic vase breathing, we're ready to put it in the context of perfection stage practice and unpack its use and significance. To do this, we must survey the process approach to the nervous system and its regulation, linking these as best we can with the findings of contemporary neuroscience and stress research. The references we've been unpacking thus far each exemplify the traditional way in which the stage for vase-breathing is set, by making reference to the *yogic* model of the nervous system. As we've seen, that model revolves around the central channel said to run vertically from crown to pelvis along the neural axis, punctuated by a series of neural complexes literally called wheels (*chakras*). Before we describe that model and its role in vase-breathing in any detail, it helps to contextualize it within the larger map of the contemplative journey of the optimal integral process.

Let's first take a step back to part 3, where we traced that journey from the gateway of initiation through the first leg of the journey, the phase of transforming our familiar perception of self and world on the creation stage. That leg of the journey led us from our encounter with a congenial mentor-archetype to a full revision of our self-image through the art of role-modeling imagery. From there, we moved to the next step: putting our new heroic self-image in motion in the time-dimension, by transforming our ordinary life history through the process of narrative self-creation. With our vision of our external body, social self, and life-world transformed in the image of our mentor-archetype's, we embarked on the next leg of the journey.

In the subtle creation stage, our journey led inward, to revise our ordinary sense of the inner world of our body, speech and mind, in the image of our mentor-archetype's extraordinary inner world and life. There we began to envision our body as manned by a new inner circle of enlightened agencies, symbolized by miniature images of our mentor-archetype's body and/or speech. We did so not haphazardly, but following a specific architecture in which each image stands as a signpost for our pending encounter with the "subtle body" of the nervous system. In some of the meditative experiments of part 3, we placed miniature images of our mentor's affirmative speech at key points in our body that lined up with key points in the vertical axis of our central nervous system. As we ended our journey in part 3, we stood on the threshold of the next leg of the journey: a direct encounter with the nervous system or "subtle body" at our core, which supports all levels, states and functions of our consciousness.[11] Once we've reached this threshold, the first leg of the journey through the perfection stage is marked by three successive gateways, representing three milestones of conscious self-regulation. Between these three gateways lie the first two sub-stages of the perfection stage, collectively known as the ordinary perfection stage. Beyond them lie three more gateways, framing the three final sub-stages, collectively known as the great perfection stage.[12]

Freedom of Body, Speech, and Mind: The "Ordinary" Perfection Stage

As you might imagine, the "ordinary" perfection stage is anything but ordinary. The gateway that separates it from the subtle creation stage is a realization known as freedom of body. It refers to the freedom won on the creation stage from our ordinary mental image and concept of our human body, outside and in. Once we're able to consistently free our minds from their habitual identification with our reified bodily self-image, as aided and measured by our ability to identify with the extraordinary body-image of our congenial mentor-archetype, we've passed through the gateway of freedom of body.

At this point we've entered the first perfection sub-stage, named after the gateway that marks the end of that stage: freedom of speech. As you might guess, this gateway is reached when we're consistently able to free our symbolic minds and neural energies from their habitual identification with reified, traumatic habits of thought and speech, along with the stress-reactive patterns of neural energy they rationalize. This realization, aided and measured by our ability to fuse our thought, speech, and energy with the affirmative thought, speech and neural energy of our congenial mentor-archetype, marks our passage through the gateway of freedom of speech.

From here we enter the second perfection sub-stage, also named for the gateway that marks the end of the stage: freedom of mind. Once we're consistently able to free our stream of consciousness from its habitual involvement with stress-emotions and instinctive compulsions, and immerse it fully and constantly in the flow of blissful openness, we've passed through the gateway of freedom of mind, and completed the journey of the ordinary perfection stage.

Inspiration, Translucency, and Communion: The Great Perfection Stage

At the end of the first leg on our journey of intuitive realization, we've reached the real source of lasting freedom and happiness, the place in which we can merge our most primal bliss with the selfless transparency of the objective clear light. From here on, the course of our odyssey shifts from journeying inwards to learning how to return to the world we came from. This final leg of our journey—the great perfection stage—covers three sub-stages on which we learn to develop a pure virtual body and translucent mind out of the blissful openness tapped in the ordinary perfection stage, then finally marry these together to build a new life of altruistic mastery able to transform our world.

Given this sweeping overview of the journey to come in part 4, we're now in a position to locate the art of sublimation and the exercise of vase breathing on that map. In particular, the technique of inner fire, enhanced by the art of diamond recitation, are the main tools we need to progress on the first perfection sub-stage, which leads to true, inner freedom of speech. And this part of our journey will be our main focus in the rest of this chapter. In chapter 11, we'll turn to the next sub-stage and the next phase of sublimation, in which inner fire and diamond recitation, enhanced by real or imaginary intimacy, lead to true, inner freedom of mind. And, in chapter 12, we'll explore the last three sub-stages of the path, in which the arts of inspiration, translucency and communion, enhanced by great seal practice, lead to the final gem-like fruition of altruistic mastery.

Tapping the Subtle Body and Mind: The Triune Model of Process Science

Now for the work of this chapter, unpacking the vase-breathing exercise which prepares us for the inner fire of sublimation, we return to Tsong Khapa's *Book of Three Inspirations*. As I said, this work explores the perfection stage based on the Tibetan Kagyu tradition traced back to Naropa, based mainly on the mother process of the *Supreme Bliss Wheel*.[13] Because this tradition is often seen as definitive when it comes to the technical know-how of sublimation practice, this work is prized for providing invaluable nuts and bolts, step-by-step instruction on the art of inner fire. Not surprisingly, our great Tibetan guide begins his instructions by referencing the same passage from the *Diamond Pavilion Process* with which we opened part 3.

If you recall, that passage insists that process practice offers the quickest, most effective path to altruism because it conjoins two elements in one mind/body technology: the wisdom of emptiness familiar from the engaged insight path and the art of role-modeling which is distinctive to the process path. In particular, when it comes to the art of role-modeling, it alludes to both stages in the process technique of "adopting ... the teacher's form": using role-modeling imagery to simulate that form on the creation stage and using the "blissful art" of sublimation to actually reproduce that form on the perfection stage. So, in the context of unpacking the latter art in this key work, Tsong Khapa sets out to explain how the blissful art depends on mastering the subtle material structure and function of the nervous system, in order to transform our stress-reactive body into a master altruist's body of blissful openness.[14]

First of all, as in the models of current neuroscience, in this model the gross anatomy of the nervous system is described in terms of a subtle material microstructure which involves four structural-functional elements: neural pathways called channels, neural complexes called wheels, neural secretions called drops and neural energies called winds. In addition, the nervous system is also seen as basically plastic, constantly changing in response to mind/body factors like intentions and actions, as well as body-mind causes like diet and lifestyle.

On the other hand, the actual map of the nervous system is strikingly different from our modern maps, more closely resembling the map the nervous system we know from *Hatha* yoga.[15] Yet while all Indic process traditions share this yogic model, the system of core neural channels and complexes we're familiar with is only part of the full triune model used in Buddhist process psychology, psychiatry and medicine.[16] In that model, the nervous system involves three nested levels of microstructure and function supporting three continuous levels of consciousness, not just the one level mapped by the familiar *chakra* map. Also, its complex structure and function varies across a whole spectrum of possible body-mind states, ranging from the defended, fragmented state of an ordinary, reactive body-mind to the completely disarmed and consciously regulated state of an extraordinary, fully integrated body-mind.

In the Buddhist process model, the three nested levels of neuropsychological structure and function are called the gross, subtle, and extremely subtle body-mind. These are akin to the three sheaths or layers of the body-mind mapped by classical yoga psychology: the outermost, physical layer sustained by food and fivefold sense consciousness; the internal, mental layer sustained by the pure neural energy and the sixth sense of mind; and the innermost layer sustained by the subtlest bliss energy inseparable from pure open-mindedness.[17]

According to the Buddhist model,[18] the gross level is supported by branching networks of neural pathways that radiate out from the central neural complexes at the mid-brow, crown, throat, heart, navel, pelvis, and sexual organ, pervading the whole body out to the periphery. Some of the networks—from the crown and heart—are said to curve downwards like the spokes of an umbrella, while others—from the throat and navel—are said to curve upwards like the spokes of an inverted umbrella, the two kinds interweaving where they touch to form two main neural circuits. This outermost layer of neural structure supports gross sensory-motor functions like gathering input from the five senses, as well as executing the movement of the limbs, trunk, neck, and head.

The subtle level of the nervous system[19] is supported by three main channels running together vertically along the neural axis, from the mid-brow and crown to the pelvis and sexual organ. While the central channel runs directly up and down the mid-line from the mid-brow up to the crown and from there down to the tip of the sexual organ, the two side channels run up from each nostril alongside it, winding around the central channel at each of the complexes, knotting off the central channel and constricting the flow of energies and drops in all three channels. The two side channels separate from the central channel below the navel, the right rejoining it at the sexual organ, the left branching off to the anus. The right and left channels, called luscious and succulent,[20] are seen as maintaining reciprocal, regulative functions based on polar energies and drops, described as solar or subjective versus lunar or objective, respectively. The central channel, called released,[21] is seen as maintaining core, vital functions, based on primal energies and drops, also described as masculine and feminine. Together, the three channels and seven main complexes of the subtle body-mind support discursive thinking and symbolic processing by the mind as a sixth sense, as well as the intentional actions of mind like complex emotions.

The extremely subtle body-mind[22] is supported at a molecular level of structure-function only accessible within the central channel, where the subtlest bliss energies are inseparable from the so-called indestructible drop and clear light mind, usually located at the core of the central channel nested deep within the heart complex. The extremely subtle mind-energy-drop is seen as sustaining the functions of primal homeostasis, reinforcement and reward, as well as interfacing with the genetic material derived from the parents' germ cells. This innermost layer of the body-mind is said to support primal, nonconceptual awareness and intuition as well as the unconscious instincts and appetites that normally drive the unconscious mind.

The Subtle Body in Action: Explaining Transitions in Mind/Body State

After describing this model,[23] Tsong Khapa reviews the way it explains alterations in mind/body state based on shifts in the distribution of neural energies and drops through these channels and complexes. In particular, he describes how such shifts support state-changes that naturally occur in daily rhythms like the wake-sleep cycle. As our mind/body state shifts from waking to dream or deep sleep, for instance, the energies and drops based in the crown complex shift towards energies and drops based in the throat and heart complex, respectively. Likewise, state-changes in the course of sexual intimacy are explained based on shifts from energies and drops based in the upper complexes to energies and drops based in the navel, pelvis, or sexual organ (the latter two called the "secret" and "tip of the secret" or "jewel" complexes, respectively). Also crucial is that these changes from more differentiated, complex states to more undifferentiated, primal states involve a progressive shift in neural energies and drops inwards, from the gross body-mind into the subtle and subtlest body-mind. In describing this neural explanatory model, he references the elegant, fourfold system of the *Wheel of Time*:

> The subject is also discussed in the system of the *Kalachakra Tantra*, wherein it is said that the *chakras* at the forehead and navel are associated with the waking state; the *chakras* at the throat and secret place are associated with the dream state; the *chakras* at the heart and jewel are associated with deep sleep; and the *chakras* at the navel and tip of the secret place (or jewel) are associated with the fourth occasion (i.e., sexual ecstasy).[24]

In contrast to these normal physiological changes in mind/body state, the changes we cultivate through process practice involve using techniques like breath-control to consciously regulate shifts in energies and drops, in order to access deeper levels of neural function and profound bliss states, which can serve as platforms on the process path.[25] This is how the process model of the nervous system helps unpack the passages we've quoted, in which the art of inner fire is said to involve controlling the energies within the side channels so we can use them to tap into the bliss-states supported by the extremely subtle energies and drops in the central channel.

Can the Triune Process Model and the Triune Brain Model Be Linked?

Before we apply this model to explain the traditional teachings of vase-breathing and inner fire, it helps to draw some correlations and distinctions between this process map of the nervous system and our modern one, so that, as scientifically educated moderns, we can more easily relate to the ideas and terms used in those teachings. As we've seen, there are clearly some family resemblances linking these very different maps: (1) the basic assumption that mental processes invariably depend on neural structures and functions; (2) the description of those structures and functions using similar explanatory elements: channels and pathways, complexes and nuclei, winds and energies, drops and neurotransmitters; and (3) the view that these structures and functions are plastic and naturally change based on shifts in mental factors like attention, intention, and action, as well as physical factors like diet, lifestyle, illness, and health. At the same time, the process and modern models seem so divergent in their view of the basic structure of the nervous system—a basically top-down, spine-centered view versus a bottom-up, brain-centered view—as to be wholly incompatible.

Of course, this divergence is only natural given the distinct sources, aims and uses of the different maps. The contemplative map based on first-and-second person meditative experience is meant to guide mind/body self-regulation from the inside out. While the brain-based map built on third-person and impersonal observation, gross anatomy, and mechanical experiment, is meant to guide medical and surgical manipulation of the nervous system from the outside in.[26] I believe it's possible to correct for this divergence and bridge the seemingly insurmountable gulf between them by considering the unique nature and structure of neural tissue.

First consider that the process map tends to locate neural structure and function where the embodied mind tends to *feel* them, while the modern map locates them where the outside observer can most easily *measure* them. Next, view this difference in terms of the microstructure of neural tissue: the process map tends to locate neural function at the terminal end of neurons, where their axons end in sensory or motor synapses; while the modern map charts neural function from the proximal end of neurons, where their cell bodies connect with other neurons through dendritic networks, forming the "grey matter" of structures like nuclei or cortex. Now consider this: while the distance between where we feel neural functions occur and where modern brain science maps them may seem large relative to the gross anatomy of the human body, on the cellular level it's usually no more than the length of one or two nerve cells. In other words, even if we think in the most reductive terms, it may be that the gap between these two maps of the nervous system is no greater than the distance from one end of a given nerve cell to the other.

Of course, some might object here that this sort of thinking is culturally insensitive and unfairly reduces a Buddhist map of mind/body states to a Western map of neural structure and function. In one sense, this objection is both unavoidable and absolutely valid. Viewing the subtle body in terms of nerve cells is certainly foreign to the process map, and assumes the explanatory models and methods of our culturally relative sciences. On the other hand, there can be little doubt that the process map is intent on explaining mental processes in the naturalistic terms of "subtle" structural and functional elements within the body that support them. Nor can there be any doubt about the use to which that map is put: to help people gain control over their mental states by understanding and manipulating the psychophysical causality of bodily structures and functions, which we would be hard pressed *not* to relate to our concept of a nervous system. The family resemblance between the process map and our modern map becomes more striking when we compare the kinds of structure and function attributed to each model.

The Subtle Body and Central Nervous System: Two Maps, One Terrain?

If we grant for now that these two culturally distinct models map the same general terrain with divergent aims and means, it may be useful to make some tentative links between aspects of the two models. First, the subtle body map seems analogous to our neural map in terms of the functions it seeks to explain. For instance, its five primary and five secondary wind-energies are said to control the things we see as governed by the nervous system: inspiration, expiration, digestion, excretion, core vital functions like heart rate and mental processing, as well as the function of the five senses. Second, the two side channels of the subtle nervous system are also said to control vital rhythms and functions we see as governed by the central nervous system, including wake-sleep cycles, rhythms of digestion, assimilation and excretion, and cycles of sexual-reproductive function. Finally, at the extremely subtle level within the central channel, the subtle body controls functions we think of as core neural functions, including: vital homeostasis, states of consciousness, levels of activation, instinctive appetites and impulses, as well as consummation and internal reward. Flowing within these channels are masculine, feminine, and mixed drops which modulate levels of consciousness, modes of activation, and degrees of sensual arousal and satisfaction.

Considering the array of functions attributed to the subtle body, it seems quite clear that this model is meant to explain many if not most of the same functions as our neural model. Given this, it seems plausible to align the major structural-functional aspects of the process triune model with the modern model of the triune brain as an organ which integrates three systems of natural intelligence—based in the primate cortex, limbic cortex, and reptilian core brain—with the basic life support system of the brainstem. Assuming the traditional process concept of the gross body-mind, for instance, we may tentatively align it in a very general way with the sensory, motor, and associative regions of the primate neocortex. The subtle body-mind, with its regulation of cognition, emotion, and autonomic rhythms, would seem to generally line up more with the prefrontal cortex and mammalian limbic cortex. And the extremely subtle body-mind, with its regulation of consciousness, instinctive seeking and primal reward, may be very generally aligned with the "reptilian" forebrain, midbrain, and brainstem. A disclaimer: this tentative alignment aims not at some sort of localized cross-mapping, but simply to show that, for general heuristic purposes, the process model has the range and flexibility to encompass the whole spectrum of neural structure and function mapped in the triune brain model.

The Process Model Applied: Mapping the Arts of Vase Breathing and Inner Fire

With this overview of the procedural and neuropsychological context for teaching the art of inner fire, we're ready to look more closely and practically at Saraha's allusive instructions, as unpacked by Tsong Khapa:

> Thus, he says that, by relying on the art of penetrating the vital points in the outer and inner body, injecting the sun and moon wind-energies into the (central) released channel and dissolving them, burning the furor (fire) and melting the enlightenment spirit, and filling the body and uniting bliss and void, you eradicate ignorance and encompass all personal instructions.[27]

Given this brief outline, perhaps the best way to explore the art of sublimation in this tradition is to review each of his four main points systematically. The four are: (1) tapping into the vital points of the central nervous system; (2) balancing the polar energies of the side channels and infusing them into the central channel; (3) kindling the inner fire of sublimation and causing the release, flow, and spread of bliss chemistry throughout the body-mind; (4) sealing the state of orgasmic bliss with the visceral intuition of emptiness.

1. Tapping into the Vital Points of the Central Nervous System

If you recall, the threshold through which we entered the first perfection sub-stage was marked by placing seed-syllables representing the mentor-archetype's affirmative speech at key points along the spinal axis where the central channel is mapped. These syllables now serve as signposts indicating the vital points—such as the crown, heart, navel, or sexual organ—at which it is said to be easiest to gain control over the energies of the central nervous system. By focusing our attention as single-mindedly as possible on syllables visualized at those points, we can begin to prime neural feedbacks that induce shifts in our neural energy, chemistry and state of consciousness.[28] But before we jump to this step, there are a number of exercises—physical and mental—said to help prepare our minds and nervous systems for success in this work.[29] So let's review these exercises under six headings, culminating in the art of vase-breathing. They are: (1) preliminaries; (2) visualizing the body as an empty, person-shaped bubble or shell; (3) breath-capacity exercises; (4) visualizing the channels of the central nervous system; (5) visualizing syllables within the channels; (6) the vase-breathing exercise.

Preliminaries: Role-Modeling the Arts of Perfection

In this context, the preliminaries typically include the first five steps in the sevenfold role-modeling practice we've explored in part 3. They are done in the format of the *Heroic Altruist* practice, with the mentor–archetype of our choice envisioned in miniature, facing forward just above our crown. The format may also be expanded by stacking figures in the historical lineage of mentors who have handed the practice down to our personal mentor, envisioned one above the other in the same form. The key steps include: admiring the mentor–archetype as embodying all refuge; conceiving the spirit of enlightenment in the process-oriented mode of a *Heroic Altruist*; and asking our role-model/lineage for blessing and guidance on the path. When this has begun to stir positive energy, the mentor dissolves through our crown and into our hearts as in the other role-modeling practices, dissolving our ordinary form into clear light until we re-emerge in stages or all at once in his/her image.

Visualizing the Body as an Empty, Person-Shaped Bubble

This second preparatory step should also be familiar. We envision ourselves in the outward form of our chosen archetype, while inside we see our bodies as hollow bubbles of pure energy and awareness. Ideally, we've already dissolved our ordinary body-image and self-sense into clear light, and re-created them in the image of our mentor–archetype. So at this point, we should feel that we're not made of gross physical tissues and organs, but rather of pure, luminous energy and awareness. Any positive imagery we associate with ourselves, such as a sun or moon-cushion, seed-syllable or archetypal physical form, we should try to see as mere reflections or manifestations of clear-light awareness, serving as transparent symbols for our enlightened mind, speech and body. Of course, if we plan to enhance our sublimation practice with imaginary or real intimacy, we need to envision ourselves in the androgynous mother-father form of our archetype, as in the six session practice of the *Master Altruist.*

Process Yoga: The Six Breath-Capacity Exercises of Naropa

Although the Indian process traditions preserved in Tibet date to well before the codification of the wide range of physical postures most of us are familiar with through *Hatha Yoga*, it does involve a smaller set of postures and breath-exercises meant to support the perfection stage art of sublimation. In particular, Tsong Khapa highlights a series of practices called the six exercises of Naropa, all meant to relax, balance, tone, and strengthen the parts of our body and nervous system involved in enhancing what we now call our pulmonary function. If we're doing these to prepare for the perfection stage, there are two initial steps we should take to clear our minds and energies. First, following the preliminaries, we should take care to envision our bodies as empty person-shaped bubbles made of clear light, appearing in the form of our chosen genius archetype. All the six exercises that follow should be practiced while maintaining this exceptional image of our bodies. Next, to clear our energies for the exercises, we should use the technique currently taught as alternate nostril breathing, known to balance and integrate both sides of our central nervous system.

We're now ready to move on to the first of the six exercises, the vase breathing practice we tried in our first meditative experiment, actually a streamlined version of the technique to be practiced in full later on. Once again sitting with back straight and legs crossed, this time we place thumbs inside our fists. We begin by breathing in through both nostrils as slowly and deeply as possible, imagining that the air fills the abdomen like a balloon, and when we're full, swallowing some saliva and sensing it move to a point just below the navel. At the same time, we gently tone the muscles of the pelvic floor as if holding in urine or doing a Kegel exercise. Now, with the air-filled abdomen very gently compressed like a balloon from above and below, we focus our minds deep inside the belly at the navel, holding the breath for as long as we can without force or straining, thinking of our body as a translucent vase of pure energy and awareness, then gently releasing the air out our nostrils. We can repeat the exercise two or six times. The remaining five exercises are all done together with this vase-breathing technique.

The second of the six is called the revolving wheel. Sitting cross legged in the full lotus posture this time, with feet placed up on the opposite thighs, we reach our hands across our bodies to hold the big toe of the left foot with the left hand and the right with the right. Straightening up the spine in its natural curvature, be sure to open the shoulders and upper chest. Now, after taking a vase breath and holding it, we rotate the trunk clockwise three times, then rotate it counterclockwise three times. Taking another vase breath if need be, next we stretch our whole trunk over as far as possible to the right, then after returning gently to center, reverse the movement as far as possible to the left. Finally, with a third vase breath, we arch the abdomen backwards, return to center and then arch it forwards, as if we were doing a seated version of the cat pose (from *Hatha Yoga*). Optionally, we can repeat the whole exercise two or six times.

The third exercise called the binding hook is also done in a seated posture, preferably the lotus, while holding a vase breath. Once again we place the thumb inside our fists, join them at the heart and extend them fully together straight out in front of the heart. Now we stretch both arms together as far as possible to the left, and as if drawing in a hook, slide the right fist back along the left arm and chest, placing it over the right breast. Then we draw back the left fist, placing over the left breast, and finally, firmly tuck both elbows into the sides of the ribs like folded wings. Now we reverse the whole movement, extending the fists from the heart, stretching them right, drawing in the left first, then the right fist, and tucking the elbows in. Optionally, again, we can repeat the whole exercise two or six times.

The fourth exercise called diamond binding begins from a kneeling posture. With spine straight, we bend the ring and middle fingers of both hands into the palm, locking them down with the thumbs while extending the index and pinky fingers out like two horns. With our hands at our sides in the binding gesture, palms facing up, we take and hold a vase breath, then stretch hands out to our sides as far as possible and raise them gradually until they join, pointing up over our heads. Now we turn the hands so their backs touch and palms face out to both sides, and reverse the movement by gradually stretching and lowering them until they touch the ground. Again, we should feel free to repeat the exercise two or six times.

The fifth exercise, the expelling breath-lock, begins by kneeling, bending forward and planting both hands on the ground, as in the cat pose. After raising the head and straightening the spine, we take and hold a vase breath. Now bow the head between the arms and forcefully push all the air from our lungs making a "hah" sound, and hold the breath out for as long as you comfortably can. After raising the head again, we gently draw a full breath in through the nostrils, stand up and shake out our legs and feet, three times each. Again, we may choose to repeat the whole exercise two or six times.

The sixth and last exercise is simply shaking the head and body all over, gently flexing all our joints, and massaging both our hands as if washing them. Of course, this general relaxation and toning could also be achieved by doing a cycle of restorative yoga postures. As in *Hatha Yoga* practice, all such physical preparation and training should be done on an empty stomach, gently and mindfully, while focusing on the breath. Unlike conventional yoga, they should be done as much as possible in conjunction with the exercise of holding vase-breaths, to train ourselves to maintain a baseline of deep, abdominal breathing and a firm yet gentle control of the breath at all times. Of course, the Tibetan masters emphasize over and over again that we must be ever-mindful to practice all these exercises—especially vase breathing—with unwavering patience and gentleness. While this is generally emphasized in most yoga practice, it is absolutely indispensable here, so as not to interfere with the progressive deepening of relaxation we need to tap into the blissful energy and chemistry of the central nervous system.

The Six Exercises: A Total Work-Out for Breath, Body, and Mind

In sum, it seems fairly obvious that these exercises are meant to relax, tone, expand, and strengthen the physical and neural structures supporting our breath capacity. In his commentary on inner fire, Tsong Khapa makes a point of presenting these exercises in detail, despite his explicit mention of the fact that many of the Tibetan traditions he calls "later" have omitted emphasizing or even teaching them as preparations.[30] Though not described in the Indian source texts and commentaries of the process tradition, like those translated into Tibetan, he says, they were clearly taught as part of the oral transmission of process practices into Tibet. His logic in emphasizing these physical exercises is that they prime the body and nervous system, and reduce the risk of mind/body stresses and strains that may occur when we dive into perfection stage arts like inner fire without basic training.[31]

For our purposes, his emphasis on these exercises underscores the fact that perfection stage practice assumes a gradual preparation of the body and nervous system that is not just mental but clearly involves the athletic enhancement of respiratory function and neurophysiological tone. In this sense, these six exercises of Naropa bear a general family resemblance to intensive systems of respiratory training from the Hindu yoga tradition, such as those taught in the context of *Kundalini Yoga* or *Sudarshan Kriya Yoga*.[32] This is noteworthy since it suggests the potential efficacy of these exercises in generally enhancing mental and physical health, as the recent studies by Dick Brown and Patricia Gerbarg clearly suggest.[33] We'll return to this later when we turn our attention to comparing Buddhist and Western views of the neurophysiology of vase-breathing and sublimation. For now, though, given this background on physical preparations for vase-breathing, we can turn to the three final preparations of mind and energy.

2. *Balancing the Nervous System: Visualizing the Channels and Complexes*

As in training through physical exercises, so in preparing the mind for vase-breathing we orient ourselves with role-modeling imagery. We then check to be sure our sitting posture is stable—ideally in the lotus posture—so it can support a straight spine, open chest, and slight head nod, as our up-turned palms rest, left over right, on our lap. Next, we prime our energy, say, by alternate nostril breathing, one or more simple vase breaths, and/or an expelling breath-lock. At this point, we follow the sevenfold mentor-bonding process up to the fifth step. Now, however, beyond simply asking for general blessings and guidance on the perfection stage path, we specifically ask our mentor, lineage, and male and female muses for support in the work of making our neural energy more positive and our nervous system more plastic. As we imagine receiving their blessing and guidance in the form of rainbow lights, a miniature duplicate of our role-model comes to our crown, melts into rainbow bliss-nectar, and flows through our crown to our heart, energizing and opening up all the channels of our nervous system.

At this point, in order to prepare for full vase-breathing and inner fire practice, we imagine withdrawing energies and drops from the peripheral channels of the coarse body-mind into the three channels of our subtle body-mind. To support these practices, we envision the three channels in a simplified and truncated form.[34] Specifically, we see the central channel as bluish in color, starting four finger breadths below the navel, just in front of where our lumbar spine would be, and running vertically up the spinal axis to the complex at the crown, where it curves down again towards the mid-brow, like the curved handle of an umbrella. Alongside it are the smaller side channels, the right red and left white, inserted into the bottom opening of the central channel below the navel and curving around and up to rejoin it at the navel, from where they run up on either side to the crown, and then diverge to end at the nostrils.

Connected with the channels, we envision the four main complexes where smaller channels branch out in a truncated way, seeing each as a lotus flower of various colors and with various numbers of petals symbolizing branch channels. The "emanation" complex at the navel, said to have a triangular shaped hub, is red, with sixty-four branch petals curving slightly upwards. The "truth" complex at the heart is envisioned as white, with a circular hub and eight branch petals, curving slightly downward. The "enjoyment" or "beatific" complex at the throat is envisioned as red, with a circular hub and sixteen branch petals, curving slightly upward. And the "great bliss" complex at the crown is rainbow colored, with a triangular hub and thirty-two branch petals curving slightly downward. The complexes are to be conceived

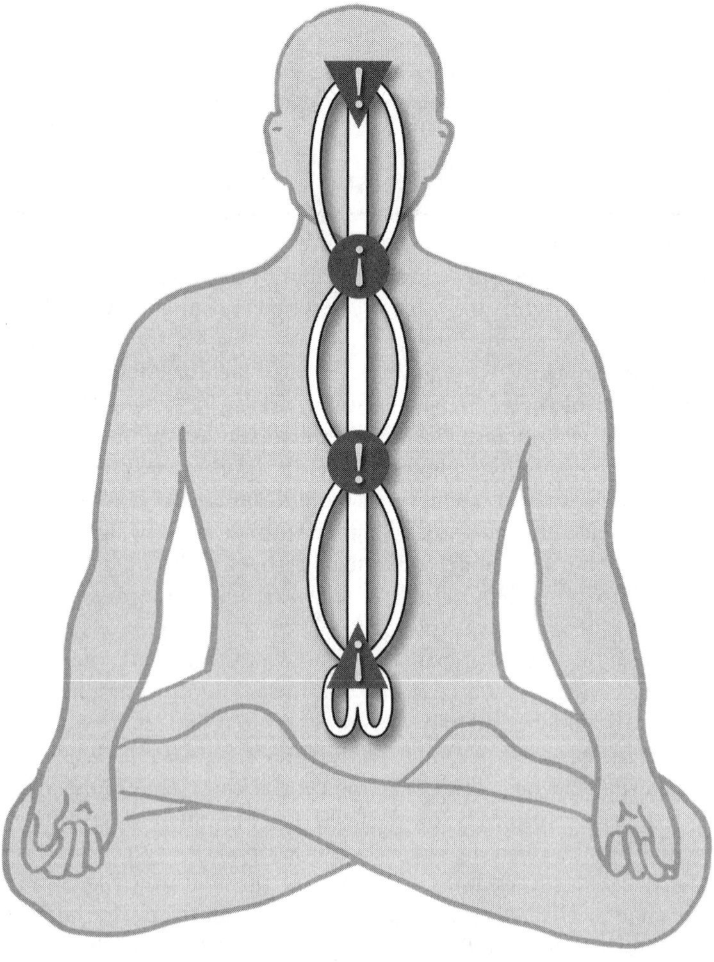

Figure 10.2 The Neural Network of Sublimation

as two complementary pairs, with the navel and throat complexes embodying feminine energy or wisdom and the heart and crown embodying masculine energy or art.

Given this setup, we begin by focusing our visualization on the point below the navel where the three channels join, and then envision the complexes in succession, starting with the navel and moving up. Eventually, the complexes should appear clearly, along with their distinct petals. If clarity doesn't come based on the complexes, we can simply envision the three channels, again starting below the navel where they converge. This detailed imagery is meant to orient us specifically to begin the work of tapping and channeling core neural energies.

From a neuropsychological point of view, there are several lines of research which would suggest that focusing repeatedly, vividly, and stably on these visualized structures along the neuraxis is likely to prime neural network connections with afferent feedbacks in the locations involved, which may increase central neural plasticity[35] and alter local chemistry[36] and metabolism.[37] So, while the appearance and configuration of the channels and complexes are mentally constructed rather than naturally occurring, they nonetheless may facilitate the development of real structures and capacities within the nervous system. Interestingly, this seeming paradox has long been recognized within the process tradition, in which the specific forms of the structures visualized are recognized as artificial constructs, yet still useful to guide practice and prepare our minds to tap and master innate structures, energies and chemistry within the nervous system. However intently or lightly we practice this preparation, eventually it leads us to the next step in setting up the full practice of vase-breathing and inner fire.

3. *Kindling the Inner Fire: Visualizing Syllables Within the Channels*

If visualizing the channels and complexes in detail picks up where we left off with envisioning the central channel in the subtle creation stage, this next preparation does the same with our initial vision of seed-syllables at key points along the neural axis, reviewed in our first meditative experiment 10.1. In describing the practice, Tsong Khapa advises a middle way between the most elaborate and most bare bones array of syllables.[38] Specifically, he suggests we visualize four, one in the hub of each of the complexes we've envisioned, but advises us to use the most abbreviated forms of the syllables we can.

Beginning with the navel, this means envisioning a version of the syllable AH which looks like a simple vertical brush stroke, slightly wider at the bottom, made of ruby red light.[39] The best visual analogue in the Roman alphabet is an upside down exclamation point, understood as an abbreviation for the exclamation AH! This stroke should be visualized four fingers below the navel, standing on a moon-cushion within the central channel in the hub of the navel complex. Then, at the level of the nipples, he suggests we envision a sapphire blue syllable HUM standing on its head, also on a moon cushion within the central channel in the hub of the heart complex. Next, at the level of the Adam's apple, we envision a ruby red syllable OM, standing upright on a moon cushion within the central channel in the hub of the throat complex. Finally, at the crown, we envision a diamond white syllable HAM, standing on its head on a moon cushion within the central channel in the hub of the crown complex.

For ease of visualization in Roman script, I suggest people abbreviate these syllables further, either to two letter transcriptions—UM, OM, AM—or, simpler, to vowels alone—U, O, A—or simpler still, to four exclamation points. This would approximate the Sanskrit and Tibetan, which allows these syllables to be written in a vertical format, condensing them into a complex character one space wide akin to single strokes, so that they all fit neatly within the straw-sized central channel and line up nicely along the vertical axis in a way that suits the visualizations to follow. All four syllables are to be envisioned as small as possible, ideally the size of a mustard seed.

A final subtlety is that all the syllables use an element of the Sanskrit alphabet to make the visualization more suggestive. In particular, certain nasal sounds like "n" and "m" are sometimes written by placing a dot above the letter preceding the sound. Since the visualization of seed-syllables in inner fire is meant to convey the image of a flame melting wax or snow, these dots are enhanced to give the letters the appearance of a flaming fire or melting drop. This is done by adding a crescent element like a brazier under the dot and a squiggle like a flame-tip (or dripping snow-melt) above the dot. Specifically, to prime the mind for vase-breathing and inner fire in this tradition, all four syllables have the threefold melting-dripping element added to their main character: the two upright syllables at the navel and throat have the crescent, dot, and squiggle pointing up like flames; and the two inverted syllables at the heart and crown have the crescent, drop, and squiggle pointing down like melting drops. This subtlety is another reason why I prefer to use exclamation points for all four, since they include a dot element which can be enhanced as in Sanskrit or Tibetan. If you choose to use this shorthand, obviously the exclamation points at the navel and throat need to be inverted, and those at the heart and crown upright, technically the opposite of the Sanskrit and Tibetan syllables.

Given the centrality of this phase in the art of sublimation, we'll survey the practice of kindling inner fire—Tsong Khapa's third point—step by step, under seven sub-headings: (a) releasing bliss; (b) adding vase-breathing; (c) mastering vase-breathing; (d) immersing energy, dissolving mind; (e) regulating bliss; (f) deepening sublimation; and (g) adding diamond recitation.

3.a Kindling in Practice: Igniting the Fire and Releasing the Flow of Bliss

Tsong Khapa advises that we take these syllables as objects of single-pointed meditation, just as we might focus on the mind in quiescence meditation or its

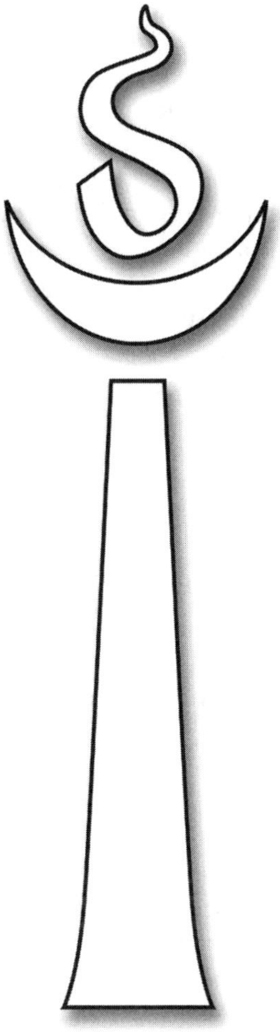

Figure 10.3 The Enhanced Ah-Stroke Syllable

ultimate emptiness in insight meditation.[40] So he reminds us that they must be engaged with a centered and balanced attention, in order to avoid the distraction that comes of applying too little effort or the dullness that comes of applying too much. He also points out that we should try to immerse our minds so fully in the syllables that we feel we *become* them, since the degree of our immersion in them will correlate with the degree of blissful flow it induces, and the degree of bliss will correlate with the amount of control we gain over our neural energy. If we run into difficulty envisioning the syllables as small as seeds, we can begin by envisioning them and the channels as larger, then gradually fine-tune their size. After briefly focusing on the three upper syllables, most of our time should be spent on the AH-stroke at the navel, the key to kindling the inner fire of sublimation.

According to the classical literature, this practice will gradually lead to being able to envision the inner anatomy of the channels, complexes and syllables as vividly and stably as creation stage practice allows us to re-envision our bodies and environment. Eventually, just by focusing stably on the AH-stroke at the navel, its radiance will increase until it begins to warm and light our body like a small, red hot flame.[41] As the flame continues to intensify, its tip and heat eventually rise up the central channel until they begin to reach the sapphire blue HUM syllable at the heart complex, melting its down-facing tip until it begins to drip like wax into the tongue of flame at the navel. This further fuels and intensifies the inner fire, causing it to rise through the heart up the central channel to the throat complex, where it ignites the ruby OM syllable until it merges with the inner fire threading up the channel from the navel. Further intensified, the inner fire finally climbs to the crown, where it reaches the inverted diamond HAM syllable, causing it to melt and drip down through the central channel towards the throat, spreading a rush of bliss as it flows. While the claim that simply focusing in this way could release a real flow of bliss chemistry may seem incredible, current mind/body research supports the power of vivid imagery to have a range of neurological effects, depending on its intensity, form and location. In addition, several studies show increased blood levels of endorphins in meditation,[42] and others show Tibetan process techniques can support the self-regulation of basic functions including neural plasticity and metabolism.[43]

Provided we carefully nurture it, the bliss induced by this practice gradually pervades the whole body, with our experience of it increasing in intensity as it spreads. Traditionally, this spread is described as a progression through four successive degrees of intensity. As the flow reaches the throat complex we experience bliss. As it reaches the heart it becomes sublime bliss. As it reaches the navel, it becomes supreme bliss. And finally, as it reaches the pelvic complex it becomes orgasmic bliss. In his review of the process, Tsong Khapa cites this description of the warming and melting of the heart from the *Perfect Union Process*:

> At the center of the heart is a lotus
> With eight petals, together with its (blissful) essence;
> The channel that runs through its center
> Has the nature of the flame of a butter lamp;
> (The lotus) resembles the flower of the water tree
> Opened in bloom, petals stretched downward.
> Residing at its center is the (concentration) hero,
> (Envisioned) the size of a mustard seed,
> (As) the indestructible syllable HUM;
> (The heat) causes the seed to melt like snow.[44]

In addition to the imagery of this sketch of sublimation, I draw your attention to the way the central channel is described: not as a solid structure like a stem, but rather as a dynamic flux of heat energy. This kind of precise naturalistic description reinforces the recognitions that the actual channels, complexes, energies and drops visualized at this stage are not seen in a naïve or reified way as gross anatomical or microscopic structures. Rather, they are projected guides to a subtle network of dynamic elements which can nonetheless be influenced by conscious control of factors like attention and breath-rhythms. This brings us to the final preparation for inner fire, conjoining all the prior mind/body practices in an integrated exercise of vase-breathing.

3b. Enhancing the Inner Fire With Vase-Breathing

Though vase breathing is included as the most basic of the six exercises of Naropa, the oral traditions of Tibetan process lineages add that combining vase breathing with the mental preparations just reviewed will facilitate and speed our developing the capacity for sublimation through inner fire. The actual technique begins on the stage set by the preparations of visualizing the network of three channels and four complexes, and planting seed-syllables inside it at the four vital points. After reviewing this background, Tsong Khapa presents the art of vase breathing as having four steps: (1) breathing in; (2) filling like a vase; (3) compressing the breath; and (4) releasing it. As with all forms of physical yoga, inner fire enhanced by vase breathing should be practiced on an empty stomach.

Of course, we begin this practice as we said above, sitting cross legged with back upright and hands in our laps, clearing our energy with alternate nostril breathing or an expelling breath-lock.

1. We breathe in through both nostrils evenly, as gently, slowly and deeply as we can.
2. As we breathe in, we engage in the next step called filling the vase. Specifically, we envision the air directly entering the side channels where they open at each nostril, and slowly filling each channel like a sausage or tubular balloon, right down to the point where they loop around in the pelvis and curve up again to meet and insert together into the lower opening of the central channel, where the ruby AH-stroke sits.
3. Before we mildly compress the air, we imagine that the breath in the side channels has begun to flow into the central channel. Now we compress by swallowing some saliva and very gently pressing the diaphragm down. As we press gently down, we envision the air within the side channels flowing into and filling the central channel so that it presses down on the AH-stoke from above. Next, we very gently tone the muscles of the pelvic floor, imagining that this stirs and presses energies from the sexual and anal areas upwards, until they enter the lower opening of the central channel and compress the AH-stroke from below. I like to compare this compression of the relaxed and distended pot-belly from above and below to gently messaging a balloon with one hand from above and

one from below. At the same time, bringing the energies from above and below together to compress the AH-stroke may be compared to pressing both middle fingers from above and below into the heart of the balloon until they make its two sides touch in the midst of the balloon. This two-way compression by inspiratory energy pressed down from above and excretory energy pulled up from below is often referred to as a "kiss." Tsong Khapa quotes the *Supreme Bliss Creation Process*:

> The energies that course above and below
> Through the mind are brought to a kiss.[45]

After compressing the energies together into this kiss, we focus on the AH-stroke while holding this vase breath as gently and as long as possible, being careful to prepare to release it well before we're feeling forced or uncomfortable.

4. In the final step, we release the compressed breath-energy like an arrow, up and out the central channel, taking care to do so as gently, slowly and quietly as possible. At the crown we imagine the air re-entering the side channels and being expelled evenly out of both nostrils.

3c. Vase-Breathing in Practice: Pointers, Warnings and Signs of Success

In summarizing this compound practice, Tsong Khapa highlights two keys: using the vase technique to bring the two energies into a "kiss" around the AH-stroke; and focusing with luminous clarity on the vivid image of the seed-sized ruby stroke within the central channel at the navel complex.[46] According to the traditional explanation, when the side channels' lower openings are open, the central channel's lower opening is closed, and vice versa. So by squeezing the air out of the side channels until they've emptied into the central channel, we've not only opened the central channel but gathered and inserted into it all the energy normally circulating in the side channels. Again, Tsong Khapa cites and reiterates the advice of prior Tibetan masters to first open and clear the channels, and then compress and hold the breath-energies in a relaxed way with extreme gentleness.

Like any contemplative learning process, this one cannot be forced, but must grow naturally through persistent yet patient preparation over time. The flow of blissful energy and chemistry aroused by this practice will not last at first, but rather will naturally tend to be quite fickle and elusive, coming and going with no clear rhythm. So, in order to cultivate this art successfully over time, we must be unwaveringly nurturing and patient, and simply keep practicing gently and devotedly no matter what, as when tending an infant or toddler. On the other hand, it's important to bear in mind that diving unprepared into such advanced practice, or using excessive or forced control despite being prepared can actually reinforce the energy of stress and trauma rather than transforming them into blissful energy and openness. This risk is comparable to that faced by those who dive prematurely into practices like *Kundalini Yoga*.[47]

As for signs of progress, when blissful energies and chemistry can be reliably released, held and savored at the vital points, it makes sense to try to stretch ourselves very gradually and try to increase their duration or intensity. The signs of success are that the AH-stroke at the navel complex is not only vivid and stable, but increasingly glows and radiates warmth and light.

3d. Immersing, Retaining and Dissolving Vital Energy Within the Central Channel

Once we've stabilized our focus on the flame of inner fire at the navel, the next step in the practice is to fully immerse our vital energies within the bliss-network of the central channel, and to be able to keep it there long enough to induce a real dissolution into clear light. Traditionally, the objective sign of having immersed the energies within the central channel is that the breath flows evenly and equally through both nostrils, without our having to exert effort to balance it. Once our vital energy has been fully immersed within the central channel, continued focus leads to a gradual calming of the normal breath-rhythm, to the point where the breath has become very subtle and slowed to a stop. This is the objective sign that the vital energy of the breath is being "retained" within the central channel, inducing a gradual dissolution of normal consciousness and full immersion into orgasmic bliss and clear light.

The depth of our retention is measured by a series of hand movements that serve as a clock: rubbing the right palm against the left three times, then snapping the fingers six times is the unit of measure, approximately five to seven seconds. The target length for the suspension of breath ranges from thirty-six units to one hundred and eight, in other words, roughly from three to twelve minutes. Traditionally, it is said that being able to retain the breath immersed within the central channel for this length of time allows us to fully master the dissolution of our mind/body elements into the clear light, whether during meditation or during actual death, a claim supported by recent research.[48] The key for us here is to be perfectly clear that taking vase-breathing to such athletic heights is not necessary in order to use it effectively to support sublimation and change. Introductory practices like vase breathing have been shown to be teachable to novices, and to have measurable mental health benefits in just a few short weeks' time.[49]

However far we take it, when we've reached a degree of immersion and slowing of our breath-energies, with or without vase breathing, it naturally leads to the dissolution of our coarse mind/body processes into the subtle and extremely subtle body-mind, a dissolution marked by the signs we simulated in the course of self-creation.

> The first sign is like a mirage,
> The second like a wisp of smoke,

The third like the flickering of fireflies,
The fourth like a glowing butter-lamp,
And the fifth (through eighth) formless sign(s)
Resemble a sky free from clouds.[50]

Though the experiences of dissolution, heat and bliss in the course of process practice may be of many degrees and kinds, they take on a special depth and intensity once we've gained some ability to immerse, hold, and dissolve the vital energies within the central channel. In cataloging common varieties of dissolution, heat, and bliss, Tsong Khapa recommends we not rest content with the superficial forms, but work towards those of greater depth, intensity and purity which involve immersion in the central channel with the help of vase-breathing.[51]

3e. Mastering Sublimation: Restraining and Reversing the Flow of Bliss

Whether we cultivate sublimation simply by focusing on channels and syllables or with the added help of vase-breathing, mastering the art of inner fire has to do with gaining control over the release and flow of bliss-energies and chemistry through the central channel. While the reason for channeling subtle energies into the central channel is to deepen dissolution and bliss, there's an added benefit to focusing on the flow of bliss through the five major complexes (the four envisioned above plus the secret or sexual organ complex). By bringing attention to the release of bliss chemistry from its source in the crown and following its flow in stages through the whole central nervous system, we can more easily practice gaining fine control over that flow. This is vital to sublimation, which requires that we master the most profound bliss states well enough to harness them towards realizing visceral wisdom on the first sub-stages and integration on the great perfection stages.

When kindling and channeling inner fire in this tradition, we practice controlling the flow of bliss chemistry through the central channel by pausing, holding and savoring it at each of the four points where we've envisioned seed-syllables, as well as at the tip of the sexual organ. By exercising our ability to stay mindful of bliss chemistry throughout its flow in this way, we not only avoid getting carried away with excitement but also gradually gain conscious control over its flow. This control is enhanced by practicing reversing the downwards flow of bliss energy and chemistry, by drawing them back up from the navel to the crown, again stopping to pause, hold and savor the bliss at each of the three higher points.[52] This art of mastering the controlled flow of bliss energy and chemistry in both the descending and ascending directions is described in a key passage form the *Diamond Rosary Process*:

Then one should teach the emerging order:
In the crown of the great bliss wheel,
It is said to be "joy";

> In the wheel of beatitude, it is "sublime joy";
> In the wheel of truth, it is "supreme joy";
> And in the emanation wheel, "orgasmic joy"—
> All these are caused to be experienced....
> (Then) in the emanation wheel there is joy;
> Sublime joy dwells in the wheel of truth;
> Supreme joy dwells in the beatific wheel;
> Orgasmic (joy in the) great bliss (wheel),
> These are declared to be (experienced) in the reverse order.[53]

Although this text belongs to the *Esoteric Community* tradition of father process teachings, also called "art" teachings, the fourfold progression and two directions all carry over into the *Supreme Bliss Wheel* tradition of mother or "wisdom" process teachings. Though initially the flow may only go as far as the source of inner fire—to the complex just below the navel—before it's reversed, this is largely to check its intensity and keep it from triggering the instinctive sexual response associated with the lower pelvic and sexual complexes. Once we've begun to control the flow of bliss this far, we re-envision the lower end of the central channel as extending below the navel through the pelvis to the tip of the sexual organ. With this, we allow the downward flow of innate bliss to naturally descend to the opening of the central channel at the tip of the sex-organ, and practice blocking its release in an uncontrolled orgasm by envisioning a sapphire seed-syllable HUM blocking the tip. If the orgasmic bliss gets out of control, Tsong Khapa recommends a forceful technique for stopping and reversing it, by focusing on the syllable at the crown, reciting the syllable HUM and trying to draw the bliss energy and chemistry back up the central channel to the crown.[54]

This technique describes the art of restraining our normal sexual response, the foundation of the work of sublimation, especially in its early stages. While we may not grasp the specifics, most of us have had some experience of trying to restrain orgasm to enhance our interpersonal experience of normal intimacy. The process practice builds on that basic mind/body competence, and opens the door to an inwards path towards psychosexual maturity, which is seen as indispensible even if we plan to integrate intimacy as an outwards path to embodied altruism. In fact, this art is so central to developing sublimation that it figures as the prime technique for tapping into the central nervous system in the other of the two main methodologies of the process tradition, the so-called father or art methodology based on the *Esoteric Community Process*.

3f. Deepening Sublimation: Combining the Arts of Mother and Father

According to the *Esoteric Community*, the five primary neural energies of the peripheral nervous system are most efficiently drawn into the central nervous system by focusing on a drop at the tip of the sexual organ. In this method, the tip of the sex organ is considered one of three vital points for gaining control of neural energies and immersing, holding, and dissolving them into the central channel. These three are called "tips of the nose," the other two being what we think of as the tip of nose and the point in the middle of the central channel at the heart complex. Within the synthetic process traditions of Tibet, this method may be seen as picking up where the inner fire technique from the mother systems leaves off. Although it requires a greater capacity for sublimation, it also supports a deeper immersion into the central nervous system, and so is used by Tsong Khapa to explain the more advanced phase of the first sub-stage leading to the gateway of freedom of speech. In explaining this methodology, he quotes this passage from the *Diamond Rosary* linking the five primary energies of the nervous system with the five families of enlightenment and the five main neural complexes which are their sources:

> Vitalizing energy stays in the heart center,
> Born from the specific (scepter) clan of the *Immovable One.*
> Evacuative energy stays in the genitals,
> Born from the *Jewel Mine* clan.
> Ascending energy stays in the throat,
> With the (lotus family) nature of *Infinite Light.*
> Metabolic energy stays in the navel lotus,
> With the (sword family) nature of *Real Success.*
> Pervasive energy stays in all parts,
> With the (wheel family) actuality of the *Illuminator.*[55]

And later in the same chapter, he cites this passage from the *Further Process* of the *Esoteric Community* tradition:

> Breath, with the nature of the five wisdoms,
> Is the reality of the five elements,
> Arising in the form of a lump,
> Imagine it on the tip of your nose.
> That five-colored jewel (drop)
> Is called "life energy" and "control."[56]

This more advanced phase is correlated with gaining access not just to the subtle central nervous system, but specifically to the extremely subtle nervous system mapped onto the "indestructible drop" in the midst of the central channel at the heart complex. The language used to map this next phase of the journey draws on the image of the core complexes not just as hubs but as points where the central channel is knotted by the side channels coiling around it multiple times. The idea here is to illustrate graphically the normal resistances which block our conscious access to deeper, more primal levels of consciousness and neural function. The insight implied in the image of the complex knots is that those resistances are maintained by the grip exerted on our body-minds by our clinging to reactive swings between extreme states of hyper-vigilance and paralysis or collapse. According to all process traditions, accessing our subtle and subtlest mind/body requires centering our minds enough not just to tap into the subtle nervous system at vital points but also to gradually unravel these knots, so that we can regulate the normally unconscious energy, chemistry and mind-states they support.

3g. Refining the Fire with Diamond Recitation: Unraveling the Heart Knot

Of all the complex knots that constrict and block off the central nervous system, it's said that the knot at the heart is by far the most primal, complex, and profound. This is usually illustrated by the image of the normal, constricted heart complex as knotted where each of the side channels wrap around the central channel three times, making a six-fold knot. In contrast, at the knots of all the other complexes, the side channels wrap around the central channel only one time each, making a double knot. Another indication of the primacy of the heart complex is the teaching that the knots at each of the other complexes must be loosened and resolved separately, one at a time, while the knot at the heart, once loosened and resolved, also loosens and resolves all the other knots at the same time. This is why, once we've been able to tap into the central channel and immerse, hold and dissolve our mind and energies into that channel, the next phase on the way to freedom of speech is to begin focusing our efforts on unraveling the heart-knot, in order to tap into the extremely subtle body-mind. Tsong Khapa quotes the *Diamond Rosary*:

> Abiding in the center of the mid-brow,
> The drop is truly taught as wind-energy,
> And is opened through the reality of affirmation.
> The practitioner, upon releasing the (heart) knot,
> Knows the reality of wind-energy.

Whether the five energies are immersed in the central channel at the "lower nose-tip" of the sexual organ or at the mid-brow complex near the "upper nose-tip," eventually the father method is to bring the drop of coalesced energies to the "middle nose-tip" at the heart, where the knots of the subtle nervous system can be fully released and the extremely subtle body-mind accessed. Once vase breathing and inner fire help us access the central channel, Tsong Khapa invokes the father process arts of focusing on the drop and diamond recitation to describe the unraveling of the heart knot and the work that follows. The art of diamond recitation involves focusing mindfully on the balanced and slowed breath which flow when mind and energy are not just immersed in the central channel, but (more or less fully) immersed within the indestructible drop mapped at the hub of the heart complex in the central channel.[57]

> Coming out from the indestructible drop, which abides in the center of the lotus in the heart-center, is the exhalation, HUM, entering inhaled there is OM, and held abiding there is the nature of AH. These depend

on the color white, etc., having the characteristic of the elemental spheres of water, etc. They occur with process of (normal breathing) through the superficial nostrils, right and (left). Thus you do the diamond recitation which effortlessly accomplishes the activities of pacification, etc., and effects the purification of all previous obscurations.[58]

Although inspiration, holding, and exhalation are aligned with the seed-syllables of the enlightened body, speech and mind—OM, AH, HUM—traditionally this alignment is seen as purely symbolic, since the "recitation" here involves simply minding and "hearing" the in-breath, pause and out-breath as the real sound of the three seed-syllables.[59] As for the alignment of the breath-energies with the elements, referred to in the preceding quote, the breath is symbolically linked with the four elements/states of matter depending on whether it flows mainly through the right nostril (air/gas), the left nostril (water/liquid), or both (fire/energy in, and earth/solid out).

The importance of these fine points is to clarify that diamond recitation helps us dissolve any dualistic distinction between the constructive activity of thought or speech—including verbal and/or visual symbols—and the non-constructive, elemental processes of breath-energy. We apply this art to unraveling the heart-knot because freedom from traumatic habits of thought, speech and imagery is needed to free our minds and neural energies from the oscillating extremes that come from reifying the binary constructs like "safe" and "unsafe." In effect, the knots formed by the side channels represent the crystallization of those symbolic habits in the form of a blocked off and fragmented pattern of neural energy and information processing. Once we've accessed the central channel and tapped into the extremely subtle heart-drop, freeing our minds from symbolic habits with the help of this ecstatic, non-conceptual mode of breath-mindfulness is vital to fully tapping and harnessing the chemistry of orgasmic bliss. To illustrate this, Tsong Khapa quotes the *Diamond Rosary*, which proclaims itself the sole source of this art:

The nature of the supreme secret
Which is not stated clearly anywhere,
That opening of the drop—
I will explain it—you listen to it!
In the sky chamber of the heart-lotus,
The intuitive wisdom scepter always dwells,
Showing truly the lower and upper,
Home of the great life and evacuative energies.
There again, in the center of the hard to open,
It is wrapped up by three (double) knots.
These defeat the evacuative energies,
Which do not succeed going upward.
These also defeat the fivefold energies:
The vitalizing, evacuative, ascending,

Pervading and metabolic wind-energies
(By splitting them into fragmented, stress-energies).[60]

4. *Sealing the State of Orgasmic Bliss with the Visceral Intuition of Emptiness*

Once we've begun to taste orgasmic bliss inwardly with inner fire, especially when enhanced by vase-breathing and diamond recitation, we've reached the point at which we can begin to practice the process form of meditation on emptiness. With our minds and nervous systems increasingly free and clear of the reified dualistic constructs and polar energies that normally block and fragment them, we're naturally disposed to realize the openness and interconnectedness of all subjects and objects, minds, and things. In particular, the Naropa tradition of mother process practice encourages us to start harnessing bliss to emptiness meditation as soon as we've been able to follow the flow of bliss in the descending order down to the tip of the sexual organ and hold it there without normal orgasm.

Although reached meditatively, this altered state resembles normal orgasm in its destructuring of normal dualistic perception of self and other, subject and object. This state makes us naturally more open and receptive to seeing through reified dualistic appearances and sensing our deeper connectedness with others and the world around us. In effect, this state—which we think of as altered though it's far older and more basic to life than our waking state—reflects that part of our psychobiology which is best suited to seeing through our normal self-limiting delusions and to perceiving intuitively the selfless nature of things which is ultimately freeing and healing. Although the tradition encourages us to apply the same analysis and insight we cultivated on the paths of self-healing and engagement, it also offers an alternate intuitive path to those unversed, based on just seeing subjects and objects from the perspective of non-conceptual bliss and openness. Tsong Khapa explains:

> At that time one must engage mindfulness of the view of emptiness to be ascertained, and must place the mind firmly there. Rest within the inseparable ecstasy and (wisdom of) emptiness. Even if you do not have a profound understanding of the emptiness doctrine, at least avoid all distraction and rest in the singular ecstasy of the experience until the absorption becomes stable, mixing this with beyond-conceptuality consciousness.[61]

These alternate paths may be compared to the divergence in contemporary affect therapies between more analytic approaches like neuro-psychoanalysis[62] and more affect-based methods like accelerated emotional dynamic therapy.[63] Though the level of access to traumatic conditioning possible through emptiness meditation based on inner fire and diamond recitation is generally much deeper than that reached by such modern therapies, the methodologies overlap.[64] In either meditative mode, the next step is to hold the deconstructive experience of inseparable bliss-emptiness or bliss-void intuition as we reverse the flow of bliss chemistry back up the central channel to the crown: experiencing bliss/void, sublime bliss/extreme void; supreme bliss/universal void; and orgasmic bliss/complete void. This then begins the final phase of sublimation, working with the four bliss-void intuitions to gradually deepen and refine our direct experience and embodied realization of the objective reality of emptiness, known on the perfection stage as the objective clear light.

In effect, the induction of stable, deep and intense natural bliss states is the bridge on this path which leads from an ordinary inference and mental perception of emptiness to an extraordinary intuition and contemplative direct perception of emptiness as clear light translucency.[65] The way this is traditionally framed is that the objective clear light of emptiness known by this path is one and the same as the ultimate objectivity of emptiness on the engaged path, but the subjectivity which knows that reality is radically different. In particular, the intuitive subjectivity of orgasmic bliss accessed by sublimation is far more profound and efficient a platform for realizing emptiness than the bliss of ordinary flow states accessed by concentrative quiescence. This is not only because its bliss is more profound and intense, and hence more disarming and deconstructive, but also because the extremely subtle level of consciousness of that bliss state supports the mind's natural capacity to immerse itself indivisibly in its object, making intuitive realization more profound, complete, and transformative.

Cultivating Bliss-Void Indivisible Wisdom Between Sessions

As with prior practices like mindfulness or quiescence-based insight meditation, such bliss-void meditation involves practice not just within sessions but also between sessions. In describing this, Tsong Khapa points out that even such profound realizations of orgasmic bliss and intuitive emptiness do not immediately translate into experiencing blissful openness or profound insight when encountering people and things in the world between sessions. Instead, we must consciously work at extending those realizations through our meditative aftermath into our daily life, as we would on the engaged insight path. So at this point he briefly introduces the key art of great seal practice, in which we practice making the universe our partner on the altruistic path by communing with all things through blissful openness:

> During the post-meditational periods one must consciously cultivate mindfulness of the experience of ecstasy and emptiness, and stamp all objects and events that appear and occur with the seal of this ecstasy and emptiness. This application causes a special ecstasy to be ignited, which one should foster.[66]

As for the end result sought by enhancing inner fire with diamond recitation, the aim is to deconstruct the whole network of mental constructions which make up our ordinary, traumatized self and life history. This is described in terms of the final extinction of stress-reactive habits called Nirvana, the final aim on the path of self-healing and the fulfillment of self-interest sought on the path of engagement. The path of inner fire and its destination is eloquently expressed in this realization poem from a Nalanda successor of Naropa's, Atisha:

> Conquer the progress of sun and moon—
> Otherwise in the door of the great sky
> The wind-sphere will not enter.
> By the yoga of opening and closing (the lower doors),
> You should compel the fierce goddess (of inner fire),
> The five Buddha (systems) and four goddess (elements)—
> You should burn them again and again.
> The ten directions' heroes and practitioners
> Gather and dissolve into the crown *chakra*.
> The four drops in the four lotuses
> Will generate the sixteen blisses.
> The self-luminous wisdom dwells
> In the center of the formful lotus navel.
> When enlightenment dwells in the jewel tip,
> You gain Nirvana like a butter lamp.
> When you win Nirvana there
> In the tip of the jewel,
> The host of notions such as self and other,
> I no longer see them at all.
> When the planet (Rahu) seizes sun and moon,
> The mind and the wind-sphere do not proceed.
> When all notions fully dissolve,
> The mind becomes pure experience of the (reality) realm.[67]

After reviewing the arts of compressing the polar energies with vase breathing and inserting them into the central channel with inner fire, Atisha describes mastering the flow of bliss chemistry and harnessing orgasmic bliss towards realizing emptiness. Deepened by the complete immersion, holding, and dissolution of polar energies (sun and moon) within the central channel (the mythical planet Rahu which eclipses them both) that blissful realization is profound enough to de-reify all constructs of self and life, yielding Nirvana through the space-like equipoise in the pure objectivity of clear light.

Of course, in its eloquence, this poetic statement seems to gloss over the reverse flow of bliss-void realization up to the crown, as well as the final phase on the way to freedom of speech: compressing the energies from above and below into a "kiss" that helps us gradually unlock and access the indestructible drop within the heart complex. This elision may reflect the fact that Atisha relied mainly on the *Death Terminator Process*, which merged arts from the mother and father traditions and influenced the Tibetan synthesis attributed to Gampopa[68] and refined by Tsong Khapa. In any case, Tsong Khapa affirms the teaching that we must practice mastering bliss-energy and chemistry at all three "nose-tips"—at the sex organ, mid-brow, and heart—and ultimately work to compress and immerse the upper and lower energy-drops into the central heart-drop. Recommending this method of using the heart complex to practice diamond recitation and reach freedom of speech, he cites this passage from the *Vow Arisal*:

> The energy gone into the heart-center lotus,
> In the likeness of a white HUM letter—
> You should visualize and be entranced with that,
> And you will not be bound by objects.
> The energy (normally) moving up into the life-cycle
> Will progress downwards into Nirvana.
> The totally non-local Nirvana
> Dwells in the heart-center lotus' anthers.[69]

Diamond Recitation: Immersing, Holding and Dissolving into the Heart-Drop

Later, Tsong Khapa explains in detail that the many colors and configurations of syllables used in vase-breathing each may be helpful for some novices. Here, he includes the intriguing array of three concentric circles of vowels, consonants and seed-syllables (like AH or HUM), visualized respectively in diamond, ruby and sapphire light, attributed to Naropa. This is of interest not just because it shows the intent of this stage not to obliterate speech but to purify and free it of conditioned habits, but also because these three rings are linked in the tradition with the three luminous intuitions—luminance, radiance and immanence—described as the fifth through seventh signs of dissolution into clear light.[70] This relates to the fact that, as we practice alternately radiating rainbow light-energies from these syllables and gathering them back to immerse and hold in the heart drop—the sapphire seed at the hub—we'll naturally experience a dissolution into clear light, marked by the signs, only now based on dissolving into the extremely subtle drop, rather than merely into the central channel. As opposed to dissolution ushered in by vertical movements of bliss-void energy-drops—descending to jewel or ascending to crown—the final dissolution here is ushered in by a radial or concentric movement into the heart-drop.

Of course, since this preparatory practice is meant to help us progress towards a diamond recitation free of verbal or visual symbols, eventually the radiating and gathering involves single-minded bliss-void focus on the flow of exhalation, inhalation and holding within the inner space of the heart-drop. The suggested setup for this practice is to envision our extremely subtle minds as a luminous moon disc floating reflected in the inner space of clear light transparency, and supporting the sapphire blue A-stroke, with the complex crescent and flame-tip elements added to the upper point or drop. As we practice dissolving into and emerging out of the clear light within this sphere, aided by diamond breathing, we gradually deconstruct our ordinary conceptuality, which has conditioned our mind and energy from very early development. Naropa explains the rationale for this deconstructive work beautifully:

> Since the various memories and mental constructions
> Arise from the (subtlest) mind as (source of) evolutionary actions,
> Meditate the affirmation wheel at the heart center,
> The base where consciousness and life-energy converge.[71]

According to Tsong Khapa, without having to purposefully hold the breath-energy within the heart-drop, simply practicing single-mindedly breathing in and out in a state of blissful immersion that loosens and unknots the heart, the inhalation and exhalation will both naturally shorten and eventually be suspended. At this point, the three phases of breath will no longer feel discernibly different, and within that suspension, will merge into the altruistic spirit of blissful openness, free from ordinary conceptuality. He cites this passage:

> By (such a) sign, (breath-)reality stays, (all) three,
> The nature of natural recitation;
> Nameless and inexpressible,
> This is the supreme enlightenment spirit.
> Those very three become one,
> And neither go nor come.[72]

Vase Breathing and Inner Fire in Light of Contemporary Science

While it is not my intention to explain away the profound arts we've been exploring in terms of modern science, it's clear that this tradition considers it necessary to explain them in terms of its own science of mind, body, contemplation, and enlightenment. Just as it would be misleading for a translator to use a modern term to translate the traditional language of these arts without comparing and contrasting the way the modern and traditional terms are used, so I have found it misleading to present these arts and their explanation without any reference to the culturally specific sciences we moderns have been taught. Of course, given the limits in our popular and scientific understanding of sublimation, any attempt to compare process models and explanations with analogues from modern science can only be provisional and hypothetical at best. Even if such comparisons are in some sense accurate or valid, as when they're somehow "tested" in a modern laboratory, this in no way means that the modern scientific account is more necessary, true or helpful to people who seriously try to put those arts into practice. Still, I've found that making careful comparisons and contrasts, however tentative, is helpful for scientifically educated minds to understand these life-transforming arts. With these caveats, let's explore how vase breathing and inner fire might be explained in terms of modern science.

Sudarshana Kriya Yoga: A Comparative Model of Vase Breathing

If we start with vase breathing and the other physical exercises which support it, our work is made somewhat easier by a growing body of modern research and thinking about the physiological effects and mechanisms of related breath practices from the yoga tradition.[73] While much of the modern research on yoga breathing practices either focuses on one specific technique or else studies them very generally as "yoga breathing," some excellent work has been done recently by my colleagues Richard Brown and Patricia Gerbarg on a rigorous system of practices which are very close to the six exercises of Naropa. So the simplest and most direct way for us to link these exercises with modern science is to draw on their research on a system called *Sudharshan Kriya Yoga*, also known as SKY.[74]

First of all, Brown and Gerbarg themselves draw comparisons between SKY and contemporary versions of Naropa's exercises taught by Tibetan masters like Lama Lobsang Palden as *Trul Khor* or *Yantra Yoga*,[75] as well as comparable practices from the Hindu tradition like *Kundalini Yoga*.[76] As for the specific exercises, SKY groups them into four: victorious breathing; bellows breathing; OM recitation; and pure vision in action. Of these, OM recitation may best be thought of as analogous to recitation of the role-modeling steps and requests leading up to the exercises, as well as a kind of basic training for diamond recitation. The other three contain most of the practices that make up the six exercises. The key elements of both systems include: alternate nostril breathing; slow nostril breathing; breath-holding; slow prolonged exhalation through the nostrils; rhythmic shoulder and arm movements; toning the muscles of the pelvic floor; tilting the head to slightly close the epiglottis; forced nostril breathing and exhalation; and activating fast movements/breathing. Taken together, these elements seem to have as similar intent and effect: to expand, flex, and tone the capacity of our whole breath apparatus, including the lungs, chest, diaphragm, and abdomen.

Naropa's Six Exercises and SKY: Two Total Nervous System Work-Outs

While I have no wish to blur the distinction in the detailed methods of these two traditional systems, I believe the comparison Brown and Gerbarg themselves make with Tibetan breath-exercises is right on target. The overall impression is that these two systems are different versions of a multifaceted, total breath work-out,[77] which has the intent of exercising, strengthening and toning our breath capacity while re-setting our breath, nervous system, and awareness towards a calmer, clearer baseline. Besides putting the six exercises from the Nalanda tradition in the general context of the Indian yoga tradition, an added windfall of this comparison is that it allows us to draw on Brown and Gerbarg's comprehensive review of the clinical benefits of such practices,[78] as well as their thoughtful summary of the current research on their likely neural mechanisms.[79]

Clinically, SKY has been shown to be as effective in treating people suffering from major depression as the antidepressant imiprimine, and almost as effective as electroconvulsive therapy (ECT).[80] In addition, other studies have shown as little as three weeks of practice to be effective in treating depression, and as little as one week of training to bring about a remission in 68 percent of people diagnosed with dysthmic disorder, a milder form of depression.[81] Still other studies have shown victorious breathing alone to be effective in relieving insomnia, test anxiety and caregiver stress. And there have also been two studies showing SKY works well in reducing the symptoms of post-traumatic stress disorder (PTSD), including one study in survivors of the Southeast Asia Tsunami of 2004.[82] Since the methods of intensive breath "work-outs" like those offered by SKY and Naropa's system are not specific to disorders like depression, anxiety, or post-traumatic stress, Brown and Gerbarg, among others, believe the research supports their general effectiveness in enhancing the healthy balance, synchrony, and plasticity of the human mind and nervous system.[83] They state their rationale for this claim quite succinctly:

> Breathing is controlled by both voluntary and involuntary mechanisms with complex feedback involving autonomic networks, brain stem nuclei, limbic system, cortex and the neuroendocrine system. The voluntary control of breath can modulate autonomic nervous system functions including cardiac vagal tone … (and) level of central nervous system activation.[84]

SKY and Naropa's Exercise System: Likely Mechanisms

When it comes to the likely mechanisms of action these methods have on the nervous system, Brown and Gerbarg initially summed their proposed model of mechanisms of the SKY breath work-out in eight points, depicted in figure 1.[85] I list these with some additions from a more recent article:[86] (1) strengthening and balancing sympathetic and stress-response systems; (2) decreasing chemoreflex sensitivity; (3) improving baroreflex response; (4) shifting to parasympathetic dominance *via* vagal stimulation; (5) synchronization of cortical areas by thalamic nuclei; (6) quieting of cortical areas involved in anticipation, planning, and worry, while enhancing cortical problem-solving through greater synchrony and integration; (7) activation of the limbic system leading to stimulation of forebrain reward systems and emotional release;

and (8) increased release of prolactin and oxytocin, enhancing feelings of calmness and social bonding. While some of these proposed mechanisms, like the increased release of oxytocin, remain to be tested, additional aspects have emerged thanks to more recent research: (9) promoting neural flexibility and plasticity through the release of brain-derived growth factor. This added point is consistent with the finding that SKY practitioners, like practitioners of Tibetan compassion practices, show EEG trains of gamma wave activity associated with high levels of cortical synchrony, neural plasticity, and nerve growth or neurogenesis.

Polyvagal Theory and Self-Regulation: A Comparative Model of Inner Fire

Given this model of the physical exercises surrounding vase breathing, we can now turn to explore current models for the art these exercises support: inner fire. While there are numerous studies of advanced process practices conducted on adepts of both the Tibetan and Indian process traditions, a wide

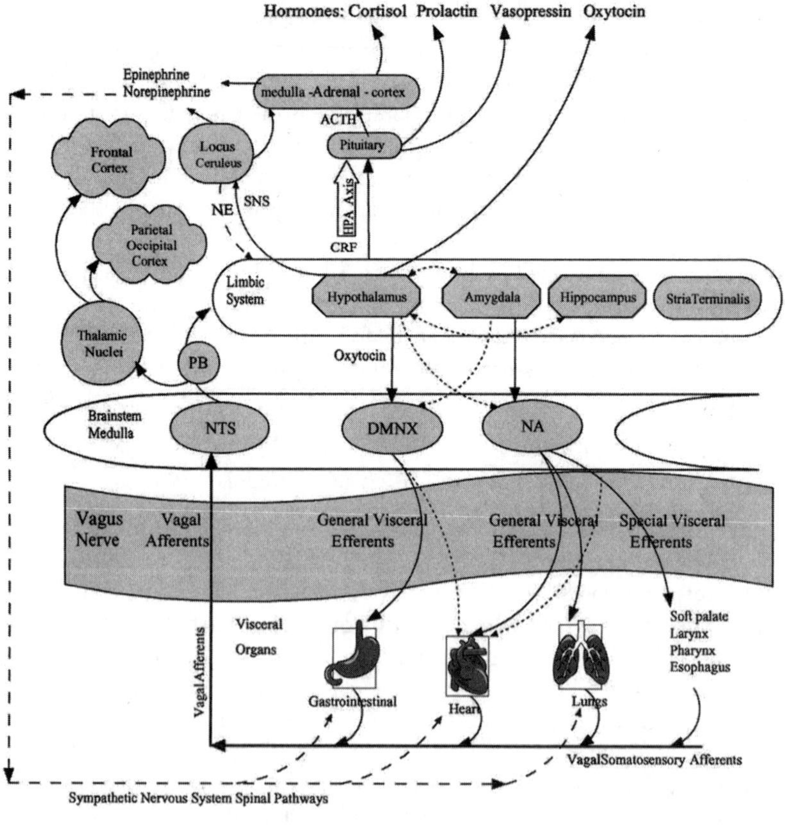

Figure 10.4 The Neural Mechanisms of Process Self-Regulation

range of models has been invoked to explain their complex physiology.[87] Also, as we learn more about the brain, especially the regulatory role of the prefrontal cortex which is distinctive to humans, we seem to be coming closer every day to a detailed understanding of the neural mechanisms of self-regulation practices like yoga and meditation. If you recall, in parts 2 and 3 I made some tentative links between the new field of interpersonal neurobiology and the theory and practice of altruism in the engaged and process traditions. Nonetheless, models which link phenomena as complex as the development of empathy and altruism to any one aspect or system of neural structure and function must inevitably oversimplify them, almost to absurdity. Despite this, since such models do circulate and become sources of partial understanding or confusion, we can't simply stand aloof and make no effort to correct or improve them.

One researcher who has spent his career helping us understand the mind/body connection is Stephen Porges. Porges has focused on correcting our very partial model of the autonomic nervous system, which stands at the crossroads between higher brain functions and the regulation of primal bodily functions. Now that we're familiar with the model of interpersonal neurobiology, based largely on the invaluable synthesis of Dan Siegel, it's time to introduce Porges' model of the autonomic nervous system (ANS). Given the subcortical structure and function of the ANS, Porges' perspective on self-regulation offers a perfect complement to cortical models. It allows us to push our tentative alignment of Siegel's cortical map with the coarse and subtle body-mind map of the process tradition to the next level. Just as the perfection stage moves our attention inwards, towards the frontier between the subtle and extremely subtle body-mind, so Porges' model of the ANS helps us appreciate the deeper connections that link higher cortical areas, by way of the limbic cortex and midbrain, to the central regulation of the primary processes of awareness and bodily function in the brainstem.

Polyvagal Theory: A Brave New Vision of Autonomic Regulation

Before we can explore a model of inner fire based on Porges' work, we'll need to draw some tentative links between his map of the ANS and the map of the subtle and extremely subtle body-mind used to guide the art of inner fire. To do this, we first need to understand some of the remarkable shifts in our conception of the ANS he has ushered in.[88] According to the twentieth century view, the sympathetic nervous system (SNS) played the leading role in the ANS, insuring our ability to mobilize in response to basic natural and higher social emotional challenges. In contrast, the parasympatheic nervous system (PNS) was presented as a mere shadow of the SNS, which simply handled the primal vegetative needs for sleep, digestion, excretion, and so on. To balance this view, Porges focused on understanding the PNS, by exploring the structure and function of its substrate, the tenth cranial nerve, called the vagus or "wanderer" since its fibers and functions range diffusely though the body.

This explains why he called his new theory the polyvagal theory. The real story begins when we look at his recognition that the vagus is not one monolithic nerve but has two main branches with two distinct origins in different but related nuclei in the brainstem, hence the word "poly," meaning multiple. This brings us to the most intriguing and relevant part of his model.

By comparing the structure and function of the vagus in humans and other animals, Porges observed that one part of the nerve—the part with a myelin sheath that serves much of the upper body including the heart, lungs, the vocal apparatus, the esophagus, and muscles of the face and neck, is actually new to mammals. Nicknamed by Porges the "smart" vagus, it controls many of the new structures and functions mammals evolved in order to live on land, raise womb born young, and avoid larger, fiercer reptile predators through social engagement and communication. This part of the vagus is what allows mammals to consciously control breathing, as well as other newer functions like vocalization, social listening and rapid shifts from states of receptive attention to active mobilization. It does this by regulating the two older parts of the ANS: the SNS, which enhances the stress-response to danger with the "fight-flight" defensive reactions, and the most primitive survival system, mediated by the older unmyelinated branch of the vagus which supports not just unconscious life-rhythms but the "freeze" reaction of fear-based immobilization as well. Based in a new brainstem nucleus (the nucleus ambiguous, NA) that migrated away from the old nucleus (the DMNX), towards the roots of the cranial nerves (V, VII, IX, XI) that control speech, sucking, swallowing, social listening and facial expressions.

The newer, "smart" vagus is crucial to mammalian life since it insures the platform for social engagement by putting a "brake" on the defensive reactivity of the SNS and providing an alternative to vagal emergency immobilization, allowing mammals to stay in a mid-range where they can cooperate with others they see as safe without reverting to either primitive defense.

The most crucial element of the theory in terms of the biology of self-regulation is the insight that these three autonomic systems—the newer "smart" vagus, the older SNS, and the oldest vagal system which we share with reptiles—are organized in a hierarchy. Within this hierarchy of ANS response, the newest, highest level mode is preferred, but only in situations perceived as safe. Once we see our environment as dangerous or life-threatening, we tend to automatically revert to "fight-flight" stress-reactivity or the "freeze" reflex of fainting or simulating death, a potentially life-threatening defense for mammals whose oxygen-hungry hearts and brains may die if breathing and heart rate slow dramatically. Porges describes his model in his recent book, *The Polyvagal Theory*, which is well worth quoting at length:

> Functionally, when the environment is perceived as safe, two important features are expressed. First, bodily state is regulated in an efficient manner to promote growth and restoration (e.g. visceral homeostasis). This is done through an increase in the influence of mammalian myelinated

vagal motor pathways on the cardiac pacemaker that slows the heart, inhibits the fight-or-flight mechanisms of the sympathetic nervous system, dampens the stress response system of the HPA axis (e.g. cortisol), and reduces inflammation by modulating immune reactions (e.g. cytokines). Second, through the process of evolution, the brainstem nuclei that regulate the (newer or "smart") myelinated vagus became integrated with the nuclei that regulate the muscles of the face and head. This link results in the bidirectional coupling between spontaneous social engagement behaviors and bodily states. Specifically, an integrated social engagement system emerged in mammals when the neural regulation of visceral states that promote growth and restoration (via the myelinated vagus) was linked neuroanatomically and neurophysiologically with the neural regulation of the muscles controlling eye gaze, facial expression, listening and prosody (vocalization).

The human nervous system, similar to that of other mammals, evolved not solely to survive in safe environments but also to promote survival in dangerous and life-threatening contexts. To accomplish this adaptive flexibility, the human nervous system retained two more primitive neural circuits to regulate defensive strategies (i.e. fight-or-flight and death-feigning behaviors). It is important to note that social behavior, social communication, and visceral homeostasis are incompatible with the neuropsychological states and behaviors promoted by the two neural circuits that support defense strategies. Thus, via evolution, the human nervous system retains three neural circuits, which are in a phylogenetically organized hierarchy. In this hierarchy of adaptive responses, the newest circuit is used first; if that fails to provide safety, the older circuits are recruited sequentially.[89]

In addition to providing a balanced view of the ANS, Porges' work is crucial for our purposes since his model is focused on the neural structure that supports the prime gateway of self-regulation in Indic contemplative science: the conscious control of breathing. The fact that the smart vagus gave mammals a means of consciously regulating the very oldest brainstem structures and functions helps explain the natural substrate for ambitious arts like those of the perfection stage. As we'll soon see, this not only involves regulating the systems mammals use for self-defense, it also involves sea-changes in the other most basic functions of life: courtship, mating, caretaking, and play. Both aspects of this profound change are key to our understanding the neurobiology of inner fire from the standpoint of modern science.

Towards a Comparative Model of Inner Fire: Polyvagal Theory and the Subtle Body

Before we can connect this new model of the ANS to the art and science of inner fire, we first need to link it with the process-oriented map of the subtle and extremely subtle body-mind. We can start by drawing some tentative comparisons between structural and functional aspects of both cultural models. For instance, the subtle mind-body map used to set the stage for inner fire depicts two side channels following and wrapping around the central channel, blocking, and knotting the five main complexes of the subtle body-mind. If we assume that these are linked with the neural axis we map onto the central nuclei of the spinal cord, brainstem, and cortex, then the two side channels could be linked with the polar structure and function of the SNS and the primitive PNS.

Like the sympathetic chain and the old, unmeyelinated vagus, the side channels modulate wake-sleep cycles, shifts from mobilization to quiescent states like digestion, as well as peripheral aspects of vital functions like respiration, circulation and excretion. Specifically, the solar or feminine right channel could be aligned with the old vagus, and the lunar or masculine left channel, with the SNS. Although the sympathetic chain and the old vagus both are bilateral structures, in fact the function of the vagus is lateralized, with the right specialized for visceral regulation. Given this linkage, the central channel would seem to be more closely aligned with the structure and function of the "smart," myelinated vagus, balancing and integrating the extremes of the two side channels and serving as the royal road to higher, conscious self-regulation.

However unlikely it seems, a tentative linkage of higher vagal control of the ANS with the structure and function of the central channel has some things to recommend it. First, if we consider the node of the heart complex where the central channel is knotted off around the extremely subtle body-mind, there is an intriguing parallel in the ways the split between its upper and lower portions and those of the vagus are represented by the two models. In Porges' model, the regulation of breath and heart rate is the point of intersection where the new, upper branch of the vagus overlaps with the old, lower branch.[90] At the same time, this crossroads is also a fork, in the sense that the structure and function of the upper and lower branches are normally quite distinct, at times even diametrically opposed. This is naturally explained by the evolutionary divergence of these two systems, reflected in the anatomical division between their two nuclei, different kinds of nerve fibers, as well as their distribution and function.

The upper or smart vagus originates in the ventral vagal nucleus (NA), and sends special, *voluntary* motor fibers to the structures of the branchial arches derived from the gill arches of earlier aquatic life—the muscles of the larynx, pharynx, mouth, palate, jaw, face, and neck—as well as to the cardiac pacemaker and the bronchi. The lower branch originates in the dorsal vagal nucleus (DMNX), and sends largely *involuntary* motor fibers to the bronchi, heart, gut, pelvis, urethra, anus, and sexual organ. Its sensory afferents, 80 percent of its fibers, use a dorsal sensory nucleus linked with the DMNX, the nucleus of the solitary tract (NTS). Despite the divergence of the new and old vagal systems, given the proximity of their nuclei and their overlap in the realm of heart-lung function, it is possible for them to become functionally integrated.

In a similar way, the origins, distributions and functions of the five main energies within the central channel also follows a biphasic pattern.[91] Two form an upper circuit, with vital energy from the heart complex circulating between the crown and nostrils, controlling circulation, inhalation, mental functions, sensation, and ingestion; and expressive energy from the throat, circulating from there to the crown and nostrils, controlling exhalation, speech, spitting, and emesis. Two form a lower circuit, with the digestive energy from the navel circulating between there and the heart, controlling digestion and metabolism; and excretory energy from the pelvis circulating down to the sexual organ, urethra and anus, controlling elimination, and sexual function. Not only do the functions of the upper and lower energies based in the central channel parallel those of the new and old vagus, but the triple knot around the extremely subtle body-mind at the heart means that their energies are naturally split, unless conscious efforts are made to unravel the heart knot and integrate them.

Next, as the modern model maps the origins of the vagus in the primal crossroads where we find the main activating system for consciousness and the nuclei of the cranial nerves to the senses, so the process model maps the origin of vital energy in the heart complex, along with the primal clear light consciousness and the origins of the five secondary energies and their channels to the senses. Last but not least, in and around the same crossroads, both models map the origins of the main neurochemicals that help regulate basic life functions; and both models divide these into opposing groups that work together to maintain a balance of activation and calm throughout the nervous system and body-mind. A special case of this balance is the convergence of activating and calming chemistry in the primary process of seeking and finding satisfaction through food, social engagement, and sex.

Before we move on, it's important to expand on the last similarity and note that polyvagal theory has a neurochemical dimension as well. In particular, it presents the role of the mammalian neurotransmitters oxytocin and vasopressin as congruent with that of the smart vagus. Specifically, these two respectively alter the function of the older calming and arousing neurochemicals—acetylcholine, serotonin, melatonin, and endorphins versus epinephrine, norepinephrine, dopamine, and cortisol—working to modulate these messengers of the primitive defense systems and override them with new forms of calm and arousal that support strategies of social engagement like empathic communication, intimacy, caretaking, and play.[92] This upgraded, mammalian version of vertebrate neurochemistry offers a parallel to the process model, in which the feminine and masculine drops of the subtle body-mind are identified as the twin "spirits of enlightened altruism." Like the chemistry of the smart ANS, these drops are understood as the neural chemistry that supports the emotional intelligence of empathy and altruism, including the prime social emotions of love, compassion, joy, and equanimity.

A Comparative Model of the Self-Regulation of Visceral Mind/Body States

Given this comparison of the process map of the subtle body-mind with the modern map of the ANS, we can now suggest a comparative, hypothetical model of the art of inner fire.

The first point of the model is that *the basis of the exceptional self-regulation mapped in the perfection stage is the conscious control of the primitive defensive systems of the ANS*, which is normally available to well-developed humans thanks to the evolution of the smart vagal nervous system. If we align the side channels with the more primitive, defensive regulatory systems of the SNS and old vagus, this is how our model translates the teaching that inner fire is kindled when the polar energies of the side channels are immersed into the central channel.

The second point in our comparative model is that the means *by which normal control of the ANS is extended is through the repeated practice of progressive methods of enhanced mind/body self-regulation, based on enhanced conscious control of the breath.* This is how our model translates the traditional teaching that the gateway to inner fire is the breath work based on vase breathing.

The third point in our comparative model is that *the prime role of breath-slowing methods like deep abdominal breathing and breath-holding in inner fire suggests that its main mechanism is to stimulate vagal sensory fibers in the chest and gut, which feedback to enhance the tone of both the new and the old vagus, simultaneously.*

The fourth point of the model is that *prolonged breath-holding stimulates still deeper vagal feedback circuits, likely including vestiges of the diving reflex developed by aquatic mammals, which signal both vagal nuclei to induce a paradoxical state of profound physical calm and heightened mind/brain arousal like that found in REM sleep, hibernating, estivating and diving mammals.*[93] Induced by the freeze-response center in the hypothalamus under the influence of the motor nucleus of the old vagus (DMNX), Porges calls such states fearless immobilization and links them to "immobilized love" states,[94] though I prefer to call them "unconditional love" states.[95]

The fifth point and main hypothesis of our model is that *consciously inducing the unconditional love system, which marries the most profound bodily calm with the most heightened mind/brain arousal, is the main psychophysical mechanism of the art of inner fire.*[96]

The sixth point of the model is that *the art of inner fire—especially when enhanced by vase breathing and simulated or real intimacy—involves mastering a gradual state-shift from the simple social engagement of the smart vagal system (supporting the courtship stage of intimacy), to a vasopressin modulated social approach mode of SNS arousal (supporting the flirting and seduction stages), and culminating in an oxytocin modulated "old" vagal state of passionate immobilization (supporting the consummation stage).*

The seventh point of the model is that *the imagery of melting and releasing the flow of masculine and feminine forms of bliss chemistry may be linked to the release of vasopressin and oxytocin*, functioning as mediators of the mixed sympathetic-primal vagal arousal of sexual excitement and intimacy, as well as modulators of the older arousing and calming neurotransmitters like norepinephrine, dopamine, acetylcholine, and the endorphins.

The eighth point of this model is that *the mastery of the biology of intimacy and consummation is not limited to courtship and mating, since the same unconditional love system is normally recruited for nursing, the basic paradigm of mammalian caretaking.*[97]

The ninth point of this model is that *mastering the biology of fearless social immobilization also provides a model for the socially engaged practice of fierce compassion*, since the same kind of mixed sympathetic-vagal activation at work in sex, love, and caretaking[98] is also involved in the socialization of aggression exemplified by rough-and-tumble play.[99]

The tenth point of this model is that *kindling the inner fire and inducing a shift to a state of ecstatic immobilization supports the insight-oriented process of extinguishing the conditioning of fearful memories and defensive reactivity from aversive learning,*[100] *as well as the formation of new, unconditional social bonds reinforced by healing visceral states and transformational affects.*[101]

The eleventh point of this model is that *unraveling the heart knot by deepening ecstatic immobilization with diamond recitation may refer to the way profoundly slowed and calmed breathing—itself conceived as a reassuring rhythm of implicit vocalization—can slow and stabilize the "common cardiorespiratory oscillator," helping to extinguish traumatic memories and reactivity in a broad range of brain regions.*[102]

The twelfth point in this model is that *by slowing breath to a near standstill in the context of ecstatic immobilization induced by inner fire, diamond recitation helps reset the three systems of the ANS—smart vagal, sympathetic, old vagal—to an optimal state of freedom from reactivity and openness to receptive, fearless and intimate engagement, experienced as the three lucid intuitions that culminate in clear light transparency.*

The thirteenth point in this model is that *given the profound slowing of heart-breath rhythm induced by vase breathing and diamond recitation, inner fire practice induces drastic reductions in oxygen metabolism and dramatic shifts in blood flow that simulate normally preconscious or unconscious state-transitions like those to orgasm, fainting, deep sleep, or death, leading to the conscious experience of signs of body-mind dissolution and reemergence like those mapped in the eightfold process of death-like dissolution and birth-like reemergence.*[103]

Vase Breathing and Inner Fire in Daily Practice

With this introduction to the arts of vase breathing, inner fire, and diamond recitation, we've surveyed the path of the first perfection sub-stage, hopefully with some sense of the gateway of freedom of speech. I've laid out the steps on the path in far more depth and detail than usual, because I believe if we have a clear view of what may lie ahead, it can serve to orient, inspire and challenge us. Again, I've taken some care to link the grand vistas of the process path to the simple steps laid out in some of its most basic introductory practices. Having linked the total nervous system work-out of vase-breathing to the simple preliminary form of the art taught in the action process practice of the *Healing Mother*, we turn now to link the profound arts of inner fire and diamond recitation to a simple practice of purifying our traumatic conditioning and reactive energies, akin to the practice of the *Heroic Altruist, Mother-Father.* Remember that if you're not currently an optimal process practitioner, this experiment is solely for liberal arts purposes, not for regular practice.

Meditative Experiment 10.2: Our Inspiring *Heroic Altruist Father-Mother*

In as peaceful and uplifting a space as possible,
With or without real offerings or images
Of the Heroic Altruist Mother-Father,
Settle into a comfortable, stable posture,
And clear your breath and balance your state
With nine rounds of alternate nostril breathing.
Now prime your energy and nervous system
By taking three or more simple vase breaths,
And, as you hold them, doing a breath work-out
Using the rotating wheel, binding hook,
Diamond binding, expelling breath-lock,
And/or total shakedown, at least once or twice.
When you've reached a balance of heightened clarity
And profound calm, recite mentally or out loud the following
Performance script, based on the purification process
Of the Heroic Altruist Mother-Father, pausing after each section
For as long as you like to hold its imagery,
Follow the recommended breath practice,
Focus on your experience, or seal in its meaning.

1. *Taking Refuge in the Four Healing Gems*
   "In a state of true confidence and radical openness,
   I take refuge in my mentor's inspiration and clarity—
   A gem-like embodiment of triple kindness,
   In the prime example of the Great Sage, Shakyamuni,
   His enlightening teaching and altruistic community
   And in all mentor-archetypes of heroic altruism.

To free myself and all sensitive beings I conceive
The altruistic spirit of pure blissful openness, and will
Develop myself and all beings as quickly as possible,
Until we gain the enlightenment to heal this world!"

1a. *Invoking the Mentor and Lineage as Heroic Altruists*
"Suddenly out of the void, six inches above my crown,
Your pure reality emits a thousand-petalled lotus
Of rainbow light, in the midst of which your translucent mind
Dawns like a full moon in water. Bubbling up from the moon
Like a fish leaping out of the water comes a sapphire light HUM,
Which instantly becomes a diamond scepter marked by HUM,
Flawless and unbreakable as your commitments and vows,
Beaming a rainbow aura everywhere that purifies
The destructive habits and instincts of all living beings,
And delights the enlightened, melting the whole multiverse
Into gem-toned light that returns and melts into the scepter
Until it dissolves and transforms into your embodied form
As the moonlight-white *Heroic Altruist*, father and mother
Of all enlightened beings and all master altruists.
Seated in meditation, facing forward, hovering
Just inches over my crown, your right hand holds a scepter,
And your left a bell, as they embrace your partner,
Diamond Pride, who straddles your lap, her arms and legs
Embracing you, holding a chopper and skull-bowl.
At ease in heavenly silks, you both bear the marks and signs
Of perfect altruism, and the living gems of transcendent virtue.
Above your head, like a string of pearls, sit all the mentors
Of your great seal lineage, up to Naropa and Tilopa,
Above whom sits the prime *Heroic Altruist*,
Mother-Father, all appearing exactly like you!"

1b. *Inviting the Mentor and Lineage to Bless Your Efforts*
"Your form glows like a cooling moon, lit from within
By the diamond OM, ruby AH, sapphire HUM
Seed syllables on moon discs at your crown, throat, and heart,
Beaming gem-lights to invite your spirit and the pure genius
Of all mentors to melt into my vision and merge as one!"

2. *Welcoming Mentor and Lineage into Your World*
"In the presence of your clarity, all experience has the taste
Of blissful openness, pervading the mind and all the senses!
I HAVE A PURE NATURE WHICH IS
THE NATURAL PURITY OF ALL THINGS!

In the crucible of the clear light of bliss, my five mind/body
Systems and elements melt and transform into healing
Elixir, the quintessence of the five pure intuitions.
OM AH HUM HA HO HREE! (3X)
Welcoming you all gratefully into my world, I offer
A sun-shower of sense delights—scented waters,
Incense, flowers, lights, music, and delicacies—
Converging toward you from everywhere, horizon and sky!
Fully and freely I share with you all my resources,
Virtues, every aspect of my intimate life—
Transformed by healing the elixir of my blissful openness,
Plus this precious earth, with its oceans, continents,
Wonders, forests, waters, and infinite web of life.
Perfectly pleased, the primordial *Heroic Altruist*
And all the mentors from Tilopa and Naropa
One at a time, melt into you and merge as one!"

2a. *Requesting and Receiving Consecration*
"Intensified by absorbing the genius of the lineage,
And enjoying the singular taste of these blissful offerings,
The sapphire HUM at your heart beams gem-lights everywhere
Inviting the five Mother-Father Transcendent Ones
To consecrate you and grant me initiation.
The couples come holding vases of wisdom elixir
Which they pour into you crown, filling your body/mind
And overflowing as an *Unshakable* Buddha crown.
MAY THE CONSECRATED VOWS
OF ALL THE TRANSCENDENT SHINE!"

3. *Fully Disclosing Faults, Limits, and Blocks*
"Regretting all the negative instincts and habits I've acquired,
All that limits and blocks me from mastering inner fire,
From the depths of my heart I regret every one of them now,
And firmly resolve with your help to avoid and unlearn them all."

4. *Vicariously Enjoying the Power of Inner Fire*
"Though all things are empty of any non-relative being,
With gratitude I enjoy your mastery of inner fire
And the power it gives you to burn blocks to pure bliss,
And refine the wisdom that yields a master's communion."

4a. *Enhancing Enjoyment with the Four Boundless Moods*
"May all beings have real happiness and its causes!

May we all be freed from all suffering and its causes!
May we all enjoy and savor all excellent things!
May we all know unwavering equanimity!" (Repeat 3X)

5. *Requesting and Receiving Blessings*
"Mentor of bliss and clarity, please bless my body-mind
With your inspiration, help me focus my awareness
And purify my energy so I can open and clear
The channels and complexes of my central nervous system,
Balance and gather my sun and moon energies into
The central channel at my navel, to ignite inner fire,
Master the flow of bliss and realize innate wisdom!
Moved by your love for me and all life, mother-father,
You enter into a full embrace and melt into bliss
That flows from your crown and sexual organs into your hearts,
Which merge into one jewel drop of orgasmic bliss-complete void,
Melting into my crown, into my central channel,
Radiating warmth, bliss, and light, so I can see and feel it
Opening and clearing the channel both frontwards to mid-brow
And downwards to my throat, heart, and navel, where I see and feel
Both side channels loop and curve back up to join into it.
Savoring the drop's warmth, bliss and light, I see and feel it
Light up and clear my crown complex, with its diamond
Exclamation point, then flow to light my throat complex,
With its inverted ruby exclamation point, then flow
To light my heart complex, with its sapphire exclamation point,
And finally flow to light up and clear my navel complex,
Merging with its inverted ruby exclamation point, until
It intensifies the navel point's innate warmth and light.
Focusing now on that ruby point, I see and feel it
Glowing with heat and light like a ruby-seed tongue of fire,
Fanned to greater heat with each breath, its starts to flare
From its brazier and point and burst from its tip into flame.
Kindled now, I take some vase breaths to ignite inner fire,
Melt and savor pure bliss and seal it with emptiness."

Now slowly draw breath in through both nostrils,
See and feel it filling both your side channels all the way down
Below your navel, and then looping up with them into your
Central channel. Nodding your head, as you swallow gently press
The remaining breath down and out your side channels, into your
Navel complex, and hold it down onto the flaming ruby-seed. now
Tone the muscles of your pelvic floor, drawing whatever sensual
Energy you've aroused

Up your central channel to your navel complex,
Holding it up to the flaming ruby seed, to meet the breath above
In a kiss. Now hold your breath and savor that kiss as long as you can,
But well before any distress, start letting it go, gently and slowly,
Up though the flaming ruby point, up the central channel to the crown,
Where it reenters the side channels and leaves out the nostrils.
As you repeat this 3, 7, or 21 times, taking care not to strain or push yourself,
See and feel the flaming ruby exclamation point at your navel
Burn and blaze more and more, until its flame-tip threads its way
Slowly up the central channel, melting the sapphire point at the heart,
Until it drips like wax into the fire, then threading up to throat,
Kindling its ruby inverted exclamation point to burst into flame,
And join the navel flame-tip until they reach the diamond exclamation point
At the crown, heating it until it too starts to melt and drip like wax,
Releasing the flow of bliss-chemistry. As it reaches the throat,
It spreads a sense of bliss and emptiness, as it reaches the heart, it spreads
Sublime bliss and extreme emptiness, at the navel it spreads supreme bliss
And ultimate emptiness, and at the sexual organ it spreads orgasmic bliss
And complete emptiness. Take care to restrain a natural release,
And instead put your mind to drawing the flow of bliss back up
From the sexual organ to the navel, spreading bliss-void, to the heart,
Spreading sublime bliss-extreme void, to the throat, spreading supreme bliss-ultimate void, and to the crown, spreading orgasmic bliss-complete void.

Finally, now practice gathering all your bliss energies and chemistry
Into the extremely subtle body-mind at your heart. First, let your lunar
Bliss melt down from your crown to your throat, spreading bliss-void,
Dissolving your solidity and sight, marked by seeing all like a mirage;
Next, draw your solar bliss up from your sexual organ to your navel,
Spreading sublime bliss-extreme void, dissolving your bodily fluids

And hearing, marked by seeing all things swirl like smoke; then
Let your lunar bliss melt from throat to heart, spreading supreme
Bliss-ultimate void, dissolving your bodily heat and smell,
Marked by seeing all things scintillate like sparklers; finally, draw
Your solar bliss up from navel to heart, spreading orgasmic
Bliss-complete void, dissolving breath-gasses and taste, marked
By seeing all things glow like a flame. At your heart level,
Withdraw your subtle energy from your outermost circle of
Distracted seeking into your sapphire exclamation, spreading
Bliss-void as its body slips into clear light, marked by a luminance
Intuition like a clear moonlit sky; next withdraw your subtle
Energy from your intermediate circle of angry defensiveness
Into your sapphire crescent, spreading sublime bliss-extreme
Void as it slips into clear light, marked by a radiance intuition
Like a clear twilit sky; then withdraw your subtle energy from
Your inner circle of share-bound isolation into your sapphire
Flame-drop, spreading supreme bliss-ultimate void as it slips
Into clear light, marked by an immanence intuition like a
Midnight sky; and finally, withdraw your subtle energy entirely
From seeking, defensiveness, and isolation into your sapphire
Flame-tip, spreading orgasmic bliss-complete void as it slips into
Your extremely subtle energy-drop and clear light, marked by a
Translucence intuition like a crystal clear predawn sky. As you
Immerse your bliss-energy completely in clear light translucence,
Observe your in-breath, pause and out breath themselves as the
Diamond recitation of OM, AH, HUM, and reflect that your
Subtlest breath-drop-mind knows no distinction between self
And other, subject and object, body and mind, and lacks even
The subtlest hint of any non-relative being, essence, nature,
Identity or objectivity (1 or 3X). Seal the process by affirming your
Enlightened pride & confidence:

"I AM THE SELF WHOSE NATURE IS
THE DIAMOND INTUITION OF OPENNESS!"

5a. *Self-Consecration: Embodying Pure Inspiration*

"From the womb of emptiness my clear light mind becomes
A vast rainbow lotus with sun and moon cushions
From which my affirmative thought bubbles up as a sapphire
Light syllable HUM, in which all my vowels and constants,
Neural energy and mind merge as one, beaming a rainbow
Aura, within which I take bodily form as the diamond white
Heroic Altruist Father-Mother, in blissful embrace,
Holding a scepter and bell, chopper and skull-bowl,
Symbolizing the union of great bliss and pure clarity!

Lit from within by a diamond OM, ruby AH,
Sapphire HUM on moon discs at my crown, throat, and heart,
I beam rainbow lights everywhere to invite all altruists
To melt into me and merge as one, while wisdom muses
And geniuses consecrate me with pure bliss-void nectars,
Overflowing as an immovable Buddha-crown."

6. *Requesting Constancy as you Practice Inner Fire*
"Recognizing this imagery as a mere simulation,
I ask you, mentor, and the whole inner fire lineage,
Please stay with me until I reach perfect mastery!
Moved by your love for me and all life, mother-father,
You instantly come to my crown, embrace and melt
Into one, indestructible drop, like a rainbow tear for joy,
Which slips through my crown and throat to melt into my heart,
Merging your blissful openness with mine, intensifying my light,
Energy and warmth until they fill me as a flame fills a lamp
And a nectar, a vase, rippling out in my actions
Until all those around me at home and on earth become
Heroic Altruists, returning a wave of joy to my heart!"
Now pause to absorb and drink in the warmth and moisture of that joy,
As long and deeply as you can, and then prepare to close the session:
"Suddenly the earth, my meditation space and my body
All return to their normal appearance, and the three syllables
Sealing my body-speech-mind melt into my heart-drop."

7. *Dedicating yourself to Embodying Sheer Brilliance*
"With any errors or omissions I've made in this practice
Out of ignorance, misperception, lack of resources, or art,
I ask you, mentor, please be patient and all-forgiving!
Any positive insight or energy I've gained through this practice
I dedicate to being always inspired by your teaching,
Until I myself become a *Heroic Altruist*,
In this very lifetime, as quickly as possible!
By mastering the arts of inner fire and diamond recitation,
May I gain the free speech to enlighten myself and all life!"

11 Inspiration—Turning Bliss to Light

> (Aryadeva says) in the Integrated Practices that, if you possess the intuitive wisdom of realizing freedom of mind through the process of knowing the instinctual natures and the three luminances, at the time of the homogenous order (of four bliss-voids), you will dissolve the wind energies that move the virtuous and nonvirtuous natural instincts and the voids will dawn in sequence and you will enter into clear light transparency.
>
> (Tsong Khapa, *Brilliant Illumination of the Lamp of the Five Stages*[1])

The Stage of Freedom of Mind: Embarking on the Process Path of Insight

Once we've begun to unravel the knot of defenses that binds our hearts, to taste and savor the bliss and clarity deep within, we're ready to embark on the next phase of our journey: using that clarity to disarm and transform the instincts that drive us. Though the methods used here are basically the same as those used on the first perfection sub-stage—inner fire, diamond recitation, and sublimated intimacy—this stage involves more profound forms of these inner and outer arts. More profound immersion in recitation and more vividly simulated intimacy or real intimacy with an actual partner help take us deeper into the subtlest layers of the mind, allowing us to expose and reform not just reactive habits learned through conditioning but the innate instincts underlying them. That is why our focus in this phase, as described by Tsong Khapa, shifts from the subjective aspect of sublimation—tapping and harnessing the progressive flow of bliss—to its objective aspect: cultivating the intuitive clarity freed by progressive realization of openness, technically realized as "emptiness" or "voidness."

On the face of it, this shift is reminiscent of the transition on the path of engagement from the stage of insight, which dispels learned negative habits, to the stage of meditation, which uproots the instincts underlying them. Though technically, that shift on the process path is not complete until the end of the third perfection sub-stage, it begins in earnest here. As we learned in chapter 10, the objective reality of emptiness that helps us cut through both habits and instincts here is the same reality as that known on the engaged path. But the art of sublimating bliss, which serves as the platform for contemplating emptiness on the process path, is fundamentally different from the engaged method of concentrative quiescence. Specifically, the insight of emptiness we cultivate on the second perfection sub-stage is a visceral insight at the subtlest level of our energy-mind, a type of intuition that is truly indivisible from the flow of great bliss tapped by inner fire and deepened by diamond recitation. This explains why Tsong Khapa closes the chapter on this sub-stage in his *Brilliant Illumination* by describing the aim here in terms that would equally suit the engaged insight path, while linking that aim to a method distinctive to the process path:

> To abbreviate the import, understanding the self habit as the cause of migrating in the egoistic life cycle and as the means of supporting the instinctual cognitive obscurations, you decisively determine the view of selflessness that eradicates the objective of the self habit. (In terms of method) you see that if you do not develop that view into the experiential actuality of great bliss you will not have completed the extraordinary cause of the wisdom of the truth body, so you generate bliss by dissolving the wind-energies that drive the instincts.[2]

Process Meditation on Emptiness: The Four Bliss-Voids and Luminous Intuitions

Traditionally, the distinctive process form of emptiness meditation depends on the alignment of the levels of emptiness insight with the degrees of bliss-void intuition tapped by inner fire, as well as with the subtlest levels of the dissolution caused by immersing our subtle energy-mind into the extremely subtle wind-mind-drop at the heart. This alignment is expressed in the identification of the four bliss-voids—bliss/void, sublime bliss/extreme void, supreme bliss/ultimate void, and orgasmic bliss/complete void—with the four luminous intuitions that mark the four final stages of dissolution—luminance, radiance, immanence, and translucence. Before we go any further, this key alignment of the bliss-voids and luminances—alluded to in our opening quote—needs some clarification. The first point to clear up is how and why these nuanced metaphors of light serve to orient us on the path towards freedom of mind. The second point is why that quote cites only three luminous intuitions, rather than four.

Pure Intuition: The Luminous Clarity of the Primal Mind

While the tradition makes a great deal of the distinctive process view of the body, nervous system and mind, the use of the metaphor of light to describe the primal nature of the mind is as old as Shakyamuni's first teaching. Though the first two noble truths of suffering and origin, and the last, the truth of the path, describe the complex nature of the mind in its compulsive mode driven by the three poisons, the third truth of Nirvana—which he pronounced "the sole, supreme truth"—describes the mind as "profound, peaceful, blissful and *luminous*." His finding that consciousness is naturally lucid awareness or primal clarity insures the fundamentally positive and radically optimistic character of Buddhist psychology, in all forms.

When it comes to the process-oriented path, the depth-psychology of the process tradition is no exception. In explaining freedom of mind, Aryadeva's *Integrated Practice* cites pronouncements from the "Lord," that is, Shakyamuni himself, which link the process view of mind with the view of classical systems of Buddhist psychology:

> The Lord said, "Mind has the character of space—free of color, shape and so forth." The Lord also explained that, "(It) should be understood through (its) characteristics of radiance and perceptiveness." Hence, the personal instruction of that (shall be) introduced: that is to say, first the radiance(s), then the prototypes (of the instinctive patterns).[3]

The Three Intuitions: Paths to Purification

Now let's consider why the luminous intuitions are listed here as three, not four. The answer to this question, on the face of it, is simple. Of the four luminous intuitions aligned with the four voids and the four final phases in the dissolution into clear light, the first three—luminance, radiance, and immanence—are grouped together, distinct from the fourth—clear light translucence—based on their distinct functions in the normal mind as well as the distinct roles they play on the path. The normal function of the first three intuitions is different from the clear light since they co-operate with the eighty instinctive patterns that drive ordinary, compulsive life, while the clear light is naturally free from such patterns and so can support either compulsion or purification. In addition, their key role in the contemplative practice of the second perfection stage is that they are the means to an end—the realization of clear light—while the clear light itself, in this context, is the end.

As for definitions of the three luminances, they are of two kinds: heuristic and definitive. The first kind, meant for novices on the second perfection stage, applies a range of terms from various systems of Buddhist psychology to help provide some provisional indications of their true nature based on familiar ideas. Nagarjuna's *Five Stages* applies three sets of heuristic terms, to illustrate their functional, cognitive, and affective nature, respectively.

The Three Sets of Three Heuristic Similes of the Three Luminances

The first of these sets compares luminance, radiance, and immanence to mind, mindset and consciousness, terms derived from the depth-psychology of Buddhist Constructivism. After critiquing any simplistic alignment of the three with the three levels of consciousness defined in that psychology—superficial consciousness, traumatic mindset, and the subconscious mind—Tsong Khapa explains that the intention here is simply to indicate that the three luminances, like the layers of mind in that system, can be fully purified through contemplative self-analysis.[4] In lieu of aligning the three with layers of mind, he aligns them with the functional aspects of accumulating normal experiences, supporting those experiences, and maintaining consciousness. Of course, in the same moment, he insists that all three luminances have all three functions to some degree, so the terminology seems to serve as a heuristic way of indicating that the three together have a quality of a depth of mind which must be successively exposed and transformed.

The second set of terms—imaginary, relative, and perfect—also derive from the deconstructive framework of Constructivist depth-psychology. According to that system, our cognition is distorted by our instincts for projecting and reifying our habitual constructs of past experience onto present reality. Those projections make up the imaginary reality we normally project onto the world and mistake for the world as it actually is. Underlying those projections is a real process of subconscious construction of conception and perception, a process referred to as the relative reality or the reality of interdependence. When, on the path of contemplative self-analysis, we deconstruct our projected, imaginary view of the world, and expose the real process of interdependent causes and intersubjective conditions underlying it, that real process now emerges as the perfected or purified reality of mind and things as they are. Applying these terms to the luminances presumably helps prepare the novice for the way the successive experience of the three deconstructs even the subtlest, intuitive sense of subject-object dichotomy involved in normal compulsive experience.

Of all Nagarjuna's heuristic similes of the three intuitions, however, the one that most concerns us is his affective simile, comparing them to the three root compulsions—attachment, aggression and delusion—respectively.[5] Of course, as we'll see when we explore them further, this likeness is complicated by the link between the luminances and the other key dimensions of the subtle mind: the neural energies and instinctive patterns. The complexity here lies in the fact that the three groups of instinctive patterns, or at least the first two, don't sprout neatly from any one root compulsion, but seem like a wild bramble of tangled instincts, positive and negative, desirous and aggressive.[6] Despite that complexity and a range of views on this topic, I've chosen to stick with the alignment cited in Aryadeva's *Integrated Practice*.[7]

More significant than that alignment per se, is the seeming contradiction Tsong Khapa resolves between Aryadeva's view of the three luminances as each aligned with one group of instinctive patterns and the view of some Tibetan medical and scholarly traditions that all eighty patterns dissolve with our coarse energy-mind into the first luminous intuition at the threshold of the subtle energy-mind.[8] The seeming contradiction stems from a contrast between the baseline condition in which a normal person's subtle luminances are unconscious and remain enmeshed with the eighty instincts, and the condition of a person on the path who, thanks to exceptional control of neural energies, remains conscious in transition through the three subtle intuitions and so is able to "dissolve" the normal instinctive patterns into them.

So if we read Nagarjuna's simile as describing the mind in its normal compulsive condition, the luminous intuitions represent layers of the subtle mind's primary cognitive process, yet they also cooperate with the reactive energies and affective functions of the subtle mind, represented by the instinctive patterns. However we group the instinctive patterns, the point of this simile is to orient us specifically to the process of insight and transformation involved at this stage. That is, to disengage our subtle minds from their normal enmeshment with instinctive patterns of compulsive life, by freeing the three intuitions from the reactive energies that fuel those patterns; and by joining them instead with the blissful openness that helps us see through and break free of instinctive compulsions.[9]

More Heuristic Similes from the Imagery of the Creation Stage

Before we delve more deeply into the art of disentangling the luminances from the instincts, we should touch on a final set of heuristic similes for them which derive not from classical Buddhist psychology but from the process imagery of the optimal creation stage. This imagery combines natural symbols used on the creation stage—moon and sun, night and day, female and male, left and right, lotus and jewel—with the linguistic symbols for the parts of the breath-cycle from diamond recitation—OM, AH, HUM—to indicate the second perfection stage experience of the three luminances. Specifically, moon, night, female, and so on combine with the in-breath sound OM to indicate luminance; sun, day, male, and so on combine with the breath-pause sound AH to indicate radiance; and moon-sun union, day-night boundary, androgeny, and so on combine with the out-breath sound HUM to indicate immanence.

Spacious, Formless Awareness: The Definitive Definition of the Luminous Mind

As for the definitive explanation of the three luminances, Tsong Khapa quotes Aryadeva's *Integrated Practices*:

> (Luminance) ... is formless, without body or speech; it is like a taintless autumn sky filled by the illumination of light rays from the moon disc, perceived in the form of the natural clarity in all things—this is the ultimate spirit of enlightenment, the first void, the wisdom-luminance.

> (Radiance) has the form of freedom from subject and object, and is without body and speech; being the perception of all things in the reality of extremely brilliant taintlessness, like the autumn sky flooded with sun rays, it is the second spirit of enlightenment, the total goodness, having the character of the second stage, that of extreme void.
>
> (Immanence) has the form of nothingness, the character of space, lacking body and speech; as if pervaded in a state of fog-bound midnight, subtle and selfless, motionless, with no movement of life-energy control; without mind, unwavering ... (it) has the characteristic mark of delusion, the ultimate void.[10]

So in a definitive sense, the three luminances are described as subtle intuitive states of pure awareness, increasingly freed from visual or auditory symbolic forms, and progressively purged of even the subtlest distinction of subject-object duality, experience or motion. But this cognitive description reflects only one of three key dimensions that define the luminances, the second and third being the activity of subtle neural energies and, coordinated with that activity, the functioning of instinctive patterns of affect. As for these two other dimensions, Tsong Khapa quotes Nagarjuna's *Five Stages*:

> With the nature of twilight, day and night,
> There are luminance, luminance-radiance,
> And likewise luminance-immanence;
> Thus the mind is said to be threefold.
> And thereby its basis is explained.
> The wind-energies, in their subtle form
> Having become fully mixed with consciousness,
> Emerging through the paths of the senses,
> Thus cause the perception of (all) objects.
> When you have luminance(s)
> Mounted on wind-energies,
> Then all the instinctual natures
> Fully arise without remainder.
> Wherever the wind energies remain,
> There the instinctual natures function.[11]

In other words, these primal, undifferentiated forms of consciousness, comingled with the reactive neural energies of stress and trauma, activate the instinctive patterns of compulsive life, which color all our mental activity, perception and experience. But while this is how the luminances function in the normal condition of unconscious life, they also can serve as powerful forces of purification and change, when they can be consciously accessed and freed from reactive energies. So Aryadeva quotes the *Intuition Diamond Compendium*:

> The consciousness which arises from brilliance—that very thing is called "mind" (and) "mentation." All things have that as their root, (having) the nature of defilement (or) purification. From that, (evolves) the imaginary duality, self and other. That consciousness is mounted on air ... From that, (one) experiences very clearly the three consciousnesses, the manifestation of the prototypes (of instinctive patterns) and the luminances. The prototypes are born from the luminance(s) as cause.[12]

Wind in the Trees: Reactive Energies and the Instincts They Stir

Interestingly, Aryadeva goes on to illustrate the causal interactions linking the luminous intuitions with the instinctive patterns they support by drawing on a classical metaphor of wind and the movements it engenders:

> The three consciousnesses (are) rootless, unlocated, foundationless, signless, colorless, shapeless, beyond the senses. Nonetheless, (they are) luminous; thus, one is aware (of them when they are) conjoined with the air (i.e. wind) element. For the same reason that the formless air-element may be perceived by inference by observing the actions (of trees and such) moving and shaking, and so on (in the wind), just so the formless luminance of (subtle) consciousness may be perceived by inference, as it is inferable from the (perceptible) prototypes such as passion, dispassion, moderate passion, and so forth.[13]

In fact, considering the definitive definition the luminous intuitions, this metaphor can be tweaked a bit to help illustrate the complex relations between the elements of subtle consciousness, energy and primal patterns (which my colleague Christian Wedemeyer translates elegantly as "prototypes"). Specifically, if we follow the analogy of the luminances with sky or space, then the analogue of the wind which must be inferred from the moving trees is actually the reactive subtle energy that normally drives the compulsive mind. And it is such reactive energy in turn that stirs up the instinctive patterns, which are the specific analogues of the moving trees.

Given this analysis, when Nagarjuna and the *Intuition Diamond Compendium* describe the three luminous intuitions as the causes of instinctive patterns, we must add the caveat that this is only true in the condition of their unconscious "defilement" by reactive stress-energy, not in the condition of their conscious "purification" by pure, disarmed bliss-energy. With this distinction between defiled and purified mind-states, our analysis of the definitive model of the subtle body-mind leads to the actual practice of the second perfection sub-stage, based on deepening forms of diamond recitation and sublimated intimacy. But before we can explore how those arts work to bring us to the realization of clear light, the gateway to freedom of mind, we should turn to consider the instinctive patterns which are the shades of attachment, aggression, and delusion to be dispelled by the brilliant light of the three luminances.

Affective Psychology in the Process Tradition: The Eighty Instinctive Patterns

As for the traditional enumeration of these patterns, both Thurman and Wedemeyer confide that Indian and Tibetan process masters seem to have attributed little importance to rectifying the precise list and count. Fortunately, my pioneering colleagues have done the work of reviewing the literature and codifying two fairly compatible lists. Though I've taken some liberties with their scholarly translations for the sake of consistency with the model of process science we developed in chapter 10, essentially I follow their presentations.[14]

As we said, the lists are organized in three groups, aligned with the three luminances—luminance, radiance and immanence—and categorized (by most experts) as attachment-oriented, aggression-oriented and delusion-oriented, respectively. Each list contains a different number of patterns, classically: thirty-three in the first; forty in the second; and seven in the third. You'll notice, as I said, that the list contains a wide range of different affective instincts, some seemingly contradictory with the primary instinct that defines their category. Of course, given the complex interconnections and polarities which characterize the nervous system as conceived in both the process subtle body and modern brain models, this should hardly be surprising.

The Luminance Intuition's Thirty-Three Attachment-Oriented Instinctive Patterns

As for the thirty-three attachment-oriented patterns aligned with luminance, I will list each with a brief description drawn from Tsong Khapa. The first three—mild, moderate, and strong detachment—refer to letting go of objects of attachment or desire. The fourth, extroversion/introversion, refers to the mind's tendency to approach objects of desire and avoid objects of fear.[15] Patterns five, six, and seven—mild, moderate, and intense grief—refer to the emotional anguish caused by the loss of an object of attachment or desire. The eighth, gentleness or benevolence refers to the mind being at ease or at peace with others. The ninth, antagonism, refers to the opposite: the combative activity of an agitated mind.[16] The tenth, eleventh, and twelfth, mild, moderate, and intense fear, refer to the fear, panic, and terror of the mind facing threatening adversity. The thirteenth, fourteenth, and fifteenth, mild, moderate, and intense craving, refer to the mind's strong longing for an object of desire. The sixteenth, dependency, refers to an addictive clinging to some sensory stimulation. The seventeenth, discouragement, refers to a disinclination to engage in positive actions. The eighteenth and nineteenth are hunger and thirst. The twentieth through twenty-second are mild, moderate, and intense sensitivity to pain, pleasure and indifference. The twenty-third through twenty-fifth, receptivity, retention, and discrimination, refer to the three capacities for social learning. The twenty-sixth, conscience, refers to an aversion to harmful actions based on personal values. The twenty-seventh, compassion, refers to a sensitivity that wishes others to be relieved of suffering. Mild, moderate, or intense love, refers to the wish for others to be safe and happy. The thirty-first, being startled or alarmed, refers to the insecurity of a mistrusting mind. The thirty-second, greed or hoarding, refers to an obsession for collecting possessions. The thirty-third, envy, refers to feeling disturbed by the good fortune of others.

The Radiance Intuition's Forty Aggression-Oriented Instinctive Patterns

As for the aggression-oriented instinctive patterns aligned with radiance, there are forty. The thirty-fourth, attraction, refers to longing for an unattained object of desire. The thirty-fifth, passion, refers to longing for an already attained object of desire. The thirty-sixth through thirty-eighth, mild, moderate, and intense joy, refer to enjoyment of pleasure. The thirty-ninth and fortieth, delight and rapture, refer to the joy of attaining a desired goal and the joy of repeatedly savoring that attainment. The forty-first, awe, refers to the intense enjoyment of something wholly astonishing or new. The forty-second and forty-third, elation and satisfaction, respectively refer to the mind's exuberance at and enjoyment of something delightful. The forty-fourth through forty-sixth, embracing, kissing, and sucking, refer to the primal urges of social bonding. The forty-seventh, constancy, refers to the mind's ability to persist without changing course. The forty-eighth, courage, refers to an impulse to undertake a positive challenge. The forty-ninth, pride, refers to an inclination towards arrogance. The fiftieth, effectiveness, refers to the urge to fully engage challenges. The fifty-first and fifty-second, covetousness and aggressiveness, refer to the impulse to deprive or dominate others. The fifty-third, enthusiasm, refers to the impulse to initiate positive action. The fifty-fourth through fifty-sixth, mild, moderate and extreme transgression, refer to the urge for increasingly violent actions towards others.[17] The fifty-seventh, hostility, refers to unprovoked aggression towards others, especially those in authority. The fifty-eighth, seduction, refers to the impulse to charm or possess an attractive person. The fifty-ninth, resentment, refers to the inclination to harbor a grudge. The sixtieth, virtue, refers to the impulse to engage in positive action. The sixty-first, transparency, is the impulse to communicate clearly and openly. The sixty-second and sixty-third, honesty and dishonesty, refer to the inclination to communicate truthfully or deceptively. The sixty-fourth, conviction, refers to a strong mindset of certitude and determination. The sixty-fifth, dispossession, refers to the inclination to stop accumulating things. The sixty-sixth, generosity, refers to the impulse to give things away. The sixty-seventh, leadership, refers to the urge to rouse more inhibited others. The sixty-eighth, heroism, refers to the urge to face inner demons like addictions and compulsions. The sixty-ninth, incorrigibility, refers to the impulse to indulge negative actions without qualms of conscience. The seventieth, deceitfulness, refers to the intent to mislead others through dissembling. The seventy-first, malevolence, refers to an inclination to indulge malice. The seventy-second, domination, refers to the urge to oppress others. The seventy-third, cunning, refers to the urge to defraud or manipulate others.

The Immanence Intuition's Seven Delusion-Oriented Instinctive Patterns

Finally, there are the seven delusion-oriented patterns aligned with the immanence intuition. The seventy-fourth, moderate attachment, refers to residual clinging to familiar objects of love and desire. The seventy-fifth, forgetfulness or mindlessness, refers to loss of memory or mindfulness. The seventy-sixth, confusion, refers to a tendency towards disorientation, distortion and error. The seventy-seventh, withdrawal, refers to an urge to stop communicating. The seventy-eighth, exhaustion, refers to a tendency towards depression and fatigue. The seventy-ninth, apathy, refers to a disinclination to act. Finally, the eightieth, dullness, refers to a tendency towards mental fogging and doubt.

Deep Cognitive and Affective Change: Accessing and Analyzing the Subtle Mind

Given this brief introduction to the process depth-psychology of the subtle mind, it's time for us to turn to the contemplative path of insight based on that model. This is where the path of insight begins in earnest on the optimal integral perfection stage: with a direct, deconstructive encounter with a range of compulsive patterns that are not acquired in this lifetime, but instinctive and innate. But before we can explore how we might understand the work of this sub-stage in terms of modern neuroscience and psychotherapy, we first need to unpack the traditional models and methods used to guide and support that work.

Perhaps the best place to start that unpacking is to revisit a distinction Tsong Khapa makes about the nature of the subtle mind: that the luminous intuitions and the instinctive patterns of the subtle mind are mutually incompatible. This insistence may seem confusing now that we've surveyed the model and map of the subtle mind in terms of the intersection of the luminances, reactive energies, and instinctive patterns. You may recall, though, the point I made in that survey: that the normal condition in which these three are enmeshed is not the condition to which Tsong Khapa's commentary is addressed.[18]

A simple way to resolve this seeming contradiction is to draw a distinction between the luminances as normally unconscious, subtle levels of mind, and the luminous *intuitions* as conscious realizations of the natural potential of the subtle mind to disentangle itself from reactive energies and instinctive patterns. Given this distinction, we only realize a luminous intuition to the extent that we have the mastery of neural energies we need to take the wind out of the sails of the instinctive patterns, and the clarity we need to expose those patterns as reactive compulsions driven by reactive energies.

Disentangling the Intuitions from the Instincts: Sudden or Gradual?

Although Tsong Khapa makes the point that the luminances can and must be freed from the instincts, by dissolving reactive energies into the subtlest mind-energy-drop at the heart, he also adds that this dissolution process is not instantaneous but gradual.[19] This raises some question about whether the disentanglement of the luminances from the instincts is gradual as well. Thurman addresses this question in a long footnote to his translation by suggesting that the instincts dissolve along with *coarse* energy all at once into the first luminance of the subtle mind, and are not compatible with the *subtle* energies that support the first three luminances leading up to the *extremely subtle* energy-mind of clear light.[20] However, such a disjunction based on different energy levels conflicts with the basic assumption that the extremely subtle mind-energy-drop is the source of both the reactive instinct-energies which drive compulsive life *and* the proactive bliss-energies which fuel enlightened life.

Given that assumption, it seems clear that the luminous mind and its subtle energies must be equally able to operate in either of two possible modes: an unconscious, compulsive mode clouded and biased by the instincts; and a conscious, enlightened mode purged and freed from the instincts. Assuming this, the process of awakening the luminous intuitions and purging the energies and instincts of the subtle mind must be a gradual process, in which luminous intuitions and bliss-void energies increase as instinctive compulsions and reactive energies are dissolved.

In effect, we can think of the luminous intuitions as *progressive degrees of clarity within the depths of the subtle mind, brought about by disentangling intuitive consciousness from the clouding and biasing influence of innate compulsions.* In this, they reflect the extension and deepening of the work of the first sub-stage, which purged our deep symbolic processing of the clouding and biasing influence of stress-conditioned memories and the reactive neural energies supporting them. In this phase, the luminous intuitions help take the process beyond symbolic processing and energy, to free the deepest affective processing of our minds from the clouding and biases of innate compulsive patterns and the reactive neural energies that support them.

So, if the goal of the first sub-stage was freeing our symbolic mind-energy to fully merge with the blissful rhythms of expressive energy cultivated by diamond recitation, the goal in this stage is to free our deepest affective mind and intuitive energy to fully merge with the blissful openness of the heart-drop, released and accessed in the final phases of diamond recitation.

Understanding this parallel is key not just to recognizing the insight-oriented aim of the second sub-stage, but also to understanding the methods that bring us to freedom of mind—to total immersion in the ecstatic translucency that is the gateway to the great perfection stages.

The Arts That Free: Diamond Recitation and Process-Oriented Intimacy

Once we clearly understand this aim—the final objective of the process-oriented path of insight—it's time to turn our attention to the arts by which it is realized: the most profound forms of diamond recitation; and the most advanced practice of sublimated intimacy. Starting with the first, Tsong Khapa spends much of his discussion of freedom of mind on reviewing and critically assessing the many traditions of advanced diamond recitation found within the classical literature and the process lineages of his day. The many methods he reviews use a broad range of arts to cultivate freedom of mind at various points along the central channel, including the navel and sexual organs, as well as the crown and heart. Some methods involve complex visualizations, others simply involve lights and syllables or no imagery. While most involve some advanced form of diamond recitation, some do not. And while some emphasize conjoining diamond recitation with real sexual intimacy, others emphasize conjoining it with simulated intimacy alone. The main point to be drawn from this review is that there seems to be no one, exclusive way to approach this profound insight path or to reach its aim, called "the mind objective."

In analyzing the range of traditional process methods for realizing freedom of mind, Tsong Khapa reiterates many of the points we've explored already in chapter 10. Wherever we find it easiest to immerse coarse mind-energy into the central channel, he emphasizes the vital importance of eventually gathering and immersing subtle mind-energy into the indestructible drop at the heart. His reason should be familiar: among all the complexes within the central channel, the heart complex plays a special role as the seat of the coarse and subtle life-support energies as well as their source in the extremely subtle mind-energy-drop. From this follows his preferred method for immersing mind and energy fully into the subtle and subtlest levels of the heart complex, namely diamond recitation, the most effective art for loosening and unraveling the heart-knot which normally blocks access to the extremely subtle body-mind.

So while he admits the potential value of methods involving other complexes like kindling inner fire at the navel—with or without intimacy—to start the descent of bliss from crown to sexual organ or to channel it back up to the crown, he locates these as introductory ways for novices to tap into the central channel. This synthetic approach uniting the arts of the mother and father traditions at different points in perfection stage practice was already well established in Tibet thanks to the *Death Terminator* lineage transmitted

Figure 11.1 Atisha, Master of the Process Art of Inspiration

by Atisha. Eventually, however we tap the flow of bliss, he recommends we learn to gather it from above and below into the heart, so we can practice tapping into the indestructible drop. He says this quite clearly:

> Thus, by the inner condition of the method of life-energy control however you do it, and by an outer condition of relying on union with a (virtual or actual) consort, the wind-energies and (blissful) enlightenment spirits are compressed into the heart center from the top and bottom of the body.[21]

So, when it comes to practicing diamond recitation at the heart, here as in the second sub-stage, the art of immersing awareness and energy fully into the subtle and subtlest body-mind involves channeling the flow of bliss-voids concentrically into and out of the indestructible mind-energy-drop. And, as we saw in chapter 10, those methods which guide this practice with elaborate or simple sets of syllables arrayed around a lotus, wheel, moon or sun disc, are seen by Tsong Khapa as preliminary means of gathering mind and energy, which should be gradually simplified and eliminated as practice progresses. The aim here is exemplified by the method transmitted from Naropa to Marpa using three concentric rings of syllables—outer vowels, middle consonants, and a seed-syllable hub—to cultivate the final immersion and dissolution process, marked by the successive dawn of the three luminous intuitions that culminate in the objective clear light.[22] Of note, most lineages within this tradition anticipate Tsong Khapa's conclusion that, in using this form of diamond recitation as preparation for freedom of speech, the wheel is first alternated with formless practice then removed entirely.

As for the final keys of practice for realizing freedom of mind, Tsong Khapa points to two indispensible "inner" conditions, conjoined with two possible "outer" supports. The two inner keys he defines are: (1) holding the energies from above and below in a "kiss-connection" at the heart; (2) "compressing" coarse and subtle mind-energies concentrically into the extremely subtle mind-energy-drop at the heart. The two "outer" supports are: (3) simulated sexual intimacy with a virtual partner, and/or (4) real sexual intimacy with an actual partner. Let's touch on each of these, one at a time.

The Two "Inner" Keys to Freedom of Mind: Kiss-Connection and Compression

When it comes to the first key, essentially Tsong Khapa is referring to the same process of gathering and connecting energies from above and below at one vital point within the central channel, as in the art of vase breathing we experimented with in chapter 10. The difference here is that the focal point of that "kiss-connection" is shifted upwards from the navel to the heart, as in our meditative experiment 10.2. He makes this quite explicit: "Here (in the context of freedom of mind), holding in kiss-connection requires that you perform vase-pressure at the heart center."[23] Of note, in discussing this key, our guide mentions the risk for novices in applying such pressure, yet assures us that, "if you know what you're doing, this is not a big hindrance." Essentially, this risk comes from the temptation to be impatient with the slow unfolding of the gentle path of gradual self-transformation and to push for "results" too hard, too soon.

As for the second inner key, the art of compression essentially involves the ability to gather, focus, and dissolve mind and energy into a vital point, in this case concentrically into the innermost essence of the heart. Essentially, this art amounts to a continuation of the work of loosening and unraveling the heart-knot with the help of diamond recitation. As this unraveling proceeds beyond the level of freedom of speech, we gradually experience a fuller and deeper immersion of coarse and subtle mind-energy into the heart-drop, made increasingly accessible by continued recitation. As at less profound levels of immersion and dissolution, this process is marked by the eight signs which culminate in the conjunction of the four bliss-voids with the concentric dawning of the three luminous intuitions, and finally, clear light translucence.

In reviewing this key, Tsong Khapa points out that when we've been able to experience the four bliss-voids conjoined with glimpses of the luminous intuitions on the path to freedom of speech, there will likely be no need for further imagery to aid the art of compression. Instead, the gradual dissolution of coarse mind-energy and subtle mind-energy into the unknotted heart will have been deep enough to give rise to the four initial signs of death—mirage, smoke, sparks, flame—and we'll go on to experience the concentric flow of bliss-voids as subtle mind-energy melts into the drop, marked by the signs of luminance, radiance, immanence, and finally clear light. Tsong Khapa quotes the *Concise Five Stages*:

> First the mirage-like experience
> Arises with its five light-rays,
> Second there is the moon-like luminance,
> And third there is embrace by the light of the sun;
> And from the night luminance there is immanence.[24]

You'll notice that, where a prior quote abbreviated the last four stages into one, this quote abbreviates the first four into "the mirage-like experience," and only implies the final experience of clear light. The focus here is on the three luminous intuitions, specifically because of their key role in the analysis and purging of the subtle mind-energy-body. Given the continuity of the experience on the two stages—freedom of speech and freedom of mind—you might wonder, "What is the difference in the work on the two stages?" We already mentioned the key distinction: while the first stage focused on unlearning defensive reactions based on the symbolic imprints acquired through personal or intergenerational traumas, this stage focuses on exposing, disarming, and transforming compulsive reactions based on innate, natural instinctive patterns. More to the point, although the literature often seems to describe these stages and their attainments as all-or-nothing events, in my view, this tradition approaches the profound work of symbolic and intuitive self-analysis they map as gradual processes involving an intricate unraveling sequence in which countless, cumulative insights are aligned with corresponding breakthroughs in emotional and energetic self-mastery.

Two Sides of One Fabric: Disentangling Learned and Innate Reactivity

In particular, though I've drawn a distinction between the two stages in terms of analyzing symbolic and non-symbolic reactive patterns, our more or less conscious, learned stress-reactions and our more unconscious, instinctive reactions are so congruent by nature and interwoven by development that disentangling them is far from simple. The enmeshment of these levels is suggested by the term reserved for the unconscious level reactions—literally "instinctive constructs"—a compound that may seem like a contradiction in terms. The first word, meaning "instinctive," "primal," or "natural" seems to clash with the second, meaning "construct," "concept," or "pattern." This tension reflects a recognition of the complex causal relationship between learned symbolic processing habits, on the one hand, and pre-symbolic, instinctive processing patterns, neural energies and chemistry, on the other. As I see it, this insight and term dovetail neatly with the psychoanalytic notion of "instinctual representatives," which Freud used to describe how higher mental and emotional patterns reflect the demands made on the conscious mind by unconscious instincts and the energies driving them.[25] Likewise, the continuity between the symbolic "speech" stage of process insight and the pre-symbolic "mind" stage also reflects Tsong Khapa's depth-psychological formula of the two-tiered analysis of conscious and unconscious defensive habits on the engaged insight path:

> Although this (unconscious, instinctive) mental habit does not hold (objects in this way) after analysis of the meaning of expressions, if the objects thus held (as objectively real) were to exist in fact, they would have to be discoverable by rational cognition that analyzes the manner of existence of the referents of conventional expressions. Therefore, since there is no contradiction between the fact that non-analytic, unconscious self-habits are the principal rational negates (of self-analysis) and the fact that the treatises contain only analytic negations (on the theoretical plane), one (should) not adhere to the notion that "the texts merely negate intellectual mental habits with their objects."[26]

Tsong Khapa clearly affirms that discursive self-analysis works because there is a structural congruence between the forms of misperception caused by conscious self-protective habits and by instinctive, unconscious self-protective patterns.

This formulation may also help explain the apparent conflict between the teaching that the instinctive patterns dissolve all at once into the first luminance and the recognition that the gradual unraveling of the heart-knot and immersion into the heart-drop involves a long process of purifying and dissolving reactive energies and instincts. The seeming conflict disappears if we assume that the conditionings layered over instincts may be resolved as early as the initial dissolution into the central channel on the way to freedom of speech, while the final disarming of the underlying instinctive patterns may only be resolved gradually as we progress to the full unraveling and immersion into the heart-drop on the way to freedom of mind. A final indication of the gradual nature of the path to freedom of mind comes in the many subtle shades of distinction traditionally made in describing the levels of realization of the clear light which is the aim of this stage, as described in this passage from the *Diamond Rosary*:

> By strong application of diamond recitation
> Having known the nature of wind-energy,
> You cut off the instinct-driving wind-energies,
> And will attain the objective in the mind.[27]

Mother and Child: Levels and Types of Clear Light

When it comes to that objective, the tradition distinguishes many levels and shades of clear light, depending on how profound and complete is the dissolution of mind and energy which leads to it. There are many profound shifts in mind/body state that may lead to a dissolution process, marked by the experience of the eight signs culminating in clear light, but each can be distinguished based on the level and depth of that state transition, as mapped onto the process model of the subtle nervous system. The dissolution caused by natural transitions from waking to sleep, waking to orgasm, or life to death lead to different (usually faint) experiences of clear light when compared with the dissolutions caused by consciously induced transitions from waking to altered meditative states.

As for meditative transitions, the dissolution caused by immersing coarse mind-energy into the central channel leads to an experience of clear light far less profound than that caused by the dissolution of coarse and subtle mind-energy into the extremely subtle, indestructible drop. And the dissolution caused by the partial dissolution of subtle mind-energy into that drop leads to an experience of clear light less profound than that caused by complete dissolution of subtle mind-energy into the fully unraveled heart-drop. Only the clear light realized in this final context has the depth, stability, and intensity which compares with the natural clear light glimpsed in the more or less unconscious process of deep sleep, orgasm, or death, while also being fully realized because of its fully entering and abiding within the stream of conscious experience.

Technically, the natural experience of clear light is called the "mother clear light" while that experienced through meditation is the "child clear light." The clear light experienced through dissolutions short of full immersion into the heart-drop is called "non-free clear light," while that experienced though full immersion into the heart-drop is the "free clear light." A realization of clear light still mediated by a mental image of emptiness is called "metaphoric clear light," while one that involves a direct intuitive perception of emptiness is the "objective clear light." And a realization of metaphoric clear light in which subtle mind-energy is less than fully immersed in the heart drop is called "penultimate metaphoric clear light," while one in which that mind-energy is fully immersed is the "ultimate metaphoric clear light." Of course, the point of reviewing these distinctions is simply to get a feel for the way the gradual and progressive nature of the first two perfection sub-stages is mapped and experientially described.

Outer Keys to Freedom of Mind: The Nine Mergers and Three Seals

The most important aspect of this traditional mapping is the idea that reaching the goal of fully immersing coarse and subtle mind-energies into the unraveled heart-drop is not normally possible by inner meditative means alone. Traditionally, in order to reach freedom of mind, it's said that most people will need to combine the "inner" methods of tapping and unraveling the heart-drop which we've surveyed with "outer" methods or conditions. The conventional wisdom is that fully unraveling the heart-knot and immersing mind-energy is only possible when we enhance the arts of diamond recitation, kiss-connection, and compression with the natural altered state of sexual orgasm or near-death experience. This insight leads to the remarkable framework of altered-state integration called the system of the nine mergers and three seals. We've already touched on the three seals, and will soon explore the art of reaching freedom of mind with the aid of simulated/real intimacy, Tsong Khapa's third and fourth keys. For now though, we need to set the stage for that discussion, by exploring the nine merger system which frames the whole methodology of self-transformation on the optimal integral perfection stage.

The Nine Mergers: A Complete Framework for State-Specific Self-Transformation

Taken together the nine mergers and three seals set out a framework for using both consciously induced and naturally occurring altered states to help us get through the gateway of freedom of mind and onto the final three perfection sub-stages. In effect, the nine mergers system is a perfection stage version of the framework of narrative self-creation you may recall as the three conversions. As the conversions set out the logic for transforming our normal perception of the nodes of the life-cycle—death, development, and life—the mergers set out the logic for transmuting our normal range of mind/body states into the living-breathing fabric of a master altruist's fully integrated body-mind.

The nine mergers come in three sets of three. Each set involves a cycle of three mind/body states which is "merged with" one of the three aspects of perfect altruism: the embodiment of truth; the embodiment of enjoyment or bliss;

and the embodiment of emanation or manifestation. What this means is that the altered state in question is used as raw material to be worked, by way of the arts of the perfection stage, into one of the three fruits of the path. In the context of the perfection stage, the three fruits or forms of embodied enlightenment, respectively, are: the objective clear light mind; the pure virtual body; and the transformation of our normal body-mind into a manifestation of their communion.

The Waking State Mergers: Waking Meditative Paths to Altruistic Mastery

The first set—the waking state mergers—map the transmuting of our meditative states into vehicles for realizing a master altruist's fully integrated body-mind. Specifically, our meditative experience of dissolution into the metaphoric clear light is merged with a master altruist's embodiment of truth; our meditative experience of the re-emergence out of that clear light in a virtual body of blissful openness is merged with the embodiment of enjoyment; and our meditative re-entry into the normal waking state after and in-between sessions is merged with the embodiment of emanation. Of course, on the traditional map, this set of mergers cannot take us all the way through the gateway of freedom of mind, and so must be complemented with the second or third set of mergers, which relate to the mind/body states of the sleep-cycle and death process, respectively.

Sleeping, Dreaming, and Awakening: Sleep-Cycle Paths to Altruistic Mastery

Since the sleep-cycle involves the natural dissolution of coarse, waking mind-energy into the formless state called the clear light of sleep and reemergence from that into the virtual body of the dream state, it is highly recommended as a platform for deepening our realization of clear light and, consequently, our ability to resurrect our body-mind as a virtual body of pure blissful openness. Tsong Khapa addresses this briefly in his *Book of Three Inspirations*:

> (In sleep yoga) one meditates upon the heart *chakra* because it is to the petals of the heart *chakra* that the vital energies naturally withdraw when one goes to sleep. Working with this *chakra* during the waking state brings familiarity with a technology that can be utilized in the sleep yogas, to be engaged when (during the process of entering into the sleep state) the subtle energies of the luscious and succulent *(side channels)* naturally begin to withdraw into the central channel and the heart *chakra*. The force of the experience of the four emptinesses in general and the clear light emptiness (metaphoric clear light) in particular will be amplified. One fixes one's meditative absorption on this clear light of sleep as intensely as possible.[28]

> The manner of the application (of this same art to dream yoga is that in the process of first retaining the clear light of sleep one cultivates awareness of the four emptinesses (luminous intuitions) of sleep. After that, when dreams occur one recognizes them as such.... If in the process of dream yoga one wishes to extend the duration of one's dreams, then before going to sleep one meditates on the throat chakra as (one did the heart) before. As soon as the mind holds to it for a moment, then within the dream sphere one engages in whatever spiritual exercises are appropriate.[29]

Bringing deep sleep into our practice in this way is what is meant by merging the sleep state with the truth body; and bringing dreams into our practice afterwards is what is meant by merging the dream state with the bliss body. And finally, waking up while bringing new levels of clarity and bliss to transform our embodied experience of daily life is what is meant by merging the sleep-cycle with the emanation body. In terms of the traditional mapping of the second sub-stage, this art may help us advance the depth and fullness of our realization of the penultimate metaphoric clear light closer towards the ultimate metaphor clear light, but cannot take us all the way there, much less to the objective clear light which yields complete freedom of mind. Nonetheless, using the sleep-cycle can help us progress toward freedom of mind and also have spin-off benefits on the way. Before we move on, two points may help flesh out the nature and use of this practice, especially of working with dreams.

First, Tsong Khapa clearly distinguishes this process method of working with dreams through inner fire from the method of simply bringing waking focus and resolve to stay lucid in the dream state. Although he lays out at length a range of techniques for using resolution alone, some from the process tradition and some not, in the end he insists that the depth, stability, and effectiveness of dream practice based on resolution is limited in comparison with the optimal integral practice based on inner fire. "To bypass the method of inner heat and instead to rely solely upon cultivating the power of resolution is like throwing away the trunk of the tree and keeping only the branches."[30] This point is relevant in distinguishing the process practice from the arts of dream-work we're familiar with from psychoanalysis[31] and lucid dreaming.[32]

Second, this tradition involves an extensive practice of working with dreams to overcome traumas, phobias and general anxiety, as well as to transmute traumatic images of ourselves, others and the world we share into ideal images of a mature altruistic self, life and object world.

> During the dreaming process whenever anything of a threatening or traumatic nature occurs, such as drowning in water or being burned by fire, recognize the dream as a dream and ask yourself, "How can dream water or dream fire possibly harm me?" Make yourself jump or fall into the water or fire in the dream. The method of training in the illusory

> nature of dreams entails that we take one of the dream objects, such as a vase or the like, and remind ourselves that, even though this object is appearing in the dream, nonetheless it is empty of the nature of its appearance. Recognize dream objects as dream objects.... On the basis of that understanding one transforms the dream world and its inhabitants into the supporting and supported *mandala* (i.e. ideal environment and archetypes). One meditates on how all these appearances are empty of true self-nature, yet manifest as illusions. Cultivate the vision of how all phenomena are a drama of ecstasy and void. These meditations are also to be applied to the waking state.[33]

Death and Dying: Near-Death Paths to Altruistic Mastery

The final set of three mergers applies to using the process of death and dying to enhance our experience of metaphoric clear light based on waking state and/or sleep cycle practice with the profound, natural dissolution of mind-energy in the course of near-death or real death. Tsong Khapa explains:

> Should death arrive before supreme enlightenment has been attained (through the gateway of freedom of mind), and one wishes to apply the yoga for enlightenment at the time of death, then (as the death process sets in) one engages in the yogas of controlling the vital energies in order to recognize the clear light of the moment of death, using the same principles that were applied in the yoga of retaining the clear light of sleep. In this way one enters into the *bardo* (transition state) experience, applies the techniques learned through the yoga of the illusory (virtual) body of dreams, and generates the *bardo* body as the illusory body of the *bardo*.[34]

So, relying on the natural dissolution of death to fully unknot the heart, access the heart-drop and deepen our experience of the luminous intuitions, we can reach not just the ultimate metaphoric clear light but the actual, objective clear light that yields perfect freedom of mind. This remarkable transformation of traumatic death into a path to enlightenment is what is meant by merging the clear light of death with the body of truth. In the transition that follows clinical death, akin to that reported by the many who survive near-death experiences,[35] the art of shaping the re-emergence into a virtual body like a dream body is what is called merging the transition state with the bliss-body of a master altruist. And finally, given the traditional view of intergenerational agency (or after near-death experience), the voluntary transmission of that virtual body as a seed of altruistic mastery into another (or our own) embodied mind is called merging re-incarnation with the emanation body of a master altruist.

If the arts of unraveling the heart-knot through meditation in the waking state or sleep cycle were not remarkable enough, this third set of mergers introduces a truly incredible science of transforming even the final transition of death. Of course, this science is integral to the process tradition, and like process dream-work, deserves a volume in itself. But while the application of process neuroscience and technology to death and dying is crucial to understanding its full scope and potential, in terms of our understanding of the perfection stage, it is also in a sense a detour. This is because the mainstream of optimal integral process practice is devoted to becoming a master altruist "in this life, as quickly as possible," to quote a traditional refrain. Even if merging the sleep-cycle with the embodiment of altruistic mastery brings us closer to unraveling the heart-knot and realizing objective clear light, we cannot actually complete our journey to perfect freedom of mind short of death without relying on the "outer" support of the first two seals.

The Virtual and Actual Seals: A Fourth Set of Mergers?

Given this, Tsong Khapa glosses over the mergers of sleep and death while discussing the freedom of mind stage laid out in Nagarjuna's *Five Stages*, but devotes much of his chapter to his remaining two keys: the two seals of simulated and real intimacy. In fact, it's not a stretch to think of these two as a fourth set of mergers, teaching us how to merge the dissolution, reemergence, and afterglow of sexual experience with the triple embodiment of a master altruist. In any case, viewed in light of the mergers, it's easier to appreciate the science behind the traditional emphasis on the sexual arts of the first two seal practices. On this, Tsong Khapa quotes the *Wisdom Scepter Compendium*:

> Just as, without thoroughly combining milk and sesamum you won't get butter and sesame butter, so, without uniting *vajra* (scepter) and lotus which thoroughly combine (male and female) practitioners, you cannot approach the three (ultimate luminous) consciousnesses (that lead to objective clear light). Through such inability to unite vagina and phallus, the concentration of great bliss is not discovered.[36]

And in the same key, the *Five Stages*:

> Of all magics, a woman's magic is most excellent.
> This clearly marks the distinct three (luminous) wisdoms—
> Attachment, detachment and that between—
> All three come from the union of the two organs,
> The connection of the scepter and the lotus.[37]

Sublimation and Sexuality: Sacred or Profane?

Given the hypothetical model of sublimation we sketched in chapter 10, we can better understand the role of sexual imagery and practices in the perfection stage arts of sublimation. Our model strongly supports the traditional insistence that sexual imagery and practices on the process path are in not meant to attract lustful students or promote indulgent lifestyles. The key role of the biology of courtship and sexual intimacy in the perfection stage is not gratuitous or pedagogical, but a simple reflection of the fact that tapping into the subtle and extremely subtle body-mind requires more profound altered states than those accessible from the normal waking state, even in the warm-blooded mode of optimal social engagement. In fact, our model suggests that mammalian forms of courtship and sexuality are the prime paradigms for the smart vagus disarming and recruiting the sympathetic and primitive vagal nervous systems into a socially engaged way of life. It suggests that the art of sublimation may be seen as a contemplative method of cultivating and extending the natural cycle of psychosexual maturity in humans, which leads from courtship to intimacy, intimacy to mating, mating to reproduction, and childrearing to caretaking and parental/extended group altruism._

As in the Jungian notion of the psyche as an androgynous being with feminine and masculine aspects—*anima* and *animus*—the process art of the virtual partner involves envisioning ourselves as embracing an opposite sex partner who embodies those aspects of integration which complement our gender-specific ideal self-image. If we identify with a feminine archetype of heroic altruism, we center our minds in the objective intuition of translucency oriented towards unconditional openness and envision our intuition partner as a congenial masculine archetype aligned with the blissful energy and chemistry of compassionate openness. On the other hand, if we identify with a masculine archetype of heroic altruism aligned with compassionate bliss-void energy, we envision our intuition partner as a congenial feminine archetype aligned with the wisdom of clear light translucency. In either case, our aim is to develop a strong enough sense of empathy, intimacy and communion that we can see things from both gender perspectives, without losing the sensorimotor experience of being fully embodied and immersed in intimate union.

The way the simulation works is that we imagine ourselves as vividly as we possibly can in our empty archetypal body being intimate with our intuition partner, also envisioned vividly as inhabiting an empty congenial body of light. Inside our body and our partner's, we envision the subtle nervous system with its three channels, four complexes and four syllables, only now we extend the three channels into the pelvis, opening out at the fifth complex at the tip of the sexual organ, blocked by a sapphire seed-syllable HUM. We imagine our two bodies, both sitting in meditation, the female on the male's lap or vice versa, with arms and legs wrapped around each other in passionate kiss, joined in full sexual communion. While the aim here is to bring the experience as much as possible to life, with all senses engaged—looking, hearing, smelling, tasting, and touching our partner as viscerally as possible—and rehearsing the mounting excitement, balancing the vividness of our simulation is the enlightened dignity which sees the transparency and emptiness of self, other, and our shared experience. Visually reflecting this balancing act between arousal and restraint, the sex organs themselves are envisioned in symbolic form, the male's as a diamond scepter, and the female's as a pure gem-light lotus, with their most sensitive points blocked by a sapphire seed-syllable.

This vivid simulation is then conjoined as an "outer condition" to enhance the "inner condition" of inner fire and diamond recitation. So, whatever sensual arousal we generate adds fuel to the fire, intensifying the energy available to draw up from the locked "lower doors" to meet the inhaled energy pressed down from above in a "kiss" around the AH-stroke at the navel or heart. Mastering the art of sublimation means that, whatever bliss we generate, is not meant as an end in itself to be indulged, but as a means to an end. And that begins when we restrain the normal sexual response and instead use that bliss as a platform to practice seeing through any and all the ordinary constructs we'd normally bring to such an experience. This includes deconstructing any sense of "myself" or "my partner;" any notion of physical identity or gender identity with a reified "body;" any construct of a discrete, identifiable "experience" to be had, or a discrete, identifiable "mind," "subject" or "self" that could have it. In describing this process of fueling inner fire by arousing the sexual response—called "the wood of the organ of truth" in the *Great Seal Drop*—Tsong Khapa quotes this compelling passage:

> By closing and opening (the lower doors),
> The energy encompasses the fire.
> With the wood of the organ of truth,
> Thereby the furor-fire burns,
> Consuming the body entirely,
> And all materials of the heap of notions.[38]

Given the general point that the seal practices are indispensible to freedom of mind in this life, he goes on to explore some of the technical questions surrounding them. Among these, two main points shed light on the links between the arts of sexual intimacy and the death and sleep mergers we just surveyed. While both points impact on both seal practices, the first mainly concerns the actual seal or real sexual partner, while the second is more relevant to the intuition seal or imaginary partner.

Tapping and Channeling Bliss with the Aid of Sexual Intimacy

The first question Tsong Khapa addresses about how the bliss of sexual arousal and orgasm is channeled in the seal practices is twofold: where should we try to tap into the central channel; and once we've done that, where and how should we channel the flow of bliss through the various complexes? The traditional response is that we can tap into the central channel at any number of vital points, including the classical three "nose-tips" or points for energy-control, at the nostrils or mid-brow, at the tip of the sexual organ, or at the heart. In addition to these three—upper, lower, and middle "doors"—emphasized in the father process there is the navel complex where most kindle the inner fire, and, as we saw in dream practice, the throat. But while we may tap into the central channel at any of these points, the release and flow of bliss chemistry is typically localized, as descending from the crown to the sexual organ, and/or as ascending in reverse order from the sexual organ up to the crown.

This is perhaps most especially true in the context of the sexual arts in the process tradition, since the downward flow of bliss chemistry from crown to jewel, and the upwards flow of sublimation from jewel back up to crown make obvious sense given the normal physiology of sexual orgasm and its restraint. Given this orientation, we would expect the vital points to be emphasized in the first two seal practices would be either the "lower door" called the "lustful" (for cultivating bliss) or the "upper door" called the "lust-free" (for practicing sublimation). Assuming this, Tsong Khapa's answer to this question and his explanation are not just surprising but also shed light on the real nature and mechanisms of the first two seal practices.

The Necessity and Efficacy of Heart-Centered Sexual Intimacy

Tsong Khapa's reply is clear: even the "outer" support of sexual practices must ultimately be applied at the heart and channel the flow of bliss-voids concentrically. Given the special role of the heart, perhaps this insistence shouldn't surprise us in itself. But, of course, applying this orientation to sexual practice, not just to meditation, sleep, and death, seems counterintuitive and is surprising. Given the many references to sexual organs in the literature, he takes pains to show that, while the flow of sexual bliss may be channeled to the "lustful lower door" and/or the "lust-free upper door" to strengthen bliss and/or sublimation, eventually it must be channeled into the middle or "medium" door of the heart, citing the following key passage from Aryadeva's *Integrated Practices*:

> From the union of the scepter and the lotus, beginning from the crown, the enlightenment spirit melts from the 72,000 channels and flows gradually though the lustful, lust free, and their medium states.[39]

Even more intriguing is his own explanation of why the heart-center must ultimately be used:

> Here you are developing the four voids of extremely great impact according to the death process, and so it is an emergent order coming from the process of compressing the wind-energies into the heart center and a reverse order coming from a process of expanding back out from the heart center. Thus, by the inner condition of the method of meditating life-energy control however you do it, and by an outer condition of relying on union with a consort, the wind-energies and enlightenment spirits

> are both compressed into the heart center from the top and bottom of the body.[40]

In other words, the heart center must be used because only when meditatively channeled there can the orgasmic bliss generated naturally by sex have the same "extremely great impact" on the subtle body-mind as the death process: fully unraveling the heart-knot in which the extremely subtle mind-energy drop is normally bound. In this sense, the intensely sublimated version of sexual intimacy practiced on the optimal integral perfection stage is in fact closely linked with the death mergers. And this link helps reveal that the form of intimacy this practice involves is as far removed from ordinary sexuality as the death mergers are from the ordinary experience of dying. Naturally, such a sublimated re-channeling of sexual arousal and bliss is only possible in the context of a mind and nervous system prepared by the meditative arts of inner fire, diamond recitation, vase kiss-connection and compression. Tsong Khapa explains:

> (Sexual practice fosters …) compression in the heart center, because, when you rely on previous habituation to the compression practice in the heart center, when you unite with the consort and practice the yoga of the two contemplations (compressing into and expanding out of the heart-drop), union with the outer consort serves as a condition for the compression of wind-energy into the heart center.[41]

Virtual Versus Actual Intimacy: The Primacy of Mind

This brings us to Tsong Khapa's second main question about process sexual practices. Is real intimacy absolutely indispensible to reaching freedom of mind in this life, or can simulated intimacy serve as well for any practitioner under any circumstances? The focus of the question is how to read an obscure passage from the *Five Stages*:

> Who finds *not* scepter-lotus (real sexual) union,
> Even superficially,
> Will (still) achieve (mind objective) once by experience,
> Due to the potency of the yoga.[42]

Tsong Khapa's remarks on this question are both surprising and significant. After dismissing misinterpretations, he supports the reading that highly receptive students may have so powerful an experience during their initiation rite that their subsequent "inner" practice combined with simulated intimacy is enough for them to realize the objective clear light. Traditionally, this is taken to mean that, without even once experiencing an external, "superficial" union with a real partner, some process students may be able to achieve the same death-like depth, stability, and intensity of clear light experience as others who rely on a real sexual partner. This reading is especially clearly developed in the commentary based on the *Wheel of Time* tradition by Tsong Khapa's main process-oriented disciple, Khedrub Je.[43] This partly reflects the distinctive *Wheel of Time* teaching that the central channel remains partly open naturally even in untrained humans, making the prospects for unraveling the channel knot(s) and fully accessing the indestructible drop(s) by meditation more promising.[44]

This reading is remarkable because it challenges yet again the widespread misconception that process practices are meant to indulge or enhance normal sex, making it unmistakably clear that the emphasis in this tradition is on the *sublimation* of sexual energy and chemistry for the sake of mind/body self-regulation and mature psychosexual development. In a sense, it also links the sexual practices back to the dream mergers, in that it underscores the possibility for fully orgasmic experiences to be mentally generated through vivid imagination, as in the normal experience of some sexual dreams. And this explains why Tsong Khapa frames the supposed necessity of relying on a real sexual partner as advice meant for novices who need or want external support tapping into the central channel to release the flow of bliss.[45]

As a corollary to this crucial question, Tsong Khapa also touches on the methods of restraining orgasm we explored in chapter 10, as vital to the art of sublimating sexual energy and chemistry. As you might expect, he also reframes these methods as specifically addressed to novices who have just begun to master tapping into the central channel and are struggling to gain control of the flow of bliss energy and chemistry. While he admits the potential value of such practices in intensifying the experience and control of bliss, he also clearly challenges any reading that overstates the importance of men restraining emission or women restraining orgasm, as if such restraint or the heightened, prolonged bliss it supports was an end in itself:

> As for this, for many who can hold (enlightenment spirit) without emission (or orgasm) … though the (practice) can be claimed to produce great excellent qualities, if there is no art of uniting this (practice) with the view of voidness that decisively ascertains reality, the purpose for generating the bliss is lost.[46]

As a final note, Tsong Khapa's take on the primacy of sublimation in the seal practices also helps explain another framework commonly used to describe their range and scope. Specifically, that's the rubric of sexual practices as complicated, uncomplicated, and extremely uncomplicated. This rubric describes the tradition, as part of the ritual matrix of these practices, for real sexual partners to use elaborate *mandala* stage settings and gatherings with costumes, masks, play dialogue, food, music, song, and dance, to help them envision/hear themselves and one another as archetypal beings rather than ordinary partners. Given Tsong Khapa's analysis of the elective and preliminary role of real sexual practice, and our comparative model of the disarming effect of positive facial imagery, speech tones and movements on the heart, we can easily understand the rationale for these audiovisual aids for novices. Tsong Khapa comments:

> As for the need for performing those, the *Integrated Practices* says that it is for the sake of not letting the mind turn elsewhere and to mutually delight each other, meaning that the mind should not deviate from great bliss, and to mutually increase the bliss.[47]

We can also readily see these as part of an organic progression to less complex ritual arts for more advanced practitioners who can leave more to the imagination, eventually leading to the most advanced, extremely uncomplicated practice that focuses simply on joining the internal process of channeling and sublimating bliss with the process of simulated intimacy.[48]

Given this look at the four keys of practice on this stage, we're almost ready to translate its remarkable means and ends in terms of modern science and psychology. But before we do, it remains for us to address the culmination of the process path of insight on this perfection sub-stage: the intuitive realization of clear light that is the gateway of freedom of mind.

Realizing Clear Light: The Gateway to Freedom of Mind

However we approach the unraveling of the heart-knot and full immersion in the heart-drop, the culmination of the path of insight on this crucial perfection sub-stage is the practice of harnessing the four deepest levels of bliss to realizing the most profound forms of the four voids, which is the final attainment of the luminous intuitions including the translucence intuition of the ultimate metaphoric clear light. Tsong Khapa stresses the fact that the aim of this practice is to realize the true nature of the mind. So he insists that it isn't enough to focus on emptiness as an afterthought to the dissolution process, in the state of orgasmic bliss and complete void. Instead, he explains the traditional emphasis at this stage on the three intuitions, rather than on the clear light, is meant to counteract any tendency to rush to clear light and gloss over the subtle mind. In fact, cultivating the emptiness insight continuously through all stages of dissolution is vital to insure both the purging of each successive layer of the mind and the cumulative development of depth and stability of insight needed to achieve the ultimate realization of the objective nature of the mind. Here is how he spells this out:

> Since you will not realize selflessness if you do not unite the bliss and void of the three wisdom-intuitions, they will not arise in the mode of nonelaboration (required to deeply realize clear light), and only the luminances themselves of white, red and black will arise. If you do unite the bliss and void of those three, in the actuality of the certain knowledge of

> the view (of emptiness) you must eliminate the subject-object dichotomy in the three luminances.[49]

It's pertinent that Tsong Khapa uses the term "selflessness" here, since it underscores the fact that the crucial point of this stage is to see through even the subtlest residue of our conscious and unconscious identification with traumatic memories and aversive mind states. So it is vital for us here not just to *see* pure, blissful openness as the objective nature of our minds, but to immerse our sense of self so completely in that nature that we dissolve any lingering confusion with or clinging to an aversive mind-state as "I" or "mine." In this spirit, he unpacks the traditional emphasis on the first three luminances, especially the third, in technical terms, explaining how the depth of our immersion in the first three bliss-voids prepares the mind for the most profound, nonconceptual realization of clear light:

> In general in the first three voids, by just the proportion of how great is the momentum of termination of wind-energies, just so dense and long are the clarity and nonconceptuality of the clear light. Especially in the occasion of immanence unconsciousness, by just how great is the momentum of the loss of consciousness, just so much is the elimination of the mind's ability to distract itself to other objects and the development of immersion into clear light itself.[50]

The "termination of wind-energies" and "loss of consciousness" he refers to in this passage presuppose the basic insights of process science that the mind-states accessed by full immersion into the heart-drop naturally involve the gradual dissolution of even subtle neural energies, to the point where even experts can expect a transient loss of consciousness. Likewise, "nonconceptuality" and the prior reference to "nonelaboration" are references to the fact that such profound states naturally involve a decline in symbolic processing to the point where we are less prone to distraction and more able to directly experience the mind and its reality, eventually without the intrusion of even the most accurate mental constructs which make prior intuitions of clear light "metaphoric."

Of course, the endpoint of the second stage is not the final realization of objective clear light without any conceptuality at all. Instead, it is an opportunity to refine our mental image as far as possible by fully dissolving disturbing energies into the blissful openness of the heart-drop. Technically, the fruit of the second stage is called the ultimate metaphoric clear light, where the mind is free from the bias of reactive instincts and energies, and so can refine its symbolic image of clear light to approximate its objective reality as accurately as possible. Tsong Khapa's point here is that when we can immerse our subtle mind-energies fully in the luminous intuitions, our awareness makes a relative break with even subtle forms of compulsive self-consciousness and self-object dualism. Once we've effectively cut the umbilical cord to those familiar frames of reference, we don't permanently lose consciousness, but, as clear light dawns, we gain the greater clarity we need to glimpse the objective nature of mind, albeit in the mirror of a highly refined intuitive image. Here are Tsong Khapa's final pointers for this radical realization:

> At the time of the arisal of clear light, except for remembering the view of voidness and focusing one-pointedly on the import of reality, you must concentrate consciousness completely, unmoved by wind-energies, without any thinking about other objects.[51]

Once again, it's notable here that Tsong Khapa not only places this realization near the extreme lowest limit of human conceptuality and mental complexity, but also still assumes and describes a continued capacity to monitor, analyze, and direct our experience with discursive thought. His words make it crystal clear that freedom of mind does not mean freedom from thought, but rather from any reactive mind-energy states that would block our total immersion in blissful openness, as well as any symbolic self-object habits that might distance us from the natural clarity of our luminous mind.

The Path to Freedom of Mind in Terms of Modern Brain Science

For a modern scientific view of the subtle body-mind at the heart of this stage, we only need to recall the comparative, hypothetical model of the central nervous system sketched out in chapter 10. Assuming this model, it makes good sense that the primal sources of consciousness and our instinctive life would both be traced to the subtle and subtlest body-mind, since we've linked these with the sub-cortical and brainstem levels where consciousness and primal instincts originate in our modern brain map. More precisely, the analysis of the subtle mind and its affective life into three types of consciousness and three classes of instincts may also be translated based on our model into systemic mind-states and instinctive response-styles regulated by the three aspects of the ANS, namely: the smart vagus, sympathetic, and old vagus systems, respectively. This tentative link would help explain why the first consciousness—luminance—is aligned with instinctive patterns related to social attachment; the second—radiance—is aligned with instincts related to survival and self-protection; and the third—immanence—is aligned with instincts related to primitive withdrawal and immobilization. The association of the immanence intuition with the old vagus is further supported by the tradition that its realization leads to a syncopal episode, since these are mediated by the old vagal freeze reflex.

Assuming this hypothetical alignment, it makes sense that learning to master these sources and instincts would involve tapping the central channel and accessing the vital heart-drop, since our comparative model has linked these steps to developing conscious self-regulation of the ANS, by enhancing our conscious control over its three sub-systems *via* the smart vagus. Specifically, this would suggest that gaining profound freedom of mind requires the art of diamond recitation, since slow breathing and breath-holding deepen the down-regulation of fearful attachment and defensive reactivity, by enhancing smart vagal control of the cardio-respiratory oscillator thought to cross-regulate sympathetic and old vagal tone. This linkage is further strengthened by the teaching that regulating states of consciousness and primal instincts at the deepest possible level requires completely un-knotting the heart complex and accessing the heart-drop, by deepening diamond recitation with kiss-connection and compression/expansion at the heart. Our comparative model would also suggest that these advanced arts of tapping into the heart may take smart vagal regulation of the ANS to the next level, by stimulating the release of oxytocin and vasopressin, which mediate the mammalian modulation of the sympathetic and old vagal systems to support fearless, playful, and unconditional social engagement.

In terms of the advanced methodology of the mergers and seals, our comparative model would suggest that the reliance on more profound altered states works by offering the conscious mind access to the primitive defensive mechanisms like sympathetic fight-or-flight reflexes and old vagal immobilization, since these are involved in various ways in REM sleep, slow wave sleep, near-death experiences, sexual courting and consummation.[52] Given that access, our model would suggest that the arts of diamond recitation, kiss-connection and compression/expansion at the heart support a progressive deepening of higher self-regulation of mind-state and instinct, mediated by both the deepening neural integration of the ANS under smart vagal dominance and by the increasing chemical modulation of the HPA axis and ANS by enhanced production and release of disarming neurotransmitters oxytocin, vasopressin, melatonin, and β-endorphin.[53]

Finally, in terms of the fruits of this path of insight-oriented self-regulation, our comparative model would suggest that the insight path of the second sub-stage helps make it possible for us to consciously access and integrate the deepest intuitions and instincts of the body-mind, by offering reproducible methods for extending the normal regulation of cortico-limbic processing mediated by prefrontal cortex to the level of hypothalamic, core brain and brainstem processing. Though such advanced levels of conscious self-regulation and mind/brain integration are not normally seen by us as accessible or teachable, a growing body of evidence gathered from process adepts and novices strongly suggests the contrary.[54]

The freedom promised by this path is a radical freedom of mind that involves not just breaking the hold of aversive conditionings from childhood or adult trauma but also breaking the grip of unconscious instincts for fear-based attachment, reactive self-protection, and primitive immobilization and withdrawal. It reflects not just freedom *from* the grip of mind-states driven by traumatic conditioning and primitive stress-instincts, but freedom *to* fully immerse ourselves in our natural potential for mind-states of intuitive clarity and blissful openness. By freeing us to make these deeply positive states our new normal, the attainment of freedom of mind would not just be an incredible boon for us as individuals, but an even more incredible revolution in our potential for unconditional social engagement, including exceptional psychosexual integration and exceptional altruism.

The Path to Freedom of Mind in Terms of Modern Psychotherapy

In terms of the insights and methods of contemporary psychotherapy, this profound level of integration of conscious and unconscious, mind and body, is hardly conceivable from the perspective of mainstream therapies. Of course, there are less conventional forms of psychoanalysis, dynamic and somatic therapies which do offer analogues for the second perfection sub-stage. Although no one modern therapy integrates the broad range of process insights and methods that clear the way to such complete freedom of mind, there are several that offer partial analogues for the inner approach of this stage, and some that offer analogues for its outer approach. In particular, the inner approach of the stage may be compared with those of the Kohutian and Lacanian schools of analysis. And the outer approach may be compared with those of Jungian and Riechian analysis.

The Inner Path of Selfless Desire: Kohut and Lacan

In terms of its inner approach, the second sub-stage resembles those schools of analytic psychology which believe we can delve deeply into what is normally the unconscious mind, and gradually eliminate unconscious self-imposed blocks to our natural capacities for clarity and love, deepening and expanding our primal interconnectedness with others. In Kohut's conception, the development of the self revolves around our natural capacity to merge with others, as the infant originally did with mother, guided by our empathic ability to see and connect with the inner life of another. With the help of attuned and "mirroring" others, Kohut believed, our tripartite minds naturally avoid the fragmented, compulsive mode of life Freud described, in which the traumatized ego is powerless over a punitive conscience and instinctive drives. At our best, our narcissism is not self-enclosing, but increasingly opening us through empathy with others to allow the development of mature self-love, healthy intimacy, and eventually the expansive mode of engagement he called "cosmic narcissism."[55] Of course, such growth involves the ability to use empathic bonds to expose and see through traumatic self-object constructs and the attachment, aversion or primitive narcissism which anchor them. The aim of this process of self-analysis is the freeing and expanding of our most profound natural capacity for unconditional acceptance, mature empathy and heroic connection to life, eloquently described by the Buddhist analyst Pilar Jennings in her recent book, *Mixing Minds*:

> He called this (optimal phase of development) the *curve of life*, in which we understand, without undue despair that we are part of a life continuum that does not start with us and will not end with us. The world is something more than our original experience, and our capacity to move into this graceful recognition, argued Kohut, is our greatest psychological achievement. With this reconciliation to impermanence and connection to the larger rhythm of life and death comes wisdom, the final transformation of our primary self-interest.[56]

In this sense, while Kohut's psychology puts "self" and "self-love" first, it does so given a view of human narcissism as naturally unitive, connective, and self-transcendent, and as capable of evolving into a cosmically loving, open agency akin to the process-oriented "self of selflessness."

Perhaps more suggestively, the deconstructive analysis of Lacan was based on the profound insight that the unconscious is not a fixed structure of mind but the product of habitual reifications of language. Given this profound insight, Lacan saw our potential to break through the reified constructs that constitute our personal unconscious and gradually come to embody our mind's primal desire to love and be loved, the source of enjoyment or *jouissance*. Although desire is one, enjoyment has masculine and feminine forms. Lacan's deconstructive approach to freeing these from the repression of self and culture revolved around the distinction of three "orders" of mental life: the imaginary, the symbolic, and the real. These three bear a clear family resemblance to the three natures Nagarjuna aligned with the three luminous intuitions.

Like the constructed which indicates luminance, the imaginary is the most dualistic and differentiated layer of mental life, driven by attachment to images of self and world signified or constructed as objects of desire. Like the relative which indicates radiance, the symbolic is a less differentiated, more subjective layer of mental life, the realm of the signifier driven by compulsive demands and by defensive repetitions of the death drive. Like the perfect which indicates immanence, the real is without differentiated subject and object, and is described by Lacan as a deconstructive immersion in the authentic other, "the essential object which is not an object any longer, but this something faced with which all words cease and all categories fail."[57] Another point of resemblance is that Lacan distinguished the constructed aspect of instincts called "drives" or "demands" from the natural aspect called "instincts" or "needs." So along with deconstructing the imaginary object-world and symbolic, signifying self, analysis clears the way to a deconstruction of drives in and through immersive dialogue with the genuine other.

Although neither Kohut nor Lacan delve as deeply into the undifferentiated, unconscious mind or offer the kinds of altered state methods that allow the level of integration sought on the perfection stage, they both assume a core level of blissful desire for selfless connectivity within the mind that bears some family resemblance to the process view of the luminous bliss-void intuitions at the heart of the subtle and subtlest mind.

The Outer Path of Sublimated Passion and Intimacy: Jung and Reich

As for the "outer" practice of sublimating sexuality, the pioneering approaches of Jung and Reich offer helpful analogues for the psychosexual methods of the intuition seal and action seal, respectively. In his contemplative model of psychotherapy, Jung incorporated not just the hermetic tradition of active imagery we compared with the art of the creation stage, but also the alchemical tradition of sublimating the instinctive energies of sex and death. This esoteric complement to Jung's more popular archetypal imagery includes some striking analogues for the profound insights and blissful arts of the second perfection stage. In his groundbreaking book, *The Psychology of the Transference*, Jung reviewed and analyzed a medieval alchemical manuscript called the *Rosarium Philosophorum*, which revolves around an imagery of deep transformation through the sexual union of opposites, called the *unio oppositorum* in Latin. In particular, he describes the images of union—some suggesting sexual merger, some suggesting death—as symbolic of the sublimation of Eros into a source of integration and creativity:

> Our pictures of the *conjunction* (sexual union) are to be understood in this sense: union on the biological level is a symbol of the *unio oppositorum* at its highest. This proves that the union of opposites in the royal art (of alchemy) is just as real as coitus in the common acceptation of the word, so that the *opus* (work) becomes an analogy of the natural (sublimation) process by means of which instinctive energy is transformed, at least in part, into symbolical activity. The creation of such analogies frees instinct and the biological sphere as a whole from the pressure of unconscious contents.[58]

In fact, after laying out the alchemical model of the mind as a mercurial fountain, whose three pipes symbolize the way the sublimation of desire dissolves and unifies the polarities of male and female, right and left, sun and moon, the text introduces the archetypes of king and queen linked in desire, leading Jung to comment:

> Meditation and speculation about the mystery of the *conjunctio* were inevitable, and this would certainly not leave the erotic fantasy untouched, if only because the pictures spring from the corresponding unconscious contents—half spiritual, half sexual—and are also intended to remind us of that twilit region, for only from indistinguishable night can the light be born.[59]

What follows is a series of eight images which map an odyssey from desire, convergence and union, through the stillness of death, and from there back through ascent and purification, to reengagement and reintegration. We can easily correlate the stages "naked truth," "immersion," and "conjunction" with the three luminous intuitions of the dissolution process; the stage of "death" is obviously linked to the clear light of death; and the stages of "ascent," "purification," and "return" with the luminous intuitions of reemergence process; all this culminating in "the new birth" linked with voluntary reincarnation.

On the level of process or mechanism, Jung links the art of sublimation, which drives this work, to the symbolism of the mercurial fountain:

> In our picture the immersion is effected by the rising up of the fiery, chthonic Mercurius, presumably the sexual libido which engulfs the pair and is the obvious counterpart to the heavenly dove (which descends on them in the fountain).[60]

In addition to the family resemblance between the fiery, three-piped fountain and the inner fire within the subtle body, the text speaks of two airs that rise from the sublimation fire to purify the mind of residues and taints,[61] as well as dew showers which descend from the heavens (like the dove), purifying the spirit for its ascent.[62] These latter images suggest links with the polar energies of the side channels fused in the art of inner fire, as well as the bliss drops that descend from the crown and help us purify the subtle body-mind.

Although Jung made only general links between some of the terms of this art and those of psychoanalysis, he did apply certain insights and methods from Western alchemy to his work with clients in psychotherapy. In particular, he used the erotic imagery of *anima* and *animus* to address the feminine and masculine aspects and energies within his clients' minds and relationships, and saw psychotherapy as a path in which therapist and client may venture together into the primal depths of the mind to undergo phases of dissolution and reemergence which foster greater self-knowledge, self-transcendence, and re-integration or "individuation." In addition to applying this profound path of psychosexual self-transcendence to the everyday work of psychotherapy, he also applied it to his archetypal approach to dream imagery and its analysis.

As for the use of real intimacy on the process path, the first pioneer of a psychosexual approach to disarming unconscious defenses and fully integrating our vital energy was Wilhelm Reich. Troubled in later life and marginalized by mainstream analysis, Reich is still recognized for his early work developing Freud's insights into the link between sexual repression, self-preservative instincts and the development of neurotic character styles. In addition, he developed a somatically-based affective approach to psychotherapy that influenced gestalt therapy, bioenergetic analysis and primal therapy, anticipating current trends in affective neuroscience and psychotherapy.[63] Finally, Reich was among the first proponents of popular sex education, and was a forerunner of modern sex therapies.

Most compelling from a comparative standpoint are Reich's ideas about the way traumatic conditioning and stress-reactivity lead to a developmental convergence of defensive character traits with somatic tensions and rigidities he called "character armor." Like the "knots" formed in the subtle body by the constricting effect of compulsive energy-swings, Reich saw character armor as anchoring reactive mood-energy states and blocking the flow of the disarming energy of blissful openness Freud termed libido and he called "orgone." Anticipating current findings that facial expressions, vocalizations, and bodily movements have a bidirectional feedback on autonomic tone and visceral affect or vegetative state,[64] he developed a method of teaching clients to practice deep, relaxed breathing, positive facial expressions, vocalizations, and movements, which he called "vegetotherapy." As part of this approach, he believed couples should incorporate practicing healthy sexual intimacy into their work disarming stress-reactive character traits and body armor, with the aim of freeing their minds and bodies to tap and integrate their full natural potential for blissful openness he called "orgasmic potency," experienced in and through "ego-orgasm." Although he pursued his pioneering work in extreme ways that obscured his contribution, his most basic insights and methods were well ahead of his time and are practiced to this day in Lowen's tradition of bioenergetic analysis[65] as well as in deep affect approaches to couples therapy.[66]

Sex, Love, and Self-Transcendence: Process Intimacy in Perspective

The very existence of an overlap between sexuality and such advanced forms of contemplative practice raises a host of questions to which I cannot do justice here. The exceptional nature of process practices may make them seem not just daunting but frankly inconceivable to most novices or mainstream readers. This is why I find our analogies with modern therapies helpful, even if those therapies are also exceptional. Yet, like an ultra high-tech breakthrough achieved in the course of space exploration, what such extremely advanced and profound contemplative arts suggest about the powerful potential link between sexual intimacy and the liberation of our minds and nervous systems from instinctive compulsions should be known to educated moderns.

More specifically, what we've learned about these practices should completely dispel the popularization of Indian *tantra* as an amped-up "secret" version of sex therapy, the *Kama Sutra* or the *Joy of Sex*. On the other hand, it should also dispel the equally unfortunate misconception of the process arts of intimacy as inaccessible, sacred mysteries, or arcane rituals. The traditional case for working with the human experience and neuropsychology of intimacy and sexuality—as one among many natural platforms for deepening self-regulation and embodied altruism—is not just relevant to all our lives, but very resonant with cutting edge research and clinical approaches to optimal psychosexual development. As such, it stands alongside the process arts and sciences of death and dream-work, as one of humanity's most complete and effective contemplative systems of mind/body self-regulation and altruistic development.

In deference to the traditional emphasis on the indispensible role of sexual intimacy in fostering the greatest freedom of mind we can reach in this life, it may help to compare the process approach to that of Emotionally Focused Couple Therapy (EFT), a recent evidence-based approach fostering couples' psychosexual development, inspired by the thought of globally minded contemplative Thomas Merton. A few passages from Sue Johnson's *Hold Me Tight* can help us glimpse the possibility of a deep dialogue between the process science and arts of intimacy and a key growth need for our alienated secular culture and lifestyle:

> The emotional bond forged here is something that many couples have never experienced, even in the midst of initial infatuation when their bodies were flooded with passion's hormones. It is similar to the joyous connection between parent and child, except that it is more complex, reciprocal, and sexual. As this conversation unfolds, partners see themselves and their lovers differently; they find themselves feeling new emotions and responding in new ways. They can now take more risks and reach for more intimacy.[67]

With this background, Johnson contrasts a mature approach to what she calls "the neural duet" of "synchrony sex" with our culture's addictive messages and habits:

> We are told that the sexual fires that burned so brightly at the start of love inevitably burn down, just as our relationships, once filled with excitement, inexorably turn into prosaic friendships. Moreover, we've been taught to see sex as an end in itself. Slaking desire, preferably with a big orgasm, is the goal. We emphasize the mechanics of sex, the positions, techniques, and toys that can heighten our physical bliss. Sex is all about immediate physical satisfaction, we believe. In fact, secure bonding and fully satisfying sexuality go hand in hand; they cue off and enhance each other. Emotional connection creates great sex, and great sex creates deeper emotional connection. When partners are emotionally accessible, responsive and engaged, sex becomes intimate play, a safe adventure. Secure partners feel free and confident to surrender to sensation in each other's arms, explore and fulfill their sexual needs, and share their deepest joys, longings and vulnerabilities. Then, lovemaking is truly making love.[68]

Finally, in exploring the global implications of her approach to teaching ordinary couples how to cultivate deep, healing intimacy, Johnson traces the source of her work to Merton, a Catholic monk who was deeply drawn to Buddhism and involved in bringing contemplation to a world of action:

> The view of love and lovemaking presented in this book fits with the thoughts of the Trappist monk and writer Thomas Merton, who believed that compassion had, in the end, to be based on "a keen awareness of the interdependence of all living things, which are all part of one another and all involved in one another." It seems that if we, as a species, are to survive on this fragile blue and green planet, we have to learn to step past the illusion of separateness and grasp that we truly are mutually dependent. We learn this in our most intimate relationships.[69]

As Johnson suggests, I've found that our most profound glimpses into the freedom of mind it takes to feel such deep interconnection come in the context of couples working on deepening their intimacy. Though even the most mature process practitioners I've worked with have yet to fully dive into the second sub-stage, many students and some of my clients with experience in the creation stage and/or readiness for the perfection stage have reported tastes or glimpses of the kind of deep, instinctive disarming which yields full freedom of mind.

Intimacy Practice for Process Novices

Even the most preliminary creation stage practice involves commitments and pledges that directly address couples' perceptions of and feelings towards one another. Two of these, however simple, are worth pointing out here. First, there is the key guideline—based on the fourteenth pitfall—to maintain the utmost respect for the opposite sex. This guideline, like the keys to lasting love Sue Johnson recommends, aims at alerting us to the need to maintain a special quality of accessibility, responsiveness and engagement with our partners. Of course, to be genuine and consistent, it also obliges us to expose and reverse any negative bias towards members of the opposite sex in general—whether cultural, familial or personal in origin—since such biases not only block our full empathy for all, but also specifically interfere with our capacity for true intimacy with our partner.

The second element of creation stage practice that addresses couples' perceptions and feelings is the guideline that lay practitioners envision their partner through the idealizing lens of the opposite gender archetype of their chosen practice. This guideline especially applies to moments of intense intimacy including sex, where we're directed to see ourselves as our chosen archetype and our partners as archetypal partners. So while process practitioners on the creation stage may be far from applying the inner or outer keys of the second perfection stage, they start right away to work on transforming their perceptions of themselves and their partners to facilitate intimacy. If we recall our comparative model of process practice from chapter 10, we would expect that this seemingly artificial tool may be helpful in blocking negative self-images and transference projections that would make us feel less fundamentally safe and open to our partner. This guideline resembles the attention paid in Jung's method of active imagery to exposing and transforming unconscious images of our *anima* or *animus* projected onto our partners, since such projections tend to block our full capacity for conscious integration and mature love.

Guidelines for Intimacy in the Mother Class of Optimal Integral Process Practices

As a final note, optimal integral practices of the mother class like the *Supreme Bliss Wheel* involve their own special set of guidelines, known as the ten exceptional pledges of mother process practice. Though we cannot give these the consideration they deserve, simply listing them here may be instructive. As you'll see, they address the process practice of intimacy far more explicitly than the ordinary commitments and pledges of the (father class) optimal integral process. (1–2) The first two pledges—initiating all physical actions with the left hand and/or foot first—is an intriguing guideline that seems to be meant to shift the normal balance of our mind and nervous system towards the more emotionally and viscerally sensitive, less defended "feminine" side of our cerebral cortex and vagal nerve. The remaining eight pledges are mostly self-explanatory: (3) see all members of the opposite sex as archetypal beings; (4) avoid intimacy with the immature; (5) contemplate emptiness during sexual intimacy; (6) learn to restrain and sublimate passion; (7) learn to sublimate sexual orgasm; (8) practice intimacy with a virtual partner and/or embodied actual partner; (9) harness intimacy towards practice communing with the universe as a partner; (10) abandon any revulsion towards the primal sensual experience of intimacy. Even though many of these pledges pertain to advanced stages and methods, they are presented to mother process novices as guidelines for present and future, with the clear intent of preparing the way for the process practice of intimacy.

Given this tradition, though it's neither possible nor practical for us in the context of our introductory survey to try to simulate the meditative experience of the second sub-stage, we may get a taste or glimpse of the insight path to freedom of mind by revising our practice of the feminine and masculine wisdom archetypes, *Transcendent Wisdom* and *Sheer Brilliance.* Observing the tradition of emphasizing the art of intimacy as the prime "outer" support for profound process insight, we'll close with a meditative experiment that joins these two archetypes into a wisdom couple. Remember, if you're not currently an optimal process practitioner, this experiment is solely for liberal arts purposes, not for regular practice.

Meditative Experiment 11: The Union of *Mother Wisdom* and *Father Brilliance*

In as peaceful and uplifting a space as possible,
With or without real offerings or images
Of Transcendent Wisdom and Sheer Brilliance,
Settle into a comfortable, stable posture,
And clear your breath and balance your state
With nine rounds of alternate nostril breathing.
Now prime your energy and nervous system
By taking three or more simple vase breaths,
And, as you hold them, doing the rotating wheel
Exercise counterclockwise three times, then clockwise
Three times, and then forward and back three times.
When you've reached a balance of heightened clarity
And profound calm, recite mentally or out loud the following
Performance script, based on the purification process
Of the Wisdom Mother-Father, pausing after each section
For as long as you like to hold its imagery,
Follow the recommended breath practice,
Focus on your experience, or seal in its meaning.

1. *Taking Refuge in the Four Healing Gems*
"In a state of true confidence and radical openness,
I take refuge in my mentor's inspiration and clarity—
A gem-like embodiment of triple kindness,
In the prime example of the Great Sage, Shakyamuni,
His enlightening teaching and altruistic community
And in all mentor-archetypes of heroic altruism.
To free myself and all sensitive beings I conceive
The altruistic spirit of pure blissful openness, and will
Develop myself and all beings as quickly as possible,
Until we gain the enlightenment to heal this world!"

1a *Invoking the Mentor and Lineage as Heroic Altruists*
"Suddenly out of the void, six inches above my crown,
Your pure reality emits a thousand-petalled lotus
Of rainbow light, in the midst of which your translucent mind
Dawns like a sunrise reflected in water.
Bubbling up from the sun like a fish leaping out of water
Comes a 3-D sapphire light exclamation point,
Resonating with the loving sound of your voice,
Beaming a rainbow aura everywhere that purifies
The destructive habits and instincts of all living beings,

And delights the enlightened, melting the whole multiverse
Into gem-toned lights that melt into the exclamation point,
Intensifying its light until it emits a rainbow
Aura in which you assume your embodied form
As *Transcendent Wisdom-Sheer Brilliance*, mother and father
Of all enlightened beings and all master altruists.
Seated in meditation, facing forward, hovering
Just inches over my crown, your golden complexion
Glows with light and warmth like the sun,
And the wisdom crown before your topknot
Holds a mini blue Buddha *Unshakeable.*
Your right hand holds the light saber of wisdom overhead,
And your left, embracing the small of your partner's back,
Holds the stem of a lotus that blossoms a wisdom text
At your left shoulder. Straddling the father's lap, you sit
As the sunrise gold *Wisdom Mother*, your arms and legs
Embracing your partner, holding a chopper and skull-bowl.
Your third eye sees with non-dual intuition,
And the wisdom tiara before your topknot
Holds a mini blue *Lady Reality.*
At ease in heavenly silks, you bear the marks and signs
Of perfect altruism, and the living gems of transcendent virtue.
Above your head, like a stack of suns, sit all the mentors
Of the great seal tradition, above whom sits the prime *Wisdom*
Mother-Father, all appearing exactly like you!"

1b. *Inviting the Mentor and Lineage to Bless Your Efforts*
"Your form glows like a brilliant sun, lit from within
By the diamond OM, ruby AH, sapphire HUM
Seed syllables on moon discs at your crown, throat and heart,
Beaming gem-lights to invite your spirit and the pure genius
Of all mentors to melt into my vision and merge as one!"

2. *Welcoming Mentor and Lineage into Your World*
"In the presence of your clarity, all experience has the taste
Of blissful openness, pervading the mind and all the senses!
I HAVE A PURE NATURE WHICH IS
THE NATURAL PURITY OF ALL THINGS!
In the crucible of the clear light of bliss, my five mind/body
Systems and elements melt and transform into healing
Elixir, the quintessence of the five pure intuitions.
OM AH HUM HA HO HREE! (3X)
Welcoming you all gratefully into my world, I offer
A sun-shower of sense delights—scented waters,

Incense, flowers, lights, music, and delicacies—
Converging toward you from everywhere, horizon and sky!
Fully and freely I share with you all my resources,
Virtues, every aspect of my intimate life—
Transformed by healing the elixir of my blissful openness,
Plus this precious earth, with its oceans, continents,
Wonders, forests, waters, and infinite web of life.
Perfectly pleased, the primordial *Transcendent Wisdom-Sheer Brilliance Mother-Father* and all the mentors
One at a time, melt into you and merge as one!"

2a. *Requesting and Receiving Consecration*
"Intensified by absorbing the genius of the lineage,
And enjoying the singular taste of these blissful offerings,
The sapphire HUM at your heart beams gem-lights everywhere
Inviting the five Mother-Father Transcendent Ones
To consecrate you and grant me initiation.
The couples come holding vases of wisdom elixir
Which they pour into you crown, filling your body/mind
And overflowing as Mother-Father Blue Buddha crowns.
MAY THE CONSECRATED VOWS
OF ALL THE TRANSCENDENT SHINE!"

3. *Fully Disclosing Faults, Limits and Blocks*
"Regretting all the negative instincts and habits I've acquired,
All that limits and blocks me from mastering inner fire,
From the depths of my heart I regret every one of them now,
And firmly resolve with your help to avoid and unlearn them all."

4. *Vicariously Enjoying the Power of Inner Fire*
"Though all things are empty of any non-relative being,
With gratitude I enjoy your perfect freedom of mind
And the power it gives you to embody pure bliss and light,
And refine the wisdom that yields your master's communion."

4a. *Enhancing Enjoyment with the Four Boundless Moods*
"May all beings have real happiness and its causes!
May we all be freed from all suffering and its causes!
May we all enjoy and savor all excellent things!
May we all know unwavering equanimity!" (Repeat 3X)

5. *Requesting and Receiving Blessings*
"Mother-Father of bliss and clarity, please bless my body-mind
With your pure intuitions, help me focus my awareness

And purify my energy so I can open and clear
The channels and complexes of my central nervous system,
Balance and gather my sun and moon energies into
The central channel at my heart, unlock my heart-drop,
Master the flow of bliss and realize innate wisdom!"

"Moved by your love for me and all life, MOTHER-FATHER,
You enter into a full embrace and melt into bliss
That flows from your crown and sexual organs into your hearts,
Which merge into one jewel drop of orgasmic bliss-complete void,
Melting into my crown, into my central channel,
Radiating warmth, bliss and light, so I can see and feel it
Opening and clearing the channel both frontwards to mid-brow
And downwards to my throat, heart, navel, and sexual center.
Savoring the drop's warmth, bliss and light, I see and feel it
Light up and clear my crown complex, with its diamond
Exclamation point, then flow to light my throat complex,
With its inverted ruby exclamation point, then flow
To light my heart complex, with its sapphire exclamation point,
And finally flow to light up and clear my navel complex,
Merging with its inverted ruby exclamation point, until
It intensifies the navel point's innate warmth and light.
Focusing now on that ruby point, I see and feel it
Glowing with heat and light like a ruby-seed tongue of fire,
Fanned to greater heat with each breath, its starts to flare
From its brazier and point and burst from its tip into flame.
Kindled now, I take some vase breaths to ignite inner fire,
Melt and savor pure bliss and seal it with emptiness."

Now slowly draw breath in through both nostrils, see and feel it
Filling both your side channels down below your navel and into
Your central channel. Nodding your head and swallowing, gently
Press the breath into your navel complex, and hold it down onto
The fiery ruby-seed there. Now tone the muscles of your pelvic
Floor, and see and feel yourself embracing your (virtual or actual)
Partner, drawing whatever sensual energy you've aroused up
Your central channel to your navel complex, holding it up to
Yhe fiery seed, to meet the breath above in a kiss. Now hold your
Breath and savor that kiss as long as you can, but well before any
Distress, start letting it go, gently and slowly, up though the fiery
Ruby point, up the central channel to the crown, where it reenters
The side channels and leaves out the nostrils. As you repeat this 3,
7, or 21 times, taking care not to strain or push yourself, see and
Feel the fiery ruby exclamation point at your navel burn and

Blaze more and more, until its flame-tip threads its way slowly up
The central channel, melting the sapphire point at the heart, until
It drips like wax into the fire, then threading up to the throat,
Kindling its ruby inverted exclamation point to burst into flame,
Sending the flame-tip up to the diamond point at the crown,
Heating it until it too starts to melt and drip like wax, releasing
The flow of bliss-chemistry. As it flows throughout your nervous
System, downwards from crown to pelvis then back up to your
Crown, And finally permeating to the core of your being at your
Heart, imagine your sense of self melting gradually Into more
Intense bliss and more perfect openness. As you try to immerse
Your awareness and energy as fully and deeply as possible into
Blissful openness, reflect on savoring and sharing that taste with
Your (virtual or real) partner, and practice letting go of patterns
Of fearful attachment, angry defensiveness, and shame-bound
Isolation, finally savoring and sharing real freedom from fear,
Anger, and shame-based blocks to communion with your partner
And the world we all share.

As you immerse your bliss-energy in translucent openness,
Observe your in-breath, pause and out breath themselves as the
Diamond recitation of OM, AH, HUM, and reflect that your
Subtlest breath-drop-mind knows no distinction between self
And other, subject and object, body and mind, and lacks even the
Subtlest hint of any non-relative being, essence, nature, identity,
Or objectivity (3 or more breaths). Seal the process by affirming
Your enlightened pride & confidence:
"I AM THE SELF WHOSE NATURE IS
THE DIAMOND INTUITION OF OPENNESS!"

5a. *Self-Consecration: Embodying Pure Inspiration*
"From the womb of emptiness our clear light mind becomes
A vast rainbow lotus with sun and moon cushions
From which my affirmative thought bubbles up as a sapphire
Light syllable HUM, in which all our vowels and constants,
Neural energy and mind merge as one, beaming a rainbow
Aura, within which we take bodily form as the sunrise gold
Brilliant Wisdom Father-Mother, in blissful embrace,
Holding a light saber and text, chopper, and skull-bowl,
Symbolizing the union of great bliss and pure clarity!
Lit from within by a diamond OM, ruby AH,
Sapphire HUM on moon discs at our crowns, throats, and hearts,
We beam rainbow lights everywhere to invite all altruists

To melt into us and merge as one, while wisdom muses
And geniuses consecrate us with pure bliss-void nectars,
Overflowing as blue Buddha and Buddhess crowns."

6. *Requesting Constancy as you Practice Freedom of Mind*
"Recognizing this imagery as a mere simulation,
I ask you, mentor, and the whole great seal lineage,
Please stay with me until I reach perfect mastery!
Moved by your love for us and all life, Mother-Father,
You instantly come to my crown, embrace and melt
Into one, indestructible drop, like a rainbow tear for joy,
Which slips through our crowns and throats to melt into our hearts,
Merging your blissful openness with ours, intensifying our light,
Energy and warmth until they fill us as a flame fills a lamp
And a nectar, a vase, rippling out in our actions
Until all those around us at home and on earth become
Wisdom Mother-Fathers, returning joy waves to our hearts!"
Now pause to absorb and drink in the warmth and moisture of
That joy, as long and deeply as you can, and then prepare to close
The session:
"Suddenly the earth, my meditation space and my body
All return to their normal appearance, and the three syllables
Sealing my body-speech-mind melt into my heart-drop."

7. *Dedicating Yourself to Embodying Non-Dual Wisdom*
"With any errors or omissions I've made in this practice
Out of ignorance, misperception, lack of resources or art,
I ask you, mentor, please be patient and all-forgiving!
Any positive insight or energy I've gained through this practice
I dedicate to being always inspired by your teaching,
Until I myself become the *Wisdom Mother-Father*,
In this very lifetime, as quickly as possible!
By mastering the arts of inner fire, recitation, and intimacy,
May I gain the freedom to enlighten myself and all life!"

12 Uniting Pure Inspiration with Perfect Clarity

> "Art" is the magic (virtual) body which is the purity of the superficial reality, and "wisdom" is stated to be the ultimate reality, it being the clear light intuition that is of one taste with that (reality). "Uniting together" is uniting (them) indivisibly in actuality.... Having made them one in the form of the great seal deity body, in the center of that vessel and essence you should meditate the form of the communion master altruist.
>
> (Tsong Khapa, *Brilliant Illumination of the Lamp of the Five Stages*[1])

There's No Place Like Home: Realizing the Great Seal in the Great Perfection Stage

This packed quote from Tsong Khapa on "the learner's communion" surveys the whole arc of the "great" perfection stage. He begins where the gateway of freedom of mind left us, emerging from the ultimate metaphoric clear light into the (still impure) personification of joy called the virtual body. He then moves through that body's purification on the third stage to its final immersion in sheer translucency called the objective clear light, gateway to the fourth stage. And finally he concludes with the fifth stage, the learner's communion, in which the now pure virtual body and the objective clear light mind are seamlessly sealed together as one. This great arc lays out the last leg of our journey together: surveying the work of inspiration, clarity and communion that yields the mature mastery of heroic altruism, the final fruition of the whole process path.

What remains is for us to see how the warp of principles and woof of practices we've already explored is woven together into the fine fabric of altruistic mastery in the course of the great perfection stage. One simple way to orient ourselves to the final challenge ahead is to recall the analogy Gelek Rinpoche has drawn between the journey of the gradual path and the epic journey of Homer's *Odyssey*. Like the journey of Odysseus, the process path first leads us far away from our familiar selves and lives, far outside our familiar map of world, to a heroic encounter with the primal forces of nature and life. Once there, it then follows us back through a return to the familiar world, only now with a newfound, heroic way of being, and a whole new relationship to everyone and everything we thought we knew. Prepared by our initial journey through the coarse and subtle creation stage, the hurdles we've had to navigate thus far are marked by the gateways called freedom of body, speech, and mind. Clearing these hurdles will effectively free us from the conditioned perceptions, conceptions and emotional states that had locked us in the armor of our compulsive self and life. Given the death to our traumatic selves we've experienced in the metaphoric clear light, we're now prepared to start the return leg of our journey, reemerging for the first time in the nascent heroic form that will eventually mature into the new body and mind of a master altruist.

Since the phase of the process odyssey we'll cover in this chapter completes the deconstruction of our reactive old self and life with the reconstruction of a new altruistic self and life, it offers us a mirror in which to review the map of the perfection stage path as well as a window through which to look at the ethics of the perfection stage. We'll begin with a brief overview to help cross-reference the contemplative map of the five stages with the ethical map of the ten stages of enlightened altruism. Then we'll look more closely at the aims and methods of the remaining three stages. Finally, we'll link these to contemporary science and psychotherapy.

Body, Speech, Mind, and Reality: Reviewing the Odyssey of the Perfection Stage

Perhaps the simplest overview of the perfection stage maps its journey into three purifications—of body, speech, and mind—plus realization of the two realities. In other words, the odyssey has two parts: gaining freedom from the jaws of compulsive life; and gaining realization of the healing mastery of reality, just as it is. If you recall our exploration of the path of engagement in part 2, you may remember the view that the true nature of things is taught in terms of two realities: the superficial conventional reality and the profound ultimate reality. And you may also recall that the path and fruit of altruistic enlightenment are both taught in ways that align with that view of reality. So, the way to master the surface reality of social consensus is *via* the path of universal compassion; and the way to master the ultimate nature of reality is *via* the path of radical openness realized as emptiness. These two paths in turn shape the final fruition of enlightened altruism, which joins the full development of compassion with the final realization of openness as its physical form body and mental truth body, respectively.

Drawing on the "noble" tradition of aligning the optimal process path with this centrist approach to the engaged path, Tsong Khapa called his chapter on the third stage "the two reality perfection stage." Assuming this tradition, his title aligns the third and fourth stage achievements of virtual body and clear light with the conventional and ultimate realities, as well as the form and truth bodies of enlightened altruism. In what follows, we'll be unpacking the parallel alignment of the engaged and process paths to altruism, focusing both on their deep resonance as well as on key distinctions.

Three Vehicles, One Compass: The Five Stages on the Contemplative Path

If we go in for a more in depth look at the way these two maps of contemplative practice and moral development are aligned, there are many different traditions about how the engaged stages and the process stages might be linked. The touchstone of these is the system of five stages on the contemplative path, which ultimately refers back to the foundations of Buddhist contemplative science in the path of self-healing. After reviewing a wide array of remarkably divergent ways of aligning the process path with the ten-stage map of the engaged path to enlightened altruism and the five stage map of the path of self-healing, Tsong Khapa reconciles them as much as possible and suggests his own approach.[2] This approach aligns the early phases of the optimal process path—initiation, coarse creation stage and subtle creation stage—with the contemplative stage of accumulation, since these involve amassing the momentum of compassion and wisdom, altruistic vision and enlightened dignity, we need to embark on the perfection stage process of intuitive realization. As for the perfection sub-stages, the first, second, and third stages—freedom of speech, freedom of mind, and virtual body—are aligned with the path of preparation, since these involve preparing the mind/body process for the direct intuitive realization of emptiness which is the gateway to the fourth perfection stage called "manifest enlightenment" or "clear light translucence."

As on the engaged path, so here too on this map of the process path, the breakthrough of direct realization of emptiness marks the beginning of the path of insight, the irreversible path to altruism, so the commencement of the fourth perfection stage is aligned with the first of the ten stages of enlightened altruism. As we build and refine great bliss and intuitive clarity on the fourth and fifth perfection stage—clear light and learner's communion—we gradually progress through the paths of meditation and mastery, as well as the ten stages of enlightened altruism. When we finally reach the perfect communion of the master altruist, we've arrived at the full maturity of a perfectly enlightened being.

With this brief overview of the contemplative map of moral development on the process path, we're ready for a closer look at the three final stages of the perfection stage: virtual body, clear light, and communion. As for the first of these, the stage alternately called virtual body or self-consecration is crucial to understanding the remarkable contemplative fruition and ethical maturation that takes place in the great perfection stage. Following the classical teaching tradition, we'll touch on four key points that illustrate the nature and function of the virtual body: (1) basic science; (2) contemplative practice; (3) qualities of experience; (4) arts of enhancement.

Virtual Body Basic Science: The Dreamlike Nature of Constructed Mind

The first key point about the virtual body is that it assumes the basic science of the subtle and subtlest body-mind laid out in our last chapter on freedom of mind. If you recall, the emphasis on that second perfection stage was the deconstruction of the learned and innate patterns that structure and drive the normal, compulsive body-mind. Once we've succeeded in disarming and dissolving these patterns into the translucent freedom called the clear light, the natural re-emergence of subtle and coarse consciousness in the aftermath awakens us to the ways in which the subtlest and subtle energy-mind structure experience and perception.[3] In effect, once our subtlest awareness has been consciously reached, our minds are no longer confused with those patterns and are free to prune and cultivate them artfully into a "new normal" body-mind state called the virtual body. So the first key point in this art is the recognition of the natural power of our subtlest energy-mind to shape our experience, as our minds normally do in a dream. In unpacking this point, Tsong Khapa cites this passage from Nagarjuna's *Five Stages*:

> All beings are powerless,
> Not born voluntarily,
> The cause of that is clear,
> Universal void, transparency.
>
> The mind that serves
> To bind fools in the life cycle,
> That same mind takes practitioners
> To the bliss lord exaltation.
>
> Here there is no birth at all,
> There is no death at all;
> So you should understand the life cycle itself,
> Constituted (only) by instincts of the mind.[4]

If we look past its technical terminology, the gist of this remarkable passage is surprisingly consistent with what we've learned from modern neuroscience. Our minds and brains are not "hard wired" but naturally and remarkably plastic. Our primary nature as humans, biologists tell us, is to be "malleable" and "educable," in other words, to be naturally natureless and free to learn. This among other things is what is conveyed by the teaching that at the root of our lives is the naturally free and open mind of clear light transparency. The term Thurman translates with the pejorative "foolish" literally means "childish," which I prefer. The point here is that the selves and lives we take to be naturally or objectively ours are in fact constructs of our selfless mind-brains, woven as in a nightmare from a network of survival instincts to which we cling for dear life. The basic science underlying the achievement of the virtual body is the fact that we naturally have the freedom and clarity to artfully weave a new mentality or subjectivity in and through which to live, by consciously choosing and shaping our instincts into a transparent agency that harnesses and guides the very best in our nature. This potential for enlightened agency is often described as the "wish-fulfilling jewel" hidden in "the jewel sack of the body."[5]

Jewel in the Sack: The Magic Gem that Holds the Five Energies

With this key potential of our subtle mind clear, there's one more fact of basic process science we need to recall in order to grasp the basis of the art of the virtual body. That is the fact, mentioned repeatedly in our discussion of freedom of mind, that the key to disarming and mastering the instinctive patterns of our body-mind is the art of controlling and harnessing the vital energies of the subtle nervous system. Tsong Khapa highlights this point with this quote from the *Diamond Rosary*:

> Than your life-energy vital essence,
> There is nothing other in the three realms;
> By the magical wind-energy, the three (life) realms
> Are seen as like dreaming (in) a dream.
>
> Birth, living, and dying,
> And abiding in the between existence,
> Whatever (states) the world constructs,
> Are the emanations of the energy of mind.[6]

As remarkable as the *Five Stages* quote above, this passage highlights the link between the neural energies of our subtle and subtlest body-mind and the activation of instinctive patterns that drive the construction of waking experience, as in normal dreaming. And this basic insight into the normal functioning of our body-mind also anticipates current neuroscience, especially findings that link neural oscillators in the basal ganglia with the wave-like construction of perception and experience in both normal waking and dreaming.[7] What is unique to the process tradition is that this basic insight becomes the rationale for a practice of dismantling our unconscious self-world construction, by dissolving the reactive energy fueling the instinctive patterns underlying it. The other side of that deconstructive work is the transformational art of conceiving the new self and world of the virtual body— the form of altruistic agency inspired by the energy of blissful openness. Consider this quote from the *Concise Five Stages*:

> Ordinary construction-instincts ...
> Are visualized as the mind of affirmation itself

(And so deconstructed through diamond recitation).
Purifying the (subtle) body purifies constructions,
Purifying wind-energy, one becomes taintless,
And manifests the wisdom superficial virtual (body) ...
The virtual body, along with its luminance,
Arises from the mere wind-energy and mind.[8]

Virtual Body Contemplative Art: Personifying Dreamy Aftermath Wisdom

Next, we need to understand the idea of the virtual body in terms of the principles of the path of altruism in both the engaged and process traditions. The *Concise Five Stages* quote above includes several key terms that can help us flesh out that idea. The first of these comes in the next-to-last line, which suggests that our subtle intuitive mind, freed from reactive energies and so untainted by instinctive patterns and traumatic constructions, is precisely what manifests the virtual body. In other words, this "body" represents a kind of mentality or subjectivity that can voluntarily engage in experience and action in the world, without being driven by the compulsions that drive the life cycle of stress and trauma.

Our second clue comes from the adjectives used to describe that subjectivity, namely "wisdom superficial." The direct reference here is back to the two reality framework of Centrist thought; the implicit reference is to its contemplative practice on the engaged path of insight. Specifically, the subjectivity that emerges from freedom of mind is "superficial" in the sense that it aligns with the reality of appearance and social consensus. It is "wisdom" because it is the process equivalent of the dreamlike aftermath intuition of emptiness, which follows after the spacious equipoise intuition of emptiness in engaged practice. In other words, of the two modes of engaged contemplation—the profound equipoise that cultivates openness and the dreamy aftermath that cultivates compassion—the virtual body is more closely aligned with the latter.

These two suggestions are enough for us to consider the meaning of the term, "virtual body." The first half of the term, "virtual," is more usually translated "illusory" or "illusion," although Thurman prefers the word "magic," evoking the human art of working skillfully with illusion. If you recall, the dreamy or illusory aftermath comes as we reemerge from formless equipoise on emptiness into the many and varied forms of appearance; it serves to remind us that things are not real in themselves, as they seem, but dawn like dreams, illusions, reflections, mirages, as part of a seamless network of infinite, interdependent causes and conditions. As you may also recall, the contemplative work of this intuition was to help give us the empathic openness and altruistic responsiveness to assume whatever form of expression or action would be of most help to those around us.

The second part of the term, "body," suggests that this art expresses or manifests the natural embodiment of an animal spirit of blissful openness, in the altruistic form of a naturally joyful subjectivity and compassionate agency. Specifically, on the process path, this manifest form of the wisdom of blissful openness relates not just to any body, but to very specific mental and physical forms. Mentally, the self-image that arises in our minds at this point is a subtler, purer form of the archetypal self-image cultivated from the creation stage right up to the prior perfection stage (as an empty bubble holding pure light-energy). However, in addition to being fully purged of any lingering associations to our old, ordinary self-image, self-concept or affective self-state, it is also now not merely "prosthetic" or "mental" but truly embodied and inspired by the subtle energy-mind of the emerging bliss-void intuitions. This new, consciously created subjectivity is thus fully primed and inspired to act as an agent of blissful compassionate wisdom, seeing all people and things as dreamlike reflections of causes and conditions ready to be purified and transformed into bliss-void energy-mind that can manifest in heroic form. Listen to this passage from the *Five Stages*:

> Again the same threefold consciousness,
> Endowed with wind-energy,
> Arises in the practitioner's form,
> Called "magic body."
>
> Thus all beings here
> Are said to be like magical illusions;
> Staying in the magical concentration,
> One sees everything as just like that.[9]

To clarify, Tsong Khapa quotes Aryadeva's comments on this, from the *Integrated Practices*:

> "The thorough realization of one's mind's reality" does not exist in the aggregates, elements, and media, but appears as mere wisdom-intuition, apprehended as the deity body fully endowed with (marks and) signs, as illustrated by the twelve similes such as magic and dream—being the body of the nature of the mentality of the enlightened.[10]

Drawing the Reed from its Sheath: Uncoupling the Coarse and Subtle Energy-Mind

As for the twelve similes of the virtual body, we'll return to them soon in exploring its lived experience. For now, I draw your attention to two features of Aryadeva's description. First, in terms of appearance, the archetypal body-image we take on at this stage is distinguished by having all the marks and signs of fully evolved and perfectly developed altruism. Second, physically, the "mind's reality" we realize at the gateway of freedom of mind is further defined as distinct from the coarse physical body-mind (of aggregates, media and elements) familiar from the waking state and ordinary sensation, as a reed is distinct from its sheath.

On the other hand, it isn't "mere mind" with no physical support or embodiment at all, but rather the "mere wisdom-intuition" of the bliss-voids, inseparable from the subtle energy and chemistry of orgasmic bliss accessed through death-like dissolving into the heart. This distinction implies a key aspect of process science: the idea that consciousness can separate itself from the level of the coarse body-mind, but is inseparable from the subtle and subtlest energy-drops. Doing this experiment fully and decisively through the profound death-like dissolution that yields freedom of mind is what proves the point and constitutes "thorough realization of one's mind's reality." Another passage from the *Integrated Practices* references a common analogy of the interdependence of subtle mind and subtle energy at advanced stages of contemplative self-regulation, namely, the simile of mind and energy as rider and horse:

> In truth, the mind is just like luminance apart from shape and color, its reality like space, hard to touch like ultimate reality. That being granted, the three luminances of mere luminosity come to depend on wind-energy, and becoming common become light; therefore, the wind-energy binds the consciousness. Then the two luminances of wisdom and art, endowed with light rays, come to arise as the illusory deity body endowed with all variety and excellence. What is its mount? It is (subtle wind-) energy, which the mind-diamond rides like a horse, traveling wherever it wishes.[11]

The Mind-Made Body, Animal Spirit, and Self-Proclaimed Identity of Joy

As we emerge from the extremely subtle, inseparable bliss-void energy-intuition of the clear light, the immanence intuition of the reemergence sequence takes the subtle energy of supreme bliss as its "mount," and that animal spirit in turn bonds with our lucid subtle awareness, setting the stage for the spontaneous co-emergence of the subsequent intuitions and energies. Called "wisdom" and "art," the radiance and luminance intuitions then naturally assume the form of our lucid, archetypal self-image, while staying bound to the emerging animal spirits of bliss-void energy and chemistry. Staying intimately bound to these altruistic spirits allows our lucid, altruistic self-image to stay inspired by the neurobiology of blissful openness that insures spontaneous compassion in all our intentions and interactions in the world.

Given this understanding of the subtle perceptual and affective dimensions of the virtual body, there is one more feature that seals the completeness and genuineness of the practice: the cognitive dimension of self-ascription or performative identification. Just as our ordinary self is the product of a social consensual designation of "self," and, just as the archetypal self of the creation stage was sealed by the enlightened dignity that identifies the emptiness insight transparent self-image as "I" and "mine," so achieving the virtual body on the third stage is sealed by our identifying the emerging inspired, lucid self-image as "I" and "mine." Because this decisive pronouncement, when correct, is what seals the achievement of the virtual body as the realized, actualized form of our previous altruistic vision of self, this stage is also called the stage of "self-consecration." Tsong Khapa summarizes:

> Likewise, when the necessary preliminaries of freedom of mind, such as diamond recitation and so forth, the inner and outer life-energy control meditations, have been consummated, that very same complete generation of freedom of mind, from the perspective of generating earth dissolving into water and so on as in the process of death, itself separates the two bodies (of coarse and subtle energy), and the self-consecration magic body is achieved from the mere wind-energy-mind of the voids. The self here is the wind-energy-mind that serves as the base of the designation thinking "I." That very thing is created as the master altruist body, which is the consecration.[12]

In cross-cultural terms, this profound and subtle shift in self-sense may be compared with the radical shift in people who've undergone near-death experiences or mind-altering conditions like euphoric temporal lobe epilepsy, except that the shift here is contemplatively induced while the shift in these medical conditions is biologically induced. We'll return to explore these analogues and basic science models at the close of this chapter, for now let's look at the finishing touches that actualize our virtual body.

Dream Body Meets Dreamlike World: The Conjunction of Inner and Outer Resolve

Despite the emphasis on self-ascription, it's vital that we recall Tsong Khapa's insistence that achieving the virtual body is nevertheless not a merely mental or internal event. This may be further clarified by the multi-dimensional context said to be vital for realizing it. In addition to the three internal, mind/body features of this complex context—pure visionary self-image, subtle energy of blissful openness, and accurate self-ascription—there are two further features that set the total context for this profound stage of attunement. Specifically, these are the external features of social consensus in an intimate dialogue with the mentor, and of organic attunement of our microcosmic development with the macrocosmic rhythms of day and night, sun and moon. These external features are conveyed in the teachings that the virtual body can only be realized in intimate collaboration with the mentor, and that it can only be fully realized and purified at the end of the third stage, at the rare moment of conjunction when our inner enlightenment aligns with the moment of predawn, the outer enlightenment of the natural world.

In explaining the former point, Tsong Khapa cites this verse from the *Five Stages*:

> The so-called "stage of self-consecration,"
> The teaching of the reality of the superficial
> That is obtained by the grace of the mentor's foot,
> And not in any other way.[13]

As for the latter, he alludes to the need to align outer and inner aspects of enlightenment in this comment on the third stage work of purifying the virtual body of subjective elements that block its full attunement with objective reality:

> Once one has attained the (fourth stage) magic body of the learner's communion, as its homogeneous continuity is uninterrupted, one is said to "live in reality," and characteristics of the "diamond body" are complete. The third stage magic body proceeds by purifying itself by realizing objective clear light; so though it is called "diamond body," it is not full-fledged, (with characteristics complete).[14]

When it comes to the contemplative art of realizing the virtual body, it involves three main practices: making a firm resolve to realize the virtual body; checking our realization against the twelve similes of the virtual body; and relying on the mergers and seals to purify and refine it. The latter two we'll cover in key points three and four. For now, the main method is to align our best motivation and full resolve to become a master altruist with the near-term objective of emerging from the bliss-void translucence of freedom of mind in the form of the virtual body. This resolution is reminiscent of one of the methods Tsong Khapa described for contemplative dream-work, except that here, as in the process form of that work, the resolution is conjoined with the arts of dissolving into clear light and fully accessing the blissful openness of the death-like orgasmic bliss/complete void mind-energy-drop. Of course, key to making this resolve in the most decisive form is the rational realization that the quickest, most effective way to realize mature altruism in this life is by way of the learner's communion; that the only way to reach that stage is to join the pure virtual body with the objective clear light; and that the only way to realize the objective clear light and purify the virtual body is to achieve the (impure) virtual body on entering the third stage. With this, we now turn to the third key point.

Recognizing the True Experience of the Virtual Body: The Twelve Similes

The teaching of the virtual body is traditionally framed in terms of twelve similes.[15] Like the illusion of a person created by magic, the virtual body appears like a fully formed human body but is made of sheer, subtle energy-mind.

Like the moon's reflection in various bodies of water, the virtual body can manifest in many mind-bodies at once. Like the hallucination of a person where there is only a shadow, it seems like a real body but in fact is not. Like a mirage, it shape-shifts moment-by-moment. Like a dream body, it is distinct from the coarse physical body and made of mere neural energy and mind. Like an echo, it comes out of one mind/body process, but appears as another. Like a spirit city, it manifests a natural and social environment that seems real but in fact is not. Like the illusion of an image refracted in a jewel, it is one body which can appear as multiple. Like a rainbow, it harnesses the body's five energies distinctly without blurring or clouding. Like a lightning bolt in the midst of a thundercloud, it emerges within the coarse physical body. Like a bubble formed spontaneously out of water, it erupts suddenly from the realization of emptiness. And like a mirror-image of a master altruist, it appears as a whole and complete human body, though it is only a reflection of subtle energy-mind. In explaining the appearance of the virtual body, Tsong Khapa quotes the *Five Stages*:

> Free from existence and non-existence,
> A well-formed heroic altruist appears,
> As if reflected clearly
> In a flawless mirror.
>
> Endowed with all the best forms,
> This body that always fascinates
> Should be shown to the good disciple;
> That is called "self-consecration."[16]

And to explain the experience, he cites this remarkable passage from the *Esoteric Community Process*, describing the virtual body as the magnetic, gemlike personification of inner radiance and luminance which dawns from the bliss-void of clear light:

> Meditate sheer diamond
> In body, speech, mind scepters,
> Elaborating body, speech and mind,
> Become like sheer diamond.
> By lights of blazing scepters,
> To the extent of a hundred leagues,
> You shine, the personification of joy,
> Adorned by every ornament;
> And the gods Brahma and Rudra
> Are never able to behold you.[17]

The mythological reference here is to the conventional Indic gods of creation and power, who are said to be unable to conceive of the ecstatic bliss and openness of the virtual body because of their resistance to dissolving their justified, though reified, pride of self in emptiness.

As for the precursors and arts besides resolution we need to emerge from clear light in a virtual body, Tsong Khapa quotes at length from the *Four Point*:

> As for the magic body, the Noble father and sons (Nagarjuna, Aryadeva and so on) claim that the "magic" is that it appears without (having) intrinsic reality, and the "body" is the (archetypal) deity body; so it is a deity body that appears without intrinsic reality. As for the originating cause, the creation stage deity-body meditation and the creation stage deity-body-upholding habit are purified by the three voids, and hence the art and wisdom deity body freshly arises uninterruptedly like a bubble bursting forth in water or like a fish leaping from a clear stream. Furthermore, the four neuter syllables dissolve into the indestructible drop, causing the drop to arise as a deity body. The mother symbolizes void, the father symbolizes vision; their mutual kiss is the taste of vision-void arising as bliss. Like the linear short A that abides endowed with the five light rays; it is the wind-energy-mind body, hence one meditates compressing down to that.[18]

The allusions here to the dissolution of four syllables into one drop, and the A-stroke that harnesses the five energies like rays reflect the arts of inner fire and diamond recitation, compressing and dissolving energy-mind into the heart-drop, since these arts culminate in the orgasmic bliss-void of ultimate metaphoric clear light which yields freedom of mind and is also the material cause of the virtual body. In quoting this remarkable passage, though, Tsong Khapa is careful to remind us again that the arts of visualization and recitation that help orchestrate the death-like transition into that most profound state of blissful openness must not be confused with the objective neural reality of that state itself, which is the indispensable material cause of the real virtual body. Consider his sober words:

> Thus, the intent of the instructions that explain the drop arising as deity body to be the creation of the magic body, and the drop and the syllable to be the magic body should be understood as meaning that the magic body is created from the subtle wind-energy-mind body indicated by those (drops and syllables); so the magic body should not be interpreted as the mere(ly imagined) deity body created from the transformation of the drop and syllable appearing in the mind's eye.[19]

In short, we must not confuse our mental image of an archetypal body, no matter how vivid, with the bliss-void energy and luminous mind which make it an actual virtual body, and which can only occur based on the death-like altered state of the ultimate metaphoric or objective clear light. Finally, before we turn to the fourth key point of this practice, we'll need to consider a special use of the similes of the virtual body which sheds more light on the practice of achieving the virtual body. Specifically, several of the similes are singled out from the twelve as especially useful or relevant to key aspects of practice. The first of these is a set of three—mirror-image, rainbow, and water-moon—which help locate the practice of the virtual body within the system of the nine mergers. In particular, the mirror-image illustrates the art of merging the disappearance of the virtual body with the dissolution into the clear lights of sleep, death, and orgasm. The rainbow simile illustrates the art of merging the reemergence of the virtual body from clear light with the resurrection of the transitional body of development in dreams, near-death and the post-coital transition. And the water-moon simile illustrates the art of merging the voluntary incarnation of the virtual body in various physical forms of embodied altruism with the emanation body in awakening, voluntary reincarnation, and the post-coital afterglow.

A fourth simile set apart from the twelve is the simile of the virtual body to a dream body. In fact, this simile is often distinguished as the most important of the twelve, for two reasons. First, it provides a clear and convincing example, accessible to all, of a body that seems fully developed but is made of subtle energy-mind. Second, it prepares us for the work of the third stage, which depends on repeatedly refining our initial, "impure" experience of the virtual body by the merger and seal practices including dream-work. This brings us to the fourth key point, the need to enhance the practice by relying on the mergers and seals.

Purifying the Third Stage Virtual Body through the Mergers and Seals

The key point here is that the initial virtual body that emerges out of the ultimate metaphoric clear light is not yet fully purified of the taints of instinctive patterns and cognitive subtle blocks that bind and impede the mind/body process. This is reflected in the terminology used to distinguish the virtual body on the third stage—as impure—compared with that which emerges from the final direct realization of clear light which is the culmination of the work of the third stage and the gateway to the fourth. Once we have finally and directly realized clear light without the need or medium of any symbolic mental image at all, the virtual body that emerges is now purged of any residual taints of aversive conditioning or compulsive instinct. That fourth stage virtual body is distinguished as "pure," and is also called the "diamond body." Since we've already explored the arts of the mergers and seals which foster the gradual refinement of the impure virtual body on the third stage, there's no need for more detail now. Here, though, are two verses Tsong Khapa cites to describe this work. The first, from the *Concise Five Stages*, focuses on the mergers:

> By the energy of the furor-fire yoga,
> The mind objective is great bliss.

Uniting dream and magic as one;
You should merge the three betweens.
Addictions become the path of wisdoms.[20]

Here, "the three betweens" refers to the mergers of emerging from clear light while awake, emerging from the clear light of sleep into dreaming, and emerging from the clear light of death into the near-death transition-state.

The second verse, from the *Diamond Rosary*, focuses on the art of uniting with the virtual and actual seals through the "conducts" of complicated, uncomplicated, and extremely uncomplicated forms of intimacy:

Knowing to separate instincts from luminance,
Then (you) should perform the conducts.
Abandoning the evolutionary body,
(You) will attain the diamond body.[21]

As for the ethical intention and developmental fruition of the third stage virtual body, the near-term objective is to purge our subjectivity of learned and innate blocks to the point that we're able to immerse our energy-minds fully and unreservedly into clear light, dispensing with the need for any symbolic image to mediate our intuition. Tsong Khapa supports this point with this verse from the *Five Stages*:

The concentration of self-consecration
And likewise the state of clear light,
Distinguished as cause and effect,
Indicate the two realities.
By the process of self-consecration,
The clear light transparence is attained.[22]

Of note, commenting on this, Aryadeva paraphrases the famous verse from Nagarjuna's foundational work on the engaged insight path, *Foundational Central Way Verses*, "Apart from realizing superficial reality, you cannot realize ultimate reality."[23]

The long-term objective of this art is to become free enough to complete the fourth stage of clear light and embark on the learner's communion, in which we master the art of embodying spontaneous compassion, personified in the magnetic form of pure blissful openness and actualized in its "magic network" of inspired interaction. In describing the emergence of the pure virtual body on the fourth stage, Tsong Khapa quotes this passage, also from the *Five Stages*:

The aim of beings may sometimes be (realized)
By the process of self-consecration,
Which yokes consciousness with (pure) wind-energy,

And releases corresponding (intuitions like) light rays.
Just as from clear stream water,
The fish leap up so swiftly,
So from the universal void clear light
The net of magic expresses itself.[24]

Finally, in reflecting on the art of the virtual body overall, in his chapter on the fourth stage of clear light, Tsong Khapa points out the exceptional role and benefits of this process art, as compared with the analogous arts of the

Figure 12.1 Tsong Khapa, Master of Threefold Process Ethics

engaged path such as deepening wisdom by quiescence-based equipoise and building compassion through the dreamy aftermath. Specifically, because of the non-dual merger of orgasmic bliss-void in clear light and the non-dual communion of lucid awareness and blissful energy in the virtual body, the subjectivity of the virtual body offers an integrated platform for combining the work of deepening emptiness insight and the work of accumulating altruistic spirit or "merit" simultaneously in one practice. So we close our look at the third stage virtual body with these words from Tsong Khapa:

> Although when orgasmic bliss takes voidness as its object, there is a door for developing a distinctive ability to purify objective obscurations through that subjectivity, in this context of the perfection stage, the magic body is (also) the substitute of the infinite stores of merit of the other vehicles. Recognizing the combination of the two is the ultimate vital key point.[25]

The Stage of Manifest Enlightenment: Becoming Objective Translucency

With this introduction to the virtual body and the work of the third perfection stage, we're ready to cross the threshold of objective clear light and embark on the work of realizing and embodying pure enlightenment. Our brief overview of this stage will survey three key points: (1) enlightenment as the perfect attunement of subjectivity with objective reality; (2) the contemplative arts that refine the fourth stage bliss body and purge the clear mind; (3) the gemlike fruition of the diamond body.

Living in Reality: The Conjunction of Outer and Inner Enlightenments

Since enlightenment involves plumbing the most profound depths of our being and is commonly considered the most interior of all human experiences, the very idea of clear light as transparency to objective reality may seem surprising. Nonetheless, the first key point we must face on this stage, called "manifest enlightenment," highlights the non-dual nature of its realization: as the simultaneous and inextricable alignment of enlightenment as a microcosmic event with enlightenment as an objective reality in the natural and social worlds. We've already encountered the multi-dimensional nature of enlightenment in discussing the complex context for achieving the virtual body, a context which involves the conjunction of physiological, psychological, natural and social conditions. Nowhere is this clearer than in the teaching of the two enlightenments, alluded to above. In the following *Five Stages* passage cited by Tsong Khapa, Nagarjuna describes this conjunction—the momentous attainment of objective clear light—as the culmination of the final death-like dissolution of the impure virtual body which yields the dawn of the fourth perfection stage of manifest enlightenment:

> (Moonlit) luminance is part of the night,
> Day where bright sun-rays spread is luminance radiance,
> Dusk is luminance immanence,
> And gradually one's instinctual natures go (away).
> Freedom from instincts is neither night, nor day, nor dusk dark,
> It is just the instant of enlightenment taught by the best mentor,
> The goal of the practitioners themselves.
> Dusk limit not ended, but its deep black darkness fully past,
> Yet the sun has not risen—this moment (before dawn)
> Is proclaimed the taintless limit of reality.
> The supreme master free from confusion
> Shows the outer enlightenment to the disciple,
> Who attains inner bliss by this
> Instant of Buddha enlightenment.[26]

As we can see, this densely packed passage touches on all the exceptional inner and outer conditions aligned in this momentous conjunction: the outer moment just before dawn; the supreme master who acts as an external guide; the inner transmutation of compulsive instincts into great bliss; the purity of the practitioner, internally free and clear; and the consensual pronouncement of that practitioner as truly embodying in that moment archetypal enlightenment. Tsong Khapa summarizes:

> Thus, since the realization of the objective clear light specifically relates to the predawn time, it is called outer enlightenment, and since the realization is accomplished by the process of the four inner voids, it is called the inner enlightenment.[27]

The Road Ahead: Refining the Jewel in the Fire of Clear Light

Although the process path is not yet at an end, and there is still more refinement and integration that lies ahead, the profound and momentous import of this achievement reflects the fact that the refined subjectivity of the virtual body at this point allows the practitioner to directly realize emptiness as objective clear light translucence. And the import of that direct intuitive realization is that it gives the mind the untainted clarity to fully and finally see through and dissolve both the subtlest, nonverbal symbolic conditionings learned in this life and the reifying instincts underlying them. As a result, this realization frees the nascent altruist from both the learned and innate forms of self-reification which bind us, galvanizing her/his progress on the rest of the path and guaranteeing her/his eventual realization of the exceptional integrity of a master altruist. Tsong Khapa explains:

> Wherefore, by this reason, by this stage of clear enlightenment, one truly attains clear light, the taintless nature of one's body, speech, and mind becomes universal voidness—the reality of transcendent wisdom that purifies the three consciousnesses, and that thought-free and inexpressible condition is the realm of Nirvana, formless, hard to know, delivered from evolution and birth, extremely clear like the light of the sun, moon, fire and jewels.[28]

Of course, in keeping with the radically non-dual nature of this personal attainment, realizing objective clear light simultaneously insures the attainment of the pure virtual body which furthers the altruistic aims of others by flawlessly expressing the supreme joy of enlightenment. It may help to recall this evocative description from the *Five Stages*:

> The aim of beings may sometimes be (realized)
> By the process of self-consecration,
> Which yokes consciousness with (pure) wind-energy,
> And releases corresponding (intuitions like) light rays.
> Just as from clear stream water,
> The fish leap up so swiftly,
> So from the universal void clear light
> The net of magic expresses itself.[29]

What the Pure Body Reveals: The Holographic Jewel Net of Clear Mind

In a sense, the pure virtual body is the jewel through which the objective clear light illumines the world. The magic net is the jewel net of Indra, king of the Vedic pantheon, an infinite holographic network of gems, each of which reflects all the others in perfect wholeness and clarity. One of the twelve similes for the virtual body, the metaphor clearly suggests to moderns the holographic network of the human mind-brain, each of whose cells is a many-faceted gem which contains and reflects the information distributed throughout the whole. And at the same time, it also suggests the holographic social network of individual human mind-brains, each of which is a microcosmic gem that reflects the macrocosmic whole, especially though the reflective magic of our mirror neurons.

In the traditional context, the metaphor suggests the way the full transparency and natural brilliance of intuitive consciousness is perfectly conducted by the gem-like network of bliss-void energy-drops which inspires and supports the virtual body. At the same time it also suggests the "magical" capacity of the virtual body's subtle energy-mind to manifest simultaneously in multiple forms distributed across multiple body-minds, like a moon reflected in many bodies of water, or a person reflected in the endless gems of Indra's net. In this sense, the objective clear light mind fully immersed in reality—known as "thatness"—is the fire that purifies the jewel of the virtual body; while the jewel mined from that light is the subtle lens which magnifies for the world its freeing clarity and truth. These two sides of the net of enlightenment are eloquently described in this brief verse Tsong Khapa cites from the adept Nagabodhi:

> The true savior, striving
> In thatness, stays hidden
> In the jewel sack of the body.[30]

Hidden within the coarse body's subtle nervous system, the mind of the master altruist lives and works in and through transparency to others and the real, reflecting its intuitive clarity through the jewel net of the pure virtual body, the neural network fully purged and opened by the spirit of altruistic great bliss.

Holistic Gathering and Concentric Dissolving: Refining Light

Given this glimpse of the transparency called objective clear light, we now consider the contemplative arts that purge the virtual body by successive immersion in its death-like light. In effect, these arts—called holistic gathering and concentric dissolving—are extensions and refinements of the arts of kiss-connection and compression used to immerse subtle energy mind into the heart-drop and so realize the ultimate metaphoric clear light and basic freedom of mind. Tsong Khapa cites this explicit passage from the *Five Stages*:

> The disciple who has gotten the private instruction,
> Then learns the two kinds of yoga:
> The process of holistic holding
> And of serial dissolving.
>
> From the head or the feet,
> Until it reaches the heart center,
> The practitioner should enter the truth limit—
> That is called holistic holding.
>
> First having made the animate and inanimate
> (Environments) into clear light,
> (The practitioner) should make (his/her own) nature such—
> That is the (serial) dissolving process.
>
> As breath on a mirror
> Completely dissolves,
> So the practitioner should enter the truth limit
> Again and again.[31]

Of course, the natural and social environments that melt into clear light in the art of dissolving are in fact the archetypal world and community envisioned on the creation stage, while the body to be held or gathered into the heart is the virtual body conceived and increasingly purged from the third stage into the fourth. Here we see an elegant application of the mirror-image simile to contemplate the waking merger of death-like dissolution with the truth body, namely: the evocative meditation that even after the body-image is gone, the subtle energy inspiring it dissolves like breath on a mirror. Tsong Khapa also cites other similes for the process including Aryadeva's simile in the *Integrated Practices* likening this art of dissolution to the process of a snowball (or "snowflake" in one translation) melting in a clear stream or pond.

In unpacking the art of gathering, Tsong Khapa references the great Indian process commentator Abhyakaragupta, who explains that "holding" or "gathering" here means that the whole virtual body, being "held" by emptiness, is gathered into the clear light void. He also points out that the gathering involves not just a mental exercise but should be coordinated with the compression of the subtle energy which fuels the virtual body into the indestructible drop at the heart, prompting the process of death-like dissolution. He cites this reference from the *Four Goddess Dialogue*:

> Always abide in the center of the heart,
> Endowed with the blaze of great light,
> Up to reaching the nine,
> Abiding in the forehead and down to the foot soles,
> Compress all that into a drop,
> Abiding into the center of that hub.[32]

Though Tsong Khapa does not comment on "the nine," we can assume that it refers to the ninth transition into clear light which culminates from the eight stage process of death-like dissolution. In any case, he does devote a good deal of attention to the fine points of these arts, unpacking a practice tradition based on visualizing the "three heroes" of diamond body, speech, and mind, nested within one another like a set of Russian dolls.

Dissolving and Gathering: The Nested Three Heroes

While different process traditions frame the actual application of these arts in various ways, Tsong Khapa reviews and integrates them, more or less as follows. Envisioning ourselves in the archetypal form of the virtual body, we take the empty shell of that body-image as the "commitment hero" personifying the diamond body, and nest within ourselves a miniature "wisdom hero" at our heart, personifying diamond speech. Finally, at his/her heart we envision the heart drop as the sapphire blue A-stroke syllable (or exclamation point), representing the "concentration hero" and diamond mind. Conjoined with this we meditate the three seed syllables of body, speech, and mind from the diamond recitation—OM, AH, HUM—as merged into the A-stroke at the heart. Given this setup, we beam rainbow lights from the A to concentrically dissolve the natural and social environments back into our body as the commitment hero; then holistically gather the energy-mind of that body from toe and head into the wisdom hero at our heart; and finally, compress them into the concentration hero A-stroke and the A-stroke into clear light. In support of this reading, Tsong Khapa cites these lines from the *Five Stages* and *Integrated Practices*, respectively:

> The magical illusion concentration (or virtual body)
> Is purified by (immersion in clear light) the limit of reality.[33]

And:

> Superficial reality is purified by ultimate reality.[34]

Finally, he summarizes, mentioning the need to conjoin these arts with the wisdom of emptiness and enhance them with the mergers or seal practice, striking a cautionary note. His illuminating comments bear quoting at length:

> Here, relying on the two contemplations and the seal (partner), at the time of repeating the fourth void, if you do not meditate by conjoining as subject and object that bliss and void of decisive insight into reality, however you accustom yourself to the four voids coming from the mere process of compressing the energy and mind, it is impossible to realize the objective clear light. Thus it is necessary to have the way of uniting bliss and void of the sages. And in that context, though many predawn-like clear skies may arise, purged of coarse dualistic appearance, the extremely subtle dualistic appearances will not be eliminated, and the direct realization of voidness coming from one taste of the two things, subjective bliss and objective reality, will not arise. Thus you must well distinguish between (the real transparence-purified virtual body) and these conditions of the magic body which have not been (fully) purified in clear light.[35]

Gemlike Fruition: Realizing the Diamond Body

In unpacking the path from the third stage virtual body, through the fourth stage of clear light and into the fifth stage of learner's communion, Tsong Khapa reviews the many ways in which commentators have aligned the story of Shakyamuni's enlightenment and the engaged path of altruism with the final steps on the great perfection stage. In particular, the attainment of the diamond body on the fourth stage is aligned with the diamond concentration which led to Shakyamuni's enlightenment:

By the diamond-like concentration,
At the time when gray (predawn) light arises,
He is adorned by the qualities of the magic (body),
Such as water-moon and hallucination,
He conquered all the devils.
The Shakya Savior well attained
The realistic unexcelled intuition,
Saving and helping beings,
He taught all (things') thatness.[36]

As on the engaged path, the devils dispelled on the process path, the four demons—compulsions, self-reification, fear of death and infantile narcissism—are dissolved along with the reactive energy and instincts underlying them at the moment of altruistic enlightenment. While on the engaged path, that begins on the first stage of enlightened altruism and is completed on the remaining nine stages gradually over multiple lives, on the process path, as in the last hours of Shakyamuni's enlightenment, this triumphant fruition takes place in the fourth and fifth stages, compressed into years, days, or even hours.

This fruition consists in repeated immersion of the pure virtual body into clear light, gradually purging it of the subtle cognitive blocks that remain even after realizing objective clear light. In this sense, even the pure virtual body of the fourth stage resembles a diamond-in-the-rough that must still be further purified by being plunged in the refining fire of objective clear light, again and again. With each immersion, the translucency of the mind to the objective reality of emptiness is further refined, and the purity and expansiveness of orgasmic bliss it can enjoy and express is amplified, effectively speeding our progress through the compressed stages of enlightened altruism. Tsong Khapa concludes by reminding us that this process of synergistic refinement of virtual body and clear light mind leads directly to the same two embodiments—of matter and truth—which yield enlightened altruists or fully enlightened beings like Shakyamuni, only far more quickly and efficiently:

> Therefore, until you have meditated on the direct realization of the import of thatness with the orgasmic great bliss, you will not attain the truth body (of objective clear light) that completely abandons the objective obscurations. And until you have attained the magic (virtual) body from the mere wind-energy cultivated by the objective clear light, you will not attain the learner's matter body. Since these are taught, that teaches that the union of bliss and void and the achievement of the magic body are the ultimate essence of the unexcelled vehicle and these two are the two extraordinary causes of the two bodies (of a master altruist).[37]

The Fifth Perfection Stage: The Communion of Superficial and Ultimate

As we near the end of our odyssey, having realized the pure bliss and clarity that are the causes of a master altruist's body and mind, we enter the phase in which our long journey reaches its final fruition. When the fully purified virtual body—real diamond body of the fourth stage—is finally and fully immersed again in objective clear light, it emerges for the first time in the integrated form which allows us to practice the learner's communion. In describing this final stage, Tsong Khapa explains why, despite the fact that both the virtual body and the clear light have been cultivated in the mode of non-dual intuition, with no distinction of subject and object, there still remains the very subtlest residue of dualism in the sense of the two—body and light—as distinct in any way. As Thurman notes, it's intriguing that Tsong Khapa explains the fifth stage work of removing any subtle distinction between the altruistic body and mind in terms that are reminiscent of how he explains the gradual convergence of the altruist's oscillating spacious and dreamy emptiness intuitions on the engaged insight path:

> In that regard, before attaining the objective clear light, when the magic body achieved from the five energies' light rays is present, the mind is not the clear light of the same taste as ultimate reality. Before attaining communion, when the clear light of the same taste as the bliss-mind ultimate reality is present, there is no superficial reality body that serves as the magic body. Thus there is no communion since these two (mental and physical, superficial and ultimate realties) are merely alternating. When the body is consummated as the superficial reality magic body called "self-consecration," and the mind is consummated as the "clear light" ultimate reality, and these combine at one time in one continuum, coming together equally without alternation, then communion is attained.[38]

Here Tsong Khapa points out that this attainment reflects the final dissolution of learned habits and innate instincts for reifying subjects and objects, people and things:

> Therefore, communion in this context is just the non-dual intuition (of emptiness) that abandons all ideas that adhere to truth-status perceived in persons and objects, along with their instinctual propensities.[39]

In addressing the question of how such a profound breakthrough and re-integration can be realized all at once after the fourth stage objective clear light, Tsong Khapa reminds us of the long path of gradual practice which gradually purged the impure virtual body of reifying habits on the third stage. And this profound fruition of such long, gradual practice also explains why, in the instant we emerge from the objective clear light, our subtle energy-mind assumes the form of the pure virtual body, now de-reified and transparent enough to merit the term, "diamond body." To illustrate this other face of communion, Tsong Khapa quotes the *Integrated Practices*:

> Therefore, by such sky-like illumination, from the store of luminances that remain the same reality as voidness, all the world realms are illumined. The actuality of the indestructible diamond body, inseparably and indestructibly together like a shadow with its subtle elements, without transmigration and uncontaminated, liberated from all instincts of addictions, accomplished in mastery of whatever one wishes, like a fish leaping from water, or like suddenly sleeping and awakening, a form of a reality body of supreme joy arises; such a form being named "great master altruist," and "freedom," since one is definitely delivered from all bonds of cyclic life.[40]

As a result of this profound breakthrough, we become able to stay fully immersed at great length in the objective clear light, since we no longer reify any other sense of self that could be lost through such immersion. On the other hand, despite this quantum leap, the path is not yet over, since subtle, preverbal intuitions of distinction between mind and body, self and object, superficial and ultimate remain to be analyzed on the fifth stage. Unlike the mainly affective blocks to subjective freedom removed by the time we enter the gateway to the fourth stage, the subtler blocks to be removed here are the remaining cognitive blocks to sheer objectivity. The purification of these subtle mental blocks is what is achieved by the twenty-three forms of communion to be contemplated on this stage, according to the *Five Stages*. Tsong Khapa specifically references the *Five Stages* on the four most crucial of these:

> Abandoning the two notions
> Of life cycle and liberation,
> When all becomes one reality—
> That is said to be communion …
>
> Having abandoned the two notions
> Of material and immaterial,
> The lord of practitioners who realizes peace—
> Thereby attains communion.
>
> The knower of thatness sequentially
> Understands self-consecration and clear light;
> And when just those become united,
> This is the stage of communion.
>
> Having critically understood apart,
> The superficial and the ultimate,

> When you truly commingle the two,
> That is pronounced to be "communion."[41]

In fact, when the subtlest blocks to these intuitions have been removed and we reach the master's communion, where clear light mind and virtual body are inseparable as two faces of one being, there may be nothing new to learn but we'll still need time to savor and deepen our integration of all we've already learned. Here too, we may choose to do that by means of the mergers or the extremely uncomplicated conduct of the seals, to deepen the impact of our prior realizations. To highlight this mastery phase of practice, Tsong Khapa quotes this eloquent passage from Nagabodhi:

> Nonconceptual, profound,
> Magnificent, the body of the enlightened;
> This is explained as the two realities,
> The superficial and the ultimate in import;
> Having analytically known them separately,
> Having then merged them into one,
> You should meditate the uncontaminated place.
> Therefore, striving you should realize,
> By the kindness of the foot of the mentor,
> When mentality comes clear by thatness,
> Then you should engage in the conduct.[42]

The Pure Conduct of the Third Seal: Partnering with the Universe

So while on the third and fourth stage we may still practice the mergers or seals to enhance our ability to impact others through "common" attainments like peace-making, building effectiveness, increasing abundance, or fierce compassion, by the time we're on the fifth stage we mainly rely on the third, great seal practice: deepening and expanding our intuitive ability to commune with the blissful openness of all beings and things. In effect, this great seal practice treats the objective reality of others and the world as a universal partner to support our work on the stages of learner's and master's communion. Combining the inner arts of gathering and dissolving into clear light with the diamond body's outward expression and manifestation of blissful openness, this great seal practice allows us to continually refine our communion with others and the world in the course "living in reality" through both meditation and action. In this sense, it not only continues the work of further dissolving any distinction between altruism of mind and body, sheer transparency and blissful agency, but also weaves our practice seamlessly into the intimate fabric of our new, everyday world.

Back from Death: Personifying Community and Embodying Inspiration

One aspect of the waking and sleep mergers that illustrates this seamless practice is the art of consciously using the diamond body—as personifying pure enjoyment—to return to and re-animate the coarse physical body supporting our practice. In effect, this art involves merging the return to normal waking consciousness with the embodiment of emanation or manifestation, essentially making our ordinary body a living emanation or tangible manifestation of the selfless objectivity and bliss-void subjectivity of the clear light and virtual body, respectively. In this sense, the entire path of great perfection or great seal practice culminates in mastering this triune art: communing with the reality of others and the world, while spontaneously personifying pure inspiration, and merging these two realities inseparably together in a perfectly integrated life that perfectly embodies mature altruism.

Dematerializing the Evolutionary Body: The Perfection Stage in the *Wheel of Time*

As a bridge to our final comparison of the great perfection stage with modern science and psychotherapy, it's time for a brief encounter with the transparent process science of the great *Wheel of Time*. As the most modern and scientific of the optimal integral process traditions, the *Wheel of Time* developed a distinctive system of theory and practice which in many ways dovetails more closely with the contemporary neuroscience of self-regulation than classical process science. Of course, there's no way we can possibly to do justice to so complex and refined a system of exceptional self-regulation in a few passing comments. On the other hand, our look at the optimal integral process tradition would not be complete without some mention of this crucial and highly distinctive system. This is especially true given our interest in fostering a deep dialogue between traditional process science and the science and psychotherapy of our day. So, as a middle way, let's take a quick look at five key points of divergence: (1) focus on transforming the physical body in this life; (2) the basic science of four drops and four states; (3) the path of dematerializing developmental energy, atomic structure, and chemistry; (4) the immediate goal of empty form and immutable bliss; (5) the final goal of neurochemical and neurostructural change.

Dematerializing the Body of Compulsive Development in This Life

The first distinctive feature of basic and contemplative science in the *Wheel of Time* is their unique view of the normal structure and function of the physical body, as well as the emphasis on transforming that structure and function within the span of a single lifetime. Among the many features of basic science that distinguish this system, three salient ones help flesh out the unique perspective it takes on the human body and nervous system.

First, while the classical science of the subtle body makes a clear distinction between the upper and lower circuits of the subtle nervous system above and below the heart, the *Wheel of Time* accentuates the difference. Instead of describing the polar side channels as simply triple-knotted at the heart, this system depicts them as completely switching sides at the heart. And instead of simply carrying breath energies and sexual drops throughout, it depicts the side channels of the lower body as normally also carrying urine, feces, semen and menstrual blood. While these distinctions may seem like fine points, they both make the *Wheel of Time* model more prescient and explicit, by more clearly distinguishing the upper and lower circuits we hypothetically linked to the new and old vagus and by depicting the normal functions of the lower circuit we linked to the old vagal system more graphically.

The second and third distinctive features of basic *Wheel of Time* basic science are closely linked, and both offer clues about this system of contemplative science. First, the *Wheel of Time* depicts all the channels of the nervous system, including the central channel, as normally open enough to conduct energies and drops, even without the unknotting work of contemplative self-regulation. Second, it describes the flow of energies and drops in everyday life as supporting a core experience of bliss even in normal functions like eating, sleeping, and sexual intimacy. In other words, it presents the difference between the central nervous system flow of bliss energy and chemistry in normal life and on the contemplative path not as all-or-nothing, but as merely one of degree. Complementing the first distinctive feature, these two effectively narrow the distance between the basic science of the human body-mind and the contemplative science of its transformation, presenting the path of self-regulation as more accessible.

The second main distinction we'll look at in this view of the contemplative path is its refined materialistic model of the blocks that obstruct our normal capacity for blissful openness. According to the *Wheel of Time*, the affective and cognitive blocks that limit our ability to experience the lasting bliss and pure openness of enlightenment in fact consist of developmental energy patterns inscribed in the wetware of our nervous system, and linked with an atomic microstructure that supports them. In this view, the complex of mind/body systems, sense faculties and action patterns we mistake for ourselves is ingrained in our nervous system by the repetition of developmental action patterns acquired in this life or transmitted from prior generations.

As a result, the contemplative path involves de-materializing this complex network of developmental structure and function, so that we can access and master our full, natural capacity for pure intuition and immutable bliss. This means that our process practice depends on having a compulsive mind/body process to purify in this life. So this tradition does *not* include a system of mergers meant to prepare us to use death, afterlife, and rebirth as opportunities to embody enlightenment. This distinctive view of the path further highlight's the close family resemblance linking the *Wheel of Time*'s approach to life and self-transformation with our view of the neural basis of development and self-transformation.

Four Drops Four States: A Complex Map of Neural Function and Change

The second distinctive aspect of *Wheel of Time* science is its hierarchical model of neural structure, function, and states of consciousness. Instead of depicting the layers of the subtle body-mind as three concentric circles centered around a single heart-drop, this system maps it into four levels, arrayed along the vertical axis of the central channel and supported by four distinct neural drops, each reflecting a dynamic balance of polar "male" and "female" neurochemistry. In an elegant mind/body non-dualism that allows this tradition to streamline the classical system of mergers and seals, each of these four drops is aligned with one of the four increasingly more profound states of consciousness—waking, dreaming, deep sleep, and orgasm—and, as in our modern brain model, with higher and lower complexes arrayed down the neural axis. So, the waking state is aligned with "body" drops at the crown and navel complexes; the dream state with "speech" drops at the throat and pelvic complexes; the deep sleep state with "mind" drops at the heart and sexual complexes; and the state of orgasm with "intuition" drops at the navel and sex-organ-tip complexes.

Purging the Four Drops of Developmental Energies and Molecular Structures

Given this elegant model, the structure of the path can be mapped out in equally clear and concise terms. Once the path is defined as purging the four drops of the developmental energies and molecular structures that block our ability to tap the four levels of bliss they support, these drops can be seen as body, speech, mind, and intuition diamonds-in-the-rough, to be purified by process practice into the four diamond bodies of enlightenment. The four altruistic embodiments achieved as the fruit of the path are the familiar three—emanation, enjoyment, and truth—plus the intuition embodiment which realizes the objective reality of ultimate truth.

Even more elegantly, this fourfold map then rolls out into the map of the stages of the path, as well as the system of progressive arts that achieve them. The arts of withdrawal and contemplation on the creation stage purify the waking state drop into the body diamond/emanation body; the arts of energy-control and retention on the perfection stage purify the dream state drop into the speech diamond/enjoyment body; and the arts of mindfulness and concentration purify the deep sleep and orgasm drops respectively into the mind diamond/reality body and the intuition diamond/truth body.

In short, this complex mapping of four states of consciousness onto a six-tiered vertical model of neural structure and an eight-drop model of neurochemistry better approximates our modern triune brain map of consciousness, with its complex vertical mapping of structures and its detailed analysis of neurotransmitters. In addition, it maps the contemplative path as a gradual journey of progressive self-regulation of deeper and more primal neural structure and function. In fact, this system models the process of self-regulation in ways that seem surprisingly modern. First, it describes the unlearning process as the progressive dissolution of patterns of developmental energy—reactive habits of body, speech, mind, and intuition—maintained by subtle molecular structures that are not innate in the mind or nervous system but acquired through intergenerational transmission and childhood development.

Second, it describes the re-learning process as the progressive mastery of the innate clarity of mind-energy and blissful plasticity of neural chemistry at the levels of the waking body, dream symbols, deep sleep mind, and orgasmic intuition. In other words, it models self-regulation as substituting conscious awareness, positive energy, and neural plasticity for mindless conditioning, reactive energy, and neurochemical resistance to learning. A final intriguing point of divergence from the classical process practices is that the *Wheel of Time* teaches students to tap into the central channel not at the navel, sexual organ, or heart, but at the mid-brow complex, where modern models of self-regulation locate the newest and highest order region for self-regulation distinctive to humans: the prefrontal cortex.

Empty Form and Immutable Bliss: The Master Altruist's Lucid Body and Mind

The fruits of the two final phases of the *Wheel of Time* perfection stage—mindfulness and concentration—are often seen as this system's distinctive forms of the virtual body and clear light mind. Their unique way of presenting enlightened subjectivity and objectivity further illustrate the prescient nature of this tradition. Combining the archetypal body-image, developed on the creation stage through withdrawal and contemplation, with the inner arts of energy-control and retention and the outer arts of real or virtual intimacy on the perfection stage, the empty form bodies born of mindfulness and concentration are analogous to the impure and pure virtual bodies of the third and fourth classical perfection stages.

Though generally similar to the subjectivity of the virtual body, the empty form body is distinguished by its emphasis on inspired intuition as free not just from reactive energies and instinctive patterns but also from the molecular microstructure that supports them and blocks our potential for blissful openness. So the body of empty form is an inspired, intuitive self-consciousness of an archetypal form of agency that is "empty of materiality," that is, devoid of reactive habit energies and their molecular imprints. Unlike our normal reactive personality, which is like an automaton maintained by the unconscious neural imprints of aversive conditioning, the empty form body is an inspired personification of purely present self-consciousness and fully actualized self-regulation, a perfect master of the art of conscious living.

As for the analogue of clear light, called immutable bliss, it represents the enlightened mind's intuitive awareness of its own primally blissful and empty nature. Innately present within the mind/body process of all living beings as the essential nature of all four states and drops, it is realized with increasing clarity and directness by the subjectivity of empty form that seeks to know it. Known as the great inspiration and the universal spirit naturally present in all beings, immutable bliss is seen as the objective nature of life, inseparable from the elemental awareness that pervades all forms of bodily matter, especially the prime element of bodily space.

Immutable bliss is realized when the subjectivity of empty form can immerse itself single-mindedly in realizing its own objective nature, until its subjective and objective aspects both share the one taste of blissful emptiness. Specifically, the spaciousness or emptiness here is the mind's recognition of its own natural freedom from any form of creation or destruction, a freedom or emptiness which is also recognized as its true "form." Like the objective clear light of the classical systems, immutable bliss opens and expands the individual mind outwards in and through communion with the blissful openness that is the unchanging objective reality of all nature and life. Incidentally, this elegant view of sublime lasting happiness as the objective reality of nature and life is the inspiration for the title of this book, sustainable happiness.

Neural Transformation through Gradual Energetic-Chemical-Structural Change

With this lightning overview of the remarkably modern science of the *Wheel of Time*, we're ready to conclude our survey with a glimpse of the way this system models fundamental mind-body change. Unlike the classic process traditions of the *Esoteric Community*, *Death Terminator*, or *Supreme Bliss Wheel*, this system maps the gradual process of core psychological change in terms of a quantitative algorithm of cumulative simultaneous shifts in neural energy, developmental microstructure, and neurochemistry. As in the classical systems, the *Wheel of Time* path from initiation and creation stage up to mastery of inner fire and sublimation through the perfection stage arts of energy-control and retention is aligned with the stages of accumulation and preparation. According to its uncommon map, though, once inner fire and sublimation have been initially mastered, we begin a process of amassing bliss-void intuition-dissolutions by drawing red female bliss drops from the sexual complex up the central channel to the crown and simultaneously drawing white male bliss drops from the crown down the channel to the tip of the sexual organ. Each pair of drops released and channeled in this way is then retained and accumulated, building two complementary "strings" or "stacks" of sublimated drops that meet at the heart and then carry on: a white, male string descending from crown to sexual-tip; and a red, female string ascending from sexual-tip to crown.

Simultaneous with the incremental sublimation of each of these drops, we experience a visceral intuition of immutable bliss and emptiness, along with the stilling of one of the reactive energies flowing with the breath and the dissolution of one of the molecular imprints that make up the neural architecture of our compulsive body and life. After 1,800 pairs of these drops have been accumulated—initially by energy-control and retention, then by the inner art of mindfulness and the outer art of intimacy—we first realize the initial, qualified empty form body akin to the impure virtual body, then gradually progress from the preparation stage to the insight stage. At that point, we realize the unqualified empty form body, directly realize immutable bliss without any need for symbolic images, and begin practicing the art of single-minded concentration.

As the ten stages of enlightened altruism are compressed into the last two perfection stages on the classical map, the twelve stages of enlightened altruism recognized in the *Wheel of Time* are compressed into the final stage of this process, by applying single-minded concentration to uniting the unqualified empty form body and immutable bliss in one taste. This final stage involves the accumulation of the remaining 19,800 pairs of drops that complete the complementary male and female strings from crown to sexual-tip and back. These drops in turn support the experience of 19,800 moments of immutable bliss and emptiness, the stilling of the same number of reactive breath-energies, and the dissolution of the remaining molecular imprints that make up the neural architecture of our ordinary, compulsive body and life.

While the *Wheel of Time* system describes the final attainment of altruistic mastery as involving the deconstruction of our coarse, material body, it also describes the union of empty form and immutable bliss that is the master altruist's body-mind as "supported" by the accumulation of the 21,600 drops within the subtle central nervous system. So we must bear in mind that the de-materialization in question is not to be taken literally, as a withdrawal from the material world into a pure world of mind. According to the *Wheel of Time*, the blissful intuition of emptiness equally deconstructs any reified construct of material form *and* any reified construct of formless mind.[43] Technically, then, the material structure of our habitual body isn't literally de-materialized, but de-reified and transformed into the "subtle," "empty," or "open" matter of immutable bliss energy and drops.

In this sense, it may be more helpful to think of this system's emphasis on dissolving the material body of reactive molecular structures as dismantling the inertia or shadow of neural imprints and conditioned habits that have been compartmentalized by repression into a body of unconscious delusion and automatized reactivity. The agency of the master altruist is not one of disembodied mind, but rather a fully self-conscious, self-actualized form of embodiment with no shadow of repressed imprints and no inertia of unconscious conditionings.

This reading would explain the distinctive centrism of this system. The *Wheel of Time*'s empty form is not formless but is said to manifest in full the life-cycle of our universe, with its stars, suns, moons, planets, oceans, continents, life-forms and atoms, seen as evolving throughout space-time in the form of its emptiness of intrinsically real creation or destruction. At the same time, his/her immutable bliss intuition is not stuck in any one form, but simultaneously manifests the non-local Nirvana of our universe, seen as immanent and pervading all beings and things through the universal inspiration and energy of great bliss present in all beings and things throughout space-time.[44] In this way, the *Wheel of Time* personifies the interconnectedness and unfolding of all our lives and minds, stretching its inspiration and intuition throughout space and time to meet and help us through the interface where our reactive suffering becomes sustainable happiness.

The Perfect Union of Inspiration and Clarity in Modern Science and Psychotherapy

This brief comparison of the classical process science of the traditional optimal integral systems with the modern process science of the *Wheel of Time* brings us to our final comparison of the great perfection stage with modern neuroscience and psychotherapy. While there is obviously no one simple model or analogy that can be drawn between this exceptional system of contemplative self-regulation and our modern science and clinical practice, it may help us all assimilate the profound and magnificent universe of this tradition if we turn our attention to four points of comparison, most of which we've already touched on.

As for basic science, I draw your attention to two phenomena that could serve as models for the virtual body and clear light mind, respectively: the life-altering neuropsychology of near-death experience; and the exceptional neurobiology of the euphoric sub-type of temporal lobe epilepsy (TLE).

As an example of a plausible model of the virtual body, the neuropsychology of near-death experience has some compelling points of similarity.[45] As in a lucid dream, but made more profound by the extreme neurophysiology of clinical brain death, many who report near-death experiences describe feeling they have a bodily sensorium and perspective separable from their gross physical body at the same time as they experience a sense of subjective continuity. After "returning" to their normal sense of embodiment, many still feel a fundamental shift in their subjectivity as it relates to their physical body and present life.

Cognitively, this often involves a shift away from a naïve self-concept based on identifying with a reified body-image, often invested with the entirety of one's primitive narcissism, including denial of death. Affectively, this shift is often accompanied by the memory of a life-altering experience of profound, inexpressible well-being and bliss, which often initiates a fundamental affective shift away from traumatic affects and towards positive feelings like trust, acceptance, and gratitude. For some, this compound cognitive-affective shift leads not just to a lighter, more transparent image and concept of self as part of something larger, but also to a new visceral energy of inspiration and sense of purpose that leave the new self feeling more empathically connected with others and the world at large.

While this model may be limited in terms of the depth of change in self-concept and core affect involved, and in terms of the reactive, biologically based mechanism of change, it does seem to provide an evidence-based paradigm for the scope and direction of self-transformation we might expect from the profound altered-state methods involved in the great perfection stage. While study of this phenomenon is still in its infancy and often obscured by philosophical debates about the nature and status of mind's dependence on matter, as the field evolves, we can expect further clarity about the range of psychological shifts involved as well as the link between phenomenology and neural mechanisms. This, along with further study of advanced process practice, may further clarify the strengths and limits of this comparison.

As for the second basic science model, the situation is similar with the emerging field of research on the euphoric sub-type of TLE. The most common source of partial complex or *petit mal* seizures, which cause internal mental events such as absences, déjà vu experiences or auras as opposed to the gross physical movements of *grand mal* seizures, temporal lobe epilepsy has long been considered related to experiences like religious ecstasies and feelings of intimate communion with all life and the world. A sub-type of these minor seizures called euphoric TLE has long received special interest for causing not disruptive symptoms but euphoric and ecstatic states, as in the celebrated case of Theodor Dosteyevski. Interestingly, in view of the positive experience and often salutary effects of this sub-type, some researchers have argued that it should not be considered a medical disorder but rather an exceptional but healthy variant.[46] In any case, the phenomenology of these states—a euphoric expansiveness, dissolution of subject-object distinctions and a deep sense of empathic relatedness—has been linked with neural markers like high frequency theta waves which they share with advanced meditation practices similar to great perfection and great seal practice.[47]

Still more important than the similarities linking this remarkable state alteration and the profound altered states called clear light is the potential parallel between the process of long-term trait change and personality change in euphoric TLE and great perfection/great seal practitioners. In effect, the qualities of experience that emerge episodically in people with euphoric TLE are known in many to gradually shift into stable qualities of outlook and temperament that remain between seizure episodes. Although some intriguing mechanisms have been suggested to explain these core changes—including conscious neural "kindling" of positive affect and conscious self-stimulation of euphoric states[48]—the fact remains that the deep, stable shift in consciousness that often comes of euphoric TLE offers a compelling model of how repeated immersion in profound clear light states over time could foster exceptional altruistic development. While here as well the depth and degree of change in euphoric TLE may be far less profound and extensive than that in the perfection stage, and the biologically based mechanism of change here differs—at least in part—from the conscious state-alterations of process practice, the experience and study of this rare condition seems to offer a plausible neurobiological model for the transformative arts of clear light and communion.

Cosmic Narcissism and the Chorion: Inspiration and Clarity in Psychotherapy

Given these analogues from basic science, we can now consider potential models of the achievement of the virtual body and clear light in the clinical context of psychotherapy. The first of these comes from the self-psychology of Kohut, which we explored briefly in chapter 11. Since Kohut sees narcissism as part of the natural symbiosis on which childhood depends, he describes a healthy path for its development that involves the gradual refinement of empathy and intimate bonding and culminates in the optimal expansion he calls cosmic narcissism. In effect, his psychology sees the self-enclosed and self-protective aspects we associate with narcissism as secondary to a more basic and vital capacity to share love. This leads to his optimistic approach to psychotherapy as supporting and modeling the art of separating the delusional and defensive aspects that pollute healthy self-love from the empathic and connective aspects that promote optimal human development.

Seen in this light, Kohut's notion of cosmic narcissism as the most transparent and expansive form of self-love bears some resemblance to the process notion of a virtual body, especially since it sees facing death as the final touchstone of whether our connection with others and the world is truly objective and inspired by love. While this vision of our potential for a kind of self-love that truly transcends the taints of shame-based self-involvement, reactive self-protectiveness, and self-indulgent attachment may not involve the alchemy of profound state-alterations like those of the perfection stage, it does presume the possibility of a different kind of alchemy. Specifically, that is the alchemy of truly and deeply intimate bonds, both within and beyond psychotherapy. Since some of these may involve the transmuting effect of truly healthy sexual intimacy, however, Kohut's notion of cosmic narcissism may in fact offer a plausible model for the transparent and inspired personification of pure joy and love process science calls the virtual body.

As for analogues of the clear light in modern therapy, these are rare indeed. Part of the back story for this involves Freud's calculated attempt to distance himself entirely from the kinds of unitive experience we moderns have learned to identify with theistic religious traditions. In this vein, his charge that contemplative states like the "oceanic feeling" are mere regressions to infantile narcissism dovetails neatly with his critique of monotheism and his larger effort to align psychoanalysis and psychotherapy with the skeptical stance of modern Cartesian science.

While interest in contemplative states is clearly on the rise among researchers and clinicians, a general suspicion of formless states remains ingrained in our received worldview and scientific tradition. Of course, surprising or not, Buddhist contemplative science shares that suspicion, while at the same time valuing formless states as purgatives for our self-limiting instincts for reifying and clinging to forms of all kinds. In any case, this background may explain why a search for models of the selfless communion of clear light has taken me far off the beaten trail of modern therapy, to the compelling thought of the feminist linguist and Lacanian Julia Kristeva.[49]

Assuming Lacan's radically critical deconstuctive view that the unconscious is merely a shadow of the reification of the language of self-ascription, Kristeva takes an exceptional view of our potential to deconstruct the self-object symbols that create the unconscious and to directly experience a conscious immersion in the real. A Lacanian take on Hartmann's "regression in the service of the ego," Kristeva's view of our potential to consciously access and integrate the formless clarity and creative openness of the normally unconscious depths assumes that recovering this primal layer of mind can have truly progressive effects on our ability to heal, grow, and commune with the other and the real. In a decidedly feminist twist that turns Freud's critique of any return to the womb on its head, Kristeva calls this hidden source of selfless clarity and connective openness "the chorion," borrowing the Greek term for the uterine tissue that creates the placental matrix for new life. In essence, her provocative move parallels Kohut's challenge to conventional notions of narcissism, insisting that there is within us all a state of selfless, formless openness that is the eternally generative source of our own self-love as well as our ability to truly love others and the objective reality they represent.

Again, this intriguing conception may seem far removed from the profound altered-states involved in the process attainment of objective clear light. Yet if we consider that Kristeva's insights and word-choice may reflect the profoundly connective state-alterations of pregnancy and childrearing, as seen from a mother's viewpoint rather than a child's, the apparent discrepancy seems to resolve. In short, her notion of the primal mind as a *chorion*, a transparent medium of connectivity to other life, we not only have a plausible model of the objective clear light, but also come full circle to reverse Freud's dated dismissal of states of "oceanic" communion. At a time when our historic rejection of emotional intelligence, along with the feminine perspective and the powerful chemistry of connective states like love, is no longer scientifically tenable, it seems high time that psychotherapy open itself to insights like Kristeva's and the intuition of the clear light.

Something For Everyone: The Public Health Impact of the Great Perfection

With that said, however exceptional the intuitions and arts of the perfection stage, as we come to the end of our journey together it is vital that we resist relegating them to the "ancient religion" museum shelf as exotic mysteries or the anthropology museum as pristine cultural artifacts. I believe the scientific and therapeutic models of even the most advanced stages of the optimal integral path help to locate this practice within the larger terrain of exceptional mind/brain integration and optimal human development.

While we may find it hard to relate to the profound alterations in states of mind, subjectivity, and sense of reality involved in this most advanced phase of process practice, the four models mentioned above make it clear that these alterations are not just for Asians or contemplative elites. In fact, in light of current research and contemporary psychotherapy, such profound shifts in personhood and consciousness are organic outgrowths of life-altering experiences that happen naturally to some if not all of us. Surviving a cardiac arrest, living with epilepsy, having a generative response to aging, a successful intimacy and the experience of childbirth—while such remarkable events and processes are hardly exotic or pristine, they do predictably catalyze dramatic shifts in our selves and lives on the same order as the inner and outer journey of the great perfection stage. What is different about the optimal integral process path is that it does not leave such radical maturing shifts to chance or the unpredictable impact of external events.

Though I've made efforts to share the genuine flavor and living context of this truly uncommon and unexcelled system of exceptional inspiration and altruistic development, the effective practice of its intuitions and methods for most requires years of building a firm foundation and mastering preliminary practices. Yet the historic transmission of this rare tradition into Tibet shows that even its most advanced methods have always been seen as vitally relevant and potentially accessible to all. As remarkable as this rigorous and profound contemplative system may be, the ways in which it was and has been made widely accessible to a largely illiterate populace is still more remarkable. The popular teachings on death and dying presented in the so-called "Tibetan Book of the Dead" are one example,[50] and the related popular teachings of the great seal[51] and great perfection practice are others.[52] Each of these traditions in its own way offers novices and lay practitioners direct access to some of the most advanced intuitions and arts of the optimal integral process. In this, they make good on the mentor's ethical obligation to meet interested students at their level and try to prepare them to progress at their own pace towards the highest levels of process practice. In addition, they also anticipate the modern tradition of the *Wheel of Time*, which tries to make optimal integral practices a transparent science which can be taught to all to guide and support a larger cultural shift towards cultivating altruism and contemplative ways of living.

Given the growing dialogue between Buddhist contemplative science and modern neuropsychology, and the unprecedented pressures on all of us to find paths to sustainable well-being, altruism, inspiration, and happiness, it seems inevitable that we too will need to find ways of raising awareness about the contemplative power tools of the great perfection stage. It's in this spirit that I've tried to guide you through the brave new world of process science and its arts of core mind/body change. In the brief conclusion that follows, I'll share my experience teaching a mainstream audience the step-by-step path that leads to this stage, by combining group classes in the old, new science of contemplative living with the individual counseling and mentoring of psychotherapy.

Conclusion

Four Paths, One Happiness—Sustainable Living Today

> The search for intimacy and universality at the same time continually forces the human mind to stretch itself in both directions. Although the two realms often appear at odds, the reality is that human beings are forever searching for "universal intimacy"—a total sense of belonging.... (Yet) the empathic predisposition that is built into our biology is not a fail-safe mechanism that allows us to perfect our humanity. Rather it is an opportunity to increasingly bond the human race into a single extended family, but it needs to be continually exercised. Lamentably, the empathic drive is often shunted aside in the heat of the moment when the social forces teeter on the brink of disintegration.
>
> (Jeremy Rifkin, *The Empathic Civilization*[1])

Taming the Hydra: De-Reifying our Blocks to Global Empathy

We began our journey together by reflecting on Freud's sober vision of the human predicament on the brink of our recent leap to global civilization. Though psychoanalysis grew out of his personal search for an approach to the human mind grounded in modern biology, and flourished in the fertile soil of his clinical work helping individual minds heal, in the end he envisioned his new science as a bridge between the stubborn facts of human nature and the escalating demands on us all to cooperate in ever-expanding social groups. Drawing on the emerging new science of human nature, and the wisdom of psychoanalysts like Freud and Kohut, Jeremy Rifkin offers a hopeful vision of humanity as naturally empathic, calling for a more "empathic" scientific method, a "distributive economics," and a "biosphere consciousness" to meet our global crisis.

While Freud and his contemporary, Albert Einstein, were most concerned with the ticking time-bomb of weapons of mass destruction in the hands of leaders and societies blind to their death-drive and caught in the grips of a science divorced from ethics, times have changed. With the fall of the Soviet Union and the era of disarmament, the time-bomb seems to have undergone a cancerous mutation and explosion. Now instead of the ghost of mutually assured destruction, we find ourselves embroiled in a Kafkaesque struggle with a many headed monster we cannot even name. One head of the hydra is the irrationality of our global marketplace, fed by an obsessive cycle of greed and panic. Another head is the dread of global and local terrorism, fed by eruptions of smoldering disempowerment and shame-rage. The third head is terror's double, the man-made beast of extreme poverty and inequality, fed by a cult of toxic envy and myopic self-involvement. A fourth head is the healthcare crisis, where lifestyle plagues like obesity and preventable world epidemics explode with the bill for our high-tech medicine, fed by mass denial of death and gross negligence in public health and self-care. And last but not least, there's the fire-breathing head of energy crisis, global warming, and climate change, fed by the ghosts of scarcity thinking, feeding frenzy, and denial of consequences.

Mythology aside, as in medicine, so in our private and public lives, where there seem to be many problems at once, we often find ourselves facing the many heads of one beast, a systemic disease with one root cause. And, as in medicine, before we can even think about the most reasonable treatment, we must arrive at a diagnosis which gives the hydra a name. If we trace the five heads of the beast we face to their roots—greed and fear, shame and rage, envy and pride, panic and denial—we recognize our human demons, the toxic emotions that drive the cycle of stress and trauma. And if we trace those roots deeper still, to the taproot that anchors and feeds them all, the diagnosis of our current condition confirms the Buddha's. At the origin of our complex crisis today is the taproot of that timeless cycle: the malignant view that we're all isolated, alien beings at odds with others in a hostile world, a delusion based on identifying and reifying our worst-case memories and instinctive stress-reactions as "me, myself, and I."

If this stubborn delusion in fact is the root of our ills, now as in the axial age of Socrates, Confucius, and Buddha, when civilization first opened its schools, then the many-headed monster we face may be just a projection of our common self-reifying demon, like the giant cockroach the antihero Gregor Samsa saw in the mirror of Kafka's surreal short story, *Metamorphosis*. This would explain why the problems it feeds seem to escalate all around us, and seem so intimately intertwined, so pervasive, and so inextricable. Locked in place by the armed-and-dangerous nature of the self-protective instinct that anchors it, our compulsive lifestyle of stress and trauma seems as close to us as our own shadow yet as inexorable as our increasing interdependence with others. Of course, as with all diseases, especially the most insidious and intractable, the prognosis depends on our choosing and using the right medicine. When it comes to mastering the self-reifying delusion and self-destructive forces ingrained in our nature by eons of evolution, do we really have choices? And if we do, what are they?

Towards an Empathic, Scientific Curriculum: The Future of Global Civilization

Rifkin's solution is education. Not just more "Enlightenment" education employing the "experience-distant" model of objective observation and disinterested problem-solving, drawn from Newton's mechanics and Darwin's biology. Why not? First of all, because its ethos of detachment, its analytic mindset, and its manipulative methods are all too likely to reinforce the very habits of alienation, cold calculation, and forced control that feed the traumatized child and cornered animal in us all. Second, because an education that promotes disembodied, impersonal knowledge cannot possibly prepare us to develop the self-awareness, empathic sensitivity, and caring responsiveness we need to disarm stress and trauma and to cultivate the adult, empathically engaged side of our nature able to live sustainably with others on an endangered planet.

So instead, citing Kohut and Maslow, Rifkin advocates education employing the "experience-near" model of "empathic-introspective" learning and caring involvement, drawn from the human science of psychotherapy. In fact, he goes so far as to urge us to take up Maslow's challenge: "I wish to raise the more radical question: can *all* the sciences, *all* knowledge be conceptualized as a resultant of loving or caring interrelationship between knower and known?"[2]

While I happily join Rifkin, Kohut, Maslow, and the chorus of Western voices who've welcomed the new science of human nature and called for an "empathic curriculum" based on current brain science and psychotherapy, I've written this book because their voice is not alone in the world and certainly not the first. Of course, the fact that Buddhist contemplative science anticipated our new empathic vision of science and civilization by thousands of years is fast becoming a commonplace among professionals and the lay public. What most of us do not yet appreciate, though, is just how important that head start may become to our future as individuals and as a global community. Highlighting the time-sensitive nature of our current crisis, Rifkin ends his book with his own challenge: "Can we reach biosphere consciousness and global empathy in time to avert planetary collapse?"[3] Heard in light of our growing awareness of how prescient Buddhist psychology was and is, it would only make sense to rephrase his challenge. "Given the pressure on us as individuals and as a species to transform not just our consciousness but our second nature, can we really afford the time it will take to re-invent the wheel of Indic contemplative science and technology?"

Renewing the Nalanda Legacy: No Time to Re-Invent the *Wheel of Time*

Nowhere is this truly global challenge more pointed than when we face the gradual curriculum evolved at Nalanda and preserved in Tibet. What is especially eye-opening, particularly for those already familiar with the benefits of *Hatha* yoga and basic mindfulness, are the comprehensive aim and scope, methodological rigor, pedagogic accessibility, and technical power of the progressive system of contemplative living and learning we've surveyed in this book. We may be aware that Buddhist contemplative science anticipated aspects of modern brain science and that Buddhist psychology overlaps in some ways with our psychotherapy. Yet who among us is prepared to find four such prescient sciences, each with its own aims and methods, nested together into a progressive curriculum geared to lay and professional students seeking a contemplative life in a stress-driven world? I for one was not. And the more I've delved into this system and applied it in my own life and work, the more convinced I've become that this timeless gem of human contemplative science and technology will increasingly be part of the answer to the twenty-first century challenge of humanity's individual and collective self-transformation.

Based on the life-altering power of this complete and rigorous contemplative science and technology, the masters of the Nalanda tradition would strongly challenge Rifkin's unexamined assumption that our empathic nature "is not a fail-safe mechanism that allows us to perfect our humanity." In fact, one way to think of the revolutionary thrust of the Nalanda curriculum, in both its engaged and process forms, is that it is a rare system of scientific self-analysis and contemplative self-transformation that allows average humans to tap and refine our social nature into just such a fail-safe, effectively perfecting our special genius for peace and altruism. And this rare ambition and still rarer achievement of human learning is another key reason why this tradition is likely to become increasingly vital to humanity at large in our current crisis.

Seeing through Seeming Obstacles: The Analysis of Cultural Preconceptions

Of course, in surveying this curriculum and trying its insights and arts on for size, we've had to touch on various preconceptions that could get in the way of our taking the lifeline it holds out to us. We've had to question our disbelief at the very idea that a "homeless community" of monks and nuns, who look to us like Greek philosopher-scientists in sunny togas or our professors in their graduation robes, may know more about how to live happily in a human mind and nervous system than our wisest psychoanalysts or our best high-tech neuroscientists. We've had to question the protestations of many of our old school scientists and clinicians who feel a need to protect their disciplines from any association with an ancient scientific tradition that is not just partly spiritual but partly religious. And, on the other hand, we've also had to question the objections of scholars and practitioners of various Buddhist or Indic traditions, who feel a need to protect the traditions they know from any association with any modern science or practice that might interpret, apply, or in any way alter them.

In response to these preconceptions and objections, I've summarized and referenced some of the mounting body of evidence from our own scientific laboratories supporting the conclusion, however surprising, that Indic contemplative scientists understand and work with the human mind and nervous system in ways that anticipate the latest developments in neuroscience and clinical practice. In addition, we've learned enough about Buddhist science and spirituality to know that it does not fit neatly on either side of the science-religion divide which has fragmented the culture of the modern West. In fact, this ancient Indic tradition, like our modern tradition of psychoanalysis, offers a clear middle way or bridge that can help open meaningful dialogue and promise to heal that divide, along with its destructive dissociation of mind from body, knowledge from experience, and technology from motivation and ethics.

Likewise, we've learned enough about Buddhist science and civilization to know that it was intentionally left open to interpretation, application, and change, and was meant to be of ongoing practical value to any and all who wished to benefit from Buddha's healing insights and methods. If Shakyamuni and his heirs shared their teachings freely with any and all who sought their help, then taking this curriculum into our minds and lives cannot be a case of "taking what is not given." In a very real sense, if we are to truly respect the intention of this rare tradition, we must take care not to impose our Western ideas of intellectual property, cultural specificity, or sacrosanct purity onto Buddhist teaching and practice. As we can see from the openness of scholar-practitioners like the Dalai Lama, the sin we may most need to avoid now is not the sin of creating a genuine post-modern, global Buddhism, but rather the sin of *not* doing so, when humanity so clearly needs it and the continued relevance of Buddhist science and civilization requires it.

Future Shock: The Challenging Vision of the *Wheel of Time* Scientific Tradition

As a final note on preconceptions, the Nalanda tradition is humbling and challenging not just in its prescient curriculum for "biosphere consciousness" and "global empathy," but in foreseeing by as much as twelve to fifteen centuries the need to embed that curriculum in an open-source matrix of empathic science and global civilization. It is no accident that the title and format of this book reflects the wisdom and blueprint of the *Wheel of Time*, since its vision of a complete, multidisciplinary science of sustainable happiness for all life on earth is the form of choice which the Nalanda tradition evolved to introduce itself to curious members of non-Buddhist cultures schooled in non-Buddhist sciences.

The *Wheel of Time* system of integrating objective physical sciences—physics, astronomy, cosmology, and semiotics—with intersubjective life sciences—physiology, medicine, psychology, ecology, and philosophy—retroactively realizes the visions of Maslow, Kohut, Rifkin, and others in our day. Much as Kohut and Maslow prescribe, this multidisciplinary system weds an objective-analytic method with an introspective-empathic method, marrying both within an overall systems-theory of total interdependence and interpenetration of animate and inanimate, organism and environment, microcosm and macrocosm. More astonishing still, this tradition had the critical sophistication and wisdom to distinguish these conventional outer and inner sciences, with their ever-progressing, ever-provisional paradigms, from its ultimate, transformational science, whose relatively constant paradigms for adapting our relatively constant natures to civilized life are meant to help scientist-practitioners develop and guide human science and technology over time with sustainable wisdom and timeless art. That transformational science is nothing other than the contemplative science of well-being, altruism, and inspiration we've surveyed in this book, designed to help ordinary humans realize and maintain our fullest and highest potentials for self-knowledge, self-regulation and self-transformation.

Translation and Transplantation: The Nalanda Institute Paradigm

Given the remarkably clear, complete, and integrated template of the *Wheel of Time*, I believe the Nalanda contemplative curriculum only needs to be translated into the language of modern empathic science and transplanted into the soil of our modern institutions of contemplative learning and healing to be fully accessible in our day. This book distils the essentials of such a translation. And it also offers glimpses into the approach I've taken to practical transplantation of its methods into mind/body medicine, public health education, and psychotherapy. The combination of the two—translation and transplantation—make up the working curriculum of the Nalanda Institute for Contemplative Science, the contemplative learning community I, my colleagues, and our students have founded as one paradigm for renewing the Nalanda legacy here and now.

The Holistic Pedagogy of Nalanda: Marrying Objective and Consensual Methods

Perhaps the best way to think of our paradigm for transplanting the Nalanda curriculum and its complex pedagogy of broad outreach and intimate bonds is as a cross between a psychotherapy institute and a progressive, engaged university. I believe this paradigm, modeled on Nalanda and its living Tibetan offshoots, provides an effective institutional base for the new empathic curriculum Rifkin is calling for. This is why I tried to convey the multidisciplinary nature and hybrid structure of the tradition and my work in this book, by including general explanations with guided meditations and references to psychotherapy in each chapter. In what follows, I'll briefly summarize the potential contributions of our transplanted paradigm of the Nalanda curriculum and pedagogy, by touching on the four main practical applications of the core four year program outlined in this book.

The Body Wheel: Sustainable Wellbeing for Individuals

Although the first horizon on the gradual path, the lasting wellbeing that comes of personal self-healing, has received a wealth of attention since the convergence of *Hatha* yoga and simple mindfulness practice with the basic science of stress-reduction, self-healing and the new positive psychology, the Nalanda tradition takes this foundational horizon of contemplative learning two steps further. First, enhancing simple mindfulness with the technique of concentrative quiescence focused on mind, the basic practice I call deep mindfulness helps ground self-healing in a more stable, profound altered state that facilitates equanimity, clarity and letting go. Second, embedding basic yoga and mindfulness in the multidisciplinary matrix of contemplative healing, by linking meditation to cognitive learning and motivational-behavioral change, insures that basic mindfulness will mature into genuine insight meditation, the engine of lasting self-healing and fundamental life change.

Another aspect of the Nalanda tradition's distinctive approach to sustainable well-being involves combining contemplative learning with individual counseling and psychotherapy. Here again, so much has been written about this confluence that it would seem nothing more need be said. Nonetheless, there are several distinctive features to the way we advocate using the modern institution of psychotherapy to support and enrich contemplative learning, in an effort to align the modern practice more closely with the traditional practice of contemplative tutoring and mentoring. First of all, instead of restricting the work to individual therapy sessions, classes in contemplative self-analysis, meditative techniques and ethical motivation and lifestyle provide an economy of scale, while also enhancing the process with active self-healing strategies, including cognitive and behavioral learning and contemplative "homework." Secondly, interpretation and cognitive learning within and between sessions is based not on the insights and methods of modern dynamic or cognitive therapy, but rather on traditional insights and methods specifically meant to support contemplative healing. Third and finally, our approach involves a direct focus on motivational and behavioral strategies that support contemplative living and learning, and is linked with extended extramural social support for overcoming obsessive-compulsive-addictive habits with the help of meditation and yoga communities, optionally enhanced by twelve step fellowship.

The Speech Wheel: Sustainable Altruism for Lay and Professional Caregivers

The second main application of the Nalanda curriculum involves using the path of social healing through proactive engagement to reduce caregiver stress and burnout, expose and clear traumatic self-habits, and embody the compassionate openness of mature altruism. While this application of Buddhist contemplative science is also familiar by now, from the work of teachers like Sharon Salzberg applying the mindfulness-based art of loving kindness, here too there are distinctive aspects of the Nalanda approach that promise to make it more reproducible and more effective.

As with our first application, building the art of concentrative quiescence into this path works to deepen basic mindfulness practice, grounding the work of radical acceptance and caretaking in a more stable, profound altered state that enhances clarity, resilience and positive affect. In addition, the distinctive practice of combining quiescence with analytic insight extends the reach and scope of self-analysis further still, allowing insight meditation to expose traumatic memories and disarm reactive instincts that distort social challenges, blocking self-efficacy and realistic compassion. Finally, the specific skills and structured practice of mind-clearing—using verbal learning, systematic methods of building compassion, the art of giving and taking on the breath, and practice guidelines to build resilience and discipline—all make step-by-step learning, gradual progress and artful mastery of sustainable altruism more easily and widely reproducible. While starting with the basic ethos of universal benevolence taught in loving-kindness, this tradition challenges us to build on that foundation by committing to awaken and develop our human genius for unconditional compassion, heroic resolve and fully enlightened altruism.

The Mind Wheel: Sustainable Inspiration for Teachers, Leaders, Coaches & Mentors

The third main application of the Nalanda curriculum involves applying the cultural healing arts of role-modeling imagery and sublimation to the work of personifying and sustaining the affirmative vision and pure passion we need to inspire others continually and sustainably. Unlike the prior two applications, this one is not just distinctive but quite unprecedented. While most contemplative traditions emphasize calming practices and some form of disengagement from mundane roles and relationships geared towards peak performance and creativity, the rare tradition of optimal integral process practice aims at tapping and harnessing pure passion in support of congenial ideals, altruistic leadership and inspired creativity. Of course, most roles of conventional authority, professional mastery or secular leadership seem to call for narcissistic traits and obsessive-compulsive "ego" energy, making them seem antithetical to contemplative ideals and practice.

The vast potential of process practice for cultural transformation lies in offering a contemplative alternative to such compulsive agency, insuring transparent, congenial styles of responsiveness, mastery and leadership inspired by the truly altruistic energy of blissful openness. Traditionally, this is framed not just as cultivating an altruistic form of human genius, but specifically as cultivating a heroic form of altruism fully compatible with the peace-making paths of self-healing and social engagement. This unique culture of balanced and engaged leadership, using inspiration and modeling rather than drive and control, is guided by the compound ethos of guarding three commitments—to self-care, altruism and creative process—at once.

The Bliss Wheel: Sustainable Happiness for Individuals, Couples & Families

Ironically, the final application of the Nalanda curriculum is at once the most challenging and the most universal. It involves applying the natural healing arts of sublimation, inspiration, clarity and communion to tap and harness the network of blissful openness at the core of our being, as the natural way to nurture true integrity, intimacy and community in all our lives. Like the work of sustainable leadership, the path of sustainable happiness aims at cultivating a form of self-regulation that can fully tap and embody our native genius for pure joy and translucency, while staying fully grounded in the paths of personal self-healing, altruistic engagement and inspired leadership. The spirit guiding this level of practice refines the ethos of guarding three commitments at once, holding out the ideal of a natural mastery and spontaneous responsiveness that fully embraces all reality and so rejects nothing and has "nothing to guard."

In this fourth application, our path comes full circle, back to our intimate personal lives, and their profound yet often invisible interdependence with the well-being and happiness of all those around us. While we moderns tend to think of happiness as a personal matter and individual right, this sage tradition, like its ancient Greek and Chinese counterparts, tends to see happiness as a communal aim and public good. Assuming the insight only recently rediscovered by our new science that human life is inexorably social and interdependent with all nature, the process-oriented teaching tradition sees bliss not as an end in itself but as a potent means to the social end of living well with and for others. This is why it applies to the increasingly pressing need in our high-paced lives for truly satisfying intimacy, seen as the natural source of all community and the wellspring of the loving chemistry of peace, care and joy.

As a final point, I mentioned "individuals" in describing this application, since this profound transformational path is not restricted to people living conventional lay lifestyles as couples with or without children. Given the possibility of practicing this path with the help of virtual intimacy or relying on the whole universe as an intimate partner, the same powerful and transformative system of psychosexual maturity is also accessible to those who choose or find themselves living a single lifestyle. This would include people who've never chosen intimacy as a life path or who've lost an intimate partner, as well as those who have chosen a celibate life as part of a spiritual vocation. The fact that this system is equally applicable to people in these life circumstances is crucial when we understand the indispensible role of transformative mind/body experiences of intimacy to developing the psychosexual maturity required for healthy, satisfying and effective sublimation.

Through the Time Machine: The Global Transmission of the Nalanda Tradition

Of course, however we engage in transplanting this rare tradition, we must also take equal care in consulting the other side of the equation. To succeed, such work vitally depends on the openness of Buddhist teachers and communities to potential shifts that might be called for in transmitting traditional teaching and practice. Such shifts range from the simple matter of translation terminology to more complex matters like conceptual interpretation and aesthetic-ritual expression, eventually touching on centuries' old methods of teaching and practice. Given this difficulty, it's no wonder my scholarly colleagues and fellow Buddhist practitioners are reticent when it comes to the very idea of not just translating the Nalanda tradition but actually *transplanting* it into living theory and practice.

Of course, at the same time, everyone concerned with the faithful translation and preservation of this rare gem of human civilization, when pressed must admit that the chaotic process of culture-to-culture transmission is nothing new to the Nalanda tradition or to Buddhist history in general. In fact, if it weren't for that process, we would now be left with nothing but a fragmentary 10 or 15 percent of the textual and oral commentary we now associate with Nalanda. And that does not even take into account the jewel network of seemingly infinite lineages of teaching and practicing almost every aspect of its curriculum.

On the other hand, if we do *not* make a serious, concerted, and sensitive attempt to renew that tradition in the course of its global transmission today, it becomes far more likely that this incomparable ancient cultural tradition will decline and disappear, as so many have. This certainly seems to be the thinking of active interpreters and translators from within the tradition, ranging from highly visible figures like His Holiness the Dalai Lama to much younger voices like Mingyur Rinpoche[4] and Dzogchen Ponlop.[5] And, as a final note, I must add that it seems highly unrealistic for us to take the transmission of this tradition into Tibet as our only historical paradigm for what lies ahead. Modern Western civilization alone is anything but the relative blank slate Tibetan culture was during that leisurely and fairly systematic process.[6] While we may want to hold ourselves to the standard of fidelity Tibetan translator-practitioners achieved with their Indian teachers and colleagues, it may be more reasonable to consider the more dynamic, bidirectional paradigm of the Nalanda tradition's transmission into China.[7]

One thing is decidedly different for both parties to today's transmission. Whether we sit on the modern Western side of receiving this rare gift to humanity or on the offering side of Tibetans sharing a gift they received from Nalanda's masters and have carefully nurtured, we are all now very obviously in the same global life-raft. No longer safely hidden in their inaccessible mountain kingdom, Tibetan refugee scholars and masters share with their

Western students a deep appreciation for the fierce urgency and awesome complexity of humanity's current global crisis.

Having been lucky enough to be present at the first *Wheel of Time* initiation given by the His Holiness Dalai Lama in Madison Wisconsin in 1981, it's clear to me how much closer we are to the birth-pains of the global civilization that teaching predicts now, as I hear from those who were lucky enough to attend the most recent *Wheel of Time* in Washington DC. On the other hand, as the *Wheel of Time* foresees, the depth and scope of our budding global empathy and biosphere consciousness has grown by such inconceivable leaps and bounds in these three short decades that it should give us all hope that its optimistic vision will in fact be borne out; that we humans will prove to have the basic genius for enlightened altruism we'll need to make the transition to sustainable happiness together as one adoptive yet all-embracing extended family.

In light of our shared predicament and emerging global consciousness, we must all be ready to look at our own familiar sense of history—past and future—through new eyes. And here is another sense in which we must challenge even the most visionary assessments and projections made by Westerners like Rifkin or Asian masters of the *Wheel of Time*. As world citizens Arnold Toynbee[8] and William Rieschauer[9] pointed out decades ago, in order to build towards a global solution for human consciousness on this planet, we must learn to see outside even our most enlightened "unilinear" perspectives. In other words, we must be open to a fresh perspective on history, seen not just through the eyes of our own chosen discipline or civilization, as Rifkin has done, but rather through the eyes of multiple converging disciplines and histories at once.

It is as if we've been accustomed to seeing our world—including its problems and potential solutions—through lenses tainted in just one color. In order for us to be prepared to come together through global empathy, dialogue, and collaboration, we'll effectively have to start seeing our world, problems and solutions in full, rainbow color. Though inexorably limited by its own traditions of history, science, and culture, the *Wheel of Time* sets a standard of global syncretism remarkable in our day, much less for the dawn of the last millennium. Its synthesis of the Eurasian sciences and cultures of its era, like the five-civilization synthesis of Tibet's integrative world medicine, should encourage and inspire us along these lines, much as the first world histories of Toynbee have inspired a new generation of comparative global historians.

In the grips of the multi-headed crisis we face today, when our most cherished values and trusted institutions seem to be part of the problem rather than the solution, it's easy enough for us to give in to cynicism and loose heart. At such times it's often vital and wise to be ready to turn to new sources of hope and direction, however doubtful those sources may seem from our familiar reference frame. Of course, we must look closely and carefully at the latest insights and breakthroughs in science, especially when the new direction they seem to indicate is confirmed and validated by trends converging from many fields at once. Yet it may be even more key to look as far afield as we can, to try to see our predicament from the standpoint of big picture trends and radically different perspectives. This is especially true when we are so close to our cultural blind spots and so embroiled in our own predicament that it's hard for us to see a pattern that points to a new way ahead.

This is one of the main reasons why I believe we must be willing to go to any lengths to compare and contrast the new directions that seem to be emerging from our cutting edge science with insights and methods developed in the face of similarly engulfing crises in other places and at other times in world history. While the depth and scope of comparison that has occupied us in this book—between our new empathic science and the contemplative science of ancient Buddhist civilization—may at times seem a matter of historical curiosity, nothing could be further from the truth. The validation and confirmation of our best diagnosis of the crisis we face in global civilization today by the deeply resonant diagnosis made by the Nalanda scientific tradition ten to fifteen centuries ago on the other side of the world is absolutely indispensible, for several reasons. The first is because clear validation from such a different cultural standpoint, using such distinct scientific methods, provides a more robust cross-check on our bearings than simply internal cross-checks; a validation that is vital because the new clues we're following are still not all totally clear or fully declared. The second is because, if indeed another civilization in a very different place and time found a solution to a similar crisis that we can reasonably apply to ours today, we can draw on precedents that can save us vital time and can also draw much needed courage and conviction from a successful outcome in the past.

However unlikely it may seem that a culture so removed from our cultural legacy and so remote in time could have anticipated the groundbreaking insights that give our best minds hope, our odyssey together has made it abundantly clear that that is exactly what we find in the Nalanda tradition of contemplative science. And if we have any lingering doubts about whether the Nalanda vision of the future challenges we humans face is truly similar to our best vision now, we need only attend closely to the astonishing futurism rolled out in the *Wheel of Time*.

So it is that, believe it or not, we find ourselves in a position not only to validate the analysis Rifkin lays out in his optimistic re-reading of the history of Western civilization, but also to help catapult his initial prescription—along with those of pioneers like Kohut, Maslow, Diane Fosha, Dan Siegel, Sue Johnson, and Steven Porges—centuries forward towards a complete, multidisciplinary human science and curriculum for contemplative living and learning, a curriculum ready made to help with the most intractable problems we face today.

Of course, we are still at the very beginning of a journey of comparative study, research, and development, a journey that will no doubt spawn many vital new insights, methods, and cross-cultural fields, transforming both our modern culture and the ancient legacy of Nalanda in the process. But as Freud alerted us and Rifkin reminds us, this is not just a journey to assure our personal well-being or to develop our ability to care sustainably for others in an endangered world. It is also an odyssey beyond the limits of our known universe, beyond the furthest reaches of what we consider possible for ourselves, others, and our world. A journey that yields the vision and inspiration we need to help usher in a new era of global civilization, in which the living gems of contemplative living and learning are as close at hand as the latest handheld miracle device, only ready to transform the inner world of our human bodies and minds so that they naturally embody sustainable well-being, altruism, inspiration, and happiness.

Notes

Introduction: Recent Breakthroughs, Timeless Methods

1. Freud, S. (1930/1962). *Civilization and its Discontents,* J. Strachey (trans.). New York: Norton & Co., 69.
2. Benson, H. (1975/2000). *The Relaxation Response.* New York: Harper Paperbacks.
3. This approach is usually traced to the work of Jon Kabat-Zin, see Williams, M., Teasdale, J., Siegal, Z., & Kabat-Zinn, J, (2007). *The Mindful Way Through Depression: Freeing Yourself from Chronic Unhappiness.* New York: Guilford Press. Yet his early studies on Mindfulness-Based Stress Reduction in anxiety, for instance, were preceded by Marsha Linehan's development of the mindfulness-based cognitive therapy she called Dialectical Behavior Therapy.
4. Goleman, D. (1995). *Emotional Intelligence: Why It Can Matter More than IQ.* New York: Bantam Books.
5. For more on Nālandā, see Joshi, L. (1964). *Studies in the Buddhistic Culture of India.* Dehli: Motilal Barnasidas, or my doctoral dissertation, Loizzo, J. (2001). *Candrakīrti and the Moon-Flower of Nālandā: Objectivity and Self-Correction in India's Central Therapeutic Philosophy of Language.* University of Michigan: University Microfilms.
6. In Sanskrit, *patha krama*; in Tibetan, *lam rim.* For a complete introduction to this unique teaching tradition and literary genre, see Pabongka Rinpoche. (1991/1993). *Liberation in the Palm of your Hand.* London: Wisdom Press.
7. For a brief introduction to this tradition, see my essay, Loizzo, J. (2009). Kālachakra and the Nālandā Tradition: Science, Religion and Objectivity in Buddhism and the West. In Arnold, E (ed.), *As Long as Space Endures.* Ithaca: Snow Lion Press.
8. The classic discussion of these themes are in Heisenberg, W. (1958/2007). *Physics and Philosophy: The Revolution in Modern Physics.* New York: Harper Perennial Modern Classics; and Bohm, D. (1975/2002). *Wholeness and the Implicate Order.* New York: Routledge. A more recent and popular treatment by Capra, F. (1984). *The Turning Point: Science, Society and the Rising Culture.* New York: Bantam Books, is intriguing because of its linking of converging paradigms in modern physics, biology, and healthcare.
9. See Goleman, D. (2009) *Ecological Intelligence: How Knowing the Impact of What You Buy Can Change Everything.* New York: Broadway Business Press.
10. See Feinberg, M. (1995). *Why Smart People Do Dumb Things: Lessons from the New Science of Behavioral Economics.* New York: Fireside; and Anielski, M. (2007). *The Economics of Happiness: Building Genuine Wealth.* New Society Publishers; and most recently, the eloquent case made by Akerlof, G., & Schiller, R. (2009). *Animal Spirits: How Psychology Drives the Economy and Why it Matters for Global Capitalism.* Princeton: Princeton University Press.

11. For a readable update by a pioneer in the field, see McEwan, B. (2002). *The End of Stress as We Know It.* New York: Joseph Henry Press.
12. MacLean, P. (1959). The limbic system with respect to two basic life principles. In *Second Conference on the Central Nervous System and Behavior.* New York: Josiah Macy Foundation, 43–59.
13. The term "axial age" was introduced by phenomenologist Karl Jaspers. See Jaspers, K. (1966). *Socrates, Buddha, Confucius, Jesus: From the Great Philosophers, Vol I.* New York: Mariner Press. A comparative treatment of the history of civilization was sparked by visionary historian Toynbee, A. (1956). *A Study of History.* Oxford: Oxford University Press, or Toynbee, A. (1976). *Mankind and Mother Earth: A Narrative History of the World.* New York: Oxford University Press. A more recent treatment focused on Asia can be found in Farmer, E., Hambly, G., Marhsall, B., et al. (1986). *A Comparative History of Civilizations in Asia.* Indianapolis: Westview Press.
14. The term "stress response" was coined in the 1950s by Hans Seyle, the grandfather of modern stress research. For a compelling recent introduction to the psychobiology of stress, see Kabat-Zinn, J. (1990). *Full Catastrophe Living* New York: Delta Books.
15. The cumulative effects of uncontrolled stress has been attributed by Bruce McEwan and others to a failure of adaptation, a process called allostasis since it involves an organism staying in balance with a changing environment much as homeostasis involves maintaining internal balance. McEwan defined the accumulated burden of poor adaptation as allostatic load, and introduced chemical measures of stress hormones as a metric to quantify the net effects of stress. For an introduction, see his book, *The End of Stress as We Know It.*
16. Discussion about this bias has been stimulated by the recent findings of Tom, S., Fox, C., Trepel, C., et al. (2007). The Neural Basis of Loss Aversion in Decision-Making Under Risk. In *Science*, 315(5811): 515–18.
17. For a compelling, more popular discussion, see Capra in *The Turning Point.*
18. For an overview of this research, see Olivo, E. (2009). Protection throughout the lifespan: The Psychoneuroimmunolic Impact of Indo-Tibetan Meditative and Yogic Practices. In Bushell, W. Olivo, E., & Theise, N. (eds.), *Longevity, Regeneration and Optimal Health.* New York: Annals of the New York Academy of Sciences.
19. See Oke, S., & Tracy, K. (2009). The Inflammatory Reflex and the Role of Alternative and Complementary Therapies. In Bushell et al., *Longevity.*
20. For a review of this literature as it relates to psychiatry, see my article, Loizzo, J. (2000). Meditation and Psychotherapy: Stress, Allostasis and Enriched Learning. In Muskin, P. (ed.), *Complementary and Alternative Medicine and Psychiatry.* Washington: American Psychiatric Association Press.
21. For a cross-section of this emerging web, here are five representative recent references: Dalman, M., Pecoraro, N., Akana, S., et al. (2003). Chronic stress and obesity: A new view of "comfort food." In *Proceedings of the National Academy of Sciences,* 100(20); Procelli, A., & Delgado, M. (2009). Acute Stress Modulates Risk Taking in Financial Decision Making. In *Psychological Science*, 20(3). Kruk, M., & Meelis, W. (2004). Fast Positive Feedback Between the Adrenocortical Stress Response and a Brain Mechanism Involved in Aggressive Behavior. In *Behavioral Neuroscience*, 118(5); Tibblin, A. (2008). *Stress, Overconsumption and Climate Change.* Lund: Lund University; Post, J. (2008). *The Mind of the Terrorist: The Psychology of Terrorism from the IRA to Al-Qaeda.* New York: Palgrave Macmillan.
22. For an excellent introduction to this teaching from the standpoint of the Tibetan tradition, see Tsering, T. (2003). *The Four Noble Truths.* London: Wisdom Press.

23. Thurman, R. (1999). *Inner Revolution*. New York: Riverhead Trade Books.
24. Tambiah, S. (1968). *World Conqueror, World Renouncer*. Cambridge: Cambridge University Press.
25. See my article, Loizzo, J. (2006). Renewing the Nalanda Legacy: Science, Religion and Objectivity in Buddhism and the West. In *Religion East and West*, 6: 101–20.
26. These resistances have been addressed most extensively by Wallace, B. A. (2007/2009). *Contemplative Science: Where Buddhism and Neuroscience Converge*. New York: Columbia University Press.
27. This idea is key to the life work of scholars who integrate aspects of psychoanalytic thought into the social sciences to arrive at something akin to what Paul Ricoeur calls *sciences de l'homme* or human sciences. Another interdisciplinary approach from the standpoint of neuroscience is the work of researchers like Francisco Varela and Richie Davidson.
28. Epstein, M. (2004). *Thoughts Without a Thinker: Psychotherapy from a Buddhist Perspective*. New York: Basic Books.
29. Saffran, J. P. (1995). *Psychoanalysis and Buddhism: An Unfolding Dialogue*. Boston: Wisdom Publications.
30. Germer, C., Siegel, R., & Fulton, P. (2005). *Psychotherapy and Mindfulness*. New York: Guilford Press.
31. Rubin, J. (1996). *Psychotherapy and Buddhism: Towards an Integration*. New York: Springer.
32. Jennings, P. (2010). *Mixing Minds: The Power of Relationship in Psychoanalysis and Buddhism*. Boston: Wisdom Publications.
33. This formula, *Om ye dharma hetu prabhava, hetun teṣam tathāgata hy avadat, teṣam cayor nirodho evam vādi, māhaśramaṇaya svaha*, was also the motto inscribed on the seal of *Nālandā Māhavihāra*, the wheel of teaching flanked by two deer, a seal which has served as the common symbol for any Buddhist *vihāra* down to the present.
34. For a fine introduction to Buddhist psychology from the Tibetan perspective, see Tsering, T. (2006). *Buddhist Psychology*. London: Wisdom Press.
35. For a brief presentation of this process, see Lati Rinpoche, & Hopkins, J. (1985). *Death, Intermediate State and Rebirth in Tibetan Buddhism*. Ithaca: Snow Lion Press.
36. Sanskrit in Shastri D. (1968). *Tattvasaṃgraha*. (Varanasi: Bauddhabharati), k. 3587: *tapācchedāca nikaśāt suvarṇam iva pānditaiḥ / parikṣyā bhikśavo grāhyam mad vaco na tu gauravāt //*. Cited in Thurman, R. (1986). *Tsong Khapa's Speech of Gold in the Essence of True Eloquence*. Princeton: Princeton University Press, 190.
37. *Majjhima Nikaya*, 63.
38. The Tibetan of this famous verse, attributed to *Matṛceta*, was kindly provided by Geshe Lobsang Jamspal: *thub rnams sdig pa chu yis mi 'khru zhing/ 'gro bo'i sdug bsngal phyag gis mi sel la/ nyid kyi rtogs pa gzhan du spo min te/ chos nyid bden pa bstan pas grol bar mdzad//* Cited in the Udanavarga and known from Tsong Khapa's Lam-rim Chen-mo, its original source within the Buddhist canon has not been found.
39. See Zysk, K. (1990). *Aceticism and Healing in Ancient India: Medicine in the Buddhist Monastery*. Oxford: Oxford University Press.
40. For a representative treatment of twin studies of mental traits, see Matthews, G., Deary, I., & Whiteman, M. (2003). *Personality Traits*. Cambridge: Cambridge University Press.
41. This comes in the context of a discussion of ego development in Freud, S. (1923/1960). *The Ego and the Id*. J. Strachey (trans.). New York: W.W. Norton & Company, 38.

42. The respective canonical sources for these analogies are the *Milindapanha*, in Warren, H. C. (trans.). (1963). *Buddhism in Translation*. New York: Harvard University Press, 234; and the *Mahāprajñāparāmitaśastra*, attributed to Nāgārjuna, chapter 12.
43. The fourth link in the twelve-fold cycle of dependent origination, *nama-rūpa*, describes the symbolic construction of self as the conjunction of name and form. While "form" In this context could mean the body as a physical object, the more critical reading refers to the crystallization of a self-concept around the first-person pronoun "I" and its coordination with a self-image or body-image referred to by the possessive pronoun "mine." It is this crystallization that Nāgārjuna refers to in his Centrist formulation of self as "mere name" (*nama-matrā*) and Chandrakīrti in his formulation of self as a mere linguistic usage (*prajñāpri-matrā*). For more, see my introduction to *Nāgārjuna's Reason Sixty with Chandrakīrti's Commentary*.
44. See my recent review, Loizzo, J. (2009). Optimizing Learning and Quality of Life Throughout the Lifespan. In Bushell et al. *Longevity*.
45. Delmonte, M. (1995). Meditation and the Unconscious. In *Journal of Contemporary Psychotherapy*, 25: 223–42.
46. Linehan, M. (1993). *Cognitive Behavioral Treatment of Borderline Personality Disorder*. New York: Guilford Press.
47. Traditional sources for this history are the records of Chinese visiting scholars Xuan-zang and Yi-jing: Beal, S. (1884/2004). *Su Yu Ki: Buddhist Records of the Western World*. Kessinger Publishing; and Takakusus, J. (1896). *A Record of the Buddhist Religion as Practiced in India and the Malay*. Oxford: Oxford University Press.
48. Linehan M., & Shearin, E. (1988). Lethal stress: A social-behavioral model of suicidal behavior. In S. Fisher, & J. Reason (eds.), *Handbook of Life Stress, Cognition and Health* New York: Wiley, 265–85.
49. Linehan M., H., & Armstrong, S. A. (1991). Cognitive-behavioral treatment of chronically parasuicidal borderline patients. In *Archives of General Psychiatry*; 48:1060–64.
50. Simpson E., Pistorello, J., & Begin, A. (1998). Use of dialectical behavior therapy in a partial hospital program for women with borderline personality disorder. In *Psychiatric Services*; 49: 669–73.
51. Segal Z., Williams, J., & Teasdale, J. (1993). *Mindfulness-Based Cognitive Therapy for Depression: A New Approach to Preventing Relapse*. New York: Guilford Press.
52. Loizzo, J., Peterson, J., Wolf, E., et al. (2010). The effects of a program in contemplative self-healing on quality of life in women with breast and other gynecologic cancer. In *Alternative Therapies in Health and Medicine*, May/June, 16(3): 30–37.
53. Peterson, J., Charlson, M., Loizzo, J., et al. The effects of contemplative self-healing on quality of life in underserved women with breast and other gynecologic cancers. In press.

Chapter 1: Deep Mindfulness and Self-Healing

1. Skt: *gambhīra śanto virajaḥ prabhāsvaraḥ prāptomi dharmo hyamṛto 'saṃskṛtaḥ / deśeya cāhaṃ na parasyajane yannuna tuṣṇī pavane vaseyaṃ /*, from Vaidya, P. (ed.). (1958). *Lalitavistara*. Darbhanga: Mithila Institute, Buddhist Sanskrit Texts, 1, 286.
2. This association has recently received international attention thanks to the Nobel prize awarded Elizabeth Blackburn for her work on the link between

stress, aging and the DNA repair enzyme Telomerase. See Eppel, E., Daubenmier, J., Moscowitz, J., et al. (2009). Can Meditation Slow the Rate of Cellular Aging? Cognitive Stress, Mindfulness and Telomeres. In Bushell, W., Olio, E., & Theise, N. (eds.), *Longevity, Regeneration and Optimal Health: Integrating Eastern and Western Perspectives.* New York: Annals of the New York Academy of Sciences. Volume 1172; 34–53.

3. My telling coalesces the account in *Lalitavistara* with re-mythologized tales from some of the Pāli Scriptures, including *The Supreme Net Scripture (Brahmajālasutta)*, 2.2ff and *About Kevaddha Scripture (Kevaddhasutta)*, 83, Walshe, M. (trans.), *The Long Discourses of the Buddha*, 75–76; 178–79. For an English version of the *Lalitavistara*, Bays, G. (trans.). (1983). *The Lalitavistara Sutra, The Voice of Buddha, The Beauty of Compassion Volume II.* Berkeley: Dharma Publishing.
4. For those of you who want a more in depth presentation based on the Nālandā tradition, see Tsering, T. (2005). *The Four Noble Truths.* Boston: Wisdom Publications.
5. Nagel, T. (1986). *The View from Nowhere.* Oxford: Oxford University Press.
6. Taoism provided Chinese civilization with a contemplative approach to life that offered an individualist counterculture to the orthodox Confucian mainstream throughout most of Chinese history. Since its outlook and methods are more compatible with those of Buddhism, Taoism offered an indigenous partner tradition for the integration of India's Buddhist contemplative science into Chinese civilization. This natural complementarity lead to a long history of mutual influence and the eventual rise of a Taoist-Buddhist synthesis in China.
7. Price, J. (2007). Cognitive schemas, defense mechanisms and post-traumatic stress symptomatology. In *Psychology and Psychotherapy*, September (80): 343–53.
8. Deikman, A. (1966). Deautomatisation and the mystic experience. In *Psychiatry* 29: 481–89.
9. Heim, C., Nater, U., Maloney, E., et al. (2009). Childhood trauma and risk for chronic fatigue syndrome: association with neuroendocrine dysfunction. In *Archives of General Psychiatry*, January, 66(1): 72–80.
10. Leitenberg, H., Gibson, L., Novy, P. (2004). Individual differences among undergraduate women in methods of coping with stressful events: the impact of cumulative childhood stressors and abuse. *Child Abuse and Neglect*, February 28(2): 181-92.
11. Bondi, C. O., Rodriguez, G., Gould, G. G., et al. (2008).Chronic unpredictable stress induces a cognitive deficit and anxiety-like behavior in rats that is prevented by chronic antidepressant drug treatment. In *Neuropsychopharmacology*, January 33(2): 320-31.
12. Kabat-Zinn J. (1982). An outpatient program based in behavioral medicine for chronic pain patients based on the practice of mindfulness meditation: theoretical considerations and preliminary results. In *General Hospital Psychiatry*, 4: 33–47.
13. Davidson R., Goleman D., & Schwartz G. (1976). Attentional and affective concomitants of meditation. In *Journal of Abnormal Psychology* 85: 23–58; and Davidson R., & Goleman D. (1977). The role of attention in meditation and hypnosis: a psychobiological perspective on transformations of consciousness. In *International Journal of Clinincal and Experimental Hypnosis* 25: 291–308.
14. This insight has been associated with a number of pioneers, including my Columbia colleague, Eric Kandel, who was awarded the 2000 Nobel Prize in biology for his work on neural plasticity in mollusks. See Kandell, E, Schwartz, J. (1991). *Principles of Neural Science.* New York, Elsevier Science; and Kandel E.

(1999). Biology and the future of psychoanalysis: A new intellectual framework for psychiatry revisited. In *American Journal of Psychiatry*, 156: 505–24.
15. Fenwick P. (1987). Meditation and the EEG. In Wes. M. (ed.), *The Psychology of Meditation*. Oxford: Clarendon Press, 104–17.
16. For a classical treatment of states of consciousness, see James, W. (1989). *Varieties of Religious Experience*. New York: Modern Library, 413–68. A more current model based on interactive systems theory is offered by Tart, C. (1980). *The Psychobiology of Consciousness*. New York: Plenum Press, 243–69. For one recent study on this, see Calm, B. R., & Polich, J. (2006). Meditation states and traits: EEG, ERP, and Neuroimaging Studies. In *Psychological Bulletin*, 132(2): 180–211.
17. Borrelli, E., Nestler, E. J., Allis, C. D., et al. (2008). Decoding the epigenetic language of neuronal plasticity. In *Neuron*, 60(6): 961–74.
18. Goleman, D. (1977). *Varieties of Meditative Experience*. New York: Dutton Press.
19. The traditional sources for the foundations of mindfulness (skt. *sṃrti-upaṣthna*, pāli. *satī-paṭṭāna*) are found in the Pāli Scriptures, especially the *Greater Discourse on the Foundations of Mindfulness* (*Mahāsatipaṭṭānasutta*). For the English, see M. Walshe (trans.), *The Long Discourses of the Buddha, op. cit.*, 335–50.
20. Brown, R. P., Gerbarg, P. L. (2005). Sudarshan Kriya yogic breathing in the treatment of stress, anxiety, and depression: part I-neurophysiologic model. In *Journal of Alternative and Complementary Medicine*. February, 11(1): 189–201; Bernardi, L., Passino, C., Wilmerding, V., Dallam, G. M., et al. (2001). Breathing patterns and cardiovascular autonomic modulation during hypoxia induced by simulated altitude. In *Journal of Hypertension*, 19(5): 947–58.
21. Stancak, A., & Kuna, M. (1994). EEG changes during forced alternate nostril breathing. In *International Journal of Psychophysiology*, 18: 75–79.
22. This tradition is reviewed in chapter 10.
23. Thondup, T. (1998). *The Healing Power of Mind*. Boston: Shambhala Press.
24. See Mikulas, W. (1978). Four Noble Truths of Buddhism related to behavior therapy. In *Psychological Record* 28: 59–67 See Mikulas, W. (1981). Buddhism and behavioral modification. In *Psychological Record* 31: 331–42.
25. Teicher, M. H., Andersen, S. L., Polcari, A., et al. (2002). Developmental neurobiology of childhood stress and trauma. *Psychiatric Clinics of North America*, June 25(2): 397–426, vii–viii.
26. For an elegant map of this traditional schema, see Tsering, *The Four Noble Truths*, op. cit., 93–97.
27. Cohen, S. (1997). *Measuring Stress: A Guide for Health and Social Scientists*. Oxford: Oxford University Press.
28. Shulkin, J., Gold. P., & McEwen, B. (1998). Induction of corticotropin-releasing hormone gene expression by glucocorticoids: implications for understanding the states of fear and anxiety and allostatic load. In *Psychoneuroendocrinology*, 23: 219–43.
29. Shulkin, J., McEwen, B., & Gold, P. (1994). Allostasis, amygdala and anticipatory angst. In *Neuroscience and Biobehavioral Revue*, 18: 385–96.
30. Goleman, D. (2010). *Emotional Intelligence: Why it Matter More than IQ*. New York: Bloomsbury Paperbacks.
31. Weems, C. F., & Silverman, W. K. (2006). An integrative model of control: implications for understanding emotion regulation and dysregulation in childhood anxiety. In *Journal of Affective Disorders*, April 91 (2–3): 113–24.
32. Morey, R. A., Dolcos, F., Petty, C. M., et al. (2009). The role of trauma-related distractors on neural systems for working memory and emotion processing in posttraumatic stress disorder. In *Journal of Psychiatric Residency*, May, 43(8): 809–17.

33. Cyders, M. A., & Smith, G. T. (2008). Emotion-based dispositions to rash action: positive and negative urgency. In *Psychological Bulletin*, November, 134(6): 807–28.
34. Grippo, A. J., & Johnson, A. K. (2009). Stress, depression and cardiovascular dysregulation: a review of neurobiological mechanisms and the integration of research from preclinical disease models. In *Stress*,12(1): 1–21.
35. Jameison, K., & Dinan, T. G. (2001). Glucocorticoids and cognitive function: from physiology to pathophysiology. In *Human Psychopharmacology*, June, 16(4): 293–302; Sapolsky, R. M. et al. (1986). The neuroendocrinology of stress and aging: the glucocorticoid cascade hypothesis. In *Endocrinology Revue* 7: 284–301; Yehuda, R. (1997). Sensitization of the HPA axis in posttraumatic stress disorder. In R. Yeduda, & A. McFarlane (eds.), *The Psychobiology of Posttraumatic Stress Disorder*. New York, Academic Press.
36. Qin, S., Hermans, E. J., van Marle, H. J., et al. (2009). Acute psychological stress reduces working memory-related activity in the dorsolateral prefrontal cortex. In *Biological Psychiatry*, July 1, 66(1): 25–32.
37. See discussion in Introduction
38. Frolkis, V. V. (1993). Stress-age syndrome. In *Mechanisms of Ageing and Development*, 69: 93–107; Epel, E. S. et al. (2004). Accelerated telomre shortening in response to life stress. In *Proceedings of the National Academy of Sciences*, USA 101: 17312–315.
39. This simile is used in the celebrated dedication of Candrakīrti's Central Way Introduction (*Mādhyamakāvatāra*).
40. In McEwan, B. (2002). *The End of Stress as We Know It*. New York: Joseph Henry Press. Bruce applies his model of allostasis as an organisms's adaptation to a changing environment to his define allostatic load as a quantifiable measure of the cumulative effects of stress on a living system. I apply that model in my review article, Loizzo, J. (2000), *Meditation and Psychotherapy*, op. cit., to suggest the possibility of an empirical model of the resistances to learning that must be dealt with in the course of meditation and psychotherapy.
41. Gruver, A. L., & Sempowski, G. D. (2008). Cytokines, leptin, and stress-induced thymic atrophy. In *Journal of Leukocyte Biology*, October, 84(4): 915–23; Engler, H., & Stefanski, V. (2003). Social stress and T cell maturation in male rats: transient and persistent alterations in thymic function. In *Psychoneuroendocrinology*. November, 28(8): 951–69; McEwen, B. S. (2003). Mood disorders and allostatic load. In *Biological Psychiatry*, August 1, 54(3): 200–07.
42. Bremner, J., Randall, P., Scott, T., et al. (1995). MRI-based measurement of hippocampal volume in patients with combat-related post-traumatic stress disorder. In *American Journal of Psychiatry*, 1527: 973–81.
43. Sivamani, R. K., Pullar, C. E., Manabat-Hidalgo, C. G., et al. (2009). Stress-mediated increases in systemic and local epinephrine impair skin wound healing: potential new indication for beta blockers. In *Public Library of Science and Medicine*. January 13, 6(1): e12; Morgan, C. A. et al. (2004). Relationships among plasma dehydroepiandrosterone sulfate and cortisol levels, symptoms of dissociation, and objective performance in humans exposed to acute stress. In *Archives of General Psychiatry* 61: 819–25; Bushell, W. C. (2005). From molecular biology to anti-aging cognitive-behavioral practices: The pioneering research of Walter Pierpaoli on the pineal and bone marrow foreshadows the contemporary revolution in stem cell and regenerative biology. In *Annals of the New York Academy of Sciences* 1057: 29–42; Klein, Z. A., Padow, V. A., & Romeo, R. D. (2009). The effects of stress on play and home cage behaviors in adolescent male rats. In *Developmental Psychobiology*. November 23. [Epublication.]

44. Anderson, V., & Johnson, L. (1997). *Systems Thinking Basics: From Concepts to Causal Loops*. New York: Pegasus Communications.
45. Govinda, A. (1961). *The Psychological Attitude of Early Buddhist Philosophy*. New York: Samuel Weiser.
46. Hunt, P. S., Fanselow, M. S., Richardson, R., et al. (2007). Synapses, circuits, and the ontogeny of learning. In *Developmental Psychobiology*, November, 49(7):649-63.
47. Carney, N., Chestnut, R., Maynard, H., et al. (1999). Effect of cognitive rehabilitation on outcomes of persons with traumatic brain injury. In *Journal of Head Trauma Rehabilitation*, 14: 277–303.
48. Dobzhansky, T., & Gould, S. (1982). *Genetics and the Origin of Human Species*. New York: Columbia University Press.
49. Aubin-Horth, N., & Renn, S. C. (2009) Genomic reaction norms: using integrative biology to understand molecular mechanisms of phenotypic plasticity. In *Molecular Ecolology*, September 18(18): 3763–80.
50. This pronouncement, frequently repeated in the Pāli canon and included in abbreviated form in the famous four epitomes of the teaching (*dharmoddāna*), is also frequently cited in the Mahāyana literature, notably in Maitreyanātha's *Ornament of Realizations* (*Abhisamayālaṃkāra*), and Nāgārjuna's *Reason Sixty* (*Yuktiśaṣṭiika*).
51. Natural liberation (skt. *sahajā-mokṣa*, tib. *hlen-skyai thar-pa*) refers to the teachings of Padmasambhava, best known from his popular classic we call The Tibetan Book of the Dead (*Bardo Thos-drol*); great perfection (skt. *mahāniṣpanna*, tib. *rdzog-chen*) and great seal (skt. *mahāmudra*, tib. *phyag-rgya chen-po*) refer to various teaching traditions that emphasize mindfulness and insight meditation on the nature of mind. All three traditions use insights and methods derived from the contemplative art and science of the Buddhist Tantras to make more advanced levels of meditation accessible to a broader, lay audience.
52. Freud, S. (2011). *The Psychopathology of Everyday Life*. New York: CreateSpace Press.
53. Demasio, A. (2005). *Descartes' Error: Reason, Emotion and the Human Brain*. New York: Penguin Press.
54. Coleman, M. R., Bekinschtein, T., Monti, M. M., et al. (2009). A multimodal approach to the assessment of patients with disorders of consciousness. In *Progress in Brain Research*, 177: 231-48; Bernat, J. L. (2009). Chronic consciousness disorders. In *Annual Review of Medicine*, 60: 381–92.
55. According to the classical definition from Vasubandhu's *Abhidharmakośa*, II.16, mind or consciousness is not its content but that which merely observes or perceives (*upalabdhi*) the presence of objects. His autocommentary explains, "Consciousness (*vijñāna*) or mind (*citta*) apprehends (*grahana*) only the thing itself (*vastumātra*); the mental [factors] (*caitasika*) or *dharmas* associated with the consciousness, that is to say, sensation, etc. (*vedanā*, *saṃjñā*...), apprehend particular characteristics, special conditions." From Pruden, L. (trans.) (1988). *The Abhidharmakośabhaśyaṃ of Vasubandhu*. Berkeley: University of California Press, 139, n.82. Conceived as a medium (*āyatana*), element (*dhātu*) or faculty (*indriya*), mind is identified as the immediately preceding moment (*samanatara-pratyaya*) in the stream of consciousness, which serves as a basis (*aśraya*) for mental perception or discursive reflection. For more on this, see chapter 2.
56. This is true in the exoteric traditions of Buddhist psychology based on the work of Vasubandhu and Asanga, where mind as a faculty is mapped onto the stream of consciousness (*cittasaṃtana*) or the fundamental consciousness (*ālayavijñāna*); it is true in the epistemological psychology of *Digñāga* and

Dharmakītri, where the mind is viewed as the organ or faculty of mental perception (*manasapratyākṣa*) and described as naturally lucid (*prakṛtyābhasa*); and it is also true in the esoteric traditions based on the neuropsychology of the Tantras, where the primary mind is mapped onto the extremely subtle bodymind identified as the indestructible drop (*akṣārabindu*). For more on this, see chapter 2.

57. El-Sheikh, M., Kouros, C. D., Erath, S., et al. (2009). Marital conflict and children's externalizing behavior: interactions between parasympathetic and sympathetic nervous system activity. In *Monographs of the Society for Research in Child Development*, 74(1): vii, 1–79.
58. For an excellent introduction to this approach to contemplative life, see Dalai Lama, H. H., & Berzin, A. (1986). *The Ganden/Kagyu Tradition of Mahamudra*. Ithaca: Snow Lion Press.
59. This approach—to go where the pathology lies—is employed in some modern therapies on the margins of the field, including Eugen Gendlin's technique of focusing; the deep affect approach of Sylvan Thompkins and Diana Fosha's accelerated experiential dynamic therapy (AEDP); and the powerful mind/body approach to cognitive therapy called eye movement desensitization reprocessing (EMDR).
60. For more on this, see Tsering, *The Four Noble Truths*, op. cit., 17–22.
61. We'll review this table and its use in detail in chapter 2.
62. The Sanskrit of this pronouncement, *sarvāsti*, was later adopted to describe the early Realist (*Sarvāstivāda*) schools of Buddhist psychology. These include the Analyst (*Vaibhaṣika*) and Traditionist (*Sautrāntika*) schools codified by Vasubandhu in his *Compendium of Scientific Teaching* (*Abhidharmakośa*).

Chapter 2: Self-Analysis, Insight, and Freedom

1. From *Treasury of Scientific Teaching* (*Abhidharmakośa*), 1.3, available in English translation, Pruden, L. (trans.). (1988–1991). *Abhidharmakosabhasyam of Vasubandhu*. Berkeley: Asian Humanities Press, 57 Pruden's version is based on the French translation of Louis de la Vallee Poussin.
2. See Wallace, B. A. (2000). *Contemplative Science: Where Buddhism and Neuroscience Converge*. New York: Columbia University Press; and Llinas, R. (2001). *I of the Vortex: From Neurons to Self.* Cambridge: MIT Press.
3. See Dalai Lama, & Cutler, H. (2009). *The Art of Happiness in a Troubled World*. New York: Riverhead Books; Williams, M., Teasdale, J., Siegal, Z., & Kabat-Zinn, J. (2007). *The Mindful Way Through Depression: Freeing Yourself from Chronic Unhappiness*. New York: Guilford Press; and Seligman, M. (2004). *Authentic Happiness: Using the New Positive Psychology to realize your Potential for Lasting Happiness*. New York: Free Press.
4. See Epstein, M. (1995). *Thoughts Without a Thinker: Psychotherapy from a Buddhist Perspective*. New York: Basic Books; Rubin, J. (1996). *Psychotherapy and Buddhism: Toward an Integration*. Berlin: Springer Verlag; Safran, J. (2003). *Psychoanalysis and Buddhism: An Unfolding Dialogue*. Boston: Wisdom Press; and Germer, C., Siegal, R., & Fulton, P. (2005). *Mindfulness and Psychotherapy*. New York: Guilford Press.
5. Freud, S., Bonaparte, M., Freud, A. (1954). *The Origins of Psychoanalysis: Sigmund Freud's Letters, Drafts and Notes to Wilhelm Fliess*. New York: Basic Books.
6. Consider the famous verse quoted in the Introduction, "Just as a goldsmith buys gold, after testing it by melting, cutting and polishing, the wise accept my words after full examination, not just out of faith (in me)."

7. This is clear from the Buddha's refusal on his deathbed to appoint a successor, in lieu of which he gave his students the injunction, "Mendicants, be an island unto yourself, a lamp unto yourself, and a refuge unto yourself, with the teaching as your only lamp and the teaching as your only refuge."
8. PS, I, 1ab: pramāṇabhūtaya jagaddhitaiṣiṇe prānamyā śāstre sugatāya tāyine //. Thurman, R. (1986). *Tsong Khapa's Speech of Gold in the Essence of True Eloquence*. Princeton: Princeton University Press, 12.
9. Alan Wallace discusses the history of introspection research in the West in his *Contemplative Science.*
10. See Loizzo, J. (2000). Meditation and Psychotherapy: Stress, Allostasis and Enriched Learning. In P. Muskin (ed.), *Complementary and Alternative Medicine and Psychiatry*. Washington: American Psychiatric Association Press.
11. See Wallace, *Contemplative Science*; and Goleman, D. (2004). *Destructive Emotions: A Scientific Dialogue with His Holiness the Dalai Lama*. New York: Bantam Press
12. Govinda, A. (1964). *The Psychological Attitude of Early Buddhist Philosophy*, 35–36.
13. *Treasury*, 1.2; Pruden, 1, 56.
14. There are many classical textual sources for this tradition, both in the Pāli and Sanskrit traditions. The Pāli tradition lists seven classics within the *Abhidhamma* canon, and was summarized in later commentaries including Buddhagosa's *Path of Purification* (*Visuddhimagga*). In the Sanskrit tradition, the early Sarvāstivāda canon was first compiled in the Jñānaprasthāna, which became the basis of later summaries including Vasumitra's *Mahāvibhāṣa*, Upaśanta's *Abhidharmahṛdaya* and the definitive *Abhidharmakośabhaṣyam* or *Treasury of Scientific Teaching* by Vasubandhu. The *Treasury* was first translated into French by Louis de la Vallee Poussin, and is now available in an English translation by Leo Pruden, based on Poussin's.
15. For an excellent and accessible introduction to this teaching tradition, see Tsering, T. (2006). *Buddhist Psychology*. Somerville: Wisdom Publications.
16. Discussed in Vasubandhu's *Treasury*, 1.4; Pruden, 1, 58–59.
17. The list of sixty four elements I draw on here, based on a Tibetan monastic textbook in the Gelukpa tradition, *Rigs-lam sgo-brgya 'byed-pa'i 'prul-gyi lde-mig gnyis-pa*, published in 1979 by the Drepung Loseling Library in Mundgod, India, differs slightly from the list in Vasubandhu's *Treasury*, based on the table of the Kashmiri Vaibhaṣika school which commissioned him to write the *Treasury*. Instead it follows the list he himself preferred, listed in his *Pañcaskandhaprakaraṇa*, cited in Pruden, 1, 333, n.190. The traditional list of unconditioned elements includes the two cessations (*nirodha*), with residual compulsive mind/body systems and without, as well as space, which I list with the physical elements, following the *Treasury*, 1.28. The conditioned and unconditioned elements are discussed in *Treasury* chapters one, two and five: *Treasury*, 1.4–48; Pruden, 1, 58–131; *Treasury*, 2.23–34; Pruden, 1, 189–206; and Treasury, 5.1–21; Pruden, 3, 767–809.
18. Discussed in chapter one of Vasubandhu's *Treasury*, 1.12–14; Pruden, 1, 68–72.
19. Discussed in chapter one of Vasubandu's *Treasury*, 1.35–36; Pruden, 1, 99–103.
20. For a sample of the classical debate over atoms, molecules and their substantiality, see Vasubandhu's *Treasury*, 2.22; Pruden, I, 184–88. Vasubandu's critique of indivisible atomic particles comes in his *Twenty Verses* (*Vimśaka*); see Anaker, S. (2002). *Seven Works of Vasubandhu: The Buddhist Psychological Doctor*. Delhi: Motilal Barnarsidas. The element of space was included in various places in different enumerations of elements, but came to play a central role in the esoteric physics of the Kālacakra tradition. See Loizzo, J. (2009). Kālacakra and the Nālandā Tradition. In E. Arnold (ed.), *As Long as Space*

Endures: Essays in Honor of His Holiness the Dalai Lama. Ithaca: Snow Lion Press. Of note, some early enumerations of the elements not only included space as a less tangible material element in its physics, but also impure consciousness (*āśrava-vijñāna*), as would the Kālacakra system later. Vasubandhu along with the Sautrāntika school considered space as a pure absence of physical resistance (*sapratighadravyābhavamātra*), while others like Katyayaniputra (in his *Vibhāṣa*) distinguished between pure, unconditioned space *per se* (*ākāśa=arūpin, anāsrava, asaṃskṛta*) and space as an impure, less tangible material element (*ākāśadhātu=āsrava, saṃskṛta, ṛūpin*).

21. For a review of the Buddhist medical science tradition preserved in Tibet, see Loizzo, J., Blackhall, L., & Rapgyay, L. (2009). Tibetan Medicine: A Complementary Science of Optimal Health. In W. Bushell, E. Olivo, & N. Thiese (eds.), *Longevity, Regeneration and Optimal Health*. New York: New York Academy of Sciences.
22. The Buddhist view of the subtle neural body is described in Lati Rinpoche & Hopkins, J. (1985). *Death, Intermediate State and Rebirth in Tibetan Buddhism*. Ithaca: Snow Lion Press.
23. Discussed in Vasubandhu's *Treasury*, 1.16–17; Pruden, I, 74–75.
24. According to the classical definition from Vasubandhu's *Treasury*, 2.16, mind or consciousness is not its content but that which merely observes or perceives (*upalabdhi*) the presence of objects. His autocommentary explains, "Consciousness (*vijñāna*) or mind (*citta*) apprehends (*grahana*) only the thing itself (*vastumātra*); the mental [factors] (*caitasika*) or *dharmas* associated with the consciousness, that is to say, sensation, etc. (*vedanā, saṃjñā*...), apprehend particular characteristics, special conditions." From Pruden, 1, 139, n.82.
25. See Alan Wallace's *Contemplative Science*.
26. Discussed in chapter 1 of Vasubandhu's *Treasury*, 1.17; Pruden, I, 75: "Of these six consciousnesses, the one which continually passes away is (called "mind" or) manas." Vasubandhu's *Commentary*, Pruden, I, n.84, 139, states: "The consciousnesses (*vijñāna*) succeed one another; they can be visual ... mental. The consciousness which disappears is the immediately antecedent cause, the support (*āśraya*) of the consciousness which immediately follows. Under this aspect it receives the name of (mind or) *manas*, (mental medium or) *mana-āyatana*, and (mental faculty or) *mana-indriya*."
27. Govinda, *Psychological Attiitude*, 134–42, explores one version of this temporal analysis, based on the *Abhidammatta-Saṅgaha*. According to this account, one simple sense impression (*pañcadvāra-vīthi*), say a glimpse of a lotus, for instance, must take a minimum of seventeen distinct moments of consciousness of nine different kinds, two of them in dependence on visual processing. Interestingly, this process begins with one preceding moment of consciousness and two moments of resonance within the experiential factors (*bhavaṅga-calaṇāni*) which precede the engagement of a fresh object. The subsequent moments come in three phases: (1) five moments of subliminal processing called awareness (*vajjaṇa*), sense-consciousness (*indriya-viññaṇam*), reception (*sampaṭicchana*), inspection (*santīraṇa*) and discernment (*votahappana*); (2) seven moments of perception or registration (*javana*); and (3) and two moments of determination or commitment (*tadārammaṇa*). After as many as several hundred thousand such disparate impressions, a process of mental construction (*tad-anuvattaka-mano-vīthi*) integrates many impressions into a synthetic cognition (*samūhaggaṇa*) of a single object. Subsequently, the symbolic mind arrives at a mental image (*attha-paññatthi-vīthi*) of that cognition, which grasps the sense or use of the object (*atthagahanna*). And finally, the discursive mind arrives at a recognition (*nama-paññatthi-vīthi*) of that image, which verbally identifies the object (*nāmagahanna*).

28. For a psychologically informed review of the neuroscience of perception, see Kissen, B. (1986). *Conscious and Unconscious Programs in the Brain*. New York: Plenum Press. For a more current overview, see Kandel, E., & Schwartz, J. (1999). *Principles of Neural Science*. New York: Elsevier Science.
29. Causes and effects are discussed in the second chapter of Vasubandhu's *Treasury*, 2.49–65; Pruden, I, 225–309.
30. Discussed in chapter one of Vasubandhu's *Treasury*, 2.62a-b; Pruden, I, 297–302.
31. The esoteric neuropsychology of the Buddhist Tantras identifies the primary mental faculty with the indestructible drop at the heart, an extremely subtle form of mind and matter in which consciousness, neural energy and neural chemistry are seen as one empirical entity, only distinguished by the application of different categories (*dngos gcig dang ldog pa tha dad*). See Cozort, D. (1986). *Highest Yoga Tantra*. Ithaca: Snow Lion Press.
32. See Llinas, R., *The I of the Vortex*.
33. Dignaga's system distinguishes two layers of all six forms of mind, secondary conception (*anumāna*) and primary perception (*pratyakṣa*); while Asanga and Vasubandhu's depth-psychology introduces two layers of mind underlying the surface six forms of consciousness, namely: the compulsive mentality (*klista-manas*) and the subconscious mind (*ālaya-vijñāna*). The neuropsychology of the Tantras also introduces two layers of mind underlying the coarsest (*rakta*) five forms of sense consciousness, including the subtle (*sukṣma*) level of reflective mental consciousness, and the subtlest (*susukṣma*) level of intuitive consciousness.
34. Discussed in chapter two of Vasubandhu's *Treasury*, 2.63; Pruden, 1, 304–05.
35. Tart, C. (1980). A Systems Model of Consciousness. In R. Davidson (ed.), *The Psychobiology of Consciousness*. New York: Plenum Press.
36. The categories and elements in the table as presented here do not coincide exactly with those defined in Vasubandhu's *Treasury*, since in that work he followed the table of the Vaibhaṣika school that engaged him to write that classic compendium. Later versions of the table generally follow the schema he himself preferred, outlined in his *Pañcaskandhaprakaraṇa*.
37. Discussed in chapter two of Vasubandhu's *Treasury*, 2.24; Pruden, 189–90, where the omnipresent factors are listed as ten, the five in our list plus those five factors listed as objective mental factors.
38. Discussed in chapter two of Vasubandhu's *Treasury*, 2.24; Pruden, 189–90, where they are subsumed into the omnipresent mental factors.
39. PS, 1.2, Sanskrit: / *pratyakṣa kalpana apodhaṃ* /.
40. *Treatise on Valid Knowledge* (*Pramānavartika*), 1. Sanskrit: / *pratyakṣa kalpana apodhaṃ abhrantaṃ* /. For a full discussion of Dharmakīrti's thought, see Dreyfus, G. 1996. *Recognizing Reality: Dharmakīrti's Philosophy and its Tibetan Interpretions*. Albany: SUNY Press; and Dunne, J. 2004. *Foundations of Dharmakīrti's Philosophy*. Boston: Wisdom Press.
41. Sanskrit, *apoha*; Tibetan *gsel ba*. For a discussion of this concept, see Dunne's *Foundations*, and Dreyfus' *Recognizing Reality*.
42. See Popper, K. (2002). *The Logic of Scientific Discovery*. London: Routledge Classics.
43. The fourteen metaphysical questions the Buddha refused to entertain (*avyākrta-vastunī*) are: (1) Buddha exists after death; (2) does not; (3) both does and does not; (4) neither does nor does not; (5) the world is finite; (6) infinite; (7) both finite and infinite; (8) neither finite nor infinite; (9) the world has a beginning; (10) has not; (11) both has and has not; (12) neither has nor has not; (13) the self is the same as the body; (14) the self is different from the body. Another version of these fourteen questions is found in *Treasury*, 9; Pruden, 1332–36.

44. Consider the classical simile of the wounded soldier, *Majjhima-Nikāya*, 63, Mahāthera *Nyāṇatiloka* (Trans.), cited in Govinda, *Psychological Attitude*, 34: "It is as if a man were pieced by a poison arrow, and his friends, companions or near relations called in a surgeon, but the man should say: 'I will not have this arrow pulled out until I know who the man is that has wounded me: whether he is a noble, a prince, a citizen or a servant', or 'what his name is and to what family he belongs,' or 'whether he is tall, short or of medium height.' Verily, such a man would die, ere he could adequately learn all this."
45. See Klein, A. C. (1998). *Knowledge and Liberation: Tibetan Buddhist Epistemology in Support of Transformative Religious Experience.* Ithaca: Snow Lion Press; and George Dreyfus' *Recognizing Reality.*
46. Ibid.
47. Tashi Tsering gives a brief glimpse of this system in his book, *Buddhist Psychology*, op. cit., chapters 6 & 7. For a fuller discussion, see Klein's *Knowledge and Liberation.*
48. Discussed in Vasubandhu's *Treasury*, 5.7–9; Pruden, 3, 776–84.
49. This affective determination is traditionally described with the rubric of twelve kinds of mind states, discussed in chapter two of Vasubandhu's *Treasury*, 2.66–73; Pruden, 1, 310–25. Govinda, *Psychological Attitude*, 99–106, unpacks a similar schema from the Pāli tradition. The essential variables determining the developmental effects of mental states are whether they are: unhealthy, i.e., directed towards compulsive aims and conditioned by the three root compulsions; healthy, i.e., directed towards healing aims and conditioned by the three root positive emotions; or neutral, i.e., not directed in either way and not conditioned by either, as in neutral, purely receptive states like immediate sense perception. These states are further differentiated based on the realms of experience in which they can operate: the realm of insatiable desire (*kamadhātu*); the realm of pure form (*rūpadhātu*); and the realm of formless absorptions (*ārūpadhātu*). And they are also differentiated based on whether they are developmentally active (*karma*), developmentally reactive (*vipāka*) or merely functional (*kriyā*), hence developmentally inactive.
50. Discussed in chapters one and two of Vasubandhu's *Treasury*, 1.4–6 and 2.23; Pruden, 1, 58–61 and 189.
51. Discussed in Vasubandhu's *Treasury* 2.25; Pruden, 1, 191–93.
52. Discussed in Vasubandhu's Vasubandhu's *Treasury*, 8.1–23; Pruden, 1215–56.
53. Discussed in Vasubandhu's *Treasury*, 8.2–6; Pruden, 4, 1219–28.
54. Discussed in Vasubandhu's Vasubandhu's *Treasury*, 8.1–23; Pruden, 1215–56.
55. Discussed in Vasubandhu's *Treasury*, 2.43–45ab; Pruden, 1, 225–38.
56. Discussed in Vasubandhu's *Treasury*, 5.1–5; Pruden, 3, 767–74.
57. From Nāgārjuna's *Reason Sixty*, 36, translated in Loizzo, J. (2007). *Nāgārjuna's Reason Sixty with Chandrakīrti's Commentary*. New York: American Institute of Buddhist Studies.
58. Discussed in Vasubandhu's *Treasury*, 5.46–52; Pruden, 3, 841–45, where the secondary afflictive emotions (*upakleśas* and *kleśamalas*) are listed as sixteen. Of these, two—rest (*middha*) and regret (*kaukṛtya*)—are found in Vasubandhu's own table (from *Pakandhaprakaraṇa*) under variable factors; while one—rage (*krodha*)—according to the commentary, includes vindictiveness (*pratigha*) cursing (*vyāpāda*) and cruelty (*vihiṃsa*), bringing the total to eighteen. The missing two in Vasubandhu's own list, forgetfulness (*muṣitamṛtitā*), distraction (*vikṣepa*) are found in an alternate list of minor compulsions (*parītakleśabhūmikas*) offered in *Treasury*, 2.26; Pruden, 194.
59. The presentation of the secondary afflictions based on this classification of the root compulsions follows the format abbreviated in Tashi Tsering's *Buddhist Psychology.* See also Vasubandhu's *Treasury*, 5.48–51; Pruden, 3, 842–44.

60. In Dharmakīrti's *Treatise on Valid Knowledge*, 3. See Dunne's *Foundations*, op. cit.
61. Actually, the three condensed rubrics of aggregates, media and elements (*skandhas, āyatanas, dhātus*) are used to introduce the discussion of elements in chapter 1 of Vasubandhu's *Treasury*. For the aggregates, see *Treasury*, 1.7–22; Pruden, 1, 61–82.
62. For Vasubandhu's discussion of the sense media, see *Treasury*, 1.23–27; Pruden, 1, 82–88.
63. For Vasubandhu's discussion of the eighteen elements, see *Treasury*, 1.28–48; Pruden, 1, 88–131.
64. As they are in Vasubandhu's *Treasury*, 1.7–48; Pruden, 1, 61–131.
65. This passage from the *King of Concentration Scripture* (*Samadhirājasūtra*) was quoted by Tsong Khapa in his *Lam rim chung ngu*, cited here in the translation by Robert Thurman, *Essence*, 131.

Chapter 3: The Lifelong Path of Contemplative Health

1. Bodhi, Bikkhu (trans.). (2000). *Setting the Wheel of Dharma in Motion* (*Dhammachakkappavattana-sutta*), in *The Connected Discourses of Buddha*. Boston: Wisdom Publications, 1843–46 (with minor revisions by J. Loizzo).
2. Phillip Rieff has continued to elucidate this complex dynamic in psychotherapy since his 1979 classic, *Freud: The Mind of a Moralist*. Chicago: University of Chicago Press.
3. John Norcross has been one of a field of researchers presenting the evidence that psychotherapy works broadly or contextually, with more riding on relationship and lifestyle factors than on therapeutic method per se. See Norcross, J. (2002). *Psychotherapy Relationships that Work*. Oxford: Oxford University Press.
4. The asylum function of Buddhist culture is especially clear in the confessional poetry of the first Buddhist monks and nuns, some of which has been beautifully translated in S. Murcott (2006). *The First Buddhist Women: Poems and Stories of Awakening*. New York: Parallax Press. Another traditional source for this is the Pāli Scripture *The Fruits of the Homeless Life* (*Sammanaphalasutta*). In M. Walshe (trans.) (1995). *The Long Discourses of the Buddha*. Somerville: Wisdom Press.
5. See L. Joshi (1964/2002). *Studies in the Buddhistic Culture of India*. New York: South Asia Books; and G. Roth (1997). *Vihara, Arama and Mahavihara*. New Dehli: Bauddha Sanskrit Kendra.
6. See Joshi's *Studies*, and my 2001 doctoral dissertation, *Chandrakīrti and the Moon-Flower of Nālandā*. Ann Arbor: UMI Dissertation Services, both of which draw extensively on the seventh century records of visiting Chinese scholars Xuan-zang and Yi-jing.
7. Paul Fulton alludes to this challenge in his contributions to the groundbreaking volume, C. Germer, R. Siegel, & P. Fulton (eds.). (2005). *Mindfulness and Psychotherapy*. New York: Guilford Press.
8. See my review of this issue, J. Loizzo. (2011). Personal Agency Across Generations: Evolutionary Psychology or Religious Belief? In *Sophia*, 50(3): 429–52.
9. These include coronary artery disease, hypertension, cerebrovascular accidents, pulmonary function, decreased wound healing, obesity, depression, violence, and traumatic injury. Here is a sampling of recent studies: Yan, L. L., Liu, K., Matthews, K. A., et al. (2003). Psychosocial factors and risk of hypertension: The Coronary Artery Risk Development in Young Adults (CARDIA) study. *JAMA*, 290: 2138–48; Williams, R. B., Barefoot, J. C., Schneiderman, N. (2009). Psychosocial risk factors for cardiovascular disease. *JAMA*: 2190–2192; Steffen, P.

R., McNeilly M., Anderson N., & Sherwood A. (2003). Effect of perceived racism and anger inhibition on ambulatory blood pressure in African Americans. *Psychosomatic Medicine*, 65: 746–50; Hardy, R., Wadsworth, M. E. J., & Kuh, D. (2006). The influence of childhood weight and socioeconomic status on change in adult body mass index in a British national birth cohort. *International Journal of Obes*ity 24: 725–34; Carrére, S., Mittmann, A., Woodin, E., et al. (2005). Anger dysregulation, depressive symptoms, and health in married women and men. *Nursing Research*, May-June; Gouin, J. P., Kiecolt–Glaser, J. K., Malarkey, et al. (2007). The influence of anger expression on wound healing. *Brain, Behavior and Immunity*, December 8; Anger expression in children and adolescents: A review of the empirical literature. Kerr, M. A., & Schneider, B. H. (2007). Anger expression in children and adolescents: A review of the empirical literature. *Clinical Psychology Review*, August 9; Kubzansky, L. D., Sparrow, D., Jackson, B., et al. (2006). Angry breathing: A prospective study of hostility and lung function in the Normative Aging Study. *Thorax*, October.

10. This bias is addressed by Buddhist psychoanalyst J. Rubin. (2004). *The Good Life*. Albany: State University of New York Press. A shift in this language is evident in recent works like Duncan, B., Miller, S., & Sparks, J. (2004). *The Heroic Client: A Revolutionary Way to Improve Effectiveness through Client-Directed, Outcome Informed Therapy*. New York: Jossey-Bass.
11. One review of this trend from a Piagetian perspective is B. Wadsworth. (2003). *Piaget's Theory of Cognitive and Affective Development: Foundations of Constructivism*. New York: Allyn & Bacon.
12. See J. Rubin's psychoanalytic reflections on spirituality in psychotherapy, in *The Good Life*, chapter 4.
13. For a review of the literature, see J. Loizzo, (2000), "Meditation and Psychotherapy." In P. Muskin (ed.), *Complementary and Alternative Medicine and Psychiatry*. Washington: American Psychiatric Association Press.
14. See my recent review, J. Loizzo (2009). Optimizing Learning and Quality of Life throughout the Lifespan. In W. Bushell, E. Olivo, & N. Thiese (eds.), *Longevity, Regeneration and Optimal Health*. New York: New York Academy of Sciences.
15. See S. Lopez, & C. Snyder. (2009). *Oxford Handbook of Positive Psychology*. New York: Oxford University Press.
16. My sources for this presentation are Vasubandu's *Treasury of Scientific Teaching*, L. Pruden (trans.). (1988–1991). *The Abhidharmakosabhasyam of Vasubandhu*. Berkeley: Asian Humanities Press, 4 Vols; and A. Govinda. (1973). *The Psychological Attitude of Early Buddhist Philosophy*. New York: Samuel Weiser.
17. This map is spelled out in the pedagogy of the gradual path (skt. *pathakrama*; tib. *lam rim*) developed within the Nalanda tradition from Bhāvaviveka (c. 500–600) to Chandrakīrti (c. 590–670), and refined and spread to Tibet by Nalanda faculty from Kamalaśīla (760–815) to Astīśa (982–1054). My presentation of this draws on the Gelukpa tradition codified by Tsong Khapa (1357–1419) and exhaustively summarized by Pabongkha Dechen Nyingpo (1878–1941) in Pabongkha Rinpoche. (1993). *Liberation in the Palm of Your Hand*. Boston: Wisdom Publications.
18. My main sources for this presentation are Vasubandhu's *Treasury*, chapters 5-8, and Ngawang Dhargyay. (1978). *The Tibetan Tradition of Mental Development*. Dharamsala: Library of Tibetan Works and Archives.
19. The Four Noble Truths are presented in Vasubandhu's *Treasury*, AK.6.2–4; Pruden, 3, 896–911.
20. See Vasubandhu's *Treasury*, AK, 4.65–81; Pruden, 2, 641–66.
21. In this sense, the first step holds us to a degree of self-knowledge and personal responsibility for our development akin to the most profound forms of self-

analysis as well as the reflective philosophies of modern phenomenology, constructivism, and existentialism.

22. For the tradition of the gradual path, see note 17, above. While most classical maps involve three scopes, defined differently for different audiences, mine follows the modern tradition of Kālachakra, making the potent methods of the esoteric Vajrayāna more transparent and accessible for the embattled lay audience of today's conflict-ridden world. See my article, Loizzo, J. (2009). Kālachakra and the Nālandā Tradition. In E. Arnold (ed.), *As Long As Space Endures: Essays on the Kālachakra Tantra in Honor of His Holiness the Dalai Lama*. Ithaca: Snow Lion Press.
23. See Dhargyey, *Tibetan Tradition*, 39–48.
24. See Vasubandhu's *Treasury*, AK, 3.8–9; Pruden, 2, 380–83.
25. For a helpful perspective on this Buddhist ethos, see Thurman, R. 1998. *Inner Revolution: Life, Liberty, and the Pursuit of Real Happiness*. New York: Riverhead Books.
26. See Dhargyey, *Tibetan Tradition*, 183–85; 187–93.
27. See Vasubandhu's *Treasury*, 4.69; Pruden, 2, 646–47.
28. Ibid., 4.26–32; Pruden, 2, 591–603.
29. See Dhargyey, *Tibetan Tradition*, 49–52.
30. Vasubandu's *Treasury*, 6.9–11; Pruden, 3, 916–21, describes the use of mindfulness to contemplate one's body as a skeleton.
31. Pabongka, *Liberation*, op. cit., 333–61, describes the nature and benefits of contemplating death in great detail.
32, See Dhargyey, *Tibetan Tradition*, 188–89.
33. This form of mindfulness, little known in the West, is front and center in the Nalanda tradition of basic mindfulness practice taught in Tibet as Natural Liberation (*hLen-grol*), the Great Perfection (*'Dzog-chen*) or Great Seal (*Phag-chen*). See Dalai Lama, H. H., & Berzin, A. (1997). *The Geluk/Kagyu Tradition of Mahamudra*. Ithaca: Snow Lion Press.
34. This tolerance (*anupalabda-dharma-kṣanti*) is one of the forms of healing insight that facilitate realization of the noble truths (*āryasatyābhisamaya*) and plant roots of freedom (*mokṣabhāgīya*). See Vasubandhu's Treasury, 6.25–28; Pruden, 3, 942–50.
35. Budwig, N. (2000). Language and the Construction of Self: Developmental Reflections. In N. Budwig, I. C. Uzgiris, & J. V. Wertsch (eds.), *Communication: An Arena of Development*. Stamford: Ablex Press; Morin, A. (1995). Characteristics of an effective internal dialogue in the acquisition of self-information. In *Imagination, Cognition and Personality*, 15(1): 45–58; Goldstein, G., & Kenen, R. (1988). Internal Dialogue in a normal population: the implications for health promotion. In *Health Promotion International*, 3(3): 249–57.
36. The new positive psychology has alerted us to the risks of reinforcing negative habits of thought and action. For an accessible introduction, see Seligman, M. (2006). *Learned Optimism: How to Change Your Mind and Your Life*. New York: Vintage Books.
37. Tibetan renaissance genius Tsong Khapa says of Shakyamuni, "Of all his deeds, his speech is supreme; and for this very reason, true sages should commemorate a perfect Buddha for this (teaching of relativity)." R. Thurman (trans). (1986). *Tsong Khapa's Speech of Gold in the Essence of True Eloquence*. Princeton: Princeton University Press, 183.
38. To explain why lying is one of the five precepts of a lay practitioner (*upāsaka*), Vasubandhu's *Treasury*, AK, 4.34; Pruden, 2, 605, states, "Because, having violated any other rule, he would lie." Within the *pratimokṣa* vows of full ordination, lying, especially in a divisive way, is the fourth of the irremediable

transgressions (*ānantarya-karma*). See Vasubandhu's *Treasury*, AK, 4.97–98; Pruden, 2, 68-682.

39. See Janik, A., & Toulmin, S. (1976/1996). *Wittgenstein's Vienna*. New York: Ivan R. Dee.
40. This view is implicit in the Buddhist view that the reality of human social and cultural life is based on social consensus (*lokaprasiddha*), linguistic usage (*prajñapti*) and mundane convention (*loka-vyavahāra*). It is given symbolic expression in Buddhist iconography, according to which Avalokiteśvara, the Bodhisattva of compassion, also called the protector of the world (*lokapāla*), is depicted as dwelling on the tip of the tongue of the Buddha Amitabha, who symbolizes the eternal light and life of the Buddhist teaching.
41. This discipline is so vital to healthy social engagement that it is one of the cornerstones of the practice of mind-training or mind-clearing, which is explored in part 2 of the book. One key line in the most popular formulation of this practice, Chekkhawa Yeshi-Dorje's *Seven Point Mind Clearing* turns the shame-blame reflex on itself: "Drive all blame into one (your own shame-blame reflex). See chapter 4.
42. Wittgenstein, L. (1953/1958). *Philosophical Investigations*. Englewood Cliffs, NJ: Prentice-Hall, 132.
43. Dhargyey, *Tibetan Tradition*, 53–57; for a more extensive treatment, see Pabongka, *Liberation*, 362–293.
44. See Vasubandhu's *Treasury*, 6.1; Pruden, 551. This is often misunderstood to mean that the natural environment is created by our mental acts, but the intent of this aspect of *karmic* theory is that our intentions and acts create our habitats and sociocultural environments.
45. Dhargyey, *Tibetan Tradition*, 183–85; 188–91.
46. Ibid., 51–52; 214–30.
47. These retreats would typically last through the whole rainy season, and were part of the discipline required to become fully ordained.
48. See Vasubandhu's *Treasury*, AK, 4.26–34; Pruden, 2, 591–607; Dhargyey, *Tibetan Tradition*, 60–63.
49. Traditionally, the various types of refuge are addressed in the context of discussing the possible scopes of spiritual practicing the gradual path. See *Treasury*, AK, 4.14–35; Pruden, 2, 580–608; Dhargyey, *Tibetan Tradition*, 60–63; 98–129.
50. See Dhargyey, *Tibetan Tradition*, 86–87, identifies six factors: (1) the degree of harm;(2) the force of intent; (3) the particulars of the act; (4) the being harmed; (5) pattern of action; (6) presence or absence of remorse and amends.
51. Vasubandhu's *Treasury*, AK, 4.73cd; Pruden, 651.
52. In this sense, Buddhist ethics anticipates recent critiques of free-market economics in ways that anticipate the findings of behavioral economics, neuroeconomics and the emerging science of global sustainability. Tideman, S. (2005). *Mind over Matter*. PDF version online at http://www.gpiatlantic.org/conference/papers/tideman.pdf.
53. Dating back to John Maynard Keynes' recognition of the role of non-reimbursed work, this unconventional line of economic thinking is currently represented in a move to replace "single bottom-line" accounting methods with more comprehensive methods based on a multidisciplinary economics of happiness like the "gross national happiness" model developed by the Buddhist kingdom of Bhutan. See Zuboff, S., & Maxim, J. (2004). *The Support Economy: Why Corporations are Failing Individuals and the Future of Capitalism*. New York: Penguin Books; and Anielski, M. (2007). *The Economics of Happiness: Building Genuine Wealth*. Vancouver: New Societys.
54. See Carnes, P. (2001). *Out of the Shadows: Understanding Sexual Addiction*. New York: Hazelden Press.

55. See Schnarch, D. (2008). Sex Therapy vs. Couples Therapy: A Distinction without a Difference. In *Sexologies,* Vol 17, Suppl: S37.
56. This tradition of facilitating lay romance and healthy intimacy is immortalized in Indian literature by the role of the Buddhist nun who serves as a go-between in a series of classical romantic comedies. See Kale, M. R. (1997). *Malati–Madhava of Bhavabhuti.* New Delhi: Motilal Barnarsidas. It is more explicit in the esoteric tradition of making sexual fantasy and real sexual intimacy an unexcelled path for spiritual evolution in the Buddhist Tantras, explored in Parts Three and Four. See Shaw, M. (1995). *Passionate Enlightenment.* Princeton: Princeton University Press.
57. For a sample of current thinking on this, see Guerri, C., & Pascual, M. (2010). Mechanisms involved in the neurotoxic, cognitive, and neurobehavioral effects of alcohol consumption during adolescence. In *Alcohol.* February, 44(1): 15–26; and Jager, G., Block, R. I., Luijten, M., et al. (2010). Cannabis Use and Memory Brain Function in Adolescent Boys: A Cross–Sectional Multicenter Functional Magnetic Resonance Imaging Study. In *Journal of the American Academy of Child and Adolescent Psychiatry,* June 49(6): 561–72.
58. Fernández–Serrano, M. J., Pérez–García, M., & Verdejo–García, A. (2010). What are the specific vs. generalized effects of drugs of abuse on neuropsychological performance? In *Neuroscience and Biobehavioral Revues*. May 6 [Epub ahead of print]; Gouzoulis–Mayfrank, E., & Daumann, J. (2009). Neurotoxicity of drugs of abuse—the case of methylenedioxyamphetamines (MDMA, ecstasy), and amphetamines." In *Dialogues in Clinical Neuroscience,* 11(3): 305–17; and Bava, S., Frank, L. R., McQueeny, T., et al. (2009). Altered white matter microstructure in adolescent substance users. In *Psychiatry Research,* 30, 173(3): 228–37.
59. For the traditional rationale for this guideline, see Vasubandhu's *Treasury,* AK, 4.29; Pruden, 2, 596; AK, 4.34d; Pruden, 2, 605.
60. For a traditional look at the ultimate refuge of mastery, see Vasubandhu's *Treasury,* AK, 4.32; Pruden, 2, 601–03.
61. Ibid., 191–93.
62. From the Buddhist standpoint, the ultimate paradigm for this non-violent approach to life lies in Shakyamuni's renouncing of his conventional role as a member of the ruling warrior class in favor of the healing, pedagogic role he chose. For a look at how this paradigm influenced Indian notions of kingship and statecraft, starting with the first Indian Emperor Aśoka, see Tambiah, S. (1968). *World Conqueror, World Renouncer.* Cambridge: Cambridge University Press; and Thurman, *Inner Revolution.*
63. For a fascinating glimpse into the application of Buddhist ethics, the second century classic *Jewel Garland* (*Ratnāvalī*) of Nāgārjuna was explicitly written by the founder of the Nālandā tradition as a letter of advice to an Indian King of the Satavahana dynasty (perhaps the second century Antivahana II, c.150) in his capacity as a minister. In it, the Buddhist monk counsels the King in great detail about how to transform the intent and execution of his conventional role so as to be compatible with his moral development and contemplative practice. In fact, he advises the King that it would be better to first try to use his position in the world to benefit society at large before renouncing it entirely for the life of a monk. See J. Hopkins (trans.) (1976/1995). *Buddhist Advice for Living and Liberation: Nagarjuna's Precious Garland.* Ithaca: Snow Lion Press.
64. See Dhargyey, *Tibetan Tradition*, 70–97.
65. Vasubandhu's *Treasury,* AK, 6.67–70; Pruden, 3, 1022–28, and n.434; Dhargyey, *Tibetan Tradition*, 191–92.
66. Vasubandhu's Treasury, AK, 2.25; Pruden, 1, 191–92, and n. 135, which references the definition of effort (*vīrya*) as endurance in healthy activity (*kuśalakryiyā*),

and cites the traditional Buddhist view that endurance in unhealthy activity is not true effort but a form of laziness (*kausīdya*).

67. Effort kicks in as a key mental faculty on the seventh and eighth of the nine stages of concentrative quiescence meditation (*śamatha*). See the table in Thurman, *Essence*, 133.
68. See Pabongka, *Liberation*, 486–505.
69. This is explained in the general presentation of life forms in Vasubandhu's *Treasury*, AK, 3.1–13; Pruden, 2, 365–91.
70. This is clear from the reflection on the last of the eight freedoms that make human life the optimal form for contemplative living and spiritual development, namely, freedom from birth as a god. See Dhargyey, *Tibetan Tradition*, 39–40; Pabongka, *Liberation*, 308–10.
71. Dhargyey, *Tibetan Tradition*, 193–95.
72. See Vasubandhu's *Treasury*, AK, 6.17–23; Pruden, 3, 930–40.
73. Ibid., AK, 6.67–70; Pruden, 3, 1023–29; Dhargey, *Tibetan Tradition*, 194–95.
74. See Vasubandhu's *Treasury*, AK, 6.18c–20a; Pruden, 3, 931–35; Dhargey, *Tibetan Tradition*, 195.
75. See Vasubandhu's *Treasury*, AK, 6.5–16; Pruden, 3, 911–29.
76. Ibid., AK, 6.25cd–27b; Pruden, 3, 943–49.
77. Ibid., AK, 6.27c–28; Pruden, 3, 949–52; Dhargyey, *Tibetan Tradition*, 196.
78. In the most traditional map of the gradual path, which dates back at least as far as Nāgājuna's *Jewel Garland (Ratnāvalī)*, IV, this shift brings us from the narrow horizon of self-improvement through ascendance (*abhyudaya*) to the middling horizon of personal freedom through transcendence (*niḥśreyasa*). See Dhargyey, *Tibetan Tradition*, 98–104; Pabongka, *Liberation*, 534–43.
79. Dhargyey, *Tibetan Tradition*, 195–97.
80. Ibid. See also Vasubandhu's *Treasury*, AK, 6.66cd–69cd; Pruden, 3, 1023–26.
81. For a concise treatment, see Dhargyey, *Tibetan Tradition*, 156–61.
82. See the discussion of the diamond-like concentration (*vajropamasamādhi*) and how saints attains Nirvana *via* the formless absorption called the peak of existence (*bhavāgra*), in Vasubandu's *Treasury*, AK, 6.44–51; Pruden, 3, 980–93.
83. Dhargyey, *Tibetan Tradition*, 98–104; Pabongka, *Liberation*, 534–43.
84. Ibid., 198–201.
85. For Vasubandhu's use of this simile in the context of his discussion of the degrees of defilement and purification, see *Treasury*, AK.633cd; Pruden, 957.
86. Ibid., AK, 7.1–8; Pruden, 4, 1087–97.
87. Ibid., AK, 6.67–70; Pruden, 3, 1023–29.

Chapter 4: Clearing the Mind for Social Engagement

1. *Ratnāvalī* (RA), 4.94–96. Skt. Hahn, M. (1982). *Nāgārjuna's Ratnāvalī*. Bonn: Indica et Tibetica Verlag, 128–30: *// yathaiva vaiyākaraṇo mātṛkām api pāthayet / buddho 'vadat tathā dharmaṃ vineyānāṃ yathākṣamam / keṣāṃ cid avadad dharmaṃ pāpebhyo uiniuṛttaye / keṣāṃ Cit puṇyasiddhyarthaṃ keṣāṃ cid dvayaniśritam / dvayāniśritam ekeṣāṃ gambhīraṃ bhīrubhīṣaṇam śūnyatākaruṇāgarbham ekeṣāṃ bodhisādhanam //.*
2. The role of Nālandā as a center for the counter-council of the *Mahāsaṃgika* community and their relationship with what would become the Mahāyāna tradition is briefly discussed in chapter 2 of my doctoral dissertation. See Loizzo, J. (2001). *Candrakīrti and the Moon-Flower of Nālandā*. Ann Arbor: UMI Dissertation Services.

3. Including the great Tibetan historian, Tāranātha. See Chattopadhyaya, A., & Chimpa, L. (trans.). (1970). *Tāranātha's History of Buddhism in India*. Simla: Indian Institute of Advanced Study.
4. Skt. Rājaparikathāratnāvalī, translated in Hopkins, J. (1998). *Buddhist Advice for Living and Liberation: Nāgārjuna's Precious Garland*. Ithaca: Snow Lion Press.
5. See Dutt, S. (2008). *Buddhist Monks and Monasteries of India: Their History and Their Contribution to Indian Culture*. Dehli: Motilal Barnarsidas. Also, a host of related studies have recently been published describing the impact of Buddhist monasticism on other parts of Asia, notably Benn, J., Meeks, L., & Robson, J. (eds.). (2009). *Buddhist Monasticism in East Asia: Places of Practice*. New York: Routledge.
6. See Joshi, L. (1980). *Studies in the Buddhistic Culture of India*. Delhi: Motilal Banarsidas.
7. For a distilled history of this debate, see the introduction to Thurman, R. (1986). Tsong Khapa's *Speech of Gold in the Essence of True Eloquence*. Princeton: Princeton University Press; and Loizzo, J., introduction. In *Nāgārjuna's Reason Sixty with Chandrakīrti's Commentary*. New York: American Institute of Buddhist Studies.
8. Loizzo, J., *Reason Sixty*.
9. This crucial turn is the subject of my undergraduate thesis, Loizzo, J. (1977). *Wittgenstein and the Mādhyamika: Preparatory Studies for a Critical Psychology*. Amherst: Amherst College; as well as the doctoral dissertation and translation study cited in note 2.
10. For an excellent overview of this lineage, its history and literature, including Chekawa Yeshe Dorje's *Seven Point Mind Clearing (bLo-sbyong tshig bdu-ma)*, see Jinpa, T. (trans). (2006). *Mind Training: The Great Collection*. Somerville: Wisdom Press.
11. Of the many editions of Chekawa's original "root" text, I'll be working from my own translation of the contemporary, annotated edition compiled by the renowned Tibetan scholar-practitioner, Pabongka Dechen Nyingpo. The edition of the Tibetan root text I've used is found in Gyatso, K. (1996). *Universal Compassion*. London: Tharpa.
12. Nietzsche's understanding of the critical role of objective knowledge and mastery of our human nature in a post-theistic world was part of the rationale for his prophecy that "Psychology will once again become Queen of the sciences."
13. This is the path of the enlightened altruist (*bodhisattva*), described in the broad range of Mahāyāna scriptures as well as in treatises like Nāgārjuna's *Jewel Garland* (*Ratnāvalī*). See note 5, above.
14. See Browne, C, & Winkelman, C. (2007). The effect of childhood trauma on later psychological adjustment. In *Journal of Interpersonal Violence*, June 22(6): 684–97.
15. See Ponce, A., Williams, M., & Allen, G. (2004). Experience of maltreatment as a child and acceptance of violence in adult intimate relationships: mediating effects of distortions in cognitive schemas. In *Violence Victims*, February 19(1): 97–108.
16. For instance, Walker, M., & Rosen, W. (eds.). (2004). *How Connections Heal: Stories from Relational-Cultural Therapy*. New York: Guildford Press.
17. Compare the recent perspective of integrative therapy, as presented in Norcross, J. 2002. *Psychotherapy Relationships that Work: Therapist Contributions and Responsiveness to Patients*. New York: Oxford University Press.
18. See Cummings, M., & Sayama, M. (1995). *Focused Psychotherapy: A Casebook of Brief Intermittent Psychotherapy Throughout the Life Cycle*. New York: Routledge.

19. See Ricard, M., & Thuan, T. (2004). *The Quantum and the Lotus: A Journey to the Frontiers Where Science and Buddhism Meet.* New York: Three Rivers Press.
20. This is clear in the traditional *abhidharma* formulation that the ordinary life-cycle consists of the compulsive mind/body systems poisoned by the afflictions (*sāśrava-upādanaskandhas*). The afflictions and their causality are discussed in Vasubandhu's *Treasury*, 5.1–5; Pruden, 3, 767–74.
21. For the social psychology of self-transformation and world-transformation in Universalist Buddhism, see Thurman, R. (trans.). (1976). *The Holy Teaching of Vimalakīrti* (*Vimalakīrtinirdeṣasūtra*) (hereafter Thurman, *Vimalakīrti*). University Park: Pennsylvania State University Press.
22. For prerequisites of successful couples therapy, see Gurman, A. (2008). *Clinical Handbook of Couples Therapy.* New York: Guilford Press.
23. While all the main ways of presenting the *Seven Point Mind Clearing* agree in dividing the pivotal second point—often called "actual practice"—into two parts, after Chekawa, two traditions emerged about the best way to present this two-edged point. Most versions opt to present the insight-oriented practice of openness first. In contrast, the version I follow, based on the later scholarship of Tsong Khapa and his heirs, presents the heart-opening practice of compassion first. In effect, this more clearly reflects the dialogical approach of Chandrakirti and Shantideva, which protect novices from misunderstanding the critical teaching of emptiness by putting the positive practice of compassion first. I believe this gradual approach is more suitable for the increasingly broad and mixed audience this teaching seems destined to draw. The New Kadam edition I use, by the Gelukpa Master Pabongka Dechen Nyingpo (1878–1941) follows three fifteenth-century editions based on Tsong Khapa's (1357–1419) reading of the text, which in turn may be traced back to Chekawa's younger contemporary, Sangyay Gompa (1179–1250). This history is documented in Thubten Jinpa's invaluable translation study, *Mind-Training.* See note 11, above.
24. See Scott, K., & Strauss, M. (2007). Denial, minimization, partner blaming and intimate aggression in dating partners. In *Journal of Interpersonal Violence,* July 22(7): 851–71.
25. See Seidel, E., Eickoff, S., Kellermann, T., et al. (2010). Who is to blame? Neural correlates of causal attribution in social situations. In *Society for Neuroscience,* 5(4): 355–50; Waldron, B., Benson, C., O'Connell, A., et al. (2010). Health locus of control and attributions of cause and blame in adjustment to spinal cord injury. In *Spinal Cord,* August 48(8): 598–602; and Zinzow, H., Seth, P., Jackson, J., et al. (2010). Abuse and parental characteristics, attributions of blame and psychological adjustment in adult survivors of child sexual abuse. In *Journal of Childhood Sexual Abuse,* January 28(1): 61–78.
26. Neumann, S., Maier K., Brown, J., et al. (2010). Cardiovascular and Psychological Reactivity and Recovery from Harassment in a Biracial Sample of High and Low Hostile Men and Women. In *International Journal of Behavioral Medicine,* July 16 (e-publication).
27. See Feiring, C., Cleland, C., & Simon, V. (2010). Abuse-specific self-schemas and self-functioning: a prospective study of sexually abused youth. In *Journal of Clinical Child and Adolescent Psychology,* January 39(1): 35-50.
28. See Van Viet, K. (2009). The role of attributions in the process of overcoming shame: A qualitative analysis. In *Psychology and Psychotherapy,* June 82(Pt 2): 137–52.
29. Skt. *atmasñeha*, Tib. *dbag ches.*
30. See Nietlisbach, G., Maercker, A., Rossler, W., et al. (2010). Are empathic abilities impaired in posttraumatic stress disorder? In *Psychological Reports,* June 106(3): 833–44.

31. For a remarkable introduction to the neurobiology of this shift, see Porges, S. (2011). *Polyvagal Theory: Neurophysiological Foundations of Emotions, Attachment, Communication and Self-Regulation*. New York: W.W. Norton & Co. We'll return to this at length in chapter 10.
32. See Der-Avakian, A., & Markou, A. (2010). Neonatal maternal separation exacerbates the reward-enhancing effect of acute amphetamine administration and the anhedonic effect of repeated social defeat in adult rats. In *Neuroscience*, August 5 (e-publication); and Burke, L. (2003). The impact of maternal depression on familial relationships. In *International Review of Psychiatry*, August 15(3): 243–55.
33. Elliot, N. (2007). *Guide to the Bodhisattva's Way of Life*. London: Tharpa, 49.
34. Of course, this analogy is no accident, since the Asian tradition of martial arts was developed by Buddhist monks of Shaolin monastery, who had to resist the attacks of robbers on their way between monasteries in rural China, and had to do so without breaking their vows to renounce violent intentions and harmful actions.
35. See Thompson, B., & Waltz, J. (2008). Self-compassion and PTSD symptom severity. In *Journal of Trauma and Stress*, December 21(6): 556–58.
36. Curtois, C., & Ford, J. (eds.). (2009). *Treating Complex Traumatic Stress Disorders: An Evidence-Based Guide*. New York: Guilford Press.
37. The insight that human nature oscillates between reciprocally inhibitory binary biological poles was central to Freud's "dualistic" theory of instincts, and has been linked with developments in neurophysiology and neuroscience by many researchers, including Doidge, N. (2007). *The Brain that Changes Itself: Stories of Personal Triumph from the Frontiers of Brain Science*. New York: Penguin Press.
38. For a traditional presentation, see Jeffery Hopkins' translation of the Gelukpa founder Tsong Khapa's commentary on the approach to compassion in Chandrakīrti's *Central Way Introduction* (*Mādhyamakāvatāra*), in Tsong Khapa (1980). *Compassion in Tibetan Buddhism*. Ithaca: Snow Lion Press. The fourfold typology clearly predates Candrakīrti, and may also be found in Thurman, *Vimalakīrti*.
39. See Decety, J., & Ickes, W. (2009). *The Social Neuroscience of Empathy*. Cambridge: MIT Press.
40. Even Freud, who was a strong proponent of the importance of love in the development of individuals and civilizations, insisted that such social emotions were naturally restricted to kin and limited by our primal narcissism and fixed destructive instincts. See Freud, S. (1961). *Civilization and its Discontents*, chapter VIII. New York: W.W. Norton & Company.
41. This is clearest in the new optimism of interpersonal neurobiology. For an introduction, see Cozolino, L. (2006). *The Neuroscience of Human Relationships: Attachment and the Developing Social Brain*. New York: W.W. Norton & Company.
42. See Wilkinson, M. (2010). *Changing Minds in Therapy: Emotion, Attachment, Trauma and Neurobiology*. New York: W.W. Norton & Company.
43. Shantideva presents his approach, which was later systematized by Tibetan scholars, in verses dispersed in various chapters of his contemplative classic, *Guide to the Enlightened Altruist's Way of Life* (*Bodhisattvacāryāvatāra*), especially chapter eight. Among the many English translations, I prefer Batchelor, S. (trans.). (1999). *Guide to the Bodhisattva's Way of Life*. Dharamsala: Library of Tibetan Works and Archives, for its rendering of the author's profound meaning; and Elliot, for its rendering of his magnificent poetics.
44. BA, 8.90; Elliot, *Guide*, 128.
45. BA, 8.94; Elliot, *Guide*, 128.

46. Legal philosopher Thomas Nagel has made a strong case for the vital importance of such a mental exercise in contemporary thought and life, arguing that we all possess an "objective self" with which we can effectively "climb outside" the myopic, creaturely limits of our own "subjective self." Nagel, T. (1986). *The View From Nowhere*. Oxford: Oxford University Press.
47. Hence the recent trend towards promoting the value and practice of empathy in psychotherapy. See Pedersen, P., Crethar, H., & Carlson, J. (2008). *Inclusive Cultural Empathy: Making Relationships Central in Counseling and Psychotherapy.* Washington: American Psychological Association; and Clark, A. (2006). *Empathy in Counseling and Psychotherapy: Perspectives and Practices.* New York: Routledge.
48. The Buddhist distinction between love and attachment has its parallel in the contemporary contrast between secure and insecure attachment. Current research supports the view that love or secure attachment promotes healthier adult relationships. See McCarthy, G., & Maughan, B. (2010). Negative childhood experiences and adult love relationships: the role of internal working models of attachment. In *Attachment and Human Development,* September 12(5): 445–61.
49. This view is increasingly shared by the mainstream of relational analysts. See Frank, K. (1999). *Psychoanalytic Participation: Action, Interaction and Integration*. New York: Routledge.
50. See the recent collaboration of Germer, C., & Salzberg, S. (2009). *The Mindful Path to Self-Compassion: Freeing Yourself from Destructive Emotions*. New York: Guilford Press.
51. For a recent review of the literature on the link between parent-child abuse and suffering in later life, see Weich, S., Patterson, J., Shaw, R., & et al. (2009). Family relationships in childhood and common psychiatric disorders in later life: systematic review of prospective studies. In *British Journal of Psychiatry,* May 194(5): 392–98. For research on the psychological mechanisms of this link, see notes 29 and 31, above.
52. For recent work on the physiology of this triggering, see Neumann, S., Maier K., Brown, J., et al. (2010). Cardiovascular and Psychological Reactivity and Recovery from Harassment in a Biracial Sample of High and Low Hostile Men and Women. In *International Journal of Behavioral Medicine,* July 16 (e-publication); and Der-Avakian, A., & Markou, A. (2010). Neonatal maternal separation exacerbates the reward-enhancing effect of acute amphetamine administration and the anhedonic effect of repeated social defeat in adult rats. In *Neuroscience,* August 5 (e-publication).
53. RA, 1.29; Skt. Hahn, 12: *// ahaṃkārodbhavāḥ skandhāḥ so 'haṃkāro 'nṛto 'rthataḥ / bījaṃ yasyānṛtaṃ tasya prachaḥ satyataḥ kutaḥ //.*
54. BA, 8.135–6; Elliot, 135.
55. See Ricard & Thuan, *Quantum and the Lotus.*
56. While some of the background for this emerging consensus comes from developments in biology, a key role has been played by mathematical models of social cooperation such a game theory. See Miller, J., & Page, S. (2007). *Complex Adaptive Systems: An Introduction to Computational Models of Social Life.* Princeton: Princeton University Press.
57. For an intriguing look at the origins of human social ethics by a distinguished primatologist, see De Waals, F. (2009). *Primates and Philosophers: How Morality Evolved.* Princeton: Princeton University Press.
58. Ebstein, R., Israel, S., Chew, S., et al. (2010). Genetics of human social behavior. In *Neuron,* March 25 65(6): 831–44.
59. In stark contrast to the atomistic bias of the modern era, the language of systems theory has not only helped explain the new findings of modern physics, ecology,

biology and anthropology, but also given us a view of living beings as naturally open, self-transcending systems. See Oyama, S. (2000). *The Ontogeny of Information: Developmental Systems and Evolution*. Durham: Duke University Press.

60. We're all deeply indebted to the groundbreaking work of Dan Siegel for forging this emerging field. See Siegel, D. (2007). *The Mindful Brain: Reflection and Attunment in the Cultivation of Wellbeing*. New York. W.W. Norton & Company.
61. Buchanan, K. & Bardi, A. (2010). Acts of kindness and acts of novelty affect life satisfaction. In *Social Psychology*, May–June 150(3): 235–37.
62. BA, 8.107–8; Elliot, 131.
63. Ibid., 8.110; Elliot, 131.
64. Talbot, J., Baker, J., & McHale, J. (2009).Sharing the Love: Prebirth Adult Attachment Status and Coparenting Adjustment During Early Infancy. In *Parenting: Science and Practice*, January 9(1): 56–77.
65. Leimar, O., & Hammerstein, P. (2010). Cooperation for direct fitness benefits. In *Philosophical Transcript of the Royal Society of London Board of Biological Sciences*, September 12 365(1553): 2619–26.
66. De Waal, F. (2008). Putting the altruism back into altruism: the evolution of empathy. In *Annual Revue of Psychology*, 59: 279–300 (hereafter De Waal, 2008).
67. Cox, K., Wilt, J., Olson, B., & McAdams, D. (2010). Generativity, the big five, and psychosocial adaptation in midlife adults. In *Personality*, August 1 78(4): 1185–08.
68. Alessandri, G., Caprara, G., Eisenberg, N., & et al. (2009). Reciprocal relations among self-efficacy beliefs and prosociality across time. In *Journal of Personality*, August 77(4): 1229–59.
69. BA, 8.111–2; Elliot, 131.
70. BA, 8.114; Elliot, 132.
71. BA, 8. 120; Elliot, 133.
72. See Avise, J. (2004). Molecular Markers, *Natural History and Evolution*. New York: Sinauer Associates
73. Jallais, C., & Gilet, A. (2010). Inducing changes in aurosal and valence: a comparison of two mood induction procedures. In *Behavioral Research Methods*, February 42(1): 318–25.
74. See Kernberg, O. (2010). Some observations on the process of mourning. In *International Journal of Psychoanalysis*, June 91(3): 601–19; and Kernberg, O. (1974). Mature love: prerequisites and characteristics. In *Journal of the American Psychoanalytic Association*, 22(4): 743–68.
75. Considerable attention is being focused on this impulse as a distinct form of altruism which ranges across species. See Nowbahari, E., & Hollis, K. (2010). Rescue behavior: Distinguishing between rescue, cooperation and other forms of altruistic behavior. In *Community and Integrative Biology*, March 3(2): 77–79.
76. See van Veelen, M., García, J., & Avilés, L. (2010). It takes grouping and cooperation to get sociality. In *Journal of Theoretical Biology*, June 21 264(4): 1240–53. Interestingly, the adaptive benefits of increased group size appear to be a factor in all social evolution, as a recent analysis of merged, non-related ant colonies suggests: Costa, J., & Ross, K. (2003). Fitness effects of group merging in a social insect. In *Proceeds of the Biological Sciences*, August 22, 270(1525): 1697–1702.
77. See Fowler, J., & Christakis, N. (2010). Cooperative behavior cascades in human social networks. In *Proceedings of the National Academy of Sciences, USA*, March 23, 107(12): 5334–38.
78. See Miller, J., & Page, S. (2007). *Complex Adaptive Systems: An Introduction to Computational Models of Social Life*. Princeton: Princeton University Press.
79. See De Waal, 2008.

80. See Leimar, O., & Hammerstein, P. (2010). Cooperation for direct fitness benefits. In *Philosophical Transcript of the Royal Society of London Board of Biological Sciences*, September 12, 365(1553): 2619–26.
81. See Pabongka, *Liberation*.
82. A recent study of parental involvement in schools illustrates this potential: Evans, M., & Shirly, D. (2008). The development of collective moral leadership among parents through education organizing. In *New Directions in Youth Development*, Spring (117): 77–91.
83. The negative link between fear-based reactions to others and social skills like empathy is explored in Nietlisbach, G., Maercker, A., Rossler, W., et al. (2010). Are empathic abilities impaired in posttraumatic stress disorder? In *Psychological Reports*, June 106(3): 832–44.
84. Hence breath-mindfulness has been found to reduce emotional stress-reactitivity in people with social anxiety: Goldin, P., & Gross, J. (2010). Effects of mindfulness-based stress-reduction (MBSR) on emotion regulation in social anxiety disorder. In *Emotion*, February 10(1): 83–91.
85. Tibetan scholar-practitioner Losang Chokyi Gyaltsan (1567–1662) alludes to this in his *Profound Path of Victors: The Gemlike Ganden/Kagyu Great Seal Root Text* (*dGe-ldan bka' brgyud rin po che'i phyag-chen rtsa ba rgyal-ba'i gzung lam*). See Dalai Lama, H. H., & Berzin, A. (1997). The Gelug/Kagyu Tradition of Mahamudra. Ithaca: Snow Lion.
86. For a contemporary introduction to the logic of philosophical analysis and contemplation in this tradition, see the introduction to Thurman, R., *Essence*. The role of logic and discursive analysis in Buddhist learning and reflection is also evident in the practice of debate that is central to the pedagogy of Tibetan monastic colleges and universities. See Dreyfus, G. (2003). *The Sound of Two Hands Clapping: The Education of a Tibetan Buddhist Monk*. Berkeley: University of California Press.
87. The classic formulation of this methodology is found in Nālandā scholar Kamalashila's (c. 760–815) *Stages of Meditation* (*Bhāvanākrama*). Victorious in the great debate at Samye, the first Buddhist monastery in Tibet, Kamalashila was pivotal in convincing the Tibetan court to adopt the gradualism of the Nālandā tradition as central to its monastic curriculum. See Demieville, P. (1952). *Le Concile de Lhasa*. Paris: Hautes Etudes.
88 For an intriguing recent study of the power of mnemonic learning, see Lubinsky, T., Rich, J., & Anderson, N. (2009). Errorless learning and elaborative self-generation in healthy older adults and individuals with amnestic mild cognitive impairment: mnemonic benefits and mechanisms. In *Journal of the International Neuropsychological Society*, September 15(5): 704–16.

Chapter 5: De-Reifying and Dismantling the Reactive Self

1. Thurman, R. A. F. (1986). *Tsong Khapa's Speech of Gold in the Essence of True Eloquence*. Princeton: Princeton University Press, 310. Hereafter Thurman, *Essence*.
2. The range of definitions of the false, reified self, nature, or identity to be negated by self-analysis in various schools of Buddhist thought has received careful attention in the comparative therapeutic philosophy curriculum of the Nālandā tradition. Systematic treatments of this range by Gelukpa scholars from Tsong Khapa to 'Jam-dbyangs bZhed-pa may be found in works like Thurman, *Essence*, and Hopkins, J. (1983/1996). *Meditation on Emptiness*. Boston: Wisdom Publications; hereafter Hopkins, *Meditation*. Reference for different approaches to

cognitive blocks. This table is based on charts in Thurman, *Essence*, 138 and Hopkins, *Meditation*, 299.

3. Nāgārjuna, *Śūnyatāsaptatī*, 61; quoted in Tsong Khapa's *Legs-bshad sÑing-po*, trans. Thurman, *Essence*, 309; see Komito, D. (1999). *Nagarjuna's Seventy Stanzas: A Buddhist Psychology of Emptiness*. Ithaca: Snow Lion Press.
4. Ăryadeva, *Four Hundred (Catuśataka)*, 6.10; henceforth: CS. Tib: *// lus la lus dbang ji bzhin du / gti mug kun la gnas gyur te / de phyir ñon mongs thams cad kyang / gti mug bcom pas bcom par 'gyur //* (1974). *Pleasure of Elegant Sayings Textbook Series*, Vol. 18. Varnasi: *Pleasure of Elegant Sayings Press. Quoted by Tsong Khapa*, in Thurman, *Essence*, 310.
5. Chandrakīrti, *Central Way Introduction Commentary (Madhyamakāvatārabhaṣya)*, 6, ad.k.28; hereafter MABh; quoted by Tsong Khapa as trans. in Thurman, *Essence*, 309.
6. MABh, 11, ad.k.31; Thurman, *Essence*, 311.
7. Wampold, B. (2001). *The Great Psychotherapy Debate: Models, Methods and Findings*. New York: Routledge.
8. Ibid.
9. Thurman, *Essence*, 311–12.
10. Loizzo, J. (2001). *Candrakīrti and the Moonflower of Nālandā*. Ann Arbor: University of Michigan Dissertation Services.
11. Philosopher of objectivity Thomas Nagel describes the tendency toward dualistic objectivist and subjectivist extremes in modern thought, attributing them both to a confusion of the forms of human understanding with reality as it is: "These errors are connected: they both stem from an insufficiently robust sense of reality and of its independence from any particular form of human understanding." Nagel, T. (1986). *The View from Nowhere*. Oxford: Oxford University Press, 5.
12. Thurman, *Essence*, Introduction, VIII, makes this distinction by borrowing Saunders and Henze's contrast between "egocentrist" and "nonegocentrist" philosophy; I expand on this by framing the family resemblance between nonegocentrist thinkers in the Buddhist and Western traditions in terms of Wittgenstein's concept of philosophy as therapy, and Freud's notion of psychotherapy as a middle way between philosophy and medicine. See Introduction, III. In Loizzo, J. (2007). *Nāgārjuna's Reason Sixty with Chandrakīrti's Commentary*. New York: American Institute of Buddhist Studies.
13. Thurman, *Essence*, translates the name of Chandrakīrti's Centrist subschool, *Prasāṅgika* as "Dialecticist," in contrast to Bhāvaviveka's opposing Centrist subschool, *Svatantrika*, which he calls "Dogmaticist," based on their methodological preference for dialectical versus dogmatic modes of reasoning, respectively. In the context of comparative psychology, I prefer the more descriptive translations, "Dialogical" and "Doctrinal."
14. Scott, G. (2004). *Does Socrates Have a Method: Rethinking the Elenchus in Plato's Dialogues and Beyond*. New York: Philosophy Education Society.
15. BCA, 8.120; Sanskrit from Vaidya, P.L. (1960). *Bodhicaryāvatāra of Śāntideva with the Commentary Panjika of Prajnakaramati*. Darbhanga: The Mithila Institute of Post-Graduate Studies and Research in Sanskrit Learning. Digital version published by the University of the West: Digital Sanskrit Buddhist Canon. Hereafter *BCA*: *// ātmānaṁ cāparāṁścaiva yaḥ śīghraṁ trātumicchati/ sa caretparamaṁ guhyaṁ parātmaparivartanam //*.
16. BCA, 8.111–12: *// abhyāsādanyadīyeṣu śukraśoṇitabinduṣu / bhavatyahamiti jñānamasatyapi hi vastuni //tathā kāyo'nyadīyo'pi kimātmeti na gṛhyate / paratvaṁ tu svakāyasya sthitameva na duṣkaram //*.

17. MA, 1.3. Tsering, T., (Ed.). (2005). *Acarya Chandrakirti Madhyamakavataraḥ*. Sarnath: Central Institute of Higher Tibetan Studies. Digital version published by the University of the West: Digital Sanskrit Buddhist Cannon. Hereafter MA: */ ātmābhisaktau tvahameti pūrvaṁ / rāgodbhave bhāva idaṁ mameti // arhaṭṭacaryāvadadhīnaloke / kāruṇyavān yo'sti namo'stu tasmai //.*
18. Nāgārjuna, Ratnāvalī, 1.28–29; Vaidya, P. L. (ed.). (1960). Madhyamakaśāstra of Nāgārjuna. Darbhanga: The Mithila Institute of Post-Graduate Studies and Research in Sanskrit Learning. Hereafter RA: */ astyahaṁ mama cāstīti mithyaitatparamārthibhiḥ / yathābhūtaparijñānānna bhavatyubhayaṁ yataḥ // ahaṁkārodbhavāḥ skandhāḥ so'haṁkāro'nṛto'rthataḥ /bījaṁ yasyānṛtaṁ tasya prarohaḥ satyataḥ kutaḥ //.*
19. BCA, 8.124: */ kaḥ paṇḍitastamātmānamicchedrakṣetprapūjayet / na paśyec-chatruvaccainaṁ kaścainaṁ pratimānayet //.*
20. Tsong Khapa cites the Kaśyapa chapter of the *Jewel Heap Scripture* (*Ratnakūṭasūtra*), trans. Thurman, *Essence*, 374: "Kaśyapa, furthermore, the central way is the genuine insight into things; it does not make things empty by means of emptiness, but (realizes that) the very things themselves emptiness ..."
21. According to traditional formulations of the twofold selflessness—of subjects and objects, persons, and things—emptiness was taught especially to emphasize the selflessness of objective things. See Tsong Khapa's summary in Thurman, *Essence*, 299–306.
22. This formulation is traditionally traced to Kamalaśīla's *Stages of Meditation* (*Bhāvanakrama*). For an excellent brief overview of the Nālandā approach to this combined contemplative method according to Tsong Khapa's *Mid-length Stages of the Path to Enlightenment* (*Lam-rim chung-ngu*), see Thurman, *Essence*, Introduction, VIII.3, 130–49. Also, see Kamalaśīla. (2011). *Meditation: The Buddhist Way of Tranquility and Insight*. London: Windhorse Publications.
23. See Thurman, R. 1986. *Central Philosophy of Tibet*. Princeton: Princeton University Press, 138, for a table comparing levels of selfless/emptiness according to different Buddhist schools.
24. Nāgārjuna explains the indispensible role of understanding emptiness in light of the teaching of two truths in his chapter on the four noble truths, "The spiritual teaching of the Enlightened relies on the (distinction of) two realities: the social, superficial reality; and the (profound) ultimate reality. Those who do not understand the difference between these two realities do not understand the profound reality of the Buddha's teaching." MMK, 24.8–9: *// dve satye samupāśritya buddhānāṁ dharmadeśanā / lokasaṁvṛtisatyaṁ ca satyaṁ ca paramārthataḥ // ye'nayorna vijānanti vibhāgaṁ satyayordvayoḥ / te tattvaṁ na vijānanti gambhīraṁ buddhaśāsane //.* Nāgārjuna's distinction also found its way into Hindu Nondualism as well; see Sprung, M. 1973. *The Two Truths in Buddhism and Vedanta*. Dordrecht: Reidel.
25. MMK, XXIV, 10: *// vyavahāramanāśritya paramārtho na deśyate / paramārthamanāgamya nirvāṇaṁ nādhigamyate //.*
26. The classical reference here is the *Transcendent Wisdom Heart Scripture* (*Prajñāparmitahṛdayasūtraṃ*). See Vaidya, P. L. (ed.). (1961). *Buddhist Sanskrit Texts, No. 17.* Darbhanga: The Mithila Institute of Post-Graduate Studies and Research in Sanskrit Learning. Digital version published by the University of the West: Digital Sanskrit Buddhist Canon: *// rūpaṁ śūnyatā, śūnyataiva rūpam/ rūpānna pṛthak śūnyatā, śūnyatāyā na pṛthag rūpam / yadrūpaṁ sā śūnyatā, yā śūnyatā tadrūpam / evaṁ vedanāsaṁjñāsaṁskāravijñānāni ca śūnyatā / evaṁ śāriputra sarvadharmāḥ śūnyatālakṣaṇā anutpannā aniruddhā amalā vimalā anūnā asaṁpūrṇāḥ //.*

27. As Chandrakīrti suggests in his *Introduction*, MA, 6.23; Tibetan in Fenner, P. (1990). *The Ontology of the Middle Way.* Dordrecht: Klewer. Hereafter Fenner: 230: *dngos kun yang dag rdzun pa mthong pa yis / dngos rnyed ngo po gñis ni `dzin par `gyur / yang dag mthong yul gang de de ñid de / mthong ba brdzun pa kun rdzob bden par gsungs //.*
28. MA, 6.175: Digital text from the Derge Tangyur published online by the Asian Classics Input Project, 213a2-3: // *mi bden bzhin du'ang rang gi byad bzhin mdzes par bsgrub bya'i phyir / de ni yod pa ji ltar de bzhin 'dir yang shes rab gdod /sby-ang par bya la nus pa mthong bar 'gyur ba'i gtan tsigs ni /'thad pa dang bral las kyang bsgrub bya rtogs zhes shes par bya //.*
29. Chandrakīrti spells out in several places his distinctive view that relative, conventional persons and things exist only insofar as they are accepted without analysis into ultimate reality, including in his critique of Bhavaviveka's Dogmaticist Centrist philosophy in PPMMV, 1. Consider this brief passage quoted by Tsong Khapa, trans. Thurman, *Essence*, 293: "... in the usage of social conventions, such a sort of analysis (as that seeking essential identity, etc.) is not employed, and further, the things of the world are (only) existent (insofar) as unexamined critically." For more, see Thurman, *Essence*, 291-99. This distinctive approach to explaining how the miundane, superficial reality of social consensus works is also elaborated in his *Introduction*, 6.158 and following verses.
30. The ocular analogy for analytic insight features prominently in the Centrist literature, as one might expect given the classical *abhidharma* theory of the mind as a sixth sense or organ of direct mental perception. This faculty is now popularly referred to in the West as the "third eye," given the depiction common iconography of Indic contemplative traditions of a third eye in the mid-forehead directly in front of the medial forebrain.

    In *Reason Sixty*, Nāgārjuna reserves the language of vision, e.g., "transcendent insight" (*vipaśyanà*), seeing reality" (*tattvadarśana*) (YS, 5, 11), "seeing relativity" (*pratītyotpādadarśana**) (YS, 48) or simply "seeing" (*darśana*) (YS, 25, 55) for the nondualistic negative faculty of insight, also called "genuine insight" (*samyagjñāna*) (YS, 10) as opposed to conventional dualistic knowledge or understanding (*parijñāna*, tib. *yongs su shes pa*), or wisdom (*prajñā*); he also develops the metaphor of "seeing with the intellect" (*blo yis mthong ba*) for the illusion-like insight (YS, 17) and of "seeing with the insight eye" (*ye shes kyi migs gis mthong*) (YS, 54). See also his *Vigrahavyāvartanī*, 11. Candrakīrti, in the *Commentary*, ad.k.17 and 54, as well as in *Lucid Exposition*, PPMMV (ed. Poussin, 373), refines the analogy further, defining the organ of transcendent insight as the "intellect" *(buddhi)* whose disease of misknowledge or reification is healed by "the eye-salve of the emptiness insight" (*śūnyatādarśanāñjana*); the analogy is sustained through much of *Introduction* MA, 6.2, where he compares the leadership of the "intellect" (*blo*) to that of a sighted person (*mig ldan*) among the blind; and 6.23, 27, 29, 105, 108, 120, where he speaks of "seeing with the intellect" (*blo yis mthong ba*); and in 6.213, "we claim that insight has the character of a direct perception" (*ye shes ni mngon sum msthan ñid du `dod*).
31. Nagel describes this process at length in his in *The View From Nowhere*, as in this passage (p. 9): "What really happens in the pursuit of objectivity is that a certain element of oneself, the impersonal or objective self, which can escape from the specific contingencies of one's creaturely point of view, is allowed to predominate. Withdrawing into this element one detaches from the rest and develops an impersonal conception of the world and, so far as possible, of the elements of self from which one has detached."
32. Gazzaniga, S., Irvy, R., & Mangun, G. (2008). *Cognitive Neuroscience: The Biology of the Mind.* New York: W. W. Norton & Company.

33. Jiang, T. (2006). *Contexts and Dialogue: Yogacara Buddhism and Modern Psychology on the Subliminal Mind.* Honolulu: University of Hawaii Press; Hopkins, J. (1996). *Emptiness in the Mind-Only School.* Berkeley: University of California Press.
34. Popper, K. (2003). *The Logic of Scientific Discovery.* London: Routledge.
35. The current neuroscience of perception gives ample support to the idea that the mind and mental images are powerfully active and usually dominant in the normal processing of sensation. See Kosslyn, S. (1996). *Image and the Brain: The Resolution of the Imagery Debate.* Cambridge: The MIT Press.
36. The Gelukpa tradition represents the final synthesis of Chandrakirti's Dialecticist Centrist philosophy with Idealist Centrist system of Asangan depth-psychology revised by śantarakṣita (740–810) and Kamalaśīla (760–815). See Sparham, G. (1993). *Ocean of Eloquence: Tsong Khapa's Commentary on the Yogacara Doctrine of Mind.* Albany: State University of New York Press.
37. Dalai Lama, H. H., & Varela, F. (2002). *Sleeping, Dreaming and Dying: An Exploration of Consciousness.* Somerville: Wisdom Publications.
38. Demasio, A. (2005). *Descartes' Error: Emotions, Reason & the Human Brain.* New York: Penguin Classics.
39. See Beauregard, M., Courtemanche, J., & Paquette, V. (2009). Brain activity in near-death experiencers during a meditative state. In Resuscitation, September 80(9): 1006–10; and Parnia, S., Spearpoint, K., & Fenwick, P. (2007). Near death experiences, cognitive function and psychological outcomes of surviving cardiac arrest. In Resuscitation, August 74(2): 215–21.
40. Van Shaik, S. (2004). *Approaching the Great Perfection: Simultaneous and Gradual Methods of Dzog Chen in the Longchen Nyingtig.* Boston: Wisdom Publications; Padmasambhava, Gyatrul Rinpoche (trans.) (1998). *Natural Liberation: Padmasambhava's Teachings on the Six Bardos.* Boston: Wisdom Publications.
41. Crane, R. (2008). *Mindfulness-Based Cognitive Therapy: Distinctive Features.* New York: Routledge.
42. Kamalaśīla. (2011). *Meditation: The Buddhist Way of Tranquility and Insight.* London: Windhorse Publications.
43. The distinctive view of the profound wisdom lineage of the Nālandā tradition preserved in Gelukpa readings of Mahāmūdra, Dzog Chen, Mind-Clearing and Natural Mind teachings is that they represent the convergence of exoteric Idealist Centrist depth-psychology and esoteric Vajrayāna depth-psychology. See Dalai Lama, H. H., & Berzin, A. (1997). *The Ganden/Kagyu Tradition of Mahamudra.* Ithaca: Snow Lion Press.
44. This is clear in the Gelukpa version of *mahāmūdra* practice presented by Lozang Chokyi Gyaltsan's (1570–1662) *Highway of All Victors: A Root Text on the Great Seal in the Gem-Like Ganden/Kagyu Tradition (dGa' ldan bka' brgyud rin po che'i Phyag chen rtsa ba rGyal ba'i gzhung lam).* For a current translation and commentary, see H. H. the Dalai Lama, & A. Berzin's classic on *mahāmūdra.* For the translation I use here, see www.nalandascience.org/pages/r-translated.html
45. BCA, 9.27: *// cittādanyā na māyā cennāpyananyeti kalpyate / vastu cetsā kathaṁ nānyānanyā cennāsti vastutaḥ //.*
46. Chokyi Gyaltsan, *Highway.*
47. YSV, ad.k.30; Loizzo, *Reason*, 182.
48. Ibid., ad. k.45; Loizzo, *Reason*, 197.
49. MMK, 24.18–19: *// yaḥ pratītyasamutpādaḥ śūnyatāṁ tāṁ pracakṣmahe / ā prajñaptirupādāya pratipatsaiva madhyamā // apratītya samutpanno dharmaḥ kaścinna vidyate / yasmāttasmādaśūnyo hi dharmaḥ kaścinna vidyate //.*

50. MA, 6.185–86; "Things' freedom from intrinsic reality the wise designate as 'emptiness.' And that emptiness in turn we accept as empty of any substantial emptiness. (Hence) the emptiness of what is called "emptiness" is said to be the emptiness of emptiness. It was proclaimed to counteract the mindset which clings to emptiness as an entity." Dergye, 213b2-3: *//chos rnams rang bzhin med pa nyid / mkhas pas stong pa nyid ces bsnyad / stong nyid de yang stong nyid kyi / ngo bos stong par 'dod pa yin // stong nyid ces bya'i stong nyid gang / stong nyid stong nyid du 'dod de /stong nyid dngos po'i blo can gyi / 'dzin pa bzlog phyir gsungs pa yin //.*
51. Thurman, *Essence*, 342–43: "In regard to [phenomena] such as a sprout, there are three perceptual habits: one holding it to be objectively existent; one holding it to be objectively inexistent; and one holding it without qualifying it in either way. If the distinction is clearly understood that all three of these habit-patterns exist in the mental process of one in whom the authentic view is generated, but that only the first and last are present in the mental process of one in whom no authentic view has been generated, then one will put a stop to the following false views: [the view] that rationality does not put a stop to all perception [controlled] by mental constructions [such as] "this is it;" [the view] that all practices before the generation of the authentic view, such as cultivation of the will to enlightenment, are but truth-habits, or sign-habits; and [the view] that after one lays claim to having generated in mind the authentic view, there will be no intentionality in all one's acts."
52. MABh, ad.k.173; translated in Thurman, *Essence*, 330.
53. For a concise discussion of Chandrakīrti's distinctive reading of the Centrist stance of positionlessness advocated by Nāgārjuna and Ăryadeva, see Thurman, *Essence*, 154–72.
54. For some intriguing contemporary views on the Socratic stance of *apioria*, including some views of that method as psychotherapeutic, see Scott, G. (2004). *Does Socrates Have a Method: Rethinking the Elenchus in Plato's Dialogues and Beyond*. New York: Philosophy Education Society.
55. This dialogical method defines the therapeutic pedagogy advocated by Chandrakīrti as the method of consequences or *prasaṅga*, from which his school derived its name. Compare the Socratic method of *elenchus* explored by Scott and his peers *in Does Socrates Have a Method,* as well as modern versions like Freud's method of free association and Wittgenstein's method of language-games. See Loizzo, *Reason*, Introduction, III.
56. MMK, 1.1-2: *// yah pratītyasamutpādaṃ prapañcopaśamaṃ śivaṃ / deśayāmāsa saṃbuddastaṃ vande vādatāṃ varaṃ //.*
57. MMK, 22.11: *// śūnyamiti na vaktavyamaśūnyamiti vā bhavet/ ubhayaṁ nobhayaṁ ceti prajñaptyarthaṁ tu kathyate //.*
58. MMK, 25.24: */ sarvopalambhopaśamaḥ prapañcopaśamaḥ śivaḥ / na kvacitkasyacitkaściddharmo buddhena deśitaḥ //.*
59. YS, 51; Loizzo, *Reason*, 125.
60. YS, 50; Loizzo, *Reason*, 125.
61. Chokyi Gyaltsan, *Highway.*
62. See H. H. the Dalai Lama and Berzin, *Mahamudra* (op cit.)
63. Nagel, *View From Nowhere*, 210, describes the perspective of objective self as resembling the omniscience of a monotheistic God: "The wish to live so far as possible in full recognition of the fact that one's position in the universe is not central has an element of the religious impulse about it, or at least an acknowledgement of the question to which religion purports to supply an answer. A religious solution gives us a borrowed centrality through the concern of a supreme being."

64. Tsong Khapa. *Lam gyi tso-bo rnam pa gsum*. "Who sees the inexorable causality of everything whatsoever, mundane and transcendent, and breaks any objectifying habits, embarks on the path that satisfies Buddhas. Appearance is inevitably relative, and emptiness, free from convictions—as long as these two (truths) appear separate, one has not realized Shakyamuni's intent. But when they coincide without alternation, at the mere sight of unerring relativity one's certainty breaks all objectifying habits, and the analysis of worldviews is complete. Further, as appearance dispels absolutism and emptiness dispels nihilism, knowing how emptiness dawns as cause and effect—you will not be impoverished by extremist views." Tib: *// gang zhig 'khor 'das chos rnams tham cad kyi // rgyu 'bras nam yang bslu ba med mthong zhing // dmigs pa'i gtad so gang yin kun zhig pa // de ni sangs rgyas dgyes pa'i lam la zhugs // snang bar ten 'brel bslu ba med pa dang // stong pa khas len bral ba'i go ba gñis // ji srid so sor rnang ba de srid du // da dung thub pa'i dgongs pa rtogs pa med // nam zhig res 'jog med par cig car du // rten 'brel mi bslur mthong ba tsam ñid nas nges shes yul gyi 'dzin stangs kun 'jig na // de tshe lta ba'i dpyad pa rdzogs pa lags //*. Dharmasala: Tibetan Cultural Printing Press.
65. Thurman, *Essence*, Introduction, VIII.3, 130–49, succinctly reviews this convergence of complementary insight modes, and alludes to the similarity traditionally drawn between this exoteric art of integrating spacious emptiness with dream-like appearance and the esoteric art of meditating simultaneously on transformational archetypes and environments as "empty appearances."
66. According to Nāgārjuna's *Jewel Garland* (*Ratnāvalī*), the spirit and path of enlightened altruism marry transcendence with ascendance, openness with compassion, truth with form. Likewise, Chandrakīrti's *Introduction* describes this spirit and path as marrying ultimate and conventional truths, unconditional and relative compassion, and the embodiment of truth and form.
67. Jinpa, T. (trans). (2005). *Mind-Training: The Great Collection*. Boston: Wisdom Publications. Hereafter Jinpa, *Mind-Training.*
68. The process of positive social emotional development through moral action has recently gained attention in the findings of positive psychology. See Seligman, M. (2004). *Authentic Happiness: Using the New Positive Psychology to Realize Your Potential for Lasting Fulfillment*. New York: Free Press.
69. See for instance, Melsky, R. (2004). Identifying with the aggressor: how crime victims often cope with trauma. In *FBI Law Enforcement Bulletin*, August.

Chapter 6: Alturism and the Path of Engagement

1. MA, 1. 1-2: *// munīndrajāḥ śrāvakamadhyabuddhāḥ / buddhodbhavāḥkhalvapi bodhisattvāt / kāruṇyacittādvayabuddhibodhi / cittāni heturjinaputrakāṇām // bījaṁ kṛpā yajjinaśasyarāśe / stadvṛddhaye vārisamā, cirāya / bhogāya pākaśca yathaiva mānya / mādau mamā'thaḥ karuṇāpraśaṁsā //.*
2. For the Mahāyāna version of the five stages, my main sources have been Dhargyey, *Tibetan Tradition*, 187-201; and Hopkins, J. (1983/1996). *Meditation on Emptiness*, 93-109. Somerville: Wisdom Press.
3. This traditional list of contemplative faculties is, not surprisingly, aligned with recent observations of the qualities cultivated by contemplative practices like mindfulness: enhanced attention; present awareness; enhanced insight; non-reactive concentration; and greater acceptance . See Baer, R., Smith, G., Hopkins, J., et al. (2006). Using self-report methods to explore facets of mindfulness. In *Assessment*, 13(1): 27–45.
4. AK, 6.67–70; Pruden, 3, 1023–29; Dhargey, *Tibetan Tradition*, 183–86.

5. The traditional list of qualities that support an altruist's life—generosity, ethics, tolerance, endurance, meditation, wisdom, technique, power, affirmation and intuition—not surprisingly aligns well with current schemas, like Gilbert's list of eight: sympathy, sensitivity, tolerance, strength, non-judgment, creativity, care and empathy. See Gilbert, P. (2005). Compassion and Cruelty: A Biopsychosocial Approach. In P. Gilbert (ed.), *Compassion: Conceptualizations, Research and Use in Psychotherapy*. New York: Routledge, 9–74.
6. Nagel, T. (1986). *The View From Nowhere*. Oxford: Oxford University Press, 11.
7. See Carr, L., Iacaboni, M., Dubeau, M., et al. (2003). Neural mechanisms for empathy in humans: A relay from neural systems for imitation to limbic areas. In *PNAS*, 100(9): 5497–02.
8. Shiela Wang explains the nature of this shift by drawing on MacLean's distinction between neural systems of self-preservation versus species-preservation. See MacLean, P. (1990). *The Triune Brain in Evolution*. New York: Plenum Press; Wang, S. (2005). A conceptual framework for integrating research related to the physiology of compassion and the wisdom of Buddhist teachings. In Gilbert, *Compassion*, 75–120; and deWaal, F. & Preston, S. (2002). Empathy: Its ultimate and proximate bases. In *Behavioral and Brain Sciences*, 25:1–10.
9. Davidson, R. (2000). Affective style, psychopathology and resilience: Brain mechanisms and plasticity. In *American Psychologist*, 1196–1214.
10. Rizziolatti, G., & Craighero, L. (2004). The mirror-neuron system. In *Annual Review of Neuroscience*, 27: 169–92; and Rizziolatti, G., Fogassi, L., & Gallese, V. (2001). Nueropsychological mechanisms underlying the understanding and the imitation of action. In *National Review of Neuroscience*, 2: 661–70.
11. See Gilbert, 2005, in Gilbert, *Compassion*, 9–74.
12. See Critchley, H., Mathias, C., Josephs, O., et al. (2003). Human cingulate cortex and autonomic control: Converging neuroimaging and clinical evidence. In *Brain*, 126: 2139–52; and Phelps, E., Delgado, M. Nearing, K., et al. (2004). Extinction learning in humans: Role of the amygdale and vmPFC. In *Neuron*, 43: 897–905. Of note, mindfulness has been shown to increase activation in the anterior cingulated gyrus. For a review, see Siegel, D. (2007). *The Mindful Brain*. New York: Norton Press.
13. See Carter, C., Botvinick, M., & Cohen, J. (1999). The contribution of the anterior cingulated cortex to executive processes in cognition. *Review of Neuroscience*, 10: 49–57; Schoenbaum, G., & Setlow, B. (2001). Integrating orbitofrontal cortex into prefrontal theory: Common processing themes across species and subdivisions. In *Learning & Memory*, 8(3): 134–47. Again, both these areas of PFC have been shown to be activated by meditation. See Siegel, *Mindful Brain*.
14. See Iacaboni, M. (2009). *Mirroring People: The Science of Empathy and How We Connect with Others*. New York: Picador Press.
15. See Bierhoff, H.W. (2005). The psychology of compassion and prosocial behavior. In Gilbert, *Compassion*, 148–67.
16. Gilrath, Shaver, & Mikulincer (2005) make the case for the benefits of such open-ended extension of empathy based on attachment theory and the mammalian psychobiology of the caregiving system. See Gilrath, O., Shaver, P., & Mikulincer, M. (2005). An attachment-theoretical approach to compassion and altruism. In Gilbert, *Compassion*, 121–47.
17. See Hoffman, M. (2000). *Empathy and Moral Development: Implications for Caring and Justice*. Cambridge: Cambridge University Press.
18. This shift has been discussed in the literature in terms of the concepts of the prosocial personality and the altruistic personality. See Bierhoff, H., & Rohmann, E. (2004). Altruistic personality in the context of the empathy-altruism hypothesis. In *European Journal of Personality*, 18: 351–65; and Bierhoff, H. (2002). *Prosocial Behavior*. Hove: Psychology Press.

19. See Gilbert, *Compassion*, chapters 9–13.
20. The origins of empathy and altruism in spousal and parental caregiving are explored in Gilrath, Shaver and Mikulincer (2005). One neurobiological model for the importance of intimate relations in altruism is the model of empathic resonance put forward by Decety, J., & Chaminade, T. (2003). When the self represents the other: A new cognitive neuroscience view on psychological identification. In *Consciousness and Cognition*, 12: 577–96.
21. Dhargyey, *Tibetan Tradition*, 191–93.
22. See Wang, S. (2005). A conceptual framework for integrating research related to the physiology of compassion and the wisdom of Buddhist teachings. In Gilbert, *Compassion*, 75–120.
23. Davidson, R., Jackson, D., & Kalin, N. (2000). Emotion, plasticity, context and regulation: Perspectives from affective neuroscience. In *Psychological Bulletin*, 126(6): 890–909.
24. This gradual process of biopsychosocial development spanning multiple lives is described at length by Nāgārjuna in the third chapter of his *Jewel Garland* (*Ratnāvalī*), Accumulating the Stores (of Compassion and Wisdom) for Enlightened Altruism. See Hopkins, J. (1998). *Buddhist Advice for Living and Liberation*. Ithaca: Snow Lion Press.
25. See Loizzo, J. (2009). Kālacakra and the Nālandā Tradition: Science, Religion and Objectivity in Buddhism and the West. In T. Arnold (ed.), *As Long as Space Endures: Essays on the Kalacakra Tantra in Honor of His Holiness the Dalai Lama*. Ithaca: Snow Lion Press, 333–66.
26. See note 22, above.
27. See Fredrickson, B. (2005). Positive affect and the complex dynamics of human flourishing. In *American Psychologist*, 60: 678–96.
28. See Urry, H., Nitscke, J., Dolski, I., et al. (2004). Making a life worth living: Neural correlates of well-being. In *Psychological Science*, 15(6): 367–72; and Infante, J., Peran, F., Martinez, M., et al. (1998). ACTH and beta-endorphin in transcendental meditation. In *Physiology and Behavior*, 35: 591–95.
29. A growing body of basic brain research shows an intimate link between self-knowledge and empathy. See Beer, J., John, O., Donatella, S., & Knight, T. (2006). Orbitofrontal cortex and social behavior: integrating self-monitoring and emotion-cognition interactions. In *Journal of Cognitive Neuroscience*, 18: 871–79; Gallese, V., Keysers, C., & Rizzolatto, G. (2004). A unifying view of the basis of social cognition. In Trends in *Cognitive Sciences*, 8(9):396–403; Decety, J., & Jackson, P. (2004). The functional architecture of human empathy. In *Behavioral and Cognitive Neuroscience Reviews*, 3(2): 71–100.
30. The importance of the development and extension of the caretaking system for social and moral development is discussed in Gilrath et al. (2005).
31. See the concept of the altruistic personality developed in Bierhoff & Rohmann, 2004.
32. See the concept of the emergence of a prosocial personality in Bierhoff (2002).
33. Skt. *Anupalabdidharmakṣānti*.
34. Some researchers refer to meditative experiences of the temporary dissolution of self-world constructs as "ipseity." See Lutz, A., Slagter, H., Dunne, J., et al. (2008). Attention regulation and monitoring in meditation. In *Trends in Cognitive Science*, April 12(4): 163–69; and Austin, J. (2006). *Zen-Brain Reflections*. Cambridge: MIT Press. This, of course, raises hard questions about the epistemological status of such experiences, a subject which generated a long debate in the social scientific study of religious experience. See Proudfoot, W. (1987). *Religious Experience*. Berkeley: University of California Press; and Foreman, R. (1997). *The Problem of Pure Consciousness: Mysticism and Philosophy*. Oxford: Oxford University Press.

35. This traditional practice opens the door to what some have called radical acceptance. See Brach, T. (2003). *Radical Acceptance: Embracing your life with the heart of a Buddha*. New York: Bantam Books.
36. Segal, Z., Williams, J., & Teasdale, J. (2002). *Mindulness-based Cognitive Therapy for Depression: A New Approach to Preventing Relapse*. New York: Guilford Press; Hayes, S. (2004). Acceptance and commitment therapy, relational frame theory and the third wave of cognitive therapies. In *Behavior Therapy* 35(4): 639–65.
37. This case has been made in an ecumenical way as a matter of global commonsense in Dalai Lama, H. H. (2001). *Ethics for the New Millenium*. New York: Riverdale Trade Books.
38. Following Robert Thurman's eloquent translation of *bodhicitta* as "the spirit of enlightenment."
39. BCA, 3.28–32, Sanskrit from Vaidya, P.L, (ed). (1960). *Bodhicaryāvatāra of Śāntideva with the Commentary Panjika of Prajnakaramati*. Darbhanga: Mithila Institute of Post-Graduate Studies and Research in Sanskrit Learning. Digital version from Nagarjuna Institute of Exact Methods, available online through University of the West. Henceforth: BCA: *jaganmṛtyuvināśāya jāt ametadrasāyanam|jagaddāridryaśamanaṁ nidhānamidamakṣayam ||28|| jagadvyādhipraśamanaṁ bhaiṣajyamidamuttamam| bhavādhvabhrama ṇaśrāntajagadviśrāmapādapaḥ ||29|| durgatyuttaraṇe setuḥ sāmānyaḥ sarvayāyinām| jagatkleśopaśamana uditaścittacandramāḥ ||30|| jagadajñān atimiraprotsāraṇamahāraviḥ| saddharmakṣīramathanānnavanītaṁ samutthitam ||31|| sukhabhogabubhukṣitasya vā janasārthasya bhavādhvacāriṇaḥ| sukhasatramidaṁ hyupasthitaṁ sakalābhyāgatasattvatarpaṇam ||32||*.
40. See Cox, S., Wilt, J., Olson, B., et al. (2010). Generativity, the big five, and psychosocial adaptation in midlife adults. In *Journal of Personality*, August 1, 78(4): 1185–208; and Hofer, J., Busch, H., Chasiotis, A., et al. (2008). Concern for generativity and its relation to implicit pro-social power motivation, generative goals, and satisfaction with life: a cross-cultural investigation. In *Journal of Personality*, February 76(1): 1–30.
41. Hopkins, *Meditation*, 96–112.
42. BCA, 5.70, Skt: *// kāye naubuddhimādhāya gatyāgamananiśrayāt / athākāmaṁgamaṁ kāyaṁ kuru sattvārthasiddhaye //.*
43, BCA, 5.77, Skt: *// sarvārambhā hi tuṣṭyarthāḥ sā vittairapi durlabhā / bhokṣye tuṣṭimukhaṁ tasmātparaśramakṛtairguṇaiḥ //.*
44. BCA, 5.99, Skt: *// yā avasthāḥ prapadyeta svayaṁ paravaśo'pi vā / tāsvavasthāsu yāḥ śikṣāḥ śikṣettā eva yatnataḥ //.*
45. Dhargyey, *Tibetan Tradition*, 195–97.
46. The evolutionary ethos of generosity is classically described in the Vessantara Jataka and other tales, and also reflected in the Mahāyāna literature of the pure land. See Inayat Kahn, N. (1985). *Twenty Jataka Tales. Inner Traditions*; and Uno, T. 1998. *River of Fire, River of Water*. New York: Image Publications.
47. Cameron, C., Loewenstein, G., & Rabin, M. (eds.). (2004). *Advances in Behavioral Economics*. New York: Princeton University Press; Penn, D. (2003). The Evolutionary Roots of our Environmental Problems. In *Quarterly Review of Biology*, Vol. 78, No. 3.
48. Bill: See Argyle, M. (1987). *The Psychology of Happiness*. London: Methuen Press; and Dalai Lama, H. H. (2009). *The Art of Happiness: Tenth Anniversary Edition*. New York: Riverhead Books.
49. RA, 5.40–41, Skt. from Hahn, M. (1982). Nāgārjuna's Rabtāvalī, Vol. 1. Bonn: Indica et Tibetica Verlag, 146–48. Henceforth: Hahn. *// yathā śrāvakayāne 'ṣṭāv uktāḥ śrāvakabhūmayaḥ / mahāyāne daśa tathā bodhisattvasya bhūmayaḥ //*

40 // tāsāṃ pūrvaṃ pramuditā bodhisattvapramodanāt / saṃyojanatrayahāes tathāgatakulodbhavāt // 41 // jāyate 'syā viapākena dānapāramitāparaḥ / lokadhātuśatākampi jambūdvīpamaheśvaraḥ // 42.

50. RA, 2.83, T. b. Hahn, 68: *// rang gi nor bdog blangs gyur na // myur du btang ba'i brtul zhugs kyis // phyag rgya bde dang 'jig rten gyi // rnam par 'dren pa ñid du 'gyur //.*
51. RA, 2.85 Tib. Hahn, 68: *// khang bzangs gding ba rgyan dag ni // bde zhing bzang ba rab byin pas // gser ni btso ma dri med pa // shin tu 'jam pa'i mdog 'drar 'gyur //.*
52. RA, 2.87, Tib. Hahn, 69: *// sñan cing dga' bar smras pa dang // legs par smras dang mthum byas pas // khyod nu dpung mgo zlum pa dang // ro stod seng ge 'dra ba 'gyur //.*
53. See Thurman, R. (1976). *The Holy Teaching of Vimalakīti*. University Park: Pennsylvania State University Press.
54. For a current discussion, see Judith, A. (2010). *Waking the Global Heart: Humanity's Rite of Passage form the Love of Power to the Power of Love*. New York: Elite Books; or see the classic by Marcuse, H. (1987). *Eros and Civilization*. New York: Routledge.
55. Though most traditional maps break the process down into finer increments, with each of the nine levels in turn subdivided into nine degrees, the system of Chandrakirti and his heirs maintain that the corresponding degrees of all nine levels of blocks—like the grossest or subtlest—are removed all at once, since a single breakthrough in insight typically resonates on all levels of the mind. See Hopkins, *Meditation*, 96–109.
56. For Vasubandhu's use of this simile in the context of his discussion of the degrees of defilement and purification, see *Treasury*, AK.633cd; Pruden, 957.
57. BCA, 3.11, Skt: *// sarvatyāgaśca nirvāṇaṁ nirvāṇārthi ca me manaḥ / tyaktavyaṁ cenmayā sarvaṁ varaṁ sattveṣu dīyatām //*
58. BCA, 3.22–4, Skt: *// yathā gṛhītaṁ sugatairbodhicittaṁ purātanaiḥ / te bodhisattvaśikṣāyāmānupūrvyā yathā sthitāḥ // 22 // tadvadutpādayāmyeṣa bodhicittaṁ jagaddhite / tadvadeva ca tāḥ śikṣāḥ śikṣiṣyāmi yathākramam // 23 // evaṁ gṛhītvā matimān bodhicittaṁ prasādataḥ / punaḥ pṛṣṭasya puṣṭyarthaṁ cittamevaṁ praharṣayet // 24.*
59. BCA, 3.26, Skt: *// tathādhunā mayā kāryaṁ svakulocitakāriṇām / nirmalasya kulasyāsya kalaṅko na bhavedyathā //.*
60. RA, 5.43–4, Skt, Hahn, 148: *// dvitīyā vimalā nāma kāyavākcittanarmaṇāṃ / daśānām api vaimalayāt prakṛtyā tṣv avasthiteḥ // jāyate 'syā vipākena śīla pāramitāparaḥ / saptaratnaprabhuḥ śrīmāṃś carkravartī jagadditaḥ //.*
61. RA, 5.45–6, Skt. Hahn, 148–50: *// prabhākarī tṛtīyā tu śāntajñānaprabhodbhavāt / dhyānābhijñānasamutpādāt rāgadveṣaparikṣayāt // jāyate 'syā vipākena kṣāntivīryādhikakriyaḥ / kṛti mahendro devanāṃ kāmarāganivartakaḥ //.*
62. This shift is an extension of the shift in affective response modes from right-sided avoidance styles to left-sided approach styles, as documented in Davidson (2000) and Davidson, Kabat-Zinn, Schumacher, et al. (2003). Alterations in Brain & Immune Function Produced By Meditation. *Psychosomatic Medicine*, 65(4): 564-570.
63. For our potential for social-emotional attunement, see Nitschke, J., Nelson, E., Rusch, B. et al. (2004). Orbitofrontal cortex tracks positive mood in mothers viewing pictures of their newborn infants. In *Neuroimage*, 21: 583–92; and Tucker, D., Luu, P., & Pribram, K. (1995). Social and emotional self-regulation. In *Annals of the New York Academy of Sciences*, 769(1): 213–39.
64. Cozolino, L. (2006). *The Neuroscience of Human Relationships: Attachment and the Developing Brain*. New York: Norton Press; Ekman, P., Davidson, R., Ricard, M., et al. (2005). Buddhist psychological perspectives on emotions and well-being. In *Current Directions in Psychological Science* 14(2): 59–63.

65. See Shulkin, J., Gold, P., & McEwen, B. (1994). Allostasis, amygdale and anticipatory angst. In *Neuroscience and Biobehavioral Review*, 18: 491–97.
66. See Sroufe, L., Egeland, B., Carlson, E., et al. (2005). *The Development of the Person: The Minnesota Study of Risk and Adaptation from Birth to Adulthood*. New York: Guilford Press.
67. To navigate the deepest stages of concentrative quiescence, we need to release the last vestiges of forced control and develop a relaxed expertise that supports an effortless, natural control of mind and body. This final shift is a prominent feature of Tibetan teaching traditions like *Dzog-chen* and *mahāmūdra*. See Hopkins, *Meditation*, 67–90; and the Dalai Lama, *Mahamudra*.
68. See Davidson, (2000); and Gustafsson G., Persson, B, Eriksson, S., et al. (2009). Personality traits among burnt out and non-burnt out health-care personnel at the same workplaces: a pilot study. In *International Journal of Mental Health Nursing*, October 18(5): 336–48.
69. RA, 5.47–8, Skt, Hahn, 150: // *caturthy arciṣmatī nāma saṃyagjñānārcrudbhjavāt / bhāvanād bodhipakṣāṇāṃ sakalānāṃ viśeṣatāḥ // jāyate 'asyā vipākena suyāmālayadvarāṭ / satkāyadṛṣṭisaṃparka samudghātakaraḥ kṛtī //*.
70. The stages of concentrative quiescence, including the faults and remedies at each stage, are described at length in Hopkins, *Meditation*, 68–90.
71. These capacities are likely mediated by practice-induced neuroplasticity and growth in prefrontal cortical areas responsible for bodily self-regulation, fear-extinction and intuitive integration of learning and reinforcement. See Siegel, *Mindful Brain*.
72. These are understood as a natural outgrowth of innate faculties enhanced by profound concentration and continued practice; and they are seen as social faculties developed to support the empathic art of communicating enlightenment. For a traditional list of the distinctive qualities of *bodhisattvas* and *buddhas*, see Thurman, *Vimalkīrti*, 155–56.
73. See Urry et al. (2004); and Infante et al. (1998).
74. See Lutz, A., et al. (2004). Long-term meditators and self-regulation of high amplitude gamma synchrony during mental practice. In *PNAS*, 101: 16369–373; and Persinger, M. (1984). Striking EEG profiles from single episodes of glossolalia and transcendental meditation. In *Perceptual and Motor Skills*, 58:127–33.
75. See Lazar, S, Kerr, C., Wasserman, R., et al. (2005). Meditation experience is associated with increased cortical thickness. In *Neuroreport*, 16(17): 1893–97.
76. RA, 5.49–50, Skt: // *sudurjayā pañcamī tu sarvamāraiḥ sudurjayāt / āryasatyādisūkṣmārtha jñānakauśalasaṃbhavāt // jāyate 'syā vipākena tuṣitālayadevarāṭ / sarvatīthakarakleśa dṛṣṭisthānanivartakaḥ //*.
77. See Doidge, N. 2007. *The Brain that Changes Itself: Stories of Personal triumph from the Frontiers of Brain Science*. New York: Penguin Press.
78. See Sotres-Bayon, F., Christopher, K., Cain, C., et al. (2006). Brain mechanisms of fear extinction: Historical perspectives on the contribution of prefrontal cortex. *In Biological Psychiatry*, 60: 329–36; Phelps, E., Delgado, M., Nearing, K., et al. (2004). Extinction learning in humans: Role of the amygdale and vmPFC. In *Neuron*, 43: 897–905; Carr, L., Iacoboni, M., Dubeau, M., et al. (2003). Neural mechanisms of empathy in humans: A relay from neural systems for imitation to limbic areas. In *PNAS*, 100(9): 5497–02; deWaal, F., & Preston, S. (2002). Empathy: Its ultimate and proximate bases. In *Behavioral and Brain Sciences*, 25:1–20.
79. While definitive trials and long-term studies have yet to be done, there is ample preliminary research in the education and training of caregivers to support the promise of such an approach. See Shapiro, S., Schwartz, G., & Bonner, G. (1998). Effects of mindfulness-based stress reduction on medical and pre-

medical students. In *Journal of Behavioral Medicine*, 21: 581–99; and Epel, E., Daubrnheimer, J., Tedlie, J., et al. (2009). Can Meditation Slow the Rate of Cellular Aging? Cognitive Stress, Mindfulness and Telomeres. In Bushell, W., Olio, W., & Theise, N. (eds.), *Longevity, Regeneration and Optimal Health: Integrating Eastern and Western Perspectives*. New York: Annals of the New York Academy of Sciences. Vol. 1172, 34–53.

80. Dhargyay, *Tibetan Tradition*, 145–46. In addition, there is an increasing number of more recent studies lending further support to these.
81. This process involves not just insight, but insight conjoined with corrective emotional experience, as in the healing of trauma. See Fosha, D. (2009). Positive Affects and the Transformation of Suffering into Fourishing. In Bushell et al. *Longevity*, 252–62.
82. A similar theme is explored in Cialdini, R., & Kenrick, D. (1976). Altruism as hedonism: A social development perspective on the relationship of negative mood and helping. In *Journal of Personality & Social Psychology*, 36: 907–14.
83. These are listed and described in Thurman, *Vimalakīrti*, 155.
84. RA, 5.51–2, Skt., Hahn, 152: *// ṣaṣṭhī tv abhimukhī nāma buddhadharmābhimukhyataḥ / vipaśyanāśamābhyāsān nirodhāvāotiouṣkalā // jāyate 'syā vipākena devarājaḥ sunirmitaḥ / śrāvakānām asaṃhārya ādhimānikaśaṃkaraḥ //*
85. RA, 5.53–4, Skt., Hahn, *ibid: // dūraṃgamā saptamī tu saṃkhyādūraṃgamānvayāt / āpadyate nirodhaṃ ca yasmād asyāṃ kṣaṇe kṣaṇe // jāyate 'syā vipākena vaśavarty amarādhipaḥ / āryasatyābhisamaya jñānācāryamahānṛpaḥ //.*
86. For an elegant introduction to the Indo-Tibetan tradition of the five contemplative archetypes of enlightenment (*dhyani-buddhas*), see Govinda, A. (1969/1973). *Foundations of Tibetan Mysticism*. New York: Samuel Weiser Books
87. A general case for the integration of our concepts of higher intelligence and emotional intelligence is made by Goleman, D. (2006). *Emotional Intelligence: Why it can Matter More than IQ*. New York: Bantam Books.
88. MA, 6.14–16.
89. RA, 5.55–6, Tib., Hahn, 153–54: *// de bzhin brgyad pa gzhon nu'i sa // mi gyo ba de mi rtog phyir // mi gyo de bzhin lus dang ni // ngag sems spyod yul bsam mi khyab // de yi rnam par smin pas ni // stong gi dbag po'i tshangs par 'gyur // dgra bcom rang sangs rgyas sogs kyis // don gtan 'bebs la 'phrogs pa med //.*
90. RA, 5.57–8, Tib., Hahn, 154: *// sa dgu pa ni legs pa yi // blo gros zhes bya rgyal tshab bzhin // gang phyir so so yang dag rig // thob pas 'di la blo gros bzang // de yi rnam par smin pas ni // stong gñis bdag po tshangs par 'gyur // sems can bsam pa dris pa la // dgra bcom sogs kyis 'phrogs pa med //.*
91. Thurman, *Vimalakīrti*, 155–56.
92. Dargyay, Tibetan Tradition, 209–13; Thurman, *Vimalakīrti*, 149, 154.
93. RA, 5.59–60, Tib., Hahn, 154: *// bcu pa chos kyi sprin yin te // dam pa chos kyi char 'bebs phyir // byang chub sems dpa' sangs rgyas kyis // 'od zer dag gis dbang bskur phyir // de yin rnam par smin pas ni // gnas gtsang lha yi bdag por 'gyur // bsam yas ye shes yul gyi bdag // dbang phyug chen po mchog yin no //.*

Chapter 7: Role-Modeling Imagery and Self-Transformation

1. This passage from the *Vajrapañjaratantra* is quoted by Tsong Khapa in the fourth chapter of his *Great Exposition of the Poetic Path* (*Ngags-rim chen-mo*). See Hopkins, J., Dalai Lama, H. H., & Tsong Khapa. (1987). *Tantra in Tibet*. Ithaca: Snow Lion Press). It is cited as translated by Jeffry Hopkins with minor revisions by the author.

2. He does so in his systematic survey of the process-oriented path, *Great Stages of the Poetic Path* (*Ngags-rim chen-mo*), which is still in the process of being fully translated. See Hopkins et al. *Tantra in Tibet* (op cit.); Hopkins, J., Tsong Khapa, & Dalai Lama, H. H. (1987). *Deity Yoga in Action and Performance Tantra*. Ithaca: Snow Lion Press; Hopkins, J. Dzong Khapa, & Dalai Lama, H. H. (2005). *Yoga Tantra: Paths to Magical Feats*. Ithaca: Snow Lion Press; and Yarnall, T. (2011). Tsong Khapa's *Great Stages of Mantra: The Creation Stage*. New York: American Institute of Buddhist Studies.
3. See Dowman, K. (1998). *Masters of Mahāmudrā: Songs and Histories of the Eighty-Four Buddhist Siddhas*. Albany: State University of New York Press.
4. For a recent review, see Ericsson, A. Kiruthiga, N., & Roring, R. (2009). Toward a Science of Exceptional Achievement: Attaining Superior Performance Through Deliberate Practice. In Bushell, W., Olivo, E, & Thiese, N. (eds.), *Longevity, Regeneration and Optimal Health*. New York: New York Academy of Sciences.
5. Hopkins, *Tantra*, chapter 3.
6. See Thurman, R. (1986). Vajra Hermeneutics. In D. Lopez (ed.). *Buddhist Hermeneutics*. Honolulu: University of Hawaii Press.
7. See Tantra for Practice. In Hopkins, *Tantra*, chapter 1.
8. See Shaw, M. (1994). *Passionate Enlightenment: Women in Tantric Buddhism*. Princeton: Princeton University Press.
9. The contemplative faculty of flow or plasticity (*praśrabdhi*), with its experiential effects of generalized mental and physical bliss, is recognized as a pivotal state-specific faculty of all states and stages of profound concentration, whether in the contemplative science of the classical scientific teaching tradition (*abidharma*) or in the equivalent in the literature of the socially engaged teaching tradition. See Vasubandu's *Treasury*, 8.9; Pruden, (op cit.), 4: 1231–35; or Asanga, Rahula, W., & Boin-Webb, S. (2001). *Abhidharmasamuccaya: Compendium of Higher Teaching*. Asian Humanities Press. For two recent studies on the physiology of euphoric states in meditation, see Harte, J. L, Eifert, G. H., Smith, R. (1995). The effects of running and meditation on beta-endorphin, corticotropin-releasing hormone and cortisol in plasma, and on mood. In *Biological Psychology*, June 40(3): 251–65; and Infante, J., Peran, F., Martinez, M., et al. (1998). ACTH and beta-endorphin in transcendental meditation. In *Physiology and Behavior* 64: 311–15.
10. For a discussion of the self-regulation of internal reward, see Loizzo, J. (2000). Meditation and Psychotherapy: Stress, Allostasis and Enriched Learning. In P. Muskin (ed.), *Complementary and Alternative Medicine and Psychiatry*. Annual Revue of Psychiatry, Vol. 19, No.1. Washington DC: American Psychiatric Association Press.
11. For physiological findings on high arousal practices from the Buddhist and Hindu Tantras, see Corby, J., Roth, W., Zarcone, V., et al. (1978). Psychophysiological correlates of the practice of tantric yoga. In *Archives of General Psychiatry*, 35: 571–77; Benson, H., Malhorta, M., Goldman, R., et al. (1990). Three case reports of the metabolic and electroencephalogaphic changes during advanced Buddhist meditation techniques. *Behavioral Medicine* 16(2): 90–95; and Heller, C., Elsner, R., & Rao, N. (1987). Voluntary hypometabolism in an Indian Yogi. In *Journal of Thermal Biology* 2: 171–73.
12. Thurman, R. (1999). Buddhist Psychology: Sophisticated Software for the Human Brain. In Dalai Lama, H. H., Benson., H., Gardner, H., et al. *Mind Science: An East West Dialogue*. Boston: Wisdom Publications; and Cozort, D. (1986). *Highest Yoga Tantra*. Ithaca: Snow Lion Press.
13. These practices are explained in the first chapters of Tsong Khapa's *Great Exposition of the Poetic Path*. See Hopkins, *Tantra*; Hopkins, *Deity Yoga*; and Hopkins, *Yoga Tantra*.

14. In the typology of tantric practice defined within the Gelukpa system codified by Tsong Khapa, there are four levels—action (*kriya*), performance (*cārya*), integral (*yoga*), and unexcelled integral (*anuttarayoga*)—we will mainly focus on practices belonging to the two lower levels of process practice. See Hopkins, *Tantra*, Vajra Vehicle.
15. This tradition has been adhered to by eminent Tibetan masters teaching in the West. See Sogyal Rinpoche. (1994). *The Tibetan Book of Living and Dying*. New York: HarperOne. Thundop, T. (1998). *Healing Power of Mind*. Boston: Shambhala; and Gelek Rinpoche, & Rosen, B. (2004). *The Tara Box: Rituals for Protection and Healing from the Female Buddha*. New York: New World Library.
16. Davidson and others explain the role of imagery in the regulation of emotion by the prefrontal cortex in terms of a shift in cerebral dominance from the negative affective avoidance style of the right hemisphere to the positive affective approach style of the left. See Davidson, R. (2000). Affective style, psychopathology and resilience: brain mechanisms and plasticity. In *American Psychologist*, 1196–1214.
17. See Klein, M. (1966). *Freud and Hypnosis: The Interaction of Psychodynamics and Hypnosis*. New York: Agora Press; and Freud, S. (2009). *The History of the Psychoanalytic Movement and the Origin and Development of Psychoanalysis*. New York: International Association of Psychoanalysis.
18. Loizzo, *Meditation and Psychotherapy*.
19. Depascalis, V., & Penna, P. (1990). 40-Hz EEG activity during hypnotic induction and hypnotic testing. In *International Journal of Clinical and Experimental Hypnosis*, 38: 125–38; and Sabourin, M., Cutomb, S., Crawford, H., et al. (1990). EEG correlates of hypnotic susceptibility and hypnotic trance: spectral analysis and coherence. In *International Journal of Psychophysiology*, 10: 125–42.
20. See Furst, L. (2008). *Hypnosis in Freud's Day. Before Freud: Hysteria and Hypnosis in Later Nineteenth-Century Psychiatric Cases*. Lewisberg: Bucknell Univeristy Press.
21. See Lazar, S., Kerr, C., Wasserman, R., et al. (2005). Meditation experience is associated with increased cortical thickness. In *Neuroreport*, 16(17): 1893–97; Davidson, R., Kabat-Zinn, J., & Schumacher et al. (2003). Alterations in brain and immune function produced by mindfulness meditation. In *Psychosomatic Medicine*, 65(4): 564–70; Stancak, A., & Kuna, M. (1994). EEG changes during forced alternate nostril breathing. In *International Journal of Psychophysiology*, 18: 75–79; Herzog, H., Lele, V., Kuwert, K., et al. (1991). Changed pattern of regional glucose metabolism during yoga meditative relaxation. In *Neuropsychobiology*, 23: 182–87.
22. Edgette, J., & Rowan, T. (2003). *Winning the Mind Game: Using Hypnosis in Sport Psychology*. New York: Crown House; Banyan, C., & Klein, G. (2001). *Hypnosis and Hypnotherapy: Basic to Advanced Techniques for the Professional*. New York: Abbot Press; Rossman, M. (2000). *Guided Imagery for Self-Healing*. New York: New World Library.
23. See Peachey, A., Gillen, J., Livingstone, D., et al. (eds.). (2011). *Researching Learning in Virtual Worlds*. Berlin: Springer Verlag; Zigmont, J., Kappus, L., & Sudikoff, S. (2011). Theoretical foundations of learning through simulation. In *Seminars in Perinatology*. April 35(2): 47–51; and Slovensky, D., & Morin, B. (1997). Learning through simulation: the next dimension in quality improvement. In *Quality Management in Health Care*, Spring 5(3): 72-79.
24. Llinas & Riary, (1998); and Llinas, R. (2002). *I of the Vortex: From Neurons to Self*. Cambridge: MIT Press.
25. For the power of mental imagery to "override" perception, see Kosslyn, S., et al. (2000). Hypnotic visual illusion alters color processing in the brain. In *American Journal of Psychiatry*, 157(8): 1279–84; and Bushell, W. (2009). Integrat-

ing Modern Neuroscience & Physiology with Indo-Tibetan Yogic Science. In Arnold, E. (ed.), *As Long as Space Endures: Essays in Honor of His Holiness the Dalai Lama*. Ithaca: Snow Lion Press.

26. See Spiegal, D. (2003). Negative and positive hypnotic hallucinations: Attending inside and out. In *International Journal of Clinical and Experimental Hypnosis*, 51(2): 130–46; Lamas, J., & Valle-Inclan, F. (1998). Effects of a negative hypnotic hallucination on ERP's and reaction times. In *International Journal of Psychophysiology*, 29(1): 77–82; and Kunzendorf, R. (1984). Centrifugal effects of eidetic imaging on flash electroretinograms and autonomic responses. In *Journal of Mental Imagery*, 8(4): 67–76.
27. See references in Kunzendorf, (1984); and Barabasz, A. (1982). Restricted environmental stimulation and the enhancement of hypnotizability: Pain, EEG alpha, skin conductance and temperature responses." In *Journal of Clinical and Experimental Hypnosis*, 30(2): 147–66.
28. See DePascalis, V., & Cacace, I. (2005). Pain perception, obstructive imagery and phase-ordered gamma oscillations. In *International Journal of Psychophysiology*, 56(2): 157–69; Spiegal (2003); and Szechtman, H., et al. (19980. Where the imaginal appears real: A positron emission tomography study of auditory hallucinations. In *Proceedings of the National Academy of Sciences*, USA, 95(4): 1956–60.
29. See chapter 5 in Kosslyn, S., Thompson, W., & Ganis, G. (2006). *The Case for Mental Imagery*. Oxford: Oxford University Press.
30. See Bushell, W. (2009); and Olivetti-Belardinelli, M., Palmiero, M., Sestieri, C., et al. (2009). An fMRI investigation on image generation in different sensory modalities: the influence of vividness. In *Acta Psychologica (Amst)*, October 132(2): 190–200.
31. See Edwards, D. & Potter, J. (2009). *Discursive Psychology*. New York: Sage; Gergen, K., & Gergen, M. (eds.), (2003). *Social Construction: A reader.* New York: Sage; and Searle, R. (1996). *The Construction of Social Reality*. New York: Penguin Books.
32. See Ruthig, J., Hanson, B., Pedersen, H., et al. (2011). Later life health optimism, pessimism and realism: Psychosocial contributors and health correlates. In *Psychology and Health*, January 1: 1–19.
33. See Bello, I., Steffen, J., & Hayashi, K. (2011). Cognitive motivational systems and life satisfaction in serious and persistent mental illness. In *Quality of Life and Resilience*, January 25; and Ein-Dor, T., Mikulincer, M., & Shaver, P. (2011). Attachment insecurities and the processing of threat-related information: Studying the schemas involved in insecure people's coping strategies. In *Journal of Personal and Social Psychology*, February 28.
34. See Meevissen, Y., Peters, M., & Alberts, H. (2011). Become more optimistic by imagining a best possible self: Effects of a two week intervention. In *Journal of Behavioral Therapy and Experimental Psychiatry*, March 2 42(3): 371-78.
35. This scholarly adaptation has been pioneered by Robert Thurman. See Thurman, R. (2010). *Brilliant Illumination of the Lamp of the Five Stages*. New York: American Institute of Buddhist Studies.
36. For a highly accessible popular introduction to this esoteric art, I often point students to Yeshe, T. (2001). *Introduction to Tantra*. London: Wisdom Publications.
37. The Sanskrti *Buddhāhaṃkāra* and *devatāhaṃkāra* are used interchangeably in the process-oriented literature.
38. Sanskrit: *Anātmatātma*.
39. In terms of the typology of pride in classical Buddhist psychology, the pride of ordinariness (*prākṛtāhaṃkāra, tha mal pa'i nga rgyal*) is closest to the pride of inferiority (*cung zad sñam pa'i nga rgyal*) I call the pride of shame. It expands

the modern concept of an "inferiority complex" or "core shame" or the "shame-based self" to include what we think of as normal self-esteem, since even a fairly positive, normal self-concept involves the negative narcissistic prejudice that we are not born with the natural potential for enlightened altruism or altruistic genius. The Noble Ăryadeva refers to this in his exposition of the practice of the *Esoteric Community Process*, "Further, this (body) of aggregates, elements and media which is predicated on beginningless ordinary pride is now taught to have a nature composed of the fine atoms of all transcendent lords." See Wedemeyer, *Lamp*, 153.

40. Jung, C. G. (1964). *The Art of Psychotherapy*. Princeton: Bollingen Press. For an eloquent contemporary introduction to this art, see the classic discussion of the personifying imagination in Hillman, J. (1976). *Revisioning Psychology*. New York: Harper and Row.
41. For an in-depth discussion of role of this art as the backbone of Tibetan Buddhist practice, see Dalai Lama, H. H. and Jinpa, T. (2009). *The Union of Bliss and Emptiness: Teachings of Guru Yoga*. Ithaca: Snow Lion Press, a commentary on a classic role-modeling practice in the Geluk tradition by the first Panchen Lama, Losang Chokyi Gyaltsan.
42. See Yancey, A., Grant, D., Kurosky, S., et al. (2011). Role modeling, risk, and resilience in California adolescents. In *Journal of Adolescent Health*, January 48(1): 36–43; and Kuutmann, K. and Hilsenroth, M. (2011). Exploring In-Session Focus on the Patient-Therapist Relationship: Patient Characteristics, Process and Outcome. In *Clinical Psychology and Psychotherapy*, March 2.
43. In a series of influential articles, Alexis Sanderson has used this term to describe both the Hindu and Buddhist Tantras. See Sanderson, A. (1985). Purity and Power among the Brahmans of Kashmir. In M. Carrithers et al. (eds.), *The Category of the Person: Anthropology, Philosophy, History*. Cambridge: Cambridge University Press; and Sanderson, A. (1994). Vajrayana: Origin and Function. In *Buddhism into the Year 2000: International Conference Proceedings*. Los Angeles: Dharmakaya Foundation. For a discussion, see Gray, D. (2007). *The Chakrasamvara Tantra: The Discourse of Śrī Heruka*. New York: American Institute of Buddhist Studies.
44. Traditionally, this approach defines the process practice of the Diamond Vehicle (*Vajrayāna*) as a fruitional effect-vehicle (*phala-yāna*) in contrast to the seminal cause-vehicle (*hetu-yāna*) of the engaged social practice of the ordinary Universal Vehicle (*Mahāyāna*). This distinction is elaborated in all the traditional literature, including Tsong Khapa's chapter, Vajra Vehicle, in Hopkins, *Tantra*.
45. Jung, *Psychotherapy*.
46. Kohut, H. (2009). *The Analysis of the Self: A Systematic Approach to the Psychoanalytic Treatment of Narcissistic Personality Disorders*. Chicago: University of Chicago Press.
47. Siegel, *Mindful Brain*.
48. The marks (*anuyañjana*) and signs (*lakṣaṇa*) of a universal being (*mahāpuruṣa*), typically numbered at eighty and thirty-two respectively, are represented in congruent ways in the iconography of the ordinary socially engaged tradition and the extraordinary process-oriented tradition. They are described in Nāgārjuna's *Jewel Rosary* (*Rantāvālī*), chapter two, as well as in the Noble Nāgārjuna's *Five Stages* (*Pañcakrama*). See Thurman, *Lamp*, 7–8.
49. Although Tsong Khapa in the fifteenth century could not have imagined the precise conditions of our age, in general, he was deeply involved in the modernization and democratization of Buddhist contemplative science envisioned in the *Kālachakra* tradition. This is clear in the way he tried to reform process-oriented education to serve as part of a socially cohesive culture for Tibet and

its highly active and individualistic people. One symbolic clue to his intention is the fact that when he set out to use the Chinese technology of block-printing to make the entire Indian Buddhist canon accessible to Tibetans with the help of his own corpus of introductory survey texts, the first work he had printed was his commentary on the *Illuminating Lamp* (*Pradipaddyotana*), the classical commentary attributed to Chandrakīrti which spelled out the way process-oriented teaching can be safely integrated within the Nālandā curriculum.

50. Codified in the initiatory rites of consecration which establish a mutual contract and set up the confidential bond which is the container for the practice. See Tsong Khapa's chapter, Preparation for Mantra, in Hopkins, *Tantra*. Berzin, A. (1997). *Taking the Kalachakra Initiation*. Ithaca: Snow Lion.
51. These are explicit in most introductions to process-oriented practice, including Hopkins, Tantra; and Lama Yeshe, *Introduction to Tantra*.
52. *Bhaiṣajyagūru* or *Bhaiṣajyarāja*. In a sense, this archetype has a special relationship to Tibetan Buddhism, since the history of the official importation of Buddhism into Tibet involved the fact that an Indian trained Buddhist doctor healed the queen of the King who later chose to sponsor that importation, Srongtsan Gampo. See Thondub, *Healing Power*, for a traditional introduction to the literature, see Birnbaum, R. (trans.) (2003). *The Healing Buddha*. Boston: Shambhala Press. For a traditional look at the practice, see Lama Zopa, & Too, L. (2001). *Ultimate Healing: The Power of Compassion*. Boston: Wisdom Publications; and see Crow, D. *Encountering the Healing Buddha* for a popular introduction to the role of this archetype.
53. In particular, I've mixed the simple encounter format of the action process practice presented by Thodub with the more popular, canonical version of the practice revolving around the seven (or eight) Healing Buddhas. The latter practice is essentially the rite of mentor-archetype bonding excerpted from the full optimal integral process practice of *Bhaiṣajyaūru*, which involves the *mandala* with thirty-eight archetypes depicted in the visual atlas of Tibetan Medicine. See Avadon, J., Bradley, T., & Gerasimova, K. (1998). *The Buddha's Art of Healing: Tibetan Paintings Rediscovered*. New York: Rizzoli Publications.
54. See Loizzo, J. Charlson, M., & Peterson, J. (2009). A Program in Self-Healing: Stress, Allostasis and Learning in the Indo-Tibetan Tradition. In Bushell, *Longevity*, 123-47.
55. See Lee, D. (2005). The Perfect Nurturer: A model to develop a compassionate mind within the context of cognitive therapy. In Gilbert, P. (ed.), *Compassion: Conceptualizations, Research and Use in Psychotherapy*. New York: Routledge, 326–351.
56. Though the steps or limbs of the sevenfold rite are usually translated with more standard ritualistic language (praise, offering, confession, congratulation, prayers, dedication), I prefer the less ritualistic and more psychologically precise colloquial terms since they help correct for a misleading analogy between this process and the communal ritualism typical of Western monotheistic worship.
57. For an object-relations approach to the transferential dimension of role-modeling practice, see Finn, M. (1992). Transitional space and Tibetan Buddhism: the object relations of meditation. In Finn, M., & Gartner, J. (eds.), *Object Relations Theory and Religion*. Westport: Praeger, 109-18.
58. Traditionally, the first line of interpretation—the analysis of the sevenfold offering (*śaptaṅgapūja*)—is presented separately from the other two lines, which serve to define the typology of practices within the esoteric (*guhya*), process, poetic or diamond vehicle (*tantrayāna*, *mantrayāna*, *vajrayāna*). This is largely to preserve the distinction between practices like the sevenfold offering that are common to both the socially engaged and process-oriented traditions, and

practices like the six session *yoga* (*ṣaṣṭaprahara-yoga*) which follow the sevenfold format but involve symbolism exclusive to the two higher levels of process-oriented practice: the integral and optimal integral process levels. The latter practice has been most widely elucidated in the context of the six session *yoga* of *Kālachakra*. See Berzin, A. (2011). *An Introduction to the Kalachakra Initiation*. Ithaca: Snow Lion Press.

59. These are: *kriya-tantra*, *cārya-tantra*, *yoga-tantra* and *anuttarayoga-tantra*, respectively. For descriptions, see Tsong Khapa's chapter on Method in the Four *Tantras*, in Hopkins, *Tantra*. The history of traditional Tantric scholarship has seen a handful of different typologies, some of which are still represented in the various systems preserved within the four schools of Tibetan Buddhism. The third class is often translated simply as "*yoga tantra*," which leads to confusion because one classification of optimal integral process practices divides them into father or method tantras and mother or wisdom tantras, often called *yogi* and *yoginī* tantras in the commentary on the mother optimal integral process practices such as the *Bliss Wheel*. See Grey, *Chakrasamvara*. Another source of confusion may be the various English translations of *anuttarayoga-tantra*, most commonly referred to more literally as "highest *yoga tantra*" or most literally as "unexcelled *yoga tantra*."
60. As we can see from the parallels between the sevenfold offering format and the six-session yoga format reserved for higher levels of process practice.
61. This contract is traditionally enacted in an initiatory ritual called "consecration" (*abhiṣeka*), which is the usual point of entry into the congenial bond of role-modeling. See Berzin, A. (2011). *Taking the Kālachakra Initiation*. Ithaca: Snow Lion Press.
62. Ebstein, R., Israel, S., Chew, S., et al. (2010). Genetics of human social behavior. In *Neuron*, March 25 65(6): 831–44; and Gilrath, O., Shaver, P. & Mikulincer, M. (2006). An attachment-theoretical approach to compassion and altruism. In Gilbert, *Compassion*, 121–47.
63. This art is elaborately described in the Dalai Lama's *Union of Bliss and Emptiness*.
64. An eloquent introduction to the art of confession using role-modeling imagery may be found in Yeshe, T. (2004). *Becoming Vajrasattva: The Tantric Path of Purification*. London: Wisdom Publications.
65. Sotres-Bayon, F., Christopher, K., Cain, C., et al. (2006). Brain mechanisms of fear extinction: Historical perspectives on the contribution of prefrontal cortex. In *Biological Psychiatry*, 60: 329–36; Phelps, E., Delgado, M., Nearing, K., et al. (2004). Extinction learning in humans: Role of the amygdale and vmPFC; Carr, L., Iacoboni, M., Dubeau, M., et al. (2003). Neural mechanisms of empathy in humans: A relay from neural systems for imitation to limbic areas. In *Proceedings of the National Academy of Sciences*, 100(9): 5497–5502; deWaal, F., & Preston, S. (2002). Empathy: Its ultimate and proximate bases. In *Behavioral and Brain Sciences*, 25: 1–20.
66. See Town, S., & McCabe, B. (2011). Neuronal plasticity and multisensory integration in filial imprinting. In *Public Library of Science One*, March 10, 6(3):e17777; and Grant, B., & Grant, P. (2010). Songs of Darwin's Finches Diverge Wwhen a New Species Enters the Community. In *Proceedings of the National Academy of Sciences*, November 23, 107(47): 20156–63.
67. See Cleary, T. (1978). *The Blue Cliff Record*. Boulder: Prajñā Press
68. Within the contemplative map of the nervous system, a recognition of the importance of the brain in neural processing is implied by calling the neural complex at the crown "the thousand petalled (lotus) complex" (*sahasrāracakra*).
69. In the traditional iconography we'll see in the visualization of the *Healing Mother, White Tara*, later in the chapter, the initiation or consecration of a

nascent or envisioned Buddha is depicted as the ritual act of goddesses pouring ambrosial nectar from all Buddhas into the crown of the nascent Buddha, until it is filled to overflowing.

70. This is implicit in the symbolism of totems like the Northwest Coast Native Americans, which consist of heads stacked one above the other, symbolizing the legacy passed down through ancestral generations. See Leach, E. (2010). *The Structural Study of Myth and Totemism*. London: Routledge.
71. The arts of immersing awareness in the sound of recitation and in the resonance after recitation are elaborately described in Tsong Khapa's discussion of the action and performance process. See Hopkins, *Deity Yoga*.
72. Skt: *Mantrayāna*. The term *mantra* is classically understood as divine, world-creative speech, as we can see from a related term *bījamantra*, reserved for the memic or semiotic essence of such speech. This emphasis on world-creative the power of speech is even more emphasized in the Vedic tradition, especially as expressed in the Upaniṣadic and Hindu Tantric cults of mantra recitation that have so influenced the Indian tradition, as reflected in popularized practices like Hatha yoga and Transcendental Meditation. See Padoux, A. (2011). *Tantric Mantras: Studies on Mantrasastra*. London: Routledge; and the philosophy of Bartṛhari in Isayeva, N. (1995). *From Early Vedanta to Kashmiri Shaivism*. Albany: State University of New York Press.
73. See Grossman, A. (1981). *Against Our Vanishing: Winter Conversations with Allen Grossman on the Theory and Practice of Poetry*. Boston: Rowan Tree Press.
74. This is why the state of flow at this point in the role-modeling process of mentor-bonding is typically used as the platform for the process-oriented meditation on emptiness, traditionally framed as the practice of the great seal (*mahāmudrā*), to be discussed in part 4. See Dalai Lama and Berzin, *Mahamudra*.
75. This unique efficacy makes process-oriented practices the definitive technology for cultivating altruism recognized within this tradition. In fact, this distinction is the source of one of the many names of this tradition, as the vehicle of method, technique or empathic art (*upāya-yāna*). This point is reiterated in all introductions to the process-oriented path, as reflected in Tsong Khapa's *Great Stages*. See the Dalai Lama's explanation in the chapter, Vajrayana, and Tsong Khapa's, Method in the Four Tantras, as well as the appendix of Quintessential Points, listing key distinctions of process methods in Hopkins, *Tantra*.
76. For a clear survey of the traditional map of path according to the optimal integral process, see Cozort, D. (1986). *Highest Yoga Tantra*. Ithaca: Snow Lion Press.
77. For Tsong Khapa's in depth discussion of the classical optimal integral map attributed to Nāgārjuna, see Thurman, *Lamp*. I say "attributed" here since modern scholars have contested the traditional claim that the authors or process-oriented classics like *The Five Stages (Pañcakrama)* and the *Illuminating Lamp* (*Pradīpoddyotana*) were the same individuals as the authors of the socially engaged classics like *Jewel Rosary* (*Ratnāvalī*) and *Central Way Introduction (Madhayamāvatara)*. For a recent discussion of this issue informed by traditional Tibetan scholarship, see Wedemeyer (2001).
78. Kosslyn, S., et al. (2006), *Mental Imagery*.
79. This shift is an extension of the shift in affective response modes from right-sided avoidance styles to left-sided approach styles, as documented in Davidson (2000) and Davidson et al. (2003); Nitschke, J., Nelson, E., Rusch, B., et al. (2004). Orbitofrontal cortex tracks positive mood in mothers viewing pictures of their newborn infants. In *Neuroimage*, 21: 583–92.
80. See the role of the "visual buffer," "object-spatial properties processing" and "associative memories" in Kosslyn's evidence-based model of imagery and perception; Kosslyn, *Mental Imagery*, 134–73.

81. See note 37, above.
82. Technically, the term "*maṇḍala-vijaya*" describes the final fruition of the entire creation stage—coase and subtle—in the capacity to use coarse and subtle role-modeling imagery to override ordinary conceptions and perceptions of both self and others, the outer and inner worlds.
83. There is good evidence to support our potential to "override" of ordinary perception in all modalities with mental imagery—visual, auditory, gustatory, olfactory and tactile. See Depascalis and Cacace (2005); Spiegel (2003); Anbar, R. (2002). You don't like the taste of your meditation? So change the taste! In *Clinical Pediatrics*, 41(3): 197–99; Szechtman, 1998; Dadds, M. (1997). Imagery in human classical conditioning. In *Psychological Bulletin*, 122(1): 89–103; and Barbasz, A., & Lonesdale, C. (1983). Effects of hypnosis on P300 olfactory evoked potential amplitudes. In *Journal of Abnormal Psycholgy*, 93: 234–36.
84. To define this synonym Tsong Khapa quotes this key passage from the *Esoteric Community Process* (*Guhyasamajatantra*), chapter XVIII, 69c–71b, In Hopkins, *Tantra*, 106 "Minds arising dependent on a sense and an object are said to be *man*, *tra* means protection. Protection by means of all adamantine commitments and pledges explained, free from the (ordinary) ways of the world, is called "the (poetic) practice of *mantra*."; Hopkins' translation with minor revisions by the author, including the substitution of "adamantine" for the untranslated "*vajra*."
85. See Davidson, (2000). This expands on a general model of balanced laterality as a general mechanism shared by meditation and psychotherapy, see Delmonte, M. (1995). Meditation and the Unconscious. In *Journal of Contemporary Psychotherapy*, 25: 223–42.
86. See Banyan & Klein, *Hypnosis and Hypnotherapy*.
87. See Porges, S. (2011). *Polyvagal Theory*. New York: Norton & Company, 58.
88. The complex links between facial expressions, emotions and the autonomic nervous system have been explored by several key figures, including: Tomkins, S. (1962/3). *Affect, Imagery, Consciousness*. Vol. 1: Positive Affects/Vol.2: Negative Affects. New York: Springer; Ekman, P. (1978). *Facial Action Coding System: A Technique for the Measurement of Facial Movement*. Palo Alto: Consulting Psychologists Press; Izard, C. (1979). *The Maximally Discriminative Facial Movement Coding System*. Newark: University of Delaware Instructional Resource Center; and Ekman, P., Levenson, R., & Freisen, W. (1983). Autonomic nervous system activity distinguishes among emotions. In *Science*, 221: 1208–10; Eberl, E. (2010). Control of gestures and vocalizations in primates. In Brudzynski, S. (ed.), *Handbook of Mammalian Vocalization: An Integrative Neuroscience Approach*. Amsterdam: Elsevier Press.
89. Sanskrit: *asādārana-purvagama*.
90. Although I share this practice mainly based on the teaching of Ngawang Gelek Rinpoche, I've combined and simplified elements from several of the traditional meditations he teaches. See Gehlek Rimpoche, N. (1998). *Teachings of the Triumphant Ma*. Ann Arbor: Jewel Heart Transcripts. In addition, to illustrate the work of the subtle creation stage and for the sake of consistency within the range of practices in this book, I've aligned the imagery of *Healing Mother* with the classical format of the *Esoteric Community* body-*mandala* built into the most common introductory practice of role-modeling imagery in the Gelukpa tradition, the *Art of Mentor-Bonding* (*Gūrupūja*), by Lobsang Chokyi Gyaltsan. See Dalai Lama, & Jinpa, T. (2009), *Union of Bliss and Emptiness*; or, for a more literal commentary, Gyatso, K. (1990). *Great Treasury of Merit*. London: Tharpa Publications.
91. Hopkins, *Tantra*, 109.

92. Cited in Ăryadeva's *Lamp that Integrates the Practices* (*Cāryamelāpakapradīpa*), translated in Wedmeyer, *Aryadeva's Lamp*, 153.
93. *Adarśajñāna, samatāñāna, partyavekṣanajñāna, kṛtyakārajñāna, dharmadhatūjñāna*. There are many process practices which feature this alchemical model of transforming the five toxic systems with the help of the five intuitive wisdoms, notably the classical text, *Chanting the Names of Sheer Brilliance* (*Mañjuśrīnamasaṃgīti*) and the lower level practices of the Sun-Gold *Sheer Brilliance* (*Mañjuśri*) and the *Transcendent Wisdom Goddess* (*Prajñāparāmitā*). See Wayman, A. (1999). *Chanting the Names of Mañjuśrī*. New Delhi: Motilal Barnasidas, which defines *Mañjuśrī* in V.18 as "the lord who personifies the five intuitions" (*pañcajñānātmako vibhuḥ*). Chapters V-X of the text cover the five intuitive wisdoms, one at a time.
94. A very elegant and accessible introduction to this alchemical model may be found in Govinda, A. (1976). *Foundations of Tibetan Mysticism*. New York: Samuel Weiser Press.
95. The body *mandala* of Chokyi Gyaltsan's *Art of Mentor-Boding*, for instance, locates the five meditational Buddhas (*Dhyāni-Buddhas*)—the *Illuminator* (*Vairocana*), *Jewel Mine* (*Ratnasambhava*), *Infinite Light* (*Amitābha*), *Accomplished* (*Amogasiddhi*), and *Immovable* (*Akṣobhya*)—with their consorts at the neural complexes of the crown, throat, heart, navel, and pelvis. See Dalai Lama, & Jinpa, T., *Union of Bliss and Emptiness*, op. cit.
96. Where seed-syllables are abbreviated into the vertical lines or bars that serve as the main form of punctuation in both the Sanskrit and Tibetan script.
97. Skt: *sadhana*, a term which has the dual connotations of the text or script which guides imagery or other process practices and of the practice itself, as does the word *tantra*, literally "loom" or "weaving," which I translate with "process." So Tsong Khapa says, "All three (basis, path, and fruit processes) are *tantras* in the sense of being objects of discussion (in books called *tantras*). A scripture taking any of these as its object of discussion is called a 'book *tantra*' discussing (such subjects)," in Hopkins, *Tantra*, 109.

Chapter 8: The Art and Science of Reconstructing Life

1. Yarnall, T. (trans.) (2011). *Tsong Khapa's Great Stages of Mantra: The Creation Stage*. New York: American Institute of Buddhist Studies. Please note: since this invaluable work is still in publication at the time of this writing, the text and page numbers of my citations from it are actually from the version of Yarnall's translation found in his brilliant doctoral dissertation, Yarnall, T. (2006). *The Emptiness that is Form*. Ann Arbor: University of Michigan Dissertation Services, 581.
2. Yarnall, *Emptiness*, 543.
3. Scherwitz, L., Graham, L., Grandits, G., et al. (1986). Self-involvement and coronary heart disease incidence in the multiple risk factor intervention trial. In *Journal of Psychosomatic Medicine* 84(314): 187–59.
4. Loizzo, J., Blackhall, L., & Rabgyay, L. (2009). Tibetan Medicine: A Complementary Science of Optimal Health. In Bushell, W., Olivo, E. & Thiese, N. (eds.), *Longevity, Regeneration and Optimal Health: Integrating Eastern and Western Perspectives*. New York: New Your Academy of Sciences.
5. McEwen, B., & Gianaros, P. (2010). Central role of the brain in stress and adaptation: links to socioeconomic status, health, and disease. In *Annals of the New York Academy of Science*, February 1,186: 190–222.
6. See Vahia, I., Chattillion, E., Kavirajan H., et al. (2011). Psychological protective factors across the lifespan: implications for psychiatry. In *Psychiatric Clinics of*

North America, March 3, 4(1): 231–48; and Ruthig, J., Hanson, B., Pedersen, H., et al. (2011). Later life health optimism, pessimism and realism: Psychosocial contributors and health correlates. In *Psychological Health*, January 1: 1–19.

7. Lati Rinpoche, & Hopkins, J. (1985). *Death, Intermediate State and Rebirth in Tibetan Buddhism*. Ithaca: Snow Lion Press.
8. Loizzo, J. (2011). The Intergenerational Transmission of Agency: Evolutionary Psychology or Religious Belief? In *Sophia*, 50(3): 429–52.
9. On the three "lower" levels of process practice—action, performance and integral—the process is not divided into stages of creation versus perfection, but into aspects of practice, namely: constructive or symbolic (*sanimitta*) versus deconstructive or non-symbolic (*animatta*), usually translated as "with signs" and "without signs." In this context, the imagery of the constructive phase may be seen as mainly fostering vivid appearance and planting seeds for the conversions of development and life into the embodiment of enjoyment and emanation; while the deconstructive phase mainly fosters enlightened dignity and plants seeds for the conversion of death into the embodiment of truth. Of course, the two forms of practice—with and without signs—are defined somewhat differently within each of the three introductory process systems; and the difference between these practices and those which make up the creation and perfection stages of the optimal integral process is even greater. For the purpose of understanding the psychology of these practices, I've avoided these fine distinctions and tried to convey their ultimate intent as elaborated in the optimal integral process, following the strategy of the Ărya commentarial tradition and the *Kālachakratantra*. See Dalai Lama & Hopkins, *Deity Yoga*, 189–203; and Dalai Lama & Hopkins, *Yoga Tantra*, 82–109.
10. Yarnall, *Emptiness*, 502.
11. The classical format here is found in Losang Chogyi Gyaltsan's *Practice of Mentor-Bonding (bLa-ma Chod-pa'i cho ga)*. See Dalai Lama, H. H., & Jinpa, T. (2009). *The Union of Bliss and Emptiness: Teachings on the Practice of Guru Yoga*. Ithaca: Snow Lion Press.
12. Fosha, D. (2009). Positive Affects and the Transformation of Suffering into Flourishing. In Bushell et al., *Longevity*.
13. White, M., & Epston, D. (1990). *Narrative Means to Therapeutic Ends*. New York: W.W.Norton & Co.
14. Freedman, J., & Combs, G. (1996). *Narrative Therapy: The Social Construction of Preferred Realities*. New York: W.W. Norton & Co.
15. Berger, P., & Luckmann, T. (1966). *The Social Construction of Reality*. New York: Doubleday Books, 89. Quoted in Freedman & Combs, *Narrative Therapy*, 25.
16. Winnicott, D. W. (1990). *Home is Where We Start From: Essays by a Psychoanalyst*. New York: W.W. Norton & Co.
17. Berzin, A. (2011). *Introduction to the Kalachakra Initiation*. Ithaca: Snow Lion Press.
18. While this fourfold initiation, based on the *Esoteric Communion* (*Guhyasamaja*) tradition, follows the paradigm of optimal integral process consecration, the rites that govern entry into the action, performance and integral process practices differ. In particular, action and performance process rites involve five knowledge consecrations called water, crown, scepter, bell and name, the last three of which are often reserved for performance process rites. In addition to these five, integral and optimal integral process rites include a vajra master consecration, which involves taking tantric vows (in addition to sutric, bodhisattva vows) for the first time and plants the seed for our being able to give process teachings to others. Finally, the optimal integral process practices combine the five knowledge consecrations and vajra master consecration within a single

consecration called the vase, and add three higher consecrations called secret, intuitive wisdom and word. This is the fourfold format followed in our meditative experiments. Though this *Guhyasamaja* format for entry into the optimal integral process differs somewhat from the sevenfold *Kālachakra* format described by Berzin (see preceding note), the two assume similar views of the mentor-student bond and the path of optimal integral practice. See Dalai Lama and Hopkins, *Deity Yoga*, 15–18; and Cozort, D. (1986). *Highest Yoga Tantra.* Ithaca: Snow Lion Press, 34–36.

19. Compare Winnicott's notion of the "holding environment" as recapitulating the interpersonal space defined by the boundary between the family and the outside world: Winnicott, D. W. (1992). *The Child, the Family and the Outside World.* New York: Perseus Publishing; and Winnicott, D., & Kahn, M. (1994). *Holding and Interpretation: Fragment of an Analysis.* New York: Grove Press
20. For a look at the traditional iconography of the *maṇḍala*, see Brauen, M. (1997). *The Mandala: Sacred Circle in Tibetan Buddhism.* Boston: Shambhala Publishers; and Rhie, M., & Thurman, R. (1991). *Wisdom and Compassion: The Sacred Art of Tibet.* New York: Harry N. Abrams, Inc.
21. This iconography seems to have entered the Buddhist Tantras from the Kāpālika cults of the Shaivite Tantras, via the Mother or Yoginī Tantras like Hevarjra and Cakrasamvara, from where they find their way into synthetic optimal integral systems like Yamāntaka and Kālachakra. See Gray, D. (2007). *The Cakrasamvara Tanta: The Discourse of Śrī Heruka.* New York: American Institute of Buddhist Studies. (Hencefroth: Gray, *Cakrasamvara.*)
22. Dawa Samdup, K., & Evans-Wentz, W. (eds.). (1957). *The Tibetan Book of the Dead, or the After Death Experience on the "Bardo" Plane.* New York: Oxford University Press.
23. Jung, C. G. (1935/1978). Psychological Commentary on the Tibetan Book of the Dead. In Hull, R. (trans.). *Psychology and the East.* Princeton: Princeton University Press Bollingen Series, 59–76. The commentary initially appeared in the first German translation of Padmasambhava's *Bardo Thodol* by Louise Gopfert-March and was later translated by Hull and included in the third edition of the first English translation (see preceding note).
24. Padmasambhava, Thurman, R. (trans.), & Dalai Lama, H. H. (1993). *The Tibetan Book of the Dead (The Great Book of Liberation Through Understanding in the Between).* New York: Bantam Books.
25. See Lati & Hopkins, *Death, Intermediate State & Rebirth.*
26. Ibid.
27. For that map, see Lati & Hopkins, *Death, Intermediate State & Rebirth*, 38–48. My simplification involves two steps. First, instead of the eighty natural structures or instinctive impulses (*svabhāvavikalpa*) dissolving all at once in a fifth dissolution which is followed by the dissolutions of the three luminous intuitions (*āloka-jñāna*) and the clear light (*prabhāsvara*), I've aligned the three classes of impulses with the three intuitions, eliminating the fifth dissolution. Second, though the three classes each include a range of impulses—positive and negative, erotic, aggressive and cognitive—I've aligned each with the three root compulsions and their antidotes, according to the root compulsion from which the preponderance of impulses in each class is derived.
28. This is a variant method of cultivating the four bliss-voids in the *Esoteric Communion* perfection stage, to be explored in part 4.
29. Especially in optimal integral process practices of the mother class, such as Cakrasamvara. See Gray, *Cakrasamvara*; and Gyatso, K. (1991). *Guide to Dakini Land: The Highest Yoga Tantra Practices of Buddha Vajrayogini.* London: Tharpa.
30. Rank, O. (1958). *Beyond Psychology.* New York: Dover Books.

31. See Klemenc-Ketis, Z., Kersnik, J., & Grmec, S. (2010). The effect of carbon dioxide on near-death experiences in out-of-hospital cardiac arrest survivors: a prospective observational study. In *Critical Care*, 14(2): R56; Beauregard, M., Courtemanche, J. & Paquette, V. (2009). Brain activity in near-death experiencers during a meditative state. In *Resuscitation*, September, 80(9): 1006–10; and Parnia, S., Spearpoint, K., & Fenwick, P. (2007). Near death experiences, cognitive function and psychological outcomes of surviving cardiac arrest. In *Resuscitation*, August 74(2): 215–21.
32. In particular, the induction of primary, image-based processing involves a shift from our primary, verbal analytic mode and life hemisphere dominance towards a more balanced or right-sided cortical dominance. See Davidson, R., Kabat-Zinn, J., Schumacher, J., et al. (2003). Alterations in brain and immune function produced by mindfulness meditation. In *Psychosomatic Medicine*, 65(4): 564–70; and Earle, J. (1984). Cerebral laterality and meditation: a review. In Shapiro, D. & Walsh, R. (eds.), *Meditation: Classics and Contemporary Perspectives*. New York: Adeline, 171–90.
33. This experience forms the basis of the method presented by Padmasambhāva as the Teachings of Great Liberation; see Thurman, *Tibetan Book of the Dead*. It also overlaps with what early meditation researchers like Banquet called "the pure consciousness experience;" see Banquet, J. (1973). EEG in meditation. In *Electroencephalography and Clinical Neurophysiology*, 35: 143–51; and, for a scholar's perspective, see Foreman, R. (1997). *The Problem of Pure Consciousness*. Oxford: Oxford University Press.
34. For the way this architecture is depicted in the *Kālacakratantra*, see Brauen, *Mandala*.
35. The tantric skull-bowl (*kāpālika*) cult of the cremation grounds is especially associated with the Kashmiri Shaivite Tantras and the Buddhist optimal integral practices of the mother class like Hevajra and Cakrasamvara. See Shaw, M. (1990). *Passionate Enlightenment: Women in Tantric Buddhism*. Princeton: Princeton University Press; and Grey, *Chakraśamvara*.
36. Images like as the famous sand maṇḍala of Kālacakra are in effect architectural blueprints for the mental construction of such a virtual residence, as in the celestial mansion of Kālacakra. See Brauen, *Mandala*.
37. Such as the solitary hero (*ekavīra*) form of *Vajrabhairava* or the solitary heroine (*ekavīrinī*) form of *Vajrayoginī*. See Gyatso, Guide to *Dakini Land*.
38. Lati & Hopkins, *Death, Intermediate State and Rebirth*, 49–57.
39. Technically, this re-constructive process is described differently within the action, performance and integral process, though I've confined my presentation here to the optimal integral sequence, for the sake of consistency and simplicity. The first two follow a sequence of six geniuses or divinities (*devatā*), called the ultimate, sound, syllable, form, seal and symbolic geniuses. The integral process follows the sequence of the five pure enlightenments, though defined somewhat differently than in the optimal integral process, namely, as the rites of mind, hero, concentration, scepter and master altruist. For the six deity sequence, see Dalai Lama & Hopkins, *Deity Yoga*, 19–35; for the integral process five rites, see Dalai Lama and Hopkins, *Yoga Tantra*, 34–56.
40. The range of variations on this theme are reviewed by Tsong Khapa in the Creation Stage section (chapter 13) of his *Great Stages of the Poetic Path*, where he settles on a reading aligning the five enlightenments with the five intuitions. See Yarnall, *Emptiness*, 570–79.
41. The scientific teaching tradition, in all its forms, has consistently seen transition states like the intermediate state (*anantara-bhāva*) and contemplative states as both supported by a subtle material body (*sukṣma-rūpa-śarira*), akin to the

dream-body (*svapna-śarira*) of the normal sleep cycle or the subtle body of apparitional beings (*upapaduka*) living hellish or heavenly forms of life.

42. Berger & Luckman, *Social Construction*, 37–39.
43. Weingarten, K. (1991). The Discourses of intimacy: Adding a social constructionist and feminist view. In *Family Process*, 30: 285–305. As quoted in Freedman and Coombs, *Narrative Therapy*, 17.
44. For Tsong Khapa's review of the literature and discussion of the numerology and symbolism of the vowels and consonants, see Yarnall, *Emptiness*, 570–77.
45. This may be compared with the shift highlighted in affective therapies like Fosha's ADP, see note 12, above.
46. This shift is emphasized in the holding and mirroring phases of relational therapy and self-psychology. See note 19, above.
47. This shift features prominently in the reconstructive work of narrative therapy. See White and Epston, *Narrative Means to Therapeutic Ends*.
48. This may be compared with the social transformational work of narrative, marital and family therapy, as described in Freedman and Coombs, *Narrative Therapy*, chapters 4–6.
49. This shift may be compared with the personal integration work of Jungian therapies and the social integration described by Freedman and Combs, *Narrative Therapy*, chapters 7–10.
50. Siegel, D. (2007). *The Mindful Brain*. New York: W.W. Norton & Co, especially Appendix III, 337–62.
51. Yarnall, *Emptiness*, 579.
52. I suggest the fierce form of the wisdom goddess in this context, unlike the more conventional peaceful form we'll experiment with below, since her chopper and skull-bowl are central to the alchemical symbolism of sublimation which figures so prominently in the optimal integral creation stage.
53. The heart of action and performance process practices revolves around what are called the four branches of recitation: (1) the self-base, re-creating yourself in the image of a genius archetype; (2) the other-base, envisioning a personal encounter with a mentor-archetype before you; (3) the mind, that is, a mind realizing emptiness which appears in the form of a moon-disc at the heart of your mentor (and yourself); and (4) the sounds, that is, the syllables of the mantra envisioned circling the rim of the moon disc(s). These four branches support the main purpose of the lower tantras: to build quiescence and analytic insight in the same spirit as the exoteric, engaged path of altruism, only by means of a more powerful meditative technology. The gist of that technology is that you meditate not just on an object, such as the emptiness of persons or things, but also on the subjectivity that realizes emptiness, which assumes the form of a genius archetype and in turn is seen to be empty. Constructive techniques like holding the breath while focusing single-mindedly on your vivid appearance and enlightened dignity as the archetype enhance concentration; while deconstructive techniques like analyzing the six geniuses back down to the clear light mind enhance analytic insight. These are further aided by three main affirmation practices: reciting the affirmation (subvocally and mentally) at the mentor's heart; reciting it (in both ways) at your heart; and hearing it resonate on a subtle level without recitation, as the impersonal sound of the syllables placed within a flame at your heart, heard from the standpoint of your mind immersed in that same flame. The last of these practices involves three aspects: abiding in fire deepens concentration; abiding in impersonal sound fosters quiescence and flow; and abiding in freedom at the end of sound sharpens transcendent insight. Collectively, these power tools speed the engaged path of altruism up to the path of insight. From that point on, further advanced requires the sublimation techniques of the optimal integral process. See Hopkins, *Deity Yoga*, 19–35.

54. This link has been most explicit in the Tantric tradition of Kaśmiri Shaivism, and commented on by scholars and translators including Alexis Sanderson and Daniel Ingalls. See Ingalls, D. (1972). *Sanskrit Poetry.* Cambridge: Harvard University Press; and Ingalls, D., & Masson, J., Patwardhan, M. (1990). *The Dvanyaloka of Anandavardana with the Locana of Abhinavagupta.* Cambridge: Harvard University Press.
55. Dalai Lama & Hopkins, *Deity Yoga.*
56. The related body language of facial expressions has been elaborately described by affective neuropsychology in recent years. See Ekman, P. (2007). *Emotions Revealed, Second Edition: Recognizing Faces and Feelings to Improve Communication and Emotional Life.* New York: Holt Paperbacks.
57. Fosha, D., Siegel, D., & Solomon, M. (eds.). (2009). *The Healing Power of Emotion: Affective Neuroscience, Development and Clinical Practice.* New York: W.W. Norton & Co.

Chapter 9: Living Altruism through Impassioned Vision

1. Thurman, R. (2011). *Brilliant Illumination of the Lamp of the Five Stages.* New York: American Institute of Buddhist Studies, 532.
2. Thurman, *Lamp*, 521.
3. Ibid., 534.
4. Bodhi, Bikkhu (trans.). (2000). *Setting the Wheel of Dharma in Motion (Dhammachakkappavattana-sutta)*, in *The Connected Discourses of Buddha.* Boston: Wisdom Publications, 1843–46 (with minor revisions by J. Loizzo).
5. Thurman, *Lamp*, 534–35.
6. See Hopkins, J., Dalai Lama, H. H., & Tsong Khapa. (1987). *Tantra in Tibet.* Ithaca: Snow Lion Press, 106.
7. Thurman, *Lamp*, 521–22.
8. This insight is especially clear in the transformational view of life presented within the *Wheel of Time* (*Kālacakra*) scientific tradition, as elegantly explained in Wallace, V. (2001). *The Inner Kālacakratanta.* Oxford: Oxford University Press. Robert Thurman also alludes to this insight in his more popular work on the process sciences, including R. Thurman (trans.). (1994). *The Tibetan Book of the Dead: Liberation Through Understanding in the Between.* New York: Bantam Books; and Thurman, R. (1999). Tibetan Psychology: Sophisticated Software for the Human Brain. In Dalai Lama, H. H., Benson, H., Gardner, H. et al., *Mind Science: An East-West Dialogue.* Boston: Wisdom Publications.
9. This exercise is based on the lucid teaching and performance script of Lama Thubten Yeshe. See Yeshi, T. (2004). *Becoming Vajrasattva: The Tantric Path of Purification.* Boston: Wisdom Publications.
10. For a look at the ten qualifications of a process mentor, see Dhargyey, N. (1978). *Tibetan Tradition of Mental Development.* Dharmasala: Library of Tibetan Works and Archives, 223–30.
11. For an extensive presentation, see Tsong Khapa, 2005. *Tantric Ethics: An Explanation of the Precepts for Buddhist Vajrayana Practice.* London: Wisdom Publications; and Dudjom Rinpoche, H. H. (1996). *Perfect Conduct: Ascertaining the Three Vows.* Somerville: Wisdom Publications, 110–47.
12. As we've said, rites of initiation or consecration (*abhiṣeka*) vary widely across different levels of process practice as well as different systems of practice within the same levels. For a brief overview of the various rites in the three introductory process systems, see Dalai Lama, H. H., Tsong Khapa, & Hopkins, J. (1981). *Deity Yoga in Action and Performance Tantra.* Ithaca: Snow Lion Press, 15–18; and for a brief presentation of the classical fourfold rite of the optimal integral

process, see Cozort, D. (1986). *Highest Yoga Tantra*. Ithaca: Snow Lion Press, 34–36. The most extensive published discussions of process initiation rites are made in the context of the distinctive optimal integral process tradition of the *Kālacakra*. Most of these, like Dalai Lama, H. H. (1999). *Kalachakra Tantra: Rite of Initiation*. Somerville: Wisdom Publications, cover only the first sevenfold rite; for a complete discussion, see Lamrimpa, G. (1999). *Transcending Time: The Kālacakra Six Session Yoga*. Somerville: Wisdom Publications, 88–140.

13. And there we'll also review the evidence for the efficacy of process methods in supporting conscious self-regulation of vital mind/body processes based in the midbrain and brainstem. For physiological findings on high arousal practices from the Buddhist and Hindu Tantras, see Corby, J., Roth, W., Zarcone, V., et al. (1978). Psychophysiological correlates of the practice of tantric yoga. In *Archives of General Psychiatry*, 35: 571–77; Benson H., et al, (1990). Three case reports of the metabolic and electroencephalogaphic changes during advanced Buddhist meditation techniques. In *Behavioral Medicine* 16(2): 90–95; and Heller, C., Elsner, R., & Rao, N. (1987). Voluntary hypometabolism in an Indian Yogi. *Journal of Thermal Biology*, 2:171–73. For two recent studies on the physiology of euphoric states in meditation, see Harte, J., Eifert, G., & Smith, R. (1995). The effects of running and meditation on beta-endorphin, corticotropin-releasing hormone and cortisol in plasma, and on mood. In *Biological Psychology*. June, 40(3):251-65; and Infante, J., Peran, F., Martinez, M, et al. (1998). ACTH and beta-endorphin in transcendental meditation. In *Physiology and Behavior*, 64: 311–15.

    For a discussion of the self-regulation of internal reward, see Loizzo, J. (2000). Meditation and Psychotherapy: Stress, Allostasis and Enriched Learning. In P. Muskin (ed.), *Complementary and Alternative Medicine and Psychiatry*. Annual Revue of Psychiatry, Vol. 19, No.1. Washington DC: American Psychiatric Association Press; and Loizzo, J. (2009). Optimizing Learning and Quality of Life Throughout the Lifespan. In Bushell, W., Olivo, E., & Thiese, N. 2009. *Longevity, Regeneration and Optimal Health*. New York: New York Academy of Sciences.

14. For a clear and concise introduction to the perfection stage, see Cozort, *Highest Yoga Tantra*.
15. This stage is the gateway to the practice traditionally called the Great Seal or *Mahāmūdra*. See Dalai Lama, H. H. & Berzin, A. (1997). *The Geluk/Kagyu Tradition of Mahamudra*. Ithaca: Snow Lion Press. The same practice is also the source of the sister practice tradition of the Great Perfection (*Mahānispanna/Dzogchen*), within the Nyingma school of Tibetan Buddhism. See Dalai lama, H. H. & Sogyal Rinpoche. (2004). *Dzogchen: The Heart Essence of Great Perfection*. Ithaca: Snow Lion Press.
16. This poses a potent challenge to preconceived notions of religious experience in general and process practice in particular as completely transcending language, literally ineffable or "mystical." For a brilliant, in depth discussion of this question in light of contemporary religious scholarship, see Yarnall, T. (2006). *The Emptiness that is Form*. Ann Arbor: University of Michigan Dissertation Services.
17. For a recent review, see Ericsson, A. Kiruthiga, N., & Roring, R. (2009). Toward a Science of Exceptional Achievement: Attaining Superior Performance Through Deliberate Practice. In Bushell et al., *Longevity*.
18. For an introduction to the emerging concept of social enterprise, see Bornstein, D., & Davis, S. (2010). *Social Entrepreneurship: What Everyone Needs to Know*. Oxford: Oxford University Press.
19. For an intriguing look at the unique strategy of the Indian Tantras and its historic distortion in Western scholarship, see Urban, H. (2011). *Tantra: Sex,*

Secrecy, Politics and Power in the Study of Religion. Berkeley: University of California Press.

20. See Bucknell, R., & Stuart-Fox, M. (1995). *Twilight Language*. London: Routledge.
21. For the classic history of Western Hermeticism, see Yates, F. (1991). *Giordano Bruno and the Hermetic Tradition*. Chicago: University of Chicago Press. For a similar art in the Sufi tradition, see Corbin, H. (1969). *Creative Imagination in the Sufism of Ibn Arabi*. Princeton: Princeton University Press.
22. Some believe they may have been largely indigenous to India while others suspect they were brought by Sanskrit-speaking Aryan tribes that migrated from Central Asia to the subcontinent. See Sanderson, A. (1985). Purity and Power among the Brahmans of Kashmir. In M. Carrithers et al. (eds.), *The Category of the Person: Anthropology, Philosophy, History*. Cambridge: Cambridge University Press; and Sanderson, A. (1994). Vajrayana: Origin and Function. In *Buddhism into the Year 2000: International Conference Proceedings*. Los Angeles: Dharmakaya Foundation. For a discussion, see Grey, D. (2007). *The Chakrasamvara Tantra: The Discourse of Śrī Heruka*. New York: American Institute of Buddhist Studies; and Padoux, A. (2011). *Tantric Mantras: Studies on Mantrasastra*. London: Routledge.
23. There are numerous passages within the principal *Upaniṣads* which clearly suggest a tradition of selective restriction of secret teachings to specific students at specific stages of development, such as *Bṛhadarṇyaka*, 6.3.12; though the most explicit is found at the end of the *Śvetaśvtara*, 6.21–23, which recommends that a good teacher teach the most advanced stages of "purification" only to specific students with devotion to a mentor "as for God." See Hume, R. (1995). *The Thirteen Principal Upanishads*. Delhi: Oxford University Press, 411.
24. The seven ornament (*śaptālaṃkāra*) system was codified in the *Illuminating Lamp* (*Pradīpoddyotana*) attributed to Ărya Chandrakīrti. See Campbell, J. (2009). *Vajra Hermeneutics: A Study of Vajrayana Scholasticism in the "Pradipoddyotana"*. Ann Arbor: University of Michigan Dissertation Services. As with the other figures of the Ărya commentarial tradition, based on the *Guhyasamajatantra*, Western scholars have contest the traditional identification of Chandrkīrti the process adept with Chandrakīrti the centrist philosopher. A critical analysis of this question based on critically reviewing modern Western and traditional Tibetan scholarship on the Buddhist Tantras may be found in Wedemeyer, C. (2001). Tropes, Typologies and Turnarounds: A Brief Genealogy of the Historiography of Tantric Buddhism. In *History of Religions*, 40(3): 223–59.
25. Thurman, R. (1988). Vajra Hermeneutics. In D. Lopez, Ed. Buddhist Hermeneutics. Honolulu: University of Hawaii Press, 134.
26. Another Western analogue to this engaged relationship to interpretation comes in the hermeneutic philosophy of Hans Gadamer, especially his view of thoughtful individuals not as mere passive recipients of tradition but "historically effective" agents of human culture. See Gadamer, H. (2004). *Truth and Method*. New York: Continuum Press.
27. An intriguing analogue to the variations in style and depth of interpretation described in this and the fourth ornament may be found in Paul Ricoeur's nuanced views of interpretation as a phenomenological art meant to "transport" the listener "into the world of the text." These notions are spelled out in the chapter on "Phenomenology and hermeneutics" in Ricoeur (1982), *Hermeneutics and the Human Sciences,* J. Thompson (trans.). Cambridge: Cambridge University Press, 101–28.
28. In this sense, the fourth ornament helps link the levels of narrative and biological truth which Ricoeur sees as constituting the "depth" of Freud's reading of the human psyche as a text. See note 27, above.

29. For an intriguing anthropological look at this topic, see Saran, P. (1998). *Tantra: Hedonism in Indian Culture*. New Delhi: DK Printworld.
30. See Dudjom Rinpoche, *Perfect Conduct,* xi.
31. Traditionally numbered at 253.
32. The ten lay precepts (known in the *Kālacakra* system as secondary pledges) include the five we are familiar with from chapter 3—no violence, deception, stealing, promiscuity, or intoxicants—plus five additional ones: respecting mentors, elders and friends, practicing the ten virtuous acts, and cultivating love and compassion. The eighteen primary pitfalls for altruists include: praising oneself, deriding others, not accepting apologies, denying the universal vehicle , embezzling donations, being divisive, disrobing monastics, extreme acts of violence, maintaining delusions, destroying homes, teaching emptiness to the unprepared, discouraging others from reaching enlightenment, causing monastics to break their vows, demeaning renunciates, exaggerating one's realizations, receiving embezzled donations, passing false judgment, and abandoning the spirit of altruism. For the forty-seven secondary pitfalls, see Dalai Lama, H. H. (1981). *Kalachakra Initiation: Madison 1981*. Madison: Deer Park, 74–75.
33. Though the five general and five special practice pledges of the families of enlightenment and the fourteen primary and ten (or twelve) secondary pitfalls are common to most optimal integral process traditions, there are also ten pitfalls specific to the optimal systems of the mother class, which we'll review in chapter 12. The *Kālacakra* abbreviates the pitfalls to seven and adds a code of conduct distinctive to heroic altruists, including five sets of five modes of action. See Dalai Lama, *Kalachakra Initiation,* 412–13.
34. According to the Gelukpa tradition, this guideline is to abstain from interfering with offerings to male and female ancestors, referring to other non-Buddhist practices. See Dalai Lama, *Kalachakra Initiation*, 413. The early Vedic tradition involved some animal sacrifice until the reform era which brought India Jainism, Buddhism, and the later Upanishads. See *Scripture About Kūṭadanta* (Kūṭadantasutta), subtitled *A Bloodless Sacrifice*, in M. Walshe (trans.). (1995). *The Long Discourses of the Buddha: A Translation of the Digha Nikāya*. Boston: Wisdom Publications, 133–42.
35. For a brief synopsis of Naropa's story, see Dowman, K. (1985). *Masters of Mahamudra*. Albany: State University of New York Press, 142–47. For the story of Marpa's relationship with Milarepa, see Lhalungpa, L. (1992). *The Life of Milarepa*. New York: Penguin Books.
36. Though traditionally addressed to male monastic audiences as a warning to restrain the emission of seminal fluid, the deeper reference of the term "spirit of enlightenment" (*bodhicitta*) to the experience of orgasmic bliss and its neurochemistry makes clear that this warning applies equally to both sexes. Given the androgynous nature of process practice and its clear intention to embrace the feminine experience of intimacy equally suggests that this pitfall will need to be restated and read in gender-neutral terms for today's mixed audience.
37. This version of the tenth pitfall follows the presentation in Dalai Lama, *Kalachakra Initiation*, 362, where this pitfall is described as "deceitful love," and defined as "relying on a poisonous influences" (*gdug-can mdza-bor bsten*).
38. Though traditionally this pitfall is listed as the twelfth, after failing to realize the depth of process teachings, I've reversed their order in this presentation to highlight the way the pitfalls follow the stages of progress on the optimal integral path.
39. Though traditionally addressed to male monastic audiences as a warning not to devalue women, the androgynous nature of process practice and its clear

intention to embrace women and the feminine perspective on spirituality and intimacy makes it only natural to state this in gender-neutral terms for today's mixed audience.

40. Though this common practice in the Geluk tradition is usually based on a different text, composed by the first Panchen Lama, Losang Chokyi Gyalstan (1567–1662) and refined by Lozang Tenzin and Pabongka Rinpoche, I've chosen to revise a form of the practice composed by His Holiness the 14th Dalai Lama and his tutor, the former Ling Rinpoche, Thubten Lungtok Namgyal Trinley, as a six-session practice of *Kālacakra*. I've chosen this as a form since it has been the form most extensively presented and commented on in English, in several volumes including Dalai Lama & Jeffery Hopkin's *Kalachakra Initiation*.

Chapter 10: Sublimation Tapping and Channeling Flow

1. Mullin, G. (1996). *Tsong Khapa's Six Yogas of Naropa*. Ithaca: Snow Lion Press, 139.
2. See Thurman, R. (2011). *Brilliant Illumination of the Lamp of the Five Stages*. New York: American Institute of Buddhist Studies, Chapter II, 94–95, where Tsong Khapa quotes Nāgārjuna's *Five Stages* (*Pañcakrama*): "To those well situated on the creation stage and yet aspiring to the perfection stage, the perfect buddhas taught this method just like the rungs of a ladder;" and Ăryadeva's *Integrated Practice (Cāryamelapika)*: "In order for beginner beings to enter into the ultimate reality, the perfect buddhas created this artful system, just like the rungs of a ladder."
3. This passage from the *Śrī-Vajradāka* is cited by Tsong Khapa in the introduction to his *Illuminating Lamp*, translated in Thurman, *Lamp*, 96.
4. Cited by Tsong Khapa from the *Sakaltantrasambhavasañcodanī-śrī-guhyasiddhi-nāma*, translated in Thurman, *Lamp*, 134.
5. Cited by Tsong Khapa from the *Enlightenment Song Treasury* (*Dohākoṣagīti*), translated in Thurman, *Lamp*, 141.
6. Thurman, *Lamp*, 141.
7. Actually, Naropa was representative of a synthetic tradition already alive in the India of his day, and he is credited with being involved in the transmission of numerous optimal integral process systems into Tibet, including the *Kālacakra*, *Guhyasamaja*, *Hevajra* and *Cakrasamvara*. For a discussion of the lineage of commentary on these teachings in Tibet, see the introduction to Mullin, *Six Yogas*. For a biography of Naropa, see Guenther, H. 1963. *The Life and Teachings of Naropa*. Oxford: Oxford University Press. For an overview of the Indian history of the mother class of optimal integral process traditions, *Hevajra* and *Cakrasamvara*, see Gray, D. (2008). *The Discourse of Śrī Heruka: The Cakrasamvara Tantra*. New York: American Institute of Buddhist Studies.
8. For the story of Tibet's great "cotton-clad" yogi, Milarepa, see Lhalungpa, L. (1992). *The Life of Milarepa: A New Translation from the Tibetan*. New York: Penguin Books.
9. Mullin, *Six Yogas*, 140.
10. For more on this prescient tradition, see Arnold, E. (ed.). (2009). *As Long as Space Endures: Essays on the Kālachakratantra in Honor of His Holiness the Dalai Lama*. Ithaca: Snow Lion Press.
11 For this phase of practice, see part 3, and Yarnall, T. (2010). *The Emptiness that is Form: The Creation Stage in Tsong Khapa's Great Exposition of Secret Mantra*. Ann Arbor: University of Michigan Dissertation Services.
12. For a systematic map of this stage, see Cozort, D. (2005). *Highest Yoga Tantra*. Ithaca: Snow Lion Press.

13. See note 8, above.
14. See Mullin, *Six Yogas*, 126–33.
15. For the history of this model, shared as a common contemplative science by many Indian traditions, see White, D. 1996. *The Alchemical Body: Siddha Traditions in Medieval India*. Chicago: University of Chicago Press.
16. See Clifford, T. (2006). *Tibetan Buddhist Medicine and Psychiatry*. New Delhi: Motilal Banarsidas.
17. See White, *Alchemical Body*.
18. Simply described following the medical system of normal structure and function in Lati Rinpoche & Hopkins, J. 1981. *Death, Intermediate State and Rebirth in Tibetan Buddhism*. Ithaca: Snow Lion Press.
19. Technically, this level alone is designated the "subtle body" (*sukṣma-śarīra*), although this technical usage is commonly used to refer to the whole triune model as well.
20. Skt. *lalana* and *rasana*.
21. Skt. *avadhūti*.
22. Skt. *susukṣma-citta-śarīra*.
23. Following Tsong Khapa, in Mullin, *Six Yogas*, 142–50.
24. Ibid., 132.
25. The triune model is adapted to explain neural structure and function in three distinct modes: the "basis" or baseline mode of normal, untrained individuals; the "path" mode in which the system is coming under self-regulation; and the "fruit" mode of individuals who have fully integrated control of their nervous system through complete mastery of self-regulation.
26. See Loizzo, J. (2009). Kālacakra and the Nālandā Tradtion: Religion, Science and Objectivity in Buddhism and the West. In Arnold, *As Long As Space Endures*.
27. In his *Illuminating Lamp*, Thurman, *Lamp*, 140.
28. The case and evidence supporting this premise were laid out at length in chapter seven, above. For a brief summary, see Bushell, W. (2009a). New Beginnings: Evidence that the Meditational Regimen can Lead to Optimaization of Perception, Attention, Cognition and Other Functions. In Bushell, W., Olivo, E. & Thiese, N. (eds.), *Longevity, Regeneration & Optimal Health: Eastern and Western Perspectives. New York: Annals of the New York Academy of Sciences*, 348–61; and Bushell, W. (2009b). Integrating Modern Neuroscience and Phsyiology with Indo-Tibetan Yogic Science. In Arnold, *As Long as Space Endures*, 385–89.
29. Tsong Khapa reviews these in Mullin, *Six Yogas*, 133–36.
30. Ibid., 133.
31. Mullin, *Six Yogas*, 136–37.
32. Brown, R., & Gerbarg, P. (2009). Yoga Breathing, Meditation & Longevity. In Bushell, W., Olivo, E., & Thiese, N. (eds)., *Longevity, Regeneration & Optimal Health: Eastern and Western Perspectives. New York: Annals of the New York Academy of Sciences*, 54–62.
33. Brown, R., & Gerbarg, P. (2005b). Sudarshan Kriya Yogic Breathing in the treatment of Stress, Anxiety and Depression: Part II, Clinical Applications and Guidelines. In *Journal of Alternative and Complementary Medicine*, 11(4): 71–17.
34. Mullin, *Six Yogas*, 142–50.
35. See the remarkable study from Richard Davidson's laboratory showing Tibetan meditators can voluntarily enter a state marked by consistent gamma wave synchrony on the EEG, characteristic of neural plasticity and cortical integration. See Lutz, A., Grieschar, L., Rawlings, N., et al. (2004). Long-term meditators self-induce high amplitude gamma synchrony during mental practice. In *Proceedings of the National Academy of Sciences*, 101: 16369–373.
36. These include elements of the imagery research reviewed in chapter 7.

37. As for metabolic changes, Benson in several studies on Tibetan practitioners of inner fire showed that they were able to generate significant reductions in basal metabolism of as much as 64 percent. Benson, H. et al. (1982). Body temperature changes during the practice of *gTum-mo* yoga. In *Nature* 295(5846): 234–46; and Benson, H., Malhotra, M. S., Goldman, R. F., et al. (1990). Three case reports of the metabolic and electroencephalogaphic changes during advanced Buddhist meditation techniques. In *Behavioral Medicine* 16(2): 90–95.
38. Mullin, *Six Yogas*, 144–50.
39. Mullin, *Six Yogas*, 64, explains his use of the term "stroke," for which he credits Chogyam Trungpa, to translate the Tibetan "*AH-tung*," which literally means "short A." The term is appropriate because the short A in Tibetan is often abbreviated by a vertical dash created by a scribe's top-down brush stroke.
40. Mullin, *Six Yogas*, 148–50.
41. Based on the same kind of mind/body feedbacks that prompt increases in local blood flow and temperature in studies of peripheral effects of vivid imagery. See Bushell, W. (2009b).
42. For two recent studies on the physiology of euphoric states in meditation, see Harte, J, Eifert, G., Smith, R. (1995). The effects of running and meditation on beta-endorphin, corticotropin-releasing hormone and cortisol in plasma, and on mood. In *Biological Psychology*, June. 40(3): 251–65; and Infante J., Peran, F., Martinez, M., et al. (1998). ACTH and beta-endorphin in transcendental meditation. In *Physiology and Behavior*, 64: 311–15.
43. See notes 38 and 40, above.
44. *Śrī-saṃpuṭa-tantrarāja-ṭikā-āmnāya-mañjari-nāma*, cited by Tsong Khapa, translated in Mullin, *Six Yogas*, 147 (with minor modifications by author).
45. *Śrī-mahāsamvarodaya-nāma-tantra*, cited by Tsong Khapa, translated in Mullin, *Six Yogas*, 152.
46. For Tsong Khapa's full remarks, see Mullin, *Six Yogas*, 152–55.
47. Groff, C., & Grof, S. (1992). *The stormy search for the self: A guide to personal growth through transformational crisis*. New York: Jeremy P. Tacher Books.
48. Miyamura, M. et al. (2002). Is man able to breathe once a minute for an hour? The effect of yoga respiration on blood gases. In *Japanese Journal of Physiology*, 52: 313–36. Heller, C., Elsner, R., & Rao, N. (1987). Voluntary hypometabolism in an Indian Yogi. *Journal of Thermal Biology* 2: 171–73; Kothari, J., Bordia, A., & Gupta, O. (1973). The yogic claim of voluntary control over the heart beat: An unusual demonstration. In *American Heart Journal*, 86(2): 282–84.
49. See Descilo, T., Vedamurtachar, A. Gerbarg, P., et al. (2010). Effects of a yoga breath intervention alone and in combination with an exposure therapy for post-traumatic stress disorder and depression in survivors of the 2004 South-East Asian Tsunami. In *Acta Psychiatrica Scandanavica*, 212: 289–300; Shannahoff-Khalsa, D. & Beckett, L. 1996. Clinical case report: efficacy of yogic techniques in the treatment of obsessive compulsive disorders. In *International Journal of Neuroscience*, 85: 1–17; and a number of other studies reviewed in Brown & Gerbarg (2009).
50. This passage from the Indian adept Luipa (assuming "Lawapa" is scribal error) cited by Tsong Khapa, translated in Mullin, *Six Yogas*, 157.
51. Mullin, *Six Yogas*, 157–58.
52. To refine this control, the flow of these four blisses is often further divided into three or four increments each, making a total of twelve "phases of the sun" or sixteen "phases of the moon." Ibid., 160.
53. This passage from the *Vajramala Tantra is quoted* by Tsong Khapa in both his *Brilliant Lamp* and *Book of Three Inspirations*. This translation is from Thuman, *Lamp*, 213.

54. Mullin, *Six Yogas*, 163.
55. Cited from the *Vajramala*, translated in Thurman, *Lamp*, 228–29.
56. Cited from the *Uttaratantra*, translated in Thurman, *Lamp*, 278.
57. Although some optimal integral process systems apply the diamond recitation to the navel complex, the *Guhyasamaja* practice is to apply it to unraveling the heart-knot. See Thurman, *Lamp*, 302.
58. Attributed to Ekādasanirghoṣa, this passage is cited by Tsong Khapa in his second chapter on freedom of speech, translated in Thurman, *Lamp*, 301.
59. See Tsong Khapa's lengthy discussion, in Thurman, *Lamp*, 303–10, especially: "Therefore, the natural sound of the three wind-energies which enter, abide and exit are taken as the three syllables," 304.
60. Thurman, *Lamp*, 312–13.
61. Mullin, *Six Yogas* 163–64.
62. A term coined by Gerbarg, P. (2007). Yoga and neuro-psychoanalysis. In Anderson, P. (ed.), *Bodies in Treatment: The Unspoken Dimension*. Hillsdale: The Analytic Press.
63. See Fosha, D. (2009). The Healing Power of Transformational Affect. In Bushell, *Longevity.*
64. For a general review, see Loizzo, J. (2000). Meditation and psychotherapy: Stress, allostasis and enriched learning. In *Complementary and Alternative Medicine and Psychiatry.* Muskin, P. (ed.), *Annual Review of Psychiatry* 20. Washington: American Psychiatric Association, 147–97.
65. Here we return to the epistemology of the path of insight explored in chapter 2, only starting out in the "extremely subtle" intuitive mode made possible through the bliss-inducing methodology of the process tradition.
66. Mullin, *Six Yogas*, 164.
67. Cited by Tsong Khapa in the second freedom of speech chapter of his *Illuminating Lamp,* translated in Thurman, *Lamp*, 346–47.
68. The Kagyud master Gampopa is credited with synthesizing the mother-centered lineages transmitted through Naropa with the more father-centered lineages transmitted through Atisha.
69. Ibid., 293.
70. Ibid., 295.
71. Cited by Tsong Khapa from the *Concise Five Stages* (*Pañcakrama-saṃgraha-prakāśa*), attributed to Naropa, translated in Thurman, *Lamp*, 293.
72. From the *Sandhi-vyākaraṇa-nāma-tantra*, translated in Thurman, *Lamp*, 337.
73. For an excellent review, see Becker, I. (2000). Uses of yoga in psychiatry and medicine. In Muskin, P. (ed.), *Complementary and Alternative Medicine and Psychiatry.* Annual Review of Psychiatry No. 20. Washington DC: American Psychiatric Press.
74. For a recent introduction and review, see Brown & Gerbarg (2009).
75. While the precise form and history of Yantra Yoga practices are distinct from those preserved in the tradition of Naropa, they are roughly equivalent and were transmitted from India more or less contemporaneously with those we've explored. See Brown, R., & Gerbarg, P. (2009), 55.
76. For the application of breathing techniques from the *Kundalini Yoga* tradition, see Shannahoff-Khalsa, D., & Beckett, L. (1996). Clinical case report: efficacy of yogic techniques in the treatment of obsessive compulsive disorders. In *International Journal of Neuroscience*, 85: 1–17.
77. A term from Brown & Gerbarg, (2009), 58: "Our hypothesis is that yoga breathing provides a neurophysiological 'work-out' that leads to greater flexibility and plasticity in the nervous system."
78. See Brown & Gerbarg, (2005b).

79. See Brown, R., & Gerbarg, P. (2005a). Sudarshan Kriya Yogic Breathing in the Treatment of Stress, Anxiety and Depression: Part I, Neurophysiologic Model. In *Journal of Alternative and Complementary Medicine*, 11(1): 189–201.
80. Janakiramaiah, N., Gangadbhar, B., Naga Venkatesha Murthy, P., et al. (2000). Antidepressant efficacy of Sudarshan Kriya Yoga (SKY) in melancholia: A randomized comparison with electroconvulsive therapy (ECT) and imipramine In *Journal of Affective Discord*, 57: 255–59.
81. Janakiramaiah, N., Gangadbhar, B., Naga Venkatesha Murthy, P., et al. (1998). Therapeutic efficacy of Sudarshan Kriya Yoga (SKY) in dysthymic disorder. In *National Institute of Mental Health and Neurological Sciences Journal*, 17: 21–28.
82. Descilo et al. (2010).
83. Brown & Gerbarg (2009), 58.
84. Ibid., 57.
85. Brown & Gerbarg (2005a), 198–99.
86. Brown & Gerbarg (2009).
87. Consider the range of models invoked in the following studies on advanced adepts: Miyamura, M. et al. 2002. Is man able to breathe once a minute for an hour? The effect of yoga respiration on blood gases. In *Japanese Journal of Physiology*, 52: 313–16; Young, J., & Taylor, E. (1998). Meditation as a voluntary hypometabolic state of biological estivation. In *News in Physiological Science*, 13: 149–53; Benson, H. et al. (1982) and Benson, H. et al. (1990); Heller, C. et al. (1987); Kothari et al. (1973).
88. In the following discussion, I've been lucky to be able to consult his own comprehensive review of his life's work, thanks to the recent release of Porges, S. (2011). *The Polyvagal Theory: Neurophysiological Foundations of Emotions, Attachment, Communication and Self-Regulation*. New York: W.W. Norton & Co.
89. Porges, *Polyvagal Theory*, 55–57.
90. Ibid., 41–48.
91. Mullin, *Six Yogas*, 144–59; Thurman, *Lamp*, 310–25.
92. Porges, *Polyvagal Theory*, 175–79; 289–95.
93. See Young, J., & Taylor, E. (1998); and Heller et al. (1987).
94. Ibid., 180.
95. See Loizzo (2000).
96. See Loizzo (2000).
97. Ibid., 196–97; 281–93.
98. Porges, *Polyvagal Theory*, 140–42.
99. Ibid., 275–80.
100. By oxytocin/vasopressin mediated effects of the smart vagus on amygdala fear circuits and on gut memories of disgust retained in the paraventricular nucleus and the motor nucleus of the old vagus.See Porges, *Polyvagal Theory*, 172–83
101. Ibid., 292–95.
102, This oscillator consists of a network coordinating the control of heart rate, breath rhythm and laryngeal vocalization through interneurons linking the nucleus of the solitary tract (NTS), the motor nucleus of the smart vagus (NA), and the nucleus of cranial nerves VII, IX, and XI. Other research suggests that this common oscillator may also include a broad range of regions involved in traumatic memories and reactivity, including the periaqueductal grey, the central nucleus of the amygdala, the hippocampus, and the anterior cingulate gyrus. Ibid., 42–43. See the work of Richter, D., & Speyer, K. (1990). Cardiopulmonary Control. In Loewy, A., & Speyer, K. (eds.), *Central Regulation of Autonomic Function*. New York: Oxford University Press.
103. In fact, several studies support this predicted neurobiology, just as subjective reports of people who've had near-death experiences, like Jill Taylor Bolte,

generally supports many aspects of the phenomenology of the eight subjective death signs. For more, see chapter 8.

Chapter 11: Inspiration Turning Bliss to Light

1. Thurman, R. (2011). *Brilliant Illumination of the Lamp of the Five Stages*. New York: American Institute of Buddhist Studies, 394.
2. Ibid.
3. Wedemeyer, C. (2007). *Aryadeva's Lamp that Integrates the Practices*. New York: American Institute of Buddhist Studies, 216.
4. Thurman, *Lamp*, 358–59.
5. Wedemeyer, *Aryadeva's Lamp*,
6. This may explain why some Tibetan scholars reverse the order, aligning luminance with aggression and radiance with attachment. It's unclear whether this reflects a transcription/translation error or a difference of opinion, since Tsong Khapa at least makes no mention of the divergence, though he seems to be closely following Aryadeva throughout his chapter on the second perfection stage.
7. While mentioning the reverse order, Tsong Khapa affirms the order—attachment, aggression, delusion—presented by Ăryadeva, referencing the *Pañcakramārthabhāskaraṇa-nāma*, attributed to *Nāgabodhi*. Thurman, *Lamp*, 372.
8. The gist of the divergence is that some of the traditions Tsong Khapa reviews portray the instinctive patterns (*prakṛtikalpana*) as incompatible with the three luminances, and hence, as dissolving all together into the first; while Ăryadeva distributes them among the three luminances, and seems to suggest that they dissolve in stages into clear light. See Thurman, *Lamp*, 363; 368–72; and especially Tsong Khapa's discussion, 373–75. The latter view seems more compatible with Nāgārjuna's simile likening the three luminances to the three root compulsions. Also, Ăryadeva supports his reading with an intriguing reference from the *Vijñāna-samkrānti-sūtra*, which expands on the established simile of the luminances as being like space. See Wedemeyer, *Aryadeva's Lamp*, 224–25, and n. 82. My reading of Tsong Khapa's resolution is that the distributive enmeshment of luminance and patterns describes the condition of a normal individual for whom the luminances stay unconscious while the early dissolution and disjunction of luminance and patterns describes the condition of an individual on the path with exceptional control of neural energies. Thurman, *Lamp*, 375, n.116, seems to be leaning towards the same reading.
9. It's hard to miss the analogy between this binary model and the basic model of Buddhist contemplative science, which distinguishes primary mental processes and (largely affective) mental functions. The analogy seems pertinent, since in both models freedom comes from disentangling the primary process of mind from mental factors that are under the influence of delusion and the other prime compulsions. Thurman, *Lamp*, 372, n. 114, agrees, but points out Tsong Khapa's dismissal of any attempt to link the two. I believe this dismissal relates to Tsong Khapa's insistence on presenting the luminances in the context of the perfection stage in light of how they operate on the path to disjoin the subtle mind from its normally unconscious instinctive patterns. As for the presentation of the subtle mind in the medical-psychiatric context of the psychopathology of everyday life or normal life-death transitions, I suspect with Thurman that the comparison is of interest and deserves further study. Interestingly, while such interest seems to be lacking in standard Tibetan medical literature, it wouldn't seem out of place in the context of the death and dying practice of natural liberation. See

Lati Rinpoche and Hopkins, J. (1985). *Death, Intermediate State and Rebirth in Tibetan Buddhism*. Ithaca: Snow Lion Press; and Thurman, R. (1994). *The Tibetan Book of the Dead: Liberation Through Hearing in the Between*. New York: Bantam Books.

10. Thurman, *Lamp*, 363–64, with the last line supplemented from Wedemeyer, *Aryadeva's Lamp*, 218.
11. Thurman, *Lamp*, 366–67.
12. Cited by Ăryadeva from the *Jñānavajrasamuccaya*, translated in Wedemeyer, *Aryadeva's Lamp*, 215–16.
13. Ibid., 224.
14. Thurman, *Lamp*, 368–72; Wedemeyer, *Aryadeva's Lamp*, 218–22.
15. Skt: *manogatam/āgatam*. Tsong Khapa cites a tradition that considers these not as separate instincts but as tendencies which cut across all the other instincts in this group. The tradition is described by him as "the followers of the Gö tradition," Thurman, *Lamp*, 369. Hence, Thurman (*Lamp*, 370, n. 113) explains that Tsong Khapa seems not to actually count these in his list.
16. Skt. *vikalpa*. Although this term has the technical sense of construction in Buddhist psychology, its placement in binary opposition to the preceding term, *saumyam*, combined with Tsong Khapa's commentary, suggest that the word is meant here in a more general sense, as descriptive of the ambivalent, oppositional tendency of a socially insecure mind.
17. Skt. *sāhasam, madhya-sāhasam, uttama-sāhasam*. Tsong Khapa traces the confusion about these three to a scribal error which replaced *sāhasa* (rapine, violence) with *sahaja* (natural). Judging from Thurman and Wedemeyer's rendering of this term as "boldness," some confusion still remains, since the Sanskrit leaves little doubt that the kind of boldness or audacity meant here is neither positive nor neutral but violent and sadistic.
18. Tsong Khapa makes this point in his chapter on freedom of mind, Thurman, *Lamp*, 374–75: "As for the yogī/nī who can develop the three wisdoms by the power of meditation on the path, s/he can ascertain those in manifestation, not inferring them from their signs. Therefore the persons who must infer luminance from the instincts are not one of these (practitioners on the path)."
19. Ibid., 375.
20. Ibid., 375, n. 116.
21. Ibid., 388.
22. Tsong Khapa reviews various methods by which this tradition approaches freedom of mind in Thurman, *Lamp*, 378–80.
23. Ibid., 382.
24. Tsong Khapa points out that this passage from the *Pañcakrama-saṃgraha-prakāśa* was cited in Ăryadeva's *Integrated Practices*, as translated in Thurman, *Lamp*, 383.
25. Freud, S. (2010). *The Interpretation of Dreams: The Complete and Definitive Text*. New York: Basic Books.
26. From Tsong Khapa's master-commentary on interpretation, *Legs-bshad snying-po*, translated in Thurman, R. (1986). *Tsong Khapa's Speech of Gold in the Essence of True Eloquence*. Princeton: Princeton University Press, 297.
27. Thurman, *Lamp*, 385.
28. Mullin, G. (1996). *Tsong Khapa's Six Yogas of Naropa*. Ithaca: Snow Lion Press, 170–71.
29. Ibid., 176–77.
30. Ibid, 181.This comment comes after a detailed review of resolution-based methods, 175–81.
31. See Freud, *Interpretation of Dreams*.

32. For a recent overview, see Wagner, R. (2008). *Lucid Dreaming: Gateway to the Inner Self.* New York: Moment Point Press.
33. Ibid., 182–83.
34. Ibid., 171.
35. A number of recent studies have shown that near-death experiences in people who undergo resuscitation is significant and surprisingly large. See Parnia, S., Walker, D., Yates, R., et al. (2001). A Qualitative and Quantitative Study of the Incidence, Features and Aetiology of Near Death Experiences in Cardiac Arrest Survivors. In *Resuscitation*, 48: 149–56; and van Lommel, P., van Mees, R., Meyers, V., et al. (2001). Near-Death Experience in Survivors of Cardiac Arrest: A Prospective Study in the Netherlands. In *Lancet*, 358: 2039–45. Although these findings have been taken by some as fuel to argue for a resuscitation of dualism, a view that conflicts with traditional process non-dualism, they are welcome in the sense that they lend empirical support to the premise that the core body-mind can support subtle and extremely subtle forms of lucid intuition in the most vegetative of altered states.
36. Thurman, *Lamp*, 385–86.
37. Ibid., 386.
38. Tsong Khapa quotes this passage from the *Mahāmūdrabindu* in his *Illuminating Lamp*, translated in Thurman, *Lamp*, 347.
39. Ibid., 387.
40. Ibid., 387–88.
41. Ibid., 388.
42. Italics added by author for clarity. Tsong Khapa cites this from *Pañcakrama*, translated in Thurman, *Lamp*, 389.
43. The definitive treatment of this subject is said to be in mKhas-grub je's commentary on the third, wisdom chapter of the *Vimalaprabhā*, which I am currently translating with Robert Thurman. See Mkhas-grub dge-legs dpal bzang-po (1983). *Dus-'khor ṭik chen. Rgyud thams cad kyi rgyal po bcom ldan 'das dpal dus kyi 'khor lo mchog gi dang po'i sangs rgyas kyi rtsa ba'i rguyd las phyung ba sdus ba'i rgyud kyi 'grel chenrtsa ba'i rgyudkyi rjes su 'jug pa stong phrag bcu gnyis pa dri ma med pa'i 'od kyi rgya cher bshad pa de kho na nyid bar byed pa zhes bya ba.* In *Yab sas gsung 'bum*, Mkhas grub (kha). Dharmasala: Tibetan Cultural Printing Press.
44. See Loizzo, J. (2009). Kālacakra and the Nālandā Tradition. In E. Arnold (ed.), *As Long As Space Endures: Essays on Kālacakratantra in Honor of His Holiness the Dalai Lama.* Ithaca: Snow Lion Press.
45. Thurman, *Lamp*, 390–91.
46. Ibid., 391.
47. Ibid., 555. Tsong Khapa discusses these conducts at length in the eleventh chapter of the *Lamp*. Naturally, given the explicit nature of these arts, which seem to have their origins in communal feasts, they've provoked a nearly endless amount of misunderstanding and speculation, scholarly and popular. Since their true intent and nature as practiced within this tradition is elaborately described by Tsong Khapa and in similar sources, as I see it this speculation, at least when applied to the Indo-Tibetan process tradition, says more about those who engage in it than about the practices themselves. Rather than indulge in projecting our own fantasies, objectifying these as exotic, cult rituals, I suggest we think of them as refined, contemplative versions of a "god and goddess theme" costume party or of the romantic rituals or love play lay couples may use at times to arouse passion.
48. For a more extensive textual discussion, see Gray, D. (2007). *The Cakrasamvara Tantra: The Discourse of Śrī Heruka.* New York: American Institute of Buddhist

Studies; and for a historical contextualization, see Shaw, M. (1994). *Passionate Enlightenment: Women in Tantric Buddhism*. Princeton: Princeton University Press.

49. Ibid., 392.
50. Ibid., 393.
51, Ibid.
52. For a discussion of the role of vagal paralysis in sleep, see Stickgold, R., & Walker, M. (2009). *The Neuroscience of Sleep*. New York: Academic Press; for the role of the ANS in near-death transitions, see Persinger, M. (1994). Near-Death Experience: Determining the Neuroanatomical Pathways. In Besette, L. (ed.), *Healing: Beyond Suffering or Death*. Montreal: Publications MNH; and for a discussion of smart vagal modulators oxytocin and vasopressin in the human sexual response, see Panksepp, J. (2004). *Affective Neuroscience: The Foundations of Human and Animal Emotions*. New York: Oxford University Press.
53. See the comparative, hypothetical model of the perfection stage in chapter ten, as well as Loizzo, J. (2009). Optimizing Learning and Quality of Life Throughout the Lifespan. In W. Bushell, E. Olivo, & N. Thiese (eds.), *Longevity, Regeneration and Optimal Health*. New York: New York Academy of Sciences.
54. Consider the range of models invoked in the following studies on advanced adepts: Miyamura, M. et al. (2002). Is man able to breathe once a minute for an hour? The effect of yoga respiration on blood gases. In *Japanese Journal of Physiology*, 52: 313-36; Young, J., & Taylor, E. (1998). Meditation as a voluntary hypometabolic state of biological estivation. In *News in Physiological Science*, 13: 149–53; Benson, H. et al. (1982). Body temperature changes during the practice of *gTum-mo* yoga. In *Nature* 295(5846): 234–46; and Benson, H. et al. (1990). Three case reports of the metabolic and electroencephalogaphic changes during advanced Buddhist meditation techniques. In *Behavioral Medicine* 16(2): 90–95; Heller, C., Elsner, R., & Rao, N. (1987). Voluntary hypometabolism in an Indian Yogi. *Journal of Thermal Biology* 2: 171–73; Kothari, J., Bordia, A., & Gupta, O. (1973). The yogic claim of voluntary control over the heart beat: An unusual demonstration. In *American Heart Journal*, 86(2): 282–84.
55. Kohut, H. (2009). *Restoration of the Self.* Chicago: University of Chicago Press.
56. Jennings, P. (2011). *Mixing Minds: The Power of Relationship in Psychotherapy and Buddhism*. Boston: Wisdom Publications, 102–03.
57. See Lacan, J. (1991). *The Seminar of Jacques Lacan: Book II: The Ego in Freud's Theory and in the Technique of Psychoanalysis 1954–1955*. New York: W. W. Norton & Company.
58. Cited from Jung, C. G. (1954). Hull, R. (trans.). *The Practice of Psychotherapy*. New York: Pantheon Books, 250.
59. Jung, *Psychotherapy*, 214.
60. Ibid., 251.
61. Ibid., 206.
62. Ibid, 271.
63. See Fosha, D. (2009). Positive Affects and the Transformation of Suffering into Flourishing. In W. Bushell, E. Olivo & N. Thiese (eds.), *Longevity, Regeneration and Optimal Health*. New York: New York Academy of Sciences.
64. See Tomkins, S. (1962/3). *Affect, Imagery, Consciousness*. Vol. 1: Positive Affects/ Vol.2: Negative Affects. New York: Springer; Ekman, P. (1978). *Facial Action Coding System: A Technique for the Measurement of Facial Movement*. Palo Alto: Consulting Psychologists Press; Izard, C. (1979). *The Maximally Discriminative Facial Movement Coding System*. Newark: University of Delaware Instructional Resource Center; and Ekman, P., Levenson, R., & Freisen, W. (1983). Autonomic nervous system activity distinguishes among emotions. In *Science*, 221:1208–10;

Eberl, E. (2010). Control of gestures and vocalizations in primates. In Brudzynski, S. (ed.), *Handbook of Mammalian Vocalization: An Integrative Neuroscience Approach*. Amsterdam: Elsevier Press.

65. Lowen, A. (1994). *Bioenergetics: The Revolutionary Therapy That Uses the Language of the Body to Heal the Problems of the Mind*. New York: Penguin Books.
66. A prime example of this is Sue Johnson's Emotionally Focused Couple Therapy (EFT). See Johnson, S. (2008). *Hold Me Tight: Seven Conversations for a Lifetime of Love*. New York: Little Brown.
67. Johnson, *Hold Me Tight*, 54–55.
68. Ibid., 185–86.
69. Ibid., 265.

Chapter 12: Uniting Pure Inspiration with Perfect Clarity

1. Thurman, R. (2011). *Brilliant Illumination of the Lamp of the Five Stages*. New York: American Institute of Buddhist Studies, 515. Note: Sanskrit terms left in translation, translated into English in passages cited here and below by author.
2. In Thurman, *Lamp*, 494–500.
3. In fact, in the medical literature, it's said that we become directly aware of the link between instinctive patterns and the three intuitions in the course of conscious reemergence from the clear light. Lati Rinpoche & Hopkins, J. (1985). *Death, Intermediate State and Rebirth in Tibetan Buddhism*. Ithaca: Snow Lion Press, 38–46.
4. *Pañcakrama*, translated in Thumrna, *Lamp*, 402.
5. This phrase occurs in a passage Tsong Khapa cites from the *Pradīpoddyotana-nāma-ṭīkā*, translated in Thurman, *Lamp*, 400.
6. Tsong Khapa cites the *Vajramala*, translated in Thurman, *Lamp*, 404.
7. Llinas, R. (2002). *The I of the Vortex: From Neurons to Self*. Cambridge: MIT Press.
8. Tsong Khapa cites the *Pañcakrama-saṃgraha-prakāśa*, translated in Thurman, *Lamp*, 422.
9. *Pañcakrama*, cited by Tsong Khapa, translated in Thurman, *Lamp*, 406.
10. *Pañcakrama*, translated in Thurman, *Lamp*, 407.
11. Tsong Khapa cites the *Caryāmelāpakapradīpa*, translated in Thurman, *Lamp*, 410.
12. Translated in Thurman, *Lamp*, 412–13.
13. Cited from *Pañcakrama* by Tsong Khapa, translated in Thurman, *Lamp*, 399.
14. Translated in Thurman, *Lamp*, 413.
15. Following Tsong Khapa's brief definitions in Thurman, *Lamp*, 414.
16. Cited by Tsong Khapa from *Pañcakrama*, translated in Thurman, *Lamp*, 423.
17. Cited by Tsong Khapa from the *Guhyasamajatantra*, translated in Thurman, *Lamp*, 416.
18. Cited by Tsong Khapa from the Four Point Treatise *(Gsang 'Dus 'Khor Lo Med Pa Don Bzhima)*, translated in Thurman, *Lamp*, 417–18.
19. Translated in Thurman, *Lamp*, 422.
20. Cited by Tsong Khapa from the *Pañcakrama-saṃgraha-prakāśa*, translated in Thurman, *Lamp*, 455.
21. Cited by Tsong Khapa from the *Vajramala*, translated in Thurman, *Lamp*, 446.
22. Cited by Tsong Khapa from the *Guhyasamajatantra*, translated in Thurman, *Lamp*, 447.
23. This *Caryāmelāpakapradīpa* passage is cited by Tsong Khapa, translated in Thurman, *Lamp*, 447.
24. Cited by Tsong Khapa from the *Pañcakrama*, translated in Thurman, *Lamp*, 507.

25. Translated in Thurman, *Lamp*, 458.
26. Cited from *Pañcakrama* by Tsong Khapa, translated in Thurman, *Lamp*, 461–62.
27. Translated in Thurman, *Lamp*, 465.
28. Translated in Thurman, Lamp, 502.
29. Cited by Tsong Khapa from the *Pañcakrama*, translated in Thurman, *Lamp*, 507.
30. Cited by Tsong Khapa for unnamed text attributed to Nāgabodhi, translated in Thurman, *Lamp*, 512.
31. Cited by Tsong Khapa from the *Pañcakrama*, translated in Thurman, *Lamp*, 467.
32. Cited by Tsong Khapa from the *Caturdevatāparipṛcchāvyakhyānopadeśapauṣṭ ika-nāma*, translated in Thurman, *Lamp*, 469.
33. Cited by Tsong Khapa from the *Pañcakrama*, translated in Thurman, *Lamp*, 472.
34. Cited by Tsong Khapa from the *Cāryamelāpakapradīpa*, translated in Thurman, *Lamp*, 472.
35. Translated in Thurman, *Lamp*, 473.
36. Cited by Tsong Khapa from *Pañcakrama*, where it is attributed to the *Lālitavistara*, translated in Thurman, *Lamp*, 478.
37. Translated in Thurman, *Lamp*, 483–84.
38. From his chapter X on communion, translated in Thurman, *Lamp*, 509.
39. Translated in Thurman, *Lamp*, 509–10.
40. Cited by Tsong Khapa from the *Cāryamelāpakapradīpa*, translated in Thurman, *Lamp*, 504.
41. Cited by Tsong Khapa from the *Pañcakrama*, translated in Thurman, *Lamp*, 508.
42. Citation by Tsong Khapa, possibly from *Pañcakrama-vṛttārthavirocana-nāma*, attributed to Nāgabodhi, translated in Thurman, *Lamp*, 513.
43. Wallace, V. (2001). *The Inner Kālacakratantra*. Oxford: Oxford University Press, 155.
44. Ibid., 150–70, especially 154.
45. For a recent review, see Carter, C. (2010). *Science and the Near-Death Experience*. New York: Inner Traditions.
46. See Bear, D., Freeman, R., Schiff, D., et al. (1985). Interictal behavior changes in patients with temporal lobe epilepsy. In *Annual Revue of Neuropsychiatry*. Washington DC: American Psychiatric Association, 190–214.
47. One case study of euphoric TLE showed rhythmic 6–8 Hz theta waves were linked with ecstatic episodes, Ciringotta, F., Tedesco, C., & Lugaresi, E. (1980). Case report: temporal lobe epilepsy with ecstatic seizures (so-called Dosteyevski seizures). In *Epilepsia*, 21: 705–10. These findings are comparable with those found among the most advanced adepts in a classic EEG study of long-term Zazen meditators, see Kasamatsu, A., & Harai, T. (1966). An electroencephalographic study of zen meditation (zazen). In *Folia Psychiatrica Neurologica Japan*, 20: 315–36.
48. One of these models comes from study of the advanced process phase of transcendental meditation, called the adept (*siddhi*) program. See Persinger, M. (1984). Striking EEG profiles from single episodes of glossolalia and transcendental meditation. In *Perceptual and Motor Skills*, 58: 127–33; and Transcendental meditation and general meditation are associated with advanced complex partial epileptic-like signs: evidence for "cognitive" kindling? In *Perceptual and Motor Skills*, 76: 80–82. The other, self-stimulation, comes from animal models and current meditation research: see Slawinska, U., & Kasicki, S. (1995). Theta-like rhythm in depth EEG activity of hypothalamic areas during spontaneous or electrically induced locomotion in rats. In *Brain Research*, 678: 117–126; and Lutz, A., Greischar, L. Rawlings, N., et al. (2004). Long-term meditators self-

induce high amplitude gamma synchrony during mental practice. In *Proceedings of the National Academy of Sciences*, 101(46): 16369–73.
49. Kristeva, J. (1984). *Revolution in Poetic Language*. M. Waller (trans.) New York: Columbia University Press.
50. Thurman, R. (1994). *The Tibetan Book of the Dead: The Book of Natural Liberation Through Hearing in the Between*. New York: Bantam Books.
51. Dalai Lama, H. H., & Berzin, A. (1997). *The Ganden/Kagyu Tradition of Mahamudra*. Ithaca: Snow Lion.
52. Sogyal Rinpoche. (1994). *Tibetan Book of Living and Dying*. New York: HarperOne.

Conclusion: Four Paths, One Happiness—Sustainable Living Today

1. Rifkin, J. (2009). *The Empathic Civilization: The Race to Global Consciousness in a World in Crisis*. New York: Jeremy Tarcher/Penguin Books, 613–14.
2. Rifkin, *Empathic Civilization*, 610.
3. Ibid., 616.
4. Mingyur, Y. (2008). *The Joy of Living: Unlocking the Secret and Science of Happiness*. New York: Three Rivers Press.
5. Ponlop, D. (2010). *Rebel Buddha: On the Road to freedom*. Boston: Shambhala Press.
6. Bushan, N., Garfield, J., & Zablocki, A. (eds.). (2009). *TransBuddhism: Transmission, Translation and Transformation*. Boston: University of Massachusetts Press.
7. Chen, K. (1972). *Buddhism in China*. Princeton: Princeton University Press.
8. For a brief look at our age from the father of truly global world history, see Toynbee, A. (1976). *Mankind and Mother Earth: A Narrative History of the World*. New York: Oxford University Press.
9. Long time American ambassador to Japan, Edwin O. Rieschauer coined the term "de-unilineraization" to describe the global need education must meet in the global age in his book, *Towards the Twenty-First Century: Education in a Changing World*.

References

Indian and Tibetan Scholarly Editions and Translations

Anaker, S. 2002. *Seven Works of Vasubandhu: The Buddhist Psychological Doctor.* Delhi: Motilal Barnarsidas.

Asanga, Rahula, W., and Boin-Webb, S. 2001. *Abhidharmasamuccaya: Compendium of Higher Teaching.* Berkeley: Asian Humanities Press.

Batchelor, S. 1979. *Śantideva: A Guide to the Bodhisattva's Way of Life.* Dharamsala: Library of Tibetan Works and Archives.

Berzin, A. 1973. *Lam Rim Man Ngag.* Doctoral Dissertation, Harvard University.

Bhagchi, S. (Ed.). 1965. *Śrīguhyasamajatantram.* Darbhanga: Mithila Institute, BST, no. 9.

Bhattacharya, K. 1978. *The Dialectical Method of Nāgārjuna (Vigrahāvyavartanī).* Delhi: Motilal Banarsdas.

Beal, S. 1884/2012. *Si-Yu-Ki: Buddhist Records of the Western World, Translated from the Chinese of Hiuen Tsang.* London: General Books.

———. 1888/2005.*The Life of Hiuan Tsiang by the Shaman Hui li.* London: Adamant Media.

Birnbaum, R. (Trans.). 2003. *The Healing Buddha.* Boston: Shambhala Press.

Bodhi, Bikkhu (Trans.). 2000. *The Connected Discourses of Buddha.* Boston: Wisdom Publications

Chakravarti, C. (Ed.). 1984. *Guhyasamajatanrapradīpodyotanañīkāsadkoñivyākhyā.* Patna: Kashi Prasad Jayaswal Research Institute.

Chang, G. C. C. 1974. *The Buddhist teaching of Totality.* University Park: University of Pennsylvania Press.

Chattopadyaya, A., and Chimpa, L. 1970. *Tāranātha's History of Buddhism in India.* Simla: Indian Institute for Advanced Study.

Cleary, J. C., and Cleary, T. 1977. *The Blue Cliff Record.* Boulder: Shambhala Publishers.

Conze, E. 1954. *Abhisamayālaṃkāra.* Rome: Serie Orientale Roma.

———. 1973. *The Perfection of Wisdom in 8,000 Lines.* San Francisco: Four Seasons Press.

———. 1974. *The Large Sūtra Perfect Wisdom.* Berkeley: University of California Press.

Dalai Lama, H. H., and Jinpa, T. 2009. *The Union of Bliss and Emptiness: Teachings of Guru Yoga.* Ithaca: Snow Lion Press.

De Jong, F. 1949. *Cinq Chapitres de la Prasannapadā.* Paris: Geuthner.

Doshi, B. J. 1967. *Candravyākaraṇam.* Jodhpur: Rajasthan Research Institute.

Dowman, K. 1998. *Masters of Mahāmudrā: Songs and Histories of the Eighty-Four Buddhist Siddhas*. Albany: State University of New York Press.
Elliot, N. 2007. *Guide to the Bodhisattva's Way of Life*. London: Tharpa Publications.
Erb, F. 1997. *Śūnyatāsāptativṛtti*. Stuttgart: Franz Steiner Verlag.
Fenner, P. 1990. *The Ontology of the Middle Way*. Dordrecht: Kluwer.
Franco, E. 1997. *Dharmakīrti on Compassion and Rebirth*. Wein: Wien: Arbeitskreis fur Tibetische und Buddhistische Studien Universitat Wien.
Gray, D. 2007. *The Chakrasamvara Tantra: The Discourse of Śrī Heruka*. New York: American Institute of Buddhist Studies.
Gyatso, K. 1999. *Ocean of Nectar: Candrakīrti's Introduction to the Middle Way*. London: Tharpa Press.
Hahn, M. 1982. *Nāgārjuna's Ratnāvalī: Basic Texts*. Bonn: Indica et Tibetica Verlag.
Hattori, M. 1971. *Dignāga on Perception*. Cambridge: Harvard University Press.
Hopkins, J. 1998. *Buddhist Advice for Living and Liberation: Nāgārjuna's Precious Garland*. Ithaca: Snow Lion Press.
Hopkins, J., Dalai Lama, H. H., and Tsong Khapa. 1987. *Tantra in Tibet*. Ithaca: Snow Lion Press.
Hopkins, J., Dzong Khapa, and Dalai Lama, H. H. 2005. *Yoga Tantra: Paths to Magical Feats*. Ithaca: Snow Lion Press.
Hopkins, J., Tsong Khapa, and Dalai Lama, H. H. 1987. *Deity Yoga in Action and Performance Tantra*. Ithaca: Snow Lion Press.
Hopkins, J., Lekden, Kensur, and Tsong Khapa. 1981. *Compassion in Tibetan Buddhism*. Ithaca: Snow Lion Press.
Hume, R. 1995. *The Thirteen Principal Upanishads*. Delhi: Oxford University Press.
Huntington, J. 1992. *The Emptiness of Emptiness*. Honolulu: University of Hawaii Press.
Ingalls, D. 1965. *Sanskrit Poetry*. Cambridge: Harvard University Press.
———. 1977. *The Dhvanyāloka*. Cambridge: Harvard University Press.
Inada, K. 1970. *The Mulamadhyamakakarikas of Nāgārjuna*. Tokyo: Hokeseido.
Jamspal, V. L., Chopel, S., and Delta Santina, P. 1978. *Nāgārjuna's Letter to King Gautamiputra*. Delhi: Motilal Banarsidas.
Jinpa, T. (Trans.). 2006. *Mind Training: The Great Collection*. Somerville: Wisdom Press.
Johnston, E. 1950. *Ratnagotravibhāga-mahāyānottaraśāstra*. Patna.
Kamalaśīla. 2011. *Meditation: The Buddhist Way of Tranquility and Insight*. Cambridge, UK: Windhorse Publications.
Komito, D. 1999. *Nagarjuna's Seventy Stanzas: A Buddhist Psychology of Emptiness*. Ithaca: Snow Lion Press.
La Vallee Poussin, L. de. 1923–1931. *L'Abhidharmakośa de Vasubandhu*. Paris: Institut Belges des Hautes Etudes Chinoises.
———. 1907–1911. *Madhyamakāvatāra de Candrakīrti*. Paris: Museon.
Lindtner, C. (Ed.). 1979. *Pañcaskandhaprakaraṇa*. Acta Orientalia 40.
———. 2011. *Nāgārjuniana*. New Delhi: Motolal Banarsidas.
Loizzo, J. 2007. *Nāgārjuna's Reason Sixty with Chandrakīrti's Commentary*. New York: American Institute of Buddhist Studies.
May, J. 1949. *Prasannapadā Madhyamakavṛtti: Douze Chapitres*. Paris: Maisonneuve.
Mullin, G. 1996. *Tsong Khapa's Six Yogas of Naropa*. Ithaca: Snow Lion Press.
Murcott, S. 2006. *The First Buddhist Women: Poems and Stories of Awakening*. New York: Parallax Press.

Oberlies, T. 1989. *Studie zum Candravyākaraṇa*. Stutgart: Franz Steiner Verlag.

Obermiller, E. 1975. *Buston's History of Buddhism*. Tokyo: Suziki Research Foundation.

———. 1933. *Analysis of the Abhisamayalaṃkāra*. London: Luzac.

Padmasambhava, Gyatrul Rinpoche, trans. 1998. *Natural Liberation: Padmasambhava's Teachings on the Six Bardos*. Boston: Wisdom Publications.

Padmasambhava, Thurman, R. (Trans.) and Dalai Lama, H. H. 1993. *The Tibetan Book of the Dead (The Great Book of Liberation Through Understanding in the Between)*. New York: Bantam Books.

Pensa, C. 1967. *Abhisamayālaṃkāravṛtti*. Rome: Serie Orientale Roma.

Pruden, L. (Trans.). 1988. *The Abhidharmakośabhaśyaṃ of Vasubandhu*. Berkeley: University of California Press.

Roerich, G. N. 1949, 1953. *The Blue Annals* (2 vols.). New Delhi: Motolal Banarsidas.

Ruegg, D. S. 1976. *La Theorie de Tathāgatagarbha et du Gotra*. Louvain.

Sakya Drakpa Gyaltsan. 1982. *Candragomin's Twenty Verses on the Bodhisattva Vow and its Commentary*. Dharamsala: Library of Tibetan Works and Archives.

Schaeffer, W. 1923. *Die Sechtzig Satze des Negativismus*. Heidelberg: Materialen zur Kunde des Buddhismus.

Schayer, S. 1931. *Ausgewahlte Kapitel aus der Prasannapadā*. Krakow:Polska Academja Umeijetnosci.

Scherrer-Schaub, C. 1991. *Yuktisaṣṭikāvṛtti*. Paris.

Shastri, Pt. C. 1934. *Vākyapadīya with the Commentary of Vṛśabhadeva*. Lahore.

Sorenson, P. 1986. *Triśaraṇasāptati of Candrakīrti*. Vienna: Arbeitskries fur Tibelische und Buddhistosche Studien Universitat Wien.

Sparham, G. 1993. *Ocean of Eloquence: Tsong Khapa's Commentary on the Yogacara Doctrine of Mind*. Albany: State University of New York Press.

Stcherbatski, T. 1972. *Buddhist Logic*. New York: Dover Press.

———. 1927. *The Conception of Buddhist Nirvāṇa*. Lenningrad: USSR Academy of Sciences.

———. 1971. *Discrimination Between Middle and Extremes*. Calcutta: R.D. Press.

Streng, F. J. 1967. *Emptiness: A Study in Religious Meaning*. Nashville: Abingdon Press.

Suzuki, D. T. 1956. *Lankāvatāra Sūtra* (2 vols.). London: Coronet Books.

Takasaki, J. 1966. *A Study of the Ratnagotravibhāga*. Rome: Instituto Italiano per il Medio ed Estremo Oriente.

Takakusu, J. 1896. *A Record of the Buddhist Religion as Practiced in India and the Malay Archipelago*. Oxford.

Tat, W. 1973. *Ch'eng Wei-Shih Lun: Doctine of Mere-Consciousness*. Hong Kong: Dai Nippon.

Tatz, M. 1985. *Difficult Beginnings: Three Works on the Bodhisattva Path*. Boston: Shambhala Publishers.

Thibaut, G. 1968. *The Vedānta sūtras of Bādarāyaṇa with Śaṅkara's Commentary*. Delhi: Sacred Books of the East, 34 & 38.

Thurman, R. 1976. *The Holy Teaching of Vimalakīrti*. Philadelphia: University of Pennsylvania Press.

———. 1984. *Tsong Khapa's Speech of Gold*. Princeton: Princeton University Press.

———. 2008. *The Ornament of Universal Scriptures*. New York: American Institute of Buddhist Studies.

———. 2010. *Brilliant Illumination of the Lamp of the Five Stages*. New York: American Institute of Buddhist Studies.

Tillemans, T. 1990. *Materials for the Study of âryadeva, Dharmapāla and Candrakīrti*. Wien: Arbeitskreis fur Tibetische und Buddhistische Studien Universitat Wien.
Tilmann, V. 1984. *Buddha und Seine Lehre in Dharmakīrti's Pramāṇavārttika*. Wien: Universitat Wien.
Tsong Khapa and Sparham, G. (Trans). 2005. *Tantric Ethics: An Explanation of the Precepts for Buddhist Vajrayāna Practice*. London: Wisdom Publications.
Vaidya, P. L. 1960. *Prasannapadāmūlamadhyakavṛtti*. Darbhanga: Mithila Institute.
Walshe, M. (Trans.) 1987. *The Long Discourses of the Buddha*. London: Wisdom Press.
Wayman, A. 1970. *Yoga of the Guhyasamajatantra*. Delhi: Motilal Banarsidas.
———. 1978. *Calming the Mind and Discerning the Real*. New York: Columbia Univeristy Press.
———. 1999. *Chanting the Names of Mañjuśrī*. New Delhi: Motilal Barnasidas.
Wayman, A., and Lessing, F. 1968. *Mkhas-grub rje's Fundamentals of the Buddhist Tantras*. The Hague: Mouton.
Wedemeyer, C. 2007. *Aryadeva's Lamp that Integrates the Practices*. New York: American Institute of Buddhist Studies.
Yangchen Gawai Lodoe. 1995. *Paths and Grounds of Guhyasamaja According to ârya Nāgārjuna*. Dharamsala: Library of Tibetan Works and Archives.
Yarnall, T. 2011. Tsong Khapa's *Great Stages of Mantra: The Creation Stage*. New York: American Institute of Buddhist Studies.

Scholarly Works in South Asian and Buddhist Studies

Arnold, E. (Ed.). 2009. *As Long as Space Endures: Essays in Honor of His Holiness the Dalai Lama*. Ithaca: Snow Lion Press.
Avadon, J., Bradley, T., and Gerasimova, K. 1998. *The Buddha's Art of Healing: Tibetan Paintings Rediscovered*. New York: Rizzoli Publications.
Basham, A. 1975. *A Cultural History of India*. Oxford: Oxford University Press.
Baura, D. K. 1969. *Viharas in Ancient India*. Calcutta: Indian Publications.
Berzin, A. 1997. *Taking the Kalachakra Initiation*. Ithaca: Snow Lion Press.
Brauen, M. 1997. *The Mandala: Sacred Circle in Tibetan Buddhism*. Boston: Shambhala Publishers.
Campbell, J. 2009. *Vajra Hermeneutics: A Study of Vajrayana Scholasticism in the "Pradipoddyotana."* Ann Arbor: University of Michigan Dissertation Services.
Clifford, T. 2006. *Tibetan Buddhist Medicine and Psychiatry*. New Delhi: Motilal Banarsidas.
Crow, D. 2000. *In Search of the Medicine Buddha. New* York: Tarcher Books.
Cozort, D. 1986. *Highest Yoga Tantra*. Ithaca: Snow Lion Press.
Dalai Lama, H. H. 1999. *Kalachakra Tantra: Rite of Initiation*. Somerville: Wisdom Publications.
———. 2001. *Ethics for the New Millenium*. New York: Riverdale Trade Books.
Dalai Lama, H. H., and Berzin, A. 1986. *The Ganden/Kagyu Tradition of Mahamudra*. Ithaca: Snow Lion Press.
Dalai Lama, H. H., and Cutler, H. 2009. *The Art of Happiness in a Troubled World*. New York: Riverhead Books.
Dalai Lama, H. H. , and Varela, F. 2002. *Sleeping, Dreaming and Dying: An Exploration of Consciousness*. Somerville: Wisdom Publications.
Dhargyay, G. N. 1978. *The Tibetan Tradition of Mental Development*. Dharamsala: Library of Tibetan Works and Archives.

Dirks, N. 1987. *The Hollow Crown: Ethnohistory of an Indian Kingdom*. Cambridge: Cambridge University Press.

Dreyfus, G. 1996. *Recognizing Reality: Dharmakīrti's Philosophy and its Tibetan Interpretions*. Albany: SUNY Press.

———. 2003. *The Sound of Two Hands Clapping: The Education of a Tibetan Buddhist Monk*. Berkeley: University of California Press.

Dudjom Rinpoche, H. H. 1996. *Perfect Conduct: Ascertaining the Three Vows*. Somerville: Wisdom Publications.

Dunne, J. 2004. *Foundations of Dharmakīrti's Philosophy*. Boston: Wisdom Press.

Dutt, S. 2008. *Buddhist Monks and Monasteries of India: Their History and Their Contribution to Indian Culture*. Delhi: Motilal Barnarsidas.

Eckel, M. 1992. *To See the Buddha*. Princeton: Princeton University Press.

Farmer, E., Hambly, G., Kopf, D., Marshall, B., and Taylor, R. 1977. *Comparative History of Civilizations in Asia*. Reading: Addison Wesley.

Gelek Rinpoche and Rosen, B. 2004. *The Tara Box: Rituals for Protection and Healing from the Female Buddha*. New York: New World Library.

Gerow, E. 1977. *Indian Poetics*. Wiesbaden: Otto Harrassowitz.

Goleman, D. 1977. *Varieties of Meditative Experience*. New York: Dutton Press.

Govinda, L. A. 1973. *The Psychological Attitude of Early Buddhist Philosophy*. New York: Samuel Weiser.

Gyatso, K. 1982. *Clear Light of Bliss*. London: Tharpa Publications.

———. 1991. *Guide to Dakini Land: The Highest Yoga Tantra Practices of Buddha Vajrayogini*. London: Tharpa Publications.

Hopkins, J. 1983/1996. *Meditation on Emptiness*. Boston: Wisdom Publications.

Isayeva, N. 1993. *Śaṅkara and Indian Philosophy*. Albany: SUNY Press.

———. 1995. *From Early Vedānta to Kaśmiri Śaivism*. Albany: SUNY Press.

Joshi, L. 1964. *Studies in the Buddhistic Culture of India*. Delhi: Motilal Barnarsidas.

King, R. 1995. *Early Advaita Vedānta and Buddhism*. Albany: SUNY Press.

Klein, A. C. 1998. *Knowledge and Liberation: Tibetan Buddhist Epistemology in Support of Transformative Religious Experience*. Ithaca: Snow Lion Press.

Lamrimpa, G. 1999. *Transcending Time: The Kālacakra Six Session Yoga*. Somerville: Wisdom Publications.

Lati Rinpoche, and Hopkins, J. 1985. *Death, Intermediate State and Rebirth in Tibetan Buddhism*. Ithaca: Snow Lion Press.

Lhalungpa, L. 1992. *The Life of Milarepa*. New York: Penguin Books.

Loizzo, J. 1977. *Wittgenstein and the Mādhyamika*. Independent Study thesis, Amherst College.

———. 2001. *Candrakīrti and the Moon-Flower of Nālandā*. Ann Arbor: UMI Dissertation Services.

———. 2009. Kālacakra and the Nālandā Tradition. In E. Arnold (ed.), *As Long as Space Endures: Essays in Honor of His Holiness the Dalai Lama*. Ithaca: Snow Lion Press.

———. 2011. The Intergenerational Transmission of Agency: Evolutionary Psychology or Religious Belief? In *Sophia: The Journal of Traditional Studies*, 50: 429–452.

Loizzo, J., Blackhall, L., and Rapgyay, L. 2009. Tibetan Medicine: A Complementary Science of Optimal Health. In E. Olivo, W. Bushell, and N. Thiese (eds.), *Longevity, Regeneration and Optimal Health*. New York: New York Academy of Sciences.

Lopez, D. 1987. *A Study of Sautrantika*. Ithaca: Snow Lion Press.

Makransky, J. 1997. *Buddhahood Embodied*. Albany: SUNY Press.

Matilal, B. K. 1971. *Epistemology, Logic and Grammar in Indian Philosophical Analysis*. The Hague: Mouton.
Murti, T. R. V. 1955. *The Central Philosophy of Buddhism*. London: Allen & Unwin.
Pabongka Rinpoche. 1991/1993. *Liberation in the Palm of your Hand*. London: Wisdom Press.
Padoux, A. 2011. *Tantric Mantras: Studies on Mantrasastra*. London: Routledge Press.
Potter, K. 1972. *Presuppositions of India's Philosophies*. Westport: Greenwood Press.
Radakrishnan, S., and Moore, C. 1957. *Sourcebook in Indian Philosophy*. Princeton: Princeton University Press.
Rhie, M., and Thurman, R. 1991. *Wisdom and Compassion: The Sacred Art of Tibet*. New York: Harry N. Abrams.
Ricard, M., and Thuan, T. 2004. *The Quantum and the Lotus: A Journey to the Frontiers Where Science and Buddhism Meet*. New York: Three Rivers Press.
Rizzi, C. 1988. *Candrakīrti*. Delhi: Motilal Banarsidas.
Robinson, R. 1979. *Buddha's Lions*. Berkeley: Dharma Publishing.
Ruegg, D. S. 1981. *Literature of the Mādhyamika School of Philosophy in India*. Wiesbaden: Harrassowitz.
Salzberg, S. 2002. *Loving-Kindness: The Revolutionary Art of Happiness*. Boston: Shambhala Press.
Sanderson, A. 1985. Purity and Power among the Brahmans of Kashmir. In M. Carrithers et al. (eds.), *The Category of the Person: Anthropology, Philosophy, History*. Cambridge: Cambridge University Press.
———. 1994. Vajrayana: Origin and Function. In *Buddhism into the Year 2000: International Conference Proceedings*. Los Angeles: Dharmakaya Foundation.
Shaw, M. 1995. *Passionate Enlightenment*. Princeton: Princeton University Press.
Sogyal Rinpoche. 1994. *The Tibetan Book of Living and Dying*. New York: HarperOne.
Sprung, M. (Ed.). 1973. *The Problem of Two Truths in Buddhism andVedānta*. Boston: Reidel.
Tambiah, S. 1964. *World Conqueror, World Renouncer*. Oxford: Oxford University Press.
Thapar, R. 1995. *Recent Perspectives in Indian History*. Delhi: Sangham.
Thondup, T. 1998. *The Healing Power of Mind*. Boston: Shambhala Press.
Thurman, R. 1999a. *Inner Revolution*. New York: Riverhead Trade Books.
———. 1999b. "Buddhist Psychology: Sophisticated Software for the Human Brain." In Dalai Lama, Benson, H., Gardner, H., et al. (eds.), *Mind Science: An East West Dialogue*. Boston: Wisdom Publications.
Thurman, R. 1981. *The Life and teachings of Tsong Khapa*. Dharmsala: Library of Tibetan Works and Archives.
———. 1986. Vajra Hermeneutics. In D. Lopez (ed.), *Buddhist Hermeneutics*. Honolulu: University of Hawaii Press.
Tsering, T. 2005. *The Four Noble Truths*. Boston: Wisdom Publications.
Urban, H. 2010. *Tantra: Sex, Secrecy, Politics and Power in the Study of Religion*. Berkeley: University of California Press.
Van Shaik, S. 2004. *Approaching the Great Perfection: Simultaneous and Gradual Methods of Dzog Chen in the Longchen Nyingtig*. Boston: Wisdom Publications.
Wallace, B.A. 2000. *Contemplative Science: Where Buddhism and Neuroscience Converge*. New York: Columbia University Press.
Wallace, V. 2001. *The Inner Kālacakratanta*. Oxford: Oxford University Press.
Wangyal, G. 1978. *The Door to Liberation*. New York: Lotsawa Press.

Weber, M. 1986. *The Religion of India*. Delhi: Munshiram Monoharlal.
White, D. 1996. *The Alchemical Body: Siddha Traditions in Medieval India*. Chicago: University of Chicago Press
Wujtasik, D. 1998. *The Roots of Âyurveda*. New York: Penguin Books.
Yarnall, T. 2006. *The Emptiness that is Form: The Creation Stage Chapter in Tsong Khapa's Great Exposition of Secret Mantra*. Ann Arbor: University of Michigan Dissertation Services.
Yeshe, T. 2000. *The Bliss of Inner Fire*. London: Wisdom Publications.
———. 2001. *Introduction to Tantra*. London: Wisdom Publications.
———. *Becoming Vajrasattva: The Tantric Path of Purification*. London: Wisdom Publications.
Lama Zopa, and Too, L. 2001. *Ultimate Healing: The Power of Compassion*. Boston: Wisdom Publications.
Zysk, K. 1991. *Asceticism and Healing in Ancient India*. Oxford: Oxford University Press.

Western Scientific and Philosophical Works

Austin, J. 2006. *Zen-Brain Reflections*. Cambridge: MIT Press.
Benson, H. 1975/2000. *The Relaxation Response*. New York: Harper Paperbacks.
Berger P., and Luckman, T. 1967. *The Social Construction of Reality*. New York: Anchor Books.
Bouveresse, J. 1995. *Wittgenstein Reads Freud*. Princeton: Princeton University Press.
Brach, T. 2003. *Radical Acceptance: Embracing your life with the heart of a Buddha*. New York: Bantam Books.
Cameron, C., Loewenstein, G., and Rabin, M (Eds.). 2004. *Advances in Behavioral Economics*. New York: Princeton University Press.
Carter, C. 2010. *Science and the Near-Death Experience*. New York: Inner Traditions.
Cioffi F. 1969. Wittgenstein's Freud. In P. Winch (ed.), *Studies in the Philosophy of Wittgenstein*. London: Routeledge & Kegan Paul.
Claxton, G. (Ed.). 1986. *Beyond Psychotherapy: The Impact of Eastern Religions on Psychological Theory and Practice*. London: Wisdom Publications.
Crane, R. 2008. *Mindfulness-Based Cognitive Therapy: Distinctive Features*. New York: Routledge Press.
Cozolino, L. 2006. *The Neuroscience of Human Relationships: Attachment and the Developing Brain*. New York: Norton Press.
Csikszentmihalyi, M. 1990. Flow: *The Psychology of Optimal Experience*. New York: Harper & Row.
Davidson R., and Davidson, J. 1980. *The Psychobiology of Consciousness*. New York: Plenum Press.
De Waals, F. 2009. *Primates and Philosophers: How Morality Evolved*. Princeton: Princeton University Press.
Decety, J., and Ickes, W. 2009. *The Social Neuroscience of Empathy*. Cambridge: MIT Press.
Deleuze, G., and Guattari, F. 1994. *What is Philosophy?* New York: Columbia University Press.
Demasio, A. 2005. *Descartes' Error: Emotions, Reason & the Human Brain*. New York: Penguin Classics.

Dobzhansky, T., and Gould, S. 1982. *Genetics and the Origin of Human Species.* New York: Columbia University Press.

Doidge, N. 2007. *The Brain that Changes Itself: Stories of Personal Triumph from the Frontiers of Brain Science.* New York: Penguin Press.

Ekman, P. 1978. *Facial Action Coding System: A Technique for the Measurement of Facial Movement.* Palo Alto: Consulting Psychologists Press.

Epstein, M. 2004. *Thoughts Without a Thinker: Psychotherapy from a Buddhist Perspective.* New York: Basic Books.

Foreman, R. 1997. *The Problem of Pure Consciousness: Mysticism and Philosophy.* Oxford: Oxford University Press.

Fosha, D., Siegel, D., and Solomon, M. (Eds.). 2009. *The Healing Power of Emotion: Affective Neuroscience, Development and Clinical Practice.* New York: W.W. Norton.

Freedman, J., and Combs, G. 1996. *Narrative Therapy: The Social Construction of Preferred Realities.* New York: W.W. Norton.

Freud, S. 1923. Recommendations to Physicians Practicing Psychoanalysis. In *Standard Edition of the Works of Sigmund Freud.* J. Strachey (trans.). London: Hogarth Publishers.

Freud, S. 1930/1962. *Civilization and its Discontents.* J. Strachey (trans.). New York: W.W. Norton.

Freud, S., Bonaparte, M., and Freud, A. 1954. *The Origins of Psychoanalysis: Sigmund Freud's Letters, Drafts and Notes to Wilhelm Fliess.* New York: Basic Books.

Gadamer, H. G. 1975. *Truth and Method.* New York: Continuum.

Gergen, K., and Gergen, M. (Eds.). 2003. *Social Construction: A reader.* New York: Sage.

Germer, C., and Salzberg, S. 2009. *The Mindful Path to Self-Compassion: Freeing Yourself from Destructive Emotions.* New York: Guilford Press.

Germer, C., Siegel, R., and Fulton, P. 2005. *Psychotherapy and Mindfulness.* New York: Guilford Press.

Gilbert, P. (Ed.) 2005. *Compassion: Conceptualizations, Research and Use in Psychotherapy.* New York: Routledge Press.

Goleman, D. 2004. *Destructive Emotions: A Scientific Dialogue with His Holiness the Dalai Lama.* New York: Bantam Press.

———. 2009. *Ecological Intelligence: How Knowing the Impact of What You Buy Can Change Everything.* New York: Broadway Business Press.

———. 2010. *Emotional Intelligence: Why it Matter More than IQ.* New York: Bloomsbury Paperbacks.

Goodmunsen, C. 1979. *Wittgenstein and Buddhism.* London: Allen & Unwin.

Greenberg, J. R., and Mitchell, S. A. 1985. *Object Relations in Psychoanalytic Theory.* Cambridge: Harvard University Press.

Grossman, A. 1981. *Against Our Vanishing: Winter Conversations with Allen Grossman on the Theory and Practice of Poetry.* Boston: Rowan Tree Press.

Habermas J. 1971. *Knowledge and Human Interests.* J. Shapiro (trans.). Boston: Beacon Press.

———. 1990. *Moral Consciousness and Communicative Action.* Cambridge: MIT Press.

Hamilton, B. 1986. *Religion in the Medieval West.* London: Edward Arnold.

Harre, R. 1964. *The Language of Morals.* Oxford: Oxford University Press.

Harre, R., and Gillett, G. 1994. *The Discursive Mind.* Thousand Oaks: Sage.

Hillman, J. 1976. *Revisioning Psychology.* New York: Harper and Row.

Hoffman, M. 2000. *Empathy and Moral Development: Implications for Caring and Justice.* Cambridge: Cambridge University Press.
Iacaboni, M. 2009. *Mirroring People: The Science of Empathy and How We Connect with Others.*New York: Picador Press.
Izard, C. 1979. *The Maximally Discriminative Facial Movement Coding System.* Newark: University of Delaware Instructional Resource Center.
James, W. 1989. *Varieties of Religious Experience.* New York: Modern Library.
Janik, A., and Toulmin, S. 1976/1996. *Wittgenstein's Vienna.* New York: Ivan R. Dee.
Jennings, P. 2010. *Mixing Minds: The Power of Relaitonship in Psychoanalysis and Buddhism.* Boston: Wisdom Publications.
Johnson, S. 2008. *Hold Me Tight: Seven Conversations for a Lifetime of Love.* New York: Little Brown.
Jung, C. G. 1935/1978. Psychological Commentary on the Tibetan Book of the Dead. In Hull, R. (trans.). *Psychology and the East.* Princeton: Princeton University Press Bollingen Series.
———. 1964. *The Art of Psychotherapy.* Princeton: Bollingen Press.
Kissen, B. 1986. *Conscious and Unconscious Programs in the Brain.* New York: Plenum Press.
Kandel, E., and Schwartz, J. 1999. *Principles of Neural Science.* New York: Elsevier Science.
Kitcher, P. 1998. *Freud's Dream: A Complete Multidisciplinary Science of Mind.* Cambridge: MIT Press.
Kitcher, P. 1993. *The Advancement of Science.* Oxford: Oxford University Press.
Kosslyn, S. 1996. *Image and the Brain: The Resolution of the Imagery Debate.* Cambridge: The MIT Press.
Kosslyn, S., Thompson, W., and Ganis, G. 2006. *The Case for Mental Imagery.* Oxford: Oxford University Press.
Kristeva, J. 1984. *Revolution in Poetic Language.* M. Waller (trans.) New York: Columbia University Press.
Kohut, H. 1972. *The Restoration of the Self.* New York: Psychoanalytic Press.
———. 2009. *The Analysis of the Self: A Systematic Approach to the Psychoanalytic Treatment of Narcissistic Personality Disorders.* Chicago: University of Chicago Press.
Kuhn, T. 1962. *The Structure of Scientific Revolutions.* Chicago: Chicago, University Press.
Kunzendorf, R. Shiekh, 1990. *A: Physiology of Mental Imagery.* New York: Baywood.
Linehan, M. 1993. *Cognitive Behavioral Treatment of Borderline Personality Disorder.* New York: Guilford Press.
Llinas, R. 2002. *I of the Vortex: From Neurons to Self.* Cambridge: MIT Press.
Lowen, A. 1994. *Bioenergetics: The Revolutionary Therapy that Uses the Language of the Body to Heal the Problems of the Mind.* New York: Penguin Books.
MacLean, P. 1990. *The Triune Brain in Evolution.* New York: Plenum Press.
Marcuse, H. 1987. *Eros and Civilization.* New York: Routledge Press.
Margulies, A. 1989. *The Empathic Imagination.* New York: Norton.
McGuinness, B. 1982. Freud and Wittgenstein. In B. McGuinness (ed.). *Wittgenstein and his Times.* Oxford: Basil Blackwell, 27–43.
McEwan, B. 2002. *The End of Stress as We Know It.* New York: Joseph Henry Press.
Moleno A. 1998. *The Couch and the Tree: Dialogues Between Psychoanalysis and Buddhism.* New York: North Point Press.

Nagel, T. 1986. *The View from Nowhere*. Oxford: Oxford University Press.
Nietzsche, F. 1965. *Twilight of the Idols*. New York: Penguin Books.
Needham, J. 1964. *Science and Civilization in Ancient China*. Oxford: Oxford University Press.
Norcross, J. 2002. *Psychotherapy Relationships that Work*. Oxford: Oxford University Press.
Oyama, S. 2000. *The Ontogeny of Information: Developmental Systems and Evolution*. Durham: Duke University Press.
Phillips, D. L. 1977. *Wittgenstein and Scientific Knowledge*. London: MacMillan.
Popper, K. 2002. *The Logic of Scientific Discovery*. London: Routledge Classics.
Porges, S. 2011. *The Polyvagal Theory: Neurophysiological Foundations of Emotions, Attachment, Communication and Self-Regulation*. New York: W.W. Norton.
Proudfoot, W. 1987. *Religious Experience*. Berkeley: University of California Press.
Rank, O. 1958. *Beyond Psychology*. New York: Dover.
Ricoeur, P. 1970. *Freud and Philosophy*. D. Savage (trans.). New Haven: Yale University Press.
———. 1982. *Hermeneutics and the Human Sciences*. J. Thompson (trans.). Cambridge: Cambridge University Press.
———. 1992. *Oneself as Another*. K. Blamey (trans.). Chicago: University of Chicago Press.
Rieff, P. 1959. *Freud: The Mind of the Moralist*. New York: Viking.
Rifkin, J. 2009. *The Empathic Civilization: The Race to Global Consciousness in a World in Crisis*. New York: Jeremy Tarcher/Penguin Books.
Roberts, R. C. 1988. The Grammar of a Virtue. In R. Bell (ed.), *The Grammar of the Heart*. San Francisco: Harper and Row, 149–170.
Rotman, B. 1995. *Signifying Nothing: The Semiotics of Zero*. Stanford: Stanford University Press.
Rubin, J. 1996. *Psychotherapy and Buddhism: Towards an Integration*. New York: Springer.
———. 2004. *The Good Life*. Albany: State University of New York Press.
Saffran, J. P. 1995. *Psychoanalysis and Buddhism: An Unfolding Dialogue*. Boston: Wisdom Publications.
Sarton, G. 1927. *Introduction to the History of Science*. Baltimore: Johns Hopkins Press.
Saunders, J. T., and Henze, D. F. 1976. *The Private Language Problem*. New York.
Schafer, R. 1976. *A New Language for Psychoanalysis*. New Haven: Yale University Press.
———. 1978. *Language and Insight*. New Haven: Yale University Press.
———. 1983. *The Analytic Attitude*. New York: Basic Books.
Scholem, G. 1995. *Major Trends in Jewish Mysticism*. New York: Schoken.
Scott, G. 2004. *Does Socrates Have a Method: Rethinking the Elenchus in Plato's Dialogues and Beyond*. New York: Philosophy Education Society.
Searle, R. 1996. *The Construction of Social Reality*. New York: Penguin Books.
Segal, Z., Williams, J., and Teasdale, J. 2002. *Mindulness-based Cognitive Therapy for Depression: A New Approach to Preventing Relapse*. New York: Guilford Press.
Seligman, M. 2004. *Authentic Happiness: Using the New Positive Psychology to realize your Potential for Lasting Happiness*. New York: Free Press.
Siegel, D. 2007. *The Mindful Brain: Reflection and Attunment in the Cultivation of Wellbeing*. New York. W.W. Norton.

Stolorow, R., and Atwood, G. 1992. *Contexts of Being: The Intersubjective Foundations of Psychological Life*. Hillsdale: The Analytic Press.
Sroufe, L., Egeland, B., Carlson, E., and Collins, W. 2005. *The Development of the Person: The Minnesota Study of Risk and Adaptation from Birth to Adulthood*. New York: Guilford Press.
Tilghman, B. R. 1991. *Wittgenstein, Ethics and Aesthetics: The View from Eternity*. Albany: SUNY Press.
Tomkins, S. 1962/3. *Affect, Imagery, Consciousness*. Vol. 1: Positive Affects/Vol.2: Negative Affects. New York: Springer.
Toynbee, A. 1957. *A Study of History*. Oxford: Oxford University Press.
Varela, F., Thompson, E., and Rosch, E. 1996. *The Embodied Mind: Cognitive Science and Human Experience*. Cambridge, MA: MIT Press.
Wadsworth, B. 2003. *Piaget's Theory of Cognitive and Affective Development: Foundations of Constructivism*. New York: Allyn & Bacon.
Wagner, R. 2008. *Lucid Dreaming: Gateway to the Inner Self*. New York: Moment Point Press.
Wampold, B. 2001. *The Great Psychotherapy Debate: Models, Methods and Findings*. New York: Routledge Press.
White, M., and Epston, D. 1990. *Narrative Means to Therapeutic Ends*. New York: W.W.Norton.
Wilkinson, M. 2010. *Changing Minds in Therapy: Emotion, Attachment, Trauma and Neurobiology*. New York: W.W. Norton & Company.
Williams, M., Teasdale, J., Siegal, Z., and Kabat-Zinn, J, 2007. *The Mindful Way Through Depression: Freeing Yourself from Chronic Unhappiness*. New York: Guilford Press.
Winnicott, D. W. 1953. *Philosophical Investigations*. New York: Macmillan Books.
———. 1958. *The Blue and Brown Books*. New York: Harper Books._
———. 1969. *On Certainty*. New York: Harper Books.
———. 1970a. *Culture and Value*. New York: Harper Books.
———. 1970b. *Zettel*. Berkeley: University of California Press.
———. 1990. *Home is Where We Start From: Essays by a Psychoanalyst*. New York: W.W. Norton.
———. 1992. *The Child, the Family and the Outside World*. New York: Perseus.
Winnicott, D. W., and Kahn, M. 1994. *Holding and Interpretation: Fragment of an Analysis*. New York: Grove Press.
Wittgenstein, L. 1976. *Tractatus Logico-Philosophicus*. New York: Humanities Press.
Yates, F. 1964. *Giordano Bruno and the Hermetic Tradition*. Chicago: Chicago University Press.

Buddhist Studies Reference Works

Asian Classics Input Project, *Derge Tanjur: Release IV*. Compact Disc edition.
Chandra, L. 1959. *Tibetan-Sanskrit Dictionary*. Delhi: International Academy of Indian Culture.
Das, S. C. 1902. *Tibetan-English Dictionary*. Kyoto: Rinsen Book Company.
Gottingen Register of Electronic Texts in Indian Languages (n.d.). www.fiindolo.sub.uni-goettingen.de/gretil.htm

Institute for Advanced Study of World Religions. 1976. *Chone Tanjur Microfiche Edition*. Stoneybrook, NY.

Kanakura, Y. (Ed.). 1953. *A Catologue of the Tohoku University Collection of Tibetan Works on Buddhism*. Sendai: Tohoku (Toh. numbers 5001-7083).

Sakaki, R. (Ed.). 1962. *Mahāvyutpatti*. Tokyo: Suzuki Research Foundation.

Tibetan Tripitaka Research Institute. 1965. *The Tibetan Tripitaka: Peking Edition*. Tokyo: Author.

University of the West: Digital Sanskrit Buddhist Canon.(n.d.) www.uwest.edu/

Yamaguchi, Z., Takasaki, J., and Yasunori, E. 1977. *sDe dge Tibetan Tripitaka bstan hgyur, dbU ma section*. 14 Vols. Tokyo: Tokyo University Press.

Tsong kha pa bLo bzang grags pa. 1956. *gSung 'Bum (Collected Works)*. Peking Edition, Tokyo: Suzuki Research Foundation.

Ui, H. 1934. *A Complete Catalogue of the Tibetan Buddhist Cannons*. Sendai: Tohoku. (Toh. numbers 1-4569).

Scientific Articles and Chapters on Stress and Meditation

Aitken, R. 1982. Zen practice and psychotherapy. *Journal ofTranspersonal Psychology* 18–22.

Alexander, C., Rainforth, M., Maxwell, V., et al. 1991. Transcendental meditaton, self-actualization, and psychological health: a conceptual overview and meta-analysis. *Journal of Social Behavior and Personality* 6: 189–248.

Anand, B., Chinna, G., and Singh, B. 1961. Some aspects of electroencephalographic studies in yogis. *Electroencephalography & Neurophysiology* 13: 452–456.

Austin, J. 1997. Stress reduction through mindfulness meditation: effects on psychological symptomatology, sense of control, and spiritual experiences. *Psychothery and Psychosomatics* 66: 97-106.

———. 1998. *Zen and the Brain: Toward an Understanding of Meditation and Consciousness*. Cambridge: MIT Press.

Bagchi, B., and Wegner, M. 1957. Electrophysiological correlates of some yogi exercises. *Electroencephalogr & Neurophysiology Suppl* 7: 132–149.

Banquet, J. 1973. EEG in meditation. *Electroencephalogr & Neurophysiology* 35: 143–151.

Barbieri, P. 1996. Confronting stress: integrating control theory and mindfulness to cultivate our inner resources through mind-body methods. *Journal of Reality Therapy* 15: 3-13.

Barr, D., Lambert, N., Hoyt, K., et al. 1995. Induction and reversal of long term potentiation by low and high intensity theta pattern stimulation. *Journal of Neuroscience* 15: 5402–5410.

Baumgartner, J., and Epstein, C. 1982. Voluntary alteration of visual evoked potentials. *Annals of Neurology* 12: 475-478.

Bear, D., Freeman, R., Schiff, D., et al. 1985. Interictal behavioral changes in patients with temporal lobe epilepsy, in *Annual Review of Neuropsychiatry.*Washington DC, American Psychiatric Association, 190-214.

Beary, J., and Benson, H. 1974. A simple psychophysiologic technique which elicits the hypometabolic changes of the relaxation response. *Psychosomatic Medicine* 36: 115-120.

Beauchamp-Turner, D., and Levinson, D. 1992. Effects of meditation on stress, health, and affect. *Medical Psychotherapy: An International Journal* 5: 123–131.

Becker, I. 2000. Uses of yoga in psychiatry and medicine. In Muskin, P. (ed.), *Complementary and Alternative Medicine and Psychiatry.* Annual Review of Psychiatry No. 20. Washington DC: American Psychiatric Press.

Benson, H. 1977. Systematic hypertension and the relaxation response. *New England Journal of Medicine* 296: 1152–1156.

Benson, H. 1996. Mind over maladies: can yoga, prayer, and meditation be adapted for managed care? *Hospital Health Network* 70: 26–27.

Benson, H., and Wallace, R. 1972. Decreased blood pressure in hypertensive subjects who practice meditation. *Circulation* 45(suppl2): 516.

———. 1971. Decreased drug abuse with transcendental meditation: a study of 1,862 subjects, in *Congressional Record,* 92nd Congress, 1st Session, Serial No. 92-1. Washington, DC, U.S. Government Printing Office.

Benson, H., Alexander, S., and Feldman, C. 1975. Decreased premature ventricular contractions through the use of the relaxation response in patients with stable ischemic heart disease. *Lancet* 2(3): 80–382.

Benson, H., Frankel, F., Apfel, R., et al. 1978. Treatment of anxiety: a comparison of the usefulness of self-hypnosis and a meditational relaxation technique. *Psychotherapy and Psychosomatics* 30: 229–242.

Benson, H., Lehman, J., Malhotra, M., et al. 1982. Body temperature changes during the practice of gTummo heat yoga. *Nature* 295: 234–236.

Benson, H., Malhotra, M., Goldman, R., et al. 1990. Three case reports of the metabolic and electroencephalographic changes during advanced Buddhist meditative techniques. *Behavioral Medicine* 16: 90–95.

Berkovich-Ohana, A., Glicksohn, J., and Goldstein, A. 2011. Mindfulness-induced changes in gamma band activity—Implications for the default mode network, self-reference and attention. *Clinical Neurophysiology* Sep 20.

Berwick, P., and Oziel, L. 1973. The use of meditation as a behavioral technique. *Behavior Therapy* 4: 743–745.

Birnie, K., Garland, S., and Carlson, L. 2010. Psychological benefits for cancer patients and their partners participating in mindfulness-based stress reduction (MBSR). *Psychooncology* Sep 19(9): 1004–1009.

Bleick, C., and Abrams, A. 1987. The transcendental meditation program and criminal recidivism in California. *Journal of Criminal Justice* 15: 211–230.

Block, B. 1977. The use of transcendental meditation as a reciprocal inhibitor in psychotherapy. *Journal of Psychotherapy* 9: 78–82.

Bogart, G. 1991. The use of meditation in psychotherapy: a review of the literature. *American Journal of Psychotherapy* 45: 382–412.

Bormann, J., and Carrico, A. 2009. Increases in positive reappraisal coping during a group-based mantram intervention mediate sustained reductions in anger in HIV-positive persons. *International Journal of Behavioral Medicine* 16(1): 74–80.

Bracha, H. 2006. Human brain evolution and the "Neuroevolutionary Time-depth principle:" Implications for the Reclassification of fear-circuitry-related traits in DSM-V and for studying resilience to warzone-related posttraumatic stress disorder. *Progress in Neuro-Psychopharmacology & Biological Psychiatry* 30(5): 827–853.

Bradwejn, J., Dowdall, M., Iny, L., et al. 1985. Can East and West meet in psychoanalysis? *American Journal of Psychiatry* 142: 1226–1228.

Brautigam, E. 1977. Effects of the transcendental meditation program on drug abusers: a prospective study. In D. Orme-Johnson and J. Farrow (eds.), *Scientific Research on the Transcendental Meditation Program*. Los Angeles, CA, Maharishi University Press, 506–514.

Bremner, J., Randall, P., Scott, T., et al. 1995. MRI-based measurement of hippocampal volume in patients with combat-related post-traumatic stress disorder. *American Journal of Psychiatry* 1527: 973–981.

Brewer, J., Sinha, R., Chen, J., et al. 2009. Mindfulness training and stress reactivity in substance abuse: results from a randomized, controlled stage I pilot study. *Substance Abuse* Oct-Dec, 30(4): 306–317.

Brown, D. 1977. A model for the levels of concentrative meditation. *International Journal of Clinical and Experimental Hypnosis* 25: 236–273.

Brown, C., and Jones, A. 2010. Meditation experience predicts less negative appraisal of pain: electrophysiological evidence for the involvement of anticipatory neural responses. *Pain* Sep, 150(3): 428–438.

Brown, D., Forte, M., and Dysart, M. 1984. Differences in visual sensitivity among. mindfulness meditators and non-meditators. *Perceptual & Motor Skills* 58: 727–733.

Brown, R., and Gerbarg, P. 2005a. Sudarshan Kriya Yogic Breathing in the Treatment of Stress, Anxiety and Depression: Part I, Neurophysiologic Model. In *Journal of Alternative and Complementary Medicine* 11(1): 189-201.

———. 2005b. Sudarshan Kriya Yogic Breathing in the treatment of Stress, Anxiety and Depression: Part II, Clinical Applications and Guidelines. In *Journal of Alternative and Complementary Medicine* 11(4): 711–717.

———. 2009. Yoga Breathing, Meditation & Longevity. In Bushell, W., Olivo, E., and Thiese, N. (eds.). *Longevity, Regeneration & Optimal Health: Eastern and Western Perspectives*. New York: Annals of the New York Academy of Sciences, 54–62.

Burnard, P. 1987. Meditation: uses and methodsinpsychiatric nurse education. *Nursing Education Today* 7: 187–191.

Bushell, W. 2005. From molecular biology to anti-aging cognitive-behavioral practices: The pioneering research of Walter Pierpaoli on the pineal and bone marrow foreshadows the contemporary revolution in stem cell and regenerative biology. *Annals of the New York Academy of Sciences* 1057: 29–42.

Bushell, W. 1998. *Imagery, bliss and healing in the Indo-Tibetan unexcelled yoga tantras*. Paper presented at the First International Congress on Tibetan Medicine. Washington DC, Georgetown Medical School.

———. 2001. Evidence that a specific meditational regimen may induce adult neurogenesis [abstract]. *Developmental Brain Research* 132: A26.

Calm, B. R., and Polich J, 2006. Meditation states and traits: EEG, ERP, and Neuroimaging Studies. *Psychological Bulletin* 132(2): 180-211.

Carlson, L., Speca, M., Patel, K., and Goodey, E. 2003. Mindfulness-based stress reduction in relation to quality of life, mood, symptoms of stress, and immune parameters in breast and prostate cancer outpatients. *Psychosomatic Medicine* 65: 571–581.

Carlson, L. et al. 2004. Mindfulness-based stress-reduction in relation to quality of life, mood, symptoms of stress and levels of cortisol, dihydrorepiandosterone sulfate and melatonin in breast and cancer outpatients. *Psychoneuroendocrinology* 29: 448–474.

Carmody, J., Crawford, S., Salmoirago-Blotcher, E., et al. 2011. Mindfulness training for coping with hot flashes: results of a randomized trial. *Menopause* Jun 18(6): 611–620.

Carrington, P. 1987. Managing meditation in clinical practice. In M. West (ed.), *The Psychology of Meditation*. Oxford: Clarendon Press, 150–172.

Carrington, P. 1978. *Clinically Standardized Meditation (CSM) Instructor's Kit*. Kendall Park, NJ: Pace Educational Systems.

Carroll, B. 1991. Psychopathology and neurobiology of manic-depressive disorders. In B. Carroll and J. Barrett (eds.). *Psychopathology and the Brain*. New York: Raven, 265–285.

Castillo, R. 1990. Depersonalization and meditation. *Psychiatry* 53: 158–168.

Choudhary, K. 1985. Meditation and tantra: a psychiatric perspective. *Dynamische Psychiatrie* 18: 276–282.

Chung, C. 1990. Psychotherapist and expansion of awareness. *Psychother Psychosom* 53: 28–32.

Ciringotta, F., Todesco, C., and Lugaresi, E. 1980. Case report: temporal lobe epilepsy with ecstatic seizures (so called Dosteyevsky epilepsy). *Epilepsia* 21: 705–710.

Claxton, G. 1987. Meditation in Buddhist psychology. In M. West (ed.), *The Psychology of Meditation*. Oxford: Clarendon Press, 23–38.

Cooper, P. 1999. Buddhist meditation and countertransference: a case study. *American Journal of Psychoanalysis* 59: 71–85.

Coplan, J., Andrews, M., Gorman, J. et al. 1996. Persistent elevations of CSF concentration of corticotropin releasing hormone in adult non-human primates exposed to early life stressors. *Proceedings of the National Academy of Science USA* 93: 1619–1623.

Corby, J., Roth, W., Zarcone, V. et al. 1978. Psychophysiological correlates of the practice of tantric yoga meditation. *Archives of General Psychiatry* 35: 571–577.

Craven, J. 1989. Meditation and psychotherapy. *Canadian Journal of Psychiatry* 34: 647–653.

Crawford, H., Meszaros, I., and Szabo, C. 1989. EEG differences in low and high hypnotizables during waking and hypnosis: rest, math and imaginal tasks. In D. Peterson and E. Wilkie (eds.), *Hypnosis*. London: Whurr, 31–40.

Daniels, L. 1975. The treatment of psychophysiological disorders and severe anxiety by behavior therapy, hypnosis, and transcendental meditation. *American Journal of Clinical Hypnosis* 17: 267–269.

Darnell, A., Bremner, J., Licino, J., et al. 1994. CSF levels of corticortopin releasing factor in chronic posttraumatic stress disorder. *Neuroscience Abstracts* 20: 15.

Das, N., and Gastaut, H. 1955. Variations de l'activite electrique de cerveau du Coeur et des muscles squelletiques au cours de la meditation et de l'extase yogique. *Electroencephalogr Clinical Neurophysiology Suppl* 6: 211–219.

Davidson, R. 2000. Affective style, psychopathology and resilience: Brain mechanisms and plasticity. *American Psychologist*, 1196–1214.

Davidson, R. 1976. The physiology of meditation and mystical states of consciousness. *Perspectives in Biology and Medicine* 19: 345–380.

Davidson, R., and Goleman, D. 1977. The role of attention in meditation and hypnosis: a psychobiological perspective on transformations of consciousness. *International Journal of Clinical and Experimental Hypnosis* 25: 291–308.

Davidson, R., Goleman, D., and Schwartz, G. 1976. Attentional and affective concomitants of meditation. *Journal of Abnormal Psychology* 85: 235–238.

Deepak, K., Manchanda, S., and Maheshwari, M. 1994. Meditation improves clinicoencephalographic measures in drug-resistant epileptics. *Biofeedback and Self-Regulation* 19: 25–40.

Deikman, A. 1966. Deautomatisation and the mystic experience. *Psychiatry* 29: 481–489.
Dietrich, A., 2003. Functional anatomy of altered states of consciousness: The transient hypofrontality hypothesis. *Consciousness & Cognition* 12: 231–256.
Delmonte, M. 1981. Suggestibility and meditation. *Psychological Reports* 48: 727–737.
———. 1984a. Factors influencing the regularity of meditation practice in a clinical population. *British Journal of Medical Psychology,* 57: 275–278.
———. 1984b. Meditation: some similarities with hypnoidal states and hypnosis. *International Journal of Psychosomatics* 31: 24–34.
———. 1984c. Physiological concomitants of meditation practice: a literature review. *International Journal of Psychosomatics* 31: 35–36.
———. 1984d. Psychometric scores and meditation practice: a literature review. *Personal and Individual Differences* 5: 559–563.
———. 1985. Biochemical indices associated with meditation practice: A literature review. *Neuroscience and Biobehavioral Reviews* 9: 557–561.
———. 1987. Personality and meditation. In M. West (ed.). *The Psychology of Meditation.* Oxford: Clarendon Press, 118–131.
———. 1988. Personality correlates ofmeditation practice and frequency in an outpatient population. *Journal of Behavioral Medicine* 11: 593–597.
———. 1989. Meditation, the unconscious, and psychosomatic disorders. *International Journal of Psychosomatics* 36: 45–52.
———. 1995. Meditation and the unconscious. *Journal of Contemporary Psychotherapy* 25: 223–242.
DePascalis, V., and Penna, P. 1990. 40-Hz EEG acitivity during hypnotic induction and hypnotic testing. *International Journal of Clinical and Experimental Hypnosis* 38: 125–138.
Descilo, T., Vedamurtachar, A. Gerbarg, P., et al. 2010. Effects of a yoga breath intervention alone and in combination with an exposure therapy for post-traumatic stress disorder and depression in survivors of the 2004 South-East Asian Tsunami. In *Acta Psychiatrica Scandanavica* 212: 289–300.
Dinardo, P., and Raymond, J. 1979. Locus of control and attention duringmeditation. *Journal of Consulting Clinical Psychology* 47: 1136–1137.
Drevets, W., Videen, T., Price, I., et al. 1992. A functional anatomical study of unipolar depression. *Journal of Neuroscience* 12: 3628–3641.
Doidge, N. 1990. Appetitive pleasure states: a biopsychoanalytic model of the pleasure threshold, mental representation and defense. In R. Glick and S. Bone (eds.). *Pleasure Beyond the Pleasure Principle.* New Haven: Yale University Press, 138–173.
Dubin, W. 1994. The use of meditative techniques in teaching dynamic psychotherapy. *Journal of Transpersonal Psychology* 26: 19–36.
Earle, J. 1984. Cerebral laterality and meditation: a review. In D. Shapiro and R. Walsh (eds.), *Meditation: Classics and Contemporary Perspectives.* New York: Aldine Publishing, 171–190.
Easterlin, B., and Cardena, E. 1998. Cognitive and emotional differences between short- and long-term Vipassana meditators. *Imagination, Cognition and Personality* 18: 69–81.
Edwards, M. 1997. Being present: experiential connections between Zen Buddhist practices and the grieving process. *Disability and Rehabilitation* 19: 44–51.

Eisenberg, D., Kessler, R., Foster, C., et al. 1993. Unconventional medicine in the United States: Prevalence, costs and patterns of use. *New England Journal of Medicine* 328: 246–252.

Elias, A. N. et al. 2000. Ketosis with enhanced GABAergic tone promotes physiological changes in transcendental meditation. *Medical Hypotheses* 54: 660–662.

Emavardhana, T., and Tori, C. 1997. Changes in self-concept, ego defense mechanisms, and religiosity following seven-day Vipassana meditation retreats. *Journal of the Scientific Study of Religion* 36: 194–206.

Engler, J. 1984. Therapeutic aims in psychotherapy and meditation: developmental stages in the representation of self. *Journal of Transpersonal Psychology* 16: 80–93.

Eppel, E., Daubenmier, J., Moscowitz, J. Folkman, S., and Blackburn, E. 2009. Can Meditation Slow the Rate of Cellular Aging? Cognitive Stress, Mindfulness and Telomeres. In W. Bushell, W. Olio, and N. Theise (eds.), *Longevity, Regeneration and Optimal Health: Integrating Eastern and Western Perspectives.* New York: Annals of the New York Academy of Sciences. Volume 1172; 34–53.

Epel, E .S. et al. 2004. Accelerated telomre shortening in response to life stress. In *Proceedings of the National Academy of Sciences USA* 101: 17312–17315.

Epstein, M. 1988. The deconstruction of the self: ego and "egolessness" in Buddhist insight meditation. *Journal of Transpersonal Psychology* 20: 61–69.

———. 1990. Beyond the oceanic feeling: psychoanalytic study of Buddhist meditation. *International Review of Psychoanalysis* 17: 159–166.

Ericsson, A. Kiruthiga, N., and Roring, R. 2009. Toward a Science of Exceptional Achievement: Attaining Superior Performance Through Deliberate Practice. In W. Bushell, E. Olivo, and N. Thiese, (eds.), *Longevity, Regeneration and Optimal Health.* New York: New York Academy of Sciences.

Fang, C., Reibel, D., Longacre, M., et al. 2010. Enhanced psychosocial well-being following participation in a mindfulness-based stress reduction program is associated with increased natural killer cell activity. *Journal of Alternative Complementaey Medicine* May; 16(5): 531–538.

Farrow, J., and Herbert, J. 1982. Breath suspension during the transcendental meditation technique. *Psychosomatic Medicine* 44: 133–153.

Fehr, T. 1977. A longitudinal study of the effect of transcendental meditation program on changes in personality. In D. Orme-Johnson, and J. Farrow (eds.), *Scientific Research on the Transcendental Meditation Program.* Los Angeles: Maharishi University Press, 476–483.

Fenwick, P. 1987. Meditation and the EEG. In West, M. (ed.), *The Psychology of Meditation.* Oxford, England, Clarendon Press, 104–117.

Ferchmin, P., and Ertovic, V. 1989. Forty minutes of experience increase the weight and RNA content of cerebral cortex in preadolescent rats. *Deveopmental Psychobiology* 19: 511–519.

Fergusson, L. 1993. Field independence, transcendental meditation, and achievement in college art: a reexamination. *Percept Mot Skills* 77: 1104–1106.

Fergusson, L, and Gowan, J. 1976. TM: Some preliminary psychological findings. *Journal of Humanistic Psychology* 16: 51–60.

Fieve, R. 1997. Bipolar II disorder and its proposed beneficial subtype bipolar IIb: a desirable disorder? In D. Dunner (ed.), *Current Psychiatric Therapy II.* Philadelphia, PA, WB Saunders, 261–266.

Finn, M. 1992. Transitional space and Tibetan Buddhism: The object relations of meditation. In M. Finn, and J. Gartner (eds.), *Object Relations Theory and Religion*. Westport, Praeger, 109–118.

Fredrickson B, 2005. Positive affect and the complex dynamics of human flourishing. *American Psyhologist* 60: 678–696.

Gackenbach, J. 1992. Interhemispheric EEG coherence in REM sleep and meditation: the lucid dreaming connection. In J. Antrobus, and M. Bertini (eds.), *The Neuropsychology of Sleep and Dreaming*. Hillsdale, NJ, Erlbaum, 265–288.

Garland, E., Gaylord, S., Boettiger, and C., Howard, O. 1992. Mindfulness training modifies cognitive, affective, and physiological mechanisms implicated in alcohol dependence: results of a randomized controlled pilot trial. *Journal of Psychoactive Drugs* Jun, 42(2): 177–192.

Gelderloos, P., Hermans, F., Ahlscrom, H., et al. 1990. Transcendence and psychological health: studies with long-termparticipants of the transcendental meditation and TM-Sidhi program. *Journal of Psychology* 124: 177-197.

Gellhorn, E., and Kiely, W. 1972. Mystical states of .consciousness: neurophysiological and clinical aspects. *Journal of Nervous and Mental Disease* 154: 399–405.

Gerbarg, P. 2007. Yoga and neuro-psychoanalysis. In Anderson, P. (ed.) *Bodies in Treatment: The Unspoken Dimension*. Hillsdale: The Analytic Press.

Geschwind, N., Peeters, F., Drukker, M., van Os, J., and Wichers, M. 2011. Mindfulness training increases momentary positive emotions and reward experience in adults vulnerable to depression: A randomized controlled trial. *Journal of Consulting Clinical Psychology* Oct, 79(5): 618–628.

Girodo, M. 1974. Yoga meditation and flooding in the treatment of anxiety neurosis. *Journal of Behavior Therapy and Experimental Psychiatry* 5: 157–160.

Glueck, B., and Stroebel, C. 1975. Biofeedback and meditation in the treatment of psychiatric illness. *Compehensive Psychiatry* 16: 303–321.

Goldin, P., and Gross, J. 2010. Effects of mindfulness-based stress-reduction (MBSR) on emotion regulation in social anxiety disorder. In *Emotion* Feb, 10(1): 83–91.

Grant, J., Courtemanche, J., Duerden, E., Duncan, G., and Rainville, P. 2010. Cortical thickness and pain sensitivity in zen meditators. *Emotion* Feb, 10(1): 43–53.

Grant, J., Courtemanche, J., and Rainville, P. 2011. A non-elaborative mental stance and decoupling of executive and pain-related cortices predicts low pain sensitivity in Zen meditators. *Pain* Jan, 152(1): 150–156.

Green, E., Ferguson, A., Green, A., et al. 1970. *Preliminary Report on Voluntary Controls Project: Swami Rama*. Topeka, KS, Menninger Foundation.

Greenough, W., and Volkmar, F. 1973. Pattern of dendritic branching in occipital cortex of rats reared in complex environments. *Experimental Neurology* 40: 136-143.

Greenwood, M., and Benson, H. 1977. The efficacy of progressive relaxation in systematic desensitization and a proposal for an alternative competitive response-the relaxation response. *Behaviour Research and Therapy* 15: 337–343.

Gross, C., Kreitzer, M., Reilly-Spong, M., Wall, M., et al. 2011. Mindfulness-based stress reduction versus pharmacotherapy for chronic primary insomnia: a randomized controlled clinical trial. *Explore* (NY). Mar-Apr, 7(2): 76–87.

Gruzelier, J., and Brow, T. 1985. Psychophysiological evidence for a state theory of hypnosis and susceptibility. *Journal of Psychosomatic Research* 29:287–302.

Halper, J. 1998. *Advanced Buddhist meditation and the internal reward system*. Paper presented at the First International Congress on Tibetan Medicine. Washington, DC, Georgetown Medical School.

Harinath, K. et al. 2004. Effects of hatha yoga and Omkar meditation on cardiorespiratory performance, psychologic profile, and melatonin secretion. *Journal of Alternative and Complementary Medicine* 10: 261–268.

Harte, J., Eifert, G., and Smith, R. 1995. The effects of running and meditation onbetaendorphin, corticotropin-releasing hormone and cortisol in plasma, and on mood. *Biological Psychiatry* 40(2): 51–265.

Hassed, C. 1996. Meditation in general practice. *Australian Family Physician* 25: 1257–1260.

Hayward, J. 1998. A dzogs-chen Buddhist interpretation of the sense of self. *Journal of Consciousness Studies* 5: 611–626.

Heath, R. 1963. Electrical self-stimulation in the brain of man. *Am erican Journal of Psychiatry* 120: 571–577.

Heide, F., Wadlington, W., and Lundy, R. 1980. Hypnotic responsivity as a predictor of outcome in meditation. *International Journal of Clinical and Experimental Hypnosis* 28(3): 58–366.

Heller, C., Elsner, R., and Rao, N. 1987. Voluntary hypometabolism in an Indian Yogi. *Journal of Thermal Biology* 2: 171–173.

Henderson, V., Clemow, L., Massion, A., et al. 2011. The effects of mindfulness-based stress reduction on psychosocial outcomes and quality of life in early-stage breast cancer patients: a randomized trial. *Breast Cancer Research and Treatment* Sep 8.

Herzog, H., Lele, V., Kuwert, K., et al. 1991. Changed pattern of regional glucose metabolism during yoga meditative relaxation. *Neuropsychobiology* 23: 182–187.

Hjelle, L. 1974. Transcendental meditation and psychological health. *Perceptual & Motor Skills* 39: 623–628.

Holmes, D. 1987. The influence of meditation versus rest on physiological arousal: a second examination. In M. West (ed.), *The Psychology of Meditation*. Oxford: Clarendon Press, 81–103.

Ikemi, A. 1988. Psychophysiological effects ofself-regulationmethod: EEG frequency analysis and contingent negative variations. *Psychothery and Psychosomatics* 49: 230–239.

Infante, J., Peran, F., Martinez, M., et al. 1998. ACTH and beta-endorphin in transcendental meditation. *Physioloical Behav*ior 64: 311–315.

Jacobs, T., Epel, E., Lin, J., Blackburn, E., et al. 2011. Intensive meditation training, immune cell telomerase activity, and psychological mediators. *Psychoneuroendocrinology* Jun, 36(5): 664–681.

Jain, S., Boswell, E., and Jain, S. 1985. Hypnosis, biofeedback, and meditation as adjunctive techniques in treating distressed families. *Revista Internazionale di Psicologia e Ipnosi* 26: 337–345.

Janakiramaiah, N., Gangadbhar, B., Naga Venkatesha Murthy, P., et al. 2000. Antidepressant efficacy of Sudarshan Kriya Yoga (SKY) in melancholia: A randomized comparison with electroconvulsive therapy (ECT) and imipramine. *Journal of Affective Discord* 57: 255–259.

Janakiramaiah, N., Gangadbhar, B., Naga Venkatesha Murthy, P., et al. 1998. Therapuetic efficacy of Sudarshan Kriya Yoga (SKY) in dysthymic disorder. In *National Institute of Mental Health and Neurological Sciences Journal* 17: 21–28.

Jang, J., Jung, W., Kang, D., et al. 2011. Increased default mode network connectivity associated with meditation. *Neuroscience Letters* Jan 10, 487(3): 358–362.

Jedrczak, A., Beresford, M., and Clements, G. 1985. The TM-Sidhi program, pure consciousness, creativity and intelligence. *Journal of Creativity and Behavior* 19: 270–275.

Jella, S., and Shannahoff-Khalsa, D. 1993. The effectsof forced nostril breathing on cognitive performance. *International Journal of Neuroscience* 73: 61–68.

Jevning, R., Anand, R., Biedenbach, M., et al. 1996. Effects on regional cerebral blood-flow of transcendental meditation. *Physiology & Behavior* 59: 339–402.

Jevning, R., Wallace, R., and Beidebach, M. 1992. The physiology of meditation: a review. A wakeful hypometabolic integrated response. *Neuroscience and Biobehavioral Review* 16: 415–424.

Jha, A., Stanley, E., Kiyonaga, A., Wong, L., and Gelfand, L. 2010. Examining the protective effects of mindfulness training on working memory capacity and affective experience. *Emotion* Feb, 10(1): 54–64.

Jones, B. M. 2001. Changes in cytokine production; in healthy subjects practicing Guolin Qigong: a pilot study. *Journal of Complementary Alternative Medicine* 1: 8–12.

Kabat-Zinn, J. 1982. An outpatient program based in behavioral medicine for chronic pain patients based on the practice of mindfulness meditation: theoretical considerations and preliminary results. *General Hospital Psychiatry* 4: 33–47.

Kabat-Zinn, J., Chapman, A., and Salmon, P. 1997. Relationship of cognitive and somatic components of anxiety to preference for different relaxation techniques. *Mind/Body Medicine* 2: 101–109.

Kabat-Zinn, J., Lipworth, L., and Burney, R. 1985. The clinical use of mindfulness meditation for the self-regulation of chronic pain. *Journal of Behavioral Medicine* 8: 163–190.

Kabat-Zinn, J., Massion, A., Kristeller, J, et al. 1992. Effectiveness of a meditation-based stress-reduction program in the treatment of anxiety disorders. *American Journal of Psychiatry* 149: 936–943.

Kabat-Zinn, J., Whitworth, J., Burney, R., et al. 1987. Four-year follow up of a meditation-based program for the regulation of chronic pain: treatment outcome and compliance. *The Clinical Journal of Pain* 2: 159–173.

Kahn, K. 1985. Vipassana meditation and the psychobiology of Wilhelm Reich. *Journal of Humanistic Psychology* 25: 117–128.

Kandel, E. 1999. Biology and thel future of psychoanalysis: a new intellectual framework for psychiatry revisited. *American Journal of Psychiatry* 156: 505–524.

Karawatt, M. 1991. Notes for a study on the active imaginationand meditation techniques. *Giornale Storico di Psicologia Dinamica* 15: 31–53.

Kasamatsu, A., and Harai, T. 1966. An electroencephalographic study on Zen meditation (zazen). *Folia Psychiatrica et Neurologica Japanica* 20:315–336.

Kasamatsu, A., Okuma, T., Takenaka, S., et al. 1957. The EEG of Zen and yoga practitioners. *Electroencephalography and Clinical Neurophysiology Suppl* 9: 51–52.

Kelly, G. 1996. Using meditative techniques in psychotherapy. *Journal of Humanistic Psychology* 36: 49–66.

Kerr, C., Jones, S., Wan, Q., et al. 2011. Effects of mindfulness meditation training on anticipatory alpha modulation in primary somatosensory cortex. *Brain Research Bulletin* May 30; 85(3–4): 96–103.

Kilpatrick, L., Suyenobu, B., Smith, S., et al. 2011. Impact of Mindfulness-Based Stress Reduction training on intrinsic brain connectivity. *Neuroimage* May 1; 56(1): 290–298.

Kim, D.H. et al, 2005. Effect of-Zen-meditation on serum-nitric-oxide activity and lipid peroxidation. *Progressive Neuropsychopharmacology and Biological. Psychiatry* 29: 327–331.

Kjaer T., Bertelson, C., et al. 2002. Increased dopaminergic tone during a meditation induced change of consciousness. *Brain Research and Cognitive Brain Research* 13(2): 255–2599.

Kozasa, E., Sato, J., Lacerda, S., et al. 2011. Meditation training increases brain efficiency in an attention task. *Neuroimage* Jul 7.

Kozhevnikov, M., Louchakova, O., Josipovic, Z., and Motes, M. 2009. The enhancement of visuospatial processing efficiency through Buddhist Deity meditation *Psychological Science* May, 20(5): 645–653.

Krivan, M., Szabo, G., Sarnyai, Z., et al. 1995. Oxytocin blocks the development of heroin-fentanyl cross-tolerance in mice. *Pharmacology Biochemistry & Behavior* 52: 591–594.

Kubota, Y., et al. 2001. Frontal midline theta rhythm is correlated with cardiac autonomic activities during the performance of an attention demanding meditation procedure. *Brain Research and Cognitive Brain Research* 11(2): 281–287.

Kuyken, W., Byford, S., Taylor, R., et al. 2008. Mindfulness-based cognitive therapy to prevent relapse in recurrent depression. *Journal of Consulting Clinical Psychology* Dec, 76(6): 966–978.

Kutz, I., Borysenko, J., and Benson, H. 1985. Meditation and psychotherapy: a rationale for the integration of dynamic psychotherapy, the relaxation response and mindfulness meditation. *American Journal of Psychiatry* 142: 1–8.

Lazar, S. W., et al, 2005. Meditation experience is associated with increased cortical thickness. *NeuroReport* 16(17): 1893–1897.

Lazarus, A. 1976. Psychiatric problems precipitated by transcendental meditation. *Psychological Report* 39: 601–602.

Lengacher, C., Johnson-Mallard, V., Post-White, J., et al. 2009. Randomized controlled trial of mindfulness-based stress reduction (MBSR) for survivors of breast cancer. *Psychooncology* Dec, 18(12): 1261–1272.

Leone, G. 1995. Zen meditation: a psychoanalytic conceptualization. *Journal of Transpersonal Psychology* 27: 87–94.

Lesh, T. 1970. Zen meditation and the development of empathy in counselors. *Journal of Humanistic Psychology* 10: 39–74.

Limb, C., Kemeny, S., Ortgoza, E., et al., 2006. Left hemispheric lateralization of brain activity during passive rhythm perception in musicians. *Anatomical Record Part A: Discoveries in Molecular Cellular and Evolutionary Biology* 288:382–9.

Linehan, M., Armstrong, H., Suarez, A., et al. 1991. Cognitive-behavioral treatmentof chronically parasuicidal borderline patients. *Archives of General Psychiatry* 48: 1060–1064.

Linehan, M., Goldfried, M., and Goldfried, A. 1979. Assertion therapy: skill training or cognitive restructuring. *Behavior Therapy* 10: 372–388.

Linehan, M., and Shearin, E. 1988. Lethal stress: a social-behavioral model ofsuicidal behavior. In S. Fisher and J. Reason (eds.), *Handbook of Life Stress, Cognition, and Health*. New York, Wiley, 65–285.

Linehan, M., Tutek, D., and Heard, H. 1992. *Interpersonal and social treatment outcomes for borderline personality disorder.* Presented at the annual meeting of the Association for the Advancement of Behavior Therapy, Boston, MA.

Liu, G., Cui, R., Li, G., et al. 1990. Changes in brainstem and cortical auditory potentials during qi-gong meditation. *American Journal of Chinese Medicine* 18: 95–103.

Liu, C., Wei, C., and Lo, P. 2009. Variation Analysis of Sphygmogram to Assess Cardiovascular System under Meditation. *Evidence-based Complementary and Alternative Medicine* Mar, 6(1): 107–112.

Loizzo, J. 1997. Intersubjectivity in Wittgenstein and Freud: Other Minds and the Foundations of Psychiatry. *Journal of Theoretical Medicine* Vol. 12, No 3; 111–129.

Loizzo, J. 1998. The psychobiology of the Indo-Tibetan unexcelled yoga tantras a learning model. Paper presented at the First International Congress on Tibetan Medicine. Washington, DC, Georgetown Medical School.

Loizzo, J. 2000. Meditation and Psychotherapy: Stress, Allostasis and Enriched Learning. In P. Muskin (ed,), *Complementary and Alternative Medicine and Psychiatry.* Washington: American Psychiatric Association Press.

Loizzo, J., 2009. Optimizing Learning and Quality of Life throughout the Lifespan. In W. Bushell and E. Olivo (eds.), *Longevity, Regeneration and Optimal Health.* New York: New York Academy of Sciences.

Loizzo, J., and Blackhall, L. 1998. Traditional alternatives as complementary sciences: the case of Indo-Tibetan medicine. *Journal of Alternative and Complementary Medicine* 4: 311–319.

Loizzo, J. Blackhall, L., and Rabgyay, L. 2009. Tibetan Medicine: A Complementary Science of Integative Healthcare. In W. Bushell and E. Olivo (eds.), *Longevity, Regeneration & Optimal Health.* New York: Annals of New York Academy of Sciences.

Loizzo, J., Charlson, M., and Peterson, J. A 2009. Program in Contemplative Self-Healing: Stress, Allostasis and Enriched Learning in the Indo-Tibetan Tradition. In W. Bushell and E. Olivo (eds.), *Longevity, Regeneration and Optimal Health: Integrating Eastern and Western Perspectives.* New York: Annals of the New York Academy of Sciences, 123–147.

Loizzo, J., Peterson, J., Wolf, E., Altemus, M., Briggs, W., Vadhat, L., and Charlson, M. 2010. The effects of a program in contemplative self-healing on quality of life in women with breast and other gynecologic cancer. *Alternative Therapies in Health and Medicine* May/Jun, 16, 3: 30–37.

Luckoff, D., Wallace, C., Liberman, R., et al. 1986. A holistic program for chronic schizophrenic patients. *Schizophrenia Bulletin* 12: 274–282.

Lutz, A., Grieschar, L., Rawlings, N., et al. 2004. Long-term meditators self-induce high amplitude gamma synchrony during mental practice. In *Proceedings of the National Academy of Sciences* 101: 16369–16373.

Lutz, A., Slagter, H., Dunne, J., and Davidson, R. 2008. Attention regulation and monitoring in meditation. In *Trends in Cognitive Science* Apr, 12(4): 163–169.

Lutz, A., Slagter, H., Rawlings, N., Francis, A., Greischar, L., and Davidson, R. 2009. Mental training enhances attentional stability: neural and behavioral evidence. *Journal of Neuroscience* Oct 21, 29(42): 13418–13427.

MacLean, P. 1959. The limbic system with respect to two basic life principles. In *Second Conference on the Central Nervous System and Behavior.* New York, Josiah Macy Foundation, 43–59.

MacLean, K., Ferrer, E., Aichele, S., et al. 2010. Intensive meditation training improves perceptual discrimination and sustained attention. *Psychological Science* Jun, 21(6): 829–839.

Mandell, A. 1979. Psychiatric aspects of sports. *Psychiatric Annals* 9: 154–160.

Marriott, J. 1996. Meditation and hypnotherapy. *Australian Journal of Clinical Hypnotherapy and Hypnosis* 17: 53–62.

Martarelli, D., Cocchioni, M., Scuri, S., Pompei, P. 2009. Diaphragmatic Breathing Reduces Exercise-induced Oxidative Stress. *Evidence-based Complementary and Alternative Medicine*, Oct 29.

Martarelli, D., Cocchioni, M., Scuri, S., and Pompei, P. 2011. Diaphragmatic breathing reduces postprandial oxidative stress. *Journal of Alternative and Complementary Medicine* Jul, 17(7): 623–628.

Mason, L., Alexander, C., Travis, F., et al. 1997. Electrophysiological correlates of higher states of consciousness during sleep in long-term practitioners of the transcendental meditation program. *Sleep* 20: 102–110.

Matousek, R., and Dobkin, P. 2010. Weathering storms: a cohort study of how participation in a mindfulness-based stress reduction program benefits women after breast cancer treatment. *Current Oncology* Aug, 17(4): 62–70.

Mattson, M. P., et al. 2002. Modification of brain aging and neurodegenerative disorders by genes, diet, and behavior. *Physiological Review* 82: 637–672.

Maupin, E. 1965. Individual differences in response to a Zen meditation exercise. *Journal of Consulting and Clinical Psychology* 29: 139–145.

Mikulas, W. 1978. Four noble truths of Buddhism related to behavior therapy. *Psychological Records* 28: 59–67.

———. 1981. Buddhism and behavioral modification. *Psychological Records* 31: 331–342.

Miller, J. 1993. The unveiling of traumatic memories and emotions through mindfulness and concentration meditation: clinical implications and three case reports. *Journal of Transpersonal Psychology* 25: 169–180.

———, Fletcher, K., and Kabat-Zinn, J. 1995. Three-year follow-up and clinical implications of a mindfulness-based stress reduction intervention in the treatment of anxiety disorders. *General Hospital Psychiatry* 17: 192–200.

Moore, A., and Malinowski, P. 2009. Meditation, mindfulness and cognitive flexibility. *Conscious Cognition* Mar, 18(1): 176–186.

Morgan, C. A., et al. 2004. Relationships among plasma dehydroepiandrosterone sulfate and cortisol levels, symptoms of dissociation, and objective performance in humans exposed to acute stress. *Archives of General Psychiatry* 61: 819–825.

Morse, D., Cohen, L., Furst, L., et al. 1984. A physiological evaluation of the yoga concept of respiratory control of autonomic system activity. *International Journal of Psychosomatics* 31: 3–19.

Murphy, T., Pagano, R., and Marlatt, G. 1986. Lifestyle modification with heavy alcohol drinkers: effects of aerobic exercise and meditation. *Addictive Behavior* 11: 175–186.

Murthy, P., Gangadar, B., Janakiranaiah, N., et al. 1997. Normalization of P300 amplitude following treatment in dysthymia. *Biological Psychiatry* 42: 740–743.

Narayan, R., Kamat, A., Khanolkar, M., et al. 1990. Quantitative evaluation of muscle relaxation induced by kundalini yoga with the help of EMG integrator. *Indian Journal of Physiology and Pharmacology* 34: 279–281.

Naveen, K., Nagarathna, R., Nagendra, H., et al. 1997. Yoga breathing through a particular nostril increases spacialmemoryscores without lateralized effects. *Psychological Reports* 81: 555–561.

Nesvold, A., Fagerland, M., Davanger, S., et al. 2011. Increased heart rate variability during nondirective meditation. *European Journal of Cardiovascular Prevention & Rehabilitation* Jun 21.

Newman, J. 1994. Affective empathy training with senior citizens using Zazen meditation. *Dissertation Abstracts International Section A* 55: 1193.

Ng, K., and Gibbs, M. 1991. Stages in memory formation: a review. In Andrew, R. (ed.), *Neural and Behavioral Plasticity: The Use of the Domestic Chick as a Model*. Oxford, UK: Oxford University Press, 351–369.

Nidich, S., Fields, J., Rainforth, M., et al. 2009. A randomized controlled trial of the effects of transcendental meditation on quality of life in older breast cancer patients. *Integrative Cancer Therapies* Sep, 8(3): 228–234.

Nidich, S., Rainforth, M., Haaga, D., et al. 2009. A randomized controlled trial on effects of the Transcendental Meditation program on blood pressure, psychological distress, and coping in young adults. *American Journal of Hypertension* Dec, 22(12): 1326–1331.

O'Halloran, J., Jevning, R., Wilson, A., et al. 1985. Hormonal control in a state of decreased activation: potentiation of argenine vasopressin secretion. *Physiological Behavior* 35: 591–595.

Orme-Johnson, D. 1995. Evidence that transcendental meditation does not produce cognitive kindling: A comment. *Perceptual & Motor Skills* 81: 642.

Orme-Johnson, D., Kielbauch, J., Moore, R., et al. 1977. Personality and autonomic changes in prisoners practicing the transcendental meditation technique. In D. Orme-Johnson and J. Farrow (eds.), *Scientific Research on the Transcendental Meditation Program*. Los Angeles: Maharishi University Press, 556–561.

Ornish, D., Brown, S., Scherwitz, L., et al. 1990. Can lifestyle changes reverse coronary heart disease? *Lancet* 336: 129–133.

Panjawani, U., Selvamurthy, W., Singh, S., et al. 1996. Effect ofSahaja yoga practice on seizure control and EEG changes in patients with epilepsy. *Indian Journal of Medical Research* 103: 165–172.

Pelletier, K. 1977. Effects of the transcendental meditation program on perceptual style: increased field independence. In D. Orme-Johnson and J. Farrow (eds.), *Scientific Research on the Transcendental Meditation Program*. Los Angeles:Maharishi University Press, 337–345.

Persinger, M. 1984. Striking EEG profiles from single episodes of glossolalia and transcendental meditation. *Perceptual & Motor Skills* 58: 127–133.

———. 1993. Transcendental meditation and general meditation are associated with enhanced complexpartial epileptic-like signs: evidence for "cognitive" kindling? *Perceptual & Motor Skills* 76: 80–82.

Peterson, J., Charlson, M., Loizzo, J., et al. 2012. The effects of contemplative self-healing on quality of life in underserved women with breast and other gynecologic cancers. In publication.

Prince, R. 1978. Meditation: some psychological speculations. *Psychology Journal of the University of Ottawa* 3: 202–209.

Richter, D., and Speyer, K. 1990. Cardiopulmonary Control. In Loewy, A. & Speyer, K. (eds). *Central Regulation of Autonomic Function*. New York: Oxford University Press.

Rosensweig, M., and Bennett, E. 1996. Psychobiology ofplasticity: effects of training and experienceonbrain and behavior. *Behavioural Brain Research* 78: 57–65.

Rubik, B. 2011. Neurofeedback-enhanced gamma brainwaves from the prefrontal cortical region of meditators and non-meditators and associated subjective experiences. *Journal of Alternative and Complementary Medicine* Feb, 17(2): 109–115.

Rubin, J. 1985. Meditation and psychoanalytic listening. *Psychoanalytic Review* 72: 599–613.

Ryff, C., and Singer, B. 1998. The contours of positive human health. *Psychological Inquiry* 9: 1–28.

Sabourin, M., Cutomb, S., Crawford, H., et al. 1990. EEG correlates of hypnotic susceptibility and hypnotic trance: spectral analysis and coherence. *Internal Journal of Psychophysioogul* 10: 125–142.

Sahdra, B., MacLean, K., Ferrer, E., et al. 2011. Enhanced response inhibition during intensive meditation training predicts improvements in self-reported adaptive socioemotional functioning. *Emotion* Apr, 11(2): 299–312.

Sasaki, Y. 1992. Developments in Zen therapy based on Zen meditation: an overview. *Japanese Psychological Review* 35: 113–131.

Schacter, D. 1977. EEG theta waves and psychological phenomena: a review and analysis. *Biological Psychology* 5: 47–82.

Schafii, M. 1975. Meditation and prevention of alcohol abuse. *American Journal of Psychiatry* 132: 942–945.

Schafii, M., Lavely, R., and Jaffe, R. 1974. Meditation and marijuana. *American Journal of Psychiatry* 131: 60–63.

Schaie, K. 1994. The course of adult intellectual development. *American Psychologist* 49: 304–313.

Scherwitz, L., Graham, L., Grandits, G., et al. 1986. Self-involvementand coronary heart disease incidence In the Multiple Risk Factor Intervention Trial. *Psychosomatic Medicne* 84: 187–199.

Seeman, T., McEwen, B., Singer, B., et al. 1997. Increase in unrinary cortisol excretion and memory declines: MacArthur studies of successful aging. *Journal of Clinical Endocrinology and Metabolism* 82: 2458–2465.

Seidel, E., Eickoff, S., Kellermann, T., et al. 2010. Who is to blame? Neural correlates of causal attribution in social situations. *Society for Neuroscience* 5(4): 355–350.

Shaffer, H., LaSalvia, T., and Stein, J. 1997. Comparing hatha yoga with dynamic group psychotherapy for enhancing methadone maintenance treatment: A randomized clinical trial. *Alternative Therapies* 3: 57–66.

Sharinahoff-Khalsa, D., and Beckett, L. 1996. Clinical case report: efficacy of yogic techniques in the treatment of obsessive compulsive disorders. *International Journal of Neuroscience* 85: 1–17.

Shapiro, D. 1987. Implications of psychotherapy research for the study of meditation. In M. West (ed.), *The Psychology of Meditation*. Oxford: Clarendon Press, 173–192

———. 1992. A preliminary study of long-term meditators: goals, effects, religious orientation, cognitions. *Journal of Transpersonal Psychology* 24: 23–39.

Shapiro, D., and Walsh, R. 1982. *Beyond Health and Normality: Explorations in Exceptional Psychological Well-Being*. New York: Van Nostrand.

Shapiro, S., Schwartz, G., and Bonner, G. 1998. Effects of mindfulness-based stress reduction on medical and premedical students. *Journal of Behavioral Medicine* 21: 581–599.

Sheline, Y., Wang, W., Gado, M., et al. 1996. Hippocampal atrophy in recurrent unipolar depression. *Proceedings of the National Academy of Science USA* 93: 3908–3913.

Shimamura, A., Berry, J., Mangels, J., et al. 1995. Memory and cognitive abilities in university professors: evidence for successful aging. *Psychological Science* 6: 271–277.

Shulkin, J., McEwen, B., & Gold, P. 1994. Allostasis, amygdala, and anticipatory angst. *Neuroscience & Biobehavioral Reviews* 18: 385–396.

Shulkin, J., Gold, P., and McEwen, B. 1998. Induction of corticotropin-releasing hormone gene expression by glucocorticoids: implications for understanding the states of fear and anxiety and allostatic load. *Psychoneuroendocrinology* 23: 219–243.

Simpson, E., Pistorello, J., Begin, A., et al. 1998. Use of dialectical behavior therapy in a partial hospital program for women with borderline personality disorder. *Psychiatric Services* 49: 669–673.

Skuse, D., Morris, J., and Dolan, R, 2005. Functional dissociation of amygdale-modulated arousal and cognitive appraisal, in Turner syndrome. *Brain* 128(9): 2084–2096.

Slagter, H., Lutz, A., Greischar, L., Nieuwenhuis, S., and Davidson, R. 2009. Theta phase synchrony and conscious target perception: impact of intensive mental training. *Journal of Cognitive Neuroscience* Aug, 21(8): 1536–1549.

Slawinska, U., and Kasicki, S. 1995. Theta-like rhythm in depth EEG activity of hypothalamic areas during spontaneous or electricallyinduced locomotion in rats. *Brain Research* 678: 117–126.

Smith, J. 1978. Personality correlates of continuation and outcome in meditation and erect sitting control treatments. *Journal of Consulting and Clinical Psychology* 46: 272–279.

Smith, J. 1987. Meditation as psychotherapy: a newlook at the evidence. In West, M. (ed.), *The Psychology of Meditation*. Oxford: Clarendon Press, 136–149.

Smith, W., Compton, W., and West, W. 1995. Meditation as an adjunct to a happiness enhancement program. *Journal of Clinical Psychiatry* 51: 269–273.

Smith, M., Davidson, J., Ritchie, J., et al. 1989. The corticotropin releasinghormone test in patients with posttraumatic stress disorder. *Biological Psychology* 26: 349–355.

Snaith, P. 1998. Meditation and psychotherapy. *British Journal of Psychiatry* 173: 193–195.

Sommer, S., and Hassed, C. 1995. Meditation-based stress management for doctors and students. *Medical Journal of Australia* 163: 112.

Spanos, N., Stam, H., Rivers, S., et al. 1980. Meditation: expectation and performances on indices of nonanalytic attending. *International Journal of Clinical and Experimental Hypnosis* 28: 244–251.

Spencer, W., and Kandel, E. 1961. Hippocampal neuron responses to selective activation of recurrent collaterals of hippocampofugal axons. *Experimental Neurology* 4: 149–161.

Stancak, A., and Kuna, M. 1994. EEG changes during forced alternate nostril breathing. *International Journal of Psychophysiology* 18: 7 5–79.

Starkman, M., Gebarski, S., Berent, S., et al. 1993. Hippocampal formation volume memory dysfunction and cortisol levels in patients with Cushings syndrome. *Biological Psychiatry* 32: 756–765.

Stek, R., and Bass, B. 1973. Personal adjustmentandperceived locus ofcontrolamong students interested in meditation. *Psychology Report* 32: 1019–1022.

Swaab, D. 1991. Brain aging and Alzheimer's disease: "wear and tear" versus "use it or lose it." *Neurobiology of Aging* 12: 317–324.

Sweet, M. 1990. Enhancing empathy: the interpersonal implications of a Buddhist meditation technique. *Psychotherapy* 27: 19–29.

Tang, Y., Lu, Q., Geng, X., Stein, E., Yang, Y., and Posner, M. 2010. Short-term meditation induces white matter changes in the anterior cingulate. *Proceedings of the National Academy of Science USA* Aug 31, 107(35): 15649–15652.

Tang, Y, Ma, Y., Fan, Y., et al. 2009. Central and autonomic nervous system interaction is altered by short-term meditation. *Proceedings of the National Academy of Science USA* Jun 2, 106(22): 8865–8870.

Taub, E., Steiner, S., Weingarten, E., et al. 1994. Effectiveness of broad spectrum approaches to relapse prevention in severe alchoholism: a long-term, randomized, controlled trial of Transcendental Meditation, EMG biofeedback, and electronic neurotherapy. *Alcoholism Treatment Quarterly* 11: 187–220.

Teasdale, J., Segal, Z., and Williams, J. 1995. How does cognitive therapy prevent depressive relapse and why should attentional control (mindfulness) training help? *Behaviour Research and Therapy* 33: 25–39.

Telles, S., and Naveen, K. 1997. Yoga for rehabilitation: an overview. *Indian Journal of Medical Science* 51: 123–127.

Tloczynski, J., and Tantriella, M. 1993. A comparison of the effects of Zen breath meditation or relaxation on college adjustment. *Psychologia Internationalis: Journal of Psychology of the Orient* 41: 32–43.

Tooley, G. A., Armstrong, S. M., Norman, T. R., and Sali. A. 2000. Acute increases in nighttime plasma melatonin levels following a period of meditation. *Biological. Psychology* 53: 69–78.

Travis, F., Haaga, D., Hagelin, J., et al. 2009. Effects of Transcendental Meditation practice on brain functioning and stress reactivity in college students. *International Journal of Psychophysiology* Feb, 1(2): 170–176.

Travis, F. 1994. The junction-point model: a field model of waking, sleeping, and dreaming, relating dream witnessing, the waking/sleeping transition, and transcendental meditation in terms of a common psychophysiologic state. *Dreaming: Journal of the Association for the Study of Dreams* 4: 91–104.

Turnbull, M., and Norris, H. 1982. Effects of transcendental meditation on selfidentity indices and personality. *British Journal of Psychology* 73: 57–68.

Urbanowski, F., and Miller, J. 1996. Trauma, psychotherapy, and meditation. *Journal of Transpersonal Psychology* 28: 31–48.

Van den Hurk, P., Giommi, F., Gielen, S., et al. 2010. Greater efficiency in attentional processing related to mindfulness meditation. *Quarterly Journal of Experimental Psychology (Colchester)* Jun, 63(6): 1168–1180.

Van den Hurk, P., Janssen, B., Giommi, F., et al. 2010. Mindfulness meditation associated with alterations in bottom-up processing: psychophysiological evidence for reduced reactivity. *International Journal of Psychophysiology* Nov, 78(2): 151–157.

Van Nuys, D. 1973. Meditation, attention and hypnotic susceptibility: a correlational study. *International Journal of Clinical and Experimental Hypnosis* 21: 59–69.

Vestergaard-Poulsen, P., van Beek, M., Skewes, J., et al. 2009. Long-term meditation is associated with increased gray matter density in the brain stem. *Neuroreport* Jan 28,20(2): 170–174.

Vigne, J. 1991. Guru and psychotherapist: comparisons from the Hindu tradition. *Journal of Transpersonal Psychology* 23: 121–138.

Walde, L. C. et al, 2004. A pilot, study of a yoga and meditation intervention for dementia caregiver stress. *Journal of Cliical. Psycholo*gy 60: 677–687.

Wallace, A. 1999. The Buddhist tradition of Samatha: methods for refining and examining consciousness. *Journal of Consciousness Studies* 6: 175–187.
Wallace, V. 1996. Buddhist Tantric medicine in the Kalacakratantra. *Journal of the Institute for Buddhist Studies* 12: 155–174.
Wallace, R., Benson, H., and Wilson, A. 1971. A wakeful hypometabolic physiologic state. *American Journal of Physiology* 221: 795–799.
Walsh, R. 1988. Two Asian psychologies and their implications for Western psychotherapists. *American Journal of Psychothery* 42: 543–560.
———. 1996. Meditation research: the state ofthe art. In B. Scotten, A. Chinnen, and J. Smith (eds.), *Textbook of Transpersonal Psychiatry and Psychology*. New York, Basic Books, 116–128.
Walsh, R., and Roche, L. 1979. Precipitation of acute psychotic episodes by intensive meditation in patients with a history ofschizophrenia. *American Journal of Psychiatry* 136: 1085–1086.
Warrenburg, S., and Pagano, R. 1983. Meditation and hemispheric specialization: absorbed attention in long term adherents. *Imagination, Cognition, and Personality* 2: 211–229.
Weber, C., Arck P., Mazurek B., and Klapp, B. F. 2002. Impact of relaxation training on psychometric and immunologic parameters in tinnitus sufferers. *Journal of Psychosomatic Research* 52: 29–33.
Welwood, J. 1982. Vulnerability and power in the therapeutic process: Existential and Buddhist perspectives. *Journal of Transpersonal Psychology* 14: 118–124.
Wenk-Sormaz, H. 2005. Meditation can reduce habitual responding, *Alternative Therapy in Health & Medicine* 11(2): 42-58.
West, M. 1987. Traditional and psychological perspectives on meditation. In West, M. (ed.), *The Psychology of Meditation*. Oxford: Clarendon Press, 5–22.
Wicklund, R. 1975. Objective self awareness. In Berkowitz L. (ed.), *Advances in Experimental Social Psychology*. New York, Academic Press 233–275.
Winterholler, M., Erbguth, F., and Nuendorfer, B. 1997. Verendung paramedizinischer Verhafen durch M5-Patienten-Patientencharacterisierung und Anwendungswhonheiten. *Fortschritte der Neurologie—Psychiatrie* 65: 555–561.
Yehuda, R. 1997. Sensitization of the HPA axis in posttraumatic stress disorder. In R. Yehuda and A. MacFarlane (eds.), *Psychobiology of Posttraumatic Stress Disorder*. New York, Academic Press, 57–75.
Yu, X., Fumoto, M., Nakatani, Y., et al. 2011. Activation of the anterior prefrontal cortex and serotonergic system is associated with improvements in mood and EEG changes induced by Zen meditation practice in novices. *International Journal of Psychophysiology* May, 80(2): 103–111.
Zautra, A., Fasman, R., Davis, M., and Craig, A. 2010. The effects of slow breathing on affective responses to pain stimuli: an experimental study. *Pain* Apr, 149(1): 12–8.
Zeidan, F., Martucci, K., Kraft, R., Gordon, N., McHaffie, J., and Coghill, R. C. 2011. Brain mechanisms supporting the modulation of pain by mindfulness meditation. *Journal of Neuroscience* Apr 6, 31(14): 5540–5548.

Glossary of Technical Terms

English	*Sanskrit*	*Tibetan*
absolute (ultimate)	paramārtha	don dam pa
absolutism	astivāda	yod pa'i lta
absorption (equipoise)	samāpatti	snyoms par `jug pa
action (evolution)	karma	las
active development	karma-vipāka	las smin
active process	kriyā-tantra	bya ba'i rgyud
adamantine (diamond)	vajra	rdo rje
affirmation	mantra	sngags
aftermath insight	pṛṣṭalabdhajñāna	rjes thob ye shes
aggregate (system)	skandha	phung po
alchemy	rasāyana	ra sa ya na
alertness (awareness)	samprājanya	shes bzhin
alienated individual	pṛthagjana	so so skye bo
altered state	avasthā, vihāra	gnas
altruism (love)	maitri	brtse ba
analysis (judgment)	vicāra	dpyod pa
Analyst	vaibhāṣika	bye brag smra ba
analytic insight	vipaśyāna	lhag mthong
anger (aversion)	krodha, dveśa	khong gro, she drang
appearance (image)	ākāra, bimba	rnam pa, snang ba
archetype (genius)	iṣṭādevata	yi dam
art (technique)	upāya	thabs
aspiration	adhimukti	mos pa
atom	paramāṇu	'dul phra rab
attention	manaskāra	yid la byed pa

English	*Sanskrit*	*Tibetan*
awareness (alertness)	samprājanya	shes bzhin
behavioral science (discipline)	vinayā	'dul ba
bias (position)	pakṣa	phyogs pa
birth (creation)	jāti, utpatti	skyes pa, `byung ba
birthless (uncreated)	ajāti, anutpanna	skyes med, ma `byung ba
blame	nindā	smad pa
bliss	ānanda	dga' ba
sublime bliss	māhānanda	che ba'i dga' ba
supreme bliss	paramānanda	mchog tu dga' ba
orgasmic bliss	sahajānanda	hlan skyes kyi dga' ba
bliss-void	sukkha-śūnya	bde ba-stong pa
block (obscuration)	āvaraṇā	sgrib pa
affective	kleśa-	nyons mong pa'i
cognitive	jñeyā-	shes byas-
bodily system	rūpaskandha	gzugs kyi phung po
body (embodiment)	kāya, deha, śarīra	lus, sku
body diamond	kāya-vajra	sku rdo rje
body of enjoyment	sambhogakāya	longs sku
of emanation	nirmāṇakāya	sprul sku
of form	rūpakāya	gzugs sku
of truth	dharmakāya	chos gyi sku
boundless (immeasurable)	apramāṇa	tshad med
cause	hetu	rgyu
causality	karmaphala	las bras
central (released) channel	avadhūti	rtsa dbu ma
Central Way	Madhyamaka	dbU ma
Centrism	Mādhyamika	dbU ma
Dialogical	Prasaṅgika-	thal bar pa'i-
Positivist	Svātantrika-	rang rgyud pa'i-
Centrist	Mādhyamika	dbU ma pa
channel (pathway)	nadī	rtsa
clear light (translucency)	prabhāsvara	'od gsal
cognition	vijñāpti, samjñā	yongs su shes pa, 'du shes

English	*Sanskrit*	*Tibetan*
cognitive science	adhyātma-vidyā	snang rigs
cognitive system	saṃjñā-skandha	'du shes phung po
commitment (pledge)	samaya	dam tshig
communion (integration)	yuganaddha	zung du 'jug pa
compassion	karuṇā	snying rje
complex	cakra	'khor lo
compound	saṃskṛta	'dus byed
compulsion (affliction)	kleśa	nyon mongs
compulsive	upadana, kliṣṭa	nye bar len pa'i, nyon mongs pa'i
mentality	kliṣṭamanas	nyon mongs pa'i yid
concentration	samādhi	ting nge 'dzin
condition	pratyāya	rkyen
conduct	caryā	bya ba
complicated	prapañcatā	spros pa
uncomplicated	niṣprapañcatā	spros pa med pa
fully uncomplicated	atyantaniṣprapañcatā	shin tu spros pa me pa
confidence (faith)	śraddhā	dad pa
conflict, argument	vivāda	rtsod pa
conscience (shame)	hrī	ngo tsha
conscientiousness	apramāda	bag yod
consciousness	vijñāna	rnam par shes pa
consciousness system	vijñānaskandha	rnam par shes pa'i phung po
(perceptual system)		
consensus	lokayaśa	'jigs rten gyi grags
consequence (effect)	phala	'bras bu
consideration	apatrapa	khrel yod
constructed (conceptual)	vikalpita	rnam brtags pa
parikalpita	kun brtags pa	
constructed nature	parikalpitalakśaṇa	kun brtags kyi mtshan nyid
construction (imagination)		
mental	vikalpana	rnam par brtags pa
social	parikalpana	kun tu brtags pa
Constructivism	cittamatrā	sems tsam pa

English	*Sanskrit*	*Tibetan*
contact	śparsa	reg pa
contemplation	dhyāna	sam gtan
contemplative perception	yogi-pratyakṣa	rnal byor pa'i mngon gsum
contemplative science	abhidharma	mngon chos
continuum (stream)	saṃtāna	rgyun
of consciousness	cittasaṃtāna	sems kyi rgyun
convention	vyavahāra	tha snyad
conventional	vyāvahārika	tha snyad pa
conventional usage	upādāyaprajñāpti	rten nas gdags pa
counteract	vyāvṛtti	bzlog pa
craving (appetite)	tṛṣṇa	sred pa
creation stage	utpattikrama	skyed rim
Creative Vehicle	vajrayāna	rdo rje theg pa
cyclic life (life cycle)	saṃsāra	'khor ba
death	bhaṅga	'jig pa
deity (archetype)	devatā	hla
delusion (confusion)	moha, avidyā	mongs pa, ma rig pa
conscious-	parikalpitāvidyā	kun btags ma rig pa
unconscious-	sahajāvidyā	hlan skyes ma rig pa
denial	apavāda	skur ba `debs pa
dependent origination	pratītyasamutpāda	rten cing 'drel bar 'byung ba
(relativity)		
depression	styāna	rmugs pa
desire	kāma, rāga	'dod pa, chags pa
determine	niścaya	nges pa
development	vipāka	rnam par smin pa
Dialogical Centrism	prāsaṅgika-mādhyamaka	thal bar pa'i dbus ma
diamond	vajra	rdo rje
body	kāya-vajra	sku rdo rje
speech	vag-vajra	gsungs rdo rje
mind	citta-vajra	sems rdo rje
recitation	vajra-jāpa	rdo rje bzlas pa
Diamond Vehicle	Vajrayāna	rdo rje thegs pa

English	*Sanskrit*	*Tibetan*
Dignity of enlightenment	Buddhābhimāna	sang rgyas kyi nga rgyal
discrimination	paricchinna,	yongs su gcod pa,
discursive meditation	savicāra-bhāvanā	dpyad sgoms
dispassion (lust-free)	virāga	'dod chags bral ba
distinction	viśeśa	bye brag
discipline	vinayā	'dul ba
doubt	vicikitsa	the tshom
dreamlike (dreamy)	svapnopama	rmi lam lta bu
drop (transmitter)	bindu	thig le
dualism	dvayavāda	gnyis su mra ba
ecstasy (bliss, flow)	sukhha, praśrabdi	bde ba, shin byang
education (discipline)	sikśā	bslab pa
effect	phala, kārya	'bras bu
effort	vīrya	brtson `grus
ego	ahaṃkāra	ngar `dzin
egoism (self-habit)	ātmagrahaṇa	bdag `dzin pa
element	dharma, dhātu	chos
emotion	saṃskāra	'du byed
emotional system	saṃskāraskandha	'du byed phung po
empathy (compassion)	karuṇā	nying rje
empathic art	upāyakauśalya	thabs gyi mkhas pa
emptiness (openness)	śūnyatā	rtong pa nyid
end (terminate)	kṣaya	zad pa
energy (wind)	prāṇa, vāyu	rlung
cardiorespiratory	prāṇa	srog 'dzin
evacuative	apāna	thur du sel ba
expressive	udāna	gyen rgyu
metabolic	samāna	me mnyam
sensorimotor	vyāna	khyab byed
Enlightened Being	Buddha	sangs rgyas pa
enlightened altruist	bodhisattva	byang chub sems pa
enlightenment	abhisambodhi	mnon par byang chub
enthusiasm	adhimukti	mos pa
entity, nature	bhāva	dngos po

English	*Sanskrit*	*Tibetan*
envy (jealousy)	mātsarya, īrśya	phrag dog
equanimity	upekṣā	tangs nyom
equipoise (absorbtion)	samāpatti	snyam par `jug pa
equiposed insight	samāhitajñāna	mnyam bzhags ye shes
ethics	śīla	tshul khrims
evolution	karma, paribhāva	las, yongs su srid pa
evolutionary (developmental)		
causality	karmaphala	las `bras
conservation	karmavipraṇaśa	las chud mi za ba
maturity	karmavipāka	las rnam par smin pa
excitement	uddhava	rgod pa
existence	bhava	srid pa
existent, being	sat	yod pa
Existentialist	yogācāra	rnal `byor spyod pa
experience	anubhava	myong ba
extinction (cessation)	nirodha	'gags pa
extreme (limit)	antagraha	mthar 'dzin
view	antagraha-dṛṣṭi	mthar 'dzin gyi lta ba
fabrication (perplexity)	prapañca	spros pa
faith (confidence)	śraddhā	dad pa
false	viparīta, mithyā	log pa, rdzun ba
view	mithyā-dṛṣṭi	log pa'i lta ba
family	kula	riga
flow (ecstasy)	praśrabdhi	shin sbyangs
fear (anxiety)	bhīta	'jigs pa
feeling (sensation)	vedanā	tshor ba
focus	ārūdhi	'jog pa
focused meditation	ārūdhi-bhāvanā	'jog sgoms
forgetfulness	asmṛti	drang med
form (matter)	rūpa	gzugs
formless (immaterial)	arūpya	gzugs med
freedom (liberation)	mokṣa, viveka	thar pa, dben pa
of body	kāya-viveka	sku'i dben pa
of speech	vag-viveka	ngag gi dben pa
of mind	citta-viveka	sems kyi dben pa

English	*Sanskrit*	*Tibetan*
generosity	dāna	byin pa
genius	bodhi, buddha,	blo, sang rgas
gradual path	patha-krama	lam rim
gross	audarika	rags pa
ground (basis)	āśraya, ādhāra	gzhi, gnas
guilt (remorse)	kaukṛtyam	'gyod pa
habit	graha	'dzin pa
habituation	abhiniveśa	mngon par zhen pa
heroic altruist	vajrasattva	rdo rje sems pa
identity (nature)	lakṣaṇa	mtshan nyid
ills (illness)	doṣa	nyes pa
illusion (mirage)	māyā, pratibimba	rgyu ma, gzugs brnyan
illusion body (virtual)	māyādeha	rgyu ma'i lus
illusory	māyopama	rgyu ma ltar
immersion	samāhita	mnyam bzhag
impermanence	anityatā	mi rtag nyid
Individual Vehicle	hinayāna	theg dman
Individualist	hinayānika	theg dman pa
inference	anumāna	rjes dpag
private	svārtha	rang don
public	parārtha	gzhan don
innate (natural)	sahaja	lhan skyes
inner fire (sublimation)	candalī	gtum mo
insight	jñāna, darśana	ye shes, thong ba
aftermath	pṛṣṭalabdha-	rjes thob ye shes
equipoise	samāhita-	mnyam bzhag ye shes
instinct	vāsanā	bag chags
instinctual (innate, unconscious)	sahaja, prakṛti	lhan skes,rang bzhin
instinctive patterms	prakṛtivikalpana	rang bzhin kun rtogs
integration (communion)	yugannadha	zung `jug
intention	cetana	sems pa

English	*Sanskrit*	*Tibetan*
interdependence	parasparāpekṣa	phan thsun ltos pa
interest	chanda	'dun pa
interpretable meaning	neyārtha	drang don
interpretation	anumāna, saṃdhi	rjes dpag, dgongs pa
empathic	paraprasiddha-	gshan grag pa'i-
introspective	svātantra-	rang rgyud kyi-
interpretive parameters	deśanakoṭi	bshad pa'i mtha
interpretive sense	saṃdhyartha	dgongs ba'i don
intersubjective	paratantra	gzhan dbang
intrinsic	sva-	rang
identity	svalakṣaṇa	rang gi msthan nyid
objectivity	svarūpa	rang gi ngo bo
reality	svabhāva	rang bzhin
introspective	pratyātma-	so so rang gi-
intuition (insight)	jñāna	ye shes
discriminating	pratyavekṣaṇā-jñāna	so sor rtog pa'i ye shes
equalizing	samatā-jñāna	mnyam nyid ye shes
executive	kṛtyānuṣṭāna-jñāna	bya bas grub pa'i ye shes
mirroring	ādarśa-jñāna	me long lta bu'i ye shes
ultimacy	dharmahdatū-jñāna	chos dbyings gyi ye shes
intuitive (mental)		
perception	mānasapratyakṣa	sems kyi mngon sum
investigation	vitarka	rtog ge
jealousy	īrṣyā	phrag dogs
jewel	ratna	rin chen
joy	tuṣya	'ga ba
judgement (analysis)	vicāra	dpyod pa
kissing	cumbana	'o byed pa
knot	grantha	msdus
heart knot	hṛdaya-grantha	snying gi msdus
life (being)	utpāda, adhigati	skye ba, `gro ba
life cycle	saṃsāra	'khor ba

English	*Sanskrit*	*Tibetan*
life form	jaṅgama	'gro ba
life systems	skandhas	phung po rnams
logic (conflict)	vivāda	rtsod pa
logician	tārkika	stog ngen pa
lovemaking	surata	rab tu dga' ba
luscious channel	lalanā	rtsa rkyang ma
lustful (desirous)	sarāga	'dod chags can
magic body (virtual)	māyādeha	rgyu ma'i sku
master altruist	vajradhara	rdo rje chang
matter, form	rūpa	gzugs
magnanimous (objective self)	mahātmā	bdag nyid chen po
materialism	ucchedadṛṣṭi	chad lta ba
meditation	bhāvanā	sgoms pa
memory	smṛti	dren pa
mental factors	cetasika	sems `byung
mental (intuitive) perception	mānasapratyakṣa	sems kyi mngon sum
mental stability	samatha	zhi gnas
mentor	guru	bla ma
merger (immersion)	dahye	bsre ba
method (art)	upāya, kauśalya	thabs, tshul
mind	citta, manas	sems
mind/body	nāma-rūpa	ming gzugs
mindfulness	smṛti	drangs nges
mindset	muṣṭi, graha	'dzin stangs `dzin pa
misknowledge (delusion)	avidyā	ma rig pa
mistaken (misperception)	viparīta	pyin ci log pa
monism	śāśvatavāda	rtag nyid smra
mutual dependence	parasparāpekṣā	phan tshun ltos pa
naïve, child	bāla	byis pa
name	nāma	ming
natural (innate)	sahaja, prakṛti	lhan skyes, rang bzhin
nature	dharma, lakṣaṇa,	chos, mtshan nyid,

English	*Sanskrit*	*Tibetan*
	svabhāva	rang bzhin
constructed	parikalpitalakṣaṇa	kun brtags kyi mtshan nyid
perfect	pariniṣpanna-	yongs grub kyi-
relative	paratantra-	gzhan dbang gi-
negandum	pratiṣedhavya	dgag bya
negation	pratiṣedha	dgag pa
pure	prasajya-	med dgag
implicative	paryudāsa-	ma yin dgag
neural energy	prāṇa, vāyu	rlung
channel	nadī	rtsa
complex	cakra	'khor lo
drop	bindu	thig le
neurotransmitter	bindu	thig le
nihilism	nāstivāda, abhāvavāda	med pa'i smra ba, dgnos med pa'i
noble	ārya	'phags pa
individual	āryapudgala	'phags pa'i gang zag
truth	āryasatya	'phags pa'i bden pa
non-analytic	avicāra	dpyod med
non-perception	anālambana	dmigs pa med pa
non-desire	alobha	'dod chags med pa
non-aversion	adveṣa	khong khro med pa
non-violence	ahiṃsā	'tshe ba med pa
nothingness	abhāva	dngos med, med pa
object	artha, ālambana	don, dmigs pa
objectification	upālamba	rnam par dmigs pa
objective self	māhātma	bdag nyid chen po
objectivity (omniscience)	svarūpatā,	rang gi ngos bo nyid,
	grahikākara, sarvājñātā	'dzin pa rnam pa, kun mkhyen nyid
obscuration (block)	āvaraṇā	sgrib pa
openness (emptiness)	śūnyatā, viveka	rtong pa nyid, rnam par bden pa
ordinary pride	sadharana-mana	tha mal pa'i nga rgyal

English	*Sanskrit*	*Tibetan*
parameter	koṭi	mtha
particular	svalakṣaṇa	rang gi mtshan nyid
partner (seal)		
action (actual)	karmamudrā	las gyi phyags rgya
intuition (virtual)	jñānamudrā	ye shes gyi-
universal	mahāmudrā	phyags rgya chen po
peace (cessation)	upaśama, nirodha	zhi ba, `gags pa
perfect nature	niśpannalakṣaṇa	yongs su grub pai mtshan nid
perception (direct experience)	pratyakṣa	mngon sum
perceptual system (consciousness system)	vijñāna-skandha	rnam par shes pa'i phung po
person	pudgala	gang zag
philosophy	yukti, vāda	rig pa, smra ba
pledge (commitment)	samaya	dam tshig
Poetic Vehicle	mantrayāna	sngags pa'i theg pa
position (bias)	pakṣa	phyogs bzang
Postitivist Centrism	svātantrika-mādhyamaka	rang rgyud pa'i dbus ma
practitioner	yogi	rnal byor
pride	māna	nga rygal
privacy	svātantrya	rang rgyud
process	tantra	rgyud
action	kriyā-tantra	byas rgyud
performance	caryā-tantra	phyod pa'i rgyud
integral	yoga-tantra	rnal 'byor pa'i rgyud
optimal integral	anuttarayoga-tantra	bla na med pa'i rgyud
Process Vehicle	tantrayāna	rgyud pa'i theg pa
profound	gambhīra	zab mo
projection	samāropa,	sgro `dogs pa
pure information	vijñāptimātra	rnam par rig pa tsam
quiescence	śamatha	zhi gnas
real	sat	yang dag pa
reality	satya, tattva,	bden pa, de nyid,

English	*Sanskrit*	*Tibetan*
reality	svabhāva	rang bzhin
superficial	saṃvṛtisatya	kun rdzob bden pa
conventional	vyāvahārikasatya	tha snyad bden pa
ultimate	paramārthasatya	don dam pa'i bden pa
realization	adhigama	rtogs pa
realm	dhātu	mkhams
of desire	kāmadhātu	'dod pa'i mkhams
of form	rūpadhātu	gzugs gyi mkhams
of formless	arūpadhātu	gzugs med pa'i-
reason	yukti, hetu	rigs pa, rtags
recognition	parijñāna	yons su shes pa
referent	artha, vastu	don, gzhi
reflection (image)	pratibimba	gzugs brnyan
refocus	anurūdhi	rjes `jog
reification	samāropa, adhyāropa	sgro `dogs pa
relaxation (sleep)	middha	gnyid
relativity	pratītyasamutpāda	rten cing `drel bar 'byung ba
released (central) channel	avadhūti	rtsa dbu ma
remedy (therapy)	pratipakśa	gnyen po
renunciation	virāga, rāgakśaya	'dod chags bral, -zad
resistance (block)	āvaraṇa	sgrib pa
cognitive	jñeyāvaraṇa	shes byas-
affective	kleśāvaraṇa	nyon mongs pa'i-
science	vidyāsthāna	rig gnas
scientific teaching	abhidharma	mngon chos
seal, gesture	mudrā	phyag rgya
seed syllable	bīja-mantra	sa bon kyi sngags
self	ātma	bdag
personal	pudgalātma	gang zag bdag
phenomenal	dharmātma	chos kyi bdag
self-centeredness	ātmasneha	bdag ches `dzin
self-habit	ātmagraha	bdag `dzin
conscious-	parikalpitātmagraha	kun btags kyi bdag 'dzin
unconscious-	sahajātmagraha	hlan skyes kyi bdag 'dzin
selflessness	anātmatā	bdag med pa

English	*Sanskrit*	*Tibetan*
self-reifying view	satkāya-dṛṣṭi	'jig lta
sense faculty	indriya	dbang po
element	dhātu	mkhams
medium	āyātana	skye mched
shame (conscience)	hrī	ngo tsha
single-mindedness	ekāgracitta	tse gcig pa sems pa
skill (art)	upāya, kauśalya	thabs, mkhas pa
social	laukika	'jig rten pa'i
social construction	parikalpita	rnam par brtags pa
spacious equipoise insight	akaśopama-samāhita-jñāna	nam mkha' mnyam bzhags ye shes
spirit of enlightenment	bodhicitta	byang chub kyi sems pa
state of matter	mahabhūta	'byung ba chen po
state of mind	mānasendriya	sems kyi dbang po
status	siddhi, siddhatva	grub ba
freedom (openness)	viveka	dben pa
subconscious	ālayavijñāna	kun bzhi rnam shes
sublimation (inner fire)	candalī	gtum mo
substance	dravya, bhāva	rdzas, dngos po
subtle	sūkṣma	phra mo
body	sūkṣmaśarīra	phra ba'i lus
mind	sūkṣmacitta	phra ba'i sems
energy	sūkṣmaprāṇa	phra ba'i rlung
success, adept	siddha	grub pa
succulent channel	rasanā	rtsa ro ma
superficial reality	saṃvṛtisatya	kun rdzob bden pa
syllable	akṣara	yi ge
symbolic sense (universal sense)	sāmānyārtha	sphyi yi don
system	skandha	phung po
bodily	rūpa-	gzugs kyi-
sensory	vedanā-	tshor ba'i-
cognitive	saṃjñā-	'du shes kyi-
emotional	saṃskāra-	'du byed kyi-
perceptual	vijñāna-	rnam par shes pa'i-

English	*Sanskrit*	*Tibetan*
technique (art, method)	upāya,	gang thabs, tshul
therapy (remedy)	pratipakṣa	gnyen po
thing	dharma, bhāva	chos, dngos po
tolerance	kṣanti	'zod pa
Traditionist	Sautrāntika	mdo des pa
transcendence	pāramitā	pha rol tu phyin pa
transcendent		
compassion	karuna-pāramitā	snying rje'i pha rol tu phyin pa
effort	vīrya-pāramitā	brtson `grus kyi pha rol tu phyin pa
generosity	dāna-pāramitā	byin pa'i pha rol tu phyin pa
meditation	dhyāna-pāramitā	sam gtan gi pha rol tu phyin pa
tolerance	kṣanti-pāramitā	'zod pa'i pha rol tu phyin pa
wisdom	prajñā- pāramitā	she rab kyi pha rol tu phyin pa
Transcendence Vehicle		
(technique)	pāramitāyāna	phar phyin theg pa
transcendent insight	vipaśyāna	hlag thong
ultimate reality (truth)	paramārthasatya	don dam bden pa
ultimate particular	svalakṣaṇa	rang gi mtsan nyid
unconscious	sahaja	hlan skes
self-habit	-ātmagraha	-bdag `dzin
uncreated	asaṃskṛta, anutpāda	'dus ma byed pa, ma skes pa
Universal Vehicle	mahāyāna	theg pa chen po
Universalist	mahāyānika	theg pa chen po pa
valid knowledge (method)	pramāṇa	tshad ma
valid inference	ānumanikāpramāṇā	rjes dpag tshad ma
valid perception	pratyakṣikānumāṇā	mngon gsum tshad ma
Victor	bhagavān	bcom ldan `das
view	dṛṣṭi	lta ba
virtual body	māyādeha	rgyu ma'i lus

English	*Sanskrit*	*Tibetan*
virtue	kuśala	dge ba
void (empty)	viveka, śūnya	dben, stong
extreme void	ati-śūnya	shin tu rtong ba
ultimate void	parama-śūnya	mchog tu rtong pa
complete void	sarva-śūnya	kun tu rtong pa
voidness	śūnyatā	stong pa nyid
wisdom	prajñā	shes rab
world	jagat, loka	'jig rten
worldview (view)	dṛṣṭi	lta ba

Index

Page locators in *italics* indicate color insert illustrations, figures, and meditative experiments. *Italicized entries* are quoted precepts from the text *Clearing the Mind in Seven Points.*